CAMBRIDGE URBAN AND ARCHITECTURAL STUDIES

9   THE MOVEMENT FOR HOUSING REFORM IN
GERMANY AND FRANCE 1840–1914

CAMBRIDGE URBAN AND ARCHITECTURAL STUDIES

General Editors

LESLIE MARTIN

Emeritus Professor of Architecture, University of Cambridge

LIONEL MARCH

Rector and Vice-Provost, Royal College of Art

VOLUMES IN THIS SERIES

The movement for
housing reform in
Germany and France
1840–1914

NICHOLAS BULLOCK
and
JAMES READ

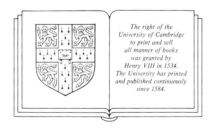

The right of the
University of Cambridge
to print and sell
all manner of books
was granted by
Henry VIII in 1534.
The University has printed
and published continuously
since 1584.

CAMBRIDGE UNIVERSITY PRESS

CAMBRIDGE

LONDON   NEW YORK   NEW ROCHELLE

MELBOURNE   SYDNEY

363,58
B 93 m

Published by the Press Syndicate of the University of Cambridge
The Pitt Building, Trumpington Street, Cambridge CB2 1RP
32 East 57th Street, New York, NY 10022, USA
296 Beaconsfield Parade, Middle Park, Melbourne 3206, Australia

© Cambridge University Press 1985

First published 1985

Printed in Great Britain by the University Press, Cambridge

Library of Congress catalogue card number: 84–1860

British Library Cataloguing in Publication Data

Bullock, Nicholas
The movement for housing reform in Germany
and France 1840–1914.—(Cambridge urban and
architectural studies; 9)
1. Housing—Germany—History   2. Housing
—France—History
I. Title   II. Read, James
363.5'1'0943   HD7339.A3

ISBN 0 521 22537 X

Contents

UNIVERSITY LIBRARIES
CARNEGIE-MELLON UNIVERSITY
PITTSBURGH, PENNSYLVANIA 15213

v

Illustrations

Acknowledgements

I have received assistance and encouragement from many, many sources. To the librarians of the British Museum, the Cambridge University Library, the Berliner Stadtbibliothek, Preussische Staatsbibliothek, the Van Pelt Library, Philadelphia and the Weidner Library, Harvard, I am indebted for the use of their resources and for their kindness and help. To 'real' historians, Geoff Eley, Tony Judt, Jonathan Steinberg and to those with an interest in architectural or planning history, David Handlin, Dean Hawkes, Wolfgang Hofmann, Robin Middleton, Stefan Muthesius and Tony Sutcliffe, I owe a major debt for encouragement and advice. I have also had generous financial assistance for my research from King's College, Cambridge, and from the Deutsche Akademische Austauschdienst. Finally, to James Read, my parents and to my extended family, particularly my four children, heartfelt thanks for their support, forbearance and patience over so many years.

N.B.

In writing a book about housing, I have been continually aware of the value of having a roof over my head. Numerous people have provided such a roof, for longer or shorter periods, and I would like to thank Bob Barnes, Sue Green, Boo Read and Greg Smith, Bob Thompson, David Thompson and, particularly, Sheila Duncker. The following organisations gave financial assistance during my research: St John's College Cambridge, Kettle's Yard Cambridge, and the Royal Institute of British Architects. I would also like to thank my parents, who provided both financial help, and a roof, especially at the start of my research.

I have made use of many libraries, and am indebted to the resources and staff of the British Library, the Cambridge University Library, the library of the Cambridge University School of Architecture, the Musée Social in Paris, the French Bibliothèque Nationale, and the public housing offices of Paris and the Seine department.

For guidance and advice, of which I hope that I have made good use, I would like to thank Tony Judt, Robin Middleton and Tony Sutcliffe. Finally, for support over many years, my thanks to Nick Bullock, Patricia Duncker, Jan and Nigel Williams, and to Frances Borzello.

J.R.

Introduction

Home Sweet Home. The importance of the home was a continual refrain during the nineteenth century, as strongly felt in France and Germany as in England. The value of the Home was displayed everywhere, in the cheap woodcuts hung up by countless working-class families, and in the samplers lovingly embroidered by girls, rich and poor; its virtues were extolled at length in those English manuals that describe the ideal of middle-class life. The Home was crucial for family life. To corrupt the Home was to threaten the family. Faced with the damaging concentration of insanitary and overcrowded housing in the growing towns and cities of the mid-nineteenth century, it was natural that attempts to improve the housing conditions of the 'labouring classes' should command widespread interest. 'As the homes, so the people.' Thus Shaftesbury, Blanqui, Huber; in England, France and Germany, the case for housing reform is one of the central elements of the debate on social reform.

Our book examines the work of the housing reform movement: the loose grouping of doctors, architects, economists, philanthropists, sanitarians and others, who attempted to improve housing conditions during the latter half of the nineteenth and early twentieth centuries. The study concentrates on developments in France and Germany, but takes as its starting point a number of themes that also emerge from the contemporary discussion of housing in England. These themes, which correspond broadly to the most important reforming interests – the sanitarians, the architects, the philanthropists – provide not only a means of focussing the discussion in what is a very wide field, but also serve as a basis for comparison between developments in one country and another. By following the way in which ideas are taken up and applied we hope to show what is common and international in the campaign for housing reform. But also by using these themes to show how ideas are transformed and modified, even rejected, in one country or another, we hope to explore the effect of national differences in, say, the form of land tenure or the structure of local government. Our discussion of housing reform necessarily cuts across traditional subject boundaries; our account leans heavily on studies by those working in other disciplines. We are conscious of the dangers of trying to treat the full range of economic, social, political and architectural issues which must be considered in a study in this field. But we remain unrepentant

1

and convinced of the need for the broad treatment that we have adopted.

The point of departure for our enquiry is the need to understand, as architects, the range of issues with which the discussion of housing is inevitably bound up. The development in Europe of the 'Neues Bauen' or 'Modern Architecture' between the wars was closely allied to an interest in the problems of housing and we reject as inadequate and misleading those accounts which seek to present these developments in mainly formal terms, as the rise of an 'International Style'. The first two conferences of Le Congrès International de l'Architecture Moderne, founded in 1928 as the standard bearer of the Modern Architecture, were devoted to the discussion of low-income housing. In the search for solutions to post-war housing problems, in the form of housing policies and the mechanisms of government intervention, the developments during the inter-war years were critically dependent on the pre-First World War movement for housing reform. This study was prompted by the desire to remind architects both of the full range of issues that have necessarily accompanied (and still must accompany) the debate on housing, and of the part that architects have played and should continue to play in improving housing conditions.

Our study starts from the premise that the development of the movement for housing reform in England, in Germany and in France had much in common. This was not only a natural consequence of the variety of contacts, both personal and informal, and institutional and official, between the three countries, but it also reflects the underlying similarities of the housing problem in London, Berlin and Paris where adequate housing simply lay beyond the means of the majority of the working classes. The artisan might be able to house his family in acceptable conditions, but the housing available to the semi-skilled and the unskilled, the vast mass of the working class, was judged by contemporaries to be expensive, insanitary and overcrowded. The essential nature of the housing problem does not change before 1914; during the period of our study the costs of decent housing remain too high for the typical working-class family. In its simplest terms the challenge that faced the reformers was: how could salubrious housing be provided in a convenient location at rents that the worker could afford? As a comparative study demonstrates, the approaches adopted to solve this problem, the programme of reform, had much in common in all three countries.

The documentation of the housing reform movement in England is now well established: the studies of Gaudie, Sutcliffe, Swenarton, Tarn, Wohl and others already provide a variety of different approaches to the subject.[1] For this reason we have chosen to concentrate on a comparative study of the developments in Germany and France. In doing so we do not ignore the achievements of the reformers in England, Certainly in the early years of the housing reform movement the ideas and practice in England were better known abroad than ideas and practice in either France or Germany; frequently the debate in England precedes that in either Germany or France. But instead of offering yet another account of developments in England we have discussed the way in which English ideas and experience were incorporated from the start in the German and French discussion of the central themes of housing reform.

Our account of developments begins with the growing sense of anxiety over housing conditions. Long before the housing reform movement there had of course been housing without drainage, water supply, ventilation or light; dwellings in which whole families were crowded into single rooms were nothing new in the 1840s and 1850s; despite the protests of the reformers the situation in London in the 1840s was probably better in many respects than it had been during much of the eighteenth century. But what Edwin Chadwick and others in England had done when they first 'discovered' the 'sanitary problem' and the 'housing problem' was to force these issues before the public's attention and to demand that something be done about it. Now there was grudging recognition that housing might no longer be just a matter of concern for the individual, but did indeed touch the interests of the whole community. Poor housing undermined the family and endangered home life, and this, by extension, threatened society as a whole. The loss of moral constraint might lead to the overturning of that fragile balance between the primitive urges of man and the civilising influence of manners, order and culture; dissatisfaction with the existing order of affairs might lead to protest and, beyond, to riot and revolution; ill-health, brought on by insanitary housing, might deprive the employer of a productive workforce or the general of a fit and able-bodied fighting force.

The insanitary housing conditions in London that were already attracting public attention in the 1840s were also to be found in Paris and Berlin, but there are local variations in the 'timetable' for housing reform in each country, particularly in the early years. In Britain the publication of Chadwick's *Report on the Sanitary Condition of the Labouring Population of Great Britain* in 1842, marked a turning point in public attitudes to conditions in which so many were forced to live. More than any preceding investigation, the case presented in the report, illustrated with a mass of vivid detail, drew attention to the existence on a national scale of conditions that most people comfortably believed to be confined to the poorest areas of the largest cities. In France the publication of Villermé's *Tableau de l'Etat Physique et Moral des Ouvriers dans les Manufactures de Coton, de Laine et de Soie* dates from 1840. But in Germany public interest in housing problems comes later. V. A. Huber's attempts to publicise the inadequacy of the housing of the working classes in the late 1840s found little response and the question did not attract widespread interest until the 1860s.

Yet, such initial differences apart, there are fundamental similarities between the development of concern for housing in all three countries: from the 1860s onwards housing is a subject of widespread public concern. Most important, in all three countries the 1880s mark another turning point in attitudes to the problem. In England, the Royal Commission on the Housing of the Working Classes reported in 1885; in Germany, the Verein für Sozialpolitik published its investigations of housing conditions in 1886; in France reformers organised the first international congress of cheap housing in 1889, and formed a national organisation, the Société Française des Habitations à Bon Marché, in the same year. All are evidence of a new attitude to social issues of which housing was a part, and also themselves gave rise to new initiatives to improve housing conditions. Earlier, solutions to the housing problem had emphasised the importance of sanitary reform and the contribution that might be made by the model dwelling companies. The conventional wisdom of the 1860s stressed the extent to which poor housing conditions were a product of the failings of the individual; as Octavia Hill put it, 'Character is the key to circumstance'. But now in the mid-1880s, in place of the almost universal belief in the efficacy of self-help, there is a recognition that the problems of housing are essentially of an economic nature, and flow from the unequal workings of society. As a result there is a new emphasis on the need for government action as the only means of changing this state of affairs. From the late 1880s onwards reformers in all three countries look to legislation as one of the key means to secure improvement.

Not only are there similarities in the timetable of the development of the movement in all three countries, but the very similarity of the nature of the housing problem in all three countries leads the debate to focus on the same basic issues. It is the major common themes of this debate, the central elements of the programme of reform and the contrasting way in which they are treated in Germany and France that form the core of our study. What, then, were the central concerns of the housing reformers?

First, there was agreement amongst all housing reformers on the vital importance of the home: it was the very foundation of a strong family life, the basis of a sound society. Well housed, the worker would be healthy, industrious, disciplined, and conscious of his stake in the existing order of society. Ownership of one's own home would further strengthen these sentiments, Samuel Smiles argued: 'the accumulation of property has the effect which it always does upon thrifty men; it makes them steady, sober and diligent. It weans them from revolutionary notions and makes them conservative.'[2]

But how was this housing to be provided? What was the ideal form of dwelling? The vision of the home for which the reformers campaigned was essentially the product of the social attitudes of the middle-class values held by the reformers themselves. In place of the reported facts of working-class life, the casual and squalid intimacy of overcrowded tenements which corroded virtues such as honesty, thrift or temperance, the reformers championed the self-contained dwellings as the key to strengthening the family. The cottage, set in its own garden, was invariably held up as the most desirable kind of home. It offered the healthiest form of dwelling, a secluded setting for the vital intimacies of family life and, at least in theory, even the possibility of home-ownership. Yet how relevant was this ideal to the vast mass of the working classes for whom it was intended? No doubt many would have chosen such a form of housing had it been accessible, but to those faced with the need to find housing within reach of work, or the necessity of taking in lodgers just to pay the rent, the reformers' ideas must have appeared an unattainable ambition.

In practice, from the very earliest days of the movement, reformers recognised that the salubrious tenement was the only practicable means of providing the ideal of the self-contained dwelling at reasonable rents in the city. Properly designed, even the tenement could provide a suitable setting for family life. Indeed the particular form of housing, whether cottage or tenement, was of less importance in creating the home than a number of other factors. Ultimately it was the self-contained dwelling, one for each family, and each with its own kitchen and hearth, that was agreed by all housing reformers as the first necessity of civilised life.

Closely related to theories about the ideal form of housing, and a second major concern of reformers, was the provision of housing that would not be injurious to health. The connection between ill-health and poor housing was recognised early on, and in England, Germany and France, anxiety over public health was one of the first and most powerful stimuli to improve housing conditions. To preserve the health of the community, sanitary and housing reformers argued that it was quite legitimate for government to intervene, a view even upheld by those like Nassau Senior generally associated with firm opposition to any extension of government activity. Indeed government might set aside the 'selfish' property rights of the few to protect the people, on the grounds argued by Shaftesbury: 'Salus populi suprema lex est'; by the end of the 1860s this principle was established in England by the Sanitary Act (1866) and the Torrens Act (1868).

Although practice might still lag behind legislative principle, the influence of sanitary reform on the housing debate can be summarised under two broad headings. First, it led to the demand for higher standards in the layout and the construction of new housing; second, it resulted in increasingly vocal demands for action to be taken to inspect and, if necessary, to regulate the use of existing housing. Calls were made for powers to enable the sanitary authorities to control over-crowding, to improve insanitary housing and, where this was not practicable, to demolish the offending properties.

In all three countries these common aims were pursued by generally similar measures: tougher building regulations and bye-laws to enforce higher standards in new housing, tighter controls of the use of existing property through a system of housing inspection, backed by tougher sanitary regulations. Naturally there are differences of emphasis, a product of the different patterns of urban growth, and the different traditions of housing from one country to another: in neither France nor Germany was there any equivalent to national legislation such as the Cross Act (1875) which gave the local authorities powers to order the large-scale demolition of insanitary housing. Yet, even without the powers conferred by national legislation, early successes could be matched by later developments: in all three countries sanitary reformers could legitimately point to a number of lasting achievements. In Germany, in particular, beset with the problems of very high density tenement housing, the sanitary reformers campaigned long and hard for tighter control over the proportion of the site that might be developed and the maximum bulk of a building. The fruits of this campaign, the zoning ordinances successfully applied in many German cities in the mid-1890s, were to have important consequences for later developments in planning both in Europe and in America.

The layout and design of housing was also an issue of continuous debate amongst housing reformers. Architects such as Henry Roberts in England, C. W. Hoffmann in Germany and Gourlier in France had been associated with the campaign for better housing from the early days of the movement. Much of this early interest in the form of housing was focussed on the problems of providing minimal but salubrious accommodation at rents that the working classes could afford. Generally the result was housing of a drab and utilitarian appearance, typified in the blocks of model dwellings erected across London from the late 1860s onwards by the Peabody Trust.

Despite the reformers' enthusiasm for the cottage, the high cost of land in central areas of large cities, and the need to provide housing within easy reach of work, inclined the debate on the most appropriate form of model housing in favour of the tenement block. By the mid-1880s the architectural profession in England, Germany and France had taken up the challenge of designing model dwellings that would combine the hygienic advantages of the cottage with the locational and economic benefits of the tenement block. However, the 1880s did also see renewed architectural interest in cottage housing, fostered both by hopes that the suburban railways would open up the cheaper land in the suburbs to working-class families, and by the new ideas about planning and housing: in England the model communities built by enlightened employers at Port Sunlight. Bournville and New Earswick all took the cottage as the starting point for the layout of the community, and it is their examples, together with the ideas championed by the Garden City Movement after 1898, which provided inspiration to housing architects in both Germany and France. Indeed, by 1914, housing reformers could point with equal pride to a successful tradition of both 'block' and 'cottage' developments. Before the First World War, Londoners were being offered cottage housing by the London County Council on suburban estates at Norbury and Totterdown Fields; even Berlin, the 'grösste Mietskasernestadt der Welt', had its cottage estates at Staaken-Spandau. Meanwhile the design of developments such as A. A. Rey's block in the Rue de Prague, the LCC Architect's Department Boundary Estate, or Messel's block on the Proskauerstrasse, showed that it was possible to provide open space, playgrounds, ample light and ventilation right in the very heart of the city: here was a vision of high-density housing very different from the utilitarian approach of the 1860s and 1870s.

The choice between tenement and cottage was not just an architectural issue, but one which raised larger questions. It was the increase in the cost of land that made the tenement block the only viable form of housing in the centre of the large city; it was the need to be within easy reach of work that tied the working-class family to housing in these central locations. It is the land question, together with the related issues of the locations of working-class housing and planning that forms the last of our major reforming themes.

How was land to be made available cheaply enough, and in the right location, to build housing that the worker could afford? In each of the three countries this issue is crucial, although the debate proceeds differently. In London the rapid expansion of the suburban railway system from the mid-1850s onwards, and the opening up of large areas of leasehold land for building provided a very different pattern of growth from the dense housing typical of Paris and Berlin. In England the Garden City Movement united those seeking a 'peaceful path to real reform' behind a programme of decentralisation of the urban population to new settlements of finite size which were to be built on land owned by the community itself.

In Germany the land question was not only widely regarded as central to the housing problem but also attracted many whose interests extended far beyond issues of mere housing. By the turn of the century a mass following was ranged behind a loosely structured programme of reform which aimed ultimately at the transfer of ownership of the land to the community. In the short term, however, land reform was identified both with reforms such as a tax on the 'unearned increment' in the value of land and with the initiation of policies of land ownership and management by municipalities such as the provision of leasehold land for non-profit housing. These policies, together with the system of city extension planning and the application of density zoning ordinances, offered the individual city the means of regulating not only the supply of land, but also the extent and the form in which it might be developed.

In France, urban growth was less marked towards the end of the century than in Germany, and the problem of land was considered less urgent. Only in the early 1900s was the question of ownership and control of land by community, either through co-operatives or municipalities, taken up in earnest. By this time the lessons of the Garden City in England, and of the land reform movement in Germany, offered to French reformers ample material on which to found a case for reconsidering the urban land question.

However, from the very first days of the movement for housing reform in the 1840s in all three countries, it was recognised that any programme of reform could only succeed if matched by an increase in the supply of new housing. This had of necessity to be a central part of the agenda for reform. Without a greater supply of new housing, hopes of reducing overcrowding, or reducing rents, of building better-designed and more salubrious housing, or reducing housing densities, all would be doomed to certain frustration. For all reformers, for sanitarians, architects, land reformers, the provision of more, of better, of cheaper housing was of central importance.

These priorities arose from the reformers' view of the existing system of providing housing. In all three countries it was clear to the housing reformers that private enterprise would, in the foreseeable future, inevitably continue to produce more dwellings than any form of non-profit housing. Throughout our period, housing reformers took for granted this central role of private enterprise; none held out the realistic hope that the non-profit sector would be able to replace private enterprise. However the failings of this system were only too obvious. Contemporaries generally judged private enterprise housing to be expensive, ill-built and subject to cyclical interruptions of supply – notably during periods of economic boom when demand for housing was greatest. Reformers in both Germany and France spoke of the quality of housing built by private enterprise in terms very similar to those employed by William Thompson:

It has been assumed by thousands who ought to have known better that private enterprise would do all that was necessary, but private enterprise unstimulated, unassisted, undirected, has hopelessly failed. It has left us face to face with a very deficient supply; it has given us the old slums, it has given us only too often acres and acres of new slums in the suburbs, jerry-built 'brick boxes with slate lids' dumped down on dust heaps and put up mainly with the object of getting a quick profit in the few years which will elapse before they degenerate into slum dwellings almost as bad as the old ones in our midst. Where the new houses are well built and on good sites they are of an unsuitable type, and the rents are so unreasonably high as to be beyond the means of one family, so they have to be sublet to other families and thus by overcrowding, with the increased wear and tear following in its train, they rapidly deteriorate and leave the housing of the mass of the people as bad in many respects as it was before. The product of private enterprise, then, is insufficient in quantity and inferior in quality.[3]

But how was the supply of new housing to be increased? Since the 1840s, reformers had been exploring ways in which housing could be provided by means that did not rely on the market mechanisms and the promise of profit so necessary to private enterprise. Early experiments in England during the 1840s with limited dividend housing companies such as the Society for the Improvement of the Conditions of the Labouring Classes and the Metropolitan Association for Improving the Dwellings of the Industrious Classes were eagerly observed in Germany and France; in all three countries employers recognised the advantages of good housing, like other social benefits such as a company health scheme, in attracting and then retaining a stable and doubly dependent labour force. The English building societies, so attractive to liberal notions of self-help, were the focus of keen interest from German and French housing reformers who sought to establish similar traditions of co-operative housing to provide for the artisan if not for the unskilled worker.

Housing reformers did not intend that these different forms of non-profit housing should usurp the role of private enterprise but they did hope that these other forms of production would stimulate the provision of working-class housing in a number of ways. Model dwellings were to demonstrate to the developer that salubrious housing could be built and let at rents that were within the reach of the working-class family; others argued that high quality non-profit housing would educate the worker to demand higher standards thus forcing private enterprise to respond.

But despite such arguments it was already clear to reformers in all three countries by the mid-1880s that government action was necessary to encourage an increase in the supply of new working-class housing. The principle of intervention by government to regulate public health, and thus by extension to exercise a measure of control over housing conditions, had been established by the 1880s in England; the Public Health Act of 1875 had unequivocally defined the duty of government in this realm. For public health this was acceptable, but the prospect of extending the role of government to involvement in providing housing, essentially an economic issue, raised fundamental questions over the legitimate role of government.

The debate over the role of government in the field of housing naturally proceeds differently in each country. The contrasting forms of government, the different relationships between central and local government, the variety of forms of local government – even within the same country – all ensured that this was so: the contrast between the centralised power of government in France and the federal constitution in Germany led naturally to a variation in each country in the role assigned to government in this field. Equally the extent of legislation in operation before the mid-1880s was very different: in England and France there already existed national legislation to control aspects of existing housing conditions; in France housing legislation dates from as early as 1850. In Prussia, by contrast, the regulation of sanitary affairs was, by virtue of the delegated police powers of the state, the responsibility of the individual local authority.

It is not surprising that the outcome of the debate on government intervention differed from country to country. In England and France the early 1890s see the introduction of national legislation which significantly extends the powers of government to assist the construction of new housing. The expansion of the non-profit sector, in England through the work of the local authorities, and in France through the Société Française des Habitations à Bon Marché, dates from this period. In Germany the situation appears, at first sight, to be very different; no national, nor even Prussian legislation on housing was passed before the First World War, despite a vigorous campaign by housing reformers of all persuasions. However, the non-profit movement in Germany did expand rapidly from the early 1890s onwards due largely to the unexpected benefits from legislation outside the immediate field of housing. The Invalidity and Old Age Insurance Act of 1890 established a source of capital for housing that was to be of enormous value in the expansion of the non-profit sector before the war. Thus despite differences in the legislation on housing, the period between the 1890s and 1914 sees a major development of non-profit housing in all three countries and, however limited the achievement before the war, the institutional structures established at this time were to provide, in each country, the foundations for post-war growth.

The account we offer seeks both to examine the programme of reform debated and proposed by the housing reformers and to judge their proposals in practice. Naturally, in practice, the results of reform often fall far short of aspiration and intention: legislation frequently proved unworkable, 'model' dwellings were generally too expensive even for the 'improvable' and 'deserving' poor, certainly the volume of housing built by 'voluntary private effort' remained pitifully small. To many the achievements of the housing reformers were too little and too late. Even in London, by 1914 all the philanthropically motivated organisations together had built under 40,000 dwellings, a contribution that seems smaller still when one considers that nearly 75,000 dwellings had been cleared to make way for the railways, while a further 5,500 dwellings had been demolished under the Cross Act to make way for the building of model dwellings. Yet the judgements passed on the reformers' achievements are often anachronistic, a product of our present values and attitudes to poverty or the role of government. To damn the reformers for failing to resolve the housing crisis that had developed in London by the mid-1880s is not only to misunderstand their aims but to misinterpret the contemporary debate on the social question.

There are some who, like Friedrich Engels, will see the whole programme of housing reform as an attempt to maintain, even to strengthen, the order of bourgeois society against the inevitable tensions generated by a capitalist society and dismiss the reformers as 'economists, philanthropists, humanitarians, improvers of the conditions of the working class, do-gooders, members of the societies for the prevention of cruelty to animals, temperance cranks, hole-and-corner reformers of every imaginable kind'.[4] No doubt fear of social unrest did serve as a spur to reforming action. But this is too limited an explanation of the motives of the reformers. It would be naive to present their work as a glorious chronicle of selfless acts of altruism; no doubt their motives were as mixed as their interests. Yet whatever their motives, the work of the sanitarians like Sir John Simon, or the search by architects for better and cheaper forms of housing did represent a serious attempt to improve housing conditions within the existing order of society. By the turn of the century even socialists were prepared to add their support to the campaign; to those with a pragmatic view, who were concerned with the conditions in which vast numbers of working-class families were forced to live, housing reform did offer the prospect of more immediate and more tangible benefits than the promise of the long-awaited 'Zukunftsstaat'.

The housing reformers may have done too little too late, their achievement in practice may be belittled as no more than the provision of better housing for a relatively prosperous few, as part of a programme which they hoped would gradually filter down to the many. But this is to overlook one of the movement's most significant achievements. Whatever the limitations in practice, their ideas, investigations and discussions were of lasting importance. Housing reformers investigated the economics of housing, they explored the design and the hygiene of the dwelling; they demanded a consideration of the problems of housing as part of the growth of cities and the expansion of the urban population. These investigations and the understanding of the problems of housing that they established were of immense importance after 1914. In England, in France and in Germany, the form of government intervention, and thus the subsequent history of housing and housing policy, was crucially determined by the debates and attitudes of the pre-war years. If we are really to understand the making of housing policy since 1914, we must look at the activities of the pre-war movement for housing reform.

Part One

The movement for housing reform in Germany 1840–1914

Recognition of the Housing Problem

1

❖◇

The emergence of the Housing Problem 1840–57

At the time when Chadwick and Shaftesbury were already turning their attention to the problems of sanitary and housing reform, the social and economic differences between England and Germany were striking. Visitors from England commented frequently on the backwardness of much of German life but also mentioned the changes that were beginning to transform the structure of German society.[1] The 1840s see the first steps towards industrialisation in Germany with the beginnings of the factory system and the construction of the first railways;[2] the 1840s also see the expansion of cities and towns with the start of the shift in the distribution of population from rural to urban areas.[3]

Most of the towns to which the rural poor moved in search of work as a result of the upheavals in rural life brought about by the enclosures and emancipation of the peasants were in many ways more like the towns of the Middle Ages than the industrial cities of the English Midlands. In Prussia in 1816, 73·5% of the population had been classed as rural;[4] in 1846, after nearly a decade of prosperity in which many cities had grown rapidly, the rural population still accounted for 72% of the total, and the 28% of the population that did live in urban areas lived predominantly in small towns, many with no more than 10,000 inhabitants, which had changed little in centuries. In 1850 the twelve largest towns in Germany had a combined population of only 1·34 million compared with Paris with a population of over a million; Berlin, the largest city in the country, had a population of only 424,570 despite a period of unprecedented growth during the 1840s.

The influx of population from rural areas created serious problems in towns and cities across the country: for many, finding work and lodging was beset with difficulties. Most of the towns were no more than market towns and offered limited opportunities for employment. Manufacturing industry generally operated on a small scale with a master assisted by a journeyman often working in his own home or in his own yard; manufacturers like Borsig, Krupp or Maffei, who were just beginning to build up their factories from small beginnings in the late 1830s and early 1840s and whose works were to expand with the boom years of the 1850s, were still very much the exception to the rule. One consequence of the small scale and relative backwardness of much of German industry was that it simply could not absorb fast enough the flood of immigrants as they flocked to urban areas. Nor could the construction of new housing keep pace with the growth of the urban population. With wages depressed by the flooding of the labour market and a shortage of housing, living conditions in the poorer areas of many cities in the early 1840s matched those that the immigrants had attempted to escape in rural areas.

These difficulties were further complicated by the economic depression of the mid-1840s. The failure of the potato harvest in 1845 and 1846, and the poor rye harvests of 1845 exacerbated the shortage of food already caused by the hot summers and poor harvests of 1842, 1843, and forced up the price of food. Prices reached a peak in the spring of 1847 and sparked off riots in a number of cities across the country, including Berlin. Concern over the condition of the poor and the associated problems of unemployment, malnutrition and inadequate housing was focussed by a number of incidents, in particular by the uprising of the Silesian weavers in June 1844; it is small wonder that by the late 1840s contemporaries should have identified 'Pauperismus' as a threatening but inescapable consequence of urban growth.[5]

Conditions in Berlin during the 1840s

These general developments can be followed in more detail in Berlin: the increase in the growth rate of the city as a result of the surge of immigration from the surrounding area, the concern for the mounting number of paupers, the deterioration of living standards during the later 1840s. As the largest city in the country, it is not typical but illustrates the scale of the social problem. Most important, we can follow in Berlin the deterioration of housing conditions that was to provoke from the mid-1840s the first concern with housing reform in Germany.

In Berlin, as in other larger cities, there was a marked increase in the number of immigrants flooding in from the surrounding countryside (fig. 1); during the mid-1840s the city was attracting an average of 12,000 immigrants a year mostly from the surrounding Mark Brandenburg but with many from more distant parts of Prussia.[6] The effect of this rapid increase in the population was to accelerate a number of processes that were already visible before the 1840s and were viewed with misgiving by contemporaries. Most significant was the increase of working-class accommodation to the south-east of the centre in Luisenstadt and in the north-west outside the walls in the Oranienburger and Rosenthaler Vorstädte (figs 2 and 3).

At the beginning of the nineteenth century the general impression of conditions in Berlin was favourable; Mirabeau described the city as 'une ville bien construite, bien percée, abondante en logements sains et commodes'.[7] During the early part of the century the central areas of Berlin – Berlin, Cölln, Neukölln and Friedrichswerder – had provided for a wide variety of uses;[8] they housed the various administrative, financial and cultural activities of the city as well as providing the principal location for manufacture of all types. Outside the city gates

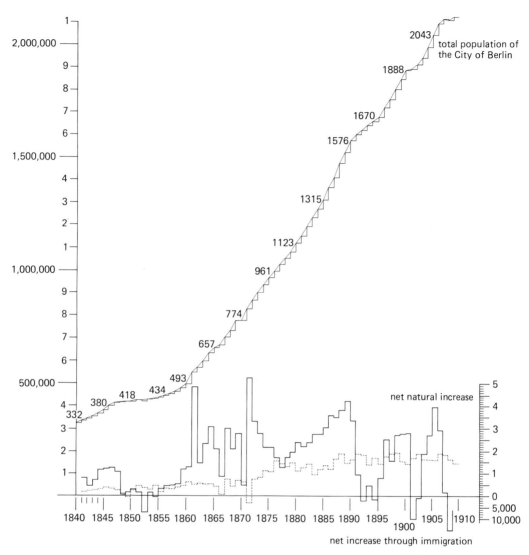

1 Population growth, immigration and natural increase in Berlin, 1840–1914

the density of development was lower, with detached villas interspersed with a number of other land uses such as market gardens, dairies, windmills, cemeteries and timber yards.

But an exception to these open, semi-rural and often genteel developments outside the city were the settlements north of the Spandauer Viertel and Friedrich Wilhelm Stadt, around the Hamburger Tor.[9] These housed a large number of working-class families and included the area called Voigtland, already notorious by the 1830s for its poverty and poor housing conditions. This district had attracted a large working-class population because of the concentrated expansion of employment in the metal working and machine building here in the late 1830s. The opening of Borsig's works in 1837 in the Chausseestrasse was followed the next year by Pflug's factory and in 1842 by Wöhlert's, in the same

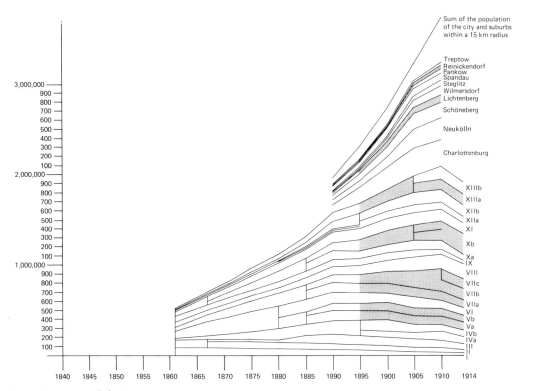

Sum of the population
of the city and suburbs
within a 15 km radius

Treptow
Reinickendorf
Pankow
Spandau
Steglitz
Wilmersdorf
Lichtenberg

Schöneberg

Neukölln

Charlottenburg

XIIIb
XIIIa
XIIb
XIIa
XI

Xb

Xa
IX
VIII
VIIc
VIIb
VIIa
VI
Vb
Va
IVb
IVa
III
II
I

3,000,000
900
800
700
600
500
400
300
200
100
2,000,000
900
800
700
600
500
400
300
200
100
1,000,000
900
800
700
600
500
400
300
200
100

1840 1845 1850 1855 1860 1865 1870 1875 1880 1885 1890 1895 1900 1905 1910 1914

2 Population growth for city
districts and selected suburbs
of Berlin 1861–1914; the
districts and suburbs shown
as shaded are those discussed
in Chapter 8.

street; in 1844 Egells also moved his plant to the Chausseestrasse while
Hoppe established his works around the corner in the Gartenstrasse. Less
dramatic in its concentration, but important as an area of employment,
was the expansion of the textile industry in the south-east of Berlin, in
the Luisenstadt and the Stralauer Viertel around which there developed
a working-class area similar in scale to that of the north-west.

As industry expanded, immigrants flooded into these areas in search
of housing within easy reach of employment. The importance of these
areas of industrial expansion for the growth of the city can be seen from
the rate at which the population outside the city walls was increasing.
Between 1840 and 1843 the population outside the walls increased by
21% while that within grew by only 7%; the same is true for the period
between 1843 and 1846. By 1846 the population outside the walls was
already one eighth of the total population, the greater part of it
concentrated in the Oranienburger and Rosenthaler Vorstädte.

To accommodate this increased population, land for housing was
required. The sale of the Royal Estates had been completed by 1835 and
did provide a flow of new land in some areas, but in others the
availability of land was held back by the difficulties in the *Separation* or
division into private ownership of common lands.[10] The Köpenicker Feld,
an enormous area of common land in the south-east of the city, and
the largest remaining area of undeveloped land within the city walls,
was only ready for development after 1840. Land in the suburbs appears

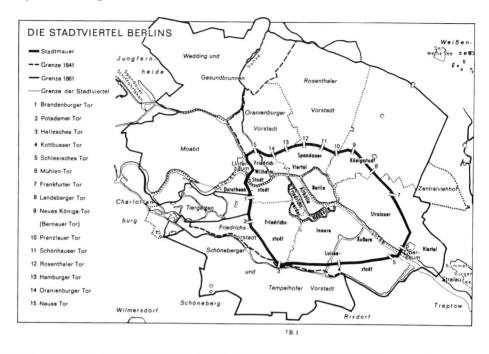

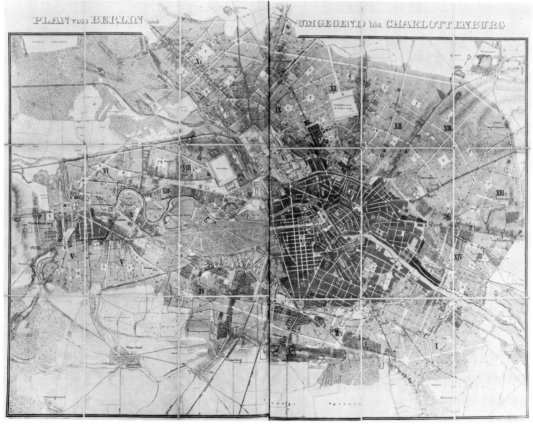

3 Berlin in the 1860s: the districts and boundaries of the city (a), and the growth of the city to 1865 by Reimer (b)

to have been made available in an irregular way, some owners sold their land while others held back, perhaps in the hope of a higher return; the result was a 'leap-frogging' pattern of growth with working-class housing being built at a higher density than was normal for the rest of the city but still interspersed with remnants of market gardens and other survivals from a semi-rural past before the 1840s.

This denser pattern of building emerged around the major areas of employment such as the Oranienburger and Rosenthaler Vorstädte, but also in the Luisenstadt and the Stralauer Viertel. While earlier developments had normally been limited to a front or 'street' block alone, those constructed from the 1840s onwards consisted of side and back buildings as well so that the site was used very much more intensively with four-storey buildings. In the north-west suburbs there was generally a differentiation between living accommodation in the street block and workshops or even small factory buildings for the metal industry which developed in the side and rear buildings; in Luisenstadt in the south-east many of the processes of the textile industry could be carried out in a domestic setting as 'out-work' and there was little differentiation between the different blocks on a site.[11]

During the early 1840s, though this more concentrated form of building was still the exception, there was a general increase in density. The average number of dwellings, or separate tenements, per plot, or development, for all Berlin rose from only 7 in 1830, to nearly 8 in 1840, and to just over 9 by 1850; this was matched by an equivalent increase in occupancy from 35 people per development in 1835, to 48 by 1850.[12] In view of the balance of new building in the suburbs to existing building in the city, we can see that the relative increase in density outside the walls to produce this average increase must have been significant.

During the 1840s demand for housing outstripped supply, producing a deterioration in living conditions in working-class areas.[13] Throughout the 1830s housing construction totalled only 8,920 dwellings, during a decade when the population rose by about 80,000; in the early 1840s production rose and between 1841 and 1846 over 2,000 new dwellings were built each year, but even this failed to keep pace with the increase in demand. In 1846, the year of peak immigration, production was down to about 1,000 dwellings. The changing relationship between supply and demand is reflected in a number of indices, for example in the rise of the number of people per dwelling from 4·93 to 5·44 in 1840, to 5·46 in 1846; and in the number of empty dwellings at any time (fig. 4). In 1840, a year of high immigration, the number of empty dwellings was low (2·4%); during the early 1840s, years of comparatively low immigration, the number of empties rose, but with the rise in immigration as the depression deepened the number of available dwellings fell back to only 2·3% of the total. The difficulties faced by working-class families in finding housing is also reflected in the rise in rents and the reduction in the number of rooms for rent below 50 Thaler per annum. As the number of empty dwellings shrank the average rents

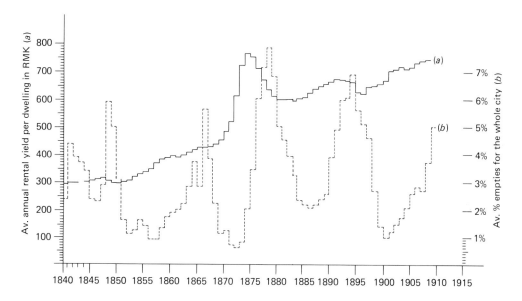

4 Average rental value of a dwelling from the *Mietssteuerkataster* (a), and the percentage of empty dwellings (b)

rose from 85 Thaler in 1830, to 98 Thaler in 1840 and to 100 in 1843; in 1847, the year of greatest pressure on the housing market, the average rent had risen to 105 Thaler.[14]

The influx of immigrants not only put pressure on the housing market, it also caused mounting anxiety over the conditions in which the greater part of the new immigrants lived. Even the *Magistrat* accused the immigrants of bringing with them their filthy rural East Prussian housing habits and of causing 'Pauperismus' in Berlin.[15] Many of the immigrants were single, and moral indignation was already awakened during the 1840s to the dangers of the system of *Schlafgänger*, whereby a lodger rented not a room but a bed, or even a share of a bed, in a room often used by the family itself.[16] The widespread poverty in Berlin during the 1840s was not simply limited to the immigrants. Nauwerk, a member of the city council working for a reform of the rent tax during the mid-1840s, estimated that over half the population of the city had an annual income of under 200 Thaler.[17] An estimate made in 1847 suggested that 180 Thaler per year was the 'poverty line' and that just under half the population lived below this level. Another index of poverty is the incidence of dwellings exempt from tax because of the low income of the tenants. In 1840 only one in every seven dwellings was exempt, but as the depression took effect the number increased so that in 1847, one in every *three* dwellings was exempt on grounds of poverty.[18]

This city-wide view of housing conditions and the incidence of poverty blurs the true horror of the worst areas. If we look at the distribution of insanitary housing, poverty and overcrowding by districts, it is clear that conditions in some districts were very much worse than conditions in the city as a whole. While the central areas remained relatively prosperous, the rapidly expanding suburbs such as the Oranienburger and Rosenthaler Vorstädte, the Stralauer Viertel, Luisenstadt and Königstadt had a much higher proportion of the population in receipt of poor relief than the rest of the city: this was the case during the 1830s and remained so throughout the 1840s. In 1840s, 40·9% of all dwellings in the Rosenthaler Vorstadt were exempt from tax on the grounds of the poverty of the tenants. In Königstadt and the Stralauer Viertel, the proportion was much lower (at 18·5% and 17·8% respectively) but still much higher than in the prosperous Dorotheenstadt where only 5% of dwellings were exempt from tax: nor were conditions appreciably better by 1850.[19]

Neither Berlin nor Germany as a whole produced a literature like that of Dickens or even Sue to describe the city in all its complexity and variety, despite the attempts of vapid imitators; nor do we have for Berlin statistical surveys of the kind already carried out in London and Paris. It is nevertheless possible to form some impression of housing conditions in the poorest parts of Berlin during the 1840s and thus to understand contemporary fear of the growth of *Pauperismus*, by considering the conditions in the tenements or *Familienhäuser* erected in the suburbs by the infamous Baron von Wülknitz in the early 1820s near the Hamburger Tor.[20]

This district, called Voigtland, had been settled as early as the mid-eighteenth century and had provided accommodation for masons, carpenters and other members of the building trades working seasonally in Berlin. In the period around the turn of the century a number of market gardeners had settled in the area (hence the name Gartenstrasse) and they had been followed by a number of weavers in search of cheap housing. The fall in the weavers' standard of living after the Napoleonic wars radically changed the fortunes of the area and from the 1820s onwards it was regarded as an area of poverty. But it was the construction of the five *Familienhäuser* between 1820 and 1824 by von Wülknitz that gave Voigtland its reputation.

The houses were built of the very cheapest materials of the poorest quality with only stud partitioning between dwellings. These dwellings were minimal in size consisting of a single room, 4 m × 7 m equipped with a stove for cooking and heating, and as many as possible were packed on to the site; the 'long block' on the Gartenstrasse, with a cellar and two storeys in the roof, had a total of six storeys containing 150 'dwellings' off either side of an unlit and unventilated corridor running the length of the block. The cellar dwellings were damp, a problem aggravated by the flooding of the court by the well, the sole source of water for the development, and the overflowing of the gutter carrying all waste and slops to a cesspit located under one of the blocks.

An army of paupers was packed into these rooms. In 1824 the 420 dwellings housed 3,800 people; numbers fell gradually in the mid-1830s but with the housing shortage of the 1840s numbers rose again. Frequently two families shared a room so that as many as 8 or 9 people were living together in about 28 m². Despite the up-turn in the economy by the early 1840s the situation still had not improved. The appalling conditions are starkly evident from the accounts in the last section of Bettina von Arnim's book *Dies Buch gehört dem König* published in 1843 which describes the families living in the different dwellings in the *Familienhäuser* seen through the eyes of a Swiss student:

In the opposite house (Gartenstrasse 92a), Room 9, lived a journeyman carpenter Gellert. I did not find him at home. His mother-in-law lay deathly sick on some straw; his wife also seemed to be very sick; she stood erect with difficulty and told me that her husband had been without work for fourteen days and had now gone out to look for bread...[21]

By the mid-1840s, as the description of Voigtland suggests, the dangers of *Pauperismus* were already being identified in specific terms: poverty, insanitary living conditions, overcrowding and poor housing. The evidence on the conditions in which the 'kleine Leute' were forced to live was readily available in general accounts of the life of the city, in the pages of newspapers such as the *Vossische Zeitung*, in medical reports and even in the reports of the *Magistrat* itself. These conditions were cause for concern. As the depression led to a deterioration of conditions and a rise in food prices, there were riots in several parts of the country. Even in Berlin itself there were riots: in late April 1847 during the four-day 'Potato Revolution' the markets had been attacked and the Royal cavalry called in to restore law and order. As the economic depression worsened and conditions for the families of the poor deteriorated, the dangers of inaction and the lack of initiative to better the situation became more real.

Huber and conservative responses to the 'social question'

Despite the terrible living conditions of so many in the late 1840s, the existence of a housing problem in Germany was at best grudgingly recognised and then only as part of the larger social question. Yet since the mid-1840s, the problems of pauperism, increased by the economic depression, had been a source of widespread concern. To those sympathetic to the plight of the poor, problems such as poverty, unemployment and poor housing were to be resolved by well-tried remedies based on alms-giving and the limited resources of charity. But to many more these problems resulted from the failings of the individual: those who drank, those who shirked work, those who lived like beasts in filthy surroundings, had only themselves to blame. To change public attitudes to these social issues was a Herculean task; nevertheless by the early 1850s a start had been made.

Early attempts to focus attention on the problems of housing have traditionally been linked with the name of Victor Aimé Huber.[22] Initially Huber was closely associated with conservative circles: his appointment in 1843 as Professor of Romance Philology in Berlin had been secured by Ernst Wilhelm Hengstendberg and Josef von Radowitz, important figures in the small circle around the king, to enable him to work for the conservative cause. In 1845, after a period of intensive preparation which included a trip to England, France and Belgium, he launched his journal *Janus, Jahrbücher deutscher Gesinnung, Bildung und Tat*[23] as a means of responding for the conservatives to the radical publications of the 'young Hegelians'.

While many in the conservative circles in which Huber moved identified the social difficulties of the mid-1840s as a threat to the existing order of society, there was a general indifference in these quarters to the problems of an urban working class.[24] Indeed, the conservative view of the State, as set out by leading writers such as Karl Ludwig von Haller or Adam Müller, excluded the possibility of the regulation of the social problem by a programme of social reform or by legislative means. They regarded the State as the natural product of social relations which had been established through history, and far removed from that artificial legal construct, the 'social contract', proposed by the liberals and those inspired by the yet more radical ideas from France. These natural social relationships were also seen to operate on the smaller scale of the family. The family was a divinely created microcosm of the natural society in which the rights and duties of the individual members corresponded to those of the different estates and the strength of the family was regarded as one of the pillars of the organic society. This emphasis on the natural form of the relationships between the different classes of society was an impediment to a programme of social reform: to seek to regulate the social problem in an artificial way by legislation, as the liberals proposed, was to tamper with the 'organic' nature of the State.

A further barrier to any initiative for a systematic programme of social reform was the unwillingness of many conservatives even to recognise the growth of an urban proletariat or to grasp that its problems were a legitimate long-term cause for concern. To many conservatives the problems of the 1840s were simply a reflection of the natural order of things, demonstrating the inadequacies of some individuals. In their organic view of society the proletariat had no place at all. Indeed many considered the proletariat as barely distinguishable from the 'criminal classes'. The rise of this class and the existence of the social question, in so far as it was even recognised, was held to be a *disease* of society, a pathological condition in which the natural relationships between estates had failed. The cure lay in strengthening traditional forms rather than social reform.

Those concerned with the condition of the poor argued, like Johann Heinrich Wichern, founder of the Innere Mission, that the proper response to social distress should be charity, the Christian responsibility of the higher estates towards those of lower estate.[25] Property enshrined the inequalities pre-ordained by God and carried with it essential obligations on the propertied classes towards the poor. The problems of poverty and distress were to be combated by a return to faith and a reawakening of brotherly love, of caritas, as in the evangelical work of the Innere Mission. Rather than elaborating a programme which would have brought immediate benefits and relief from the worst aspects of industrialism, the principal concern of Wichern and his followers was to win those in distress away from the threat of the socialist doctrines spreading from France and back to faith. Only by this recovery of faith could the social problem be solved.

Already by 1848, however, Huber recognised that this conservative ideal could offer no effective means of resolving the social problems of the working classes of the huge industrial cities he had seen for himself on his visit to England in 1844 and where the degrading housing conditions of the workers had already attracted his attention. In letters to his wife, and in *Janus*, he had set out his reactions to visiting the industrial areas of Birmingham and Manchester where he saw the workers flooding exhausted out of the factories at the end of a shift and keenly felt their sullen rejection of the whole social system that made such misery possible. To Huber, even in the mid-1840s, the situation in England was a terrible warning of events to come; Germany had to learn from the English example if she were to avoid the same damaging mistakes. The evils of English conditions where 'the greater part of the factory owners serve only Mammon and the workers work only to fill their stomachs'[26] had to be replaced on the one hand by an awareness of the factory owner of his obligations to his workers, and on the other by a strengthening of the ability of the worker to survive economically by combining together.

By 1848, though still maintaining his links with Wichern and the Innere Mission, Huber was drifting away from conservative circles – he ceased to edit *Janus* in this year – and began to explore a new approach to the social problem. Central to this was the formation of what he called 'latent associations'. Huber's ideas on associations came partly from his trip to England in 1844 and partly from the limited German experience of the time. While in the north of England, he had admired the work of the building societies and the idea of co-operation had left a deep impression on him.[27] Nearer home, Huber was familiar with the efforts of G. S. Liedke to develop co-operative associations in Berlin. Working in the area North of the Hamburger Tor (which included Voigtland) Liedke had successfully launched a savings society which enabled working men engaged in seasonal trades to 'put money by' during the period when they were in work in anticipation of the 'off season'.[28] These ideas were taken up by Huber but combined, in the form of the 'latent association', with the idea of leadership and management of the societies by the educated and upper classes during a transitional period, or at least until the working classes had learnt how to organise themselves. This form of the association, as described in pamphlets such as *Selbsthilfe der arbeitenden Klassen durch Wirtschaftsvereine und innere Ansiedlung*,[29] was to combine the drive of self-help with the ideal of help from 'above', even from government: 'The individual standing alone, be he ever so strong, is powerless against the tide of hard times and unemployment – alone he cannot stem or stay the flood, nor build a dam to protect the spot on which his cottage stands, but together with his neighbours, and under strong leadership, he can strengthen the

dam...raising its level so that both he and his companions are safe.'
In this form, the association was to be central to Huber's ideas on social
reform in a wide variety of fields and was to be extended to 'every branch
of the economy of the working man's family'.[30]

The application of these ideas to housing was a natural priority and
a discussion of the way that the association could be used to improve
housing conditions, strengthening the family and family life, already
appears for the first time in an article 'Über innere Colonisation'
in *Janus*[31] in 1845, extended and clarified in his pamphlet *Selbsthilfe*.
Huber starts from the assumption that current responses to the social
question are not enough, charity and the giving of alms cannot resolve
a problem of such magnitude: 'the propertied and ruling classes labour
under the dangerous conceit that there is no basis for the social
question...[and behave] as it if were possible to distance oneself from
the whole issue by simply maintaining the values of tradition...'[32] In
place of this complacency he urges the affluent and powerful to assist
and encourage the workers to help themselves. Associations were to be
formed which would provide well-constructed housing either in the
centre of cities at high density near existing employment or in the
suburbs as cottage housing near new industry. Here family life was to
flourish uncontaminated by the dangers of the industrial city. The
assistance of the propertied classes was to take the form of buying shares
or standing surety for loans for the housing. While it would be beyond
the ability of any single working man to take out a large enough loan
to build housing, the rents that the members of the association could
afford should, taken together, be sufficient to pay both interest and
amortisation of a loan without difficulty.

The programme that Huber set out looks forward to the intentions that
lay behind the Berliner gemeinnützige Baugesellschaft. It reflects
attitudes to social problems that combine elements of both conservative
and liberal thinking. He rejects the idea that charity could resolve the
social problems of the time but still looks to the propertied classes and
their sense of obligation to provide capital and leadership for the associations; he lays great stress on the individualist virtues of self-help but
argues that without help from 'above' the associations stand little
chance of success. He was convinced that a programme of action which
went beyond mere charity was necessary. By the end of the decade
Huber was alreading moving towards the views of those in liberal circles
who believed that a programme of social reform was essential.[33]

Liberal attitudes to the social problem

In contrast to the arguments of those such as Carl David Rau and John
Prince-Smith[34] who urged the case for economic individualism and free
enterprise, there were a number of liberals who were convinced of the
need for a programme of social reform to counteract the worst excesses
of the social problem. While Prince-Smith might dryly define pauperism
as 'the condition of men...whose needs are not in balance with their

productivity, and who cannot therefore subsist without the help of others',[35] the editors and authors of the *Staatslexikon* (a 'political dictionary' and one of the most important formulations of the political liberal view before 1848) Friedrich List, Karl Rotteck, Karl Theodor Welcker, Robert von Mohl and others were setting out a different view of liberalism. In opposition both to the conservative ideal of the organic state and to those liberals who urged the minimum of government they called for a State, ordered on rational principles, which would intervene in social issues if necessary and which might go so far as to fix minimum wages or launching programmes of public works.

The 'social liberals' form a loose group which included, besides those associated with the *Staatslexikon*, academics like Karl Biedermann, industrialists like Friedrich Harkort and Gustav Mevissen who had first-hand experience of industrialisation and its consequences and even doctors like Rudolf Virchow and Solomon Neumann; their views do not form a single unity but share a number of common themes. Most did not doubt that industrialisation and the freedom of trade would lead to greater prosperity in the long run, but there was widespread agreement that it was the present workings and structure of society, rather than the failings of the individual, that gave rise to the problems of mass poverty and pauperism. Through no fault of their own, whole classes might be thrown into unemployment and poverty from which they would be unable to rescue themselves except with the assistance of others. The range of remedies offered varied but a central element of all proposals was a programme of legislation; first, to offset the causes of poverty by introducing old-age pensions, insurance schemes for the sick and the disabled and a form of graduated income tax; second, to restrain the power of the factory owner to exploit his work-force by prohibiting the use of child labour, to outlaw insanitary and dangerous working conditions and even, in the proposals of Mohl and Mevissen to fix minimum wage levels.

As a complement to legislative action, the social liberals also sought to encourage the formation of different types of co-operative associations which would help the working man to help himself, co-operatives for savings, for manufacture and for purchasing which would enable the working man to rise above the vagaries of the trade cycle and to compete on the open market using all the benefits of size that helped the owners of factories or capital. Yet other associations were to be founded for purposes which included sanitary improvement, prison reform and education; for many, as for Harkort, education and training was a key to the development of the individual's maximum potential, an essential requirement if he was to compete effectively in a free market.

The range of interest of the social liberals is exemplified by the diversity of the work of the Central Verein für das Wohl der arbeitenden Klassen (CVWaK)[36] founded in 1844 by a number of industrialists concerned at the shadow side of industrialisation and at the growing unrest in certain parts of the country, particularly the rising of the Silesian weavers earlier that year. Launched during the celebration of industrial progress at the Berlin Trade Fair, it set out to provide a framework to enable those who had benefited from the recent development of industry to help the labouring classes; it was intended to provide a defence against the influx of 'socialist' ideas from France: a satisfied labour force clearly offered a better surety against these dangerous ideas than censorship. It was organised as a series of local societies, many of which, for example the Cologne branch, were very active; the work of these local societies was then co-ordinated and communicated by a Centralverein in Berlin which was also responsible for publishing the society's journal the *Mittheilungen* (later *Der Arbeiterfreund*)[37] which provides an uninterrupted record of the interests of the reforming liberals through until 1914. The foundation of the society was widely greeted, Harkort hailed its programme as evidence of the coming of a new attitude to the social problem: 'We stand on the eve of great progress in social relations. The mighty spirit of association is ready through brotherly love to close the broad gap which separates the lower from the upper classes',[38] even the Kaiser made a grant of 15,000 Thaler to encourage the Verein's work.

The programme of the Society during the 1840s illustrates well the application of the ideas of the social liberals in practice. The principal emphasis of the society's work was to encourage the formation of a variety of co-operative associations to enable the working man to help himself; one of the most important tasks of the Centralverein was to inform the various local societies of successful applications of co-operative or other reforming ideas in different fields across the country. But equally important, at least before the 1850s, was the discussion of a variety of different legislative measures to improve the conditions of the working classes.

To organise this wide range of interests, the scope of the association's work was subdivided into a number of specialised areas; in 1850 fourteen areas of interest had been identified, each the responsibility of a small committee.[39] Most important was the interest of the Society in the economic position of the worker and the extent to which this could be bettered by co-operation and the encouragement of thrift. Within this broad field there were separate sub-committees which dealt with savings banks, old age and illness insurance and a whole range of applications of the principle of co-operative saving schemes. The importance of education as a crucial element of social reform was reflected in the number of committees concerned with educational matters and with distributing the information gathered by the local societies. In addition to the work of the Society in these two major fields there were other committees concerned with particular aspects of the social problem: with the prison system, factory conditions, child employment, the conditions of agricultural labourers and, finally, with public health and, significantly, the problems of housing.

Even in the 1840s the Society's interest in housing focusses on the application of the co-operative principle to the provision of working-class accommodation. This was a natural extension of the ideas of the Society and parallelled those of other liberals such as Faucher, who had already published a pamphlet on the subject, *Die Vereinigung von Sparkasse und Hypothekenbank und der Anschluss eines Häuserbauvereins*, in 1845.[40] This extension of the co-operative idea was particularly appropriate at a time when the families of even well-paid workers were finding it difficult to rent adequate housing in Berlin, a problem already revealed in studies of the local society in Berlin during the 1840s.[41] It was also a recognition of the need to secure good housing as a means of improving both the economic and moral conditions of the working classes; without a proper home setting, how could the family flourish? Huber, for example, maintained that a clean, healthy and decent house constituted the starting point and necessary precondition for any wider programme of social reform. If the working man was to own his home, an ideal that the English building societies showed was within the reach of some, then co-operation and association was the only way.[42]

The Berliner gemeinnützige Baugesellschaft

The first and one of the best documented of the early housing societies that resulted from these initiatives was the Berliner gemeinnützige Baugesellschaft,[43] the first non-profit building society in Berlin. It provides the most complete illustration of the application of the ideas on housing reform to emerge during the 1840s, and the protracted history of its foundation, together with the frustrations that accompanied it and the opposition that it aroused, convey vividly the savour of housing reform in practice.

As early as 1841 C. W. Hoffmann, *Landbaumeister* in the service of the Prussian court, suggested at a meeting of the Berliner Architektenverein that architects should be encourage to submit designs for working-class housing at the Verein's monthly review of work with a view to stimulating interest in the construction of housing for the lower income groups. The Verein dismissed the suggestion on the grounds that this form of housing was unworthy of architectural consideration, so Hoffmann raised the issue in slightly different form, launching, together with Gerichts-Assessor Gäbler and Bauingenieur Wilhelm Emmich, both active members of the CVWaK, a scheme for a co-operative housing project; but this idea, too, foundered for want of support.

In 1846, stirred by Huber's article 'Über innere Colonisation' and by the mounting concern for the housing conditions of the poor, Hoffmann again turned to housing, this time founding the Verein zur Verbesserung der Arbeiterwohnungen. The Verein served as a rallying point for a number of different reforming interests with a conservative Christian background united by the common concern for the 'improvement of the moral conditions of the poorer classes and their preservation from misleading and incendiary tendencies'[44] by means of building improved housing.

After extended debate within the Verein on the best way in which to provide housing, Hoffmann launched the Berliner gemeinnützige

Baugesellschaft (BgB) in February 1847 with the publication of the pamphlet *Die Aufgabe einer Berliner gemeinnützigen Baugesellschaft*; by November, with the assistance of a steering committee consisting of Hoffmann, Gäbler and Liedke, the statutes of the society had been agreed. In mid-1848 Huber joined the Verein offering his services to edit the Verein's journal *Concordia, Blätter der Berliner Gemeinnützigen Baugesellschaft*; with the aid of his efforts a wider membership was attracted. But this period of progress was followed by a series of delays in obtaining Royal assent to the statutes. Eventually, however, this was resolved by the intervention of Schöner, a court official, whose attention had been caught by Hoffmann's pamphlet and who was eventually able to interest the King in the proposals. With Royal support at last, progress was again swift; by October the statutes had been approved.

The form of organisation finally agreed was that of a joint stock company with a dividend limited to only 4%, a decision that was to attract criticism from liberal circles in later years. This choice represented something of a compromise between the desire to initiate from above the setting up of an organisation along co-operative lines, as suggested by Huber, and the difficulties caused by the lack of any form of legal status or protection that faced the co-operative movement in general: a difficulty that was magnified by the large sums of money necessarily involved with a project of this scale. The stock company which was to raise the capital for the project was to be complemented by a tenants' co-operative which was to enable the BgB to realise its primary goal of helping deserving artisans to acquire a home of their own: 'eigen-thumslose Arbeiter in arbeitender Eigenthümer zu verwandeln'. The form of this co-operative was simple: when all the dwellings in a particular block had been let, the tenants were to be formed into an association each buying an initial share; by paying the monthly rental the tenant would amortise the loan and service the initial capital, finally acquiring the dwelling at the end of a 30-year period.

From the start, the aim of the BgB was to provide housing only for the respectable working-class families with the chance of home-ownership as well. Tenants were to be restricted to those who had lived in Berlin for five or more years, who were known to be of good character, hard working and respectably married. The company was to provide a means for the artisan to get his 'foot on the ladder' and thus to rise in society; there was no suggestion that the BgB was to help the poor. This bias towards the artisan is clearly reflected in the occupations of the tenants: of the 147 heads of households in 1851, only 55 were classed as hand or factory workers or journeymen, while 56 were classed as artisans and another 20 as officials or functionaries.[45]

Considerable publicity was given to the BgB from 1848 onwards both through the company's own journal *Concordia* and the *Mittheilungen* of the CVWaK which presented the BgB as a paradigm for general emulation. The original membership list shows the extent of the company's support amongst the upper classes of the time; it included the names of men like Alexander von Humboldt, Friedrich Karl von

Savigny, Ernst Litfass, August Borsig, ministers, high officials, army officers, bankers and religious leaders of the major denominations, even a number of Freemasons.[46] Of great value, both socially and politically, was the enthusiasm of the King, who bought 2,000 Thalers worth of shares and gave an annual contribution of 200 Thalers.

Despite this support, the company did not win the backing that its promoters had expected. This may have been due in part to the delays in launching the company: the first annual meeting was only held in January 1849, two years after the first pamphlet. By this time, as Hoffmann sadly remarked, the enthusiasm for building and the willingness to subscribe money for building working-class housing had been damaged by the revolutionary events of March 1848. Another deterrent to investors may have been the low level and the uncertainty of the return on capital which would have reduced the attractiveness of the venture to investors, apart from those acting for philanthropic reasons. But even more disadvantageous was the opposition of the greater part of the Berlin press which reflected the views of the property owners and rate payers so well represented on the Stadtverordneteversammlung and misrepresented the company and its intentions to middle-class readers. The representatives of the property interests on the city council rightly interpreted the programme of the BgB as an indictment of the housing from which so many of their fellow landlords profited so handsomely. They therefore refused to support the company or to ease the task of the BgB in any way and financial support from the City of Berlin was conspicuous by its absence.

Nevertheless by October 1849 the first 20 dwellings on the Ritterstrasse were ready for occupation. By March of the following year, all the dwellings in the block were let and the first tenants' co-operatives started. By July the buildings on the Michaeliskirchstrasse, the Wollanckstrasse (renamed the Lothringer Strasse and now the Wilhelm-Pieckstrasse) (fig. 5) and the Alexandrinenstrasse were also ready and by the end of 1850 93 dwellings were completed and nine tenants' co-operatives had been formed. By 1851 over 700 people were being accommodated in the housing provided by the company, which by this time comprised 16 'fore' buildings and 6 rear buildings together with 21 associated workshops.[47]

It is true that the finished buildings did not correspond exactly to the ideals that Huber had originally laid down in *Die Selbsthilfe*. The plans for building cottage housing had not yet materialised, nor had the common facilities, the library or the kindergarten; more damaging to the basic aims of the company were the difficulties with the tenants' co-operatives: no new co-operatives were formed after 1850 and the future of those already formed seemed shaky. But much had been achieved. The quality of the dwellings was high, the tenements were light and generous in size, each with living rooms of 20 m² and a kitchen with ample cross-ventilation. The annual rents of between 20 and 75 Thaler were regarded as very reasonable; indeed compared with an average rent in the city in 1850 of 99 Thaler, they represented

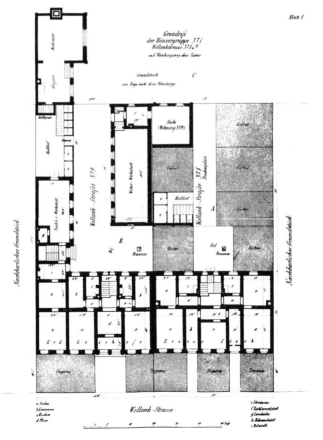

5 C. W. Hoffmann's design
   for the buildings of the
   Berliner gemeinnützige
   Baugesellschaft on the
   Wollankstrasse (now the
   Wilhelm-Pieckstrasse)

extremely good value.[48] As confirmation of the viability of the original idea, Huber and Hoffmann could still claim with justification that a number of the tenants' co-operatives were still functioning. By the mid-1850s the principle of achieving home-ownership through co-operative associations could be shown, with qualifications, to be feasible even in Berlin.

Housing and the social problem in the 1850s: the loss of momentum

The combination of the conservative social policies of the reactionary 1850s and the economic expansion of the years between 1850 and 1857 provided a context for the discussion of the social problem which was very different from that of the late 1840s.[49] In contrast to the harsh economic climate of 1846–8 when the early industrial advances seemed threatened as banks and firms faced collapse, and when pauperism seemed to be increasing without check, the 1850s saw a new expansion of the economy and the first real progress towards industrialisation. But the benefits of this expansion were unevenly distributed. Pockets of intense poverty remained, the proportion of the population supported by poor relief alone continued to cause concern, even in areas like the Ruhr or in Berlin where the new economic expansion was most rapid. Despite the mood of business optimism and the increase in the demand for labour as new jobs were created, the rise in the real value of wages was eroded by rising prices. Hammerow's optimistic view of the economy of the period must be complemented by Kuczynski's pessimistic interpretation which even shows a fall in average real incomes for the period 1850–7 to its lowest level for the whole period between 1840 and 1866.[50] Nevertheless the prevailing mood appears to have been one of economic optimism, at least for the future. Investors looked forward to a favourable future as they bought stocks and shares; the haunting fear that nothing could check the spread of pauperism gradually receded.

The economic optimism of the 1850s could not dispel anxiety over the social question, but in the changed context the issue appeared less threatening. Conservative awareness of the urban poor advanced beyond the point that it had reached in the 1840s, but this still did not lead to a new approach to the social question. Friedrich Julius Stahl considered that the social question and issues such as pauperism were still to be resolved within the framework of charity and the obligations of property: 'To cloak property relationships with supervisory power and an obligation to the propertyless is the only solution to the social question, if indeed it can be solved. There is no other.'[51] Even those more in contact with the realities of contemporary urban life produced no practicable programme of reform, despite attempts of a number of conservative writers and journalists with the *Kreuzzeitung* and the *Fliegende Blätter*, notably Hermann Wagener, to provide a greater understanding of the difficulties faced by the poor. During the 1850s they offered a detailed discussion of poverty, of living standards, even housing conditions, and kept the social problem before the eyes of its readers, but to no avail. The conservative view continued to emphasise the importance of general principles as a response to these specific problems: the return to faith and the strengthening of an organic society were to solve the whole variety of problems facing the working classes.

The liberal response was no more positive. Although the 1850s was a time of political trial for the liberals, many among their circles benefited directly from the expansion of the economy, and the arguments of those who had pressed for free enterprise and unrestrained individualism were greatly strengthened. Writers such as Prince-Smith and Otto Michaelis could now point to the recent turn of events as evidence to show that the miseries of the late 1840s were merely a passing phase of necessary, if painful, adjustment. As the fears of pauperism diminished, the concern for the shadow side of economic progress and the negative consequence of industrialisation receded. In the more favourable economic climate of the 1850s the reforming programmes of the social liberals looked anachronistic when compared to the apparent clarity and vigour of arguments in favour of economic individualism, and these views acquired yet further prestige and plausibility when combined with the 'scientific' theories of the social Darwinists. The new emphasis on self-help and co-operation is well represented by figures like Herman Schulze-Delitzsch whose views on co-operative associations allowed no room for the paternalistic assistance and leadership from the upper classes that Huber had urged:

Anyone who claims the right to assistance, even be it from the State, immediately places himself under the authority and supervision of another and thus surrenders his independence. This is to capitulate, to despair of one's own powers; indeed this is the more wrong and the more unnecessary since co-operation has already demonstrated that the workers can help themselves, if they but set about it in the right way, and that they do not stand in need of help from anyone.[52]

An optimistic discussion of the benefits of co-operation and the possibility of its application for the resolution of different aspects of the social problem now dominated liberal thinking.

Whatever the justification for the general impression of an improvement in living standards, it is clear that housing conditions did not in fact improve. In Berlin the 1850s did not see anything to compare with the flood of immigrants to the city of the previous decade; but even this slow rate of population increase was difficult to house. In the mid-1850s when the desperate need for capital was reflected in interest rates higher than at any time during the 1840s, the building industry, with its relatively low rates of return, could not attract enough capital to build. The result was that the rate of construction of new housing remained, of necessity, low. For the period 1850–5 average annual increase in the number of dwellings was a third of that in the early 1840s.[53]

Not surprisingly, with so few dwellings being built, the pressure on the housing market increased, as can be seen from fig. 4, to the point where the number of empty dwellings fell below the levels of the worst years in the 1840s; in 1853 only 1·1% of all dwellings were empty, compared with 2·3% for 1847; by 1857 the situation was even more serious with 0·9% – only 769 dwellings – empty in the whole city. The housing crisis was reflected in the increases in the average rent for the city as a whole; this rose from the low point of 295 M per year to which it had sunk in 1850, to 346 M per year in 1857.[54] This increase may have been unexceptional in comparison with the increases in other prices over the same period but for the lower income groups, the 'kleine Leute', of large cities, this led to a real deterioration in conditions as even the most miserable dwellings were rented by families desperate for somewhere to live.

Although the idea of a general 'housing problem', to be met by a programme of 'housing reform', was still not current during the 1850s, the seriousness of housing conditions did find a reflection in the increasing numbers of studies concerned with particular aspects of the housing shortage. Conservative journals now drew their readers' attention to the housing shortage, and the inadequacies of housing provided the setting for a variety of cartoons (fig. 6); mounting anxiety over housing was also reflected in the *Mittheilungen* of the CVWaK. This interest is typified by an article by E. Knoblauch,[55] 'Warum werden in Berlin nicht mehr Gebäude mit kleinen Wohnungen gebaut?', published in 1855, which emphasises the growing public unease at the inability of the building industry to build adequate housing for the working class, or even for the middle class. Emmich, an active member of the Berlin branch of the CVWaK and an original member of the BgB, made a more detailed examination of the housing market in the same year, looking closely at housing costs and rents, and concluded that it was impossible to provide adequate working-class housing within the context of a free housing market.[56]

How should we judge the discussion of housing during the 1850s? The picture that emerges is a fragmented one. The work of the BgB has traditionally been hailed by historians as the start of the housing reform movement in Germany. It illustrates the extension of the ideas of self-help and co-operation to yet another field as well as demonstrating a general interest in the problems of housing; but in practice it remained an isolated positive response to the problems and was increasingly moribund from the mid-1850s. There is, it is true, a growing concern for the housing conditions of the lower income groups, particularly as the pressure on accommodation built up through the decade. But the investigations that are carried out are still seen in isolation, as separate studies of aspects of life in an urban society where all is not well. At this time these problems are still pictured as part of the general social question. Despite the mounting interest in poor housing conditions by architects, doctors and others, the individual studies that they produce do not yet appear to have been seen as part of some larger 'housing problem', distinct from the social question. This remains the case right up until the end of the period of prosperity of the early 1850s. It is only with the economic crisis of 1857 and the acute housing shortage that

6 Contemporary perceptions
of the Housing Problem.
The caption reads:

'Wilhelm, where are you lodging?'

'Nowhere at the moment. Because my landlord tried to raise the rent for the third time, I moved into the Thiergarten for the summer; but now it is too damp and the ground is too cold because there's no heating, still, I'm going to wait there until they have finished this project for building cheap housing.'

'But haven't you been able to get any form of accommodation in some public building?'

accompanied it that the connection between these separate issues is seen to be essential and that the debate about the 'housing question' emerges as a pressing social issue in its own right. The economic crisis brought on a housing crisis: while rents rose higher than ever before, the proportion of empty dwellings slumped to 0·9%, the lowest it had ever been, and remained at that level for two years. The time had now come for Huber and others concerned with the social problem to follow the example of English reformers and to alert public consciousness to the threat of poor housing to both family and home by forcing general recognition of the 'housing problem' that had long existed.

'Oh yes. But they won't give you a key for the Litfass columns*, and in a letter box you get collected every hour; I'm just on my way to the Council to see if they can direct me to some convenient water pipe where at last I might be left in peace.'

* Litfass gave his name to the columns used for displaying advertisements in Berlin, he was also a member of the Committee that backed the founding of the Berliner gemeinnützige Baugesellschaft.

2

◇◆◇

The first debate on the Housing Problem, 1857–72

By the beginning of the 1860s Huber was quoting Shaftesbury's descriptions of the 'housing problem' in London as equally applicable to conditions in Berlin: 'I do not hesitate to state that nineteen twentieths of all evil has its roots in these (terrible housing) conditions; their removal must be the ambition and the wish of every true friend of our country and our people... Indeed for many thousands of families the 'home' of which we are so proud, has no meaning. The man who contrives to exist (in such misery) with his wife and children cannot lay claim to be the head of a family; he is simply the biggest pig in the sty.'[1] Most important, Huber was trying to impress on his contemporaries that the 'housing problem' was no longer something remote, a particularly English affliction, but an evil that was, at that very minute, degrading and corrupting thousands of working-class families in cities all over Germany. In contrast to the views of the 1850s, it was now clear to Huber that there was indeed a housing problem in Germany; but what had brought about this change in thinking?

To Huber, returning to Berlin in 1857 fresh from his impressions of the achievements of Robert Ashley in London and Jean Dollfus in Mulhouse, the inactivity over the housing crisis in German cities must have appeared intolerable.[2] To allow these conditions to persist was an affront to humanity; spurred on by what he had just seen abroad he argued vehemently for a committed assault on the problem in the manner of the English housing reformers, 'Brougham, Russell, a D'Israeli, a Derby, a Morpeth, a Dickens and others – not forgetting that the whole English reform movement in this field proceeds under the auspices and the patronage of a German prince, Albert, the Prince Consort.'[3]

From 1857 onwards, interest in the housing crisis had quickened. As a member of the committee of the Evangelischer Verein in Berlin, Huber lectured early in the year on the subject, identifying the housing problem as a major social evil and presenting it as more than just a component of the larger social question.[4] Nor was Huber's a lone voice. From 1857 the *Mittheilungen* of the CVWaK began to show a sustained interest in the problems of housing. Indicative of this is a study by E. Krieger of conditions in the notorious cellar dwellings in Berlin.[5] Drawing not only on the limited data for Berlin but also on English and

French sources, Krieger investigated in detail the incidence of disease in areas where cellar dwellings predominated and recognised that the only means of avoiding the use of these dwellings by the poor during a shortage of housing was by some form of legislation to control the natural inclination of both tenants and landlords to continue to use unfit housing. The removal of the breeding grounds of diseases such as cholera which threatened the health of the whole city he regarded as ample justification for legislative intervention and something that should be championed by a movement for reform.

The following year saw the publication of further articles on the same theme; the CVWaK carried an account by Emmich of housing reform and the housing problem in England, complete with illustrations of the Prince Consort's Cottages exhibited at the Great Exhibition, and provided detailed reports on the work of Henry Roberts in England and Edouard Ducpétiaux in Belgium. In 1859 Huber published an extended account of the housing problem in France and England and means taken to combat it;[6] Emmich contributed another article discussing the progress of the BgB and the other means available to relieve the current housing difficulties in Berlin.[7] Medical journals too, for example the *Monatsschrift für Sanitätspolizei*, were equally active in exposing the inescapable connection between poor housing, disease and high mortality rates.[8] By the early 1860s the housing problem had become the focus of attention of a number of different reforming interests: the housing reform movement, in all its diversity, was under way.

Early writings on the Housing Problem: *Concordia*

Typical of this early debate about housing as a problem in its own right are the two influential articles that Huber wrote in 1861 for his own occasional periodical *Concordia*. These articles are worth examining not only as being amongst the first extended discussions on the subject but also because they present the problem and possible means of relief in terms that were to be frequently repeated throughout the coming decade.

The first article, 'Die Wohnungsfrage: Die Noth', presents a description of the inadequacies of the existing situation. In contrast to previous studies which had dealt with isolated issues relating to housing, Huber confronts his contemporaries with a housing problem of whose existence he considered most people in Germany to be unaware: "What has this continual reference to English conditions to do with us? Surely there can be no housing problem here in Germany!' The tone of impatience in the questions and the statements of our readers can best be rendered thus.' He attacks the naivety of those who could persist in supporting the 'monstrous illusion that in Germany the housing shortage has yet to become socially damaging... Germany must learn from the example of England before time runs out.'[9]

By pointing to the achievement of the English reformers and contrasting this with the inadequacy of responses in Berlin, Huber hoped to stimulate the German conscience into action. The vital importance of a good home for the moral salvation of the working classes is vigorously advanced: 'Certainly it would not be too much to say that the home is the communal embodiment of family life. Thus the purity of the dwelling is almost as important for the family as is the cleanliness of the body for the individual. Good or bad housing is a question of life or death if ever there was one.'[10] Huber, writing at a time when overcrowding and particularly the number of *Schlafgänger* in Berlin was rising, emphasised good housing as an essential basis for a strong family life.

The dangers of inaction are also portrayed. Huber echoed the warnings of those like Wichern and Wilhelm Riehl who saw the corrosive consequences of poor housing to the family. Bad housing would damage family life, striking at one of the stabilising elements of society, dissolving the bonds between parents and children, loosening the ties of marriage, thus creating a spiritual and moral vacuum. Huber illustrates the effects of bad housing with a dramatised account of the fall of a noble worker and his family; in this cautionary tale the dangers of drink for the father, the corrupting presence of the *Schlafburschen* for the purity of the daughter and the mother's illness caused by the damp and overcrowding are vividly, if mawkishly, portrayed.

In the second article, 'Die Hülfe', Huber discusses different ways in which the inadequacies of the existing situation set out in the first article could be remedied. The range of solutions offered is drawn largely from English sources and of course from Huber's own experience with the BgB. For Huber the principal causes of the housing shortage are the failure and inadequacies of the method of housing development and construction; efforts of the reformers must therefore be concentrated here. Charity he dismisses as a wholly inappropriate solution: 'Housing Reform cannot be carried out on the basis of voluntary charity, even if the necessary material means (namely money) were available, which currently they are not; social and moral reasons combine to suggest that such a solution is wholly ill-suited to this field.'[11] Instead, he argues that the most effective means of attack would be to bring about reform by ensuring proper competition in the housing market. The task of the reformers was to stimulate the building of 'model' dwellings at reasonable rents to force private landlords to raise the standards of their housing. The 'model' dwellings were to be built either by co-operative associations, both those assisted from above and those founded on self-help, of the form Huber had been describing since the mid-1840s, or by companies conceived along the lines of the BgB, or even by large employers whether a private company, the city or the State. For Huber the only limitation on the potential of these ideas was the ignorance of the propertied classes, and those who might contribute the capital, of the true state of affairs. If they could but see the terrible conditions in which so many hard-working and decent families were forced to live, Huber had no doubt that the capital for these projects would be forthcoming. Thus one of the most important tasks for the housing reformer was to publicise the housing problem and to bring it to the centre of the public debate on the social question.

For Huber the resolution of the problems of housing was of fundamental importance to the solutions of the social problem. Unless some improvement could be made, he argued, the position of the working classes would go from bad to worse: 'The present housing conditions of the worker, of the poor, of the great mass of the people, are already one of the greatest and most pressing social evils of the present, and, as the population increases, will become worse and worse unless this evil is immediately and effectively controlled by vigorous and far-reaching counter-measures.'[12]

Liberal attitudes to social problems in the 1860s

Despite this burgeoning awareness of the existence of a housing problem, the starting point from which the question was approached was scarcely different from those of the 1850s; only in the early 1870s do new attitudes begin to emerge. This continuation of the views of the 1850s is clearly reflected in the discussions of the housing problem in the CVWaK and at the annual meetings of the Kongress deutscher Volkswirte (KdV), a body founded in 1857 and concerned predominantly with economic issues approached from the standpoint of economic individualism and free trade which Cobden and Bright had established as the Manchester brand of liberalism. These two organisations are the most important fora for the discussion of the housing problem but the issue was taken up by a number of other bodies. Both the Vereinstag deutscher Arbeitervereine (VdA) and the Vereinstag deutscher Erwerbs- und Wirtschaftsgenossenschaften (VdEW) provided a platform for the discussion of the housing question and both were active in their support for the co-operative housing movement. The VdA published Friedrich Albert Lange's book *Jedermann Hauseigenthümer* in 1865,[13] an appeal for housing co-operatives very closely modelled on the form of the English building societies; at the meetings of the VdEW, Ludolf Parisius, who was also active in the CVWaK and KdV, elaborated the ideas on co-operative housing associations that were to be published in 1865 as 'Die auf dem Prinzip der Selbsthülfe beruhende Baugenossenschaft'.[14] Membership of the different groups overlapped considerably, with many, for example Schulze-Delitzsch, Adolph Lette, and even Huber, taking an active part in both the KdV and the CVWaK. While the interests of the KdV were more specifically economic than those of the CVWaK, the attitudes of the two groups, as evident in their journals the *Vierteljahrschrift für Volkswirtschaft und Kulturgeschichte* (*VfVK*) and the *Arbeiterfreund*,[15] were broadly similar at least until the mid-1860s. Thereafter there is some divergence of views: the members of the KdV remain true to the *Manchesterismus* of Faucher and Prince-Smith, while the members of the CVWaK, perhaps as a reflection of the social liberal

origins of the Society, supported, with growing enthusiasm, the case for
State intervention.

In the early 1860s, self-help, with its natural extension in the
principle of co-operation, remains the cornerstone of liberal approaches
to the social problem for members of both the KdV and CVWak. In an
article, 'Die sogenannte Arbeiterfrage', Prince-Smith urged the case for
economic individualism with all the conviction of the Manchester
school:

> Work and save! Let need drive you forward; let the benefits ahead of you
> redouble your energy, let it increase your determination to tread the first steps
> towards the satisfaction of your economic needs – let it give you strength to do
> what no member of your family has ever achieved in a thousand years, namely,
> to save something from the daily struggle for survival with which to advance
> yourself both spiritually and economically. Economic success awaits only those
> who help themselves.[16]

The same views, though perhaps less extremely phrased, were shared
by members of the CVWaK. Summarising the history and development
of the Society, Lette, president of the CVWaK and also a member of the
central committee of the KdV, placed the same emphasis on the
importance of self-help in dealing with social problems:

> The Central Verein recognised from the very start that a sure and lasting success
> in improving the conditions of the working classes can never be won with help
> from outside or above, least of all with the help of charitable institutions or the
> rich; this has always proved inadequate for the task. The improvement of these
> conditions can only be brought about through the moral and economic efforts
> of the working classes themselves, through self-help, through co-operative
> action by the workers and through their recognition that, first and foremost,
> it is every individual who is responsible for his own moral and economic
> well-being.[17]

For both groups, co-operation was a central article of faith, a means
to ensure that even the working man could compete in the free market
created by the removal of economic restrictions. Both the KdV and
CVWaK were vigorous in urging the adoption of the ideas of Schulze-
Delitzsch, Liedke, Friedrich Wilhelm, Raiffeisen and others on co-
operative savings banks, co-operative ownership of the means of
production and co-operation in purchasing. The same message of
co-operation was proclaimed equally strongly as a defence against the
economic difficulties brought on by ill-health, old-age and death.

Yet despite the common ground shared by the members of the two
groups, it is possible, even in the early 1860s, to detect differences in
emphasis between those who urged that the virtues of self-help alone
would triumph, a view championed more strongly amongst the membership of the KdV, and those who were convinced of the need for some
form of leadership or intervention to promote self-help, a view held by
a number of members of the CVWaK.

The former view was stated with bravado by Prince-Smith. In 'Die
sogennante Arbeiterfrage' he bitterly attacked the attempts of reformers
to better conditions of the working classes by meddling with economic

processes, likening them to quacks and charlatans. Instead, he argued that the workers should in fact be grateful for the advances in industrialisation which provided opportunities for employment thus permitting an increase in wages which would eventually lead to an improvement, rather than a deterioration, in living standards. Given this optimistic view of the nature of economic progress, Prince-Smith did not hesitate to assert that success lay open to those determined enough to succeed.

The opposing view was less forcefully argued. But the need for some positive action to improve the lot of the working classes, a continuation of the ideals of the social liberals of the 1840s, was urged by the CVWaK in a number of fields. Even in the writings of the Classical economists such as Nassau Senior and J. R. McCullough, public health and education had been viewed as areas in which 'the non-intervention principle' might legitimately be set aside. In the *Arbeiterfreund* this point of view was argued in a number of articles calling for State intervention in education and far more vigorous action by the sanitary authorities in the field of public health. Indeed by the mid-1860s the need for some form of legislative control of housing was recognised by the CVWaK as desirable. In calling for some form of action on housing, Lette was not only recognising the housing question as an issue in its own right but also the necessity for intervention in such social problems.[18]

The liberal debate on housing and the triumph of *Manchesterismus*

In presenting the problems of housing as an area in which reform was needed and an issue with which the CVWaK should be concerned, Huber and others were raising for general discussion a potentially divisive issue. To demand recognition and intervention for the housing problem was to suggest that private enterprise, self-help and co-operation were not sufficient to meet the problems of housing. Liberals associated with the KdV denied that housing was in any way an issue of general concern and considered that it should be viewed like any other commodity to be distributed by the 'natural' laws of the market.

To many in the CVWaK, however, the issue of housing reform did appear more pressing. The Verein had attempted to educate and lead by example, but after 20 years of activity the benefits of this approach were meagre; the most exciting development was the work of the BgB but this had been at best a limited success and the problems of housing were getting worse not better. The call for some more radical approach, the possibility of intervention through legislation, seemed at this stage a natural response to those concerned with social reforms and one that had been tried with some apparent success in England. Naturally to the economists such as Prince-Smith, Faucher, Michaelis and others determined to hold a 'Manchester' line on economic and social policies, this was a damaging confusion. Intervention of this form or, worse still, charity would, they argued, only put off the time when a natural solution would impose itself.

These issues were brought to a head in the debate between the two sides at the annual meetings of the KdV in the mid-1860s. In 1864 the Kongress had briefly considered the question of housing for the first time, emphasising the importance of good housing – 'a healthy and suitable dwelling is the starting point for all moral and material well-being'[19] – and the co-operative as a means of providing it. The need for further consideration of the matter was accepted and a committee including both Huber and Faucher was formed, under the chairmanship of Lette, with a roughly equal balance of reforming and 'Manchester' views to solicit the opinions of members of both the KdV and the CVWaK on the housing problem.[20] The response, though less dramatic than the committee had hoped, included papers by well-known figures in the housing reform circles – Huber, Hugo Senftleben, Reinhold Klette, Carl Brämer and Ludolf Parisius.

From the start of his contribution, 'Über die geeignetsten Massregeln zur Abhülfe der Wohnungsnoth', Huber makes plain his support for reform, and ends by raising the fundamental issue of intervention: 'What attitudes, what rights, what role, what duties do the State and its subsidiaries, the municipal and other civil or spiritual bodies, intend to adopt in relation to the reform of housing conditions?'[21]

Huber's response to his own question is cautious and hedged around with qualifications, but he concludes that some form of intervention by the State is not only permissible, but indeed necessary: he urged State intervention both in legislative control of sanitary conditions in existing housing and, more novel, State intervention in the building of new housing where the State was itself an employer. In defiance of the individualist tenets he argued the pressing need for reforms of this kind because of the failure or private enterprise and *laissez-faire* policies to provide adequate working-class housing, as had been so obvious in the housing shortages of the late 1840s and again in the late 1850s.

Huber's views did not, however, reflect the general tenor of the views of the KdV, or even those of the CVWaK. It is true that the housing problem was recognised as a cause for concern by most – some even conceded that neither the unregulated free-play of market forces nor unassisted self-help offered certain solutions. But, even so, few were willing to follow Huber in his cautious call for State intervention. The bulk of the articles in the *Arbeiterfreund* still emphasised the virtues of self-help and the achievements that might be won through co-operation, looking to the example of the English building societies. The articles by Parisius and Brämer, an influential figure in the Verein and, later editor of the *Arbeiterfreund*, both praised the achievement of the English building societies as a triumphant vindication in practice of the principles of self-help.[22]

Certainly the discussion at the 8th annual assembly of the KdV favoured the line urged by Brämer and Parisius rather than by Huber. Support for co-operative housing associations was overwhelming and even the achievements of the BgB were pilloried as being tainted with charity and a threat to the spirit of free enterprise: 'the charitable character of the existing building companies has had damaging consequences; it is this form of charity that has prevented private speculation from coming to grips with the housing problem'.[23]

The final resolutions of the annual meeting with their emphasis on economic freedom and self-help reflect the mood of the Kongress: removal of all limitations on the economic freedom of the building industry; support for housing societies and companies run on purely economic basis and total opposition to any form of charity; support for co-operative housing associations which were to build cottage housing intended for home-ownership.

In the autumn of 1865 the CVWaK set up its own committee, consisting of Lette, Prittwitz, Brämer, Parisius and Oberregierungsrath Wehrmann, to look into the problems of housing in more detail.[24] Its findings show that at this point the differences between CVWaK and KdV were not great. Brämer, for example, clearly recognised the ineffectiveness of private enterprise, but still refused to agree that the possibility of State intervention was any more acceptable than charity. For him, the role of the CVWaK should be to collect and disseminate information on housing conditions, on forms of co-operative action in housing and on detailed aspects of housing design. Moritz Carl Ernst von Prittwitz, an army man better known for his book on fortifications, recommended nothing more original than a detailed study of the optimum forms of workers' housing and the desirability of the old-fashioned ideal of encouraging the workers to become home-owners: 'Become Capitalists! This is the A to Z of all material improvements in the conditions of the labouring classes. Only thus can these classes be helped to save at all. The ways and means by which they are encouraged are of less importance than the fact that they should be encouraged to save.'[25]

The need for radical solutions to the housing problem was not considered. The committee's recommendations again emphasised the role of the CVWaK as a means of collecting and disseminating information, including technical data, on successful experiments throughout the country, and urged the CVWaK to encourage the building of good quality housing for rental as well as owner occupation. Perhaps with the improvement in housing conditions the urgent need for a new approach had passed. Any hint of State intervention was still being dismissed by Brämer as 'contradicting the history of the Verein and, above all, offending aginst the generally accepted notions of the nature of the State'.[26] The seriousness of the problems, documented accurately for the first time by the statistical information now becoming available in Berlin and other cities, was recognised, but there was no willingness to advance beyond the ideas of the 1850s in seeking a solution. Education, self-help and co-operation were still the accepted solutions.

The strength of *laissez-faire* principles was already evident in these recommendations of the CVWaK, but the triumph of these views was celebrated at the Hamburg meeting of the KdV held in August 1867.

The resolution before the Kongress unashamedly stressed the virtues of private enterprise:

The housing problems of urban areas can only be solved successfully by ensuring that private enterprise builds such housing as demand dictates, especially low cost and smaller dwellings which take due account of the necessary sanitary requirements determined by the State. The present interventionist activities of private individuals, housing companies and other such organisations should recognise this and seek to restrict their activities simply to ease the difficulties of the present transitional period.[27]

Faucher's opening to the proceedings was a provocative assertion of the *laissez-faire* view: 'Surely we can agree this resolution without more ado. All the resolutions agreed by any congress of economists must inevitably lead to the conclusion that the housing problem must be solved by private enterprise, and the task of the State should be limited to ensuring the maximum freedom for private enterprise and easing the difficulties of the present moment.'[28]

During the discussion Lette, with limp support from Brämer and a few others, put forward a case for limited intervention both by the propertied classes and by the State in certain circumstances and defended the record of the BgB. But clearly the weight of opinion was in favour of Faucher, Michaelis and others such as one Timmermann who argued that it was capital and not humanitarian ideals that built housing. The failure to follow *laissez-faire* principles, according to this view, far from helping, would reduce in the working man the desire to improve his own conditions:

There is no longer a workers' problem and there should no longer be a housing problem. Each is worth his own wage and it is up to him how much of this he spends on housing. To say that housing is too expensive is only to compound the illusion that it lies in the power of the State or somebody else to provide better housing than people can afford. It is our duty to emphasise to the worker that his dwelling can only be as good as the money he pays for it.[29]

In the emphasis put on private enterprise and self-motivation as a basis for improving housing, the KdV signalled the lack of sympathy for efforts of those like Huber who believed that some form of leadership from above was desirable. To the KdV even this was tainted with charity and was therefore unacceptable.

Engels' attack on Sax and the liberal approach of the 1860s

The voices of Faucher and the other Manchester liberals were not the only ones raised in opposition to the reforming efforts of Huber and the others concerned with housing reform. An attack from an entirely different quarter was launched by Friedrich Engels in the early 1870s. The members of the KdV denied the existence of a housing problem and dismissed efforts at reform as helpless tinkering with the natural forces of the market. Engels, too, dismissed the activities of the reformers as pathetically ineffectual, a form of 'social quackery', but for very different reasons. For Engels the housing problem was simply another manifestation of the fundamental ills of a capitalist society; the only solution to the problem was not to tamper with issues like housing, but to attack the central issue, to seek the overthrow of capitalist society itself.

Engels' view on the movement for reform during the 1860s are set out in his scathing attack on a book by Dr Emil Sax, *Die Wohnungszustände der Arbeitenden Classen* (1869)[30] in a series of newspaper articles published in 1872 in the *Volksblatt* and later reprinted as *Zur Wohnungsfrage*. After its republication in 1887 it was to serve as the 'official' SPD view on the question of housing until the end of the 1890s. Sax's book is, ironically, now remembered chiefly for being the victim of Engels' attack and its original contents forgotten; however, as one of the first extended studies of the subject it provides a very useful summary of the attitudes to housing in the late 1860s, a point conceded even by Engels himself. The first part of the book establishes, at some length, the causes of the housing problem and the importance of good housing, particularly cottage housing when owned rather than rented, as a basis for a healthy economic individualism. This section ends with an extended discussion of the benefits of decentralisaton of cottage housing around existing towns near new small-scale industry. The second part of the book considers ways in which new housing could be provided. Housing by the employer is viewed with cautious approval, the idea of the 'latent association' as proposed by Huber is hailed as a short-term solution, while for the long term, Sax favours the co-operative housing association as the ideal, despite its limitations; indeed, the work of the BgB is attacked as being 'gemeinschädlich' (damaging) rather than 'gemein-nützig' (beneficial). The book is a useful summary of the approach favoured by the KdV; it is competent but familiar.

To Engels, Sax's book is nothing more than a tirade of flatulent pomposity empty of theory and understanding: Sax, as a bourgeois, is imprisoned within a system of thought that makes it impossible for him, and of course for other liberals too, to understand the real causes of the housing problem: 'Whence then comes the housing shortage? How did it arise? As a good bourgeois, Dr Sax is not supposed to know that it is a necessary product of the bourgeois social order.'[31] Robbed of a real understanding, Engels argues that Sax is forced to explain the housing problem as a series of moral failings:

Whoever declares that the capitalist mode of production, the 'iron laws' of present-day bourgeois society, are inviolable, and yet at the same time would like to abolish their unpleasant but necessary consequences, has no other recourse but to deliver moral sermons to capitalists, moral sermons whose emotional effects immediately evaporate under the influence of private interests and, if necessary, competition.[32]

The solutions to the housing problem offered by Sax are briskly dismissed. The liberal ideal of home-ownership he dispatches as a snare to fetter the worker, robbing him of the freedom of movement necessary to sell his labour most profitably. The idea of the 'latent association' and Huber's 'drivelling' ideas, are denounced as a confusion which leaves the worker at the mercy of the employer, offering the worker at best a 'revocable title of ownership'. The benefits of housing provided by the employer are dismissed as a form of economic serfdom. Finally, the liberal ideal of raising the 'so-called propertyless classes' to the level of the bourgeoisie, he attacks as totally unrealistic, as implausible as the hope that 'all the soldiers of the French army, each of whom carries a marshal's baton in his knapsack since the days of Napoleon, can be turned into field marshals without at the same time ceasing to be private soldiers'.[33] For Sax's hopes of government intervention he sees no prospect. More aware of the limitations and inadequacies of English sanitary legislation in practice than most of his German contemporaries, Engels considered the State as no better than a defender of the existing order of society:

It is perfectly clear that the existing State is neither able nor willing to do anything to remedy the housing difficulty. The State is nothing but the organised collective power of the possessing classes...If...the individual *capitalists* deplore the housing shortage, but can hardly be persuaded even superficially to palliate its most terrifying consequences, then the *collective* capitalist State will not do much more.[34]

Engels' trenchant analysis of 'bourgeois' approaches to the housing problem was to influence socialist thinking on the question of housing reform for some time. By his rejection of any hope of improvement in the conditions of the working classes in the short term, and by his insistence on the need for the establishment of the *Zukunftstaat* before fundamental reforms were possible, Engels frustrated the possibility of a new approach by those who, in his terms, had most to gain from an improvement of conditions. Had the opportunity to harness the energies of the working classes to winning an improvement in the inadequate housing conditions of countless familes been sacrificed to theoretical purity? Or was Engels' analysis a tough and realistic assessment of the likelihood of winning a real improvement in housing in the Germany of the late 1860s and early 1870s?

CVWaK and the continuing interest in housing reform

Although the KdV had clearly rejected the call for interventionist reforms in housing at the annual assembly in Hamburg in 1867, Huber's arguments did find a sympathetic reception in the CVWaK as is reflected in the balance of articles in the *Arbeiterfreund* under the editorial policies of Brämer, whose views had changed since the early 1860s. By the end of the decade the differences between KdV and CVWaK on the social question were substantial and there is only the briefest of reports in the *Arbeiterfreund* after 1867 of the activities of the KdV and the annual congresses.

An important stimulus to the CVWaK's interest in reform was the increased availability and accuracy of the statistical information on housing conditions in the 1860s. During the 1850s isolated studies had gathered considerable amounts of information on particular aspects of

the housing question as German investigators had adopted the methods
of their English or French colleagues. But these individual studies had
not provided a sufficiently general picture of the problem to mount a
convincing attack on the predominant Manchesterist doctrine. In the
1860s, however, the position changed. In 1863, the Berlin Statistical
Office under the direction of Dr S. Neumann, an important figure in
public health reform and a member of the CVWaK, produced the
pioneering report *Die Berliner Volkszählung vom 3 Dezember 1861*, which
contained, for the first time, detailed city-wide information on housing
conditions for a German city of this size.[35] This first publication was
followed by further reports on Berlin and soon the lead shown by Berlin
was taken up by other cities such as Königsberg (1864), Frankfurt
(1864), Hamburg (1867) and Leipzig (1867).[36]

As a result of these initiatives, a considerable body of information on
housing conditions in the larger cities was available by the late 1860s.
Combined with other sources, particularly medical statistics, this
evidence, with its emphasis on the lack of improvement in conditions,
suggested that the economic optimism of the Manchester liberals was
unwarranted. From the late 1860s, spurred on by the growing availability
of statistical evidence, the CVWaK was firmly for encouraging reform
through intervention. Huber sharply dismissed the KdV's hopes of
solving the housing problem by private enterprise as no more plausible
than the notion that slavery would be stopped by the slavers or the
plantation owners. The same view is clearly reflected in the extended
series of articles, *Die Bedeutung und der Fortschritt der Wohnungsfrage*, by
Senftleben published in the *Arbeiterfreund* between 1868 and 1870. In
these, Senftleben attacks the failings of *Manchesterismus*: 'The theory
that private enterprise might be capable of balancing supply and demand
is merely abstract economi: doctrine which can find but barren soil in
the daily life of the mass of the people. The vain attempt to spur the
factory or agricultural worker to save what he can and thus to improve
his standard of living by buying his own home...is a dubious
proposition.'[37] In place of the approach of the KdV, he reiterated Huber's
conviction that 'the personal interest of the propertied and educated
classes in the domestic life of the poor and the ignorant, on the one hand,
and the pioneering influence of enlightened legislation, on the other are
essential for a reform of the present housing conditions'.[38]

3

⬥◇

Boom, depression and the second debate on the Housing Problem 1872–86

By the mid 1880s the attitudes of many reformers to the problems of housing had changed out of all recognition. In place of the *laissez-faire* approach of the KdV, the Verein für Sozialpolitik (VfSP), an association founded in 1872 which included a considerable number of leading academics, had started to elaborate a programme of social reforms which envisaged a greatly increased role for government.[1] In 1886 the Verein had discussed the housing question for the first time. To Professor Gustav Schmoller, one of the most influential members of the VfSP, not only were housing conditions in urban areas a cause for grave concern, but intervention, in the form of both regulatory legislation and encouragement for the building of working-class housing, was imperative to prevent a repetition in German cities of the savage bestiality of the Paris Commune:

The time for inaction is past; we can no longer afford to sit with our hands upon our knees. A new age knocks a stern warning on our door.

The propertied classes must be shaken from their slumber: they must finally be made to realise that even if they make the greatest sacrifices, that these, as Chamberlain recently said in London, are but a limited and very modest premium with which to buy protection against the epidemics and the social revolution which must surely come, unless we can prevent the lower classes of our great cities being reduced to an animal and barbaric existence by the awfulness of their housing conditions.[2]

The views of Schmoller and the VfSP stand in opposition to the predominant Manchesterism of the mid-1860s and the views of the KdV who had been happy to abandon the question of housing to the forces of the market. What had produced this change in opinion?

The change in attitudes towards housing after 1872 must be seen against the background of two developments which caused a major shift in opinion on the social question: first, the fundamental changes in the economy after 1872; second, the beginnings of State intervention in the social question, in part a response to the rise of a radical socialist party. By the 1880s a new generation had emerged amongst those concerned with the social problem whose views were very different from the reformers of the 1860s. This new grouping, centred on the VfSP, generally supported the idea of action by the State in the sphere of social reform and welcomed new initiatives such as the compulsory insurance legislation of 1883. But before exploring the VfSP's involvement with housing reform, we must first consider the effects of the boom years of the *Gründerzeit* and the depression that followed on the housing conditions and contemporary perception of the housing problem.

Rosenberg characterises the prevailing mood of the period 1850–72 as optimistic;[3] by contrast, he describes the period between 1873 and 1896 as a time of extended economic depression when belief in the optimistic liberal nostrums of the 1860s collapsed, as a time when new attitudes had to be developed in the field of social policy. Certainly this was true of housing, and nowhere was the necessity of creating this change more dramatically illustrated than in Berlin.

The growth of population in the late 1860s and early 1870s was less rapid in Berlin than in a number of smaller towns and cities where the demand for housing during the boom swamped the limited stock of existing housing. But it was in Berlin, the centre of banking, and also of speculation, that the convulsive effects of the swing from boom to depression were most dramatic. It was here that the vulgar swagger and prosperity of the parvenu speculator was contrasted most sharply with the harsh life of the working-class families forced to 'camp' in inadequate tents and hovels on the Tempelhofer Feld. It was in Berlin that the crash of the housing market, and the flood of forced sales and bankruptcies, was most sudden. It was here, with the destruction of the annuities of respectable widows and the speculative fantasies of the 'small men', the café waiters and the domestic servants who had sunk their savings in property, that panic at the market's collapse really took hold.

Boom and depression on the housing market in Berlin

One of the principal causes of the housing shortage during the late 1860s and the boom years of the *Gründerjahre* was the rapid growth of population attracted by the employment opportunities within the city. Throughout Germany economic expansion was matched by a correspondingly sudden increase in the urban population; by 1871 the urban population of Prussia represented nearly 35% of the total.[4] In Berlin the consequences of economic growth were quite as drastic. The growth of population, illustrated in fig. 1, which had slackened during the 1850s, surged ahead in the 1860s to an annual level of nearly 20,000, easily topping the level of any previous period.

The Austro-Prussian war of 1866 led to a brief collapse in the rate of immigration, but this was followed by a return to even higher levels of immigration for 1867–9. Again, the Franco-Prussian war led to a reduction in the numbers drawn to the city, but in the next year, 1871, a massive number of immigrants were attracted by the spectacular boom fired by the handsome terms of the peace settlement. From this peak – 1871 was the year of highest immigration for the city in its history – the level declined, to remain constant at about 20,000 per year through to the end of the century, with a trough between 1876 and

1878 during the worst years of the depression. Significantly, after the mid-1870s the rate of natural increase in the population rose to over 10,000 for the first time; this natural increase balanced the fluctuations in the number of immigrants resulting in a smoother rate of growth.

But aggregate population figures for the whole city obscure the extent to which growth was concentrated in particular areas. Indeed one of the most important consequences of the growth of the late 1860s and early 1870s was that it led to acceleration of the differences in housing conditions between working-class and other areas of the city.[5] It was the working-class districts on the outskirts of the city, both in the north-west and the south-east, that bore the brunt of the population expansion before the 1880s. It was here, as development failed to keep pace with population growth, that the housing shortage led to the *Wohnungsnoth*, or housing crisis, that contemporaries described with such horrified fascination.

The growth of the late 1860s and early 1870s fell mainly on the suburbs outside the old city walls despite the poor transport facilities linking suburb to centre (figs. 2 and 3); even the outer suburbs, areas like Moabit and Wedding which were to receive the bulk of the expansion of the late 1880s and 1890s, show signs of rapid if small-scale growth. Sadly, however, suburban expansion did not necessarily mean better housing conditions. A number of areas were developed as 'Villa quarters', for example the exclusive suburb of Westend, but districts such as Wedding were settled from the first as working-class areas and immediately developed to as high a density as the building code permitted.

Despite important changes in the house building industry and the way that development was organised, an issue to which we return later, housing construction could not keep pace with the population growth and from the late 1860s to the mid-1870s there was a shortage of adequate working-class housing. For contemporaries it was the concentration of the building industry on large dwellings, where huge profits were to be made, instead of on smaller tenements that was as much to blame for the housing crisis as the growth of population.[6] The glut of empty dwellings on the housing market during the war in 1866 was quickly followed by a prosperous period when demand rose and the number of empty dwellings fell. By 1869 there was already an extreme shortage of housing, a situation belied by the official statistics which included many virtually unusable dwellings.[7] During the early 1870s, as demand surged, the availability of dwellings fell rapidly (fig. 4). Even the official statistics show that the percentage of empty dwellings in the city had fallen to the crisis level of 1.1% by 1870. By 1873, it was down to 0.6%, the lowest figures ever before the First World War. By October 1872, there were approximately 800 families without shelter and many families were living in tents and sheds on the Tempelhofer Feld and other open spaces around the outskirts in conditions similar to those of the Italian railway workers of the 1840s, whose housing had become a byword for wretchedness.[8]

This period of furious economic expansion was followed by a sudden crash. Now, in the recession that followed the boom, the crisis conditions in housing eased. With the slump, employment slackened, immigration fell and with it the demand for housing. In 1876, for the first time in eight years, the percentage of empty dwellings passed 3% and increased steadily until 1879, when it reached 8·6%, the highest vacancy rate before the war. Not until 1885 did it again slide below 3%.

Closely related to this dramatic reversal in the availability of dwellings was the level of rents. Rent levels during the 1860s had remained relatively stable, but drifted gradually upwards (fig. 4). From the early 1870s there was a rapid increase in response to demand, but by 1876 they were already falling, although, restrained by the 'ratchet' effect of prices, they fell only slowly, so that it was not until 1881, with 5% of all dwellings empty, that rents were again down to their 1872 level in both large and small dwellings.[9] Rents and the number of empty dwellings indicate in only the crudest terms the workings of the housing market, but a broad assessment of housing conditions can be made from the vast mass of statistical data available on housing and housing conditions from 1861 onwards by using the following four indicators: the size of dwellings, the occupancy of the dwelling, the composition of the household and the density of development. Most important, by comparing these statistics and the complementary morbidity and mortality rates from the medical statistics for working-class areas with those for the rest of the city, it is possible to appreciate how much worse conditions were in working-class areas than in other quarters.

Consider first the data on the size of dwellings set out in table 1. For the city as a whole, the number of dwellings with one or no heatable room[10] shows little change during the period between the late 1860s and early 1880s, apart from an increase during the years of housing crisis such as 1871; if anything, there is a gradual improvement and the number of dwellings with no heatable rooms declines. But the situation in the working-class areas differs in a number of important ways. Taking data for 1875, we can see that in the working-class areas of the north-west where metal working encouraged a divorce between work-place and residence, the proportion of small dwellings was higher than for the city as a whole. In the south-east, however, where dwellings were larger and the distribution of sizes broadly similar to the rest of the city, both the proportion used for business purposes (table 2) and the occupancy rate were higher than for the city as a whole.

The data on occupancy, set out in table 3, reveal the same difference between conditions in working-class areas and the rest of the city, set against a gradual drift towards better conditions over the whole period between the 1860s and the 1880s but with temporary reverses in this general trend during the periods of high economic activity. Thus for the whole city the average number of inhabitants for a one-room dwelling fell from 4.3 in 1867 to 3.9 by 1880 and to 3.75 by 1885, and this long-term improvement continued on into the twentieth century. In working-class areas overcrowding was higher than in the city as a

Table 1 *The percentage of dwellings of different sizes for selected districts of Berlin*

	Size of dwelling expressed in number of heatable rooms						
	0	1	2	3	4	5–7	6
1861							
City of Berlin		49.1	25.2	12.0	5.1	5.3	1.6
X, XI		64.7	24.3	7.3	1.4	0.7	0.2
V		42.4	29.8	16.7	5.3	4.1	0.7
VII		56.5	27.6	9.7	2.6	2.1	0.4
1867							
City of Berlin	1.5	49.1	25.8	11.5	5.1	5.4	1.6
X, XI	2.1	61.9	25.4	7.5	1.9	0.9	0.3
V	1.6	44.9	28.5	14.3	6.0	4.0	0.7
VII	1.6	56.9	28.2	8.1	2.5	2.2	0.5
1875							
City of Berlin	1.5	51.3	25.3	10.4	4.6	5.4	1.5
X, XI	1.3	61.6	25.2	7.9	2.3	1.2	0.2
V	1.3	46.6	27.4	12.5	5.1	4.4	0.5
VII	1.8	57.0	27.9	8.0	2.0	2.3	0.2
						5+	
1880							
City of Berlin	1.26	49.8	26.5	10.6	4.6	7.07	
X, XI	1.5	57.8	27.1	9.1	2.5	1.7	
V	1.1	50.9	26.4	11.7	4.7	4.8	
VII	1.4	58.3	27.3	7.7	2.7	2.2	

X. XI The Oranienburger and Rosenthaler Vorstädte
V Luisenstadt
VII Stralauer Viertel
Sources: 1861, 1867, 1875: Thienel, *Städtewachstum* p. 394: 1880: *Stat. J. Berlin*, vol. 10 (1884), p. 87.

Table 2 *The percentage of dwellings used for business purposes in selected districts of Berlin*

	1861	1867	1875	1880
City of Berlin	21.1	21.4	16.6	18.2
X, XI	13.1	14.5	12.5	14.1
V	19.4	21.1	17.3	20.2
VII	21.6	23.4	17.5	17.3

Sources: 1861, 1867, 1875: Thienel, *Städtewachstum*, p. 393; 1880: *Stat. J. Berlin*, vol. 10 (1884), p. 87.

whole, but not substantially so: for smaller dwellings, only the Stralauer Viertel had a consistently higher occupancy rate per dwelling than the city as a whole. But in the large dwellings the occupancy rate in working-class areas was generally higher than the rate for the whole

Table 3 *Occupancy levels for dwellings of different sizes in selected districts of Berlin*

	Size of dwelling expressed in number of heatable rooms						
	0	1	2	3	4	5–7	6+
1861							
City of Berlin		4.3	5.1	5.2	5.8	6.4	9.7
X, XI		4.5	5.3	5.5	6.2	8.2	6.0
V		4.5	5.2	5.1	5.7	6.2	8.9
VII		4.5	5.5	5.5	6.6	7.0	8.1
1867							
City of Berlin	2.7	3.9	4.6	4.9	5.2	6.1	8.9
X, XI	2.6	3.9	4.5	4.9	5.2	6.6	29.0*
V	2.7	3.9	4.8	4.9	4.6	6.1	8.7
VII	2.8	3.9	4.7	5.1	5.8	6.1	5.8
1875							
City of Berlin	3.0	3.9	4.7	4.9	5.4	6.0	8.2
X, XI	3.7	3.9	4.6	4.9	5.6	6.6	10.4
V	3.0	3.9	4.7	4.8	5.4	6.0	7.7
VII	3.2	4.0	4.8	5.1	5.6	6.2	7.6
1880						5+	
City of Berlin	3.11	3.51	4.4	4.67	5.12	6.02	
X, XI	3.21	3.49	4.57	4.44	5.19	6.18	
V	3.04	3.51	4.41	4.72	5.33	6.6	
VII	3.24	3.60	4.52	5.10	5.35	6.09	

* Statistical error, cf. Thienel, p. 392.
Sources: 1861, 1867, 1875: Thienel, *Städtewachstum*, p. 392; 1880: *Stat. J. Berlin*, vol. 10 (1884), p. 8.

Table 4 *The percentage of families taking in 'Schlafleute' (A), and the percentage of the population living as 'Schlafleute' (B) for selected districts of Berlin*

	1861		1867		1875		1860		1885	
	A	B	A	B	A	B	A	B	A	B
City of Berlin	20.3	8.3	16.0	6.3	21.0	8.3	15.3	5.2	17.6	6.6
X, XI	21.0	7.6	14.9	5.4	22.3	8.5				
V	24.5	10.8	19.1	6.3	23.5	9.8				
VII	22.0	8.3	18.3	7.2	25.0	10.0				

Sources: 1861, 1867, 1875: Thienel, *Städtewachstum*, p. 388; 1880, 1885: Reich, *Wohnungsmarkt*, p. 133.

Table 5 *The number of people per plot for selected districts of Berlin*

	1875	1880
City of Berlin	57.9	60.6
X, XI	74.2	77.2
V	73.3	76.0
VII	73.4	77.6

Source: 1875, 1880: *Stat. J. Berlin*, vol. 8 (1882), p. 78.

city; here the composition of the household is more important than a simple measure of the occupancy.

The composition of the household, particularly the number and type of lodgers, was a source of special concern to housing reformers who were quick to emphasise the dangers of taking in lodgers and the threat they posed to family life and the home.[11] In Berlin the two most common types of lodgers in the mid-1870s were the *Einmieter*, or *Untermieter*, the subtenants who enjoyed the use of a separate bed, perhaps even a separate room, and who would probably remain with the same family for a considerable period, and the casual lodgers, the *Chambregarnisten*, *Burschen* and *Schlafgänger*, who simply rented a bed, or part of a bed, for the night and would change addresses frequently, lodging with different families on different nights, and enjoying only a very limited relationship with the 'host' family. From the lodger's point of view, the system had the disadvantage that he was generally without a 'home' during the day.[12] However for the 'host' family, *Schlafgänger* provide an essential supplement to family income representing an economic benefit rather than the moral liability suggested by the reformers.[13]

There was however a progressive decline both in the number of lodgers and the number of families taking them in from the 1860s onwards (table 4), although this general trend was reversed during the housing crisis of the early 1870s: in 1867, in the whole city, 16% of all families took in *Schlafleute*; in 1875 this figure rose to 21%; by 1885, however, the proportion had fallen again to 15.3%. Both the number of families taking in casual lodgers and the proportion of the population living as *Schlafleute* were higher in working-class districts than in the whole city: this was true of the working-class areas in both the north-west and the south-east, although there were more lodgers in these latter districts; in 1875 in the Stralauer Viertel, one in ten of the population lived as a *Schlafgänger* and nearly one in four of all families took in lodgers.

Finally, consider the increases in the density of development between the 1860s and the 1880s. This question became a matter of great concern to reformers as the connection was established between medical and sanitary problems and the lack of ventilation and sunlight caused by high-density development. There was a general reaction against the four- and five-storey blocks of housing so typical of low-cost urban

Table 6 *The percentage of buildings having a 4th and 5th floor and above for selected districts of Berlin*

	1875		1880	
	4th flr	5th flr	4th flr	5th flr
City of Berlin	17	0.12	20.2	2.2
X, XI	36	0.12	27.6	4.0
V	46	0.34	25.2	3.1
VII	39	0.16	27.8	2.6

Sources: 1867, 1875: *Stat. J. Berlin*, vol. 3, 187, p. 80; 1880: *Stat. J. Berlin*, vol. 8, 1882, p. 83.

development from the mid-1860s on, an antipathy expressed in the derogatory term *Mietskaserne*, or 'rent barracks'. It was the relentless effect of block after five-storey block which shut out any impression of nature so completely, and the ruthlessness with which the process of speculation ensured that every square metre of space was put to profitable use, that contemporaries found so oppressive.

The density of development was measured in terms of the number of people per plot or development (table 5) and records a gradual increase in density from the mid-1860s to the turn of the century.[14] The extent to which this density was achieved through higher building can be traced in the changing proportion of the number of dwellings on each floor: in 1861, 20% of all dwellings were located on the third and fourth floors; by 1880 this category accounted for 30.1% of all dwellings, while 12% of all dwellings were now on the fifth floor. As plots increased in size, the proportion of dwellings giving on to the minimal courts allowed by the building code and frequently lacking adequate ventilation and light increased: in 1861, only just over a quarter of all dwellings were located in court buildings, by 1880 this proportion stood at just over a third and by the turn of the century, just under half of all dwellings were in court buildings.

Naturally the density of development in working-class quarters, the areas of more recent construction, was higher than in the centre of the city (table 5). In 1861 densities in the rapidly growing areas such as the working-class suburbs of the north-west or the south-east were between 10 and 20 people per plot higher than in the central areas; by 1885, the contrast between the density of working-class areas and the whole city was even more pronounced and in working-class areas such as Luisenstadt the proportion of sites with more than 200 people was well over double that for the city as a whole. Equally, the percentage of buildings having more than four floors was substantially higher in working-class areas than in the rest of the city (table 6).

No attempt to contrast the conditions in the working-class areas with those of the whole city could be complete without at least a passing

Table 7 *Mortality rates for children of under one year, as a permille of live births, for selected districts of Berlin*

	1875	1880
City of Berlin	34.1	32.7
X, XI	36.7	35.0
V	38.8	35.9
VII	36.0	36.3

Source: 1875: *Stat. J. Berlin*, vol. 4, 187, p. 44; 1880: *Stat. J. Berlin*, vol. 8, 1882, p. 32.

reference to the host of other statistics which emphasise the deprivation of these working-class quarters. Even the most casual inspection of the sanitary and medical statistics shows how much greater was the probability of falling ill for the residents of working-class districts such as Luisenstadt or Wedding with one of the host of epidemics that swept through these areas, or how much less favourable the chances of their living to the same age as the inhabitants of the more prosperous quarters. The contrast in the high infant mortality rates for working-class districts with those of the rest of the city is striking (table 7): in 1875 in Luisenstadt the mortality per thousand rate for children of under one year was 38.8, while in the more affluent area of Friedrichstadt it was 29.2; five years later in 1880, the situation was little better.

The terms in which reformers described the conditions of the poor have their exact parallels in the English literature of the time. The Innere Mission produced men like Stadtmissionär Böckelmann whose descriptions of the housing of the poor is interchangeable in its awfulness with the accounts given by the Rev. Andrew Mearns of the London poor. Böckelmann describes conditions in a tenement block in the St Simeon's area in the early 1880s in the following terms:

It is inhabited by 250 families or groups, amongst them live 17 common law couples, 22 prostitutes, 17 unmarried couples, and four wives who have deserted their husbands. On one corridor alone there are 36 dwellings. The window glass is nearly everywhere replaced with paper, wood or cloth. But if the exterior of the house is hardly attractive, how much less so is the interior... There is hardly a family that has the use of two rooms and those that do have only a larger room and a tiny kitchen; the average size of room is 16′ × 10′. Here one sees one or two beds, chairs, certainly not a sofa or a day-bed, a small iron stove, and that is all. Overall things are so bad that they cannot get worse. In addition the sheer filth of these dwellings must be mentioned. I find beds, if they can be called that, which are jet black with dirt. I thought that in such a room as I have just described there could be no room to sleep at all: on seeing a family with five children and only one bed I wondered where they could all possibly sleep. Four of them slept in one bed, the others on the floor, either on straw, or on piles of old rags. Nor should you imagine that there is always just the one family that lives in such a room; no!, here and there, there are two, indeed I even know of cases of three families living together in one room, who in addition have four children amongst them, and of these, three are still forced to sleep in their cradles.[15]

The accumulation of statistical evidence from studies carried out by the statistical offices such as those under Hermann Schwabe in Berlin or Moritz Neefe in Breslau[16] together with eyewitness accounts, some of them dramatic, others more objective in tone, of the housing conditions of the poor revealed only too clearly that the housing crisis of the *Gründerjahre* was not a unique state of affairs. In the mid-1880s the working-class family was once again finding it more difficult and more expensive to secure adequate housing. What was obtainable would be smaller, more likely to be shared with outsiders and more probably high up in one of the rear courts of a much higher density development than would have been the case 20 years before. In the mid-1880s, as the depression eased and the rate of immigration into the cities again increased, the availability of dwellings again fell below 3% and the rents rose once more to the levels of the early 1870s. To the reformers the need for action was clear: the housing crisis of the boom years of the early 1870s was still too fresh in people's minds to allow the housing question to be left to 'market forces'.

Changes in attitudes to the Social Question during the 1870s

By the end of the 1870s the need for some kind of government action on the social question had been recognised and accepted with a willingness that would have been unthinkable only ten years before. This new readiness to countenance government intervention was intimately linked to two important developments: on the one hand the rise of an active and radical socialist party and Bismarck's responses to this, and on the other the emergence of a new generation of thinkers on social and economic issues grouped around the VfSP who accepted and even applauded the government's social policies.

Bismarck's social policies, together with his anti-socialist legislation, were conceived as a two-pronged attack on the social democrats. At Gotha in 1875, the 'Lassalleaner' of the Allgemeiner Deutscher Arbeiterverein, founded by Ferdinand Lassalle in 1863, had joined forces with the more radical Sozialdemokratische Arbeiterpartei, founded in 1869 by Karl Liebknecht and strongly influenced by Marx, to form the combined Sozialistische Arbeiterpartei Deutschlands with a programme of radical democratic measures and contacts with the First International. Bismarck's response to this threat was the 'Zuckerbrot und Peitsche' social policies of the late 1870s and the 1880s. The whip was the anti-socialist legislation of 19 October 1878, while the carrot was represented by the 'State socialist' programme of compulsory insurance legislation for old age, sickness and accidents, initiated in 1883 and substantially complete by 1890. The effect of these policies was far-reaching. In contrast to the situation in the 1860s when social reform had been the concern of a few groups such as the CVWaK, often operating in opposition to the conventional wisdom of the time, Bismarck's social policies, however distasteful to some the link with the anti-socialist legislation, now established the principle of government intervention in social affairs.[17]

The reaction to Bismarck's policies of the older generation of those who, like the CVWaK, had been concerned with the social question before the 1870s was ambivalent. To members of the CVWaK the principal objection to the government's policies was not the offensiveness of State intervention, but the consequences of outlawing the socialists. There was little sympathy for the communist position, but to legislate against the socialists was to go too far. This view is clearly expressed in the editorial stance of the *Arbeiterfreund* under Viktor Böhmert who set out his views on the matter in 1876 in an article, 'Die sociale Frage im Reichstage und vor dem Reichskanzler'.[18] Here he argued that the new legislation could never resolve the problems which gave rise to socialism. He considered the only way forward was to provide better education in the widest sense for the worker; in this way the worker could then be led constructively forward along the path set out by the Society since the late 1850s. To Böhmert the anti-socialist legislation was hopelessly divisive, throwing class against class and almost certain to make the solution of the social question – the only real means of defeating the socialists – more difficult in the long run.

But to many of the leading members of the VfSP like Schmoller and Adolph Wagner government policy was seen in a positive light and the government's insurance legislation was regarded as a step in the right direction. The notion of a strong State actively intervening in an attempt to right the social problem was certainly compatible with the position that Schmoller had advocated from the first meetings of the VfSP; Brämer clearly expressed this view in his summary of the discussions at the first annual conference in Eisenach in 1872:

> They call for a powerful State which, opposing the egotistical interests of different classes, will make and administer our laws with justice, and will protect the weak and help the poor. They see the 200-year-long battle that the Prussian civil service and the Prussian Monarchy have successfully fought for equality before the law, for the curbing of the benefits and legal privileges of the upper classes, for the emancipation and the improvement of the lower classes, as the greatest heritage of our German State and one which we must never fail.[19]

In 1876 in an article 'Die soziale Frage und der preussische Staat' he had restated his views and again emphasised his enthusiasm for a vigorous bureaucracy as the agency best placed to resolve the rival claims of the different and often conflicting elements of society.[20] While those with a more traditional liberal background and those on the radical wing of the Verein, like Lujo Brentano, did not support the government's policies, the views of Schmoller and Wagner predominated. During the 1880s, Schmoller maintained this position emphasising the need for government intervention in social matters to improve conditions for the working classes in order to deny the socialists a foothold.

With this growing acceptance of the principle of State intervention in social matters, the authority of Schmoller and other members of the VfSP who shared the same convictions, was substantially increased. Although the VfSP had consciously chosen not to pursue a political role on the grounds that this would inevitably compromise the impartiality of its investigations, the prestige of its members and the close contact that they enjoyed with government lent considerable weight to its findings. The views of the Verein were a powerful element in forming a new consensus towards questions such as protectionism or the social problem. While the KdV had ridiculed the prospect of State intervention in social matters as a perversion of the natural laws of economics, the leading figures of the Verein were now urging just this as the best way forward.

Silence on the Housing Question 1872–85

Yet what is surprising, in view of the rejection of *laissez-faire* attitudes and the growing acceptance of the need for government intervention, is that the housing question should have been ignored so completely by social and economic thinkers between the early 1870s and the mid-1880s. In 1872 at the Eisenach meeting of the VfSP, Ernst Engel had identified housing as one of the most pressing of the social problems for the Verein to examine.[21] Yet it was 14 years before it did so. Why was this? After the 15 years of debate from the late 1850s onwards, why was there an apparent loss of interest in the subject until the mid-1880s?

Any attempt to explain this fading of interest in terms of changes in housing conditions after 1875 alone must appear mechanistic. Nevertheless, the effect of the depression of the late 1870s and the 1880s was marked and only marginally offset by the rallying of economic forces between 1879 and 1882. As economic activity declined, the pressure on the housing market eased and the number of empty dwellings increased (fig 4). The depression saw not only an end to the housing shortage but also a fall in rents at a time when real wages were rising. If we accept Ashok Desai's estimates of real wages, it is clear that those in employment now found themselves rather better off.[22] The average rental value of a dwelling fell significantly from the high point of the early 1870s right through until the early 1880s, from an average annual rent of 757 M down to 597 M; by 1886, rental levels were still as low as they had been in 1880. Both Kuczynski and Desai show a fall in real wages from 1875 to 1880, but one which was slower than the fall in rents, and both show a rise from 1880 to 1885.[23] For those in work, the mid-1880s must have marked a substantial improvement in housing conditions, at least by comparison with the boom years of the *Gründerzeit*.

While pressure on housing was thus reduced, the attention of those concerned with the social question was busily employed elsewhere. The rise of socialism and the response, in the form of Bismarck's anti-socialist legislation, remained issues of absorbing importance: the *Arbeiterfreund*, for example, devoted a whole special issue to the subject in 1879. From 1881, attention was also focussed on the compulsory insurance legislation, provoking a series of extended articles in Schmoller's *Jahrbuch für Gesetzgebung und Wirtschaft* and a debate on the extent to which State intervention in social matters was justified. In the VfSP, the contractual relationship between employer and employee and the question of trades unions attracted considerable attention; these issues and the question of taxation led to extended debate. In view of the length of this agenda of social reform, much of which demanded urgent discussion, the lack of interest in housing at this time should not come as a surprise.

A further reason for the loss of interest in the housing question during the 1870s is the death or withdrawal from active involvement of the earlier generation of reformers who had contributed so much to the debate in the 1860s: Huber, for example, had died in 1869. With the loss of the 'old guard' interest waned despite the discussion of housing at the Eisenach conference of the Verein in 1872. Engel's address to the Verein, later expanded and published as *Die moderne Wohnungsnoth* (1873),[24] contributed little to the general debate which had not already been said by Sax. The range of solutions that he offered did not go beyond the ideas that Huber had been canvassing in the mid-1850s; they certainly did not reflect the fresh approach that the Verein was urging in other fields.

Very little was published on the housing question between the early 1870s and the mid-1880s,[25] and what did appear was mainly a continuation of the ideas of the older generation. In 1882 the new journal *Arbeiterwohl*, founded by a group of Catholic industrialists based on the west around Aachen and München-Gladbach, ran two extended articles on the causes of the housing problem and ways of solving it.[26] But the ideas set out there amounted to little more than a reiteration of the solutions urged by Huber and Sax, though there was perhaps more emphasis on the duty of the employer to house his employees: a product of the industrialists' own experiences in providing for an expanding labour force. Nor did the study by Reichardt, *Die Gründzüge der Arbeiterwohnungsfrage*[27] break new ground. The benefits of the cottage and home-ownership are praised, the evils of the *Mietskaserne* castigated, the same ways of building new housing are considered, enthusiasm for State intervention remains limited. These accounts are little more than competent and up-to-date reiterations of the conventional wisdom of the 1860s; they offer nothing new. They certainly do not suggest how the housing problem could be considered from the point of view of those who grasped the significance of the government's intervention in social policy heralded by the compulsory insurance legislation, and the new attitudes to social issues that it created. This was to be the task of the Verein für Sozialpolitik.

Why the VfSP should have turned to consider the question in 1886 is not clear. Certainly Johannes Miquel, *Oberbürgermeister* in Frankfurt from 1880–90, who initiated the Verein's investigation in the field of housing gave no explanation for the Verein's new-found interest in the subject in his introduction to the VfSP's publications nor during the debate on the Verein's investigations.[28] Yet despite his reticence on the matter, Miquel's role in initiating the study was an important one. He played a prominent part in receiving the Verein in Frankfurt in 1883 when the idea was first put forward, and was made a member of the organising committee. How he became interested in housing is obscure but his work on the reorganisation of the system of support for the poor in Frankfurt may provide a clue.[29] Despite opposition from the Trustees of the old Frankfurt Charities, which now functioned haphazardly, Miquel was able by 1883 to carry through the reform of the city's charities. Indeed, Miquel regarded this achievement as one of the most important of his time in Frankfurt and these reforms may well have provided the impetus for the study of housing. Karl Flesch, Miquel's assistant in these reforms and a collaborator on the Verein's housing study, described how in pressing the case for the reform of the charities it was necessary to assemble information on the living conditions of the working classes and this may have driven home to Miquel the importance of housing as a critical element in the family life of the worker. He certainly considered the improvement of housing conditions as a practical way in which to demonstrate both his own and the government's concern for the working classes and thus as a beneficial way of counteracting the damaging effect of the anti-socialist legislation.

Another possible influence on the revival of the Verein's involvement in housing was the considerable interest shown in Germany in the spate of English investigations into housing that began in the early 1880s. The growing clamour in the press for government investigation of the conditions so dramatically revealed in Mearn's *The Bitter Cry of Outcast London*, had led to the formation of the Royal Commission on the Housing of the Working Classes. German reformers had long been interested in English sanitary legislation, especially the Torrens and the Cross Acts, but the setting up of the Royal Commission and its proceedings were watched with special interest as is clear from the reports in the *Arbeiterfreund*, the *Schriften des Vereins für Sozialpolitik* and the *Jahrbuch für Gesetzgebung und Wirtschaft*.[30] Paul Felix Aschrott, the principal interpreter of the English housing and social reform scene for these journals, was continuously at pains to point out how English investigations and experience could be directly relevant to the German context. Given the concerns of the VfSP to investigate and publicise areas of the social problem where action was needed, the example of the Royal Commission must have impressed the members of the Verein; it would hardly be surprising if this had spurred members of the Verein to undertake a similar study of its own.

The Verein's investigation of housing

In 1885 the VfSP finally turned to consider the problems of housing; the results of the investigation were published in the summer of 1886 and discussed at the Verein's annual meeting in Frankfurt in September 1886.[31] The publication took the form of a series of reports of varying quality and length prepared by individual towns and cities on local housing conditions, together with an introduction by Miquel, a discussion of the law related to housing by Dr C. E. Leuthold, reports on housing reform and legislation in England and France, and, most important, a statistical section comparing details of the different cities in 42 tables, assembled by Neefe from the data submitted by the statistical offices of the individual cities.

The survey carried out by the Verein was of importance for two reasons. First, because of the standing of so many of the members of the Verein as academics outside the arena of party politics, the results, put forward without the motive of obvious self-interest, were seen to have a valuable quality of objectivity. Second, these surveys presented the details of the housing problem with a wealth of information and clarity that had never before been available. Information on some individual cities had been available since the mid-1860s; Neumann's and Schwabe's surveys of Berlin and the kind of data collected in the *Statistisches Jahrbuch der Stadt Berlin*, first published in 1874, presented such information for Berlin, but these could easily be dismissed as atypical. Now, for the first time, the nation was confronted by a devastating picture of housing conditions across the country. Schmoller, reviewing these reports, emphasised how little was known before:

These dwellings of the worker and the poor, the habitations of the greater part of the population of our present large industrial cities, are never visited by the civilised members of our society – apart that is from the constable, the bailiff, the almsgiver and the priest; the doctor hardly goes at all, as the poor cannot pay. This misery is never seen by the propertied and educated classes, indeed they do not wish to see it.[32]

For the first time the problem had been brought out into the open; it could now no longer be avoided. A considerable volume of information on housing conditions in individual cities had been available before, but in this fragmented form it did not have much impact. Now, brought together on a common *comparative* basis, it was no longer possible to shrug off the problems of housing as a local or a temporary aberration. In contrast to the image of the worker as 'Reichsfeind', feeding on socialist doctrine and poised ready to destroy society, the worker was now seen as a patient and long-suffering victim of economic progress. Many shared the surprise expressed by Schmoller that human values could survive such conditions:

To put the psychological truth bluntly: conditions are so horrific that it is to be wondered that the consequences are not more terrible. It is only because a great part of the working classes are still able to maintain in these vile dens a store of moral values, of religious conviction, of decency left from earlier days, that the worst has not yet come to pass.[33]

The statistical material assembled by Neefe drew attention both to the extent of the awfulness of housing conditions, and to the extent to which the housing market had changed since the early 1860s, the first time for which systematic statistical data are available.[34] His statistical tables show the rapid growth of the urban population during the late 1860s and the early 1870s and demonstrate how this outstripped the land available for development, resulting in a significant increase in the density of building in every city. It was this change, represented by the emergence of the *Mietskaserne* block as the norm for urban housing and very much a product of the new form of housing development, that was identified by contemporaries as one of the most damaging aspects of the housing problem. It was already recognised that in Berlin the density of housing was high in the 1860s and had continued to rise ever since, but what was not appreciated and was now revealed by the Verein's investigations was the extent to which, by the 1880s, this same form of speculation had produced housing of almost equal density across the whole country.

The survey also revealed the inadequacy of the miserable arrangements within these blocks: the minute size of dwellings in which the bulk of the urban population now lived and the extent to which these were over-crowded. As if to mock the belief in economic progress and the optimism of the 1860s and the early 1870s, housing conditions were now shown to be little better than those in the *Familienhäuser* described by Bettina von Arnim nearly 40 years before.

Some comfort might be drawn from the limited improvement in the size of dwellings: there had been a slight decrease in the percentage of dwellings with one heatable room since the housing crisis of the *Gründerjahre*. But in Berlin, for example, conditions generally did not appear to have improved since the 1860s, and in other cities small dwellings were as large an element of the total stock as in Berlin; only in the west were conditions better.[35] The information on rents and length of occupancy only reinforced this alarming picture. The data on rents, fragmentary though these were, confirmed Schwabe's 'law' that the proportion of income paid on rent increased as income decreased, and showed this to be true for other cities besides Berlin.[36] Other tables showed a significant rise in the number of *Schlafgänger* as rents rose, suggesting the importance of casual lodgers to many working-class families as a means of supplementing income to meet higher rents. Yet other data, on the average length of tenancy, revealed the very high mobility of the lowest income groups and the frequency with which the poorest families were forced to move, either by doing a 'midnight flit', to avoid the seizure of their possessions for non-payment of rent, or as a result of being ejected.[37]

The conditions portrayed in the survey may have come as a surprise to the members of the Verein, but the conclusions were clear. That conditions were so universally bad across the country had to be seen as an indictment of the traditional liberal attitudes to the social question and of the achievements of private enterprise in house building; the unwillingness of private enterprise to build for the lowest income groups where rent losses were highest, maintenance impossible and profit margins unpredictable, had to be recognised. To redress this situation the Verein strongly urged the case for State intervention, keenly aware of the threat of political violence as the penalty for inactivity.

From the start, Miquel advocated government intervention, 'Die starke Hand des Staates und das Einschreiten der Gesetzgebung',[38] as the only means of overcoming the failings of the existing situation. Comparing the situation in Germany with that in England or France, where legislation to control housing conditions had already been enacted, Miquel demanded the introduction of national housing legis-lation, a 'Reichsgesetz über das ungesundes Wohnen', which would not only extend the provisions for the control of new building, but would, for the first time, make it possible to control the use of existing housing. Following the precedent of national legislation regulating the terms of employment, the new housing law was to contain provisions governing the terms of the rent contract, controlling the liability of the tenant in the event of non-payment of the rent, and clearly setting out the duties of the landlord. The new law was also intended to impose limitations on the use of buildings which were in poor structural repair, where lighting was wholly inadequate, or where the building could be shown to be a risk to public health; as in the Torrens Act, provisions were to be made for the community to expropriate properties which did not comply. Finally, limits were to be imposed on overcrowding by means of some index related to health; the one most favoured was based on the volume of air per person.

To provide for the great increase in the demand for low-cost housing that it was assumed would result from the imposition of such legislation, Miquel pressed for a very substantial increase in the volume of new building both by private enterprise and by municipal and state govern-ment. Employers were urged to provide housing for their own employees and the state and the municipalities were reminded of their special duty to set an example in this field. With both supply and demand stimulated in this way, Miquel argued that housing conditions would improve: gradually, as the supply of housing came to match demand, inadequate dwellings would be driven off the market, forcing the quality of housing upwards while rents would stabilise at an acceptable level.

During the Verein's debate on the investigations, the same emphasis on the need for government intervention was made by other speakers. Pastor Friedrich Franz Ludwig von Bodelschwingh, spokesman for the interests of the Christian Evangelical movement, stressed the moral dangers of poor housing: the dissolution of family life and the attractions to drink to the poor of both sexes as a means of escape from desperate housing conditions.[39] But most of all, he emphasised the connection that he had himself observed between poor housing and anarchism, claiming that the Paris Commune was a direct product of the terrible housing conditions that followed Baron Haussmann's grandiose planning projects for the reshaping of central Paris. For Bodelschwingh, good housing, particularly the benefits of home ownership, was an excellent bulwark against socialism.

A similar position was taken by Schmoller in his influential review of the Verein's investigation published under the title 'Ein Mahnruf in der Wohnunsfrage'. He called for help 'from above' to guide the working classes to a better life and to remove the dangerous conditions that fostered the growth of socialism. Pointing to the failure of traditional means of maintaining order – the school, the church, the apprenticeship system and military service – he concluded that unless reform was immediately set in train, socialism and anarchy would take over:

Like the group of Spanish Colonists in Central America who, thrown back on their own resorces when cut off in the jungle, sank back to the cultural standards of the surrounding Indians, so our present society ineluctably forces the lower classes of the urban proletariat, by the inadequacy of their housing conditions, to regress to a level of barbarism and bestiality, of depravity and violence from which their forefathers escaped long ago. I can safely say that the gravest threat to our society comes from this quarter. The doctrines of social democracy and anarchism are only dangerous when they fall on ground that is already defiled and degraded.[40]

The roots of the housing problem were considered by Schmoller to lie in the failure to build sufficient housing to accommodate the rapid growth of the urban population during the preceding 30 years. To counter this state of affairs Schmoller demanded a number of immediate reforms: the education of the worker to want better housing, the emulation of the work of English organisations such as the Peabody Trust and the individuals like Octavia Hill in German cities, and action by the State to provide housing for its own employees, a programme very similar to that urged by Miquel.

To Schmoller it came as no surprise that the working classes showed so little interest in good housing and preferred to spend their money on more immediate pleasures. How could they know better? They had never been presented with an alternative. But new housing would change this. In place of the present image of the worker, brutalised by his hideous way of life, he drew a picture of the way that the worker might live:

As he focusses his energies on the drawing up of a plan to link present with future, as he divides his house into different rooms each with its own purpose, as he gives to every member of his family and to every activity its place, he not only strengthens his inner being but binds his animal passions, through domestication he civilises his way of life.[41]

At the debate on the investigation in Frankfurt in September there was a sense of achievement and of promise. Miquel was able to claim that the undertaking had been a great success as it had dramatically reawakened interest in the problems of housing: 'The principal task that the Verein has set itself, namely to attract the attention of the educated classes, of the economists, of the civil service and, indeed, of public opinion generally, and thus to provoke discussion on the appropriate measures to be taken by the State, the community and the individual, has been thoroughly successful.' Summing up the discussion at the conference, Miquel closed the debate with the Verein unified in its approach to the problem, apart from differences of opinion, occasionally strident, with representatives of the Verein für Haus- und Grundbesitzer. This show of unity appears to have pleasantly surprised Miquel who must have been expecting a more hostile reception for such strong demands for State intervention. The Verein agreed to press for national legislation on housing, to urge the municipalities to assist all forms of non-profit housing, to help in the provision of cheap transport to housing built on cheaper land away from the central areas of cities and to undertake, along with the individual states and the Reich, the housing of their own employees as a first step to reduce pressure on the housing market. As the conference closed, there was a sense of excitement for the future and a calm determination to implement the conference resolutions; to many it appeared that with this exposure of the housing problem, a new start could now be made. To rounds of applause Miquel closed the proceedings saying:

> If the forces of propertied and manufacturing capital can be convinced of (the existence of the housing problem), then people here in Germany are human and patriotic enough to make any sacrifice. These housing conditions are not the result of indifference, but the consequences of a lack of knowledge and a lack of understanding.[42]

At least the housing problem had been recognised, not just by the few sanitarians or clergymen whose work took them into the poorest city districts but by a far wider public. From 1886 the question could no longer be ignored or dismissed. But now that there was agreement that something should be done, how was the problem to be approached? How were conditions to be improved? What were the measures that government should enforce?

Answers to these questions had long preoccupied doctors and sanitarians, architects and engineers, and others concerned with housing. The enquiry of the VfSP had spurred these investigations forward, but in nearly every case these central interests, the major themes of our enquiry can be found to have attracted attention as early as the 1850s. Since then, a programme of reform had been gradually elaborated, establishing, for example, a consensus on the ideal form of dwelling, the minimum sanitary requirements for working-class housing, or ways and means of checking the rise in the value of land that forced up the costs and thus the rents of even the smallest dwellings. It is to this varied, occasionally contradictory, programme of reform that we turn in the next section.

The programme for reform

4

◇◇

The reformers' ideal

From the earliest days of concern with the problem of housing, reformers had attacked the conditions they saw around them, drawing a comparison between existing buildings and what they felt to be an ideal form of housing. Despite the variety of different points of view, despite the range of different kinds of reforming interests, there appeared to be a consensus that the ideal was the single house and its garden; preferably it should be a detached house but it was acceptable even in terrace form. Free of the complications caused by the need to share common stairs, corridors, toilets and courts, the family would be strengthened and better able to resist the damaging pressure of modern urban life. Much of the enthusiasm for the house or 'cottage' stemmed from the benefits to family life that the reformers were convinced could only be preserved in the setting of the individual house. The ideas conveyed in the phrase, 'An Englishman's home is his castle' of the security and the privacy of the house for family life were central to the support for the house rather than the tenement.[1] Throughout the German literature on housing reform, from the 1850s to the First World War, there are continual references to the English 'cottage' – untranslated and printed in Latin rather than Gothic script – as an ideal setting for home life; undaunted by the incongruity of its literal sense, the German reformers proposed the cottage as a castle for the defence of the family.

In contrast to England where by the 1840s there was already a literature which urged the case for the 'block',[2] it is rare in Germany before the 1890s that anyone spoke in favour of the tenement and the benefits of high-density living in blocks of flats. For most people the tenement block, so often referred to in derogatory terms as the *Mietskaserne* or, literally, rent barracks, rather than simply as *Mietshaus*, represented the source of the evils of the housing problem. The most vigorous attacks on the *Mietskaserne* date from the 1870s when the massive property speculation and the unprecedented expansion of Berlin and other cities had transformed housing conditions, but even the earliest discussion of housing problems such as that by Bettina von Arnim (quoted in Chapter 1) identified the conditions in tenement housing as worse in Berlin than elsewhere.

However, in presenting the tenement as less desirable than the cottage, the reformers were also passing judgement on the most common form of housing, at least until the 1890s, being built in urban areas by the reforming organisations such as the BgB and other public housing associations. This inconsistency between ideal and practice can be easily understood; the ideal of the individual cottage house remained an absolute goal: it was to be the kind of housing provided in the best of all best possible worlds. The tenement, however, remained the only feasible solution for housing for the working classes. Reluctantly the reformers came to accept that the working classes had to live within convenient reach of employment often located in the centre or inner suburbs of cities where high land values made the construction of cottage housing totally uneconomic at rents that the working-class family could afford.

We must therefore consider two ideals: one the 'absolute' ideal of the individual cottage; the other, the feasible ideal of the 'model' tenement embodying the demands of the sanitarians and architects for higher housing standards which was championed with greater vigour from the 1890s onwards.

The cottage ideal

In England, as enthusiastic reformers reported,[3] not only was the cottage the norm for working-class housing in many cities but those directly concerned with housing reform, such as Henry Roberts, were building what appeared to be improved cottages for renting to working-class tenants. The example of the model dwellings built for the Great Exhibition in 1851, which were widely (but misleadingly) reported in Germany as workers' cottages,[4] was followed by the housing also built by Roberts for the Windsor Royal Society for Improving the Conditions of the Working Classes in 1852.

In France the cottage ideal, albeit in 'back-to-back' form, was well represented already by the mid-1850s by the Cité Ouvrière at Mulhouse. Even 30 years after its inception, this scheme continued to stimulate interest in German housing reform circles.[5] Under the leadership of Jean Dollfus a number of Mulhouse industrialists had subscribed sufficient capital to launch the building of a working-class quarter from 1853. The typical dwelling, which was widely copied elsewhere on the continent especially in Germany, was planned as one house containing four dwellings placed together in a cross. As a contrast to the first improved working-class tenements provided in Paris by the Cité Napoléon, built by the early 1850s the reformers in France could see before them the realisation of the cottage ideal and draw encouragement from its apparent success.

Despite the enthusiasm of Huber and others for the cottage there appears to have been little awareness of German achievements in this field. The cottage housing traditionally provided by employers like the mines in rural and semi-rural areas was ignored by early reformers,[6] and even the cottage housing built as part of a continuation of local tradition in areas such as the north-west, exemplified by the work of the Verein für kleine Wohnunge in Bremen, appears to have attracted little attention.[7] Indeed there appear to be no well-known examples of 'improved' cottage housing in an urban setting in Germany until the 1870s. It is true that the BgB had built a number of cottages on the Bremerhöhe in 1852, but these attracted little interest and proved difficult to rent.[8] In the absence of successful examples at home, discussion turned either to foreign developments, particularly Mulhouse and the English tradition, or was conducted in abstract terms, often unfettered by the demands of practicability.

The case for the cottage, commanding as it did almost universal support, was presented in a variety of ways. However, three themes in particular emerge early on in the debate as being of central importance: the value of the cottage for family life, a case often supported by reference to a supposed Germanic tradition and in terms of a defence of morality for the working classes; the importance of home-ownership, a benefit only really possible for cottage houses, an argument often presented in relation to a discussion of self-help; finally, the sanitary benefits of the cottage by comparison with the overcrowded, airless, noisy and densely built tenement block.

Family life and the cottage ideal

An argument that found universal favour was the importance of the individual house for the quality of home life. Elaborated by Huber in the mid-1840s, it was taken up with enthusiasm by liberals like Faucher in the 1860s and again by Schmoller and others in the 1880s. Huber's writings in *Janus* as early as 1845 emphasise the need to save the proletarian family through better housing: 'The duty of any organisation wishing to help the proletariat must return continually to its main task: the founding and fostering of a Christian family life amongst the proletariat'.[9] Only if the working-class family were thus secured would the fabric of society again be stabilised; failure to act might lead to political unrest, a case already argued in France by Blanqui after the disturbances of 1848 and frequently repeated by housing reformers in Germany and England over the next 40 years.[10]

Inspired by the writings of Robert Owen and Charles Fourier, and drawing on the tradition of Old Germanic settlements, Huber proposed the founding of new communities in which the land and dwellings would be held in common, while the individual family lived independently in separate houses, not as part of a larger community in a communal block like Fourier's *phalanstère*: 'it is axiomatic that we should demand as first priority the English cottage system; rightly understood and carefully executed, it is the only means of securing for the working-class family the independence that it needs without at the same time excluding the real benefits of association'.[11]

Huber accepted that the detached cottage might be expensive for the worker but insists that as more dwellings were assembled under one roof so the independence of the family was eroded, with inevitable physical and moral consequences. The *Familienhäuser*, or tenement form of housing, he dismisses as inferior: 'the cottage alone ensures the possibility of providing the cleanliness and order so necessary to the physical and moral well-being of the family'.[12] Co-operation might mean shared wash-rooms, common reading-rooms and other such benefits of association, but it did not mean the sharing of the necessities of family life; the kitchen and the hearth were to be firmly located as the focal point within each individual family house.

Well acquainted with the work of the English philanthropic housing companies, Huber did not doubt that the tenement could be made habitable by the standards of the reformers, but the cottage remained his ideal, a point he emphasised in his references to the *cité ouvrière* at Mulhouse.

The case that Huber and others presented in the narrower context of housing reform was supported in more general terms by writers defending the traditional values of a German way of life like Wilhelm Riehl. His attack from a conservative standpoint on the liberal society that he saw developing in the 1850s included a volume devoted to the family, *Die Familie*, 1854, the second part of which, entitled 'Haus und Familie', concentrated on the relationship between family and house. To Riehl the house was a form of physical analogue of the family: just as the extended family with its dependents was a product of a long German tradition so the 'ganze Haus' was the product of a long parallel tradition of house building. To pervert or debase the form of the house was to tamper with the very existence of the German family.

While Riehl's principal target was the manners of the new liberal bourgeoisie with their Frenchified ways, the ideal that he elaborated lent strong support to the cottage ideal. The cottage was portrayed as part of the rural tradition of the 'organic' house in which even the poorest members of the community could live, secure in the certainty of traditional values around them. To preserve the family in modern times, cottage housing was essential: 'it should be one of the first aims of the newly created non-profit housing societies to work for the benefit of the less fortunate, by building model dwellings in which the family is again taken as the natural scale for the house. These societies should draw courage and remember that their mission is a social one; they should not build tenement blocks, however well appointed, but real family houses, little houses conceived and built from the inside out.'[13]

To Riehl the dangers of the *Mietskaserne* or *Familienhäuser* were only too clear:

Family life ceases and the egotism of the individual fills every cranny. The work (of the non-profit housing associations) shall be cursed, not blessed, if they build blocks of tenements, 'hotels' for workers, instead of houses for families. It would not be surprising if gradually the architecture of the tenement block does not lead us all to the barracks of socialism; the poor man can bear this living together in a mass community even less than the rich man... Architecturally even the central areas of our cities have been made to look like the courts or closes of some Jewish Ghetto.[14]

But these fears were not restricted to the conservatives alone. For many, fearful of aspects of the new industrialised urbanised society, the cottage represented a vital link with a German past. Edward Wiss, a prominent member of the Kongress deutscher Volkswirte (KdV), writing in the 1860s, emphasised the extent to which the cottage, a product of an old Germanic way of life, should be preserved. Quoting Freytag, he contrasted the towns of roman origin, 'walled places...prisons and destroyers of men', with the individual house, the original German form of settlement: 'these were the dwellings of the free men of the different German peoples...everywhere we see the free-standing house, the house of the free man, lodging only one family, as the original way of living that was common to our forefathers'.[15] The cottage was presented as a product of the Germanic and Saxon culture that lived on in England; to build cottages was to assert the strength of this tradition unsullied by contact with the Latin south and to replant it in German soil.

Home-ownership and the cottage

Another major theme in the case for the cottage, pressed with such vigour during the first debate on the housing question, was the benefit of home-ownership which was associated so much more directly with the cottage than the tenement. Faucher's articles on housing reform, with their extended discussion of the English cottage tradition, championed demands for ownership of cottage housing for the working classes, and at the KdV's annual conference in 1864, proposals for home-ownership linked with this form of housing were unanimously endorsed. Writing in 1865, Parisius reaffirmed his belief in this ideal:

We believe that this preference, innate in all German peoples, for the fixed and permanent, but particularly for one's own house, is a characteristic which it is highly desirable to preserve. The savings of a worker bent on self-improvement cannot be invested more wisely or more usefully than in his own house. Owning his own house strengthens the independent life of his family, and a strong and virtuous marriage; it encourages cleanliness, regularity and discipline; it calls forth the 'homely' virtues; it facilitates the raising of children in good moral and physical health; it protects them and keeps them free from bad company and temptation. But, in addition, the knowledge of owning something that the thief cannot carry off, of being master of even a small patch of land, provides the workers with a stake in our whole society.[16]

To many reformers the possibility of home-ownership was the highest reward for the virtues of self-help and thrift. It was presented as an incentive to control expenditure and moral excess, as the just return for those who lived according to Smilesian precepts. To the individual it offered a freedom from the speculative market and a financial independence from rent and landlord; to society, the home owner with a stake in society would provide a valuable counterweight to the forces of the mob or the commune. Revolutionary excess, they argued, would be unattractive to those who, through home-ownership, had 'a stake' in the existing order of society.

So well established was the connection between the cottage ideal and the benefits of home-ownership, that Engels characterised this as the principal bourgeois solution to the housing question: 'the essence of both the big bourgeois and the petty bourgeois solution to housing question is that the worker should own his own dwelling.'[17] These comments were prompted by Sax's enthusiastic advocacy of home-ownership and its benefits: 'Whoever is fortunate enough to call a piece of land his own has reached the highest conceivable stage of economic independence; he has a plot of land on which he can rule with sovereign power; he is his own master...he becomes a capitalist and is safe-guarded against the dangers of unemployment or incapacity to work... He is thus raised out of the ranks of the propertyless into the class of the property owners.'[18] In this way it would be possible to create a 'diligent, skilled, willing, contented and devoted working class'.

Despite the changes in attitude during the 1870s, the cottage ideal and its association with home-ownership still retained its attraction in the 1880s. Erwin Reichardt, writing in 1883, recognised that many working-class families would find home-ownership impossible either because of the cost of buying a house or because of the need to move from city to city to find work. Nevertheless, the benefits of the ownership of a cottage were still obvious to him: 'The satisfaction of the need for housing by the erection of cottages and the ownership of these by the working classes is without question the most desirable goal for the reform of our housing conditions'.[19] Owning a home offered the worker the chance of permanently bettering the lot of his family to whom he could leave his house: 'The conviction will grow in him that there is indeed a more peaceful way to achieve a higher standard of living: from former social democrat he turns to become a defender of property and order'.[20] The test of this ideal in practice at Mulhouse was for Reichardt a vindication of this point of view.

Writing in 1886, Schmoller reiterated the view held by many that housing was a direct indication of the state of civilisation of a society and that family life in a cottage should be the lot of all; indeed only if the worker felt he had a stake in society, best represented by the home about which he deeply cared, could he be successfully incorporated into society and the threat of political unrest removed. Perhaps in deference to the growing realisation that home-ownership was beyond the means of the bulk of the working classes, Schmoller places less emphasis on the details of ownership and more on the enjoyment of the use of the cottage. For Schmoller 'it is the cultivation of the garden and the house – not agriculture – that binds mankind firmly to a settled way of life; it is the creation of the house for the single family that first generates a real family life...[It is thus that the worker] develops his own inner life, firmly limiting his lower urges and subordinating himself in this domestication to an orderly mode of life. With his home he builds an altar to morality and decency'.[21]

The cottage and the healthy home

The third major argument used in making the case for the cottage was the enormous hygienic advantages that the cottage appeared to offer over the tenement block. In the 1880s, as the density of housing increased in the developing cities, particularly Berlin, the cottage appealed more keenly still as a haven from the threat to both moral and physical well-being represented by the housing conditions in the *Mietskaserne*. In contrast to the high-density tenement block which came to symbolise, even if it did not necessarily harbour, the worst housing conditions, the obvious advantages of low-density cottage housing or other forms of 'offene Bauweisen' (open forms of building) were repeated annually from the 1880s onwards at the annual conferences of the Verein für öffentliche Gesundheitspflege (VföG).[22] This association, which brought together doctors, sanitarians, engineers, architects and municipal leaders, formed the central forum for the discussion of public health and sanitary matters in Germany from its formation as an independent section of the Versammlung deutscher Naturforscher und Ärzte in 1867, and was to play a most influential role in the movement for housing reform. It was the continued pressure from the VföG that led to the introduction of standards of density zoning which in practical terms was one of the most effective means of ensuring the development of cottage housing from the mid-1890s onwards.

The block did not have to be associated with unhealthy housing. But the cottage offered an easier resolution of the sanitarians' requirements. Tenement blocks could be built in such a way as to lower mortality rates and to ensure the levels of ventilation and isolation demanded by medical science in the 1870s and 1880s; as the evidence of Charles Gatliff, Secretary of the Metropolitan Association for Improving the Dwellings of the Industrious Classes, and others showed, the high-density 'model' tenements in London could actually be more salubrious than the worst cottage housing.[23] But the superiority of the cottage, *ceteris paribus*, was evident. Given the authority of miasmatic theories of disease, the threat of the *Mietskaserne* to health was clear: each family risked infection from its neighbours by the seepage of 'vitiated air' from one dwelling to another; for this reason alone the piling up of so many families on one site was a threat to health. In addition the lack of adequate drainage facilities and the frequent concentration of polluted air from the toilets in the cramped space of a court was regarded as providing the ideal breeding ground for disease. In a paper to the VföG in 1875. Dr W. Strassmann attacked the combined effect of vitiated air and vitiated ground, together with high density building as the cause of the high mortality rates for cities like Berlin, claiming that life expectancy was so reduced by the *Mietskaserne* as to be lower than in even the largest cities in England and America.[24] By comparison with the typical tenement dwelling which gave on to a mean court where ventilation, let alone sunlight, was almost impossible, how obvious were the benefits of the cottage, where all rooms could be so easily lit and cross-ventilated.

At its annual conferences from 1875 until the 1890s, the VföG was vigorous in its support of the cottage system of housing. At the Munich conference of 1875,[25] the first time that the control of the density of new development was considered, the benefits of an 'open' system with free-standing housing were agreed and adopted by the VföG. Speaking during the debate on the need to control the construction of high-density housing, Dr Kuby of Augsburg expressed the feelings of many when he declared that: 'There cannot now be the slightest doubt of the great hygienic advantages – light and ample ventilation – conferred by the pavilion and, even more so, by the villa system of layout.'[26] Standing alone, open to the beneficial effects of ventilation, the cheering effect of sunlight and surrounded by fresh air, the cottage was presented as immeasurably superior to all other forms of working-class housing. Just as hospital design was dominated from the 1850s by the demands of ventilation, resulting in the system of isolated 'pavilion' planning of ward accommodation, so the healthy home came to reflect the same priorities; the advantages of the cottage were unassailable.

Nearly 20 years later, essentially the same view still dominated the sanitarians' view of the ideal form of housing. Although various sanitary reforms and changes in the building regulations had started to prevent some of the worst excesses of the *Mietskaserne*, the strength of the cottage ideal remained as potent as ever. In the crucial debates at Frankfurt in 1893 and in Würzburg in 1894[27] at which the VföG debated and approved the system of density zoning, the support for the cottage system of housing for the areas of new development in the outskirts of cities was of central importance. Speaking at the Würzburg debate, Franz Adickes, *Oberbürgermeister* of Frankfurt and an influential voice in the field of city government, described the sanitarians' ideal:

As the ideal dwelling for the purposes of our present objectives we would most readily choose a dwelling which offers a fully independent family life, granting both children and adults a comfortable home and the setting for flourishing improvement. Perhaps the matter is best defined by its opposite. The antithesis of the ideal is the heaping up of dwellings in a block, it is immaterial whether it consists of a 'street' building alone, or rear and side buildings as well. Here, there can be no independent life for the individual family. Stairs, hall, court and children's playground – everything must be shared with others, physical and moral contamination spreads, the gossip and jealousies of neighbours sow the burgeoning seeds of discord and the landlord quickly assumes the role of tyrant...if the one family house and the multi-storey house are not direct opposites, then the rent barracks and the family house are, and that only the latter can serve as our ideal is something that I do not need to elaborate in this setting.[28]

By 1914, the range of examples of cottage housing in Germany was sufficient for the reformers to assess the benefits of the ideal in practice. In the decade before the war, the *Siedlungen* and *Gartenvorstädte* built by employers and non-profit housing associations demonstrated how the cottage ideal could be combined with the new approach to planning, inspired by Camillo Sitte, the champion of aesthetic values in city planning, to create a model workers' community. Most liked what they saw. Indeed for those who could afford it, or for those who did not find living in a tied cottage on a company estate restrictive or irksome, the ideal of the cottage lost little by translation into reality. The Margaretenhöhe estate started in 1910 by the Margarete Krupp Stiftung in honour of Krupp's wife, exemplified the realisation of the ideal: with its well-built houses and their gardens laid out on streets that led down to the market place, its physical form suggests those qualities of the stable communities of medieval market towns that served as sources of inspiration for its design. The pattern of daily life, salubrious and comfortable, broken occasionally by the weddings and the fêtes illustrated in the Krupp publications describing the estate, seemed to answer fully the reformers' programme of purifying and strengthening the elements of family life that risked destruction and degradation in the *Mietskaserne*. At the Margaretenhöhne the cottage idea was there for all to see and to admire.[29]

The block

In contrast to the wealth of literature written in support of the cottage ideal, there is little written in favour of the tenement as an ideal, or even as an acceptable form, of working-class housing before the 1890s. Although English and French examples of what might be accomplished in this way were known to German reformers through the *Mittheilungen* of the CVWaK and other publications, these examples appear to have generated little enthusiasm. Even the housing built by the BgB in the central working-class areas of Berlin was presented not as a conscious attempt to pursue the block as an ideal, but as a compromise; it reflected both the desirability of providing housing for working-class families in central areas close to the location of employment and the high cost of land in these areas. Despite its failure to provide home-ownership as originally intended, the project was often referred to in the later literature with affection, as one of the earliest achievements of the housing reform movements in Germany. But it did little to inspire similar attempts elsewhere. Reviewing Germany's limited achievements in the field of housing reform in 1886, Schmoller was scathing in his reference to the work of the BgB and its occasional followers: 'In Germany the housing companies we have had up to now have been nothing more than petty bourgeois experiments.'[30]

Before the end of the 1880s only an occasional voice could be heard pressing the benefits of the *Mietskaserne*. Rudolf Eberstadt, one of the most influential voices on housing reform at the turn of the century, quotes, with a clear indication that he regards it as both mistaken and naive, Hobrecht's defence of the block in his pamphlet *Über die öffentliche Gesundheitspflege* of 1868.[31] Here Hobrecht argues that the tenement block offers unique opportunities for combining the dwellings of the poor and the rich on the same site, thus ensuring that the lower classes are uplifted and encouraged towards a more moderate way of life by the genteel manners of their betters, while the rich are reminded of the duties of Christian charity towards their inferiors (whose life style they can see at first hand), offering soup and cast-off clothing as a social bridge between classes.

By the early 1890s, however, the crude polarisation of the debate on the ideal form of housing in which the overwhelming benefits of the cottage were contrasted with the horrors of the block, had been replaced by a more informed discussion. While the cottage still remained for most the ideal form of housing, it was now conceded in circles such as the CVWaK or Centralstelle für Arbeiter-Wohlfahrtseinrichtungen (CAW)[32] that the costs of the cottage in an urban setting placed it beyond the reach of the bulk of the working classes, both because of the costs of construction and because of the high cost of land within easy reach of working-class areas of employment.

Doubts over the viability of the cottage ideal can be found in a number of contributions to the debate on housing around the end of the 1880s and the beginning of the 1890s. Spurred on by the recommendations of the VfSP for an increase in the construction of new housing along the lines of the English limited dividend housing companies, housing reformers looked afresh at the potential of the block. The Deutscher Verein für Armenpflege und Wohltätigkeit (DVfAW)[33] set up a committee under Paul Aschrott to examine ways of building cheap working-class housing in the city centre. In its report, which was clearly influenced by Aschrott's detailed knowledge of English developments, the committee recommended the construction of blocks of 'model' tenements as the only possible solution and engaged the architect Alfred Messel to prepare a design.[34] The Verein zur Verbesserung der kleinen Wohnungen in Berlin showed the same interest in the block; originally founded in 1888 together with the Frauenverein Octavia Hill to rehabilitate and administer existing property using the voluntary assistance of middle-class women to collect rent in the way pioneered by Octavia Hill, the Verein found this form of housing too limited and too expensive, and in 1890 decided to embark on the construction of 'model' tenement dwellings to the design of Messel, who had been a committee member of the Verein from the start.[35] Even the sanitarians were moving towards a grudging acceptance of the block; Fritz Kalle, a liberal industrialist closely associated with the DVfAW, the VföG and the VfSP, spoke at the annual conference of the VföG of the desirability of providing tenement housing along the lines of the English 'model' dwellings movement in 1890.[36]

The social and economic benefits of the block were championed with vigour by Heinrich Albrecht at the first conference of the CAW in 1892. He challenged the applicability of the much-vaunted English cottage prototype to German conditions:

Our German workers live very differently from the English. Even in circumstances where there is no compulsion to do so and where the situation does not demand it, they will choose to live in huge tenement blocks where hundreds of families live in the same building, rather than living in isolated and scattered cottages. Our Berlin worker, for example, has no conception of the pleasures of a more spacious or healthy way of life – by comparison, the advantages for him of living in the big city where shopping is easy and housing is cheaper, are greater. All too soon the husband will miss his pub and the wife her shopping...[37]

These preferences of the German worker led Albrecht to question the benefits of the cottage ideal. In locational terms the cottage, placed in the outskirts, was impractical for most of the working class, and for women making an often important contribution to the family budget through temporary and casual work, a location near the centre of the city close to the market for this kind of labour was essential.

But in addition to these difficulties, Albrecht considered the cost of the cottage form of housing a major stumbling block. He emphasised how few were the workers who could actually afford their own dwelling, even on the favourable basis on which many reformers had based their calculations; he argued that many had assessed the costs of ownership without taking into account the whole picture, leaving out items such as the various taxes or underestimating the running and transport costs. Albrecht particularly attacked the simplistic assumptions of the Berliner Baugenossenschaft and others who unrealistically held out the promise of home-ownership. In urban areas he demanded tenements for rent at prices the working-class family could afford.

Stimulated by this new interest in the block, architects were also reconsidering the positive merits of this form of housing, particularly in Berlin. The emergence of a new interest in the tenement is exemplified by a series of articles by Theodor Goecke in the *Deutsche Bauzeitung*[38] in 1890. Writing with a sense of brisk realism and showing an awareness of the typical housing costs and working-class incomes, he strongly asserted the benefits of living in the centre of the city for the working classes: 'No, the worker prefers to be surrounded by the hustle and bustle of the city; he enjoys the excitements of the streets; he takes fullest advantage of the size of the community in satisfying his needs; and it is here that he finds his pleasures.'[39]

To meet these legitimate demands of the working man, working-class housing was not to be conceived simply as cottages on the outskirts of the city but as properly planned tenements in the centre. Thinking of the problems which faced the workers in Berlin, Goecke urged architects to look at the work of the model housing companies in London and their achievement, praising the combination of well-designed and salubrious housing at reasonable rents. Demonstrating his case with a series of designs with large courts, rather than the English system of separate parallel blocks, Goecke argued that the demands of sanitarians could be met as well in tenement housing as in the cottage and at a cost that put it within the reach of most working-class families. The case advanced by Goecke for the rethinking of the design of the tenement block was powerfully supported by the work of organisations such as the Verein zur Verbesserung der kleinen Wohnungen and the Berliner

Spar- und Bauverein, founded 1892, who employed architects of
national standing to experiment with the design of working-class tenements in the centre of Berlin.

By 1900 the results of this initiative were impressive. In place of the
traditional *Mietskaserne* built as a speculative venture with its minimal
courts and miserable dwellings, or even the tenement blocks built after
the review of the Berlin building code in 1887, architects such as Messel
were able to design housing that offered benefits that the cottage
housing in the outskirts could not match, but without the disadvantages
of the traditional *Meitskaserne* form. On the Proskauerstrasse, the
Berliner Spar- und Bauverein built a block of flats (see fig. 25), finished
in 1898, which exemplifies this new approach.[40] In place of the minimal
dwellings, often divided by a communal corridor, huddled around courts
which were little more than light-wells, Messel planned the dwellings
around a huge planted court of over 40 m in width. All the dwellings
were self-contained and had a view on to this court and on to the street,
thus ensuring cross ventilation as well as adequate lighting, and even
sunlight. Approached in this way, the tenement could clearly offer many
of the benefits traditionally associated with the cottage.

But the achievements of Messel and others in designing these large
developments was not limited to improving the quality of the individual
dwelling. In the Proskauerstrasse, as in similar large developments
carried out by non-profit organisations, the block could provide facilities
such as kindergartens, wash- and bathrooms, common-rooms and
meeting rooms, all as part of the development, and organised on
co-operative principles in a way that was rare on cottage estates.

The potential offered for the development of a true 'genossenschaft-
liches Leben' was hailed as a real benefit of the block system of housing.
Albrecht, reviewing five years of the work of the Berliner Spar- und
Bauverein, a co-operative closely associated with the CAW, drew
attention to the extent to which the facilities provided by these large
developments provided an ideal setting for co-operative life and the
edification and advancement of the working classes: while the form of
the cottage estate did not preclude the same benefits, the accessibility
of the facilities in the block encouraged tenants to take part in the
activities arranged for the community.

The range of activities organised by many co-operatives was extensive,
often surprisingly so. In the Proskauerstrasse, in addition to the benefits
of the kindergarten run by the Frauenverein Octavia Hill, the restaurant,
bakery and facilities such as the wash- and bathrooms, the Spar- und
Bauverein arranged Christmas festivities and a range of activities
explicitly intended to prove more attractive to the working man than
the 'Kneipe', or pub, and other unwholesome dissipations.[41] In the
Sickingenstrasse, a bequest from former members of the same co-
operative made it possible to start a reading-room and a library. A series
of popular lectures on scientific subjects, a number of musical
entertainments, amateur dramatic events and museum visits,
systematically covering all the 'most treasured collections of our city',

were arranged by the co-operative. The musical entertainments, for example, appear to have been quite ambitious: under the direction of Herr Königlicher Musikdirektor C. Mengwein, differences between the natural desires of the membership for popular music and the demands of edification were tactfully resolved and the Committee for the Organisation of People's Productions produced the whole of Bach's St Matthew Passion as their first enterprise. To commentators such as Albrecht and Dorothea Jacobi it was benefits of this kind that further strengthened the case for the block.[42] The dwellings in a model development such as that on the Proskauer Strasse were not only financially and locationally more suitable for working-class families: this kind of housing could claim to offer moral and other advantages that might even surpass those associated with the cottage ideal.

The conventional wisdom after 1900

But despite the arguments of those who urged the case for the block as the most appropriate form of working-class housing for large cities such as Berlin, and the difficulties that faced most workers in renting, let alone buying, a home of their own, the conventional wisdom maintained the benefits of the cottage as ideal even through into the period between the two world wars.

Eberstadt, regarded as one of the most authoritative voices in the debate on housing, unequivocally affirmed his support for the cottage.[43] The *Mietskaserne*, the product of an artificial and distorted system of financing, was unacceptable under any circumstances; the *Mietshaus* might be acceptable in an urban setting; the detached single family house might not be viable in every situation, but for Eberstadt it was the ideal for which the housing reform movement should unswervingly aim. The same view was reiterated in *Die Wohnungs- und Siedlungsfrage nach dem Kriege*, a book edited by Carl J. Fuchs in 1917 and providing a valuable summary of the pre-war debate with contributions from nearly all the best-known members of the movement.[44] Though the tenement block might be the most appropriate form of housing in some circumstances, the cottage ideal that Huber and Faucher had supported so long before still remained the unchallenged ideal.

From the 1840s to the First World War, these ideals brought together reformers who approached the problems of housing from very different points of view. By the start of the first debate on housing in the 1860s, the desirability of cottage housing rallied economists, architects, land reformers and others to the common cause. Even in these early days the battle for sanitary reform was an essential part of the reformers' campaign; the image of the 'healthy home' was a potent ideal for which to fight.

5

❖❖

Public health and housing reform

In England the campaign for sanitary reform provided one of the first and most powerful stimuli to consider the problems of housing. Edwin Chadwick's reports and activities in the late 1830s and early 1840s initiated a concern for public health which was to lead eventually to the introduction of legislation that did much both to control insanitary housing already in use and to ensure proper standards of construction for new housing. Between the 1840s and 1880s housing and sanitary reform remained closely entwined. Much of the strength of the movement for sanitary reform was due to the success of its challenge to the principle of 'non-intervention' by government in this field: even in the 1830s political theory recognised the need for government action to protect the health of its citizens quite as much as their physical safety; public health measures could not be carried out by the individual, they necessarily involved the activity of government.[1] Despite the jealousies of local government at interference from London and despite the difficulties of prodding recalcitrant vestries into controlling the most insanitary properties, the principle, and to some extent the practice, of government regulation in the field of public health was established by the mid-1860s.[2] By 1868 the Torrens Act had even established the right of government to control what the individual landlord did 'behind his own front door'.

In Germany the relationship of sanitary to housing reform is broadly similar to that in England, but the 'timetable' is different. In Germany, too, sanitary reformers establish the principle of government intervention and the need to regulate and cleanse the slum areas of the cities; the Germans were taken with the same enthusiasm for 'washing and splashing, and twirling and rinsing, and spongeing and sopping, and soaping and mopping'[3] insanitary housing and other sources of disease as in England, only later. But in Germany the first cholera epidemic produced no figures of the stature of Chadwick, and, despite the agitations of sanitarians like Carl Ignaz Lorinser in Berlin and Philipp von Walther in Munich and the spate of cholera regulations promulgated in individual cities, there was no unified movement for public health reform equivalent to the Health of Towns Association. It was not until the late 1840s with the work of Neumann and Virchow in Berlin that there is evidence of a comparable movement for public health reform in Germany.[4]

86

By the 1870s, however, the movement for sanitary reform, under the leadership of Max von Pettenkofer in Munich and Virchow in Berlin, had begun to transform conditions in a number of German cities. In 1869 the first system of sewering had been started in Danzig and the completion of the first phase in December 1871 was hailed by the VföG as a major step forward in sanitary reform.[5] After an extended campaign, enlivened by the slogan 'From the toilet to the river in half an hour', Frankfurt embarked in 1867 on the construction of a system of sewering and a proper system of water supply, which was at least partially complete by 1871, built to the designs of William Lindley, an English engineer who had worked in Hamburg.[6] After a tireless campaign by Virchow and others it was finally agreed to construct a system of sewers in Berlin in 1875;[7] by the end of the seventies this system of water-borne drainage had reached Rixdorf, and by the mid-1880s it was operating in Charlottenburg and Schöneberg. But such progress was by no means universal. As late as 1892, Hamburg was still drawing its water supply *untreated* from the Elbe, a state of affairs abruptly ended by the outbreak of cholera in that year.[8]

The hygiene of the individual dwelling before the mid-1870s

This first round of sanitary reform resulted in a number of improvements which were relevant to housing conditions; a most obvious example was the removal of 'nuisances' such as the foetid middens and cesspits whose stench had infected the stale air of the densely populated courts of the working-class areas of cities like Berlin. But it did not necessarily follow that advances in sanitary reform at this city scale had any direct bearing on the sanitary conditions in the individual dwelling. Indeed for contemporaries the development of city cleansing, canalisation, water supply and sewage disposal were considered separately from the hygienic problems of the dwelling.

There were a number of reasons why this was so. Current understanding of the spread of a variety of diseases such as cholera, dependent on the *Grundwasser* theories of Pettenkofer, emphasised the need to clean up the city and the surroundings of the house.[9] The need to control the moisture and the degree of pollution in the ground, to regulate the 'hygiene of the ground', was thus of prime importance for the whole community. By comparison, regulation of the conditions within the individual property was seen to be a private affair. The resulting balance of interest is well represented in the literature on public health. Before the 1870s, there is only scant mention of the problems of hygiene within the dwelling, while at the same time there is, by contrast, a flood of articles on the problems of canalisation, the merits of rival systems of sewage disposal (including a pneumatic system insistently championed by a Herr Lieneur), ways of assessing the quality of soil under housing and on the level of the *Grundwasser* for different cities at different times of the year.

The predominant liberal ideology of the time also suggested grounds for opposing control of conditions within the individual house more actively than for the city as a whole. The conditions of the individual dwelling were regarded as the affair of those who lived there. It was they who would suffer first from negligence, they would benefit first from cleanliness and care. In terms of the prevailing view, the choice of living in insanitary housing was regarded as a choice for the individual: if he wished, why should he not be entitled to pay a lower rent for unwholesome property in order to spend more freely on other goods?

To the landlords, vigorously championed by the Haus- und Grundbesitzer Vereine and powerfully represented in municipal government in Prussia through the three-class system of voting, attempts to regulate conditions 'behind the front door' of individual properties were deeply offensive. Sanitary reform threatened the income of the landlord: the prospect that the number of rooms packed on a site should be reduced, might mean a reduction in the number of tenancies; to ensure ventilation it might be necessary to build larger courts – a further loss of income; restrictions on cellar and roof dwellings might again close off valuable sources of income. It is not surprising that demands for higher standards of hygiene in the dwelling were regarded as a frontal attack on the freedoms of property. Here, where the health of the community could not be shown to be directly at risk, the case for reform was resisted more strongly than the case for canalisation and water supply. The landlord could always attempt to pass on the costs of reform to his tenants. Thus to the tenants the consequences of public health reform and agitation for higher standards of housing would be as unwelcome as for the landlord, especially if it meant higher rents, or the closure of insanitary property. A number of landlords even argued ingenuously that to close the cheapest dwellings, on the grounds that they might be insanitary, was to make the lot of the poor even worse.

Although municipal authorities came to accept, during the 1860s, the necessity of sanitary reform at the level of the city, the same authorities were less willing to regulate even grossly insanitary conditions in housing, although the necessary powers to do so already existed.[10] This however did not pass unchallenged. Prompted by the acute housing shortage of the late 1850s to set aside the habits of mind born of a *laissez-faire* approach, discussion of the insanitary conditions of working-class housing in Berlin begins at this time. Pressure for increased control over conditions in the individual dwelling develops gradually, stimulated by interest in the housing problem and by studies of insanitary housing, particularly cellar dwelling.[11] This new approach is exemplified in the study by E. Krieger in 1855, 'Über die Kellerwohnungen in Berlin', which stressed how the damaging effects of insanitary housing weakened the health of the poor and thus their ability to compete in the labour market. In this study, Krieger fiercely attacked the foulness of conditions in Berlin's cellar dwellings. No doubt aware of Pettenkofer's research in Munich, he warned of the dangers of a heavily polluted *Grundwasser* and the consequences of the frequent flooding in the deep cellars of the older working-class districts in Berlin with foul smelling and filthy water. In the survey conducted by the *Sanitätspolizei* in 1850, not a year of heavy flooding, one in ten of the dwellings inspected had standing water up to a depth of 66 cm. In view of these conditions it is hardly surprising that cellar dwellings, more than any other form of housing, should have been so closely associated with higher rates of morbidity and mortality, especially from water-borne epidemics. For Krieger, the 'physical deterioration of the present populous generation' and the threat to the larger community justified the closure of housing like this. It was not only 'the right, but the duty' for the authorities to intervene. But Krieger also recognised the frustrations of taking this course of action using the powers of the *Sanitätspolizei*; to condemn insanitary property at a time of housing shortage, when less than 1% of all dwellings were empty, was only to aggravate the housing shortage.

Like Krieger, Huber and the few others who opposed the *laissez-faire* views of the KdV regarded sanitary reform as an essential part of the programme for the improvement of housing condition. In *Concordia* Huber pointedly drew attention to the anomaly that those selling tainted food were liable to arrest and a stiff fine, while there appeared to be no real penalty for those landlords renting 'tainted' dwellings and he called 'without more ado, for criminal proceedings against the sale (of housing) on the same grounds as that for the sale of stale meat, fish or bread'.[12] But to Huber, and to other housing reformers, legislation alone was not enough. Real improvement was only to be achieved by educating the worker into wanting a higher standard of housing. Only then, argued Huber, would the worker be willing to spend less on beer and more on rent, and thus free himself from the damp, dark hovels inhabited by so many poor families.

This emphasis on self-help and the corrective power of education, even in sanitary matters such as these, was given yet greater prominence in the views of the Manchester liberals. For Sax, exponent of the conventional liberal wisdom on the housing question in the late 1860s, the question of hygiene was of great importance: 'the first and most important question is without doubt the arrangement of the dwelling in accordance with the demands of hygiene'.[13] Drawing widely on evidence from England, France and other countries, he argues that the cost of insanitary housing, both in human suffering and in economic terms, is too great to bear. But despite his manifest horror at these conditions, his hopes for improvement were founded only on the power of encouragement and education. The builder was to be encouraged to include proper water supply, drainage, water closets, even gardens, and to ensure a minimum volume of air per person. More than Huber, Sax stressed the need for education and the formation of the worker's desire to improve his own conditions: 'it depends essentially on the worker himself whether standards of hygiene are fulfilled and maintained'.[14] For Sax the key to improving housing conditions lay with the tenant himself. This, he argued, could never be a task for government.

The regulation of new building, sanitary reform and planning before 1875

Between the late 1860s and the mid-1870s, there is a change in attitudes to sanitary reform which is quite as significant as the parallel changes in approach to the social problem which led to the formation of the VfSP in 1872. Sanitary reform in the 1860s had focussed on the question of drainage and water supply and on the cleaning of the city. But by the mid-1870s the mood had changed. Now sanitarians did not hesitate to call for stringent controls on new development and the regulation of conditions in existing housing. The VföG, along with other professional groups like architects and engineers, looked to English legislation and demanded that stronger measures be made available to regulate new development;[15] a new consensus rapidly appeared which held that it was no longer sufficient to leave the control of these matters to the forces of the market or the self-interest of the individual tenant.

The most important cause of this change in attitude was the expansion of the urban areas in Germany during the period of hectic economic activity in the late 1860s and early 1870s. Berlin, as we have seen, grew very rapidly during this period; other cities and towns in Germany experienced a period of equally explosive growth. Contemporaries saw all too clearly the effect of this expansion on the conditions in German cities. Strassmann, introducing the discussion at the VföG of proposals for tighter control of development in urban areas, was firmly convinced that this sudden growth of the population of the cities was the central cause of the obvious decline in the sanitary conditions in urban areas.[16]

Existing arrangements to control this rapid growth had proved themselves inadequate. It was now recognised that the pressing need to prepare city extension plans to accommodate this growth could no longer be conveniently fitted into the framework of delegated powers which had enabled James Hobrecht to prepare the plan for Berlin between 1859 and 1862 at the request of the *Polizeipräsidium*. For some time the Prussian cities had exercised the authority, through the police powers delegated from the state, to control building, granting permission to develop sites and ensuring minimum standards of protection against fire and structural stability. In 1850 the powers of the police to regulate the layout of new streets had been confirmed and in 1855 these powers had been further widened to enable the police authorities to draw up extension plans for future developments; it was under these powers that Hobrecht had prepared his celebrated plan for the development and expansion of Berlin. But by the early 1870s there was considerable dissatisfaction with this system of planning. Objections arose both from the financial and legal difficulties of putting extension plans into practice and from the form of development that resulted from many plans.[17]

Many municipalities found the cost of implementing extension plans was punitive. The legal framework necessary for compulsory purchase of the land had been based on legislation originally developed for railway building and took little account of the land needed for anything but the roadway itself. In addition the cities were often faced with extortionate demands for compensation for land acquired in this way. Finally, the municipality had to meet the whole of the costs of paving and servicing the new streets while owners of the adjoining land, many of whom were the beneficiaries of inflated claims for compensation, gained handsomely from the increase in the value of the land due to improvement.

Housing reformers and architects were also highly critical of the form of development that this system of extension planning produced and the outcry over Hobrecht's plan for Berlin exemplifies the reaction of many to the results of these early experiments in planning. Werner Hegemann was later to refer to it having been drawn up with 'child-like insouciance' by Hobrecht who, he claimed, had no previous experience in the matter to qualify him for the task.[18] Its huge squares and wide boulevards were specifically demanded by 'higher authority' to emulate the scale and grandeur of Haussmann's work in Paris. But more serious than the inflated scale of the plan was its effects on the form of housing. The wide streets and deep plots that Hobrecht obligingly inked over the map of Berlin rapidly resulted in a much denser form of development than was common during the 1850s or early 1860s. The building regulations of 1853, illustrated diagrammatically in fig. 7, which controlled the bulk and dimensions of buildings throughout the 1860s and 1870s provided that the height of the building should be related to the width of the street (up to a maximum of 22 m) and that the minimum size of court should be 5.60 m².[19] The consequence of applying these controls to the street widths and plot depths laid out by Hobrecht was to guarantee a much denser form of building than had existed before, with higher buildings inadequately ventilated by small deep courts which were described as having proportions that closely resembled those of the riding boots of a Prussian Officer.[20]

During the early 1870s both sanitarians, architects and engineers, and the representatives of municipal government joined forces to demand a new approach to planning and a new legislative framework to enforce it. The leading members of the emerging planning profession, such as Hobrecht, Baumeister, with the backing of authoritative medical figures like Virchow and organisations such as the Verband deutscher Architekten- und Ingenieuren Vereine now sought the right of the individual city to draw up its own extension plans and to control and administer the development of the area within its boundaries. Demands for legislation granting more comprehensive powers to control develop-ment and the form and construction of new building had been voiced at the Versammlung deutscher Naturforscher und Ärzte in 1872;[21] they were repeated at the annual conference of the Verband deutscher Architekten- und Ingenieuren Vereine in Berlin in 1874,[22] and at the annual conference the VföG in Danzig in 1874[23]. It was this campaign which was to result in the passing of legislation crucial to the future

1853 The maximum height of the building (A) was determined by the street width (12 m minimum to 22 m maximum) measured to the opposing building line; the minimum court dimensions (B) were fixed at 5.60 m × 5.60 m giving a minimum court area of 31.60 m².

1887 The maximum height of the building (A) was determined as before and the number of habitable storeys limited to 5. The roof storey was generally set back at an angle of 45°, but this might be increased to 60° if the resulting increase in overall height was equal to or less than half the height of the roof storey set back at 45°. Court size was set at a minimum of 60 m², although for corner sites a minimum of 40 m² was permitted; the minimum court dimensions (B) were fixed as the height of the building less 6 m.

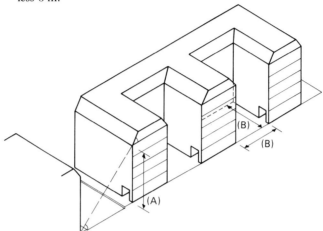

1897 The maximum height of the building (A) was determined as before, but provisions were made to allow a more elaborate treatment of the façade with turrets, balconies, gables and bays. Minimum court area (in building zone 5) was increased to 80 m², but corner sites were still permitted a minimum court size of 40 m². Minimum court dimensions could now take advantage of combining courts on adjacent sites: the minimum dimension for combined courts (B') was fixed as the minimum court dimension for a single court (B) plus ⅓B to take account of the advantage conferred by the adjacent court.

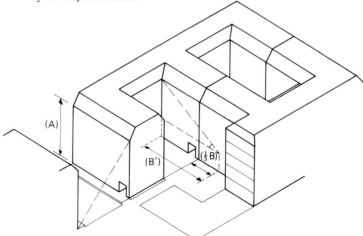

7 Simplified and diagrammatic representation of building bulk controls in the Berlin building regulations of 1853, 1887 and 1897

of planning in Prussia: the *Enteignungsgesetz* of 1874, which provided
compulsory purchase powers, and the *Fluchtliniengesetz* of 1875, which
provided the local authority with powers to regulate street lines, and was
hailed by Eberstadt as the Magna Carta of the German cities.[24] Although
the powers granted to the cities by these acts fell far short of the hopes
of the planners and the sanitary reformers, they did establish the legal
framework of planning in Prussia until after the First World War. While
this campaign and the debates in the Landtag over this new legislation
led on to the larger questions of planning and the development of local
government in Prussia, the discussion of sanitary reform that
accompanied it has direct relevance to the movement for housing
reform. The debates in the VföG on the regulation of new development
provides us with a valuable illustration of the new approach adopted
by the sanitary reformers and its significance for housing reform.

The demand for more comprehensive sanitary and public health
provisions to regulate new buildings formed an essential component of
the campaign for the control of new development. The importance of
these issues in the new 'science' of planning is clearly reflected in
Baumeister's influential book, *Stadt-Erweiterungen* (1876),[25] which was
to serve as the handbook for planners throughout the 1880s; indeed,
a whole chapter was devoted to the discussions of the control of new
building on grounds of public health. The mainspring of the campaign
was the VföG which called for an incisive and interventionist approach
to the regulation of housing: 'It is here that the inadequacy of action
by the individual without the support of public health regulations is most
clearly exposed. The individual may make the greatest sacrifices and the
greatest efforts to provide the most salubrious dwelling for himself and
his family; but he must, nonetheless, remain powerless if his neighbours
oppose him. He alone cannot ensure the hygiene of the ground, the air
and water; nor can he, alone, ensure the provision of sufficient light.'[26]

The form that control of new building should take was first discussed
at length by the VföG at the annual conferences in Danzig in 1874 and
Munich in 1875. At Danzig, a first set of draft regulations which already
signalled a recognition of the problem of the individual building were
submitted for discussion by Strassmann and von Haselberg with the title
'Anforderungen der öffentlichen Gesundheitspflege an die Baupolizei
auf neue Stadtteile, Strassen und Häuser'. The need for greater control
by the municipality of the form of housing in new developments was
emphasised from the start. With growing pressure, arising from changes
in the structure of the housing market, to build as cheaply and as
densely as possible, the need to extend the concern of the *Baupolizei*
beyond what Hermann Schwabe called their 'fixation with fire' and to
cover questions of hygiene was readily agreed. The addresses by the
main speakers at the conference with their grim recitation of the
mounting mortality rates and declining life expectancy of the poor, and
the discussion that followed, reflected a sense of urgency and the desire
for action to avert what appeared to be the increasingly rapid
deterioration of conditions in the poorer areas of big cities. The

connection between the increasing density of housing built during the boom of the *Gründerjahre* and the decline in standards of public health seemed inescapable.

The *Mietskaserne*, in which as many tiny tenements as possible, lit only from small airless courts, were packed on to a site, was singled out as the main cause of this unhappy state of affairs:

Gentlemen: if it is true, as the statistics for at least some time past appear to show, that the denser the form of housing, the less healthy are the rooms in the lower storeys, then it must inevitably follow that, with the increase in the number of densely developed sites, this must be related to a deterioration in the standards of health. But the dwellings on the fourth floor and above are not only damaging to health because of the effect they have on the well-being of those living lower down; they themselves are unhealthy. To establish this, a single fact must suffice; in dwellings on the fourth floor and above there is a terrifying incidence of infant mortality, indeed it is half again as high as for all other types of dwellings.[27]

The paper by Schwabe, 'Einfluss der verschiedenen Wohnungen auf die Gesundheit ihrer Bewohner',[28] drove home the same argument: the failure to control the dense *Mietskaserne* form of building led to significantly higher mortality rates in the worst dwellings, particularly those located in the roofs and cellars. Nevertheless, although there was agreement on the need for action, there was a feeling at Danzig that the draft regulations presented to the conference still said too little about the details of how development was to be controlled.

In 1875 at Munich matters were taken further with discussion now divided into two sections, in recognition, as Georg Varrentrap explained, of the extent to which the subject had expanded; a division was drawn between the demands for control of hygiene on the level of the district or town on the one hand, and on the level of the individual building on the other.

This was not to deny the interdependence of the two scales: the build-up of toxic agents in the ground resulting from failure to drain the city might easily affect conditions in the individual dwelling; equally, the morbific matter originating in the individual dwelling might, if not disposed of quickly and effectively, endanger the health of a whole district by contaminating the soil, the air and the water. This separation was recognised by the VföG from 1875, was of great importance as a measure of the new concern with controlling what happened 'behind the front door'.

The concern with the larger scale focussed on regulations to control the general layout of the city: the preparation of the city extension plan; some form of zoning for different land uses; the relation of street layout to the orientation and the form of the site; the provision of canalisation, water supply and open green space, and, most important, means to control the height and density of new building. This last issue, which remained a topic of burning importance until the turn of the century, was of direct relevance to the problems of housing because it affected so immediately the provision of ventilation, sunlight and other requirements of the hygienic dwelling. These demands for control of density, closely linked to the reformers' insistence on the 'cottage' as the ideal form of housing, acquired a significance that extends beyond the realm of public health alone. While issues of public health were not forgotten – the VföG remained one of the most important fora for the debate – the density of development and the virtues of an 'open' form of housing also became, after the mid-1880s, a subject of central importance in the discussion of the 'Bodenfrage', or the urban land question.

The second group of recommendations concerned the hygiene of the individual building and included the need to avoid building on sites where the *Grundwasser* was known to be high; to connect every new building to the sewage system and water supply; to provide all dwellings with a toilet ventilated directly to the outside air; to ensure adequate space between buildings and courts of sufficient size for a given height of building; to ensure adequate drinking water; and a number of provisions, particularly for cellar and roof dwellings, to ensure the construction of healthy housing.[29]

The importance of the association's recommendations was not so much their novelty; many were of course already incorporated in the building regulations of individual cities and even of some states, but the adoption of these as a minimum basis for legislation. The early 1870s saw the birth of a new attitude towards sanitary matters. The campaign for new planning legislation in Prussia sought to secure the transfer to the municipalities of responsibility for supervising the development of urban areas; the sanitary reformers were now demanding that the cities should take equally seriously their responsibility for the control of the sanitary conditions both within the dwelling and for the city as a whole.

The healthy home

Before turning to consider how far this programme of reform was implemented in practice after 1875, we must review contemporary understanding of the mechanisms of disease and the way in which hygienic controls were meant to work. Only by understanding what contemporaries thought made a house healthy – or unhealthy – can we grasp the significance, perhaps curious to us now, of certain proposals.

Contemporary understanding of the hygiene of the dwelling is set out with authority in the range of handbooks which deal with hygiene and the construction of working-class housing. These include not only books for architects such as Rudolf Manega's *Die Anlage von Arbeiterwohnungen* (1871)[30] and the relevant sections in Josef Durm's massive *Handbuch der Architektur*(1883–1907),[31] but also the encyclopaedic treatment of the subject in Hugo Wilhelm von Ziemssen's *Handbuch der Hygiene* (1882–1910)[32] or the slightly later Theodor Weyl's *Handbuch der Hygiene* of 1896–1901.[33] These same ideas were also presented more accessibly in the form of popular lectures and pamphlets produced by leading figures in the world of public health such as Pettenkofer and Virchow. They not only spoke to an extraordinary variety of societies and gatherings, but also contributed articles on the subject to the popular periodicals that were to be found in middle-class homes.[34] Thus Josef von Fodor's *Das gesunde Haus und die gesunde Wohnung* (1878)[35] or Hermann Schülke's *Gesunde Wohnungen* (1880)[36] present contemporary views of the hygiene of the dwelling in a very accessible form, though without the graphic immediacy of Thomas Teale's illustrated classic, *Dangers to Public Health: a Pictorial Guide to Sanitary Defects* (1879).[37] Written in a popular format, these books were intended for use by practitioners rather than for scientific consumption. Nevertheless, authors such as Fodor, an active member of the VföG and Professor at the Institute of Hygiene in Budapest, were clearly not prepared to sacrifice rigour to popularity.

The starting point for the discussion was the benefit, both physical and moral, to be obtained from living in a healthy home. On these advantages all were agreed: 'A good, comfortable home is a powerful means of shaping the economic and moral ways of its occupants; a healthy, comfortable home is the essential foundation for a healthy, comfortable family life.'[38] Not only would the family be stronger, the breadwinner would be more capable of earning and the lot of the wife less wearing if the home were sanitary. There were moral advantages too: returning to a well-kept, clean and salubrious dwelling, the head of the household would not be tempted to go out in search of the pleasures of the *Kneipe*.

However, what made a home healthy turned on how people understood the operation of a disease. At the time of the agitation for reform of the building regulations, miasmatic theories in their particular German form, with the emphasis on the importance of the hygiene of the soil, dominated the sanitary discussion. Prescriptions for control naturally reflected these concerns. From this understanding of disease, it followed that the most important counter-measures were general cleanliness, fanatical insistence on ventilation, avoidance of dampness and, from the mid-1880s onwards, an enthusiasm for the germ-killing effects of sunlight. The demand for cleanliness, though of the greatest urgency, and stressed in manuals of home management, was not of immediate importance to the design and construction of dwellings, although the disadvantages of certain materials, for example parquet flooring, which was claimed to harbour dust and thus, potentially, disease, were pointed out to architects. More important as a determinant of design was the overriding concern with ventilation. If disease could spread through the air, then *Bodenluft*, or air from the ground (whose existence had been demonstrated in the mid-1850s by Pettenkofer)[39] could rise and carry disease into the dwelling. Having removed all dirt with which these elements might combine to produce disease by vigilant cleanliness, the only other course of preventative action was to dispel the 'vitiated' air as quickly as possible by efficient ventilation.

But, in addition to the attack from miasmas and dust entering the home from outside (a problem that would be greatly reduced by 'city cleansing' activities of the municipality), the inhabitants and their activities within the home constituted yet further hazards to health. A human being consuming energy was regarded, by analogy with a bonfire, as giving off carbon dioxide or 'human smoke' and thus exhausting the supply of oxygen within the room; as fire cannot burn without oxygen, nor could man live without fresh air. Pettenkofer had shown in experiments in the mid-1850s that a healthy man might consume 5–6 m³ of air per night while simply sleeping.[40] The need for adequate ventilation for all rooms of the house was therefore obvious both to provide fresh air and to remove the 'tainted' air. If this was necessary in a normal dwelling, it was regarded as even more vital in the dwellings of the poor where over-crowding was the norm and where the close and foetid atmosphere, regarded as a terrible warning of the presence of disease-generating elements, left even hardened sanitarians and doctors faint. Gas fittings and heating stoves might further pollute the air of the dwelling. Fodor warned that failure to remove the build-up of polluted air might lead to harsh headaches, spells of dizziness, loss of appetite and fainting. More seriously, where this air combined with the specific elements of disease, he argued that there was real danger of either 'sudden cessation of the vital functions' or, after the polluted air had settled on the 'delicate tissues of the lung' of a slow erosion of physical efficiency and a lingering death.[41]

The answer to these dangers was efficient ventilation. In the design of the dwelling, the position and the size of the windows and the height of the room were considered to be of great importance in ensuring an adequate supply of fresh air. Ratios of floor area to window size were investigated and the positioning of the windows to provide cross ventilation was heavily emphasized. The pursuit of adequate ventilation also led to demands that designers should allow sufficient space around dwellings to prevent any obstruction to the free passage of light and air. 'Licht und Luft' became a popular slogan, a rallying cry for sanitary and housing reformers alike. Minimum court size, previously determined by the fire-fighting requirements of horse-drawn, man-powered pumps, was now required to be larger to provide better lighting and more air to the growing number of dwellings that gave on to courts.

Ventilation was as important in the construction as in the planning of the dwelling. The impermeable construction of the floor or the tanking of a cellar with asphalt might do much to prevent the entry of noxious miasmas, but the only prudent course of action was for the designer to promote maximum ventilation. Based on research by Pettenkofer in the late 1850s[42] on the porous nature of building materials, the VföG was still in the mid-1880s reiterating the need to provide construction of permeable materials in order to ensure ventilation as a hygienic necessity. As a result of Pettenkofer's studies, dampness in walls was identified not just as an agent capable, in combination with dirt, of fostering disease, but as an impediment to ventilation, caused by the filling up of the 'pores' of brickwork or plaster with water vapour. It was for this reason that the use of dwellings before they were fully dried out was castigated as a threat to health. As late as 1885, the VföG investigated the effect of damp, newly finished dwellings on health and concluded that the reduction of ventilation caused by damp was a hazard to health.[43]

The healthy dwelling needed adequate light as well as air. By the early 1880s the benefits of adequate natural light, particularly sunlight, were being championed by sanitary reformers and this led naturally to demands for an even more open form of building. Manega reported as early as 1871 that the work of Professor Schönbein on the benign effects of ozone, resulting from the combination of oxygen and light, especially sunlight, was already attracting attention.[44] The germ-killing properties of ozone and its supposed ability to drive out 'vitiated' air was seen as an essential justification for the demand for minimum levels of lighting.[45] The hygienic value of the warmth of sunlight and the need to take account of this in planning was elaborated in an important article by Vogt, 'Über die Richtung städtischer Strassen nach der Himmelsgegend und das Verhältnis ihrer Breite zur Häuserhöhe', in 1879, on the orientation of residential streets and the relationship of the width of these streets to the height of the adjoining buildings (fig. 35).[46] On the basis of experiments that he had carried out over a 13-year period in Bern on the striking difference in the mortality rates for dwellings which received adequate sunlight and those that did not, Vogt concluded that the warming power of the sun's rays was of great value in drying out damp dwellings and in ensuring thorough ventilation by convection. He therefore recommended that the layout of housing, like hospitals, should not only be planned on the 'open' or pavilion system but should be so arranged as to draw maximum benefit from insolation. He investigated this question in detail, taking account of the movement of the sun, the angle of the sun's rays and a range of alternative orientations and finally concluded that the optimum orientation was to be achieved by laying out streets on a north–south axis and by reducing to a minimum the amount of housing placed in streets running east–west.

Within the home, the concerns of the sanitarian are best exemplified by the design and the planning of the toilet. The advantages of the WC in facilitating the removal of human excrement and domestic wastes from the dwelling as quickly as possible are easily understood, particularly when one remembers that contemporaries viewed smell as evidence of a threat to health. But these advantages were partly offset by the dangers of connecting the dwelling to the sewerage system; to do so increased the danger of allowing vitiated air and morbific gases to pass from the sewer into the dwelling. The VföG considered the question of sewer gas as a threat to health at the annual conference in 1881.

In an article 'Über das Eindringen von Canalgasen in die Wohnräume' (1881), Dr Lissauer of Danzig explained clearly the nature of contemporary concern: it was not simply the unpleasant smell from the sewer that caused anxiety but the fear of introducing into the dwelling 'the tiny elements of so-called infectious diseases whose existence has yet to be proved'.[47] A malfunctioning or poorly designed toilet could only too easily become the bridgehead for disease within the home. Finally, after extended debate, the VföG concluded that there existed no proof of the connection between sewer gas and diseases such as typhoid, cholera or other zymotic diseases and in the following year Isidor Soyka contemptuously dismissed the claim that the sewer gas theory provided an explanation of the spread of such diseases.[48] But the design of house drainage and sanitary fittings remained a source of immediate interest among sanitarians.

New housing after 1886: the campaign for more open development

There was, however, a sharp contrast between the sanitarians' ideal of the healthy home and the standards to which most new housing was built – to say nothing of conditions in existing housing. The realisation of this ideal depended both on achieving a more open form of housing than was being built in cities like Berlin and on raising the quality of new construction. To do this it was necessary to enforce minimum standards of planning, sanitation and construction through the building regulations and to ensure their enforcement in practice. For many sanitarians the path to reform was to press for state-wide, even nation-wide, minimum standards to replace the confusion that existed in Prussia, for example, where each municipality enforced its own regulations in the manner it saw fit.[49] This was an issue which had long been dear to many sanitary reformers; as early as the late 1860s there had been pressure for national legislation on sanitary matters and demands for a *Centralgesundheitsamt*.

From the mid-1870s, largely at the urging of Baumeister, attempts had been made by the Verband deutscher Architekten-und Ingenieuren Vereine to gain acceptance for this idea of a national building code, but with little success.[50] Baumeister's work culminated in the publication of his proposals for a *Normale Bauordnung* in 1880, which included sections dealing with the control of the density of new building, city extension plans, sewerage and water supply and also the hygiene of the individual dwelling.[51] But his ideas found no widespread enthusiasm and his proposals remained without sponsorship. Nevertheless, the need for reform of the *Bauordnungen* was clear and articles in the *Deutsche Bauzeitung (DBZ)* during the 1880s emphasise the frustration of the architectural and engineering profession at the provisions of the outdated regulations still in force in many parts of the country;[52] in Berlin, for example, the code of 1853 was still the principal instrument of control and was wholly inadequate to deal with the new scale and the new technology of building.

The attitude of the VföG to Baumeister's proposals was mixed: it was recognised that reform was needed, but there was concern about the viability of a single code that would have to legislate for circumstances as different as those in Königsberg in East Prussia and Constanz on the Bodensee.[53] Yet to dilute the regulations to ensure a general minimum standard acceptable across the whole country ran the risk of advancing little beyond the controls already available. In 1886, the VföG had already formulated general guidelines to regulate the development of new areas of cities under the heading 'Stadterweiterung, insbesondere in hygienischer Beziehung', and had pressed, for both economic and hygienic reasons, for low-density housing to be built in these new areas.[54] But the association had not resumed the battle for the reform of the building regulations.

In 1887, after long years of disagreement between the municipality and the *Sanitätspolizei* on the administrative framework of control, the new Building Ordinances for Berlin were finally published.[55] Sadly, after so much anticipation the results were disappointing. In a review of the new Regulations, Baumeister concluded that in the hygienic field they offered little advance on existing controls, and drew attention to the effects they might, and subsequently did, have in *increasing* rather than controlling the density of housing in the Berlin suburbs where the Berlin regulations had not previously applied.[56] In the provisions governing the design of the dwelling the new regulations were evasive on a number of crucial points of detail; on the vital question of ventilation, the new code simply called for the provision of windows of 'adequate' size. But, despite Baumeister's strictures, the revision, as illustrated in fig. 7, represented a real advance in the control of density of development, at least by comparison with the provisions of the code of 1853. A maximum of only 66% of the site could be developed, the minimum court size was increased from 28 m² to 60 m² and the maximum building height was fixed at five storeys. In the field of drainage and water supply the new code also represented a significant step forward, reflecting both advances in sanitary technology and the willingness of the municipality to impose control in such a sensitive area. But this progress in Berlin had been slow. Without the spur of national legislation, there was little hope of widespread adoption of similar measures.

By 1888, however, the attitude of the VföG to the building regulations had changed. Stimulated by the publicity given to the housing problem by the VfSP and responding to the call for national or at least state-wide legislation to control housing, the VföG, vigorously urged on by Miquel, took up the challenge of reforming the building regulations at the annual conferences in Frankfurt in 1888 and Strasbourg in 1889.[57] At Strasbourg detailed technical questions of the appropriate form of control were debated and Strauss, a lawyer from Gladbach, and Hartwig, an architect from Dresden, put forward a series of proposals, significantly entitled 'Reichsgesetzlichen Vorschriften zum Schutze des gesunden Wohnens'. As finally adopted by the Verein, the resolution included the following proposals: control of the density of development and the drawing up of extension plans; measures to ensure adequate ventilation of the dwelling, such as minimal court dimensions, minimum street width in relation to building height; measures to ensure proper drinking water and toilet facilities; each dwelling to be provided with its own toilet ventilated through to an outside wall and connected to an adequate system of drainage. Further controls were to ensure minimum height of rooms, minimum window sizes in relation to the size of room and further restrictions on the use of cellar dwellings. Finally, a number of important recommendations were made to provide control of the use of housing, an important advance which Miquel attributed in part to French achievements, particularly the work of du Mesnil.[58] A minimum volume of air per person was to be fixed in order to limit overcrowding and the municipal authorities were urged to enforce these provisions by a system of inspection, forbidding the renting of dwellings that failed to comply with these standards.

The recommendations made by the VföG at Strasbourg went further than before in specifying the range of technical issues to be treated in the *Bauordnungen* and provided a basic set of requirements for inclusion in all subsequent debates on the technical aspect of the code.[59] Indeed the range of controls considered necessary remains basically the same until 1914. While there are significant changes in medical science and the understanding of the mechanisms of disease, the emphasis in the building regulations remains firmly fixed on traditional problems like fire and structural safety and the preoccupations of the sanitarians with the problems of ventilation, light and drainage.

The concern with ventilation and with lighting focussed attention both on the relationship of the dwelling to other dwellings and the space around the building, and on the internal planning of the dwelling.[60] Both Baumeister and the VföG wished to determine the separation between buildings such that the distance between the opposing blocks should be equal to their height. However, in practice the range of variation was enormous. In many cities minima and maxima were imposed both on street width and on building height. In Berlin and elsewhere further local variations abounded to take account of the towers, turrets and other details of elevational treatment that architectural fashion demanded towards the end of the century.

The size of the court was of equal if not greater concern and the VföG and other bodies demanded that they should be larger. By the end of the 1890s minimum dimensions for the court were fixed by the building regulations while the area for the particular case might be calculated on a proportional basis from the size of the plot; it might be determined according to some geometric rule; yet again, it might be fixed by some combination of the two forms of control. In some cities changes in the regulations were introduced to make it possible to take advantage of shared courts between adjoining sites.

Closely related to the question of the spacing between buildings was the height of the buildings and the maximum number of floors permitted by the regulations. Both Baumeister and the VföG had recommended that habitable rooms be built no higher than the fourth floor but in many cities, particularly in the east, five floors of habitable rooms were permitted.[61] Much of the early sanitary concern in the 1850s and 1860s had focussed on the dangers to health of cellar dwellings and as a result most *Bauordnungen* by the 1870s contained provisions to control the use of cellar dwellings as tightly as possible. Baumeister wished to prevent their use as separate dwellings altogether;

but, bowing to the demands of practice, both he and the VföG were prepared to allow their use as habitable rooms subject to stringent constructional standards. Roof dwellings were regarded as being almost as damaging to health as cellar dwellings, because of the heat in summer and the lack of ventilation, and many building codes sought to limit the use of roof-space for habitable rooms either partially or totally.

The culmination of the sanitary reformers' campaign to limit the density of new development was the introduction of a system of density zoning in a number of cities in the mid-1890s. The idea of a *gestaffelte Bauordnung*, or a form of differential density control for different areas of the city, had been put forward by Baumeister during the crucial debates at Frankfurt and Strasbourg:

> It is unthinkable that in a large city such as Strasbourg one and the same regulation should be suitable for both the oldest and the newest parts of the city. Different regulations must be made...and each authority must consider whether it should choose quite different and, from the point of view of public health, more demanding regulations for the outskirts and suburbs of our cities.[62]

But it was not until the early 1890s that the potential of these ideas was seriously examined. In 1893 at the annual conference of the VföG in Würzburg, Franz Adickes, Miquel's successor as *Oberbürgermeister* in Frankfurt, and Baumeister presented a set of proposals, 'Die unter-schiedliche Behandlung der Bauordnungen für die Innere, die Aussen-gebiete und die Umgebung von Städten', which provided for the first time for different densities of development in different parts of the city by limiting either the number of residential floors or the amount of the plot that could be developed. Although these proposals appeared as a new approach to the control of density, Adickes was able to point to the successful application of the same principles in practice. As *Bürgermeister* of Altona a simple version of these proposals had been tried as early as 1884. In Frankfurt regulations of this form had been tried in 1891 and the regulations for Berlin drawn up in 1892 had made successful use of this same principle.[63]

But these proposals had a significance that went beyond merely ensuring adequate 'Licht und Luft'. In introducing them, Adickes stressed that this regulation would make it possible for the municipality to exercise much more active control over the price and use of urban land. Reminding the conference 'that the real enemy of the ideal form of layout is in practice the price of land',[64] he looked forward to the way in which this new form of density control would reduce the price of land in the outskirts of cities. He called on the cities to control high-density housing through the building regulations, and argued that limitation of this form would reduce land prices, thus opening the way to a more open and a healthier form of housing. The gains made in the name of public health would also, he claimed, result in lower housing costs and lower rents. These proposals were greeted with great enthusiasm and the association resolved to consider a more detailed submission at the next annual conference.

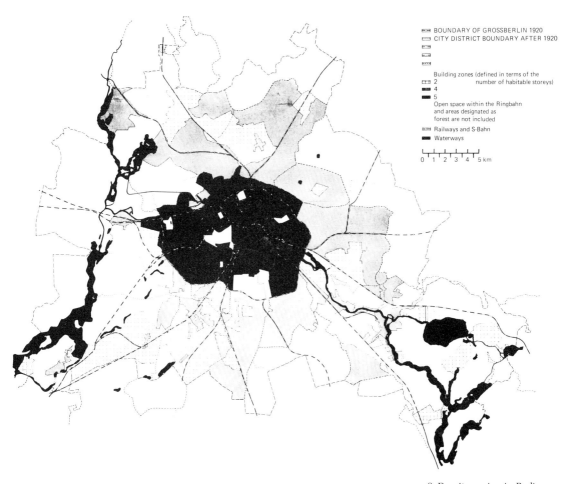

BOUNDARY OF GROSSBERLIN 1920
CITY DISTRICT BOUNDARY AFTER 1920

Building zones (defined in terms of the
number of habitable storeys)
2
4
5
Open space within the Ringbahn
and areas designated as
forest are not included
Railways and S-Bahn
Waterways

0 1 2 3 4 5 km

8 Density zoning in Berlin
after the regulations of 1892

In 1894, Adickes presented a more fully developed version of the same set of proposals, backed up by the technical knowledge and experience of Baupolizei-Inspector Classen and Baurath Hinkeldyn.[65] Basing his proposals on the regulations drawn up for Berlin and its suburbs in 1892 (fig. 8), Classen set out details of the way in which the new form of controls would be implemented. He pressed for the setting up of three different classes of density or zones; in each zone, the height of the building would be fixed as would the proportion of the site that might be developed. This would range from 50% of the site in Class I, to 30% utilisation in Class III, a specific encouragement to 'open' forms of building. Hinkeldyn elaborated on proposals made by Goecke for a clear differentiation in width between different types of streets (fig. 9).[66] Like Goecke, Hinkeldyn argued that residential areas carried less traffic than the main arteries of the city and could therefore be made narrower. This would make it possible to limit the maximum permissible height of building in residential areas, thus providing further support for a more open form of housing in the city.

Significantly, Adickes referred at some length to the support that

9 Diagrammatic illustration
of the relationship between
streets of different widths
and the bulk of adjoining
buildings.

Schnitt nach A B

The main traffic streets, both 22 m wide, are fronted by buildings of the
maximum permissible height; within the grid of these main streets the
residential streets carrying less traffic can be reduced in width to 15 m or even
to 9 m, thus ensuring a less dense form of development.

economists with an interest in the land question were now offering to
the VföG's campaign for more open building. Adopting the arguments
that Eberstadt had set out in his book *Städtische Bodenfragen*,[67] Adickes
argued that the campaign for lower densities not only held out the
promise of a healthier form of housing, but also offered a chance to strike
at the profits of those who speculated in land. If the rental return for
a given site could be calculated from the expected returns from the
largest number of tenements that could be fitted on to that site, then,
according to Eberstadt and his fellow economists, a reduction in the level
of site utilisation would ultimately lead to a reduction in land values.
To the VföG assembled at Magdeburg it seemed as if the reforms for
which the association was campaigning offered a means of striking at
the very base of the housing problem.

    The members of the VföG had cause for enthusiasm. The success of their agitations can be measured by the speed with which these proposals were adopted not only by German cities, but even abroad. Already by 1895, only a year after the recommendations had been first approved, Baumeister was able to record that over 50 cities of more than 15,000 inhabitants had chosen to adopt the new form of density zoning regulations and a further 36 had already made specific provisions for some form of zoning for low-density 'open' housing.[68] By the turn of the century there were already rumblings of opposition from property interests who saw these measures as an unwarranted infringement of their traditional rights.[69] But by 1900 the veterans of the sanitary campaign for 'Licht und Luft' could point with pride to the more open form of the new development that was already being built in the suburbs of cities like Berlin.

The determination to reform the building regulations in the late 1880s and the achievements in practice were of considerable importance. Advances such as the reduction in the level of site utilisation, the increase in minimum court sizes or the requirement that all dwellings should have their own ventilated toilet, won in the changes to the building regulations in Berlin in 1887 and again in 1897, do not make dramatic reading. But they did pave the way for the rethinking of attitudes to the block. If the block could be 'tamed', if the necessary light and ventilation could be guaranteed by the building regulations, then many of the objections to tenement housing, formed by the image of the *Mietskaserne* housing thrown up during the speculative boom of the early 1870s, would fall away. As Messel's work showed, the reform of the building regulations might make it possible for an architect of ability, working for a client who did not build just for profit, to construct working-class housing in the centre of the city which would not only be as healthy as the cottage but would be cheaper, and better located as well.

The regulation of existing housing after 1886: overcrowding and *Wohnungsinspektion*

Even the best designed and the most hygienic housing would quickly become insanitary if overcrowded; slums were the product of poverty, decay and bad management: they were not built. To win a real improvement in the insanitary housing conditions of the poor, the sanitary reformers wished to ensure that housing was not only built better and more soundly, but that its use was controlled with equal stringency.

The question of regulating the conditions in existing housing had long been an issue for sanitary reformers. Even the early cholera regulations had made provision for the removal of nuisances and disinfection and white-washing in the dwellings of the sick.[70] Despite the power of the sanitarians, the right of the landlord to use his property as he saw fit remained largely unchallenged throughout the 1860s; as we have seen, it was only in the 1870s that the VföG seriously attacked the problems of the hygiene of the individual dwelling with recommendations to strengthen the provisions of the building regulations. Even then the chances of approving measures to control the use of existing housing seemed remote.

However, in the late 1870s the problems of controlling the conditions of common lodging houses encouraged the VföG to examine the question of the use of existing housing for the first time. In 1878, a Dr Goldthamer reported at length in the influential *Vierteljahrschrift für gerechtliche Medizin und öffentliche Sanitätswesen* on the appalling in-sanitary conditions in many of the lodging houses and hostels in Berlin, a large number of which were associated with bars and inns.[71] It came as no surprise to Dr Goldthammer that the mortality rates from disease such as cholera and typhoid in these doss-houses were substantially higher than in other forms of housing in the same parts of the city.

Yet to the frustration of the sanitarians, control in Berlin over this form of licensed housing lay outside the jurisdiction of the sanitary authorities. There was nothing to compare with the English legislation such as the Common Lodging Houses Act of 1853 and the provisions of the Public Health Act of 1875; only in times of epidemic were special regulations enforced to control such housing. Goldthammer pressed urgently for the transfer of the supervision of sanitary conditions in this form of housing back to the *Sanitätspolizei* and set out a minimum list of sanitary regulations including: separation of the sexes; limitation of overcrowding; provision of a minimum volume of air per person; provision of washing facilities; regular cleaning and whitewashing of the sleeping quarters and the requirement to notify the authorities of any cases of infectious diseases such as cholera or typhoid.

In 1879 the issue of lodging houses was raised, as a matter of urgency, at the annual conference of the VföG at Stuttgart and the Verein approved regulations for their control which contained the greater part of Goldthammer's original proposals. The debate that accompanied the presentation of Moritz Pistor's paper[72] clearly revealed the determination of the Verein to see the introduction of some form of control not only for lodging houses, but for other forms of existing accommodation such as hostels as well.

However, as in so much related to housing, a new initiative in this field had to wait until after 1886. At both the Frankfurt and the Strasbourg conferences the VföG passed recommendations seeking to control not just new dwellings, to which we have already referred, but also the use of existing housing, limiting the freedom of the landlord and tenant to operate as they pleased. Dampness and inadequate ventilation were to be grounds for refusing permission to use a room for habitable purposes; a minimum volume of air per person was to be used as a basis for controlling overcrowding. Finally, along the lines of English legislation, the community was to be granted the rights, backed by powers of compulsory purchase, to repair or even demolish and rebuild insanitary property. The possibility of embarking on a programme of *Sanierung*, or slum clearance, akin to the demolitions carried out under the Cross Act, was not beyond the bounds of the proposed law.

At the annual conference of the VföG in 1891 in Leipzig, Josef Stübben and Erich Zweigert, the *Oberbürgermeister* of Essen, considered in more detail how to implement the recommendations concerning the use of existing housing passed at the conferences of 1888 and 1889.[73] They recommended the setting up of municipal housing departments to control and supervise the housing in each city, a major innovation and a clear extension of the role of municipal government. These were to be responsible for regular inspection of housing and the collation of housing statistics to identify insanitary properties; they were also to be responsible for bringing to book those who let insanitary accommodation, and the closing of housing which did not comply with the municipality's standards of hygiene.

Aware of the difficulties, but drawing inspiration from similar regulations introduced in France[74] and from the Torrens and Cross Acts in England, Stübben and Zweigert elaborated the legal basis for their proposals. Both concluded that the majority of the powers that they had demanded for the *Wohnungsämter*, or housing departments, were already available to the police in Prussia,[75] and that what was needed was not so much new legislation as an act of political will to make such a system of control possible.

The recommendations of the VföG soon found a limited application in practice. In Hesse, in July 1893, state legislation was introduced to set up *Wohnungsämter* and to provide a system of supervision of dwellings and lodgings in communities with a population of over 5,000. In Prussia, Düsseldorf introduced a *Polizeiverordnung* in November 1895 to control the use of dwellings under the existing police powers and was followed by Essen in 1889; other states, Hamburg (1898) (where the cholera epidemic of 1892 had been a powerful spur to action), Saxony (1900), Bavaria and Württemberg (1901) and Baden (1907) soon followed the lead taken by Hesse.[76]

In Prussia, however, no state legislation was successfully passed to provide a system of housing supervision and inspection, although articles providing for a system of housing inspection were included in both the Prussian Housing Bill of 1904 and that of 1913.[77] In some areas in Prussia, particularly in the Rhineland and the west, the authorities of individual *Regierungsbezirke* introduced police regulations to provide for a system of housing inspection and in a number of cities the municipality was also able to do so under the existing police powers. But the absence of state legislation left many cities still without a *Wohnungsamt* in 1914. Nevertheless, by the war, a system of municipal housing inspection had been introduced in a number of the larger Prussian cities; using the advisory powers of the municipality, housing departments were operating in Düsseldorf, Essen, Berlin, Cologne, Charlottenburg, Aachen, Breslau, Cassel and Elberfeld. In a number of other cities in the west of the state, Bonn, Barmen and several Rhenish cities, the inspection of housing was carried out using the powers of the police.[78]

Falling between the municipality and the delegated police powers of the state, the administration of the system of housing inspection emphasises the difficulties that lay in the path of attempts to improve housing conditions without the backing of state legislation. In Berlin, for example, the municipality had unsuccessfully sought to persuade the state government to confer on it the necessary police powers to deal with housing matters generally; the city was therefore forced to fall back on implementing an advisory system of inspection.[79] In a number of Prussian cities the housing inspectors were regarded as being akin to officers of the welfare department, their role limited to visiting, inspection and advice, almost in the manner of Octavia Hill's assistants. Indeed a number of housing departments chose to employ women as housing inspectors for these reasons.[80] In most cities, housing inspection was more a question of advising tenants, or even landlords, on the dangers of insanitary accommodation and overcrowding, than of exercising the statutory powers for which the VföG was campaigning.

The opposition of property interests to the programme of sanitary reform grew as the conference recommendations of the VföG began to find application in practice. By the turn of the century, assured of very full representation in both local and state government in Prussia by the three-class system of voting, it was fighting attempts by municipalities to control both new development through the system of density zoning and the regulation of conditions in existing housing through housing inspection. In Mannheim the density controls proposed by Baumeister and introduced by the municipality under Oberbürgermeister Beck in 1901 were challenged in court and the local authority forced to modify its controls; similar cases came up in Prussia and in other states.[81]

But opposition by the property lobby to density controls and the regulation of conditions in existing housing was not total. Owners of existing housing were understandably less troubled by the density controls than landowners and builders. Many property owners were not unhappy to see attempts to control the most insanitary housing. The image of the slum landlord living in luxury from the exploitation of misery and profiting from decaying accommodation was distasteful (however appropriate) to many members of the Haus- und Grundbesitzer Vereine and recognised as a political liability. Thus in 1905 at the VIII Prussischer Haus- und Grundbesitzertag it was agreed to support the system of housing inspection proposed in article 5 of the Prussian Housing Bill and the introduction of minimum sanitary standards put forward in article 4.[82] Although the opposition of the property interests was one of the reasons that the Bill did not become law, the fact that the provisions for the control of density of new development and the regulation of existing building were written into the Bill in the form that they were indicates not only how far public health reforms had been adopted by the government, but also how far the government judged these controls to be acceptable to the different interest groups affected by the bill. Even in the much weakened and reduced form of the Prussian Housing Bill of 1913 these articles were still retained albeit in less specific form.

The sanitary reformers had not achieved all they had demanded, practice frequently lagged behind the letter of the regulations; but the campaign of the VföG had been immensely successful. The standards of design, layout and construction of new property had been thoroughly improved through changes in the building regulations; a start had been made with the regulation of existing property; in a number of cities overcrowding was being investigated by municipal housing departments; at the level of the city, development in new areas was less dense and more open. These successes now provided the context within which better, healthier housing could be built. But the benefits of these higher standards had to be paid for. As the inspectors from the housing department closed insanitary dwellings or prevented families from sharing accommodation to reduce overcrowding, the costs of housing rose. How were the poor to meet the costs of sanitary reform? Better construction, larger courts, proper toilets, running water on every floor: all these improvements had to be paid for. By the turn of the century, the designer of working-class housing faced a formidable challenge: was it possible to design housing that took full advantage of the achievements of sanitary reform and to build it at prices that placed it within reach of the working classes?

6

◇◇◇

The design of working-class housing

The early development of the design of working-class housing in England, France and Germany is heavily indebted to the movement for sanitary reform. Effective ventilation, good lighting, adequate heating – the concerns of the sanitarians – together with considerations of cost and the demands of local tradition are the factors that shape the design of both cottage and tenement block. For Rudolf Manega, writing in 1871, the requirements of the working-class dwelling were 'economy, firmness (stability and durability), commodity (efficiency), fitness for health and finally, in last place, beauty'.[1] The contribution that the architect could make was limited. In Germany, architectural interest in this field begins only in the 1870s and the involvement of the profession on any significant scale dates from the 1890s.

In England, architects like Henry Roberts and Henry Darbishire were exceptions. They made an important contribution even in the early days of the movement for housing reform with their work on the design of 'model' tenement buildings. Roberts' housing for the SICLC, the Society for the Improvement of the Conditions of the Labouring Classes, at Streatham Street was viewed in favourable terms by the profession and the lay press, and his model dwellings for the 1851 exhibition, erected under the patronage of Prince Albert, attracted widespread comment both at home and abroad. His book *The Dwellings of the Labouring Classes* (1851) was translated into French at the request of the President himself and by 1852 it had already been translated into German; his designs were equally well known to reformers abroad and were published in German journals.[2] But one of the most important aspects of this contribution was to show that there were real benefits in economy, convenience and hygiene to be gained by reconsidering the design of the dwelling rather than simply trusting to tradition.

In Germany, however, the early efforts of the housing reformers produced nothing as memorable as Roberts' housing planned on the open staircase principle or Muller's housing at Mulhouse with its cruciform planning. Reformers in Germany were familiar from the 1850s onwards with developments in England and France through journals like that of the Central Verein für das Wohl der arbeitenden Classen and from the international conferences and congresses. But the advances in foreign practice were not immediately incorporated into

110

German work. The buildings of the BgB, the first significant achievement of the movement for housing reform, were salubrious but unadventurous in design; C. W. Hoffmann's position and influence on the committee of the company did not result in a design of any originality.[3] He produced a lavishly illustrated folio of drawings to accompany a text describing the project, but architecturally there was little to distinguish what was built from the mass of speculative housing being built in Berlin at the time, apart from a willingness to reduce the amount of accommodation packed on to the site.

The first development of the BgB was built on the Wollankstrasse in Wedding in 1849–50 (fig. 5). The development of the site generally followed the recommendations of Huber who, despite his enthusiasm for the cottage, had recommended in *Selbsthilfe* the building of tenement housing for the working classes in urban areas where land values were high. In line with the tradition of multi-storey, low-income housing in Berlin,[4] the building was organised in two blocks with three tenements opening off the staircase in the main block and two in the smaller block; in the main block there were five floors, in the smaller block only four. The limited toilet facilities and the water supply, in the form of a well, were located in the courts which were also shared with workshop accommodation. The design of the block on the Michaeliskirchstrasse, built very shortly after, uses the same plan type but here three blocks each with two flats opening off a stair, a typical *Zweispänner* plan, are placed side by side; again both toilets and water supply are located in the court. Comparison with contemporary English designs is not flattering:[5] although the space standards of Roberts' designs for the Great Exhibition Cottages are too generous, the outside stairwell and the planning of kitchen, internal water-closet and dust chute, which all give on to the well-ventilated open-air landing, is more sophisticated than Hoffmann's designs. Even compared with the more straightforward buildings of the Metropolitan Association for Improving the Dwellings of the Industrious Classes the design and the standards of the buildings of the BgB appear backward; in the former, the flats are larger, there is better ventilation of both kitchen and WC, and water supply and toilet are provided within each dwelling.

On the Bremerhöhe on the outskirts of the city, the BgB was able to build a number of cottages in 1852. But even here the results are unexciting; the planning is asymmetrical, but for picturesque, not for practical purposes. Indeed the most interesting aspect of the project is the extent to which the BgB followed Huber's ideas, building cottages only in the outskirts where the lower land values made this possible.

The forms of tenement and cottage housing, 1850–80

The buildings of the BgB naturally invite comparison with the work of the limited dividend housing companies in England. But in Germany this form of 'model' housing remained very much the exception until the 1890s. Summarising developments in housing design up to 1871,

Manega could find no German examples worthy of note and was thrown back on to English and French examples from the 1850s. The occasional examples of this type of building before the later 1880s, for example the housing built in Frankfurt by the Frankfurter gemeinnützige Baugesellschaft during the late 1860s (fig. 10) or the project by the H. J. Meyer Stiftung in Leipzig Lindenau are, like the housing of the BgB, similar in most respects to the form of speculative housing of the time. Occasionally something new is tried; in the development by the Johannesverein in Dresden every dwelling was provided with the means for cross ventilation by an ingenious but curious system of light-wells (fig. 11) But the very limited number of 'model' tenement blocks built in Germany simply did not provide the opportunities for experimentation that existed in England.

The economic constraints – on the one hand the high cost of construction and land, on the other the desire to keep rents down as low as possible – forced German reformers to accept that it was impossible to do much more within the existing framework of financing and building control than to provide tenement housing which satisfied minimum standards of hygiene. It was only in the late 1880s and the early 1890s, when the demands of the VfSP for a new approach to housing combined with the changes in the building regulations which enforced larger courts and more open forms of development, that the approach to the design of the tenement block became more adventurous.

A more important contribution to the design of working-class housing before 1890 was made in the field of cottage housing. Large numbers of cottage estates were being laid out by the co-operatives and by those employers who needed to provide for a large workforce, as in mining and metal-working, in rural or semi-rural surroundings where no other housing was available as in the examples from the Ruhrgebiet illustrated in fig. 12. Typically this form of housing, though probably better constructed than purely speculative housing, might be barely distinguishable from the normal forms of housing in the area. But it was the design of these estates that provided the focus for the debate on the design of the working-class dwelling before the 1890s.

By comparison with the wealth of material on the sanitary aspects of the dwelling, little was published on the design of working-class housing before the interest of the profession was aroused in the 1890s. Much of what was written was by engineers, surveyors and sanitarians and it is symptomatic that the fullest discussion of the time, *Die Anlage von Arbeiterwohnungen* (1871) by Manega, should have been written by an engineer who was secretary to the Austrian State Railways. The book, dry and purposeful in tone, provides a useful review of housing design during the late 1850s and 1860s, the time of the 'first debate' on the housing problem; it summarises the 'state-of-the-art' in Germany as the Paris Exhibition of 1867 had done for housing in France.

The book is divided into four parts and opens with a discussion of the sanitary requirements of the working-class house; the approach is

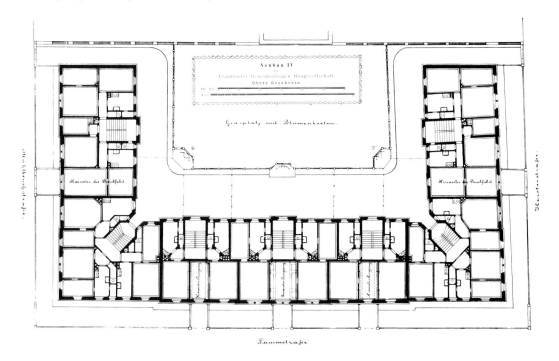

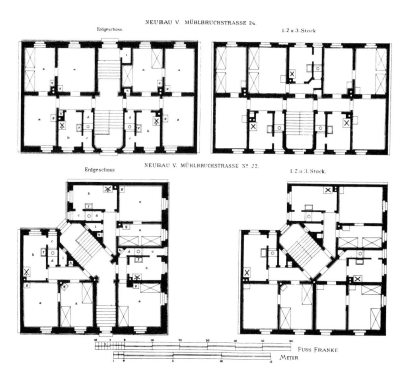

10 Housing built by the Frankfurter gemeinnützige Baugesellschaft on the Dammstrasse and Mühlbruchstrasse in 1868: (above) site layout and ground floor plan; (below) upper floor plan of typical tenement and corner unit

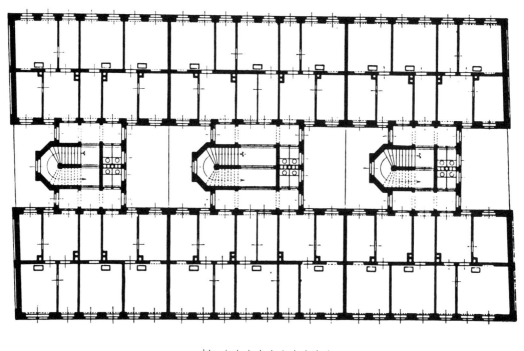

Obergefchofs.

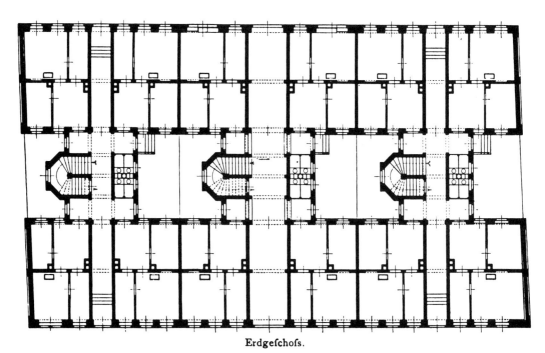

Erdgefchofs.

Häufergruppe des Johannesvereins zu Dresden.

Arch.: *Richter.*

11 Housing by the
Johannesverein in Dresden,
1887

12 Housing built by the mining companies: (above) the Eisenheim estate at Oberhausen-Osterfeld, 1844 and (below) at Dortmund-Sölderholz, 1850–70

similar to that of the sanitary reformers with the same emphasis on ventilation, heating, lighting and drainage, illustrated with frequent reference to English and French sources. In the second section Manega discusses different forms of construction in relation to their cost; throughout, considerations of economy are given great prominence. The final brief section of the book reviews an assortment of facilities that might be provided when planning a working-class housing estate: a library, washing facilities, a crèche, even a communal fire fighting service.

The most interesting and the largest section of the book is one which deals with questions of 'commodity' or the appropriateness of different types of housing. Manega opens with an assertion of the benefits of the cottage ideal and the 'isolation' which it provides, but concedes that in practice the ideal can rarely be achieved. In place of this absolute, he therefore argues, on the basis of the 'principle of isolation', that the fewer people who live under one roof the healthier and more contented they will be. From principle he proceeds to example. He examines a range of different forms of housing, the cottage, the terrace and, finally, the block, illustrating the different forms with English, French and, occasionally, German examples. The greater part of the chapter is devoted to a section on 'groups of houses' which includes semi-detached houses, terraces and 'cross'-planned houses. This type of development he regards as most suitable for general use because this form unites the economy of the block with the hygienic and moral benefits conferred by the 'principle of isolation' to be found in the cottage. By comparison, the discussion of tenement housing is brief and limited mainly to a discussion of English 'model' dwellings, indeed, for Manega the success of Roberts' designs for the SICLC with their open communal staircases lay in the way that they made it possible to retain the benefits of 'isolation' even at the high density of the tenement block.

The approach set out in the book, similar to that of other articles and pamphlets of the time, is simple and utilitarian.[6] It is the manual of an engineer approaching a problem which must be resolved in the most economical way possible, subject to the constraints of hygiene, solidity, and the demands of the 'principle of isolation'. It is not an approach that seeks to encourage architectural ingenuity; it reflects perfectly the approach to the design and layout of working-class housing that had developed in practice since the early years of the century by employers such as the mines.

For the most part this type of housing was the product of the strictest economy, both in planning and construction.[7] The house form was very simple: detached or semi-detached cottages, occasionally terrace housing in regions like the north-west. The internal planning of the house probably owed much to tradition and, particularly in rural or semi-rural areas, might include provision for a pig or a cow. One of the very few examples of the successful incorporation of a new 'designed' solution within this tradition was the 'cross' plan or Mulhausen Grundriss which Muller had pioneered at Mulhouse, despite difficulty with cross-ventilation it found widespread application in the 1860s and 1870s because of its economy (fig. 13). Construction, and therefore appearance, frequently differed from local vernacular tradition – a fact bemoaned by architects like Paul Schultze-Naumburg around the turn of the century. The cheapest materials were used, even if they had to be imported from outside the region; thus the importation of slates and machine-made tiles frequently resulted in a shallow roof form which was cheaper and used less timber, and looked very different from the high thatched or tiled roofs of the vernacular in many regions.

The strength of this tradition is evident from the range of examples that can be found throughout the nineteenth century. The tradition of state provision of housing for miners in the Prussian mines, which extends back to the first quarter of the nineteenth century, exemplified this approach. The housing built by the Königlich Preussiches Ministerium

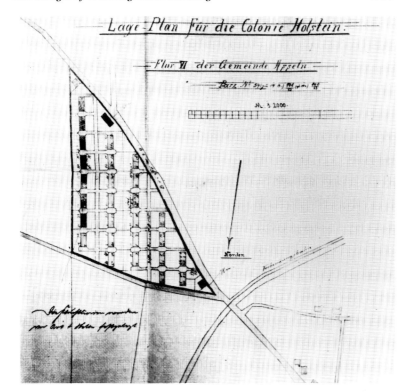

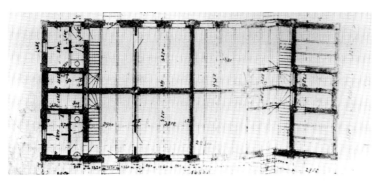

13 Typical German application of the Mulhouse 'cross plan': Kolonie Holstein, Dortmund, built by the Phönix Aktiengesellschaft für Bergbau during the 1870s: (above) site plan, (middle) elevation, (below) plan

14 Housing for railway
workers at Laienhausen near
Hanover: a four-family unit
on the 'cross plan'

Vorderanficht.   Seitenanficht.

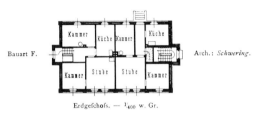

Bauart F.   Arch.: *Schwering*.

Erdgefchofs. — $^1\!/_{400}$ w. Gr.

für Handel und Gewerbe in mining areas such as the Ruhr, the
Saar and Silesia reveals a typical pattern of wide frontage detached or
semi-detached housing, the former especially common for 'premium'
housing.[8] Of the simplest and most utilitarian form of brick construction
with a shallow pitched roof of slate or tile, each house normally had
its own garden, together with accommodation for a pig, to provide a
supplement to the family budget. Similar housing was also built by the
individual states, and later by the Empire, for employees such as railway
workers living away from areas of existing settlements (fig. 14).
Well-publicised examples of such housing include the accommodation
built for workers at the main railway depot at Laienhausen near Hanover from 1877; housing was either semi-detached or planned for four
families to share a single house, with two dwellings on each floor, each
approached by a separate staircase.[9] Equally well known as an example
of improved housing for the employees of the Empire was that built for
the workers at the Imperial Torpedo Factory at Friedrichsort.[10] This was
planned on a much larger scale than most of the housing built by private
employees. The approach to site planning is typical of the period before
the 1892s, with a regular grid-iron layout focussed on a small area of
green space as a concession to the notions of community and healthy
recreation. There is no regard yet for issues such as orientation which
were to become so important after the turn of the century. Status within
the factory was directly reflected in the form of accommodation:
semi-detached houses were provided for the foremen and the more
skilled workers while the rest lived in houses containing four dwellings,
two to a floor.

   The same workers' 'cottage' tradition is equally apparent in much of
the 'improved' working-class housing built between the 1850s and the
late 1860s by private industry. The estate built by Villeroy and Bosch,
the ceramic goods manufacturers at Mettlach,[11] frequently cited by
housing reformers as an ideal, shows the same regimented array of
houses planned with no concern for orientation or the other niceties

of site layout which were to occupy architects after the turn of the century. Here, despite the opportunity for the individual employee to build his own house, uniformity and systematisation were ensured by requiring everyone to choose their design from a limited number of type plans provided by the employer. Even in south Germany the form of housing built by private industry was similar; the Augsburger Kammgarnspinnerei[12] built housing with plans and site layout which were quite as regimented and utilitarian as anything north of the Main.

Krupp's housing before 1890

The approach to the design of 'improved' working-class housing before the 1890s is well illustrated by the housing built in Essen by Krupp for his workforce in order to keep pace with the massive increase in business which resulted from the surge of armament production and the economic expansion in the 1860s and 1870s.

As early as 1861, the firm had built a group of ten houses for the works' foremen and senior skilled workers, planned as single-storey houses with rooms in the roof space and laid out in terrace form. However the first significant attempt to provide housing for a larger section of the workforce dates from 1863. Two hundred and nineteen temporary dwellings were hurriedly thrown up on the Westend site, now in the centre of Essen,[13] in a series of parallel blocks in the systematic manner of contemporary town extension plans dominated by the rigid geometry of the building line. Built with masonry ground floors and a wooden superstructure, this housing was utilitarian in conception and minimal in provision.

The expansion of 1863 seems to have provided sufficient accommodation to meet demands until the next surge of expansion in the early 1870s. The war with France and the economic boom of the *Gründerjahre* enabled the firm to grow even more rapidly and new housing related to the factory site was again urgently required. The next development on the Nordhof estate (1871) was again built as temporary housing and wooden construction was used with an unusual system of external staircase access to give each dwelling its own separate entrance (fig. 15). Site planning remained as harshly geometrical as at Westend, although a small landscaped area was provided for recreation. At last however between 1871 and 1873, Krupp laid out his first 'non-temporary' housing on the Schederhof (1871) and Baumhof estates (1872). On the Schederhof Krupp claimed that the design followed 'with reverence' the form of the original Krupp *Stammhaus*, while the site planning remained strictly orthogonal.[14] On the Baumhof estate the approach to site planning is similar but the houses are now closer in appearance to the traditional local working-class housing built by the mining authorities, with two-storey blocks each with two flats per floor, or with four two-storey dwellings planned on the 'cross plan' (fig. 16). Here, as if to emphasise that this was not temporary housing, construction was no longer in wood but in brick with a decorative string-course and

15 The Nordhof estate,
Essen, 1871

greater formal emphasis on the entrance gates. In other respects it is still entirely utilitarian in appearance.

While the Baumhof estate was located at some distance from the factory on cheaper land and could thus be built to a lower density, the Kronenberg estate, where development started in 1871, was adjacent to the factory on more expensive land and shows the way in which economic constraints such as land values influenced architectural form. Here in place of the two-storey housing used on the other estates, the housing is in the form of three- and four-storey blocks. But despite this, the approach to the planning of the block still remains based on the primitive 'cross plan' giving four dwellings per floor. In the design of this housing there is no evidence of any reference to English work on housing with its emphasis on the 'through' plan which would have been applicable in this situation. The construction and appearance of the housing on the Kronenberg estate is similar to that used at Baumhof but simply inflated in scale. The site planning, too, continued the systematic geometric approach of the earlier developments, but now with greater generosity, providing a considerable area for planting and even individual gardens.

Because of its size – it housed over 1,500 families – and the facilities it provided, which included a church, a school, a co-operative shop and wash-houses, the Kronenberg estate (fig. 17) can be seen to represent the most complete realisation in Germany to that date of the reformers' view of a purpose-built working-class community. It invites comparison with achievements in France or England not of the early 1870s, but of the 1850s, with the housing built by employers such as Jean Dollfus at Mulhouse or Sir Titus Salt at Saltaire. Like these, the community is

16 The Baumhof estate,
Essen, 1872–3, site plan and
view of typical block

17 The Kronenberg estate,
Essen, 1872–4, site plan and
view of typical block

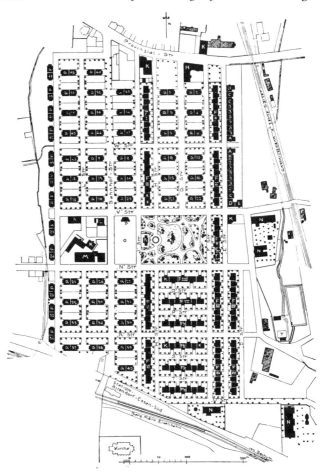

made up of a number of individual houses assembled on a purely additive basis. They share certain common facilities, church, shop and school, but there is no attempt to exploit in architectural terms the idea of community in the layout of the site. There is no similarity with the earlier tradition of planned communities like those of Owen and Fourier, nor do these estates look forward to the interest of planners in the 1890s in the forms of natural communities like the villages and small market towns of the Middle Ages. On the level of both the individual dwelling and the estate, the approach to the design of working-class housing remains utilitarian; architectural questions are ignored.

Developments from 1890

From the beginning of the 1890s there is evidence of a change in the attitudes of the profession towards the design of housing. By the turn of the century architects of national reputations had become involved in the design of working-class housing. Messel and Goecke are closely associated with attempts to reconsider the design of the tenement block; Herrmann Muthesius, Richard Riemerschmid and Karl Henrici are concerned with a new approach to the design of the cottage and cottage estate. From the early 1890s architects viewed the design of working-class housing as a matter of immediate concern.

There are a number of reasons for this. First, much more 'improved' housing was being built by non-profit organisations, such as the co-operatives, who were not just building for speculation and wanted high-quality housing. The demands of the VfSP for a vast increase in the volume of housing on the lines of that provided by the Peabody Trust and the limited dividend companies in London had stimulated a response in Berlin and other cities. By the end of the 1880s organisations including the Verein zur Verbesserung der kleinen Wohnungen and the Deutscher Verein für Armenpflege und Wohltätigkeit began to consider how to set about the construction of housing in the working-class districts of the city. Even more important in the long run was the assistance given to the co-operative movement. In 1890 legislation limiting the liability of co-operatives was introduced and this, in combination with the availability of finance from the local state insurance boards, led to a rapid expansion of the whole non-profit housing movement.[15] This expansion of the production of new housing naturally created an enormous opportunity for architectural work of all kinds.

But no less important were the changes in the attitudes of the profession towards the role of the designer in society. From the 1890s onwards architects no longer considered the design of housing as being below the dignity of the profession. In England, domestic architecture, even on a modest scale, had attracted the abilities of architects of reputation since the 1850s. Moreover, as a result of the impact of the values of the Arts and Crafts movement, to which German architects and designers had responded with enthusiasm, the designer now addressed himself with interest to the design of everyday objects. The design of the dwelling was naturally seen as the most important extension of these attitudes, as the culmination of these interests and certainly as deserving of the careful and considered treatment of the designer and architect. Housing was no longer regarded simply as a utilitarian exercise worthy only of the surveyor, nor as a frustrating battle over cost in which the architect sought to preserve his artistic freedom. From the 1890s the design of the working-class dwelling was accepted as a problem in its own right, not simply as a middle-class villa to be constructed to a small scale on a tight budget, nor merely as a utilitarian building thrown up without thought.

This new level of concern is evident in the work of a number of organisations around the beginning of the 1890s. In the Vereinigung Berliner Architekten (VBA)[16] the issue of designing suitable housing for the working classes in Berlin was discussed extensively in 1891 in relation to the problem of tenement buildings. The same theme was also examined by the Centralstelle für Arbeiterwohlfahrtseinrichtungen (CAW).[17] In the same year this organisation mounted a large exhibition with the help of the VBA of designs for working-class housing which concentrated on the range of accommodation being built by employers and by various non-profit organisations for working-class tenants. This exhibition, the extended reports published by the CAW[18] to accompany it and the conference held to mark its opening, taken together with accounts of the debates within the VBA, form a valuable review of current developments from which it is possible to separate out the main lines of approach to the design of working-class housing.

Although there were a number of intermediate forms of housing, the debate can be divided broadly into the discussion of the design of the 'cottage' on the one hand, and the design of the tenement block, or *Mietshaus*, on the other. Now, in contrast to the limited and grudging approval of the tenement block in the early days of the housing reform movement in the 1850s and 1860s, there was general acceptance of the need to build improved tenement housing in large cities, even though this might be at odds with the reformers' ideal of the family living in its own home, standing in its own garden. For the mass of workers living near their work in the centre of large cities like Berlin, the well-designed tenement block was now regarded as the only viable solution, a view that was plainly stated in the VBA's public statement on the housing problem:

In view of the fact that local circumstances in Berlin and the traditional habit of the working-class population make it most improbable that a preponderance of the latter can be accommodated in the foreseeable future in separate houses, the task of perfecting the most suitably designed tenement block for working-class tenants becomes a matter of some urgency. This is particularly so as, here in Berlin as indeed elsewhere, the question has received but little consideration from architects, who have instead concentrated their powers of invention on the planning of detached and semi-detached houses for one or two working-class families.[19]

This did not imply an abandonment of the earlier cottage ideal. This was simply the qualification of early unrestrained enthusiasm; however much the design of the tenement block might be accepted, the ideal still remained the cottage.

The design of the *Mietshaus*

It is in Berlin, more clearly than anywhere else, that we can see the evolution, illustrated in fig. 18, of the form of the block in response to the reformers' demands for a new approach. From the typical *Zweispänner* plan of the 1860s with two flats on each floor, the blocks of flats or *Mietshaus* had, by the late 1880s, been developed by private enterprise to provide a number of different forms for different social and economic groups. Thus the typical working-class form, found principally in areas such as Moabit and Wedding to the north, and in Friedrichshain and Kreuzberg to the east and south-east, might, depending on the frontage, contain anything between 4 and 20 dwellings on one floor. These would be planned either side of a common corridor which would be unlit and unventilated except through the individual dwellings; some dwellings would be cut in two by the corridor, the largest dwellings would be undivided and placed at the end of the corridor (figs. 18 and 19). In the 'front' buildings, those which faced on to the street, kitchens were normally placed on the court side of the corridor; in the 'back' buildings, kitchen and main room might be adjacent. Toilets were either placed on each landing or, more commonly, in the court; by the 1880s most dwellings had their own water supply and a number, even in working-class districts, had their own water closets.

During the 1880s, as a result of the deep sites laid out in the development plan for Berlin, the number of courts per plot increased and, with this, the number of dwellings located in the side and back buildings, a form of development illustrated at its worst in areas such as Wedding (fig. 21).[20] Dwellings in these side buildings were regarded as particularly insalubrious. They were normally arranged with two flats per landing, but with ventilation on one side only; in another common arrangement, for example that illustrated by Eberstadt, the side building might simply contain rooms extended out from the main blocks in an attempt to cram the maximum number of dwellings on to the site.

The provisions of the *Bauordnungen* of 1887 had done something to limit the density to which a site might be developed, but the internal planning of the block, particularly in the working-class *Mietskaserne*, remained untouched. During the 1890s, housing was still being built in which the common corridor was planned in such a way that it divided the typical two-room dwelling. It was this tradition of inadequate housing where 'home means nothing more than a place to cook' that Goecke attacked in his call for a redesign of the *Arbeitermietshaus*, in his articles in the *Deutsche Bauzeitung* of 1890.[21]

Well aware of the different components of the housing problem, the economics of the processes of development, the rents that the working

18 Schematic representation of the development of the Berlin *Mietskaserne* type from the early *Zweispänner* of the 1850s

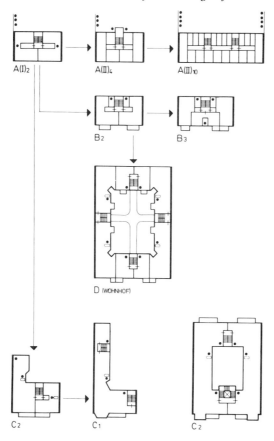

A(I)₂   A(II)₄   A(II)₁₀

B₂   B₃

D (WOHNHOF)

C₂   C₁   C₂

A(I)   Typical early *Mietshaus* form with internal, unventilated toilets or toilets located in the court

A(II) Minimum standard working-class tenements with 4–10 dwellings per floor and with toilets on the landings or in the court

B   Artisan or lower middle-class housing: self-contained dwellings with balconies and internal, ventilated toilets

C   Middle-class flats: well-equipped, self-contained dwellings with bathrooms and internal toilets, balconies and bay windows, and, as in type C1, servants accommodation with separate access

D   Large court developments typical of many built by the non-profit housing movement during the 1890s and early twentieth century to the same standards as housing of type B

●   WCs

classes could afford and the acceptance in the eastern cities of the high-density form of living, Goecke urged a reconsideration of the design of the tenement block. He called for working-class housing to be built to standards acceptable to the reformers and at tolerable rents, rather than repeating yet again the call for cottage housing in the suburbs. Indeed, approached in the right way, he argued, there was no reason why the *Mietshaus* could not be made every bit as hygienic as the cottage.

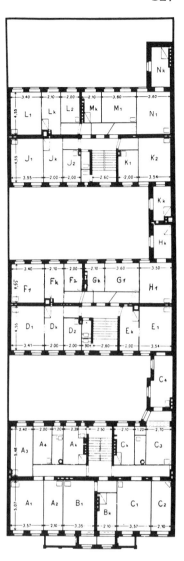

19 Plan of a typical Berlin *Mietskaserne* around the turn of the century. Each set of rooms with the same letter represents one dwelling.

In the designs that illustrated his argument (fig. 22) Goecke demonstrated ways in which a number of the problems of the earlier type of block could be overcome. By maintaining the *Zweispänner* type, by careful and systematic planning of the corner and by increasing the number of staircases, he was able to produce designs in which the common corridor did not divide the individual flat, even on plots with wide frontages. At the same time, he was able to provide a distribution of flat sizes that matched working-class demand, with many two-room dwellings, a number of larger flats, and a scattering of one-room dwellings. At rents which he estimated to be within reach of the working-class family's budget, his designs provided self-contained dwellings, each with its own toilet and with waste-chutes associated with each staircase; each flat, except the corner flat, was to be provided

20 View into the court of
typical Berlin *Mietskaserne* of
the turn of the century

with a balcony and each was to have its own kitchen equipped with
a stove. One of the most obvious benefits of Goecke's designs was the
way that courts on adjoining sites could be combined to give, in place
of the two separate light-wells so common in Berlin, a real court
providing not only adequate ventilation, but even a usable open space
for children's play or planting. Most important, Goecke argued that all
this accommodation could be provided at the kind of rents that the
working class could afford and in areas where working-class housing
was required.[22]

The result of Goecke's call for a reconsideration of the design of the
tenement block together with the interest in housing issues that had
been awakened by the VfSP's survey of housing and even the concern

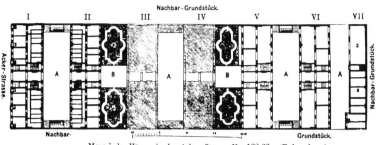

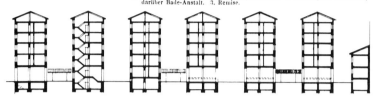

Meyer'sche Häuser in der Acker-Strasse No. 132/33. (Erdgeschoss.)

A. Höfe. B. Gärten. I—VI. Wohnhäuser. VII. Verwaltungsgebäude. 1. Dampfmaschine. 2. Wohnung des Verwalters, darüber Bade-Anstalt. 3. Remise.

21 The Meyers Hof development on the Ackerstrasse, Wedding: plan, section and view through the street entrance into the succession of courts

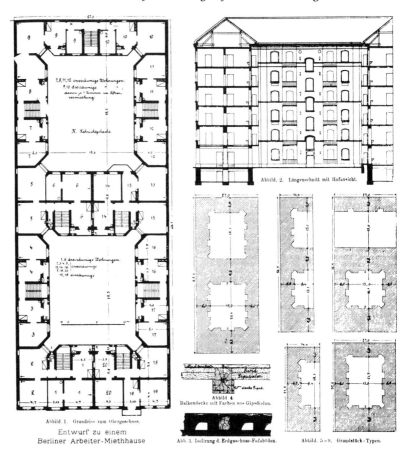

Entwurf zu einem
Berliner Arbeiter-Miethhause

1.   Plan of typical upper floor
2.   Section and view into court
3.   Ground floor construction
4.   Intermediate floor construction showing sound insulation
5–9. Alternative site layouts

of the new Kaiser, Williem II, in social matters (which we discuss in
chapter 12) led the Vereinigung Berliner Architekten to arrange a
number of colloquia on the question of working-class housing which
brought together a wide number of the interested parties in Berlin,
including representatives of the Handels Ministerium.[23]

Much of the discussion touched on economic and social aspects of the
housing problem, but the debate naturally centred on the problems of
designing working-class housing. One of the central issues in the debate
was the problem of dealing with the larger sites in Berlin that resulted
from the road layouts in new areas; in the normal form of speculative
development this tended to lead to very deep developments with many
courts opening back off a single street façade. This form of housing was
exemplified at its worst by the notorious Meyers Hof development in
Wedding which contained more inhabitants (over 2,000) than any
other development in Berlin. In more general form, however, the

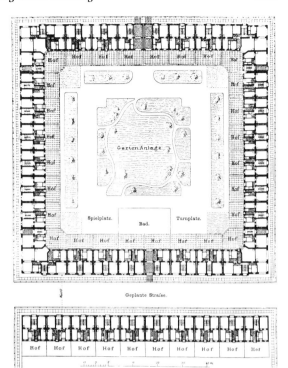

23 Alfred Messel's first site plan for the Weissbach'sen development planned by the Verein zur Verbesserung der kleinen Wohnungen

scale of the problem was reflected in the continuous rise in the *Behausungsziffer*, or the population per site, from the 1870s through to the decade before the First World War (see tables 5 and 6). To counter this problem the Association recommended the parcelling up of development land in the outskirts of the city in such a way that the maximum depth of block should not exceed 80 m, allowing a depth of 40 m for each plot, and the case for smaller plots was pressed with some urgency in an attempt to reduce the number of back and side buildings.[24]

Closely related to the problem of the deep block was the growing concern to open up the court area in working-class developments to ensure more light and air in response to sanitary concern about health and the vital need for ventilation. In contrast to the limited dimensions of the court in traditional working-class housing, the discussions of the VBA publicised the way in which architects such as Messel were already experimenting either with combining the courts of adjacent properties, or with using the large scale of plots on the outskirts of the city to ensure much more generous courts than would normally have been possible. Already in his first designs (fig. 23) for the development of the Weissbach'sen estates for the Verein zur Verbesserung kleiner Wohnungen in 1890,[25] Messel was experimenting with the design of a court large enough to contain planting and gardens on a scale fundamentally different from the miserable minimal courts of the typical *Mietskaserne* built by private enterprise at the time. Looking to English examples, Messel set out to offer something akin to the London

24 Alfred Messel's
development on the
Sickingenstrasse for the
Berliner Spar- und
Bauverein, 1895

Abbildung 427.

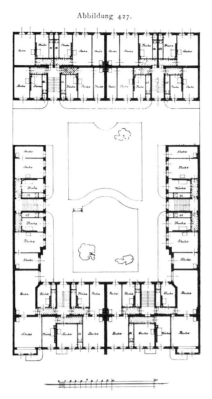

residential 'square' as a model for urban living, rejecting the court of light-well proportions normally associated with the tenement block as wholly unsatisfactory. Nor were the financial consequences of these higher standards necessarily disadvantageous. Messel claimed that the return for the Verein would be very close to that which would have been possible with the traditional form of development.

As a reflection of the enthusiasm of the VBA for these large courts, one of nine recommendations made at the 1891 meeting on the housing problem, was to change the *Bauordnungen* of 1887 in such a way that the developer could maintain the level of the side buildings at the same level as the front building, thus allowing him an increase in floor space, if he were to combine the court on his site with that of his neighbour. In the final recommendation by the Association the emphasis on increasing the size of courts was even more direct: 'Building Societies and Housing Associations concerned with the welfare of the working classes must regard the provision of gardens and green space within their developments as an issue of the greatest importance; it is something that should be held up as a model for imitation by private enterprise.'[26]

The initiative towards housing with larger courts started by Goecke and Messel in 1890 was to find its first successful realisation in the design for the housing built by the Berliner Spar- und Bauverein on the Sickingenstrasse in Moabit finished in 1895.[27] This organisation, which included amongst its founders leading housing and land reformers such as Heinrich Albrecht and Damaschke, could afford to put greater emphasis on quality than most of the private enterprise developers and set out to build a 'model' development. The development designed by Messel shows what could be done by combining the courts in adjacent developments to give a single large-scale court of 23 m × 38 m, which was planted and even contained a play space for children in a Kindergarten run by the Verein in the court behind the independent back building. Despite the size of this open space, the rents were claimed to be no higher than normal, although this was attributed in large part to the low rate of interest at which the Verein had been able to borrow its capital.

This approach was carried forward by Messel, working for the same organisation, in the design for the development on the nearby Proskauerstrasse (fig. 25); here the site was even larger, permitting an internal court whose largest dimension was 40 m. The internal planning of the flats carried on the tradition of improvement to which Goecke had attached so much importance, with the result that each dwelling was entirely self-contained and possessed its own WC. But in addition to the flats, the Spar- und Bauverein also built on the same site a library, six shops, a pub, washing and bathing facilities, a kindergarten which was able to use the large court as a play area, and a meeting hall which served as a focus for the life of the community.

Messel was to develop these same ideas in the design for the housing finally built by the Verein zur Verbesserung der kleinen Wohnungen on a

25 Alfred Messel's development on the Proskauerstrasse for the Berliner Spar- und Bauverein, 1897–8

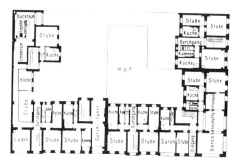

26 Alfred Messel's development on the Kochhannstrasse and the Weissbachstrasse for the Verein zur Verbesserung der kleinen Wohnungen, 1899–1905

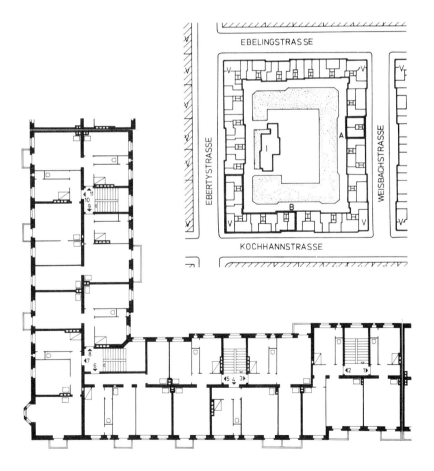

block at the intersection of the Kochannstrasse and the Weissbachstrasse (fig. 26).[28] This project, which had evolved from Messel's early experimentation in the 1890s, was built between 1899 and 1905, and shows a way of overcoming the problems of high-density housing which was a source of such concern to the sanitarians and the VföG. Messel showed how an architect could turn to advantage the new system of density zoning, introduced to Berlin in 1892, and how this could be used to transform the tenement block from the airless and lightless *Mietskaserne* of the 1880s and earlier into an entirely new environment. Here the tenant was offered the advantages of a location near the centre of the city together with the benefits of a self-contained *Zweispänner* flat, capable of being fully cross-ventilated, and giving on to a generous planted court or 'square'. In addition the Verein provided certain common facilities for bathing and washing, and a kindergarten; these common facilities were run by the Frauenverein Octavia Hill which also provided evening lectures, and classes in home economics, and Christmas festivities, thus creating a focus for the life of the community.

The achievements during the 1890s of such organisations as the Verein zur Verbesserung der kleinen Wohnungen and the Berliner Spar- und Bauverein, together with architects such as Goecke and Messel had shown that working outside the market framework of private enterprise, the non-profit housing sector could take advantage of density zoning to provide an attractive environment, even in the centre of the city. Now, during the expansion of non-profit building after 1900, experiments with different ways of providing more light and more air, and with providing at least the minimum amount of sunlight by opening up the forms of the block, are pursued with equal vigour and ingenuity.

The rents in developments of this kind were generally beyond the reach of working-class families, although those of the dwellings behind the extravagant façades of developments such as the Versöhnungs-Privatstrasse were not more than those in other non-profit housing (fig. 27). But these experiments were nevertheless of importance for the development of high-density housing for the working class. First, the architectural quality of the layout did much to rid high-density housing of its associations with the *Mietskaserne* and the taint of poverty. Second, the solutions to problems of site layout with which architects were experimenting here could, and indeed did, provide a useful testing ground for working-class developments funded by the non-profit housing movement generally.

By 1914, Berlin architects like Messel, Paul Mebes, Albert Gessner, Paul Jatzow, Paul Kolb and others had confronted, and to some extent 'resolved', the architectural and sanitary, if not the economic problems of high-density low-cost housing. In other cities too, in Hamburg, Leipzig and elsewhere, the design of such housing was being actively explored.[29] In place of the gross inadequacies of the typical *Mietskaserne* of the 1870s and 1880s, much of the limited amount of 'improved' working-class housing built between the mid-1890s and 1914 showed that, despite the loyalty of most housing reformers to the ideal of the

27 Non-profit housing in
Berlin: the Nürnberger Hof
of the Versöhnungs-
Privatstrasse
development by the
Vaterländischer Bauverein in
Wedding, 1903–4

'cottage', housing of high quality could be provided at high density even in the centre of the city. Through this work in Berlin a new ideal was elaborated which was well suited, if not to the problems of low-income housing, then at least to the work of the non-profit associations which began to play an increasingly important part in housing the better-paid artisan and clerk from the mid-1890s onwards.

The design of the cottage after 1890

As in the design of the *Mietshaus*, so in the design of the cottage the 1890s represent an important period of transition. By the end of the decade the cottage had become a topic of interest, even for architects of national reputation. In place of the utilitarian approach employed in the design and layout of the Krupp's early estates such as that at Baum-hof or the housing built by the Navy at the torpedo workshops near Kiel, architects now approached the design of the cottage with new interest. Before the 1890s it had been shrugged off by most designers and architects as insignificant, together with a number of other more modest design problems. But now in Germany, as in England, the cottage provided a new challenge to designers. Closely related to this search for an unpretentious setting for family life was the new respect for traditional design and craftsmanship and the traditional forms of vernacular building. The enthusiasm for vernacular forms and the qualities of design to be found in the village and the small market towns

28 The Agnetapark estate, Delft, Holland, 1888–92: site plan and typical four-family block

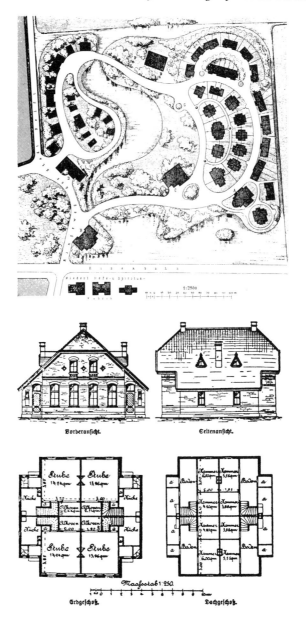

A lodging house
B general stores
C director's house
D planned school
E social centre

F children's playground
G bandstand
H boathouse
I land for future expansion

of rural Germany, evident in the work of architects like Theodor Fischer or Paul Schultze-Naumburg, found a focus in the design of the cottage and the layout of cottage estates. In place of the rigid geometry of the site plans of the 1870s, architects now sought to exploit the topography of the site, respecting existing buildings and planting, often seeking to recreate the qualities that they admired in the architecture and forms of the small towns of the past.

The first steps towards this new design of the cottage and the housing estate are taken in the late 1880s and early 1890s. An early example of the new development is the layout of the Agnetapark at Delft in Holland planned in 1888 (fig. 28).[30] It was widely illustrated in contemporary discussions of housing layout and admired as a model of what could be achieved by taking advantage of the natural features of the landscape and combining this with an informal layout for the housing. More widely publicised in Germany was the layout of the first phase of the Altenhof estate in Essen prepared by Robert Schmohl, who had just been appointed architect to the Krupp estates. Previous attempts to obtain a site plan by competition in 1892 had produced no advance on traditional geometric layouts.[31] Built to provide housing for retired or injured employees of the firm, the Altenhof estate was under construction from 1893 onwards and was thus started at the same time as the Alfredshof also for Krupp estate, a late example of the old approach.

The comparison between the two, illustrated in fig. 29, is instructive. Both were laid out as cottage estates away from the centre of the city and the factory where land was cheaper. The site plan of the Alfredshof embodies the conventional approach of the 1870s with its rigid geometry. Hermann Hecker suggests rather cryptically that it was laid out during the period when Schmohl was taking over the direction of the firm's architectural and planning affairs, and that therefore it represents perhaps the residuum of earlier ideas.[32] However, in the design of the individual dwellings there are already changes that are the result of Schmohl's arrival (fig. 30). The picturesque handling of the roofscape and the wooden framing of the upper storey are very different from the treatment of the housing on the earlier estates; in contrast to the simplicity of the roofs in, say, the Baumhof estate, the ridge of the roof on a number of blocks is designed in the shape of an H giving the most varied roof treatment possible and the variety of two gables on the street elevation. However traditional the geometrical site planning, the design of the individual houses looks forward to later developments.

At Altenhof the approach to the design of the home is similar but the site plan is treated in a very much freer way. With its curving streets and the picturesque disposition of the cottages in relation to the street, it already looks forward to the site planning of the period after the turn of the century. With this picturesque approach to design and with each dwelling standing alone or semi-detached, the estate gives the impression of being a scaled down version of middle-class villa developments rather than a factory housing estate. Looking back on the developments of the 1890s in *Kleinhaus und Kleinsiedlung*, Muthesius was highly critical of this kind of housing which appeared determinedly picturesque and 'which to our present sensibilities has something unnatural about it'

29 Developments in site
planning: the first phase of
the Altenhof estate
1892–1900 (above), and the
first phase of the Alfredshof
estate, 1893–6 (below)

(fig. 31).[33] Here the strongly modelled groupings, appropriate perhaps
for the villa, result in an approach which is openly at variance with the
scale of the houses; they are too small for the 'villa aesthetic' foisted
upon them. The traditional virtue of economy that had always been an
essential constraint on the design of working-class housing is completely

30 Developments in the design of the dwelling: overseer's house (left) and house for four families (right) on the Alfredshof estate, 1893–6

31 The Altenhof estate, first phase, 1892–6

abandoned. With their bays, their turrets, their dormers and their corners, these houses are much less economical than the kind of planning, often based on terrace layouts and probably of English inspiration, that was to follow, and decidedly very much more expensive that the simple 'cross' plan typical of working-class housing of the 1870s.

The extent to which Schmohl's Altenhof scheme was typical of the current approach to working-class housing can be judged from the projects entered for the competition for the estate. Clearly the organisers were looking for something of the nature of Schmohl's plan as it was one of the conditions of the competition that designs should avoid a 'dry uniformity' and seek instead to give a 'variety of elevations to enliven the appearance of the street'; to assist competitors in the quest for variety, they were urged to build detached or semi-detached housing only.[34] The entries nearly all give the same impression of a miniature villa colony, aping at a reduced scale the turrets and towers of the villas of Grunewald and the other villa suburbs of cities like Berlin in the 1890s. The only entries to avoid this effect were those that continued the utilitarian traditions of the 1870s or those, for example Tschar-mann's, that were simpler in design and, according to Muthesius, already owed their inspiration to developments in England.

The approach exemplified by the first phase of the Altenhof estate was not unique – comparable estates were being laid out by other large manufacturers by the mid-1890s – but it did represent a first and decisive break with the earlier tradition of utilitarian planning. However, around the turn of the century there is another change of approach, away from the fussy qualities of estates such as these, towards simpler designs and a greater interest in vernacular models with their emphasis on economy of means and materials.

One of the first examples of this new direction is the initial stage of the Margaretenhof estate at Rheinhausen (fig. 32) built by Schmohl for Krupp in 1903. In place of the visual autarchy of the Altenhof estate, the dwellings here are grouped in terraces, a form of housing more common in England than Germany, and related in an orderly way to the street. The houses are planned as narrow frontage terrace houses and are simple in plan and elevation without the bays and corners of the Altenhof housing; the choice of materials is equally simple, the houses being rendered and the number of materials kept to a minimum. The planning of the site, based on the formal square, Krupp Platz, in the middle of the estate is less advanced than later estates where the effect of topography and orientation on site layout is more important. Nevertheless, here was a new approach to the design of the cottage estate.

The speed with which these ideas were taken up is evident in a number of housing layouts illustrated in the new periodical *Der Städtebau*, the first journal dedicated solely to planning, launched by Sitte and Goecke in 1904.[35] In place of the diminutive villa type of housing of the 1890s we can now see in estates such as the Margaretenhöhe in Essen by Metzendorf (see fig. 36), or in the housing designed by Henrici for the

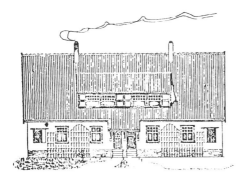

32 Terrace of four houses
from the Margaretenhof
estate, Rheinhausen am
Rhein, 1903–5

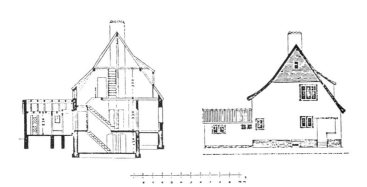

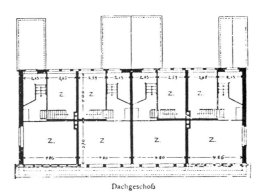

Dachgeschoß

Erdgeschoß

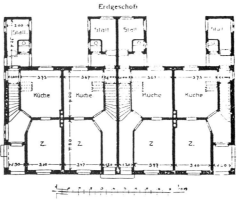

Abb. 218 und 219.

33 Karl Henrici's project for workers' housing for the state mining authorities at Kurnow: site plan (above) and view of housing (below)

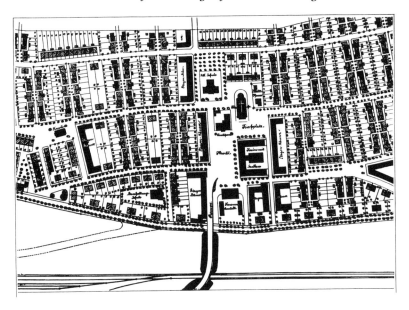

Kurnow mines (fig. 33), a new formal vocabulary evolved specially for
working-class housing. What were the ideas that lay behind this new
approach?

Fortunately, the 14th Annual Conference of the Centralstelle für
Arbeiterwohlfahrtseinrichtungen in 1905 took the design of working-
class housing as its subject and provides us with a valuable summary
of the current debate, enabling us to identify the most important
elements of the new approach.[36] The participants at the conference
included Muthesius, Riemerschmid, Henrici and Schulze-Naumburg,
leading architectural figures of the time; their contributions emphasise
the importance now attached to the subject by the profession as a whole.

One of the most powerful influences on the design of the small house
was, as Muthesius explained,[37] an admiration in Germany for the work
of the English 'Free School' architects like Norman Shaw, William
Nesfield and Philip Webb. Even the work of the younger generation of
architects like William Lethaby, Charles Voysey, M. H. Baillie Scott and
Barry Parker and Raymond Unwin was well known through publications
like the *Studio* and the *Building News* before the publication of Muthesius's
authoritative three-volume study *Das englische Haus* between 1904–5.
In the field of working-class housing, too, German architects like
Muthesius and Riemerschmid looked to England, to developments like
Bedford Park, Bourneville, Port Sunlight and New Earswick, for demonstrations of a new 'way forward' that avoided both the utilitarian values
of earlier approaches to the design of workers' housing, and the
artificiality that they considered typical of so much of nineteenth
century design: 'In the history of the artistic design of workers' housing,
Port Sunlight will always be honoured with the highest recognition. For
it is here that the gates to a new world were first opened; in place of
the dismal appearance of utilitarian buildings we were shown a new
vision; in place of the misery associated with the barren rows of
workers' terraces we find joyfulness and homeliness'.[38]

The sympathy for the values of the craft tradition of the past, evident
in the work of the English 'Free School' architects, was already to be
seen in the work of German architects such as Fischer whose Kohlen
Insel project for Munich draws on forms from the German towns of the
Middle Ages. Equally powerful support for this approach was to be found
in the Heimatschutz and Dürerbund lobbies who were committed to
the defence of traditional German cultural values and were represented
at the conference by Schultze-Naumburg. Comparing 'good' and 'bad'
examples of housing (fig. 34), a technique already used in his studies
Kulturarbeiten, he urged a return to German vernacular tradition, in
place of the 'rootless' mass housing of the present, claiming 'only from
tradition can we expect salvation'.[39] He presented the small farmhouse
with its simple dignity and sensitive and economical use of materials
as the most appropriate prototype to follow in housing the worker. His
description of this paradigm echoes exactly the ideal pursued by the
early housing reformers:

This is our task: to create comfortable, healthy and economical living space set
in a small garden, with a veranda for sitting outdoors in the summer-time, with

34 Paul Schultze-Naumburg:
'good' (above) and 'bad'
(below) examples of cottage
housing

rooms that are well lit and well ventilated but warm in winter. For all this, there
stands before us the inspiring example of the German farmhouse as it still existed
well into the nineteenth century, and as it still exists today, in sufficient quantity
to establish its viability as a prototype.[40]

The relevance of Schultze-Naumburg's views for current attitudes to
design is clear. He clearly supported the trend away from picturesque

confusion in planning and in the handling of elements such as the roof and the elevations of the house. It is significant that he should have singled out Schmohl's design for housing on the Margaretenhof estate as an example of the 'good', contrasting this with the drabness and utilitarian uniformity of the housing of the earlier estates and the fussiness of the first stage of the Altenhof estate of the 1890s as examples of the 'bad'.

Another major and related influence on the layout of working-class housing, and one represented at the conference by Henrici's paper,[41] were the ideas of the younger generation of planners who developed and adapted the ideas of Camillo Sitte. Since the publication of Sitte's book *Der Städtebau nach künstlerischen Grundsätzen* in 1889,[42] the engineers' stock response to city planning, the unrelieved grid-iron plan, had been under attack. Sitte urged architects and planners to remember the great achievements of 'city building' of the past when aesthetic and spatial values had predominated over mere technical questions like traffic circulation and drainage. The success of his ideas was dramatic. This new emphasis in planning gained widespread attention not only in Germany, but in France and England too; from 1904 *Der Städtebau*, provided under the editorial policy of Sitte and Goecke an influential platform from which to campaign for these ideas. Already by the turn of the century, Sitte, Henrici, Goecke and others interested in exploiting the new approach, were able to demonstrate their ideas in city extension plans for Dessau, Munich and a number of smaller cities.[43]

In housing these ideas were widely influential. The introduction of density zoning in the mid-1890s led to the laying out of many low-density suburbs, frequently referred to after the turn of the century as *Gartenvorstädte*. These areas, often developed by non-profit housing Associations, offered, along with the housing being built by large employers, a rich field for the application of these new ideas on planning. Illustrated widely in *Der Städtebau* before 1914, the plans of these estates (see fig. 33) by architects such as Henrici, Jansen and Pützer show how great was the contrast with the approach to layout and planning in the 1890s. The square, for example, is no longer a patch of rear garden, but more like the market square of a small town; it provides a spatial focus for the estate and the surrounding buildings. The surrounding buildings, perhaps the co-operative store, the school, sometimes a church, sometimes housing built to a higher density than elsewhere, now enclose and control the space of the square. Planning of housing and street is now carefully considered together and freed of geometrical constraints. The street now leads the viewer through the estate or to the main square, in the way that the planners claimed had been achieved in medieval towns like Buttsted; the layout now responds to the lie of the land, saving construction costs and enabling the planner to take advantage of aspect as well as orientation.

Yet even within the approach to planning that had evolved by the end of the 1900s we can identify a number of different stages of development. Whereas the layouts of the early 1900s often contained a variety of curving streets, in a self-conscious avoidance of any rigid geometry, later projects avoided such obvious devices, looking for greater simplicity and introducing curved streets only where the terrain made this desirable. Indeed by the end of the decade, housing layouts were again coming to have a formal simplicity and a regular order about them, but one which was far removed from the utilitarian grid-iron planning of the 1870s. Even at low densities, the emphasis was now on the planning of groups of houses, sometimes around a court, or around the end of a cul-de-sac, arranged to take account of orientation and site. The results are often very similar to Parker and Unwin's housing on the Pixmore or Bird's Bill sites at Letchworth.

An important reason for the move towards a simpler and more regular layout was the emphasis that was now placed on questions of sunlight and orientation, and on roads. In both England and Germany, handbooks on housing are invaded by diagrams showing the position of the sun at each season and the resulting optimum orientation and carefully drawn sections through roads of different classes giving details of construction and cost.[44]

As we have seen in our discussion of sanitary reform, the problems of orientation for sunlight had received some attention from Vogt and others by the early 1880s (fig. 35).[45] But the utilitarian and rigidly geometrical approach to site planning still used in working-class estates before the 1890s, took no account of orientation. Even in the design of the dwelling it was frequently overlooked: the traditional 'cross' plan favoured by many architects before the 1890s ensured inferior orientation for at least one of the four dwellings. But with the growing emphasis put by sanitarians on the benign effects of sunlight the question was treated more seriously and by 1890 Christian Nussbaum, one of the leading contributors to the technical side of the architectural debate on housing reform, was arguing that orientation had become a question of cardinal importance in site planning and demanded that every dwelling should be oriented to receive direct sunlight.[46] It was certainly treated as one of the principal determinants of site planning by Muthesius in *Kleinhaus und Kleinsiedlung*. By the end of the 1900s, good practice demanded that residential streets should, where possible, be laid out on a north–south or, ideally, north-west–south-east axis; layouts with streets running east–west were to be avoided, although the disadvantages of a north-facing orientation might be overcome in the planning of the house type. The overall effect of this concern with orientation was to strengthen still further the trend towards regularity in housing layouts.

This trend was reinforced by the reconsideration of the design of roads in residential areas.[47] As a result of the demands of the VföG during the seventies and eighties road layout had often been generous with a uniform width of road enforced throughout a development to ensure adequate ventilation in the manner of the English bye-law street; during the 1890s the 'writhing' roads of picturesque site layouts had further increased the cost of roads in an estate. To reduce these costs architects

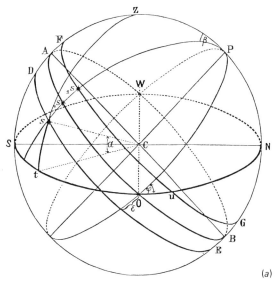

(a)

35 Adolf Vogt: studies of insolation and its relationship to residential street layout

(a) using the descriptive power of solid geometry. Vogt calculates the angle α of the sun's rays for different times of the year (EsD for the shortest day; Os_0 A for the equinoxes; us_1 F for the longest day) for different latitudes falling on the position of an observer C standing on a plane OSWN (which also represent the four points of the compass – Ost, Süd, West, Nord).

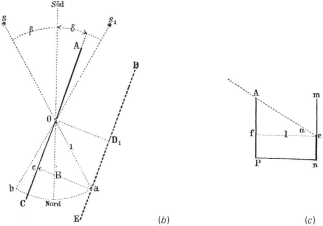

(b)   (c)

(b) from this projection of the sun's path Vogt shows how the height and spacing of opposing parallel buildings can be arranged to ensure an absence of overshadowing. If 0 is the position of a pole casting a shadow 0a of length 1 then a building whose front lies on AC of height 1 will cast a shadow bounded by the line DE. Using different values for α, this can be generalised to give the minimum spacing between AC and DE to avoid overshadowing of DE for any orientation of AC, described in relation to South by δ, and for the position of the sun at any time of day described by β.

(c) Vogt's method can also be used to calculate the height of shadowing cast on the wall of an opposing building. If AP and mn represent the position of two opposing terraces (in section), then the maximum height of shadow, e, on mn can be calculated for the shortest and the longest days of the year for buildings of different orientations.

36 Further developments in
site planning: the
Margaretenhöhe estate, Essen
(above) and the Krupp estate
at Emscher-Lippe (below)

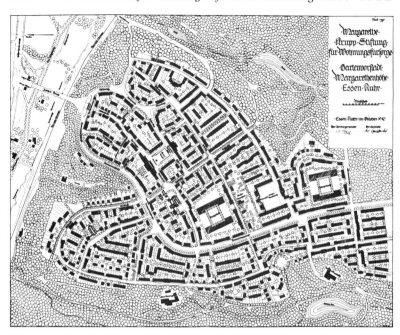

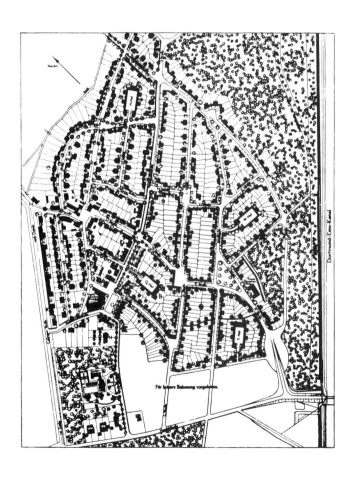

such as Muthesius now argued for a clear hierarchy of roads in which the width of road would reflect the volume of traffic using it: thus the distributor road to an estate would be wider than the roads serving the individual houses. In contrast to estates such as the Margaretenhöhe estate started in 1910 where the width of road was constant throughout (fig. 36), later estates such as that at Emscher-Lippe planned just before the war by Schmohl show a clearer hierarchy of roads, an attempt to differentiate between distributor and purely residential streets, and, according to Muthesius, substantial savings in road costs.

The design of the dwelling

The rethinking of housing design around the turn of the century was not just limited to the issue of planning and appearance. Like Parker and Unwin in England, the German architects concerned with housing reform also turned their attention to the design of the individual house.

One of the difficulties besetting the architect in dealing with the redesign of the cottage was the wide range of variation in patterns of living across the country.[48] Thus in the east the tradition was to have a 'living kitchen' rather than a 'cooking kitchen'and a parlour as was more common in the Rhineland. Despite a consciousness of these regional variations, which were often viewed with strong affection by the members of the Heimatschutz organisations, there appears to have been a consensus, around the turn of the century, on an ideal layout for the cottage. Indeed the German debate has close parallels with the discussion of the subject in England. Until this time, architects had appeared to view the design of the working-class dwelling as simply a question of reducing the scale of the villa. At the scale of the workers' cottage this normally resulted in incongruous planning, with small, pokey rooms and over-generous circulation, and the waste of a considerable volume in the roof space of turrets and towers. However from the turn of the century onwards, we can see a new architectural interest brought to bear on the task of designing an appropriate working-class dwelling.

Central to this discussion was the way in which the kitchen was to be used.[49] Because of the concern, for sanitary reasons, with dampness and the steam which were an unavoidable consequence of the cooking and washing carried on in the kitchen, reformers were anxious to separate those processes which generated steam, dampness and smells from the other living activities of the family. Equally, however, the reformers recognised the attractiveness of the living kitchen for the family both during the day, when the mother could keep an eye on the children while doing her housework, and in the evening when it provided a meeting place for the family after the husband was back from work and the children were back from school. Most important, in cold weather, it made it possible to use a single heat source for cooking, warming water and heating the main space of the house, an obvious advantage: 'the higher the price of fuel and the colder the climate, the longer the kitchen will be used as the main living room'.[50]

The solution favoured by most reformers, from Nussbaum writing in 1901 to Muthesius writing in 1918, was the construction of a small scullery where activities involving water and washing could be concentrated away from the main living kitchen. This made it possible to retain the living kitchen but without its most obvious drawbacks. With the introduction of gas cooking before the war (35% of dwellings in Berlin had gas in 1910), it was even possible, for those who could afford it, to remove the 'cooker' with its steam and cooking smells to the scullery and thus to elevate the tone of the family's main living room still further. In housing reform circles in England the debate on the rival virtues of the 'cooking' and 'living' kitchen resulted in the same concensus. In most LCC cottage estates, houses were built before the war with a living kitchen and a small scullery. Significantly there was little support among German architects for the cooking kitchen which was to become an almost universal feature of the housing built by the progressive architects of the next generation during the late 1920s. Nussbaum was emphatic in his condemnation of this arrangement:

The attempt to offer cooking kitchens to people who are used to living in the kitchen in the hope of educating them to a 'higher' way of arranging their lives, has failed everywhere. Indeed experience has shown that these endeavours have invariably had the very opposite of the effect intended. Instead of raising the standard of hygiene in the home, it has reduced it, because people insist on using their cooking kitchens as their principal family room, a role for which it is neither large enough nor properly equipped.[51]

Closely bound up with this question was the provision of a 'gute Stube' or parlour. Clearly where only a cooking kitchen was provided, a separate living room was essential, but reformers like Muthesius also argued, despite the increase in costs, for the provision of a parlour:

Here the housewife has a small empire free from the hustle and bustle of her daily routine. The best furniture, a wedding gift, lives here too; here all is clean, pretty and neat; here the woman of the house receives her friends, here she proudly sits and chats with them. This is the room for special days...the room on which she lavishes all her love and attention...and which lifts her above the cares of life, fulfilling the desire for higher and beautiful things that beats in every breast, even in the poorest.[52]

The question of the 'living' kitchen and the provision of the parlour were the most widely debated issues in the internal planning of the house. But on other issues, the number of bedrooms, the need for ventilated larders, the demand for a water closet within the dwelling, the reformers held equally strong views. One of the important consequences of these views was the increase in the amount and the kind of accommodation that was now felt to be necessary even for the working-class family.

In 1871, Manega had calculated, on the basis of the volume of fresh air required per person, that a family with three children would need 52 m^3 cubic feet of air, or a floor space of about 20 m^2. Divided into two small bedrooms to ensure separation of boys from girls, and a large living kitchen in which the parents would sleep, this area would be sufficient for the family's needs.[53] But by the turn of the century, recommended standards had substantially increased for both cottage and tenement housing. Nussbaum and Weissbach and Mackowsky summarise the accommodation that a worker's cottage should contain and their recommendations are generally supported by Muthesius and by the *Zeitschrift für Wohnungswesen*. A cottage was to have a floor area of up to 60 m²; this was to be broken down into a living kitchen of 15–20 m² with a scullery and at least two bedrooms; to this there might be added a parlour, a third bedroom and, in all probability, an internal water closet. By contrast, a much lower standard of 32·5 m²–44 m² was recommended for tenement dwellings.[54]

The relationship between these standards and practice was not as remote as might be expected. These recommendations seem to have corresponded broadly with the size of 'improved' working-class flats as built in Berlin at the time. In Messel's development for the Berliner Spar- und Bauverein on the Proskauerstrasse when rents at 207–336 M for a two-room dwelling and 246–504 M for a three-room dwelling were comparable with other rents in the district, the area and facilities provided were in line with Weissbach and Mackowsky's recommenda-tions; here each two-room dwelling measured 31 m² and consisted of living kitchen, hall, larder, WC and bedroom.[55] In the development built by Messel for the Verein zur Verbesserung der kleinen Wohnungen on the Kochhannstrasse, standards were slightly higher; a two-room dwelling had an area of 39 m², a three-room dwelling, 60 m².[56] In cottage estates the variation in the size of houses was wider, but in general most cottages illustrated in the literature on housing reform before 1914 were larger than the standards recommended by Nussbaum or by Weissbach and Mackowsky. Many of the cottages built by employers and non-profit housing bodies were over 70 m²; none of those illustrated by Muthesius in *Kleinhaus und Kleinsiedlung* was under 65 m², and a number were as large as 85 m² and over.[57] Indeed the space standards of the housing built by the various reforming and non-profit housing organisations were generally higher than those available on the open market, and the housing reformers could claim with sound justification to be providing better standards all round than private enterprise.

The costs of better housing

The reformers' demands for better construction, higher space standards, for more open planning, for more light and more air, were of critical importance to the costs of new housing. How far costs were increased by the higher standards and the other proposals put forward by the reformers for 'improving' housing is difficult to judge.[58] Costs varied significantly from region to region, from urban to rural areas within each region and for different types of construction and specification; moreover there are significant variations in costs from one year to another. But, although it is difficult to follow in detail the way different proposals affected cost, it was inescapable that higher standards and the better housing provided by the non-profit housing movement and others would lead to higher building costs.

Naturally higher space standards, internal WCs, first-rate construction and open-site planning cost money and in pressing for them the reformers faced a dilemma. To maintain high standards was to run the risk of raising the costs of new 'improved' housing beyond the means of the very people for whom it was intended; to accept lower standards was to threaten the benefits for which the reformers were campaigning.

There were however a number of ways in which costs could be reduced. Different forms of financing, cheaper money, new sources of capital, and other ideas could be used to reduce the costs of housing to the tenant; from the 1890s onwards, there are important developments in this field. But housing costs could also be reduced in another way which had attracted keen attention since the early days of the first debate on the housing question: by reducing the cost of the land on which housing was built. Since the 1860s, land values had risen in Berlin and elsewhere; after accelerating sharply during the boom of the *Gründerzeit*, prices were still rising in the 1890s. To many it was the burden of the high land prices that produced the unacceptable *Mietskaserne* form of housing and which blocked the road to a real reform of housing conditions; it was the selfish profits of the speculator in land, the unscrupulous directors of the land companies, which condemned working-class families to live in the insanitary housing in working-class districts. Improved housing too had to bear the 'unjust' burden of high land prices. Messel's Prosskauerstrasse development was built in Friedrichshain, a working-class area where land values were relatively low, but even here land at 50 M/m² was nearly equal to the construction costs at 55 M/m².[59]

Most reformers saw the *Mietskaserne* as the inevitable product of the speculation in land that appeared unavoidable with the German system of urban land tenure. To many the problems of housing could not be resolved by tampering with the forms of housing alone; the housing question could only be settled by striking at the way in which land was developed. Improving the quality of new housing necessarily involved a frontal assault on the land problem.

7

◇◇

Housing reform and the Land Question

The problem of land, its value and its price, forms of land tenure and the process of the development of land, were regarded as having a very much more important influence on the housing problem in Germany than in either England or France. In these countries the land question, though acknowledged as significant, was never seen to be central to the debate on housing reform; here it was the related question of decentralisation that attracted more attention, championed by Frédéric Le Play in France and by Ebenezer Howard and the Garden City Movement in England. In Germany the sudden rise in land prices and the speculation in land that followed during the boom of the *Gründerzeit*, first focussed public attention on the land market. Speculation in land and the fortunes made by a few were easily presented as one of the causes of the housing problem: thereafter the housing problem and the land question were frequently linked.

The influence of land values and forms of land tenure on the cost of housing was a subject of interest right from the start of the movement for housing reform. In his earliest essays on housing, Huber had raised the question of decentralisation and land, and had commented explicitly on the attraction of founding new communities on cheaper land outside existing cities.[1] But these proposals were conceived less as a response to the problems of land or its shortage than as a means of providing employment for the unemployed and the victims of pauperism in the city. It was clear to Huber that undeveloped land outside the city was cheaper but the thought that land prices in the city were the product of an 'unnatural' process does not seem to have troubled him.

The Land Problem in the 1860s, Faucher and the 'Monopoly' Theory

It is in the 1860s that the effect of land prices on housing first becomes a source of concern. Faucher and the Manchester Liberals would not admit that the housing problem was a source of general concern; however, the idea that the value of land was not determined by the workings of a free market but manipulated by landowners who exploited their position of monopoly, was deeply disturbing. Faucher's anxiety was provoked by the changes in the land market that took place in the early 1860s. It was then that methods of land development were established which were to culminate in the great speculation in land and property of the *Gründerzeit*. In Berlin these transformations in the land market and the growth of the speculation were precipitated by two changes: first, new developments in the process of preparing land for building and, second, the publication of Hobrecht's plant[2] of 1862 announcing the 'stock' of land that was to serve the city for the next hundred years – an open invitation to speculation.

Stimulated by the need to provide 'ripe' building land more rapidly than ever before to house the population boom of the early 1860s, new methods of financing and development were introduced. Until this time development had generally been small in scale and undertaken by the builder who would have arranged his own financing through a system of private mortgages.[3] In the early 1860s this changed as money became available for the first time through public mortgage banks. This was a crucial development, as it provided the necessary means to channel the increasing volume of risk capital on to the property market on a larger scale than heretofore. The first mortgage bank in the city was founded in 1862; in 1863 and again in 1867 the Prussian state laid down guidelines for the conduct of public mortgage banks and in 1867 the City of Berlin launched its own municipal mortgage bond office, the Berliner städtische Pfandbriefamt. From only one mortgage bank in 1862, the number had risen to 10 by 1869 and by 1874 the number had shot up to 26.

Equally important was the rise of the *Baugesellschaften* or, more properly, land companies at around the same time; it was their activities that particularly alarmed contemporaries and attracted the odium of later housing and land reformers. They were generally set up as joint stock companies to develop land and their success was heavily dependent on the flow of capital from the recently founded mortgage banks. By the end of the 1860s there appear to have been some 60 in operation in Berlin and between them they bought up large amounts of the land around the city required for the realisation of Hobrecht's development plan. J. A. W. Carstenn, a Hamburg businessman referred to as the 'Napoleon' of land speculators had, by the early 1870s, bought up over 1,700 hectares of land in Lichterfelde and Wilmersdorf – equivalent, Voigt claimed, to 20% of the total area of the city at the time.[4] Carstenn appears to have acquired the taste for land speculation in England and Voigt adds that there were a number of land companies with English backing working in the city during the 1860s and early 1870s.[5] In the suburbs to the west and south, the land companies seem to have aimed at a type of development closer to the suburbs of London than was common in Berlin, with speculation based on the sound return expected from middle-class villas and artisan cottages linked by railway to the centre. These hopes were raised by the growth of a suburban railway service from the late 1860s; Carstenn's station at Lichterfelde, the first suburban station built to serve a particular development, was opened in 1868. But in the north and the north-east of the city developments were at a higher density. Here the wide streets and deep plots of Hobrecht's new plan offered unparalleled opportunities for the construction of blocks of tenements five, sometimes even six, storeys high. Those who could buy land at agricultural prices could count on a massive profit from the sale of property whose value would reflect the expected rents from the maximum number of tenements that could be packed on to these large sites. Faucher describes the first emergence of this kind of development in the city.

One is confronted in the open fields to the south, the east and the north of the city by streets of four-storey houses; they are frequently without any form of paved connection to the rest of the city but are filled from basement to roof with a teeming mass of humanity, it is here that the greatest decline in housing is to be found – in Luisenstadt most of the dwellings do not even have their own kitchen.[6]

During the 1860s and early 1870s the expansion of the land market under the influence of these new developments was very rapid. Throughout the 1850s the annual rate of registration of land transfers had never exceeded 1,000; by 1860 it had risen to 1,161 and by 1863, it had reached 2,852. Data after the 1860s are available in different form, but, taking the figure of recorded sales, the speed of the market's expansion is equally apparent; in 1868 there were 292 recorded sales of undeveloped land and 634 sales of developed land, by 1872 sales of undeveloped land had risen to 1,162, while sales of developed land stood at 3,735.[7] Evidence on the increase in land values is fragmentary, but Voigt suggests that building land was being developed in the early 1870s at prices that were anywhere between 10 and 50 times the value of agricultural land.[8] It was the success of the land companies during the 1860s and early 1870s that attracted public attention. The operations of companies such as the Nordend Gesellschaft seem from contemporary accounts to have been characterised by the boldest and most ingenious frauds practised on avaricious and gullible shareholders at a time when the primitive development of company law offered only limited redress.[9] Thereafter the activities of the land companies were invariably tinged in the public mind with a glow of wickedness, an image that persisted until after the turn of the century.[10]

Concern at this state of affairs was loudly voiced by Faucher. In two rambling articles 'Die Bewegung für Wohnungsreform' (1866) and in a separate shorter article, 'Über Häuserbauunternehmungen (1869),[11] he set out ways of reforming the system of development that he saw around him and striking at the cause of the deterioration in housing conditions. Much of his thinking was inspired by his visits to England where he had been most impressed by the low-density terrace housing of the London suburbs which, in his view, contrasted so favourably with the new buildings in Berlin.

Faucher believed that the rise in land prices, and thus the deterioration of housing conditions, was due to the speculative activities of the landowners who were holding the rest of the community to ransom.

They enjoyed what Faucher describes as a position of 'monopoly' through their ownership of the limited supply of urban land and the supply of building land immediately around the outskirts of cities like Berlin: 'The monopolistic ring of building land which surrounds building enterprise everywhere like a giant corset has our cities, as it were, in the bag.'[12]

To counter these evils, Faucher proposed a solution intended to strike directly at the mechanism of the monopoly. Rather than tinker with details of the existing situation, such as modifying the tax system on urban property, he advocated a bold new strategy which would work through the market. A national housing development company was to be set up to develop land along the lines of Carstenn's companies in Hamburg and Berlin, or H. Quistorp's in Berlin Westend. The company was to buy up and prepare as much land as possible for development both in cities and around the outskirts of cities, where land prices would be lower. Following the example of the speculators of the 1860s who had courted the favour of the railway companies, Faucher argued that the railways would make it possible to attract the right kind of pioneers to live in the new developments – significantly he calls his ideal project 'Hubersfeld' – while enabling them to continue working in existing cities. The housing in these new developments was to be built along the lines of the English building societies thus minimising the amount of capital required by the parent company. Most important, by flooding the land market with vast quantities of housing land, the monopoly in land would be destroyed and the value held by the speculators in the existing cities would fall, making it possible to build cottage and terrace housing similar to that which he had admired so much in London.

Despite the enthusiasm with which Faucher had preached the cause of decentralisation and the virtues of 'Hubersfeld', his plans were never taken up. Nevertheless his analysis of the 'monopolistic' workings of the land market and the damaging effect on land values of Hobrecht's approach to planning were influential in forming later ideas on the land question.

His attacks on Hobrecht's plan were taken up by others like Engel and Bruch,[13] who denounced the naivety of Hobrecht's enthusiastic copying of Haussmann's Parisian boulevards and the unprecedented chances offered by the plan to the land speculators. From his position as director of the Prussian statistical office, Engel repeated with more detail the warnings that Faucher had already given in general terms:

Is it not true that the future inhabitants of the houses (built on land with an inflated value) must bear on their shoulders, without the possibility of eventual relief, the interest of those millions so easily made by a fortunate few? Every 100 Thaler per square perch places a never-ending burden on a family dwelling of 17–20 Thaler of extra rent per year.[14]

The painful lessons learnt from the 1862 plan were also summarised for future planners by Baumeister, he warned against too detailed a specification of the city's future shape: 'If planning is restricted in the first instance to the main streets, there will be fewer 'future façades' and land values will be less artificial. Agricultural land will not simply be labelled 'ripe' building land. Land values will generally be lower and more regulated by natural factors...'[15]

But Faucher's analysis of the relationship between the land market and the housing problem was not immediately taken into the mainstream of housing reform. Sax made no mention of the land question, nor did Huber or those writing in the *Arbeiterfreund*. Engel, familiar with the housing problem in Berlin through his statistical work, did emphasise that the high cost of urban land was a direct cause of the *Mietskaserne* form of housing and, though he rejected Faucher's *laissez-faire* attitudes to the housing problem, he adopted his analysis of the land market without reservation.[16] But Engel's interest was the exception rather than the rule. The high cost of land was recognised as one of the barriers to cottage housing, but it was not yet identified as one of the principal causes of the housing problem. Perhaps the concern of the land speculators of the 1860s and 1870s with villa housing in the suburbs meant that the land question remained outside the immediate area of concern of those interested in the problems of working-class housing. Perhaps too, the ferocity of the 'Krach' in 1873 with the ruin of all but 6 of the 70 land companies at work in the city was viewed as a sufficiently powerful deterrent to future speculators. Certainly the land market remained depressed for some time. The volume of trading in undeveloped land fell and many of the sales after 1873 were forced by foreclosure;[17] throughout the period 1876–9, there was an annual decrease in the average rental value of developed sites and in 1880, the first year when the number of forced sales was markedly down, the number of sales of land was only half what it had been in 1868. In Prussia the new planning powers granted to the cities in 1875 may also have affected the land market. The *Fluchtliniengesetz* of 1875 placed the control over the growth of the cities firmly in the hands of the municipalities; arrangements for compulsory purchase of land for streets were no longer beneficial to the landowner and the cost of developing new streets was now shifted to the developer. Whatever the reasons, it was not until the late 1880s and the early 1890s that housing reformers turned to consider the question of land and its effect on the housing problem.

Henry George and the Bund deutscher Bodenreformer

During the early 1880s the discussion of the land problem and its relationship to housing was extended beyond the analysis provided by Faucher and others in the 1860s by new ideas on the way that land should be used and valued. In this debate we can identify a number of different but frequently interconnected groups who start from very different positions and assumptions but share common policies. The two groups whose ideas have most relevance to the housing problem are, on the one hand, the land reformers, inspired by Henry George and led initially by Michael Flürscheim, later by Adolf Damaschke, and on the other the professional economists such as Rudolf Eberstadt and Andreas Voigt.

The *Bodenreformer*, or land reformers, saw in the present use of land the source of many, some would have said all, the evils besetting society.[18] They were thus committed to a thoroughgoing reform of existing forms of land tenure, and, if need be, of society itself; to this group the problems of housing, though an important issue, would only be solved, along with the other ills of society, by the successful resolution of the land question. The economists approached the question from a different point of view and were frequently contemptuous of the universal panacea offered by the land reformers. The economists believed that more limited reforms to the existing situation would suffice and concerned themselves with specific issues such as the relationship between building form and land values, and land values and rent. Yet, despite the distance between the two groups, there were a number of people, like Professor Adolph Wagner, one of the founder members of the VfSP, who were held in high respect by both camps. Furthermore, despite their differences, both land reformers and economists were united in their support for certain policies. Both groups gave strong support to the VföG's campaign for a new approach to regulation of the density of residential development through the building regulations; both groups supported the call for the introduction of a tax on the increase in the value of land, the *Wertzuwachssteuer*; both sides were active in pressing for more ambitious programmes of land purchase and control of land by the municipalities. As Damaschke's immensely popular books, *Die Bodenreform* and *Die Aufgaben der Gemeindepolitik*,[19] showed, it was not difficult to absorb the specific arguments of the economists in the all-embracing campaign mounted around the turn of the century by the Bund deutscher Bodenreformer (BdB); equally, the broad based support of the BdB was of great value in mobilising public opinion in favour of the more specific reforms advocated by the economists.

The *Bodenreformer* drew their ideas from a variety of sources, but most influential were the writings of the American prophet of land reform, Henry George whose book, *Progress and Poverty* (1879),[20] developed ideas he had first published in 1871. In this book George addressed himself to problems more general than housing or land alone and his German followers displayed the same diversity of interests. Rather than follow this range, it is useful to concentrate on the most influential sources of the ideas that formed the attitudes of the BdB, in order to explain why the Bund supported policies like the *Wertzuwachssteuer* or the greater involvement of the local authorities in the land market, which were of direct importance for housing.

In his account of the German land reform movement, Heinrich Freese, leader of the movement from 1890 to 1898, links the first development of a broad-based movement for land reform to the impact of George's ideas in the 1880s;[21] *Progress and Poverty* was first translated into German in 1881.[22] By 1886, under the leadership of Michael Flürscheim, owner of a steelworks in Baden, George's German followers had formed themselves into an organisation, the Land Liga (in 1888 to become the Bund für Bodenbesitzreform). In 1898, Adolf Damaschke, a former primary school teacher, took over the leadership of the Bund (in 1898 renamed the Bund deutscher Bodenreformer), greatly expanding the membership and preparing a mass campaign for land reform; by 1914 the movement claimed a membership of over 13,000,[23] compared with only 139 when Damaschke became leader. Damaschke's most important contribution was as a leader campaigning and popularising the aims of the BdB; as Dorothea Berger Thimme's recent study makes clear he had great charismatic powers, although the ideas that he presented so successfully were not his own but drawn from a whole variety of other sources. This is typified by his free adaptation for German consumption, of Henry George's message, and his specific interpretation of the ideas of Adolph Wagner.

Michael Flürscheim differed from George in the method by which he wished to transfer the ownership of land from private hands back to the community. George had proposed a 'single tax' which would be levied on the unearned increment of the value of land; this, he claimed, would have the benefit of leaving productive capital invested in industry free from tax so that it might increase the prosperity of all, unburdened by the dead weight of rising land costs.[24] In contrast, Flürscheim advocated a system of transfer in which bonds issued by the government would be exchanged for land. The viability of these proposals turned on optimistic assumptions of the relative rates of interest of these bonds *vis-à-vis* other forms of investment, but the proposals did have the virtue that the method of transferring ownership of land to the community appeared less radical and more plausible than the means proposed by George. Even though these proposals lacked the simple appeal of the 'Single Tax Gospel', they were enthusiastically received and, promoting these ideas through the periodical *Deutsch Land*,[25] launched in 1887, the Liga launched a campaign for the transfer of land from private to communal ownership.

It came as a considerable surprise to the members when, barely a year after the Liga's foundation, Flürscheim announced the abandonment of his earlier ideas on the means of transferring land to communal ownership, because of a miscalculation of the likely attractiveness of the proposed government land bonds.[26] More important for the development of land reform in Germany than this painful realisation, was Flürscheim's heretical change of programme. He now appeared ready to tolerate the continued private ownership of land, but on condition that the 'unearned increment' in the value of land be made over to the community through taxation at the time of transfer along the lines of the *Wertzuwachssteuer* already suggested by Adolph Wagner in the 1870s. It was under the banner of these new policies that Flürscheim called for the foundation in September 1888 of the Bund für Bodenbesitzreform. The articles of the Bund emphasised the communal ownership of land as the only acceptable form of land tenure in the long run but recognised the importance of 'taxing away the increment of income earned through increased urban land rents' as the first practicable step. The Bund still retained intact the distinction, derived from George, between 'false' and 'productive' capital – Flürscheim endows terms like 'compound interest' with diabolical meaning – but put its faith in the education of public opinion in the hope that this would lead to such widespread revulsion with the activities of property speculators and others playing the market in land that the *Wertzuwachssteuer* could be introduced without serious opposition.

The first demand in Germany for the introduction of such a tax is normally credited to Adolph Wagner. With Flürscheim, he represents the second principal source of the economic ideas incorporated in the programmes of the Bund für Bodenbesitzreform. Wagner's demand for the introduction of the *Wertzuwachssteuer* was, however, part of a larger critique of society extending well beyond the immediate concern with land and land reform that characterises Flürscheim's work. In demanding the reform of a variety of areas of economic activity, municipal finances, the form of stock company and the form of ownership of the railways, Wagner, one of the founding fathers of the VfSP, was developing a tradition of economic thought going back to earlier German economists such as Johann Karl Rodbertus. This had emphasised, in clear contrast to the English classical school, the role of the State in balancing the conflicting demands of the different sectors in the community: in place of the 'invisible hand' of Adam Smith and the limitations on government activity that he had demanded, the State was charged with active intervention in economic affairs for the benefit of the whole community.

In 1875–6 Wagner had published his *Grundlegung*,[27] the first volume of what was to be a standard economic textbook for a generation, in which he set out these ideas attacking the individualist attitudes of Faucher, Prince-Smith and the *Manchesterrschule* of the KdV. In place of 'naked self-interest' he demanded that the State take an active part in preserving the economic interests of future generations and in resolving the most glaring injustices of the *Soziale Frage*. Although a leading Conservative in his political affiliations – he was leader of the Conservatives in the Prussian Abgeordnete Hause and he strongly supported the landed interests in their demands for economic protection – his enthusiasm for State intervention made him a valuable source of theoretical support for Land Reform. Not only did he take part in a number of the annual congresses of the Bund für Bodenbesitzreform but in 1900 he was elected an *Ehrenmitglied* of the Bund, the supreme honour, for his contributions to the cause.[28]

In his section on Individualism in his *Grundlegung*,[29] Wagner provides a critique of private property that was to be of value to those who urged the case for municipal and communal intervention in land, although he is careful to draw a distinction between the need for this in urban areas where the landlord benefits at the expense of the community and in agricultural areas where he claims that the landlord is engaged in 'productive' activity. The starting point for this discussion is an attack on the absolute property rights enshrined in the *Manchesterschule's* ideology: in place of these absolute rights and their corollary, the system of mortgages and the capitalisation of land, all of which he denounces as a product of the society of economic liberalism, he presses for a return to older German forms of tenure in which property and land were held for periods of limited duration akin to the English system of leasehold. For many forms of economic activity, however, the leasehold system provides too short a period of tenure to give an adequate return, with the result that investment might be cut short. In place of such a leasehold system he therefore urges the transfer of ownership of land, and property, to the community, be it the state or the municipality.

From the development of this theoretical position Wagner moves directly to a series of practical policies. Arguing that it would be impossible and naive to expect a transfer of private property to the community in the short term, he draws up a series of measures which would take from the urban landlord and property owner the unearned benefit that he derives from the improvements made by the community as a whole. The most important of these measures was to be the *Wertzuwachssteuer*, a form of taxation that he himself had first proposed, to the consternation of so many, during the debate on the *Kommunalsteuer* question at the fifth annual congress of the Verein für Sozialpolitik in 1877.[30] Why, insisted Wagner, if the municipality could own and run gasworks, tramways, waterworks, slaughterhouses and other services regarded as necessary to the functioning of the community, could it not secure the ownership of the most vital resource of all for the development of the city, the land needed for future growth? Municipal control of land was a natural extension of the activities of the cities in other fields.

Published in 1890, Flürscheim's book, *Der einzige Rettungsweg*, shows the merging of the ideas of Henry George's German followers with the ideas of Adolph Wagner. The analysis of the ills of society are still taken from George, but the policies for reform now incorporate Wagner's ideas. In place of Flürscheim's original proposals for the exchange of bonds to achieve municipal ownership of land, the municipality was to take over the ownership of land for the community by a programme of land purchase and the introduction of a tax on the increased value of land at sale. The ideas that Flürscheim outlined here, with a clear avowal of the debt to Wagner, provide the basis for the programme of the BdB during the 1890s. After Damaschke had taken over the leadership of the Bund in 1898, it was his simplified presentation of these ideas, uncomplicated by the details and realities of the particular situation, that made it possible to attract a mass following with support from the most varied quarters, uniting as he put it: 'the priest, the freethinker, the Pan-Germanist, the Zionist, the monarchist and the democrat'.[31]

The economists and the urban Land Question

In contrast to the attempts of the Bund für Bodenbesitzreform to resolve
all the ills of society by means of land reform, the economists with an
interest in the land question were much more explicit both in their
analysis of the way in which the current form of land development based
on the *Mietskaserne* lay at the root of the housing problem, and in their
assertion of how these differences could be put right. Best known of this
group is the economist Rudolf Eberstadt, one of the professors of
economics at the university in Berlin; his authoritative *Handbuch des
Wohnungswesens und der Wohnungsfrage*, first published in 1909, was
regarded as the standard work on housing before the First World War
and such was its reputation that, despite the very changed circumstances
after the war, a new edition was published in 1922.[32] While the Bund
drew so much of its inspiration from Henry George's writings, Eberstadt,
a student of Schmoller and the historical school, based his plans for
reform on a series of detailed empirical investigations of the workings
of the existing methods of development. These were focussed largely on
Berlin, but also drew on evidence from Düsseldorf and the Rhineland.
Städtische Bodenfragen, published in 1894, brought together four essays,
three of which had already been published elsewhere.[33] Even so its
impact was immediate: overnight it created a reputation for Eberstadt
as the authority on housing and the land question.[34] The significance
of the position that he adopted was quickly recognised by those like the
VföG concerned to control the spread of the *Mietskaserne* and his
analysis welcomed as a weapon for use in the campaign. His study also
stimulated further investigation of the urban land question, and a
number of other economists, including the brothers Paul and Andreas
Voigt, Karl von Mangoldt and Adolf Weber published studies on the
subject.

To a modern view, however, their discussion must appear curious
because of the indifference to the issue of location that has come to
dominate more recent interest in the subject. The absence of any
systematic consideration of location in the debate in the 1890s and early
1900s is particularly curious in view of von Thünen's study, *Der isolierte
Staat*,[35] and Alfred Weber's work on industrial location, *Über den
Standort der Industrien*, published in 1909,[36] which refers back to von
Thünen's early work. Weber's approach with its emphasis on theoretical
analysis contrasted sharply with the empirical 'historical' approach
of Eberstadt and the Voigt brothers, and it was Weber who was to
give the study of urban land and its value a new direction. In retrospect,
the debate on the urban land question in Germany around the turn
of the century remains little more than an appendix to the mainstream
of economic thought, but with its concern over the *Mietskaserne* form of
housing it was of crucial importance to the debate on the housing
problem.

The situation that provoked the concern of the economists in the
1890s was very different from that of the early 1860s and 1870s. In

Berlin and elsewhere the operations of the property market ran at a much larger scale than before.[37] In place of the small land companies and the newly founded mortgage banks of the *Gründerzeit*, development was now carried out by substantial public companies backed by major banking combines. The number of mortgage banks had barely increased since the 1860s but the scale of their operations had expanded enormously in the late 1880s; in 1889 alone the number of new mortgages increased by 18.2% and the amount mortgaged had increased by nearly 10% since the previous year and more than 50% since 1884. These developments were viewed with misgiving. Voigt, for example, bitterly regretted that the mortgage banks were able to attract nearly all the capital destined for the property market, forcing out the small property investor.[38] Parallel to the expansion of the credit institutions, there were similar changes in the form of the land companies. In place of the flamboyant activities of the companies in the 1870s, the new companies were run on much more orthodox lines and, after 1891, took advantage of new legislation to become limited liability companies. Another important change since the 1870s was the links between land companies and the large banks. Many of the land companies which failed in 1873 had been taken over by the banks; by the 1890s banks like the Deutsche Bank, Darmstädter Bank and the Berliner Handels-gesellschaft had established control over a number of land companies; the connection that Voigt described between the Deutsche Bank and the Kurfürstendamm Gesellschaft operating in Charlottenburg was typical of many at the time.[39] As a result of this large-scale backing, the volume of construction increased significantly. While the majority of the companies of the early 1870s would have developed a site or two at a time, Voigt reports that the new companies of the late 1880s were laying out a whole street at a time, each development financed by a single mortgage bond series.[40] One of the consequences of this increase in size was to favour the large developer whose costs, due to the advantages of the economies of scale, were lower.

This expansion of the property and land markets during the late 1880s was fuelled by the shortage of other forms of investment; there was now no competition for capital from the railway companies as there had been in the 1860s and 1870s, and the new-found respectability of the land companies further encouraged investors. In Berlin the result was a boom in construction to accommodate the rapid growth in population during the late 1880s. In 1889, the city's population rose by 56,799, the largest single annual increment in the natural increase in the history of the city and a year in which more migrants flocked to the city than in any year since 1871. With demand running high, developers were quick to take advantage of the new opportunities opened up by the development of the Ringbahn, or suburban railway, around Berlin in the early 1880s and the reform of the fare structure in 1891, which attempted to encourage working-class use of this form of transport.[41]

But it was not this boom in construction, so much as the type of

37 View c. 1900 from the
Grunewald towards
high-density housing on the
outskirts of Charlottenburg

housing that provoked the attacks of the housing reformers. Unlike the
speculation in land in the 1860s and 1870s which had been based, predominantly, on villa building, this boom was based on the construction
of *Mietskasernen*. Under the provisions of the 1887[42] building regulations
it became possible, for the first time, to build the typical five-storey block
of the centre city in suburban areas like Schöneberg, Charlottenburg,
Rixdorf and Wilmersdorf which figure in Heinrich Zille's photographs of
Berlin life (fig. 37). The developers of the late 1880s and 1890s exploited
these regulations to the full, twisting to their own advantage even the
special regulations for areas zoned for villa building in order to pack the
maximum number of dwellings on to a site. Even the revised regulations
of 1892, which provided for different levels of site utilisation for different areas of the city, did little to restrict the density of housing within
the city and in suburban areas within the Ringbahn and Charlottenburg,
all of which now fell under the control of the Berliner Hochbauordnung.
Only for the outer suburban areas was any limitation of density possible.
The extension of the *Mietskaserne* form of housing was also aided and
abetted by other factors. The achievements of the sanitary reformers in
introducing water-borne drainage and a water supply in Rixdorf in the
late 1870s, in Charlottenburg and Schöneberg in the mid-1880s and
in Wilmersdorf and Friedenau slightly later, had removed real difficulties
frequently associated with high-density housing.[43] A further stimulus
to high-density housing was provided by the unwillingness of the local
authorities to release land for new development because of the considerable cost to the local authority (despite the development costs paid

by the developer) of new roads, services and drainage, all requirements enforced more vigorously as a result of the regulations of 1887 and 1892.

Fuelled by the rising property market land prices rose from 1887, and trade in undeveloped land rose to even higher levels than those of 1872.[44] New dwellings were being built faster than at any time since the mid-1870s and the sale of developed sites proceeded more rapidly than at any time since 1872. Capital flowed into the mortgage banks from insurance and pension funds raising the level of lending to extravagant heights, frequently beyond the levels covered by the value of the property; Voigt reports that older properties in Charlottenburg were being heavily mortgaged with first mortgages representing 60.5%, second mortgages 20.5% and third and subsequent mortgages 19.2% of all borrowing.[45] The value of many properties was artificially inflated by private fire companies who offered higher valuations than those approved by the municipal *Feuerkasse* in the hope of attracting higher premia. Many properties, heavily mortgaged and overvalued, were sold to unsuspecting purchasers with the recommendation that the price was 'unter der Feuerkasse' or mortgaged no higher than the *Feuerkasse*'s valuation. As the trebling of the rate of forced sales in the mid-1890s showed, many of these investments were precarious in the extreme.[46]

It was this property boom, already fading after 1890, that focussed the attention of the economists such as Eberstadt and the Voigt brothers on the relationship between the operations of the property market and the housing problem. Eberstadt's ideas on the subject are presented in a variety of publications, and in most general form in the *Handbuch*, but the approach set out in all these publications was attacked by his critics as being typical of the work of the historical school and making up in detail and anecdote what it lacked in theory and system. The challenge to Eberstadt's ideas by others, but especially by Andreas Voigt, provoked intense debate in both academic and professional circles over the 'urban land question' and its relevance to the housing problem which lasted well on into the 1900s.

Eberstadt's starting point was the view that the current forms of high-density housing were the product of the processes of speculation:

> From the preparation of raw building land to the occupation of the finished dwelling, the form of the development of our cities and the whole trade in land values has been taken over by the processes of speculation. The division of land into sites ripe for development is a question of speculation. The form of layout, the form of the building and the production of housing are all determined by the processes of speculation. The ownership of land and property are in the hands of the speculators: they also control the supply of capital for building and the system of the Grundbuch.[47]

In terms not so far removed from the despised Henry George, he argues that this kind of speculation is not of the wholesome type so necessary for economic life generally, but of a form that seeks to make a profit from manipulating money alone: it is thus damaging rather than beneficial for the economic interests of the community. Eberstadt maintains that the land market has wholly different characteristics from those of other goods: first, land can be mortgaged; second, in the land market, prices are always rising; finally, the market is not controlled by the balance of the forces of supply and demand, but instead by the effective monopolies enjoyed by the owners of urban and suburban land.

Eberstadt first considers the value of building land: it is partly a product of the expected return in rents, partly a product of the speculative form of development by which land is brought on to the market and prepared for building, and partly a product of its location. Because of the building regulations, higher densities are to be expected in the outskirts; this leads to a higher return on land, but, as rents in these peripheral areas rise, the rents in the centre, where accessibility is higher, also rise by the same amount.

The high densities of the *Mietskaserne* are inextricably related to this increase in the rise of land values. Indeed Eberstadt presents the *Mietskaserne* as the mechanism which drives up land values, and dismisses as fools those who suggest that this form of building might actually reduce costs per dwelling, and, therefore, rent. Instead, basing his argument on Ricardo, he argues that it is the very high expected return on a site developed with the high-density *Mietskaserne* form that drives up the price of land: 'This dense form of building works entirely to the advantage of the site owner, or, to put it more abstractedly, to force up land values.'[48] As a result, land values are so high that only the densest forms of building can be built, completely excluding the possibility of open space, so necessary for health, and the cottage form of housing.

This system of exploitation was maintained by the limited availability of suitable building land; Eberstadt claimed that the supply of land was carefully controlled by a cartel of land owners, land companies and banks to secure a selfish advantage at the expense of the community. Furthermore he maintained that these institutions were sufficiently powerful to maintain this economic control in both boom and depression. The result was a continuous rise in the price of land and a form of housing that benefited the speculator while condemning many to live in the misery of unhygienic tenements.

For Eberstadt, the sale of the finished building to its eventual owner was only one step in a long chain of speculative activity, extending from the purchase of 'raw' agricultural land through to the management of the dwellings after sale. For him, this whole process was distinguished by the unreasonable profits that were made by economic parasites. He claimed that, starting with the first sale of agricultural land as building land, the value was artificially inflated as it was sold from land speculator to speculator; in his description of the process he drew attention to the scale of the profits to be made, particularly by the first purchaser of agricultural land, and played down the cost of road building and other development costs that were required of the developer by the *Fluchtliniengesetz* of 1875. Although his critics charged that Eberstadt lacked any systematic data on which to base his assertions, he illustrated his argument with a number of examples, which, the reader was assured, were typical of everyday practice.

Eberstadt singled out, as the weakest and most damaging aspect of this chain of activity, the sale of the plot ready for building to the builder, portrayed as generally nothing more than a 'man of straw' without capital.[49] The dangers that arise here are, he claimed, a direct product of the absence, in the system of registering a loan in the *Grundbuch*, of any division between money intended for building and that intended for the purchase of land. As a consequence, the land companies were able to inflate the price of a plot by misdirecting capital that should have been used 'productively' for building to pay for the site. In a transaction with a builder who had his own capital, this would not have been possible; but with a 'capital-poor' builder, typical of the residential building industry in Berlin during the 1890s which we discuss in Chapter 8, Eberstadt claimed that the land company could take advantage of the situation by arranging the mortgage, often doing so through its own parent bank. Having spent much of this first mortgage on the purchase of the site, the builder, Eberstadt claimed, would then be forced to find the *Baugeld*, or construction money, from a second and even a third mortgage. To increase the maximum amount that he could borrow in this way he would take every opportunity to increase his mortgage limit, using techniques like the overvaluation of the future value of the finished building through fire insurance companies prepared to overlook the niceties of property valuation in return for large insurance premia.[50]

Eberstadt contrasts the security enjoyed by the land company with the financial dangers to which the builder is exposed during this period of development. The former was always well protected by the security of the *Grundbuch* in which its charge was entered first, while the builder had to take second place at a time when he was very much more exposed to the difficulties of the market. He had to pay a higher rate of interest for this *Baugeld* than was paid by the 'unproductive' money used in the purchase of the site. It was common practice in Berlin in the 1890s for the builder to finish paying off his suppliers and his workforce only when the building was finally sold.[51] Throughout the whole period of construction and through until the sale of the building, the builder remained exposed to every fluctuation in interest rates and was faced with certain bankruptcy if demand should fail, as it had done in the mid-1870s, leaving him with an unsaleable building. Even if he were successful in selling the finished building, Eberstadt argued, his profit had to remain minimal because of the large percentage already taken by the land speculator on the sale of the site.

Eberstadt's view of the processes of development as nothing more than a series of shaky speculations, in which each percentage point change in the rate of interest and each suspicion of a slump threatened the whole rickety structure, was founded on a view of the land speculator operating in a market in which he enjoyed a monopoly, thus ensuring him the upper hand. This view of the monopolistic functioning of the land market, already established by Faucher, was greatly elaborated in a study of the urban land problem, *Die städtische Bodenfrage* (1907)[52] by Karl von Mangoldt of the Deutscher Verein für Wohnungsreform. In this, Mangoldt attempted to systematise the theory of the so-called monopoly of land-ownership in the limited area of 'ripe' building land surrounding the city – already referred to by Faucher as the Schmaller Ring or 'thin ring'[53] – as the cause of high land prices. Assuming that there is uninterrupted growth of the city, he claims that the increase in the population must be housed in this 'thin ring'. Demand for land in this area is therefore high. But supply is limited; the prospect of developing beyond is unattractive, either because it is too remote from transport, or because it is too expensive to provide roads and drainage. The result is the rise in land values. Defending his position against the attacks of those critics like Adolf Weber and Andreas Voigt who denied the existence of any such 'thin ring', Mangoldt insisted that the shortage of land in this critical area was also aided and abetted by the policies of the local authorities. Much of the blame for the present land problem he placed on the system of city extension planning and the inept attempts of the municipality to control development, which further limited the supply of new land. In addition, he argued that the political pressures of property interests on the planning authorities contributed to the slowing down or, occasionally, the complete restriction of the supply of new land, in order to maintain the level of land prices. He claimed this was achieved in practice by delaying the drawing up of development plans and by postponing the provision of roads and services which were expensive for the authority.

Mangoldt allowed that the costs involved in the development of land, the contribution to roads and service costs, and taxes, together with the high cost of buying out the holders of small key plots, were high; but not high enough, he insisted, to justify the action of the land owners in the 'thin ring' in using the leverage of their monopolistic position to drive up the price of land. But to this must also be added the actions of the owners of land immediately outside the 'thin ring'. He argued that they too withheld land from the market until its value would have risen to that of the land within the 'thin ring', thus compounding the problem of the supply of land and strengthening the monopoly. To explain the inflated value of urban land, claimed Mangoldt, it was no longer necessary to posit some vague notion of an 'all embracing speculation'; the actions of the land owner in the 'thin ring' were cause enough of the high cost of urban land.

The views of Eberstadt and others who regarded the increase in residential land values as the product of a 'malignant and unnatural' process of speculation stand in sharp contrast to the views of Andreas Voigt. Andreas Voigt and his brother Paul, killed in a climbing accident in the summer of 1900, were authors of a number of studies of the development of Berlin; Paul Voigt's study *Grundrente und Wohnungsfrage in Berlin und den Vororten* (1901) provided an extended and detailed account of the growth of the city and its suburbs, which drew attention to the importance of changes in accessibility due to the development of the transport system and the impact of commercial and industrial land uses on land values. Andreas Voigt assembled from notes the contribution that his brother had planned for the VfSP's investigation into the housing question, 'Bodenbesitzverhältnisse, das Bau- und Wohnungswesen in Berlin' (1901),[54] but he is better remembered as the co-author with the architect Paul Geldner of *Kleinhaus und Mietskaserne* (1905). In this book he sharply attacked the prevailing orthodoxy, singling out Eberstadt for particularly bitter criticism. Even now the vehemence with which the two opposing views were pressed can be sensed in the acrimonius exchanges in the *Jahrbuch für Gesetzgebung*[55] unaffected by the feeble attempts of C. J. Fuchs and other academics to see 'fair play' and referee the encounter. So heated were the exchanges that a court case was only just avoided.

Much of the exchange between the two camps was merely vituperation and academic name-calling, but the clash did originate in real differences of approach to the question of land values and the related issue of the relationship between building form and rent levels. On some issues both were agreed: both Andreas Voigt and Eberstadt accepted as a starting point Ricardo's theory of rent in which, in its simplest form, the value of the land was determined by the rents that the land would yield. But from here on they differed. Eberstadt argued that the new development plans, the building regulations and the resulting *Mietskaserne* made it possible to fit a much larger number of dwellings on to a site than before; this resulted in an increase in the value of the land. In a later version of this argument, in the *Handbuch*, he claimed that the system of financing and the chain of speculative activity involved in housing resulted not only in an increase in land value, but also in an increase in the rents charged for the individual dwelling as the owner was forced to raise rents in order to cover fluctuations in interest rates.

Voigt starts with Ricardo too, but argues that the increase in the value of land is not a product of the increased density of residential building but the result of the expansion of the whole city and particularly the result of the higher rents paid by industrial and commercial uses:

> It is crucially important to oppose the theory which makes land speculation the cause of *every* increase in the price of land, by showing that the increase in land values today is clearly *not* caused by speculation for the most part. It is instead the necessary and inevitable result of a completely objective process, the ever more intensive use of land, evident in the vertical dimensions of our buildings and the increase in the number of floors.[56]

He dismisses the 'monopoly' theories of Eberstadt and Mangoldt as irrelevant to the discussion of land values, challenging the assumption that the dealer can afford to allow land to remain economically fallow for an indefinite period in the hope of a return. By comparison with the profits to be made from other forms of investment, he argues, the returns on land are actually low, particularly when the long period over which the profit is made is taken into consideration. Indeed Voigt's study of the proportion of the total cost of housing attributable to land emphasised that in working-class residential areas this might only account for between 28% and 33% of the total cost although in commercial areas this might be very much higher.[57]

Having argued that land values are neither the product of the *Mietskaserne* nor excessive, he then turns to show that the *Mietskaserne* is in fact the best means of keeping rents down when building on high-priced land. The basis for this case is the assumption, supported by data taken from practice and estimates calculated from the *Deutsche Baukalendar*, that building becomes cheaper as the number of floors rises to four or five storeys. Voigt seeks to demonstrate that this reduction in construction costs combined with the operation of the property tax, make 4–5 storey building more economical than other forms of development and result in lower rents. Thus for Voigt, the *Mietskaserne*, far from being an instrument to increase rents, actually serves to moderate them.[58]

For Voigt, the developer and the land company were necessary agencies in the creation of the city; they merely operated with land and housing as others did with other forms of production. He accuses Eberstadt of grossly exaggerating the gains made by speculators by concentrating only on the profits made during the *Gründerjahre* or the boom years of the late 1880s, and by failing to take account of the period of time over which these profits were made. According to a study made by Edward Wagon, the return on land in Berlin between 1884 and 1900, a period which included the boom of the late 1880s and early 1890s, was only 1.5%, which barely equalled the profit made by manufacturers of table linen.[59] Voigt ridicules Eberstadt's suggestion that most builders were men without capital and dismisses his account of the process of development as entirely fanciful, and credible only by those who wish to believe the worst of the speculator, a figure who, he claims, Eberstadt makes the scapegoat for all the problems of housing.

Accusing the misguided followers of Eberstadt of increasing rents by their uncritical advocacy of the cottage ideal, the most expensive form of housing to build, Voigt presses the case for the hygienically designed tenement block. He calls for architects to pay greater attention to reducing building costs as the most effective means of reducing rents and ends the book with a description of a large development, the Goethe Park in Charlottenburg, as an illustration of what can be achieved even on the high-priced land near the centre of the city.

But despite the attention that Voigt's argument attracted, the consensus appears to have favoured the views of Eberstadt and those who regarded the current forms of development as the result of a damaging process of speculation.[60] Voigt, along with more obvious champions of the interests of property like Siegfried Ascher and Georg Haberland, remained one of the few defenders of the existing situation. The housing reform movement united with the land reformers in attempting to change the existing processes of development and the land market as a vital step in the battle for better housing.

The programme of reform from the 1890s to the First World War

To review the range of reforms put forward in an attempt to resolve the land question would be a daunting task; the interests of the *Bodenreformer* alone would lead us well beyond the discussion of the housing question. Their programme concerned both urban and rural land; there were frequent debates and articles in the *Jahrbuch für Bodenreform* on a host of other subjects ranging from protecting the workers in the building industry to more exotic interests such as land reform in Israel and the supposed benefits of land reform to the inhabitants of Germany's colonies.[61]

Equally, there were a number of subjects which one might have expected the *Bodenreformer* to have discussed or at least to have formed part of the agenda for land reform, but which remained neglected. Issues such as decentralisation and the provision of cheap transport, which attracted widespread attention in France and England, received little attention as part of the debate on the housing question in Germany. In England no discussion of the question of land and the housing problem would be complete without reference to the Garden City Movement. But in Germany the Deutsche Gartenstadtbewegung,[62] despite its impact in architectural circles, remained relatively insignificant and overshadowed by the achievement of other organisations such as the Bund deutscher Bodenreformer or the Verein für öffentliche Gesundheitspflege, and, in the field of physical planning, by the work of Sitte and his followers. In England, the Charity Organisation Society had urged the provision of cheap transport as a means of providing access for the working-class family to cheap land on which housing could be build to let at low rents; great things, too, were expected of the Cheap Trains Act of 1883. But in Germany, there were only occasional references to the benefits that might flow from cheap travel.[63] In his paper for the VfSP's enquiry into housing in 1900, Adickes identified the value of public transport as an attractive way of providing access to cheaper land for housing[64] and the matter was raised at the Verein's debate in 1901. But Eberstadt's discussion of the theme in the *Handbuch* is cursory, a mere 12 pages devoted largely to a review of developments in London and New York. Despite the completion of the Ringbahn in 1882 and the introduction of lower fares in 1891,[65] the cheap trains in Berlin still did not lead to the formation of working-class suburbs like those which grew up outside north and east London along the lines of the Great Eastern Railway. For the most part, the working man in Berlin lived near his work in the north-west or the south-east. Only when the new industries started to move further out during the late 1890s to take advantage of the accessibility provided by the railway did the worker travel further to work.[66] To housing reformers in Germany, cheap transport was a desirable means of making more land available for development but it was not a high priority. Too often in practice the planning and investment in public transport appeared to offer more effective assistance to the property lobby than to the working class in their search for cheaper housing. In Berlin, for example, the only major expansion of the underground system out into the suburbs took place between 1910 and 1913 in the prosperous western residential districts. This was undertaken by the underground line owned by the municipalities of Schöneberg and Wilmersdorf and served to increase property values dramatically; moreover, the fare structure on the new line was a further powerful deterrent to those with less than middle-class incomes.[67]

More important than these issues was the introduction of the density zoning regulations in the mid-1890s as a result of the campaign by the VföG; to many land reformers this was the first real advance. At the meeting of the VföG at Magdeburg, speakers had welcomed the support of Eberstadt's economic insights and ideas on the urban land question in the campaign for a more open form of housing.[68] To Eberstadt the system of density zoning for which the VföG was battling was the first real control to be imposed on the activities of the speculator. This view was held equally strongly by the BdB. Damaschke identified the new system of density regulation as 'the most important means to combat the damaging inflation of land prices',[69] and the demand for the general introduction of these measures was an important part of the Bund's programme of action.

But the question of density zoning was no longer such a live issue after the 1890s; the VföG's campaign had led to its successful intro- duction in a number of cities, both large and small.[70] To gain an impression of the activities of the different groups concerned with land reform, the *Bodenreformer*, the economists, the planners and municipal leaders, we must look at the issues which dominated the debate on the land question before the First World War. Two are of particular interest: the demand for a sales, or land transfer tax on the 'unearned' increase in the value of urban land and the campaign for the cities to develop a municipal land policy. Both issues were of direct relevance to the housing question; both measures offered the possibility of controlling land values and hence housing costs and rents. The importance of the two topics is clearly reflected in Adolf Damaschke's immensely popular book on the urban land question, *Die Aufgaben der Gemeindepolitik*, in which the first part is devoted to a discussion of municipal taxation and property, and the second to the question of the communal ownership of land.

Taxation and land reform

The emphasis on the introduction of a new form of taxation on urban land was natural. Land reformers of all convictions were keen to see the community benefit in some way from the increase in the value of land that the community itself created, rather than let this value fall into the hands of the land speculator as untaxed and unearned income. It is hardly surprising that a tax on this 'unearned income' should be an important focus of these different interests.

From reading the literature on land reform, it would be easy to form the impression that the *Wertzuwachssteuer* (WZS) was the only tax on land and property to be introduced in Germany apart from a general property tax, the equivalent to our English system of the Rates. But even before the turn of the century, a number of attempts had been made to enable cities to tax the increased value of property. In 1893 a number of important reforms had been introduced in Prussia while Miquel was Finance Minister by the legislation of 14 July, known under the portmanteau title of the *Kommunalabgabengesetz*.[71] The act was intended to help the finances of the communes, *Gemeinden*, by increasing their income, both by ceding to them a number of sources of taxation formerly used for state taxes and by reassessing existing sources of income; in particular the law encouraged the *Gemeinden* to look to taxes on property as a source of revenue. Significantly, the law was presented as enabling legislation leaving the details of taxation to be worked out to suit the requirements of the individual city.

Until 1893, the principal tax on land and property had been that of the law of 21 June 1861 which was based on a system of valuation that had become entirely obsolete by the 1890s. Land, for example, was taxed not on its actual yield, but on a potential yield assessed at the time when much of the land in urban areas in the 1890s was still in agricultural use; little had been done to revise these early assessments. Buildings were taxed in an equally outmoded way; the taxes which were assessed every 15 years were levied at the level of 4% on the average return over the preceding 10 years, providing only a feeble weapon with which to tax the very rapid growth of building values in large urban areas.

The legislation of 1893 provided the opportunity to change this. After a number of false starts, during which several different forms of taxation, including a tax on building land, were tried experimentally but without success, most of the cities introduced a modified form of the existing method of taxation on land and property. But these differed crucially from the system of taxation before 1893 in being based on the 'common' or the sale value; the new method of assessment did not necessarily lead to a higher return but its defenders claimed that it did provide a more equitable distribution of the tax load. In particular it had the advantage that land kept off the market was now generally liable for tax, thus removing an anomaly that had long infuriated land reformers. It also provided the means to control the speculators' practice, attacked by Eberstadt, Mangoldt and others, whereby a plot of prime building land was taxed as a cabbage patch leaving the owner to collect the massive and unearned increment in value created by the community when finally sold.

As might be expected in view of the contribution to these tax reforms made by Miquel and Adickes, both of whom were at one time *Oberbürgermeister* of Frankfurt, this city was one of the first cities in Prussia to introduce new measures under the act, giving a lead to other Prussian authorities.[72] Land was classified according to a number of locational and land-use characteristics and was taxed at 0.3% of the aggregate sale value of the class to which it belonged; housing was taxed at 4% of the previous year's rental, buildings with high rent yields were taxed at a higher rate.

The ability to tax unused land was an important step forward, but reformers looked to further control of land speculation and the land market from the introduction of an *Umsatzsteuer* or a property transfer tax under the provisions of the 1893 law. This was a form of taxation that some cities such as Frankfurt had used from the early years of the century but which other large Prussian cities only introduced after 1893. Berlin, for example, first levied the tax in 1895; here, shortly after its first introduction, the tax was generally assessed at the rate of $\frac{1}{2}$% on the sale price of building and developed land; undeveloped land was initially assessed at 1% of the sale price, but from the turn of the century the level of assessment rose to 2% of the sale price.[73]

Imposed directly on the sale price, this tax represented a real advance in taxing the profits made from land and property. But the tax urged most keenly by the land and housing reformers was the (WZS) which many cities were able to introduce by using the general provisions of the Kommunalabgabengesetz which governed the system of local taxation. Ever since the early days of the land reform movement under Flürscheim, this had figured as a key element of the programme, and it remained till the First World War one of the most important 'planks' of the BdB platform. In the early 1890s, Wagner joined the BdB in pressing for the tax as part of a wide range of measures aimed at reforming the existing structure of land tenure. But it was not until the later 1890s, with the growth of the BdB, that there was mass support for the WZS. The significance given to it is well illustrated by the place it occupies in Damaschke's writings: in one of his most popular books, *Die Bodenreform, Grundsätzliches und Geschichtliches* he places the WZS as the most important measure in his discussion of land reform in urban areas.[74] In the BdB's programme it occupied an equally central position. One of the favourite examples of the success of land reform, referred to countless times by the BdB, was the introduction of a tax on the unearned increment in the value of land in the German colony of Kiau-Chu in 1898. The tax was imposed on the hapless Chinese landowners by the Navy Department at a rate of 33% and hailed as a great success by the BdB who proudly congratulated Tirpitz and the Navy on following the Bund's programme and thus preventing the inroads of the land speculator and preserving for the community the rightful profit of improvement.[75]

Writing in 1902, Damaschke expressed the hope of seeing the idea of the WZS realised in Germany in the city of Ulm, one of the first cities to seek corporate membership of the BdB and one which had already won a reputation for adventurous land and housing policies under the direction of H. von Wagner.[76] But the first city to introduce the tax in practice was Frankfurt am Main. Adickes, whose contribution to new developments in tax reform, land policy and city management was crucial and who represented a worthy continuation of the tradition that had started with Miquel, won acceptance from the *Magistrat* for the tax in 1904. He rejected as too unwieldy the idea favoured by Mill and others of a periodic valuation of all land and property as the basis for assessment, and introduced the tax as a levy on profits at the time of sale of property and both developed and undeveloped land. The form of the tax adopted in Frankfurt was a minimum levy on the sale price against which might be set the costs of improvements, calculated on a sliding scale taking into account the recency of the sale and the price of the property.[77]

The introduction of the WZS at Frankfurt was followed by its adoption in broadly similar form in a number of other cities: in 1905 Cologne and Gelsenkirchen adopted it, by 1907 Dortmund, Bremen, Kiel and a number of the *Vororte* in Berlin had followed suit. By 1911, 650 *Gemeinden* (out of a total of 76,000) had introduced some form of WZS, although its adoption in larger cities was less rapid; Berlin only introduced a WZS of similar form to that of Frankfurt in 1910. As the tax became more widespread, a range of local variations grew up; the tax for Breslau was cited by Dawson as typical of many.[78] Here the first 10% of the increment was free from taxation, an increment of between 10% and 20% was taxed at 6% of the excess of the price over that at the previous change of ownership and so on with a maximum levy of 25% of the increment where this was greater than 100%.

Following on from the successful introduction of this form of tax in individual cities, the BdB turned its attention, under Damaschke's orchestration, to agitation for a *Reichswertzuwachssteuer*.[79] Damaschke had raised the issue in 1908 and by 1910, after a furious campaign of agitation, a draft of the law had been prepared. In 1911 it became law. The new law appropriated half of the tax on the unearned increment for the state, leaving 40% for the local authorities and 10% to the Reich: provision was also made that those cities who had already stated to levy the tax before 1911 should retain their original income. However in 1913 after only two years' trial, the *Reichswertzuwachssteuer* had been repealed. The debate over the introduction of this tax is an issue which is more relevant to the complex question of the tax structure of Germany and the difficulties of apportioning taxes between federal, state and local government, but it does serve to illustrate, as Berger-Thimme points out, the confusion, and occasionally the conflict, between reforming intentions, political opportunism and reform in practice. Many of the reformers themselves viewed the introduction of legislation for the whole Reich in this field as quite inappropriate. To them it appeared, not as powerful and benign legislation by the Reich, in the manner of the *Reichswohngesetz* for which housing reformers had campaigned and which was to have overruled the selfish interests of property at city or state level, but as an example of fiscal opportunism remote from the very different circumstances and needs of different cities.

The value of the local WZS was also a source of debate amongst land and housing reformers. Eberstadt, for example, clearly felt that the emphasis placed on it was unwarranted and that as a measure with which to attack the problems of the high costs of land, and thus housing, it was misdirected.[80] He claimed that it failed to touch on the crucial issue of limiting the means and security for borrowing money for land and property and would therefore have little effect. He also feared that the substantial revenue that the tax brought in would reduce the enthusiasm of the local authority to continue pressing for lower prices for land. Nor was Eberstadt alone in this view. Summarising the effect of the WZS during the First World War, Sembritzki emphasised that its effect was impossible to assess, largely because of the depression which strongly affected the land and property market towards the end of the first decade of the century.[81] On the basis of the evidence available he held back from making the optimistic generalisations so typical of the BdB; he concluded that the claims of the BdB for the effectiveness of the tax and its influence on land values could not be substantiated.

How the various taxes introduced after 1893 affected land values is difficult to assess. However, contemporaries did feel that the new taxes were more equitable in effect and it was clear that the community did derive a substantial benefit from the transactions in land and property. The general effect of the reforms after 1893 was to increase substantially the tax revenue from property and land. The total tax revenue from property and land in cities such as Frankfurt and Cologne rose from 6.8% and 11.3% respectively in 1894/5, to 27.4% and 28.3% by 1910. However the importance of the general tax reforms brought in by the *Kommunalabgabengesetz* of 1893, as against the measures championed by the land reformers, is clear from the small proportion of this increase due to the *Umsatz-* and *Weertzuwachssteuer*. In Berlin, for example, in 1910 the income from the WZS represented only 3.7% of all tax revenue from property and land.[82]

Municipal land policies

Taxing the 'unearned increment' in the value of land was one approach. But potentially more successful as a means of overcoming the damaging effects of urban land speculation, and more widely supported, was the growing interest, from the 1890s onwards, in encouraging the development of a systematic land policy for German cities. If the municipality, in the role of large landowner, could exercise significant pressure on the land market, the reformers held high hopes that it would be able to challenge the way in which other landowners used their supposed 'monopoly' of the market. Supporters of a municipal *Bodenpolitik* or land policy argued that a determined programme of municipal land purchase would lead more effectively to communal control of the benefits of land than any other policy.

The fact that the community once enjoyed the common ownership and use of much of the land in Berlin, for example, was still alive in the memory of some at the time of Faucher's writings, when the conventional wisdom supported the sale of the common and crown lands to individuals and private enterprise. Reformers like Andreas Voigt turned to historical precedent to underline the acceptability of the communal ownership of land:[83] he reminded contemporaries that at the beginning of the nineteenth century the greater part of land in Berlin was not in private hands, and that the sale of the crown lands from 1808, forced by financial need, was eagerly justified by liberal ideology. Common land was split up and the monarchic domains sold off rapidly until 1835, the pace then slowed until 1850, but thereafter speeded up again, until by 1866 virtually all land, with the exception of a number of areas of the Royal Domains such as Dahlem and Grunewald had been sold to private owners.

In the early 1870s the wisdom of selling off communally owned land was challenged, though too late to be of significant effect in Berlin. At the first meeting of the VfSP the case for municipal ownership of land was aired by Adolph Wagner. With the growing popularity of Henry George's writings in the 1880s and the launching of the BdB, the demand for communal ownership of land grew rapidly. It now became a central policy of the land reformers to encourage the municipal ownership of land. Housing reformers encouraged the municipalities to use this land for housing purposes by making land available, sometimes at advantageous terms, to the housing associations and co-operatives whose activity was beginning to expand in the 1890s.

Nor was it difficult for the German cities to take up this challenge. Contrary to English practice, which would have made it necessary for towns to seek special powers to do so, German cities had long possessed powers to buy land. Many already had large holdings of land by the 1890s, both within their city boundaries and outside, reflecting a policy of land purchases that pre-dated the BdB's propagandist activities. Frankfurt was exceptional in the proportion of the city's area owned by the municipality; by 1897 this amounted to 49.4% of the total. But other cities, too, held substantial stocks of land; many owned over 30% of all land within the city boundaries and still more outside, as a reserve for future use.[84]

From the late 1880s onwards, the BdB had pressed for further extension of municipal ownership of land and there appeared to be widespread agreement among the whole spectrum of reformers, from the BdB to the Social Democrats, that substantial increases in municipal land ownership would provide a powerful means of controlling the speculation in land prices. Indeed this very view had been put to the municipalities by the Prussian government in a circular to *Regierungspräsidenten* of the different provinces from the ministers of trade and commerce, education and the interior in March 1901, urging them to increase their land holdings and to make them available to the non-profit housing movement:

A judicious communal land policy is of far-reaching importance for the better adjustment of housing conditions. The existing evils have their chief source in unhealthy land speculation, which in part can only be combated by changes in legislation. A powerful means of checking this speculation is, however, available at present in the acquisition of as much landed estate as possible by those communes whose continuous growth converts the surrounding agricultural and garden land in ever-increasing measure into building land. The manner in which land so purchased, which as a rule should permanently remain in the hands of the commune, should be used for building – whether the commune itself, either directly or through contractors, should erect dwellings upon the land and either let or lease them, must be left for each commune to decide for itself.[85]

One of the most important issues for the success of municipal land policies was for the cities to retain control of the land that was released for building. By the turn of the century many cities were offering municipally owned land for the building of non-profit housing to break the 'economic stranglehold' of the land speculator. But the success of this policy depended on the continued exclusion of the speculator even after the construction of the housing; if the housing could be bought up later on, the benefits of the policy would be lost. German cities and the land reformers were therefore most anxious to complement these land acquisition policies with a series of measures which would enable the city to retain a degree of control of land, even after it had been made available for some approved purpose. The idea of some form of leasehold system, or some provision to buy back the land once it had been sold, was therefore a natural and vitally important development of the cities' land policies.

The principle of leasing was of course thoroughly familiar to English reformers, as were its advantages. But in Germany, although there existed a form of leasing both in old German law and in Roman law, the Superficies, the system of leasing land had almost died out in urban areas.[86] In the early 1870s there was sporadic interest in the English leasehold system: Eberstadt mentions that Hobrecht in 1872 had attempted to revive its use to make land available for the development of Berlin, but to no avail. It was only in the 1890s that there began a sustained interest in this system of land tenure. The BdB strongly supported the leasehold system: in 1899, it had invited one of its members Professor Rudolph Sohm to investigate the possibilities of using a system of leasing for urban land and to draw up a draft statute providing for this.[87] From then onwards the demands for legislation to establish a system of leasehold land tenure, the *Erbbaurecht*, became an important part of the BdB's campaign.

However the first significant translation of these ideas into practice dates from the introduction, by Adickes, of a form of leasehold contract in Frankfurt in 1900 to make municipal land available for non-profit housing.[88] From this date the leasehold system was adopted by a large number of cities, states and other organisations as a means of making land available without selling it. The existence of a method of leasing which would provide a generous source of land for non-profit housing was an important contributory factor in the movement's success. However the introduction of the leasehold system created problems of financing development both for the non-profit sector and for private enterprise because the normal system for loans was modified by leasehold tenure. This might be overcome for the non-profit sector as it was in Frankfurt by the creation of an *Erbbaukasse*, or special fund for loans to development on leasehold land. But, for the traditional developer, building on leasehold land presented considerable difficulties in raising capital.

The problem of retaining control of municipal land even after it had been developed could be approached differently. In Ulm, under Oberbürgermeister H. von Wagner, the city had started in the early 1890s to build housing for sale subject to the condition that the city should have the right to buy back the property at any time during a given period, fixed first at 15 years, but from 1902 onwards, at 100 years.[89] This right could be exercised if the owner were to resell his house, if the owner were to mortgage his house without the city's approval or if the property were to become neglected and dilapidated. Wagner argued that by making municipal land available on these terms it was possible to capture all the benefits claimed for the leasehold system, but with the added advantage that those buying acquired the freehold of their properties with all the additional benefits that this conferred.

Despite such advances made in the control and management of municipal land, many local authorities still faced difficulties in assembling a stock of land, finding themselves thwarted and frustrated by owners who refused to sell, often in the hope of forcing a wholly inflated price for their land. Housing reformers, land reformers and municipal leaders, therefore, all joined in a campaign for the introduction of a number of further powers to enable the municipalities to manage the land within their boundaries in the most efficient manner and to ensure the orderly development of the city along the lines of the town-plan. Most important of these were the powers of expropriation and redistribution (*Umlegung*) or amalgamation (*Zusammenlegung*) of plots of land.[90] The powers necessary to appropriate land for streets and for the general provision of traffic were already well established: in Prussia the *Fluchtliniengesetz* of 1875 and the *Enteignungsgesetz* of 1874 made provision for this and similar measures existed in other states. Where expropriation was carried out, compensation was paid; in some states, as alternative to compensation, a landowner faced with compulsory purchase enjoyed the right to demand another property or site of equivalent value and as close to the original location as possible.

However, while these powers could be used to secure land for roads in future extension plans and also to provide the powers for driving new streets through existing areas, no provision for expropriation existed for more general purposes such as the provision of land for housing. In a situation where a single owner was holding the development of a whole 'block' to ransom by refusing to sell, the municipality was powerless to act. Although by 1900 legislation granting general powers of *Umlegung* had been passed in Hamburg (1892), Baden (1896) and Saxony (1900), in Prussia progress was very much slower.[91]

Here the first attempt to translate the principle of *Umlegung* into practice was made by the indefatigable Adickes in Frankfurt am Main.[92] The difficulties that he faced give some measure of the strength of the property lobby, particularly in the lower house, and their opposition to such measures: in 1893 Adickes presented a first draft proposal to the Prussian Herrenhaus, where, after modification, it was accepted and handed over to a special committee of the Abgeordnethaus where the power of the property lobby was concentrated, only to be rejected. However, presented again in 1901 in very much reduced form it finally became law under the title of 'Lex Adickes', with an application limited to the city of Frankfurt alone. Indeed it was not until after the First World War that these powers were made available for Prussia as a whole.

The results of the campaign for land reform were unevenly distributed. In Berlin, for example, the programme of land purchase and the development of a municipal *Bodenpolitik* was slow and unsure. By 1900 the city owned 34.8% of the area within its boundaries, even the municipalities surrounding the city proper owned no more; Charlottenburg owned 32.8%, Schöneberg 32.5%, but most, like Neukölln, owned less than 20%.[93] Without the driving leadership of an Adickes or a Wagner, and caught from the turn of the century onwards in an increasingly complex debate over the relationship of the city proper to its hinterland and the adjacent communities, Berlin, like many other cities, was unable to follow the example of Ulm or Frankfurt.

Attempts to incorporate more land, started in the 1870s, were checked with the creation in 1906 of the independent cities of Schöneberg, Rixdorf, Lichtenberg and Wilmersdorf.[94] The campaign for a 'Gross-Berlin', the unification of all the different local authorities into a single larger body, publicised by the Architektenausschuss Gross-Berlin in its competition for a plan for the whole conurbation,[95] drew attention to the difficulties of planning for transport, utilities and housing and land policies across the borders of the different authorities. Reinforced by differences in per capita income, these boundaries were jealously guarded and provided a barrier to attempts to develop a city-wide land policy, particularly where this was for non-profit housing. As in the case for the London County Council cottage estates, well-to-do suburban communities in Berlin bitterly opposed attempts to provide housing for working-class families employed elsewhere. In Tempelhof, the authority rejected plans put forward by the Berliner Spar- und Bauverein for a development of artisan housing to accommodate workers in the beer industry in Schöneberg. It did so on the grounds that it was not its duty 'to provide for the workers of other far better endowed authorities' in an area which would otherwise 'be developed for residential purposes by inhabitants with higher and therefore more taxable incomes'.[96] However, despite problems of local opposition and the fears of wealthy municipalities like Charlottenburg, the Zweckverband Gross-Berlin was established in 1912, to achieve some measure of co-ordination between the different authorities to promote common policies for the acquisition of municipal land, planning, transport, building regulations and other issues directly related to the interests of the land reformers. But without the power to undertake planning and initiate action, it remained a largely advisory body, a sad reflection of the desire to obtain the benefits of planning without a willingness to pay the political costs of doing so.

However, in some cities such as Frankfurt or Ulm the results were impressive. In Frankfurt the provisions of Lex Adickes had led to a real extension of the powers of the city. The programme of municipal land purchase was equally successful: by 1906 the city owned more than half the land within its boundaries: Freiburg in Baden owned 77.7% of its administrative area.[97] The benefits of these land policies for the non-profit housing movement were significant; in Frankfurt the use of municipally owned land for non-profit housing was actively encouraged both before and after the First World War. The city's housing programme of the 1920s under Ernst May, which was to attract world-wide attention between the wars, was greatly helped by the pre-war land policies that the city had pursued under Adickes. Here was an atypical but convincing demonstration of what could be achieved by a vigorous municipal *Bodenpolitik*.[98]

Land reform, together with the other elements of the programme of housing reform, the sanitary campaign and the determination to improve the design of working-class housing, was directed at creating an environment in which better housing would be possible. If implemented, the reformers' proposals would have led to more salubrious, more economical and better designed housing, planned more openly on cheaper land. But to strike at the heart of the housing problem all were agreed that it was not enough simply to encourage better housing, it was vitally important to build more, and methods of increasing the supply of new housing form the necessary complement to the elements of the reformers' programme that we have considered so far.

Reform and the provision of new housing

8

❖◇

Housing by private enterprise

Central to the programme of housing reform was the recognition that the existing forms of housing production were inadequate to provide suitable housing for the working classes at rents they could afford. From Huber onwards there had been calls for changes in the existing situation and for the exploration of new methods of financing and developing housing. If other sources of capital could be found for housing, which would be free from the fluctuations of the market and the unquenchable desire for profit, would it not then be possible to provide sufficient housing to the right standards and at the right price? In England, in Germany and in France this was one of the basic themes of housing reform from the early 1840s through to the years before the First World War. Only if sufficient new housing could be built could overcrowding be reduced and unhealthy housing controlled; only with a massive increase in the number of houses available could the market provide housing at rents low enough for the working-class family.

But how was this to be done? There was always the hope that the existing system of housing production might be reformed. In the early days, Huber and others had believed that the model dwelling movement, on English lines, might encourage, even compel, private enterprise into providing housing of higher quality. The public health and sanitary reforms of the 1870s and 1880s were aimed at ensuring that even the housing built by private enterprise did not fall too far short of the standards of the model dwellings. Minimum standards had been raised. But this had, if anything, only increased the cost of housing. The problems of securing an adequate supply of housing by private enterprise still seemed as remote to members of the VfSP in 1886 as it had during the first debate on housing during the late 1850s and 1860s.

The reformers had long tried to encourage the growth of other forms of housing production. They had looked to sources of capital from outside the traditional capital market. They had turned instead to the principles of self-help and co-operation, to philanthropy, and even to the self-interest of the employer. These attempts form as important a theme in housing reform in Germany as in England or France. But to understand the reformers' analysis of the failing of private enterprise, to appreciate the way in which their proposals were intended to improve matters, and, finally, to judge the success of reformers' proposals in practice, we must first examine the operations of the existing system of housing production.

Private enterprise housing in Berlin at the turn of the century

To understand the forces that produced the conditions in Berlin was, as Emmy Reich argued in her study of the Berlin housing market, to understand in general terms the full range of forces that generated the housing question.[1] The failings of private enterprise had been evident since the late 1840s, but by narrowing down to Berlin our examination of the provision of housing by private enterprise during the period around the turn of the century, we can not only observe the system in its 'mature' forms, but compare this with the non-profit sector when this sector was already growing rapidly. Because of its size and its position as the capital city of the Empire, Berlin is clearly atypical, but it provided a focus of attention as central for the concerns of the reformers in Germany, as did London for the English reformers or Paris for the French. In Berlin the housing problem was regarded as being as acute as anywhere else in the Empire, perhaps even more so. We start by considering the different elements of the supply side of the market: the supply of land, the building industry, the system of property ownership and the capital market, and their effect, first, on the volume of new dwellings coming on to the market at any time, and second, the costs at which they were produced and then rented.

The supply of land for residential building

The way in which land was supplied for housing was an issue of central importance to the analysis of the causes of the housing problem offered by reformers like Eberstadt and his followers. But how did land costs determine the total cost of the building? While the price of land in Berlin was generally high, as Eberstadt and others rightly asserted, the value of land varied sharply between different areas for different uses, and, contrary to the widely held contemporary opinion, its value appears to have increased less rapidly than did other components of residential building.

Some indication of the proportion of total building costs represented by the cost of land is given by Andreas Voigt in 'Die Bodenbesitzver-hältnisse, das Bau- und Wohnungswesen in Berlin'[2]. In contrast to the later studies which based their findings on data drawn from a number of individual cases, Voigt was able to arrive at an assessment of the relative cost of the land by identifying the cost of building construction and subtracting this from the total value of the property. The estimation of building costs he based on the valuation of the *Feuerkasse*, a valuation used for insurance purposes to calculate the replacement cost of the building;[3] the value of the property he derived from the municipal tax or 'common' value as registered in the *Mietssteuerkataster*. While Voigt

Table 8. *Land costs as a percentage of total development costs (A), and cost in Reichsmarks per square metre of land (B), for selected districts of Berlin*

	1880		1895	
	A	B	A	B
City of Berlin	49	149	62	261
Va ⎱ Vb ⎰	22	34	33	88
VIIa ⎱ VIIb ⎰	28	54	45	125
Xb	29	31	34	82
XIIIa	18	15	47	27

Va   Luisenstadt jenseits des Kanals (westlich)
Vb   Lunsenstadt jenseits des Kanals (östlich)
VIIa   Stralauer Viertel (westlich)
VIIb   Stralauer Viertel (östlich)
Xb   Rosenthaler Vorstadt (nördlich)
XIIIa Gesundbrennen
Source: Voigt, 'Bodenbesitzverhältnisse', pp. 254–60.

admitted that these assessments were both subject to error, he felt justified, nevertheless, in using them as a foundation for his calculations. Basing his study on these assumptions, Voigt constructed a general ranking of land costs as a proportion of total building costs for the different districts for the whole of Berlin. From these tables the differences between commercial and residential districts emerge clearly. So too do the differences between working-class and other residential districts.

This ordering of land values was naturally reflected in the proportion of total building cost due to land (see table 8). For the city as a whole, in 1895, land accounted for 62% of the total development costs, but in working-class districts this value was lower: in the Stralauer Viertel it was 45%, in Wedding and Gesundbrunnen 47%, in Luisenstadt (jenseits des Kanals) it was 33%, while in Moabit it was only 28%, a value comparable to the lower estimates of Heinrich Höpker (29%), Siegfried Ascher (28%) and Georg Haberland (27%).[4]

Voigt's study also reveals something of the changes in the value of land during the economic cycle. Using an extended time series he was able to confirm the general expectations of his contemporaries and to support the general proposition that the value of land moved cyclically with economic activity, rising rapidly during periods of economic expansion and rising only very slowly, if at all, during periods of recession. But while Voigt confirmed the conventional wisdom in this respect, the evidence of his researches challenged widely held views on the damaging effect of the high cost of land on the housing problem.

Voigt's study, along with later studies such as Ascher's, emphasised that in Berlin it was not the land so much as characteristics of the house building industry, particularly the increase in construction and financing costs, that caused costs to rise during the late 1890s.[5]

The building industry

By comparison with the rapid development in the scale of the land companies and the mortgage banks, house building remained, even after the turn of the century, a relatively small-scale and primitive branch of industry. Nevertheless between 1890 and 1907 the size of general contracting firms did increase, reflecting in part the greater scale of residential developments in this period. Thus in Berlin in 1890 there was no building firm employing more than 200 workers, but by 1895 there were 20 and by 1907 the number had risen to 31; by 1907, 25% of all firms employed more than six workers compared with the situation in 1890 when only 15% did so.[6]

The structure of the residential building industry was criticised by many contemporaries for encouraging inefficiency and bad management and the industry's operations were regarded as corrupted by malpractices of every conceivable kind. Reich comments on the attractions to the unscrupulous of the dramatic profits that could indeed be made during a boom: 'the chance of making large profits at no great personal risk attracts the adventurous and the dubious into this branch of industry.'[7] Reviewing the collapse of the Berlin building industry in 1912, Dr M. Rusch emphasised the danger to labour and building material suppliers from the incompetence and greed of residential developers many of whom operated without professional training of any kind.[8] Neither qualification nor capital was required for residential building. Working together with a land company, the builder himself needed only to raise sufficient capital for the *Baugeld*, or construction costs; even the financing of this could be spread over a considerable period. Thus our typical Berliner 'Baulöwe' (literally 'building lion') would have to pay only a third of the costs of building materials on ordering, a third on commencement of construction, while the final third had only to be produced on the sale of a building. In many cases building workers were not paid until a second mortgage had been obtained, or until the sale of the completed building to an owner.[9] But despite the occasionally huge profits and the very limited resources required, the average gains for residential construction were estimated to be low. The dividends of 10% reported by the very few companies which were properly registered and published their accounts were the exception, a view shared by Reich and Ascher.[10] However high the profits made during the short period of building activity between 1902 and 1906, long-term profits were low; certainly during the depression that set in after 1907 large numbers of builders went bankrupt.

The primitive and precarious nature of the house building industry was reflected in two important ways in the cost and volume of housing built in our period. First, wages rose rapidly but without an equivalent increase in productivity, thus leading to higher overall production costs.[11] Second, given the under-capitalisation of the industry, its financing was critically dependent on the cost of capital and the fluctuating state of the capital market. Ascher estimates the increase in the overall construction costs of new residential building in Berlin to have been from 180–270 M/m² in 1890 to 195–290 M/m² in 1900 for the simplest standards of construction and finish.[12] Setting aside the very limited effect of the higher standards demanded by tougher building regulations, the most substantial portion of this increase was caused by the rapid rise in wages in the building industry from 1893 onwards. Examining the wages of a number of trades, Ascher concluded that wages generally in the industry had increased by as much as 60–70% from 1895 to 1910.[13] But this increase in wages can be shown to have been offset by a less rapid increase in the cost of materials and components. This was due in large part to a far greater efficiency in the fabrication and supply of materials: not only were components such as doors and windows now commonly manufactured off site in greater quantities and, in real terms, more cheaply, but innovations in the production of materials such as bricks also reduced costs. While the price of materials such as bricks, cement and tiles varied with demand, naturally rising at times of peak construction, the general trend was downwards.[14]

The cost of production must also include the developer's cost in financing the purchase of the site and the period of construction. Although these were often no more than 10% of the total construction costs, this, given the way in which residential development was financed, might well be the margin between profit and failure, particularly as these costs (represented in fig. 38) varied sharply with the state of the capital market. The rate for borrowing for first mortgages, generally used to pay off the cost of the site and protected by the security of the *Grundbuch*, would be low but the substantial amount and the period over which the loan might be required could result in considerable expense. To these costs had to be added the cost of borrowing the *Baugeld*. Because of the system of payment for materials and labour, both the level and the period of the loan would be far less than the full costs of construction. However, because of the high risk involved in this phase of development, interest rates for *Baugeld* were generally 1%, occasionally as much as $2\frac{1}{2}$%, above the rates for first mortages. Taking as an example the financing of a development in 1910, Höpker concluded that the financing costs might account for about 10% of total production costs, but, in periods of high building activity during a boom when money would be more expensive, these costs could rise to nearer 15% of the total.[15]

Taken together, the different components of the construction costs of housing amounted, according to Andreas Voigt's study, to approximately 40% of the total cost of housing production in 1895 for the whole city. In working-class areas the proportion was substantially

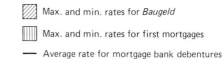

38 Interest levels for the different types of capital used in residential development

◫ Max. and min. rates for *Baugeld*

▥ Max. and min. rates for first mortgages

— Average rate for mortgage bank debentures

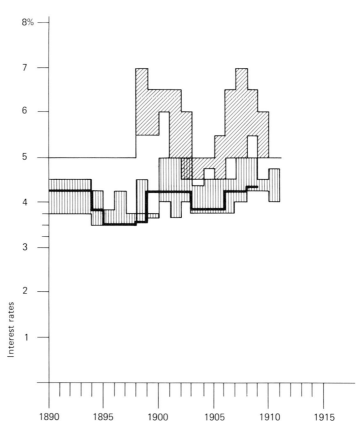

higher, nearer 60–70%.[16] Furthermore, these costs tended to increase in line with general economic activity, rising relatively more rapidly than land at a time of economic expansion, thus pushing up rents. But despite the influence of these costs on rents, rent levels at any point in time were ultimately dependent on the costs of financing the ownership of housing.

Investment in residential property

The ownership and management of property in Berlin during our period appears to have been as fraught with the constant risk of bankruptcy and forced sale as the construction of housing. Nevertheless the attraction of investing in residential property was high. Home-ownership was very limited by the 1890s so that demand for rented accommodation was high – indeed 97.7% of all dwellings were rented.[17] Investors were drawn into the housing market as landlords by the promise of handsome profits to be made either through managing property as a source of regular income, ideal for those seeking a 'steady' return, or, more aggressively, by realising the value of the house as a speculative venture. In contrast to the wealth of literary sources on the subject, there is little statistical information on the social and economic characteristics of residential landlords, but data collected by the statistical office of Charlottenburg in 1906 gives some substance to the image of the landlord as the personification of the petty-bourgeois.[18] Even to the small business man, the shopkeeper or the respectable widow, investment in property held out the promise of a secure income together with the chance of a golden 'nest egg' on sale.[19]

However, despite these attractions in theory, the chances of maintaining this level of income were affected in practice by a number of complicating factors, particularly at the lower end of the market. During a period of economic expansion it might not be difficult to keep flats let, and rents could always be raised to meet the extra cost of higher interest rates, although it should be remembered that for every 1% increase in mortgage interest rates, rents had to rise between 10 and 15%. But, in a recession, the landlord would have no such room for manoeuvre. As the proportion of empty dwellings in the city increased, it would be correspondingly more difficult for the landlord to let his flats – he might have to reduce rents in order to attract tenants. As income declined it would be increasingly difficult to meet the interest payments on a house which might be as much as 96% mortgaged, even though interest rates might come down during a slump. The difficulties faced by landlords in a depression can be inferred from the level of forced sales: during the depression of the early 1890s, they accounted for 20–25% of all property sales.[20]

The task of realising a substantial profit on the sale of a property was even more fraught with complications. In the long term, the rise in the value of land due to the growth of the city was generally sufficient to produce an increase in the value of most properties. Thus it should have been possible to sell any property at the right point in the economic cycle to make enough to pay off the mortgage and still retain a handsome profit. But in practice there were difficulties in managing property over the period necessary to show a real increase in the value, and the chances of making a substantial profit were certainly dependent on the fluctuation of the economic cycle and the changing state of the capital market.

The capital market

The difficulties faced by the builder in finding *Baugeld* during a boom, or by the landlord in meeting his mortgage payments during a slump, were only symptoms of the larger problem of securing capital for residential development and for working-class housing in particular. These difficulties sprang essentially from the low profitability of housing when compared with other forms of investment. It is this which determined the behaviour of the institutions which provided capital for housing and their operation at different stages in the economic cycle.

Because of the limited capital possessed by most developers and landlords, nearly all money invested in housing was borrowed on the capital market. The principal source of finance was the mortgage banks.[21] Until the 1890s they were almost the only source, but during the 1900s their share of the total declined, until by 1914 it was just over 40%. As their share of lending contracted, the activities of the savings bank and life insurance companies expanded. However, the operations of the mortgage banks still serve as a typical illustration of the behaviour of these institutions.

Unlike the building societies in England, the mortgage banks raised money not from the investment accounts of large numbers of small borrowers, but from the sale of debentures.[22] Money raised in this way was then lent in the form of mortgages to developers or owners of property. In general, mortgages were arranged for a period of ten years and were lent in aggregate at a slightly higher rate than the mortgage debenture rate – the difference was normally less than 1%, but occasionally it went higher. The rates at which individual mortgages were lent depended not only on the state of the market, but on the type and security for the loan and even on the area of the city in which the loan was to be made. Loans on first mortgages were lent at rates between 1 and $1\frac{1}{2}$% lower than second mortgages, while the rate for *Baugeld* might be as much as $\frac{1}{2}$–1% up on this again. Variations in the rates for different types of loans are illustrated in fig. 38. Mortgages for working-class and suburban housing were generally $\frac{1}{2}$% more expensive than those for the better quality housing in the west of the city that was favoured by the mortage banks.[23] Generally the mortgage banks tended to concentrate on the less risky first mortgages, leaving the provision of second mortgages and *Baugeld* to private investors. The balance of lending between the different types of mortgages is suggested by Paul Voigt's studies of lending in Charlottenburg in the 1890s.[24] On old property, first mortgages accounted for 60.5% of the value, second mortgages for 20.25% and other forms of loans for the rest. On new property the balance was 78.5% for first mortgages and 14.4% for second mortgages.

Of great importance were the changes in these mortgage rates over time and the relationship between these rates and the operations of the rest of the money market. An understanding of the operations of the mortgage banks at different points in the economic cycle is of key importance in investigating both the cost of borrowing, and thus the effect of financing on rents, and the volume of capital that was available for residential development at any time. Given the relatively low return on housing, even during periods of expansion when the housing market was strong, the extent to which mortgage rates could rise was limited and this naturally limited the rise of the debenture rate. Thus the attraction of these debentures and, in consequence, the flow of funds into the mortgage banks did not rise even during a period of economic up-turn. By contrast, during a depression, when the housing market was weak and demand for mortgages low, the mortgage banks would attempt to protect the value of their debentures, even buying up debentures when their price fell. The consequence of keeping the price of debentures up in this way was that the interest rate remained relatively stable.

The resultant stability of rates in relation to the economic cycle contrasts clearly with the fluctuation in share prices; the debenture rate resembles much more closely the rates for bonds and state and federal securities. The consequence was a flow of funds into the mortgage banks which lagged behind the economic cycle. When the general interest rates were low, as in periods of recession, the debenture rate was relatively high and money flowed into the mortgage banks; conversely, at times when the economy was high, the debenture rate was, relatively, low and the mortgage banks found it difficult to attract money. Thus, when the housing market was strong, the demand for mortgages could not be satisfied. This anti-cyclical availability of money for residential development was of some importance for the cost and the supply of housing, and leads us on to a more detailed discussion of the effects of the economic cycle on the housing market in this period.

The Berlin housing market 1895–1910

How effectively did these different elements of the production side of the housing market combine together to supply housing for the working classes? Was it reasonable to hope, as did some reformers, that the failings of the existing situation might still be corrected, or was the system of supply, as others believed, so inherently unstable and so inadequate as to be incapable of producing a steady supply of dwellings at reasonable rents? To answer these questions we must view the relationships between the demand for housing and the different agencies involved in its supply – the capital market – against the different phases of the economic cycle.

Consider the period between 1895 and 1914. In her description of the housing market during this period, Reich identifies three separate phases of activity.[25] The opening period, after the sharp recession of the early 1890s, is characterised by economic expansion, which was the result of the growth of heavy industries such as metalworking, engineering and electrical engineering. This phase appears to have lasted until late 1898, when the economy began to falter. The second period begins with the crisis of 1900 and two further years of economic difficulty. But by 1903, economic recovery was already under way, led by foreign trade, much of it with the USA. This phase of expansion continues until 1907, the end of our second period. The third period, starting in 1908, is principally a period of deepening recession which continues beyond 1910 to the war.

This macro-economic cycle has an important bearing on the population growth of the city, which represents the most effective, albeit crude, measure of aggregate housing demand. The period that we describe is still one of general population growth, both for the city of Berlin and for the surrounding area, although this growth is now a product more of natural increase than of immigration. But, as the variation in migration illustrated in figure 1 demonstrates, the cycle of boom and slump still affects the demand for housing. In times of prosperity, the increase through migration might still be substantial; in years of peak migration like 1905, this could rise to 39,564. Equally, in periods of depression the population might still decline; in 1908, a year of declining employment prospects, 20,854 people left the city. Generally, however, the growth of population, at 13% during the period 1895–1900, was double that of the preceding five years.

The demand for housing was a product not only of economic forces, but also of the changing pattern of population distribution within the metropolitan area of Berlin (fig. 2).[26] Within this area the growth of population was not evenly distributed. Most obvious was the increasingly rapid growth of the suburbs and the outer districts of the city at the expense of the inner areas. On the one hand, non-residential land uses forced housing out of central areas, and on the other, the relocation of industry further out, the so-called 'Randwanderung' to the Ringbahn, led to the outer districts becoming more attractive for working-class housing. This period sees a rapid growth of outer working-class districts such as Wedding and Gesundbrunnen to the north and the Stralauer Viertel to the south-east and an equally significant growth of the suburbs. In 1895, the population of the suburbs formed only 17% of the total population of Greater Berlin, but by 1900 this had risen to 29%, and by 1910 to 45% of the total population of the metropolitan area. Thus, during the period under consideration, demand was not only rising, but new housing was now required in the outer districts of the city and in the suburbs. How effective was private enterprise in providing for this demand, particularly for working-class housing?

Certainly private enterprise was ill adapted to meet the fluctuations in the demand for housing in the years before the First World War. It is above all the constraints imposed by the predominant pattern of economic activity, not demand, that determined the number, and type, of new dwellings that were built: production inevitably lagged behind the demand created by a rise in economic activity, while in a recession many developers found themselves putting newly finished dwellings on to a falling market. Thus, between 1895 and the war the housing market oscillated between over-provision and under-provision. A measure of the variations in supply and demand is given in figures 39 and 40. In the first phase of our period, supply greatly exceeded demand, resulting in a period of low-level production. This was then followed, around the turn of the century, by a period of acute shortage which, slowly, encouraged an increase in production levels which rose for the first half of the 1900s. But by 1907 the level of production was again falling as the economy as a whole began to falter and with it the demand for housing. After 1912, the entire system of private enterprise in Berlin was convulsively shaken by bankruptcies and liquidations, caught again by over-production and falling occupancy rates. By 1914 the inability of the existing system of housing production to react to, let alone

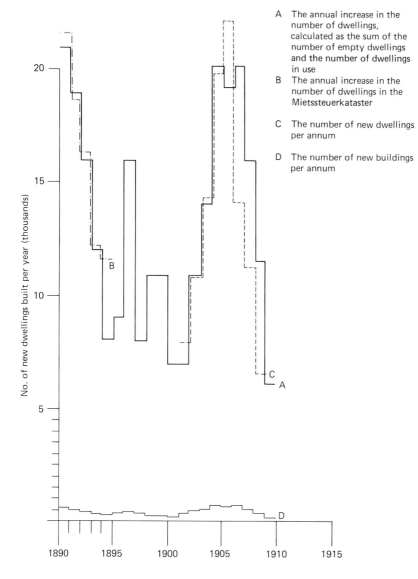

A The annual increase in the number of dwellings, calculated as the sum of the number of empty dwellings and the number of dwellings in use

B The annual increase in the number of dwellings in the Mietssteuerkataster

C The number of new dwellings per annum

D The number of new buildings per annum

39 Estimates of the production of new dwellings

anticipate, demand must have been painfully obvious.[27] But if private enterprise could not even respond adequately to the general city-wide demand for housing, how could it hope to provide for the needs of working-class families at the bottom end of the market where the problems of management had always been extreme, and where profit margins were slimmest? To investigate the housing that was provided by private enterprise for the lower income groups, we must now look in more detail at conditions in the working-class districts and suburbs of Berlin.

40 The percentage of empty
dwellings and the level of
rents in Berlin 1890–1910

A1 and A2 The average return on a dwelling (for all dwellings and rooms)
is used as a proxy for rent

B The percentage of empty dwellings

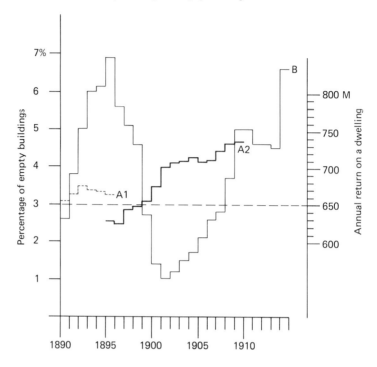

Housing conditions in working-class areas of Berlin

How do housing conditions in the predominantly working-class districts
and suburbs compare with those in the rest of the city and with other
suburbs? To simplify the comparison we have chosen to focus on a
limited number of areas where the concentration of those with unskilled
and semi-skilled occupations was highest.[28] Within the city we have
selected six such districts (illustrated in fig. 41) located in the north-west
and north where metalworking and engineering were still the predominant forms of employment and in the eastern areas where
employment was more diverse with clothing, wood-based trades and the
building industry as major employers but still with about 10% of all
employment in metalworking. Of the suburban areas we have chosen
Rixdorf, Lichtenberg and Weissensee, which lie to the south and east,
and Reinickendorf which lies to the north of the city.[29]

Consider first the density of development, an issue which lay close to
the heart of many reformers. In the working-class areas the density of
housing was far higher than the average for the whole city (table 9).
In 1905 only 25% of all sites in the city as a whole housed over 100
people, in working-class areas this figure was higher and if we consider
the percentage of plots housing more than 200 people the difference
between working-class areas and the city as a whole is even more

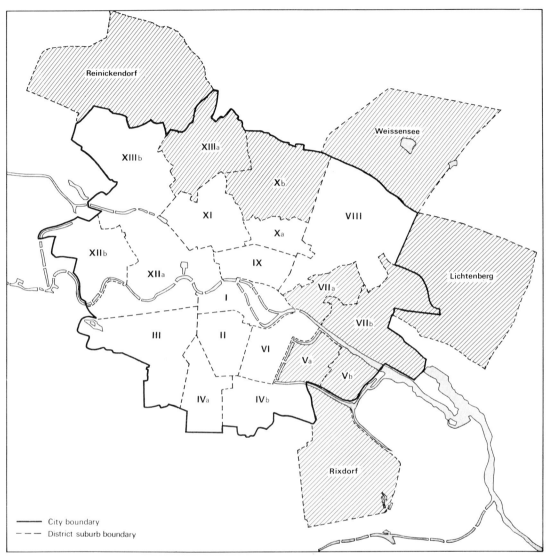

KEY

I	Berlin, Cöln, Friedrichswerder, Dorotheenstadt
II	Friedrichstadt
III	Friedrich und Schöneberger Vorstadt
IVa	Friedrich und Tempelhofer Vorstadt (westlich)
IVb	Tempelhofer Vorstadt (östlich)
Va	Luisenstadt jenseits des Kanals (westlich)
Vb	Luisenstadt jenseits des Kanals (östlich)
VI	Luisenstadt diesseits des Kanals, Neucöln
VIIa	Stralauer Viertel (westlich)
VIIb	Stralauer Viertel (östlich)
VIII	Königsstadt, Königsviertel
IX	Spandauer Viertel
Xa	Rosenthaler Vorstadt (südlich)
Xb	Rosenthaler Vorstadt (nördlich)
XI	Oranienburger Vorstadt
XIIa	Friedrich–Wilhelmstadt, Tiergarten, Moabit (östlich)
XIIb	Moabit (westlich)
XIIIa	Gesundbrunnen
XIIIb	Wedding

41 Diagrammatic map of the boundaries of city districts and selected suburbs of Berlin just before the First World War; the districts and suburbs referred to in Chapter 8 are shaded.

Table 9. *Residential density for selected districts and suburbs of Berlin:*
(a) the percentage of plots with different residential densities, (b) the
average number of people per plot ('Behausungsziffer')

	(a) Percentage of plots with different densities expressed in number of inhabitants			(b) Average number of people per plot
	1–100	101–200	207+	
1900				
City of Berlin	74.7	22.2	3.0	77
Va	68.0	28.6	3.3	90
Vb	45.2	43.1	11.5	120
VIIa	75.2	21.2	3.4	83
VIIb	50.7	44.1	5.1	103
Xb	44.3	48.5	7.1	114
XIIIa	66.8	27.2	6.0	84
Reinickendorf	99.7	0.3	0	17
Rixdorf	74.0	24.3	1.5	69
Weissensee	100	0	0	15
Lichtenberg	86.6	11.8	0.8	54
1905				
City of Berlin	74.0	23.0	2.9	77
Va	71.4	26.4	2.1	84.5
Vb	51.7	39.5	8.7	111.2
VIIa	75.0	18.7	2.6	78.2
VIIb	57.1	40.6	2.1	100.8
Xb	46.2	47.8	5.8	111.5
XIIIa	65.7	27.4	6.7	86.3
Reinickendorf	97.8	1.8	0.1	
Rixdorf	71.7	27.1	0.1	
Weissensee	97.0	2.6	0.3	
Lichtenberg	88.0	11.3	0.6	

Va	Luisenstadt jenseits des Kanals (westlich)
Vb	Luisenstadt jenseits des Kanals (östlich)
VIIa	Stralauer Viertel (westlich)
VIIb	Stralauer Viertel (östlich)
Xb	Rosenthaler Vorstadt (nördlich)
XIIIa	Gesundbrunnen

Source: (a) *Stat. J. Berlin*, vol. 32 (1913), pp. 265–7; vol. 33, p. 146, (b) *Stat. J. Berlin*, vol. 27, (1903), pp. 198–9; vol. 33, p. 147

marked. In the suburbs the density was generally lower, reflecting the lower cost of land in the smaller suburbs like Weissensee and Reinickendorf. But already in the larger suburbs, like Rixdorf with a population of nearly 150,000, the average number of people per site was close to that for the city of Berlin.

Not only were the working-class areas developed more densely, the

Table 10. *The percentage of dwellings (without business premises) of different sizes for selected districts and suburbs of Berlin*

	Size of dwelling expressed in no. of heatable rooms					% of small dwellings with 0–2 rooms
	0	1	2	3	4+	
1905						
City of Berlin	1.1	49.3	29.8	10.8	8.8	80/2
Va	1.2	58.4	27.3	8.7	4.4	86.9
Vb	1.1	69.8	20.4	5.8	2.9	91.3
VIIa	1.2	53.0	28.3	10.0	7.5	81.5
VIIb	0.8	54.7	32.8	8.5	3.2	88.3
Xb	0.9	51.4	32.2	11.6	3.9	84.5
XIIIa	0.7	55.1	33.8	7.4	3.0	89.6
Reinickendorf	0.3	43.9	41.7	11.0	2.7	85.9
Rixdorf	0.5	50.5	38.3	7.8	2.7	89.3
Weissensee	0.9	55.0	34.3	7.3	2.2	90.2
Lichtenberg	0.6	54.1	35.7	7.3	2.0	90.4
1910						
City of Berlin	1.7	47.2	32.6	10.2	7.3	81.5
Va	2.0	69.8	20.8	4.9	1.8	90.8
Vb	2.7	58.9	27.0	7.7	3.5	93.3
VIIa	2.7	53.2	28.3	9.5	5.8	84.2
VIIb	1.9	50.9	37.6	7.1	2.3	90.4
Xb	1.9	50.4	38.9	7.1	1.4	91.2
XIIIa	1.9	57.2	33.6	5.4	1.7	92.7
Reinickendorf						
Rixdorf						
Weissensee						
Lichtenberg						

Sources: 1905: *Grundstücks-Aufnahme* 1905, pt 1, pp. 70–8; 1910: *Grundstücks-Aufnahme* 1910, pt 1, vol. 2, pp. 48–9.

Table 11. *Household composition for selected districts of Berlin*

	Percentage of dwellings with:	
	No lodgers	*Schlafleute*
1910		
City of Berlin	82.3	10.2
Va	80.9	13.1
Vb	85.9	11.0
VIIa	79.0	14.0
VIIb	88.1	8.9
Xb	88.4	8.3
XIIIa	86.1	10.8

Source: Stat. J. Berlin, vol. 32 (1913), pp. 968–76.

Table 12. *The percentage of empty dwellings for selected districts and suburbs of Berlin*

	Percentage of empty dwellings		
	1900	1905	1910
City of Berlin	0.6	1.5	5.0
Va	0.2	0.5	3.8
Vb	0.4	0.5	3.9
VIIa	0.5	1.0	4.9
VIIb	0.4	3.1	5.7
Xb	0.4	1.2	7.9
XIIIa	0.3	2.5	8.9
Reinickendorf	0.5		
Rixdorf	0.5		
Weissensee	2.0		
Lichtenberg	0.3		

Sources: 1900: *Stat. J. Berlin*, vol. 27 (1903), p. 200; 1905: *Stat. J. Berlin*, vol. 29 (1905), p. 104; vol. 33 (1916), pp. 144–5; 1910: *Stat. J. Berlin*, vol. 32 (1913), p. 303.

dwellings themselves in these districts were also smaller (table 10). If we compare the proportion of dwellings with one and two rooms for the city as a whole with the proportion in our six working-class districts, this difference emerges clearly: four of the six districts and three of the four suburbs have about 10% more of these smaller dwellings than the average for the rest of the city.

In working-class areas in both city and suburbs, dwellings were not only smaller but were more frequently used to take in *Schlafleute* than dwellings in the rest of the city (table 11), although the number of such lodgers, an issue of close concern to reformers, fell after 1890 and continued to decline until after the war. Generally during a housing shortage accommodation in working-class districts was in shorter supply than elsewhere in the city but during a depression occupancy levels in these districts might fall rapidly as people left in search of work. During the acute housing shortage at the turn of the century when the proportion of empty dwellings stood at 0.6% for the whole city, the shortage was still more acute in working-class areas (table 12): in Luisenstadt, for example, only 0.2% of all dwellings were empty. With people trying to save money by moving to smaller and cheaper dwellings, the pressure on housing in these areas was intense. Even in the suburbs where the proportion of empty dwellings was slightly higher than in the city as a whole, the shortage in working-class areas was more acute, indeed almost as critical as in the city districts.

Even when aggregate figures show an overall balance between demand and supply there might still be very considerable variation between the availability of housing and demand in different working-class areas. Thus in 1908 when, overall, 3.42% of all dwellings were

Table 13. *The average rent levels per dwelling in selected districts and*
suburbs of Berlin

	Average rent (in Marks) for all dwellings			Average rent for a 2-room dwelling
	1900	1905	1910	1910
City of Berlin	443	465	464	427
Va	(351)*	357	367	428
Vb	(281)	324	334	425
VIIa	(392)	385	394	414
VIIb	(321)	355	363	409
Xb	(280)	340	361	419
XIIIa	(270)	300	321	379
Reinickendorf	201	287		
Rixdorf	256	328		
Weissensee	203	261		
Lichtenberg	231	289		

* The figures in parentheses are calculated by taking the differentials in the
annual rental value for each district (from the *Mietssteuerkataster*) and multiplying this by the average rent for the whole city.
Sources: 1900: Calculated from *Stat. J. Berlin*, vol. 27 (1903), p. 200–1; 1905:
Grundstücks-Aufnahme, 1905, pt 1, pp. 43, 70–8; 1910: *Grundstücks-Aufnamme*
1910, pt 1, vol. 2, pp. 48–9.

empty, the number of empties in Luisenstadt was right down to 1.9%.
Here, as a result of demand for land for other uses, there had been a
net decrease in housing, forcing population to the outer districts and
the suburbs. In Gesundbrunnen, however, the number of empties was
as high as 6.8%, reflecting the volume of new building in the suburbs:
in Wedding, for example, the number of empty dwellings in 1910 was
more than double the 1903 total.

As might be expected, the rents paid for a dwelling at any time varied
between districts and according to size and location; even within the
same development rents varied from the fifth floor in a back court to
the first floor looking out over the street.[30] As we have seen, the rent
for the same dwelling also varied with the availability of housing
generally. Nevertheless, average rents in working-class districts were
lower than elsewhere but not markedly so (table 13). In 1910 the rents
for both a one-room and a two-room dwelling in Gesundbrunnen, where
the number of empties was high, was around 12% lower than rents for
the whole city. But in other more central working-class areas, like
Luisenstadt where demand was higher and the number of empties was
lower, rents might be equal to, or even slightly above, the average for
the whole city.

Nor were the rents for working-class dwellings necessarily lower in
the suburbs. Average rents, over all sizes of dwellings, for the suburbs,
compared with average rents for Berlin, did tend to suggest a lower level

in the suburbs than in the city (table 13). But this was not always the case. Data cited by Reich show that the rent in 1905, when there was no shortage of housing, for a single-room dwelling in Rixdorf, one of the larger suburbs, was actually marginally higher than the average rent for an equivalent dwelling in the city.[31]

Hermann Schwabe, when director of the Berlin Statistical Office, had formulated the 'Schwäbisches Gesetz'[32] relating income to rent in 1868, but comprehensive data on household income and expenditure necessary to investigate the issue systematically were not available before 1914. However, some information on the subject, though contradictory and not strictly comparable because of differences between 'per capita' and 'household' income, is provided from two sources, first, the information collected for the income tax returns and from average rents and, second, a number of surveys of household income and expenditure carried out by the statistical offices of a number of cities and the Reichs statistical office itself. Most interesting for our purposes are the two surveys carried out by the Berlin Statistical Office in 1900, both based on samples of semi-skilled households where the head of the household was typically a carpenter or sales assistant.[33] Both groups had a similar 'per capita' income which was below the mean per capita income for the whole city and both groups spent nearly the same proportion of income on rent, But, significantly, both groups spent a lower proportion (16.35–17.6%) of income on rent than might have been expected from other contemporary studies.

Complementary to these findings are those based on the use of income tax data. Ascher, for example, adopts this latter approach.[34] Using aggregate income tax data for the city he arrives at an average income per inhabitant which he then compares with the average rent for all dwellings. On this rather abstract basis he calculates that in 1900 the average proportion of income spent annually on rent was 19% for an average per capita income of 605 M. And for 1910 he optimistically estimated that average expenditure on rent had declined to 17% on a per capita income of 782 M.

But the relative optimism of Ascher's figures and the data obtained from the family income and expenditure survey were challenged by others.[35] Kuczynski, director of the statistical office in Schöneberg, produced figures in 1911 to show that in Schöneberg those with annual incomes of 12,000 M were paying as much as 32.4% of their income in rent. To Schwabe's original axiom, 'the lower the income, the higher the rent', he added 'the smaller the dwelling, the higher the rent'.[36] Kuczynski's findings may have been distorted by the particular circumstances in Schöneberg, one of the wealthier suburban municipalities to the south-west of Berlin, but in his concern over the portion of income paid in rent by the poorer families, he echoed the anxieties of the housing reformers generally.

The reformers' belief in the truth of Schwabe's axiom was typical of their assessment of the housing provided by private enterprise. Not only was the existing system of housing production unable to respond to

42 Housing conditions in the centre of Berlin, illustrations from a survey of conditions carried out by the Verein Wohnungsreform in the 1920s

demand, the housing that it did supply was inferior (figs. 37 & 42). That the smallest, most crowded, most densely built dwellings should be, in addition, the most expensive in relative terms was damning evidence of the inability of private enterprise to offer adequate housing for the working classes.

The failure of private enterprise to provide for the worker's family had been one of the foremost concerns of the housing reformers from the earliest days of the movement. In his celebrated 'Mahnruf in der Wohnungsfrage' in 1886, Schmoller was only repeating what Huber and others had already been arguing in the late 1840s and the 1850s. Schmoller warned:

The real cause [of the housing problem] lies in the fact that for 30 years the working-class population has been piling up in our large industrial cities; not enough housing has been built for these people and it is in their nature to accept the depression of their housing standards all too easily...Everywhere the increases in rents for the dwellings of the poor have been beyond measure...But even so the private developer will only set himself about the task of laying out working-class districts and building working-class housing in an unwilling and fitful way and on a completely inadequate scale...[37]

For Schmoller and the housing reformers, the real way to overcome the difficulty was to look beyond the existing system of building housing for profit to alternative ways of developing and to alternative sources of capital:

In addition to the purely speculative forms of private enterprise, there are here in Germany a number of other possible and very effective agencies whose work it must be our first task to encourage. In this respect I refer to:
(1) the housing work of the individual employer...
(2) the housing co-operatives of tradesmen, artisans and workers...
(3) those enterprises, directed by the educated and propertied classes, the housing trusts, the limited dividend housing companies...[38]

It is to these alternatives to housing by private enterprise that we turn in the following chapters. We examine first the provision of housing by the employer for his employees and the reformers' assessment of its value. We then consider the most important alternative to the provision of housing by private enterprise, the public utility non-profit housing sector, or *gemeinnützige Bautätigkeit*, the housing provided by the limited dividend housing companies and the co-operative housing movement.

9

Housing by the employer

In Germany as in England the tradition of the employer, either private or public, providing housing for his employees has a long history. Much of the housing built by English employers during the early years of the industrial revolution to house mill and mine workers in areas away from existing settlements was primitive and utilitarian. But already by the mid-nineteenth century, Sir Titus Salt had created at Saltaire a more positive image of what the employer could do. The 'model' developments at Port Sunlight, Bournville and New Earswick, continue this tradition. What Lever, Cadbury and Rowntree could do for England could be done in Germany too, and by the end of the 1890s similar 'model' estates were to be seen rising in different parts of Germany. Set beside much of the housing built by private enterprise, the quality of the accommodation built by these employers by the turn of the century was to exert a powerful influence on the ideals of the housing reform movement.

Albrecht, Kalle, Jäger and Schmohl all trace back to the middle of the eighteenth century a tradition of miners' housing built by both public and private employers.[1] In the Silesian coalfields developed under Frederick II and, later, in the Saar, the Prussian mining authorities provided miners with a premium, a low-interest, sometimes a free, loan and free or cheap land on which to build.[2] When completed the house became the property of the miner but this ownership was subject to certain overriding constraints in favour of the employer: most important, the employer retained the right to re-purchase the house and to limit the manner in which it was used. An alternative method of providing housing, favoured by private employers, and one which was to become more important from the mid-1860s with the increase in the rate of industrial growth, was for the employer to build housing himself and then to rent this to his employees.

Reformers and housing by employers before 1886

Surprisingly neither of these forms of providing housing seems to have attracted the attention of reforming circles such as the CVWaK, although the principle of the employer housing his own workforce was already recognised by the 1850s. Indeed before the 1860s, with the exception of the housing being built at Mulhouse, the importance of the employers' contribution seems to have passed unremarked.

During the period of the first debate, the attitudes of reformers towards housing provided by the employer remained ambivalent. To those like Huber, and even to Sax, the employer's contribution to the solution of the housing problem was essentially to offer assistance 'from above' as at Mulhouse.[3] Writing in 1869, Sax was still pressing the case for 'latent associations', led by the employer, to build housing out of a concern 'for the physical, economic and moral well-being of his workers'. The benefits to the employer were clear: 'This interest brings its own economic returns through success in creating and securing a brave, skilled, determined, peaceful and decent workforce. In this manner the full perspective of a vigorous and far-reaching approach to the problem of housing is thrown open to view'.[4]

To the reformers, the role of the employer was thus a special case of the general attitude required of the propertied classes in approaching the housing problem. The employer, whose wealth was a product of the work of his employees, had an even greater duty, in addition to the spur of self-interest, to assist in providing housing either through limited dividend housing companies or enterprises such as the Berliner gemein-nützige Baugesellschaft. Clearly this was a very different approach from that of the mining authorities and employers like Krupp for whom housing was a necessary investment to ensure the operation of the factory, whatever the interpretation offered for public consumption.

Members of the Kongress deutscher Volkswirte (KdV), however, held the view that in the long run this system of housing would prove unsatisfactory. Citing the example of employers' housing in Düsseldorf, Parisius argued that the self-interest of the employer resulted in the construction of housing to progressively lower standards as employers attempted to save money.[5] To the members of the KdV the goodwill, and even the most generous estimates of the self-interest of the employers were only a poor substitute for the strength of co-operation and self-help.

Nevertheless, the expansion of the economy in the mid-1860s and the increasing rate of industrialisation produced an urgent need for housing in areas of industrial growth, forcing employers to build. Away from the large cities, in the semi-rural areas such as the Ruhr, for example, the employer had of necessity to provide housing for his employees and in general the quality was higher than that provided by private enterprise in the cities.[6] In the Saar and in Silesia the growing workforce in the mines continued to be housed along the lines already established. But parallel to the continuation and expansion of this old tradition, the 1860s also saw a rapid growth in the volume of housing rented by the employer. Although this had only started in a tentative way in the 1840s, Albrecht was able to report by 1900 that this form of employer housing was very much more common than the older 'indirect' form.[7]

There were, however, important distinctions between the kinds of employers who could (and would) build for their workers. Naturally the distribution of this housing varied widely between regions and for different types of employer. In urban areas few employers built housing for their employees on any large scale. In Berlin, for example, even Borsig who certainly commanded the resources to do this, had difficulty in housing his foremen and supervisors because of the cost of land; in general the workforce of the metal industry in the north-west of Berlin lived in housing rented on the open market.[8] For many employers the cost of providing housing was prohibitive; at about 4,500 M per dwelling, building even a few houses required substantial capital. For all but the large employer the difficulties were obvious: it would probably be necessary to build in order to expand the workforce at a time of industrial growth when money would be most expensive and desperately needed to expand the firm's activities. Building housing would divert money which would be more suitably used for increasing production. Moreover, during the slump, the employer might not only have to face his factory working below capacity, and even standing idle, but also meet the cost of maintaining factory housing. Some of this housing might well be empty as hands were laid off with a down turn in production. The economic disadvantages to all but the largest employers must have been considerable.

Reviewing the achievements of the employers in providing for their workers, Reichardt concluded that the criticism of German employers during the 1860s that, by comparison with foreign employers, they were not doing enough to house their workers, was probably justified.[9] But by the 1870s he argued that this was no longer true; during the expansion of the economy in the late 1860s and early 1870s, both the State and private employers had invested heavily in housing. Täglichsbeck records a rapid increase in investment in housing for miners by the Prussian mining authorities between 1865 and 1874.[10] Krupp started to build rapidly during this same period. In 1863 the company built 219 dwellings, but the main surge of expansion comes, predictably, with the boom years of the early 1870s: between 1871 and 1873 the company added 2,199 dwellings to its stock, an astonishing achievement in such a short time. Although on an unparalleled scale, these efforts were not unique. Reichardt quotes a survey carried out by the Prussian state in 1875 which showed that of the 4,850 employers who participated in the survey, 34% were already engaged in assisting their employees with their housing in some way.[11]

Employers' housing after the 1880s

The growing concern for the housing problem during the mid-1880s and the debates of the VfSP placed fresh emphasis on the role of the employer in providing housing for his workforce. Miquel's hopes for the employers' contribution contrasted with the reservations of earlier reformers on the suitability of housing built by the employer.[12] Schmoller too urged the employers to increase the amount of housing they built.[13] He urged the employer to help his workers to help themselves by supporting and encouraging various forms of voluntary housing organisations and, concerned at the possible 'blameworthy dependence' that might result from living in accommodation rented from the employer, he championed the system of loans to the employee to enable him to build his own house. The VfSP and other associations who opposed the *laissez-faire* attitudes of the *Manchesterschule*, and called for an active response to the housing problem, now combined to remind the employer of his duty to provide housing for his workers.

In groups like Verein Arbeiterwohl, composed largely of Catholic industrialists, which had long taken a stern view of the duties of the employer towards his employees, the VfSP's call for the employer to take on the responsibility of housing his workforce was hailed as an endorsement of the Verein's existing attitudes.[14] In the early 1880s, the journal *Arbeiterwohl* had carried articles enthusiastically describing the housing built by various employers. The Verein's support for the VfSP's programme was unqualified and the Verein campaigned for increased action on this front during the late 1880s and early 1890s. The *Arbeiterfreund*, the most authoritative voice of reforming liberalism, now too urged the same approach.

The founding of the Centralstelle für Arbeiterwohlfahrtseinrichtungen (CAW) in 1891 reflects the same conviction.[15] This organisation, based in Berlin, and founded with the support of government ministers like Freiherr von Berlepsch, brought together reformers like Albrecht and employers like Heinrich Freese concerned to provide well-equipped facilities for the lower paid. The first conference of the organisation, Die Verbesserung der Wohnungen in April 1892, focussed specifically on the contribution that could be made to the problems of housing by the employer.

The aims of the employer in providing for the welfare of his employees must be to ensure that they remain efficient and contented at their work; only thus can he secure both productive and willing helpers. To achieve this goal, a number of considerations must be satisfied which are both external and internal to the mind and the emotions of the individual. But above all the employer must attempt to create a healthy setting for family life. This is the first consideration in providing both for the worker's own welfare and happiness and for that of his children, the coming generation. Of central and critical importance for the development of family life is the manner in which the worker's family is lodged. Thus the concern for the working man's home must be one of the most important social duties of the employer.[16]

Again the achievements of Krupp exemplified the response of private employers to the need to provide for an expanding workforce. The company had built nothing since 1873 and during the 1870s the workforce had actually contracted; however, by the early 1890s production had increased and the workforce had expanded to the point where new housing was again required. In 1893 construction started on the Altenhof, Alfredshof and Friedrichshof estates and by 1910 a further 2,406 dwellings had been added to the 3,659 built before 1891. Forced to build housing of necessity, the quality of the company's accommodation was high. The terms on which this housing was rented were clearly better than equivalent housing on the open market in Essen at the time and, whatever reservations workers may have had about being tied to their employer, Finanzrath Gussman, speaking for the firm, could claim with pride in 1892 that demand for this kind of housing had always exceeded supply.[17] The regulations that governed the use of the company housing were comprehensive but not obviously more draconian than those for similar developments elsewhere;[18] in many respects the regulations resembled those enforced since the early nineteenth century by the Prussian mining authorities. Indeed in some respects Krupp was more generous than other employers and the housing was certainly of the highest quality.

By the end of the 1890s Krupp's achievement was no longer the lone example of employer-built housing as it had been in the 1860s and 1870s; other companies were building substantial numbers of dwellings for rent, notably BASF (509 dwellings), the Farbwerk Meister, Lucius and Bruning (442 dwellings) and Villeroy and Bosch (324 dwellings).[19] In most cases not only was the quality of housing high for low rents, but the provision of housing was complemented by other facilities such as wash houses, bath houses, co-operative shops, schools and sometimes even medical facilities.[20]

Parallel to the expansion in the volume of housing being built by private enterprise was the increase in the amount of housing built by government at all levels for its own employees. Already during the 1870s various government departments such as the railways at Reich and state level had followed the lead of the mining authorities and started to build housing for their employees in areas where suitable housing was not already available.[21] After 1886 this development gathered strength and in the mid-1890s there was an increase in the funds allocated by government at all levels to the housing of those in government service. However insignificant the contribution in real terms, government could now point to these measures as evidence of a willingness to act on the housing question. But the achievements of the Reich reflect the limits of this new initiative. Little was built except by those departments, such as postal services, railways and forestry, which needed to provide housing in districts where this was not readily available.

From 1901 onwards, the Reich government had also set aside additional funds, the *Wohnungsfürsorgefonds*, in the budget of the Ministry of the Interior, to contribute towards the cost of housing Reich employees.[22] By 1903, 10 million Marks had been earmarked for this purpose and, although threatened in 1911, the annual estimate was actually doubled in 1912. In judging the scale of this contribution, however, it is important to remember that the annual allocation was not sufficient to cover the construction costs of even 500 dwellings.

The contributions of the individual states to the housing of their employees was of comparable scale. In Prussia too, the initiative to expand the provision of housing for government employees dates from the mid-1890s, when the law of 13 August 1895 established the principle of allocating an amount for housing those in government service.[23] But again the volume of housing built remained pitifully small;

the funds were sufficient to provide, at most, for the construction of 2,500 dwellings.[24]

Other states were also preparing similar arrangements for their employees by the turn of the century.[25] From 1900 onwards, Bavaria, for example, had greatly extended the system of housing its railway employees by not only providing housing in areas where no alternative housing could be found, as it had before 1899, but by also providing loans to non-profit organisations. By 1903, 5·4 million Marks had been spent to provide 1,266 dwellings, enough for 19% of all railway employees, and similar provision was made by other ministries. From 1902 onwards, as a result of a circular by the State Treasury, limited funds were also made more generally available to government employees as in Prussia.

Finally, from the mid-1890s municipal government became involved in providing housing for city employees, although this development was not widespread. In Berlin, for example, the proposal that the city should house its own employees was rejected by the employees themselves as creating an undesirable dependence on their employer.[26] But in other Prussian cities housing was already being provided by 1900; Albrecht cites the example of eight large cities.[27] Normally provision was only on a limited scale and then only for skilled workers in municipal enterprises such as the tramways, or the gas and electricity works. In other states, such as Bavaria, the situation appears to have been comparable.[28]

In contrast to the inactivity of most cities, there were a number which had long provided housing for their employees. But it was the work of Ulm and especially Frankfurt that attracted the attention of the reformers and was held up as an example of what could be achieved. Municipal support of this form for the housing of the city's own employees might appear to shade almost imperceptibly into the offering of a general subvention to the non-profit sector, a question to which we turn later. But the fact that the city was assisting the housing of its own employees, albeit indirectly, appears to have been regarded as sufficient defence to counter any charge of an indiscriminate and general subsidy of non-profit housing. Indeed with first Miquel and then Adickes as *Oberbürgermeister*, Frankfurt's commitment to the programme of the VfSP and its willingness to shoulder the responsibility of the employer for housing needs no explanation.[29] The city first became engaged in the provision for its own employees in 1889; by 1915 it had provided 467 dwellings. But in addition to this direct form of provision, the city was also very active in encouraging various forms of non-profit organisations to provide housing for its employees. By 1914 the city had made very substantial loans to the non-profit housing sector, largely for the housing of its own employees. Nearly every non-profit organisation had received some support from the city for this purpose. The Volks Spar- und Bauverein, for example, the largest co-operative in the city, had received loans amounting to about 25% of its total capital from the city, sufficient to finance about 250 of its 927 dwellings. In addition the city purchased shares, provided guarantees for payment of interest on loans and, from 1900, provided leasehold land for non-profit organisations.

The value of the contribution of employers' housing

How did the housing reformers view the provision of housing by the employer? On the one hand, there were those who denounced it as a means of serving his own interests – in rural areas a necessary part of investment in manufacturing; on the other, there were those who still regarded it as a form of altruism inspired by the desire to improve the lot of the worker. On balance, however, it appears that most reformers accepted that employers acted largely out of self-interest, but considered that they took a large enough view of their own interests to realise that a contented, well-housed and healthy workforce was a good long-term investment. Opening the debate at the CAW conference in 1892, Fritz Kalle expressed a view that reflected the opinions held widely in reforming circles: 'The aim of the employer in working for the welfare of his workers must be to ensure that his workers are efficient and happy in their work so that he finds them not only productive but willing.'[30] Twenty years later Eberstadt still regarded employers' housing as a bridge between employer and employee: 'from a mere tool of the employer it had become a social and a social-political achievement of consequence'.[31] Contemporaries such as Kalle, Albrecht and other reformers accepted the need to harness the self-interest of the employer to raise the standards of housing. Kalle strongly emphasised the benefit to the employer of helping his workers in this way: 'This must not be taken to imply in any way that this approach is uneconomic; far from it. Experience has shown us that, both in direct economic terms and indirectly, the factory owner derives a substantial benefit from this kind of policy'.[32] In arguing this case the reformers were concerned to win employers to their view of the value of good housing and to pillory the large numbers of employers who did nothing. To reformers such as Kalle the paternalistic concern of the employer was a healthy development by comparison with the days of the *Manchesterschule* in the 1860s when dealings between factory owners and their employees were harshly and impersonally fixed by the market alone. For those urging the case for this form of housing, the employer was cast in the role of a father providing for his family:

The whole way of life of the employer must justify his position of authority, as does the father in his family; the way in which he exercises his powers must awaken in his inferiors the belief that he has their interests at heart. If this feeling can be created, it will inevitably lead to mutual affection; in place of the consciousness of the separate classes, a sense of unity will prevail. The acceptance of authority will be willingly achieved, a triumph without bitterness; the ground will thus be prepared for the improving activities of the employer.[33]

To Kalle, as to many reformers, there was nothing to be deplored in the paternalistic way in which Krupp pursued his self-interest. There was nothing inconsistent in building housing of the highest quality and controlling it with 'firm' management.

However, the employer had to weigh the benefits of providing housing for rent or for home ownership through a system of loans. The attraction of home ownership to the employer was summarised by Kalle as follows: it might not be cheaper but he could expand his workforce, though not always as fast as if he built for himself, without the burden of planning and administering the construction. Most important, he was freed from the problem of the management and maintenance of rented property. To the worker there were also benefits. He could choose the design of his own home and arrange the costs to suit his own pocket. To the reformers it appeared that society, too, would gain; as the worker became a home owner, he joined the stable ranks of those with a stake in the existing order of society.

But against these benefits had to be set a number of substantial disadvantages. Where the employer provided housing for home-ownership, the most important was the inexperience of most workers when faced with the problems of building. Many employers might give help by providing designs for 'model' dwellings or the services of the company's surveyor.[34] But many feared that, if construction costs rose and the worker found himself in difficulties, the house would pass into the ownership of an outsider beyond the employer's control, although in practice this concern appears to have been largely unwarranted.[35]

Compared with the system of home-ownership the risk of renting accommodation appeared less. Frequently this form of housing offered the advantage of high quality and low rents. The annual rents quoted by Gussman for Krupp's housing look surprisingly low:[36] in 1892 the rent for a two-room dwelling on the Westend or Nordhof sites (admittedly built originally as temporary or emergency accommodation) was between 60 and 90 M per year; on other sites it was between 90 and 109 M; for a three-room dwelling it was 120–162 M and for a four-room dwelling, 180–200 M. Schmohl reported that at these rents the income from renting was insufficient to cover the cost of repairs and maintenance and management so that interest and amortisation charges were carried in effect as a subsidy by the firm.[37] Not surprisingly, at these rents the housing was much cheaper than that available in the rest of Essen: In 1903 a Kruppianer paid only approximately 14% of his income on housing while those renting on the open market with an income of up to 600 M paid between 25–30% and those with incomes between 660 and 1,050 paid 20–25% of their income.[38] But the burden of management and maintenance, with all the friction between employer and employee that this entailed, was greater. Furthermore it was obvious, even to those in reforming circles, that many employees deeply resented the dependency on the employer that was forced on them by renting 'works' housing. Nowhere was this dependence of the employee more painfully obvious than in the rent contract specifying the terms of tenure with all its restrictions, particularly the grounds on which the worker might have to vacate his dwelling.[39] On Krupp's estates no tenant might offer goods for sale from his house, only lodgers who were employees of the factory were allowed and there was some attempt to restrict overcrowding; surprisingly, however, on the cottage estates tenants were allowed to keep pigs, goats, hens and rabbits. Most important were the grounds on which a tenant could be ejected; if, for any reason, the worker ceased to be employed in the factory, he was required to leave his house; equally, persistent disturbance of his neighbours, or other forms of anti-social behaviour, could also lead to eviction. All the main estates had supervisors who had the power to report the rowdy and disruptive tenants. Nor were these regulations left unenforced. In 1889, 21 families out of 3,700 were evicted for ill-discipline; however, only 12 families were evicted in 1890, and only 10 in 1891.[40] Displeasure to the employer at work for either disciplinary or political reasons, even the membership of a trade union, could lead to the loss of employment and thus loss of the worker's home. If the worker died and his son was not employed by the same employer, the widow was forced to choose between remarrying another employee, accepting a lodger nominated by the company or moving out altogether. In some firms eviction followed on the same day, in most firms, however, 14 days notice was given.[41] Companies allowing a period of 6 weeks between the worker leaving their employment and requiring him to leave his employer's house were viewed as exceptional. Significantly Krupp increased the period before eviction from 14 days to 12 weeks on some estates, at least by 1892, apparently in keeping with local practice.[42] No doubt it is desirable that the myth of Krupp as a benign employer altruistically serving the interests of his workers should be exploded. But we must also remember that the standards by which Krupp's housing was judged were different from our own; the terms on which accommodation was rented on the open market were harsh, as Flesch pointed out,[43] and will appear unbelievably so to those accustomed to the protected tenancies and 'fair' rents of today.

Yet even to some contemporaries, this threat of eviction, though justified, undermined much of the good that the employer could achieve in providing good housing. To Albrecht, for example, the statements made by employers who claimed to value the salubrious home as the means of nurturing and strengthening family life conflicted openly with the ease with which the family could be evicted:

All beneficial influences, which an ordered way of living, inseparable from homely comforts, effects upon a worker's family will be seen as no more than illusion if they cannot be matched by a degree of permanance; if the worker is compelled without ado to change his home when he changes his job then there can be no question of this necessary permanence.[44]

This degree of dependence was damaging, whatever other benefits the worker might gain through housing provided by his employer.

To the employers the quality of housing provided by many employers was a model for general emulation and the scale on which employers could build was impressive. By 1898 Albrecht estimated that 143,049 dwellings had been built, sufficient to provide dwellings for 18 in every 1,000 workers in the Reich at the time, a remarkable achievement.[45] Neither the scale nor the quality of this achievement could be ignored. But how relevant was this form of housing to the reformers' view of the housing problem? By far the greater part of the housing built by the employers was in rural areas where no alternative accommodation existed; even if the reformers could accept the paternalistic spirit in which the housing was offered and the manner in which it was administered, this form of housing offered no real hope of improving the housing conditions in the cities, the reformers' central concern.

By 1900, the emphasis on the contribution of the employer, stressed so strongly a decade before, attracted less interest. In the VfSP's review of the housing problem in 1900, housing by the private employer might still be welcomed, but now the value of this form of assistance for the housing problem in the cities was recognised as negligible. The government might be eager to advertise the volume of housing that it was building as an employer to distract attention from its record on housing reform in general. But the scale of government achievement in the cities, the states and the Reich was limited; it no longer met the demands of the housing reformers for more far-reaching action. For many workers employed by small employers, for the self-employed and for the large number in casual or occasional employment, not to mention the problems of the unemployed, this form of housing could provide no solution. To solve the problems of housing in large cities, other alternatives were vitally needed.

10

◇◇

Non-profit housing before 1890

In Germany the search for a way of providing housing without appealing to the profit motive of private enterprise or the self-interest of the employer dates from the first days of the movement for housing reform. The reformers' first initiatives had been bound up with attempts to launch a non-profit housing society in the early 1840s, and the foundation of the Berliner gemeinnützige Baugesellschaft in 1847 had done something to draw attention to the housing problem in Berlin. But important though it was, the BgB did not provide an enduring paradigm. For inspiration for later ventures, reformers turned to other sources, particularly to England where the work of the limited dividend housing companies and the achievement of the building societies exemplified alternative forms of non-profit housing.

By 1900, the distinctions between these different forms of non-profit organisation appeared to be of only limited significance. To Albrecht, reviewing the different kinds of organisation providing housing, it was natural to include the work of joint stock companies, limited liability companies, housing trusts, housing societies and co-operatives, under a single heading.[1] Earlier, however, the differences between these various types were regarded as having greater significance. During the first debate on the housing question in the late 1850s and the 1860s, the distinctions corresponded to very different views of the way in which social issues should be approached. On the one hand, there were those like Huber and others associated with the *Arbeiterfreund* who urged the responsibility of the propertied classes for the less fortunate and campaigned for assistance 'from above' to better their lot. On the other hand there were those associated with the Kongress deutsche Volkswirte (KdV) who championed the case for self-help and economic individualism. For the former, limited dividend companies such as the BgB appeared as the most appropriate means of providing housing; to the latter, the housing co-operative, or the *Baugenossenschaft*, was the chosen vehicle of progress.

In this search for different forms of organisation to provide housing, the achievements of the housing reformers in England were an obvious source of inspiration. The *Arbeiterfreund* carried articles on both the English limited dividend housing companies and the co-operative building societies from the late 1850s on,[2] and the *Vierteljahrschrift für*

217

217

Volkswirtschaft und Kulturgeschichte was enthusiastic in its coverage of the work of the English building societies.[3] The English limited dividend companies offered an obvious example for emulation; the building societies were an equally potent example of what could be achieved through 'self-help'. Nevertheless, the relationship between developments in the two countries must be viewed with caution. In England, the limited dividend companies built housing for rent, while the building societies built primarily for home-ownership; in Germany, however, the first company, the BgB, was intended from the start to encourage home-ownership, while many of the co-operatives built for rent.

The choice of the joint stock limited dividend company as a form for non-profit housing in the early days was made on essentially pragmatic, not ideological, grounds. Although the English building society was an attractive paradigm, the difficulty of establishing a co-operative at this time in Germany was considerable because it possessed no firmly defined legal status.[4] However, legislation already provided for the joint stock company so that establishing such a company was relatively straight-forward, and therefore attractive to housing reformers. But, although the reasons for choosing the company form were thus essentially practical, the form of the company, particularly where dividends were limited, was soon associated, as in England, with 'help from above'. This was to result in a separation between company and the co-operative approach which during the 1860s came to correspond to an ideological division and which was to last through until the mid-1880s. Although this distinction was increasingly irrelevant from the turn of the century onwards, the mood of the debate in the 1860s can only be grasped if we consider the development of the company before 1886 in separation from that of the co-operative.

The non-profit housing companies before 1886

During the 1860s most members of the KdV, and even part of the membership of the CVWaK, remained hostile to the work of the limited dividend companies. At the KdV's conference in 1866, the limited dividend company was attacked as a thinly disguised form of charity: 'certainly housing associations and companies need no justification; but they are completely misguided if they see their work, or like it to be seen, as being of a charitable nature'.[5] However, true to his belief in the need for assistance 'from above', Huber strongly supported this form of organisation and in *Concordia* he called for immediate action by companies operating with a limit on dividends along English lines.[6] Applauding the work of the Society for Improving the Conditions of the Labouring Classes and the Metropolitan Association in London, he drew a clear distinction between housing provided on this basis and charity which he denounced as an unacceptable basis for social reform. In his submission, 'Über die geeignetsten Massregeln' prepared for the KdV conference. Huber again pressed this line of attack.[7] He championed the benefits of the joint stock company with limited dividend as the ideal means of building housing for the working classes, presenting this as a transitional form, necessary in the current situation before the formation of true co-operatives. The limitation of dividends was a particularly contentious issue. In opposition to the views of most members of the KdV, Huber stressed the need for a limitation on dividends paid to share holders in order to be able to reduce the costs of the housing they supplied. To Huber this was not charity. He drew the essential distinction between the work of the limited dividend companies and charity in terms of the level of dividend paid on shares. If this was reasonable – Huber regarded 4% as reasonable – then the company was not simply offering charity.

However, despite the publicity given to the BgB, and the work of various foreign housing companies, the growth of the limited dividend companies in Germany was slow. This is clearly revealed in the discussion of the achievements of housing reform in the *Arbeiterfreund* in 1865, particularly in the report 'Bericht über die in Deutschland bestehenden Baugesellschaften' by Brämer. In this survey he could find only eleven active limited dividend housing companies;[8] all those for which information was available had been founded after the BgB, the majority in the 1860s, and all were of limited scale, having built fewer than 100 dwellings.

Though larger than most, the Frankfurter gemeinnützige Baugesellschaft (FgB) illustrates the work of these companies during the 1860s and 1870s.[9] The company had been founded towards the end of 1860 by a group of Frankfurt am Main reformers led by Dr Georg Varrentrap, one of the prominent figures in sanitary reform at the time, to provide healthy and well-built dwellings 'for rent to members of the lower classes of good reputation'. The company was to pay a maximum dividend of 4% and provision was also made to enable the tenants to buy their dwellings as easily as possible, though not on terms below the cost price.

By the end of 1873 the company had built 53 buildings containing 235 dwellings and accommodating 1027 people. The rents for the dwellings were claimed by Varrentrap to be between 30 and 50% *below* the rents of comparable quality on the open market. But even so, the company's rents were still sufficient to cover not only a 4% return on capital, but also to produce a further return of $1\frac{1}{2}\%$ for repairs, supervision, management, and other such expenses . In his review of the company's activities in the *VföG* in 1874 Varrentrap emphasised the achievements of the company's work and its contribution to the housing market in Frankfurt:[10] the benefit to working-class morality, the benefits to the health of the community, the benefits to employers of a stable well-housed workforce. He also stressed that it was only through the work of such a company that the less well paid artisan could gain access to such housing and that it reminded the more affluent classes of their duty to help their less fortunate fellow-citizens. Dividing the city's population into twelve parts. Varrentrap suggested that the role of the company was to provide housing for the eleventh, rather than for the poorest, the twelfth part. Not only had the eleventh just sufficient income to be able to afford the minimum of sanitary accommodation, but there was the added benefit that, by providing new housing for this group, better accommodation would eventually become available to the poorest by a process of 'filtering' or 'levelling up'.

No other city in Germany could match the volume of non-profit housing built in Frankfurt before 1886 where the FgB and the Frankfurter Bau- und Sparverein,[11] a second non-profit company, had together built over 600 dwellings. Many large cities remained without a limited dividend housing company even after the mid-1880s.[12] In Berlin the combined achievement before 1886 of the BgB and the Alexandra Stiftung totalled less than 450 dwellings and no new non-profit organisation, housing company, society or trust was established between the foundation of the Alexandra Stiftung in 1856 and the mid-1880s.[13] By 1886 the achievement of the non-profit companies in Germany lagged far behind the work of those in England.

The origins of the housing co-operatives

Compared with the uneven and often disappointing achievement of the limited dividend companies, how effectively did the co-operative housing movement meet the hopes of many housing reformers for a substantial increase in the volume of non-profit housing before 1890? In the field of co-operative housing, as with the limited dividend companies, the example of England was of crucial importance: the achievement of the English building societies led German reformers to hope that the *Baugenossenschaft* might flourish on German soil too.

In Germany the ideas of co-operation and association were first linked to the programme of savings banks and to production co-operatives in the writings of Liedke and Huber in the early 1840s.[14] But the first systematic exercise in co-operative self-help is generally linked with Schulze-Delitzsch's work in Delitzsch between 1848 and 1850.[15]

The distinctions between the *Vorschussvereine*, or self-help loan associations, set up by Schulze-Delitzsch and the variety of similar associations that already existed in Berlin by the same time are important for a general understanding of the parallels and distinctions between the development of English and German attitudes to the co-operative. Crüger suggests that these early associations in Berlin were really nothing more than instruments of charity through which the needy were given access to money in the form of interest-free loans of indefinite duration.[16] This type of association, drawing its inspiration and leadership from 'above', was very different from the friendly societies and burial clubs in England which, true to the vision of self-help, were largely made up of small groups of artisans and even unskilled workers associating for mutual advantage.

To Schulze-Delitzsch and to the members of the KdV, this English form of co-operative with its emphasis on self-help was greatly preferable. In pamphlets published in the early 1850s and in his book *Vorschuss-Vereine als Volks-banken* of 1855, Schulze-Delitzsch set out the basis for a co-operative movement, which, like that in England, was to be based on self-help and mutual interest.[17] The *Vorschussverein* that he proposed for Delitzsch was to attract capital by paying commercial, or at least near commercial, rates of interest, often as high as 10% per annum, and those seeking to take advantage of the credit offered by the association would in turn pay to service the loan.[18]

The success of Schulze-Delitzsch's ideas in Delitzsch and in Eilenburg were followed up during the 1850s by the founding of similar associations elsewhere.[19] By 1860, the application of these ideas in practice and the declaration of support by the KdV for Schulze-Delitzsch's programme at the first congress in Gotha in 1858 had established in Germany a co-operative movement, based on 'self-help and mutuality' with Schulze-Delitzsch as its leader.[20]

The debate over the form of the co-operative before 1867

With the growth of the popularity of the co-operative idea in general, it was only natural that this principle should soon be applied to housing too. In the search for a suitable form for the housing co-operative, German observers turned enthusiastically to England for inspiration; initially, however, the differences between the different English forms and the simple idea of the *Baugenossenschaft* led to some confusion.[21] In the early English terminating societies the members of the society joined in order to build and the later distinction between borrowing and lending members was non-existent, or at least much less evident. In this form the building society answered to its name and did indeed exemplify the application of the principles of mutual co-operative and self-help. It was this form that German observers found most immediately recognisable; the *Baugenossenschaft*, too, was centrally concerned with building housing for ownership by its members. But to German eyes the more advanced form of English permanent society appeared essentially as a co-operative for raising and paying mortgages, or as a form of savings bank lending on the security of housing. As Sax explained: 'The English *building societies* are not at all what the name "building society" or "co-operative building society" might lead one to believe, they are better described in German as "house purchase societies"...The "building society" is for one part of its membership a savings bank, for the other a loan association.'[22]

However, even in the mid-1860s, the term *Baugenossenschaft* was still used in a very flexible manner. It normally implied something like a terminating society and suggested reliance on mutual self-help, but it was used indiscriminately by writers on housing reform like Brämer who used it in an article in the *Arbeiterfreund*, 'Die nützliche Baugenossen-schaften in England', to describe any form of non-profit organisation.[23]

However by this time it was already clear that the *Baugenossenschaften* were to develop away from the form of philanthropic organisations such as the BgB, along the lines envisaged by Schulze-Delitzsch in his programme for co-operative action. At the annual conferences of groups such as the KdV. the Vereinstag deutscher Arbeitervereine and the Vereinstag deutscher Erwerbs- und Wirtschaftsgenossenschaften, there was strong support for these developments.[24] Progress in this direction was further supported by a number of influential publications, particularly Parisius' discussion of the co-operative and his review of the progress of the various non-profit organisations in Germany, 'Die auf dem Prinzip der Selbsthülfe beruhende Baugenossenschaften', and F. A. Lange's 'Jedermann Hauseigenthümer' (1865) which Dorothea Jacobi identified as one of the most influential publications on the subject in Germany.[25] The book emphasised the debt of the German movement to English ideas and was itself closely modelled on Theodor Jones' book *Every Man His Own Landlord, or How to Buy a House with its Own Rent* (1863).[26]

Much of the material on the co-operative published before 1865 was just a documentation of developments in England, France and Germany, often in rather general form. Neither Huber nor Brämer, for example, two of the most frequent contributors on the subject, said very much about the detailed form of the co-operative, although it must have been evident by then from English experience that it was very much these 'details' of management that decided between the success or failure of a society. But here at last were publications which actually explained how to start and run a housing co-operative. Lange in his book attacked the problems of running the co-operative on a day-to-day basis, rather than questions of high principle. He set out crucial details such as the size of the monthly payments, and the current and future values of shares. Parisius' ideas too were widely influential on the form of the co-operative. Rather than building tenements for rent, he argued that the self-help co-operative should concentrate on the supply of cottage housing for home-ownership. This, he concluded, on the basis of an accurate understanding of the workings of both the terminating and the permanent societies in England, was best done by the latter type with as large a membership as possible. By advocating the permanent form he hoped to gain advantages from the membership of those who joined to save, and thus to overcome both the problems of the long lead-time required to assemble capital before building, and the difficulties created should members leave the co-operative, a problem that was almost insoluble with a limited membership. In addition he urged that co-operatives should have the power to borrow money for building – a right only granted to the English societies in 1856 – and that such loans should be secured on the liability of individual members of the co-operative committee. Much of the value of Parisius' account was due to his willingness to discuss the details of administration and management: ways of resolving the problems of allocating houses to members, the payment of the dividend, the dissolution of the co-operative and other practical difficulties.

The result of these publications and debates on the housing co-operatives in the mid-1860s was to promote a wave of public interest in the subject. According to Vossberg, it was Parisius' report that really convinced Schulze-Delitzsch of the enormous potential of applying the principle of co-operation to housing.[27] Engels' attack in *Zur Wohnungsfrage* on the expansion of the co-operative movement can be seen as a measure of the co-operative movement's new-found success.

But despite this new level of interest in self-help housing associations, the number of successful applications of the co-operative principle remained very limited. The only *Baugenossenschaft* founded on self-help principles that Parisius could find in Germany was the Häuserbau-Genossenschaft von Schiffszimmern in Hamburg.[28] Founded in 1862 at the instigation of C. F. Balzer, director of the Hamburger Volksbank, the co-operative had built 48 houses on land leased from the state for artisans and craftsmen employed in the shipyards. But the difficulties encountered here were typical of those facing the co-operatives in general. Most serious was the difficulty of raising capital for building because of the lack of security for a mortgage. In Hamburg the problem was only overcome when Balzer was able to intervene, obtaining the necessary loan from five local business men on the future security of the houses themselves.

The root of these problems was the anomalous legal position of the co-operative, an issue emphasised by Parisius: 'Without the rights of a corporation or the status of a legal entity, not even possessing the rights of a trading company, the co-operative, as determined by the common agreement of the law of every German state, can neither acquire nor sell property, nor sue or be sued.'[29]

With neither a clear status nor any limit on liability, the obstacles to securing capital seemed insuperable. These difficulties did of course face co-operatives of all types, but for the housing co-operative the problem was greater than for most because of the high value of the 'goods' in which they 'traded' and because of the length of time over which it was necessary to spread this activity. The early co-operatives had been set up under the provisions of the Allgemeine Landrecht which, though adequate for many, did not suit the housing co-operative which needed to borrow money on a larger scale than most; to wait for the gradual increase in capital through weekly contributions was too slow to permit anything but the most limited activity.

The need to redefine the legal status of the co-operative was, however urgent, not particular to the housing co-operatives alone. The problem had already been considered by Schulze-Delitzsch at the beginning of the 1860s. At the annual conferences of the Verband Schulze-Delitzschen Genossenschaften in Mainz (1864) and Stettin (1865) the question of reform had been pressed.[30] But it was not until 1867 that legal recognition was at last granted in Prussia. Although this was rapidly followed by recognition in a number of separate states, it was not until the law of 4 July 1868 that legal recognition was finally granted to the co-operative in all the states of the North German Bund.

At last the co-operatives were considered as legal entities, a right already conferred on the English building societies in 1836 and strengthened in 1864. They now enjoyed the right to own property and sue although the question of liability still remained unsolved. For many forms of co-operative this was not an issue of pressing importance and even for the housing co-operatives it must have appeared a small obstacle in the optimistic climate of 1868. Their newly acquired legal status and, along with it, the ability to borrow capital must have appeared a great step forward. With enthusiasm for the co-operative movement in liberal circles still high the prospect for the co-operatives looked bright.

The development of the *Baugenossenschaften* 1868–89

As so often in the history of housing reform, this promise was not immediately realised. Indeed during the next 20 years the fortunes of the housing co-operative declined rather than advanced. Many of these difficulties were a product of the economic climate of the period. Both the boom economy of the early 1870s, with rising construction and land costs, and the stagnant economy of the following depression years when it was difficult to attract members and capital, presented the co-operatives with real difficulties.

But there were other reasons too for the slowing down of the rate of co-operative house building. The rights won in 1868 were important, but the liability of the individual members of the co-operatives still remained unlimited. This was largely as a result of Schulze-Delitzsch's insistence on the mutual nature of the co-operative. He argued that by leaving the liability unlimited, each and every member remained responsible for the fate of the co-operative and the activities of the rest of its members, thus avoiding a form of organisation with a few leaders and a large inactive membership. But for the housing co-operative this did nothing to remove the substantial disincentive of financial responsibility for those wishing to form a co-operative and borrow capital from outside. The capital necessary to start a co-operative could be obtained by borrowing only if, true to the ideal of self-help and mutuality, all the members accepted collective responsibility for the loan. Until this question of liability was overcome, the financing of the housing co-operative would remain an impediment to growth.

The dangers of the situation before 1889 are illustrated by the tragic saga of the Pforzheimer Baugenossenschaft.[31] Founded in 1872 with a membership of nearly 200 workers, the co-operative built 42 houses for owner occupation. But with the depression which hit the jewellery business, the main employer in the city, many of the purchasers were unable to keep up the repayments on their houses. In 1876 no dividend was issued on paid-up shares which at this time had a face value of 600 M. In the next year the whole membership was faced with the daunting task of paying a supplementary levy of 253 M to cover the increasing interest charges on the co-operative's capital, in the meantime the value of the co-operative's assets fell to below half their original cost price. But worse was still to come. In 1879 it was resolved at a stormy meeting to sell the houses which had been repossessed from owners unable to continue their monthly repayments. The sale took place, but at a striking loss and resulted in a further levy of 699 M per member being raised.

But even this was not sufficient to right the situation. In 1881 the co-operative was faced with collapse, a situation complicated by the decision of 137 members to leave the organisation. Faced with the need either to declare bankruptcy to prevent those leaving from evading their mutual responsibility, or of finding yet further funds, another management committee was appointed which, miraculously, was able together with an external committee of enquiry to persuade a number of individual members to find the necessary sum. Even so the cost of these difficulties to the individual was crippling: for a member with a paid up share of 500 m, the loss was 2,250 M, a figure equivalent to between two and three times the annual income of most members. The only consolation was that by avoiding bankruptcy the remaining 130 members were not reduced to total destitution.

This failure to limit liability and the harsh economic climate of the 1870s was identified by later champions of the co-operatives as the main barriers to growth. Plans to follow the example of the Hamburg co-operative in Karlsruhe, Freiburg im Breisgau, Munich and Mannheim had to be abandoned[32] and in Berlin, for example, a number of co-operatives, established during the first flush of enthusiasm, failed to survive the crisis of 1873/4.[33] The form of the co-operative that had evolved during the 1860s faced overwhelming difficulties in the depression years of the mid-1870s and beyond. During this period the successful co-operatives were those in which the method of acquiring capital did not involve borrowing large sums of money with all the attendant complications of liability. This problem was approached in two ways, and in both cases success depended on accumulating capital from the limited contributions of a large membership.

One way forward was suggested by the application by Christian Hansen in Flensburg from 1878[34] of the principles first tried successfully in a Danish society, the Arbejderner Byggeforening founded in 1865 in Copenhagen.[35] Central to the success of this Copenhagen society was the low weekly subscription and the large membership. Unlike the Hamburger Häuserbauverein, the Copenhagen example was indeed based on self-help. Here the capital was contributed directly by the substantial membership, not by borrowing. The entrance premium was 2 krone and the weekly contribution was fixed as low as 35 öre. Paid over a ten-year period, it gave the member a share of 20 krone; the number of these shares was limited to ten per member. Each paid-up share entitled the owner to take part in a ballot to determine the ownership of a dwelling. Those not wishing to take their chance in the ballot could choose to withdraw their savings on a monthly basis. For those leaving their savings in the co-operative there was an annual dividend paid from the remainder of the annual income after the transfer of 10% of the income to a reserve fund. The success of the organisation is indicated by the rapid growth in membership and the number of dwellings that it built. In 1867 there were already 222 members. By 1877 this had risen to 7,460 and by 1884 to 12,643; by this time the co-operative had built 523 dwellings while still paying a dividend of 90 öre on each paid-up share. But the significance of the venture for later developments lay in the speed with which the co-operative was able to build up a mass-membership without the need to contract large loans on the open market with the burden of liability for the membership.

The other approach was represented by the type of co-operative based on the principle of the 'Spar- und Bauverein'.[36] This form of society sought to combine the benefits of a savings club with the provision of housing for rent. The member paid a low premium and a low weekly contribution into a savings account and received in return a proportionate share in the benefits of the profits from renting. Once the member had saved enough for a share he was entitled to enter the ballot for a dwelling. If successful he rented a dwelling which remained the property of the society rather than acquiring the property for himself, securing a number of advantages both to the tenant and to the co-operative. The tenant was not saddled with the burdens of ownership nor tied to a particular location; the co-operative was able to avoid the dangers which so distressed housing reformers, of seeing non-profit housing sold on to the open market for private profit. Here was a new point of departure which, by reducing costs, opened up the benefits of co-operative housing to many who had previously been excluded because of the high costs of home-ownership.

The first example of this new type was the Hannover Spar- und Bauverein founded in 1885 with only 70 members.[37] The purpose of the Verein was originally to collect the weekly rents and to guarantee payments to the landlord in return for lower rents and better housing. But in the event this idea proved unacceptable to the local landlords and the association resolved instead to build housing on its own account. After bitter argument, the association declined offers of help 'from above' from local philanthropists, despite its limited membership and resources, and decided to press ahead with the purchase of a plot of land which exhausted the association's assets. But at an even more stormy meeting the members finally managed to raise enough capital from their own resources to start building. By October 1886 the first eight dwellings were ready for occupation; the Verein had survived its most difficult period. By 1891 it had built 133 dwellings and had a total membership of 1,580; by 1900 this had increased to over 3,300.

Although the early success of the Verein depended on the personal resources of what must have been a number of relatively affluent artisans, the key to its success was again the size of the membership and the small weekly contribution. Paying a contribution of 30 Pfennig per week the member was entitled to establish a savings account and to benefit from the annual dividend earned from the society's rents which generally amounted to a return of 4% on his savings. When he had

saved the 300 M necessary for a share he was then able to enter the
ballot for a dwelling. The choice of tenant for the flats was then decided
by lot and the rents were generally a third lower than the average for
similar housing in the rest of the city. Significantly the Verein only
borrowed money on mortgage to expand its activities after it had
acquired limited liability in 1889. Until that time it had been able to
operate with unlimited liability by using only the contributions of its
substantial membership.

Despite developments in Flensburg and Hanover little co-operative
housing was built before the 1890s. In Berlin the achievements of the
co-operative movement remained very limited before 1889.[38] The only
positive note was the foundation of the Berliner Baugenossenschaft in
May 1886 based on the principles of Hansen's experiment in Flensburg.[39]
In 1886, Hellwig, a Berlin builder, had approached the CVWaK with
plans to start a society on Flensburg lines in Berlin and the year after,
with assistance from Schrader and Wolgemut the co-operative was
launched. The Berliner Baugenossschschaft was, however, extremely
fortunate in its early existence in being able to secure a loan of 36,000 M
'from a generous and helpful philanthropist' at $3\frac{1}{2}\%$. This enabled it to
start building without delay. With this help it built two houses during
the first year despite having a membership of only 58. By 1887 the
membership had risen to 103 but even so its ability to build remained
restricted. Only with the introduction of limited liability in 1889 could
it secure capital from outside on a large scale and thus expand its
activities substantially.

The call for expansion of the non-profit sector

By 1886, the achievements of the non-profit sector were dishearteningly
small. The reformers' early hopes of the limited dividend companies had
clearly been disappointed, and the isolated successes of a few co-
operatives could not blind the reformers to the very limited achievements
of the movement as a whole. During the late 1870s and early 1880s
co-operative house building had actually declined. Writing in 1883,
Reichardt ended his review of co-operative housing in Germany on a
sombre note;[40] Jäger recorded that the number of societies had risen to
50 by 1879, but then fell again to only 28 in 1888 and concluded his
account by pointing out the painful fact that by 1888 the movement
had only built 110 dwellings in the whole of Germany.[41] This meagre
achievement was due in part to the general down turn of the economy
after the early 1870s. But it also reflected the problems, particular to
the housing co-operative, which we have already identified: the lack
of any restriction in the liability of the membership and the resulting
difficulties in borrowing capital.

However at the VfSP conference in Frankfurt, a vigorous call was
made to reverse this sorry state of affairs. As a necessary complement to
demands for tighter regulation of housing, the Verein agreed to call for
a substantial increase in the volume of housing built by employers and

by the non-profit sector. Now in contrast to the prevailing lethargy of the 1870s, there was a recognition of the need for urgent and incisive action. The notion of providing housing through charity remained as unacceptable as ever, but the old suspicion of the activities of the limited dividend companies as little more than charity was at last replaced by an unequivocal demand for the propertied classes to discharge their duty towards the less fortunate members of society. The limited dividend companies provided the ideal vehicle to carry forward these new hopes.

At the Frankfurt conference both Miquel and Schmoller urged the case for the company with great vigour, demonstrating the help it could offer in housing the less well paid as a natural complement to the co-operative with its better-paid membership. Looking to English examples, Miquel exhorted the companies to take on a more active role in building new housing.[42] Schmoller was even more emphatic about the need for help from above: attacking the feeble German record of 'vegetating lethargy' in this field, he urged his fellow countrymen to match the English example:

Can we in Germany not match this achievement because we are not yet fallen into such a desperate situation as already exists in London and the great English manufacturing cities?... Now is the time for us to tackle this matter on a large scale, with plenty of capital and with architects of the highest ability. There are few more pressing tasks which face us; in our fight against the degradation of our labouring classes, the crippling increases in the costs of housing and the unhealthy level of rents in our large cities, the founding of large associations and companies, firmly based on humanitarian values, offers the easiest and surest remedy.[43]

Nor was there any loss of interest in the co-operative. There was no longer the same absolute faith in the value of 'self-help' as a panacea for social problems, the hope that the mass of the working classes could finance their own housing ceased to command serious interest. But housing reformers still looked to the co-operative to fulfil an important role, and after the mid-1880s the terms of this contribution were more carefully defined than in the 1860s. Schmoller's views were typical of many members of the VfSP and other housing reformers by the mid-1880s. His assessment of the difficulties facing the co-operative movement was realistic: he recognised the problems of raising capital and the difficulty of unlimited liability. Yet for certain types of families, 'an elite of the working class,...the industrious small workshop master, the foreman and the clerk', he argued that the co-operative had an important, if restricted role.[44]

Nor was the VfSP alone in pressing for a vigorous and rapid expansion of the non-profit sector, particularly the work of the limited dividend companies. The CVWaK showed keen interest in the VfSP's proposals and members of the Berliner Lokalverein founded the Verein zur Verbesserung der kleinen Wohnungen in 1888 to provide more housing for the lower paid in response to the call made by Miquel and Schmoller.[45] The programme of the VfSP was also taken up by the Deutscher Verein für Armenpflege und Wohltätigkeit (DVfAW) which debated at length during the late 1880s and early 1890s the possibility of founding a limited dividend housing company to provide housing for the lower paid.[46] Similar ideas were debated by the Verband katholischer Industrieller und Arbeiterfreunde, a body based in the west around Aachen and München-Gladbach with close links to the Zentrum party and big business. At the general meeting in 1888 Franz Brandts had proposed that the Verband should attack the problem in ways similar to those urged by the VfSP: legislation to control the use of existing housing, balanced by an increase in the volume provided by employers and the non-profit sector, particularly by an expansion of the work of the limited dividend housing companies.[47]

The attention focussed on the housing problem by the VfSP's enquiry and the Verein's call for an increase in the supply of new housing did much to revitalise interest in the non-profit housing movement. In Berlin evidence of this new sense of purpose can be seen in the foundation of a number of limited dividend housing companies and housing co-operatives in the late 1880s.[48] But the great expansion of the non-profit movement in the 1890s was dependent above all on resolving the problem that had plagued both the limited dividend companies and the co-operatives from the start: the supply of capital. It is the resolution of this question with government assistance and the related, and increasingly contentious, issue of government intervention that dominates the debate on the non-profit sector after 1890.

11

◇◇

Non-profit housing after 1890

Shortage of capital was recognised as the greatest single barrier to the expansion of the non-profit sector for which housing reformers had been calling since the mid-1880s. Hopes that limited dividend companies would attract sufficient funds to make a real impact on the housing problem could no longer be seriously entertained. Equally the growth of the co-operatives lagged far behind that of the building societies in England. Despite societies based on the Flensburg and Hanover models, the unlimited liability of the individual member still acted as a deterrent to investment and barred the way to any large scale expansion.

Neither 'self-help' nor assistance 'from above' had proved sufficient to create a healthy non-profit sector. However, was there now a possibility that government might be induced to go beyond the mere regulation of housing, as demanded by the VfSP and the VföG, and offer assistance to the housing companies and co-operatives? In reforming circles this possibility attracted growing interest in the late 1880s and early 1890s and centred in particular on expanding the use of the funds held by the regional insurance boards, set up under the invalid and accident insurance legislation of the 1880s, to provide capital for building working-class housing.

The possibility of using the funds of the regional insurance boards was first established by the Invalidity and Old Age Insurance Act of 1890.[1] To judge from the debate in the Reichstag on this issue in 1889, it would appear that this was not, at the time, regarded as an important innovation and certainly not as sanctioning a major extension of government activity into the supply of cheap housing.[2] The inclusion of these provisions, which appeared almost accidental, was made as a result of a proposal by Karl Schrader, a member of the Freisinnige Vereinigung, of the CVWaK and also of the management committee of the Berliner Baugenossenschaft. During the second reading of the Invalid and Accident Insurance Bill Schrader had urged the use of the funds for the benefit of the working classes and had included among the possible uses for these funds, 'as an example, the building of workers' housing'. This was a problem with which he was already familiar through this work on the committee of the Berliner Baugenossenschaft which in 1886 had encountered great difficulty in raising money for a development in Cöpenick, being dismissed as too small a

230

project by the big banks and viewed with mistrust by the small banks.[3] Despite the subsequent importance of the measure, little attention was paid to Schrader's proposal during the debate; its acceptance was readily agreed at the urging of Staatssekretär Karl Heinrich von Boetticher, the government spokesman and himself probably sympathetic to the problem of workers' housing,[4] as a measure which might be of value in addressing the problems of housing. It was not regarded as extending the role of government; indeed, Schrader presented the idea as a means of strengthening the co-operative tradition of self-help, arguing that the insurance contribution paid by the working man, though administered by the State, should be used for his own benefit.

Gradually, from 1891 onwards when the law came into effect, funds from this source, at lower rates of interest than were available from commercial sources, were lent to non-profit housing associations to build working-class housing subject always to a maximum limit on the lending by any one board to a quarter of its funds. By 1891 it appears that the non-profit housing associations in the Rhineland were already able to borrow money from the regional board based in Düsseldorf, largely as a result of the urging by the *Oberpräsident* and the *Regierungspräsidenten* in the province.[5] The Hanover board was also lending money for the construction of working-class housing from the same date.[6] But probably more typical of the views of the majority of the insurance boards was the opinion expressed by Dr Freund from Berlin. At the CAW conference in Berlin in 1892, he reported on plans to use the funds for working-class housing but emphasised the need for caution in view of the uncertainty, at this early stage, of the rate of flow of money into the insurance funds and the level of claims that the funds would have to meet.[7]

Despite this cautious approach to the management of the funds, it soon became clear that they had enormous potential as a source of capital for housing. It was the flow of capital from these sources that transformed the fortunes of the non-profit housing sector during the 1890s. But before examining the details of this rapid expansion, it is important to consider the impact of this new-found availability of capital both on the form of the company and the co-operative, and on their respective roles within the non-profit sector.

The limited dividend housing companies after 1890

Under the provisions of the Invalidity and Old Age Insurance Act of 1890 the limited dividend companies, like other non-profit housing societies, were to be offered support from the regional insurance funds of most regions on terms which, if not always as generous as those for the co-operatives, were still better than those on the open capital market.[8] Now, with access to funds from this source, it looked as if the perennial difficulty of attracting investors who would accept a limited return on their capital had at last been overcome. By 1890 the limited dividend housing companies seemed poised ready to expand the scale

of their operations enormously. Despite these advantages the success of
the company in housing the lower paid worker and his family appears to
have slowed again after the initial surge of interest in the mid-1880s.
This may perhaps be due to the growing feeling in reforming circles from
the early 1890s onwards that government should play an increasingly
important part in the provision of housing, replacing the philanthropic
ideal that had led to the founding of the limited dividend housing
companies. In part the decline of the company was also a by-product
of the growing success of the co-operative movement from the early
1890s onwards, which also provided for the artisan and those workers
of 'good reputation' in steady work, just the type of tenant favoured
by the limited dividend companies. With the co-operatives concentrating
on housing the artisan, often in 'cottage' housing in the suburbs, the
main alternative open to the limited dividend companies was to provide
housing for the less well paid where it was most needed, in central areas
conveniently near large areas of employment.

   Thus, of necessity, the work of the companies started from the 1890s
onwards to centre, like the work of the various trusts, on the provision
of housing for those with a lower income than the artisan, the
day-labourer and the unskilled worker for whom co-operative housing
was still too expensive. Since the 1850s, trusts such as the Alexandra
Stiftung had concerned themselves with housing these less well paid
families but their work had always been viewed with strongly qualified
enthusiasm by reformers because of the suspicion that they were in
effect offering charity with its supposedly corrosive effects. But after
1890 this became increasingly the role of the companies too. Of the new
companies founded after 1890, the two largest, the Aktienbaugesellschaft für kleine Wohnungen in Frankfurt, and the gemeinnützige
Baugesellschaft für Aachen und Butscheid, both concerned themselves
with the lower paid worker.

   This emphasis on the provision for the less well paid is exemplified
by the work of one of the largest limited dividend housing companies
in the country, the Aktienbaugesellschaft für kleine Wohnungen in
Frankfurt (ABG).[9] Founded in 1890 by Karl Flesch and Johannes Miquel
with support from a number of other Frankfurt notables, it sought to
provide housing for large families and those who could generally afford
only 20–25 M per month in rent. Costs had therefore to be kept to an
absolute minimum. To achieve this the most common dwelling
size – 42% of all its stock were flats containing a living kitchen and one
other room – were rented at 14–27 M per month and larger flats with
an extra room, making up a further 30% of the stock, were rented at
22–38 M per month, which compared very favourably with rents on
the open market for similar dwellings in the rest of the town.

   The speed and the scale on which the ABG operated reflected the
strength of the charitable tradition in Frankfurt; after only 24 years it
had constructed 1,578 dwellings housing 7,171 inhabitants, thus
making it one of the largest single companies in the country. As might
be expected with such low rents, the bulk of the tenants (61%) were

factory workers and of these just under 50% were unskilled workers; significantly 12% of the tenants were listed as being out of work, or as being widows. A further indication of the concern to help those who found difficulty with housing was the considerable number of larger flats for families with an above average number of children. But despite this concern with the poorer members of the community, the ABG still managed to pay the maximum dividend allowed by its statutes (its limitation to $3\frac{1}{2}$% was a further reflection of its philanthropic nature) and to retain sufficient income to pay for the repairs, management and other costs.

Although the work of the ABG was directed towards housing the less well paid, it did not attempt to help 'the poor'. But after 1886, a number of companies tried to house those at the bottom end of the economic scale by applying the ideas and methods of Octavia Hill. One of the first companies to do so was the Verein zur Verbesserung der kleinen Wohnungen (VVkW) in Berlin which was founded in November 1888 by a number of members of the CVWaK.[10] The Verein was founded to demonstrate that Miss Hill's ideas could be applied in Berlin to provide hygienically acceptable housing and still to show a return of 4%. By 1889 the VVkW had already bought existing property in the Eisenbahnstrasse and the Pückelstrasse. Although there is no information on the type of tenant who was accommodated here, it was reported that these properties were able to show a return of $6\frac{1}{2}$% when managed along the lines established by Octavia Hill in London. Here in Berlin too, 'lady visitors', members of the Frauenverein Octavia Hill, collected the rents and attempted to establish that 'benign and beneficial contact between visitor and tenant' that was so crucial a part of Miss Hill's system.

But although the Verein found that the management of property could pay its way if the properties remained in their existing condition, it could not afford the costs of the alterations necessary to ensure lighting and ventilation to the standards considered adequate in reforming circles. By 1890 its members were already calling for a reappraisal of policy, urging that the Verein should consider the possibility of building new dwellings. This, it was argued, would be cheaper than rehabilitation, a case already championed by Paul Aschrott at the annual conference of the DVfAW in 1890.[11] Finally, combining forces with the DVfAW in 1890, the Verein was able, by 1898, to start building to a design by Alfred Messel on a site donated by the financier Valentin Weissbach.[12]

The block built to a new design by Messel provided not only 388 dwellings (of which 40% were single-room dwellings) but a kindergarten and a bath house in which the tenants could enjoy a weekly bath, free of charge. Both the architectural quality of Weissbachgruppe development and the achievements of the Frauenverein Octavia Hill in organising the bath house, kindergarten and other 'amusements intended to foster the feeling of community amongst the tenants of the development' were hailed as a success.[13] Unable to extend its activities before the war because of rising construction costs, the VVkW was able, nevertheless, to keep rents down in its existing accommodation. In 1905 the annual rent for a single-room dwelling was 216 M, or about 40 M less than the rent for an equivalent dwelling on the open market and certainly of better quality.[14]

The achievements and the difficulties encountered by the VVkW are perhaps more typical of the fortunes of the limited dividend companies than the successes of the ABG. True, the achievement of the ABG up to 1900 was not unique; its achievement could be matched by a number of other companies and trusts.[15] The Gladbacher Aktienbaugesellschaft had built 1,000 dwellings; the Verein für das Wohl der arbeitenden Klassen in Stuttgart, 558; the H. J. Meyer Stiftung in Leipzig, 529, and the Gemeinnütziger Bremer Bauverein, 468. Nevertheless the scale of the operations of the majority of limited dividend companies by 1900 was very limited. Albrecht shows that only 12,718 dwellings had been built by all the companies, trusts and societies working across the whole country, less than a third of the English achievement.[16] In Frankfurt, the work of the ABG and the other companies had made an appreciable contribution to the housing stock of the city; Cahn estimated that by 1915, 7.2% of all dwellings in the city had been built by non-profit organisations and that of these 48% were built by limited dividend companies. But Frankfurt was the exception.[17] In Berlin, as we have seen, the achievement of the companies over a 60-year period was pitifully small. By 1914 all the different forms of limited dividend companies, societies and trusts together had produced only 2,817 dwellings, less than 25% of the *annual* volume of residental construction by private enterprise between 1902 and 1907.[18]

But how else was housing of acceptable standards to the reformers to be provided for the lower-paid working-class family? In providing a high proportion of one-room dwellings the VVkW was attempting to cater for the lower paid like so many of the limited dividend companies. Indeed by 1900 these companies had developed in a very different direction from that envisaged at the time of the first initiatives in the 1850s. Instead of building for the artisan of 'good reputation' the companies were now attempting to help the day-labourers, the porters, the cab-men and other unskilled workers.

In offering housing to tenants, like this, the companies were still charged with offering charity 'from above', even by those familiar with their work. Jacobi, for example, compared in unflattering terms the loss of independence and initiative amongst the tenants of the housing companies, to whom decisions made by the management on the running of the house were simply 'handed down', often in inflexible terms, to the vigorous interest in management encouraged by the co-operatives.[19] Yet, despite these criticisms, the role played by the company was one that could not easily be undertaken by other forms of organisation. However limited in quantitative terms, the limited dividend housing companies and the trusts alone operated at the lower end of the housing market.

The housing co-operatives after 1890

Before 1890 the growth of the co-operative housing movement had
been held back both by the absence of a limit on the liability of the
individual member and by the related problem of raising capital. By
1890, however, solutions to these problems were to hand: first, under
the provisions of the Invalidity and Old Age Insurance Act of 1890
capital could be borrowed from the regional insurance funds; second,
the liability of the individual member of the co-operative was limited
by the legislation of 1 May 1889.

There had been opposition to the lack of any limitation on liability
even before 1868, but it was not until 1881 that the co-operative
movement had resolved to press for changes in legislation in order to
limit liability, breaking at last with the fundamental principle of
mutuality set out by Schulze-Delitzsch.[20] Despite divisions within the
movement, a majority favoured a radically new departure and by 1888
a bill had been placed before the Reichstag proposing, amongst other
changes, the introduction of limited liability for members of co-operatives.
On 1 May 1899 the new legislation was approved. With this organisational barrier removed and new sources of capital, there were again
hopes that the work of the housing co-operatives would expand.

In the expansion of the co-operative movement after 1890 we can
distinguish three principal types of co-operative: the traditional type that
built for home-ownership, the Spar- und Bauverein form that built for
rent, and a third type, the Beamtenwohnungsverein, or white-collar
housing society, that first emerged after 1890 but was to expand rapidly
before 1914.

The work of the co-operatives of the traditional form, often based on
the Flensberger Arbeiterbauverein, continued to expand after 1890. By
1900 Albrecht estimated that they had built around 3,000 dwellings
for home-ownership, about half as many as the number of co-operative
dwellings built for rent.[21] This level of expansion certainly continued
up to the war. Summarising the situation in 1916, the rather incomplete
statistics assembled by Albrecht show that 12,700 dwellings had been
built for home-ownership and that this accounted for something like
40% of all co-operative building.[22]

In Berlin this form of co-operative was represented by the Berliner
Baugenossenschaft which rapidly increased the scale of its operations
after acquiring limited liability in 1889 and borrowing from the regional
insurance funds.[23] By 1900 the membership had increased to 1,042 and
213 houses had been built for home-ownership with a further 200 for
renting in the city centre to working-class members. By 1909 just over
1,000 dwellings had been built for ownership and 616 were now being
rented.

The Berliner Baugenossenschaft was an exception in providing
low-priced housing for rent; this was normally provided by the Spar-
und Bauvereine modelled on the pioneer society in Hanover. By 1900,
their activities had increased even more rapidly than that of the

traditional type of co-operative and accounted for around 60% of all co-operative housing.[24] By 1916 they were still maintaining this share of total production, having built around 20,000 dwellings for rent.[25]

In Berlin a Spar- und Bauverein had been founded as early as February 1892, one of the first half dozen in the country.[26] The inspiration for this had come from Albrecht and the circle around the Centralstelle für Arbeiterwohlfahrtseinrichtungen, but despite this exalted 'patronage' its organisation was based more directly on the principle of self-help than that of the Berliner Baugenossenschaft. Closely modelled on the Hanover example, the entrance premium and the weekly cost of the housing were held low and the co-operative rapidly built up a large membership; by 1894 membership had reached 1,097. Significantly in 1899, 76.8% of the membership was composed of 'workers', apprentices, shop assistants and junior clerks.

But as the shortage of the late 1890s grew worse, demand for the Spar- und Bauverein's housing rose sharply. By 1902 the membership was already 2,565, very nearly double that of 1899. The growth of the membership made it possible to build on a larger scale and by 1905 the Verein had built 511 dwellings. By 1913, the number had reached 1,560, more than any other non-profit organisation building for working-class families in the city of Berlin. Rents were low. In 1905 the average rent for all dwellings were nearly as low as those of the VVkW, a valuable indication that the Spar- und Bauverein type of co-operative could really reduce costs to a level comparable to rents in the limited dividend companies.[27]

Finally, an important area of growth of the co-operative movement before 1914 was the work of the Beamtenwohnungsvereine or the housing societies for clerical and white-collar workers, often in government employment.[28] The first co-operative of this type had been founded in 1892 in Kassel and was followed by the establishment of similar co-operatives in cities across the country with the backing of private insurance and pension funds as well as those from the regional insurance funds. By 1900 there were 14 white-collar housing co-operatives and by 1908 this figure had increased to 150 with a membership of 42,134.[29] By 1916 the number of co-operatives had grown to 69; they had built nearly 1,400 dwellings, nearly all for rent.[30]

This type of organisation was also well represented in Berlin.[31] Founded in 1900 at a time of acute housing shortage by a civil servant, the Beamtenwohnungsverein zu Berlin was an immediate success and by 1906 the membership had topped 10,000, an exceptionally rapid increase. With an adequate supply of capital assured from regional insurance boards and the Reich *Wohnungsfürsorgefonds* and a large membership, the Verein was able to build quickly and on a large scale. The first dwellings were opened in 1901 in Steglitz, and by 1914 the total number had reached 3,300, about twice as many as that built by the Spar- und Bauverein.

However, housing provided by the Verein cost appreciably more than that built by other co-operatives. Both the entrance premium and the rents were higher than those of the Berliner Spar- und Bauverein and of those of the Vaterländischer Bauverein, a society founded with trade union backing in 1902; the average rent in the Beamtenwohnungsverein was 598 M per annum, nearly 200 M more than that of the former and still 100 M more than that of the latter society.[32]

The level of the rents in the housing provided by the different forms of co-operative leads directly to the question of the membership for which each type of society could cater. This issue was of central importance. Berfore 1890 there was a general impression that the co-operative could only provide, as Schmoller argued, for an elite of the working class.[33] In the days when liability was unlimited and capital difficult to borrow it was only the best-paid workers and those in regular year-round employment who could afford the regular contribution demanded by a society, and could undertake to maintain this over the time necessary to complete payment on a share, a period often as long as 25 years. There were often long delays between the founding of a co-operative and the building of the first house and, depending on the luck of the ballot, it might be necessary to wait for years to obtain a house even after having fully paid for a share. For those in a precarious financial position, the benefits of the co-operative, however advantageous in the long run, lay beyond reach.

After 1890 the risks associated with co-operative membership were reduced and capital was easier to borrow. These benefits, combined with the two forms of society more accessible to the lower paid, should, in principle, have made it possible for even working-class members to join. But how far did this extend co-operation in practice?

The membership of the Beamtenwohnungsvereine was generally confined to the better-paid clerks and government employees and even included a considerable number of middle-class tenants. The average cost of a dwelling in this type of housing was higher at 5,563 M against 3,747 M for dwellings built by all other forms of co-operatives.[34] This very general picture is confirmed by evidence for individual cases. In Frankfurt, for example, the rents in the Beamtenwohnungsverein were near the top of the range for small flats in the non-profit sector, and significantly this form of society provided a higher proportion of larger and more expensive flats than any other non-profit organisation.[35] In Berlin, too, rents for dwellings of this sort were at the top end of those in the non-profit sector.[36]

For other forms of co-operative the situation is more difficult to assess. On the one hand we have the general impressions of contemporaries, Albrecht, Jacobi, Jäger and others, who were familiar with the movement. On the other we have the isolated studies of particular organisations. From these accounts it is clear that co-operative housing could be offered at rents as low as those in any other non-profit organisation, even in large cities where costs were high. We have seen that the Berliner Spar- und Bauverein's rents were as low as those of the VVkW and in 1898 Albrecht had reported that just over 75% of the tenants of the society described themselves as 'workers' rather than skilled workers or artisans.[37] But it appears that these examples must have been the exception rather than the rule. Contemporaries generally believed co-operative housing to be expensive and restricted to the skilled worker, although the evidence for this was impressionistic and anecdotal.

This view is supported by Jacobi's sketchy investigation.[38] After examining the characteristics of membership of the co-operatives in several cities in different parts of the country, she claimed that in 1900 around 25% of the membership of the co-operatives was made up of unskilled workers; by 1910, however, she concluded that this group had declined to negligible proportions. She concluded: 'Those living in co-operative housing are part of the elite of the working classes, they are generally skilled and nearly always well-paid workers'. For Jacobi, membership of a co-operative was frequently a product of the same attitudes and values that were to be found in those active in the trade unions.[39]

Co-operative housing was generally regarded by housing reformers as being too expensive for the great mass of the working classes to provide 'the solution' to the housing problem. But it was viewed as the most effective and desirable way of increasing the supply of new housing. Indeed once this could be done, it was argued that pressure on the housing market could be reduced and thus a start would already have been made with housing the lower paid. For many housing reformers, the way forward lay, therefore, in expanding housing production through the co-operatives and the non-profit sector as a whole.

The expansion of the non-profit sector during the 1890s

The funds of the regional insurance boards were of immense potential value to the non-profit sector: here, at last, lay a possible answer to the long-standing problems of raising capital. But how were these funds to be used and what kinds of housing organisation were to benefit? Would private enterprise be eligible too? On what terms would the funds be loaned? Would they be at interest levels substantially below the open capital market?

During the 1890s these questions were the subject of extended debate both in housing reform circles and amongst the administrators of the regional boards; inevitably the use of the funds to support the non-profit sector raised the larger question of government intervention in housing, particularly the propriety of offering assistance for non-profit housing in apparent competition with private enterprise. Unlike England or France, neither the Reich nor Prussia passed general housing legislation before the First World War; there was thus no unambiguous clarification of government intentions, or duties, in this field. The use of the funds depended on local initiatives and the attitudes of the individual regional boards.

Despite the absence of any unified policy, the volume of loans from the insurance funds increased dramatically from small beginnings in

1891, throughout the decade and on into the 1900s. From the mid-1890s onwards much of the literature on housing reform is filled with reports, generally couched in a style of restrained and sober optimism, which document the successes of the reformers' campaign to expand the non-profit sector. However, the enthusiastic interpretations of the results of this campaign offered by the reformers should not obscure how limited the achievement remained in absolute terms.

The total number of houses built by 1890 by all non-profit organisations was no more than 13,109 for the whole country.[40] But the number of dwellings built in the ten years between 1890 and 1900, was as high as 10,666, 80% of the production during the previous 40 years. Significantly, the major part of this increase was accounted for by the work of the housing co-operatives. Before 1890 the total production of the co-operatives was only 1,302 dwellings. By 1900 production, even excluding the figures for the Beamtenbangenossenschaften, had risen to 9,838 dwellings, an increase of 750%. Moreover, by 1900 many of the new co-operatives had only just started operating so that a truer indication of the expansion of the movement is the 202 new co-operative societies founded during his period. By comparison, growth of all other forms of non-profit housing societies was much less dramatic: the total production of new housing by all other types before 1890 was 11,807 dwellings, while during the decade before 1900 only a further 1,595 dwellings were added to this stock.

If we turn to examine the position at the end of the 1900s, the growth of the co-operative relative to the rest of the non-profit movement is even more pronounced. By 1912 the number of co-operatives had risen to 1,173, from only 385 in 1900;[41] by 1914 the number had again increased to 1,538. This expansion contrasts sharply with that of other forms of non-profit organisations. Albrecht estimated, in very rough terms, that by 1917 the number of all non-co-operative non-profit organisations was around 180: compared with the 80 in existence in 1900, at most an increase of 25%. Furthermore, the membership and the number of houses built by the co-operatives was rising even more rapidly than the number of societies: only 3,449 dwellings had been built by 'reporting' co-operatives in 1901, but by 1909 this figure had risen to 13,344. By 1914, as a crude measure of activity, the co-operatives were housing around 40% of their membership in 21,002 dwellings.

The national figures give a general indication of a healthy rate of growth but there were important variations between different parts of the country, and between urban and rural areas. There were areas, such as Mecklenburg or Ostpreussen, especially in the east of the country, which were still poorly provided with non-profit housing of all kinds in 1914.[42] In 1895, of the 95 co-operatives then operating in Prussia, just under half were to be found in 3 provinces, Hanover, Westphalia and the Rhineland. In 1900 the concentration in the west was yet more marked: the co-operatives in the three provinces accounted for 56·8% of all the co-operatives in Prussia. By 1914 Westphalia had 139 co-operatives, the Rhineland 122 and Hanover 64; Berlin, by comparison had only 19. By 1916 the 183 co-operatives in the Rhineland alone had built 21,500 dwellings, about double the total production of the whole non-profit sector in Berlin.

The housing co-operatives were also unevenly divided between urban and rural areas.[43] By 1900, of the 385 Prussian districts with a population of over 10,000, the 278 urban areas had 427 housing co-operatives while the 107 rural districts had only 38. By 1914 most larger cities had some form of co-operative organisation, although the level of activity varied considerably between one city and another. In 1914 in Altona, co-operative membership per 1,000 inhabitants was 345 and in Hanover, 237, but in Berlin it was only 104. Despite the rapid growth of the non-profit sector its unevenness was cause for concern.

Non-profit housing and State aid

How can this be explained? Part of the answer must lie with the new sources of capital; it was, after all, this more than anything else that transformed the fortunes of the movement before 1914. The largest single source of capital was the regional insurance funds but finance was also available from a variety of pension funds, both public and private. But throughout the whole period between the early 1890s and the war, the regional insurance funds remained the main source of capital for non-profit housing. The overall balance from different sources is difficult to estimate but by 1909 the ratio of loans from the insurance boards to those from pension funds of all forms was about 9:1.[44] More detailed information on the capital sources for different areas confirms the overwhelming importance of the regional insurance funds. In the Hanover region, for example, they accounted for about 60% of all capital invested in non-profit housing between 1891 and 1900[45] and in the Rhineland for about 66% of all loans to the non-profit sector in 1900.[46]

The value of the regional insurance funds to the non-profit sector lay not only in the volume of funds, but also in the advantageous rates at which these funds could be borrowed. These depended on the kind of organisation to which the loan was being made and on the type of security.[47] For non-profit organisations backed by the further security of municipal, regional or Reich guarantees, the rate was lowest, in most cases 3%, compared with 4.75%–5% on the open market. Arrangements for amortisation varied from board to board: in the Rhineland loans were amortised at 2% annually, but in many other areas the rate was lower. In 1910, however, the *Reichsversicherungsamt* sought to establish a uniform approach to financing through the insurance boards and a minimum rate of interest of 3.5% and an annual amortisation rate of 1%–1.5% was established for all regions. But even at this rate capital from the insurance funds remained about 1% cheaper than loans on the open market. The extent to which use was made of the insurance funds varied sharply from one part of the country to another. By 1903 the differences in the lending between regions was already quite clear.[48] Generally the level was higher in the west than in the east; while the Hanover and the Rhineland boards had lent 16.3 and 21.7 million Marks respectively, 12 of the 31 regional boards had lent less than 1 million Marks. Niederbayern had lent only 44,000 M and the Mecklenberg board had made no loans at all. Besides Hanover and the Rhineland, only two regions, Saxony and Baden, had lent over 5 million Marks. The Berlin board had only lent 2.9 million Marks.

The difference remained as clearly marked in 1914 as before, and determined to a large extent the growth of the non-profit sector in the different regions. By the end of 1914, 64% of the total volume of loans had been made by only six regional boards:[49]

Rhineland	84.3 million Marks
Westphalia	61.2 million Marks
Saxony	53.4 million Marks
Hanover	49.0 million Marks
Baden	36.3 million Marks
Württemberg	28.3 million Marks

While most boards had lent up to 50% of their resources, a number had lent far less. The insurance boards in Berlin, Unterfranken and Brandenburg had lent only 7% of their resources, while in Mecklenburg loans to all forms of non-profit housing amounted to less than 1% of the board's resources. But why was so much more non-profit housing built in the west than in the east? And how could these inequalities be avoided?

To many reformers like Brandts and others who had called during the 1890s for some supervisory body for housing at regional level,[50] the achievement of the non-profit sector in areas like the Rhineland or Westphalia lay in the strength of the Landes- und Provinzialvereine für Kleinwohnungen, the regional housing associations. It was their task to encourage, promote and co-ordinate housing, particularly non-profit housing, in each region. The Rheinischer Verein zür Förderung des Arbeiterwohnungswesens, founded by Brandts in 1897, was the first of this type of society and was soon followed by others, encouraged by the Prussian directive of 1901, in Hesse-Nassau, Westphalia, Hanover and, finally, in 1913 in Berlin.[51] These societies had five principal functions: to assemble literature, drawings and other information on housing matters; to serve as a means of communication with the authorities, the non-profit organisation and other interested parties; to arouse public interest in the problems of housing; to ensure a flow of capital to non-profit housing and to establish the financial viability and suitability of non-profit groups; finally, to support all forms of attempt to counteract the housing problem and to encourage a higher standard of housing and a better level of home-keeping.

Much of the success of the Rheinischer Verein was due to the close links that Brandts was able to establish between the society, the officers of the regional insurance fund and the local provincial government, the administrative unit for housing matters in Prussia. But in many areas there was no equivalent association. In Berlin the foundation of the Gross-Berliner Verein für Kleinwohnungswesen had to wait until 1913. But despite the reputation of its members, it was established too late to be effective before 1914, and only came into its own during and after the war.[52]

An explanation of the success of the non-profit sector which focusses on the role of the regional housing associations runs the risk of confusing cause with effect. Much of the work of the associations was concentrated in areas such as the Rhineland where there was already a strong co-operative tradition; their success was due in large measure to the character of the areas in which they operated. The housing co-operatives, like the early English co-operative building societies in the 1840s, flourished in areas like the Rhineland where there was a large number of skilled workers, artisans and others who could afford to join a co-operative and recognised the advantages that it offered.[53] Even after 1890, the cost of co-operative housing limited access to the better paid. In these terms the concentration of the housing co-operatives in areas such as Westphalia, the Rhineland and Saxony where industrialisation and urbanisation were well advanced, rather than in the east, is no more surprising than the strength of the early co-operative building society movement in towns like Leeds, Bradford, Halifax and Sheffield.

But given the significance of the character of the different regions for that work of the co-operatives, and therefore for the most important part of the non-profit movement, how effective could the non-profit sector be as a general source of housing for the working classes? How far were other forms of Reich, state or municipal government assistance able to offset the disadvantages suffered by the poorer regions and the poorer members of the community? The contribution made by national government was limited. As we have seen, provision was made for housing some of the employees of the Reich such as the postal and railway workers, and the *Wohnungsfürsorgefonds* had been set aside for housing low-paid employees in government service where no other appropriate form of housing was available. The housing paid for by these funds was frequently supplied by the non-profit sector. But if the total allocation from these sources are set beside the contribution of the regional insurance funds then the niggardly effort made by the Reich by 1914 is clear; the *Wohnungsfürsorgefonds* for the whole country amounted to less than half of the loans already made by the regional insurance board in the Rhineland alone.[54]

Nor were other forms of assistance offered by the Reich in the non-profit sector of greater value.[55] Limited help was offered by providing building land, often on the newly established leasehold system of tenure.[56] Only after legislation in June 1914 was the Reich also able to offer security, of up to 90% of the value of the housing built, for non-profit housing developments: too soon before the war to have any appreciable effect.

The contribution made by the individual states was hardly more impressive.[57] In Prussia, as in the Reich, support for non-profit housing was very largely a product of the desire to provide housing for state employees. The same was broadly true for Bavaria and Saxony. In only a few states had funds been allocated for non-profit housing for 'public utility': in Bavaria from 1908 to 1916, 10 million Marks had been set aside for public utility non-profit housing; in the same year Hesse had allocated money for similar purposes; in Saxony expenditure for this type of housing was finally approved in February 1914. But in Hesse and Saxony this form of assistance by the state was trivial; only in Bavaria did state funds for public utility non-profit housing rival the level of those from the regional insurance funds.

It is true that the Prussian government had urged the cities to support the non-profit sector in two ministerial directives sent in March 1901 to the *Oberprasidenten* of the different provinces, no doubt as part of the manoeuvring over the proposed Prussian Housing Bill.[58] These were followed by a series of more local directives regulating housing matters mainly for areas in the Rhineland and in Westphalia, and in August 1902 a further ministerial directive was sent to all regional *Prasidenten* calling for a substantial improvement in housing conditions by expanding the work of the non-profit sector by all possible means. But the initiative for adopting these recommendations rested with the different local authorities. Thus in the absence of state-wide measures, an account of support for the non-profit sector in Prussia must inevitably be presented in terms of the actions taken by the individual authorities.

A general survey of the measures adopted by these different authorities, 'Förderung der gemeinnützigen Bautätigkeit durch die Gemeinden', prepared by Beck, *Bürgermeister* of Mannheim, for the VfSP's enquiry into housing in 1900 provides an invaluable summary of the extent of the actual level of support for the non-profit sector during the 1890s.[59] Just over half (50.4%) of all authorities in the survey had done nothing at all by 1900. Nor were these simply a collection of small towns in which the problems of housing were irrelevant: they included Breslau, Posen, Altona and Bremen to mention only a few.

Beck identifies fifteen different ways in which the authorities had helped the non-profit sector and records under each heading the authorities who had offered such assistance. These different forms of support can be divided into three main categories. The most frequently mentioned was assistance with the acquisition of land; this might be through the planning process (6.2% of all the 260 authorities), through incorporation (4.6%), through the use of compulsory purchase powers (1.27%), through the establishment of new access to cheaper land through public transport (5.5%) or, finally, through transferring municipal land to the ownership of non-profit societies (15.8%). The second most frequent category was the tax and financial advantages offered to non-profit societies; this included reducing the development charge for paving and sewering (12.7%), the purchase of non-profit society shares by the municipalities (9.2%) and agreement to stand surety for loans to non-profit development (5.8%). Finally, a number of municipalities offered to assist by providing, free of charge, the services of municipal employees (13.4%) or by reducing the costs of cottage housing, the most common form of co-operative housing, through modification of the building regulations. The overall achievement, meagre in 1900, had not improved by 1914. Despite official encouragement progress remained slow: by 1909, only 9 cities with a population of over 50,000 had made cheap land available and only 16 had granted a reduction in development costs. The only positive note was the increased willingness of local authorities to stand surety for loans and by 1912, 65 cities had agreed to do so.

But within this generally rather gloomy picture there were again sharp differences in the level of support offered in each region. In general the municipal authorities in the west, particularly in the Rhineland and Westphalia, had done very much more to help than elsewhere. Seven pages of Beck's survey were devoted to the work of the authorities in the Rhineland, compared with only six for the whole of the rest of Prussia and more space was devoted to a discussion of developments in Frankfurt am Main than anywhere else.

In Frankfurt, backed by the determination of Adickes and a tradition of municipal interest in housing affairs that extended back to Varrentrap's initiatives in the 1860s, support for non-profit housing of all forms flourished right up to the First World War. In addition to the city's land policies and the introduction of the *Erbbaurecht*, the leasing of urban land, both of which benefited the non-profit societies, the Frankfurt authorities actively assisted in encouraging and financing non-profit societies.[60]

By 1915 with substantial municipal loans combined with loans from the regional insurance funds, from local pension funds and other local sources of capital such as banks and local charities, strengthened by the substantial funds paid up by members of the co-operatives – a sign of the relative affluence of the city – the non-profit organisations in the city were able to build 5,507 dwellings representing 7.2% of all dwellings in the city and housing 6.3% of the city's total population.[61]

True to Adickes' principles this achievement was founded 'auf streng wirtschaftlicher Grundlage'.[62] Nor did the city enter into direct or 'unfair' competition with private enterprise. Money was lent by the city at rates of interest which were the same as or slightly higher than the regional insurance funds.[63] The city assisted non-profit housing, but itself built only for its own employees.[64]

However by the turn of the century there were already a small number of local authorities who were prepared to embark on the more radical policy of building and managing non-profit housing for use, not just by municipal employees, but by working-class families generally.[65] This policy was anathema to many of the more traditionally minded housing reformers,[66] but it is clear from Beck's discussion of the subject that he and a number of younger and more radical spokesmen for the cities viewed this course of action as legitimate where other forms of enterprise were unable, or unwilling, to build sufficient working-class housing.

To Beck and others like Wagner and Brandts, the production of new housing lay clearly within the competence of the local authority. Charged with responsibility for the needy and those without housing, and already engaged in running enterprises such as gas, water, electricity, tramways and similar undertakings, it appeared illogical to oppose the building of housing by the cities.[67] If the municipality could manage to build hospitals for the sick, why should it not build housing for the healthy? The local authority not only had the ability to do all this, but could do it more cheaply and more efficiently than private enterprise. Freed of the need to make a profit, and unhampered by conflicts between self-interest and the good of the community, the municipality was ideally suited to do so.

But if few cities were actively willing to help the non-profit sector, even fewer were willing to build on their own account. By the war, according to a survey carried out by the Kaiserliches statistisches Amt, only 15 out of 106 cities under investigation had built any housing for rent.[68] Even amongst these the scale of these municipal initiatives was very limited. Only 5 had built over 100 dwellings, the others had all built fewer, and only Düsseldorf had built as many as 420 dwellings.

It is against this background that we must view the achievements of the very few cities like Ulm who actually started to build for the working class in general.[69] The city had begun building tenement housing in 1888 for its employees but it was not until 1896 that cottages were first built, significantly not for rent but for sale to any worker living in the town. A number of conditions were attached, the most important of which was the right of the city to the resale of the house or a share of any profits that might be made on its sale. Even with these controls the council found it impossible to retain the desired level of control and yet more stringent conditions were imposed on the third series of cottages built by the city. Here restrictions were placed not only on the terms of any sale of the property, but the use to which it might be put.

The experiences of Ulm in building housing for owner-occupation, with all its attendant difficulties, represented one direction in which municipalities could proceed in building for themselves. Another and simpler alternative was for the city to build housing for rent along the lines pioneered by Düsseldorf.[70] As in Ulm, Düsseldorf too had first become engaged in building housing for rent for its own employees at a time of housing shortage caused by the effects of the recession around 1900. Having started in this way the council then proceeded to build housing for rent to the working classes generally, constructing 143 dwellings on the site of a disused gasworks. Financed through the Rhineland insurance funds it was possible to keep the monthly rents to an average of 10.87 M per room, which was far lower than equivalent rents on the open market. Even more important as evidence of the council's concern for the lower income groups, was the construction of housing for large families who were 'poor but not destitute'. Here rents were lower still at 6–8 M per room per month, so low in fact, that they did not cover costs, with the result that the council actually agreed to subsidise the rents for these dwellings.

The non-profit sector in Berlin 1890–1914

Many of the reformers' hopes during the 1890s for a significant improvement in housing conditions turned on increasing the supply of new housing and, as we have seen, there were high hopes that the non-profit sector might answer these aspirations. In some areas, such as the Rhineland, sufficient housing had been built to make a real contribution to the housing market, especially for the artisan and the skilled worker. But if the non-profit movement were to fulfil the wider hopes of the reformers it was necessary to demonstrate that it could also provide housing, not only in the prosperous communities of the west, but also in the large industrial cities of the east and, above all, in Berlin.[71]

Berlin had of course been the birthplace of the non-profit movement in the late 1840s, but progress since then had been slow.[72] By 1890, the city could boast only four non-profit societies and of these, two, the BgB and the Alexandra Stiftung, had built little since the early 1860s; after nearly 50 years the BgB now managed only 369 dwellings and the Alexandra Stiftung only 235. Of all four institutions, only the Berliner Baugenossenschaft was actively building and by 1890 it had built only 40 single family houses.

During the 1890s the non-profit sector in Berlin expanded slowly by comparison with developments elsewhere. Some explanation for this may be found in the mounting opposition of the property lobby who sought to oppose the movement through their powers in city government (Jäger claims that 66% of the Stadtverordneteversammlung were property owners),[73] in the cautious approach of the insurance board in Berlin under Dr Freund, and, finally in the low level of housing demand in the city during the 1890s following the building boom of the late 1880s. By 1900 neither the BgB nor the Alexandra Stiftung had built much more and the VVkW had still not finished its development on the Weissbachstrasse. Only the co-operatives had started, gradually, to build. By 1900 the Berliner Baugenossenschaft had built 213 dwellings and the Berliner Spar- und Bauverein had built 227 dwellings.[74]

Eventually the acute housing shortage around the turn of the century stimulated the various non-profit organisations to action.[75] By 1902 two new co-operatives had been established: the Vaterländischer Bauverein, launched by trade union and Christian nationalist interests, and the Berliner Beamtenwohnungsverein. By the end of 1903 the volume of all non-profit housing was rising rapidly. The return for the end of 1903 in the statistical year-book shows 2,531 non-profit dwellings in Berlin and just under half (1,075) had been built by the co-operatives.[76] By the end of 1905 total production had risen to 3,754, although a major part of the housing built by the co-operatives (2,610 dwellings) was now built by the new Beamtenwohnungsverein (1,128 dwellings) for the more affluent market.[77]

This pattern of building did not change significantly before the war.[78] By the end of 1913 the three limited dividend companies had built 1,356 dwellings. By 1914 the ten Arbeiterbaugenossenschaften had built between 5,500 and 5,600 dwellings, and to this should be added the construction of a further 290 dwellings and 333 rooms in non-profit lodging houses. The work of these co-operatives was almost matched by the growth of the Beamtenwohnungsvereine which, starting in Berlin in 1890, had built around 3,700 dwellings by 1914.[79]

As a crude estimate of the total volume of non-profit housing built in the Berlin area before 1914 we can assume that together the different types of organisation including the Beamtenwohungsvereine, built in the order of 11,000 dwellings. As a proportion of the total stock of housing in the city this achievement lagged far behind that of Frankfurt and behind that of cities in the Rhineland. If the total number of dwellings built before 1914 by the seven principal organisations working within the city of Berlin (excluding the Beamtenwohnungs-vereine) was around 7,500 and the total number of dwellings in the city was around 600,000,[80] then the non-profit sector cannot have built more than 1.25% of the total stock, and this is probably a generous estimate. If we consider the equivalent figure for the whole Berlin area, including the surrounding municipalities and suburbs, the comparison is even less flattering.

What conclusion can be drawn from this achievement in Berlin? Indeed how significant was the contribution of the non-profit sector generally before 1914? Certainly it was more typical of the general achievement across the whole country than that of Frankfurt. On the basis of data for 1910 for the Rhineland Jacobi rather optimistically concluded that the non-profit sector had built as much as 5.7% of all new housing.[81] Albrecht, one of the champions of the non-profit sector, summarised the achievement before the war in more cautious terms, arguing that only in exceptional circumstances did production rise as high as 4% of the total volume of housing construction, and he stressed that in most cities the proportion was as low as 1%–2%.[82]

How should we judge the development of the non-profit sector before 1914? To critics like Eberstadt who looked to a restructuring of the operations of the open market as the only real source of improvement in housing conditions, this was simply confirmation of the essentially limited nature of the non-profit sector. But to defenders like Albrecht, despite the limited volume of production, much more had been won: a framework of housing provision had been established outside the open market and free from the profit motive of private enterprise. Certainly by 1914 the non-profit sector had not yet achieved the goals set by its more ambitious proponents. In one or two cities the reformers' expectations of the early 1890s may have been realised and sufficient housing built to exercise a beneficial effect on the housing market. In some regions, urged on by the regional housing associations like the Rhein-ischer Verein, and working closely with the regional insurance boards, much had been achieved even before the war. But in most areas this was not the case.

Yet even this limited achievement had led to heated debate on the acceptability of government assistance to non-profit housing. To the representatives of the property lobby, the Verband Haus- und Grund-besitzervereine, the government had already gone too far in favouring the non-profit sector at the expense of private enterprise. Attacking government support for the co-operative movement, Grävell, a spokes-man for property interests, denounced government policies as barely distinguishable from revolutionary socialism.[83]

To most reformers, however, the disappointing results of the non-profit sector was the inevitable and frustrating outcome of the government's equivocal and prevaricating attitude to housing. If the supply of new housing was to be significantly increased, then positive government assistance was essential. Since the early 1890s the absence of clear central government policy on housing had revealed itself in the very uneven successes of the non-profit movement, and indeed to the whole programme of housing reform; how else, but by national legislation and national direction, would it be possible to overcome the resistance of municipal and even state government to proposals for reform? By the turn of the century, the call for government action, both to regulate and to stimulate the provision of housing, already audible in 1886, was louder than ever. But opposition to these measures was stiffening. As policies to assist the non-profit sector, and to control the use of land and property took effect, the property lobby, well represented in local and state government in Prussia, mobilised to defend its interests more actively. During the 1890s the housing question becomes more than the mere interest of social reformers; it enters the realm of politics.

12

◇-◇

The campaign for national housing legislation 1886–1914

The VfSP's endorsement of Miquel's call for legislation to regulate the use of existing housing during their first discussion of the housing question in 1886 represented a clear break with the attitudes of the 1870s when most still argued that the existing powers of the sanitary authorities were far reaching enough. This call for national legislation met with widespread support. From 1886, the demand for 'regulatory legislation' forms one element common to the programmes of all the major associations concerned with housing such as the VföG, CVWaK and Verband Arbeiterwohl; the same speakers can be seen making similar points and supporting the same resolutions as members of different societies and associations with very different confessional and geographical backgrounds. Again and again there is the same emphasis on the need for regulatory legislation and calls for new initiatives in the production of new housing. During the 1890s, however, debate on the role of government was no longer restricted to the limited proposals made and championed by the VfSP or the VföG in the late 1880s.

In these earlier proposals the role assigned to government had been essentially 'regulatory'. Government was to be granted the power to limit or regulate the rights of property (and the rights of the tenant) in the interests of public health and the interests of the community: if passed, these provisions would have given to the Reich many of the powers that central government had acquired in England between 1866 and 1875. Now, citing the example of Bismarck's social legislation of the 1880s as a precedent, reformers demanded an extension of the role of government beyond mere regulation and began to campaign for a more active role for the State which might even include the provision of new housing in competition with private enterprise. Naturally the use of the funds of the regional insurance boards formed an important issue in the debates over this larger role for government.

As early as 1892 the case for a more ambitious role for government and for the use of the regional insurance funds as part of a deliberate government policy of assistance to non-profit housing was set out by Dr A. E. Schäffle and Paul Lechler in a pamphlet *Nationale Wohnungsreform*.[1] Their programme, which was to receive extensive publicity during the next decade – in 1896 a special session of the Evangelical Social Congress was devoted to their proposals[2] – is of interest as an influential statement of this new approach.

249

The starting point for their programme was the inability of either private enterprise or the existing forms of non-profit organisations to provide sufficient working-class housing. Along with the introduction of regulatory legislation of the form proposed by the VfSP and the VföG, they urged that both the states and the Reich should make capital available for new housing. Funds would be distributed through a national mortgage bank, or *Baubank*, whose bonds would be guaranteed by the State; the sale of the bonds would provide the capital for housing and although institutions such as the local authorities, local savings banks and insurance funds would have no direct connection with the *Baubank* they would be encouraged to buy its bonds. Loans for housing would generally be made to non-profit organisations such as co-operatives for the construction of working-class housing, but if these measures failed to ensure the building of sufficient low-income housing, Schäffle and Lechler proposed that a State-nominated body, the *Baukommission*, would take over the task, providing housing for rent. They argued that rents would be lower than those for housing built by private enterprise both because of the lower rate at which the *Baubank* would lend money and because costs would be related to construction costs, not the market. In addition, to help the lower-paid tenants, the rent would include a weekly contribution to an individual savings account to be used to tide tenants over illness or periods of unemployment. To administer these arrangements there would be a series of regional *Baukommissionen* staffed by government and honorary officials, and to co-ordinate the work of these regional boards a national housing department or *Reichswohnungsamt* was to be established.

These proposals were soon followed by others of a similar nature. In 1896, the year in which Schäffle and Lechler put their programme before the Evangelisch-Soziale Kongress, Max Brandts put forward proposals at the annual general meeting of the Verband Arbeiterwohl which went beyond those of Schäffle and Lechler.[3] An influential figure in housing circles in the Rhineland because of his position as director of the regional insurance board based in Düsseldorf, Brandts demanded more active measures from the cities to encourage the building of single family housing, through more imaginative use of the building ordinances, municipal property taxes and municipal land policies, more effective use of the powers of the municipalities under the provisions of the Fluchtliniengesetz and the extension of public transport to ensure easier access to cheap land. At the level of the states, he called for the setting up of a Generalkommission für städtischen Grundbesitz, a regional board for municipal land, which was to have fulfilled many of the functions of the *Baubank* proposed by Schäffle and Lechler, but would also have co-ordinated housing with the development of municipal land policies. The *Generalkommission* was to receive funds from the regional insurance boards or from the state government along the lines of the Prussian Law of 1895 providing capital for housing low-paid state employees.[4] Approved societies would be able to borrow up to 70% of their requirements from the Kommission and were to be given the right to call on cities, the *Kreis* and local co-operative organisations for a further 15% of their capital requirements, thus guaranteeing sufficient finance. Calculating the average cost of a dwelling at 4,000 M, Brandts estimated that, taking the resources of the regional insurance boards alone, it would be a relatively straight-forward matter to finance the construction of 1,500 dwellings a year in the Rhineland alone.[5]

Thus, by the mid-1890s, there was already strong support for a more active role for government in the field of housing. Government was now being asked to offer economic assistance to non-profit housing organisations in the form of capital at rates of interest that would be lower than those generally available to private enterprise. It is true that there was not yet widespread demand for government to build on its own account, but it is clear that Brandts, Schäffle, Lechler and others, such as Latscha and Teudt,[6] were calling for much more than the regulatory powers demanded in the late 1880s. Moreover the demands that they made won extensive support. Their proposals were taken up by the reforming associations and endorsed in the resolutions of the Evangelisch-Soziale Kongress and the Verband Arbeiterwohl with its strong Catholic connections, and within two or three years were supported by both the Protestant and Catholic trade union movements,[7] by the Katholische Arbeitervereine Süddeutschlands in 1899 and by the Gesamtverband der evangelischen Arbeitervereine Deutschlands in 1901.

The proposals championed by Brandts and Schäffle and Lechler were also being tried in practice, albeit on a very limited scale. In the Düsseldorf area of Rhineland the *Wohnungspolizeiverordnung* of 31 May 1893 had initiated early measures to supervise conditions in existing housing, including a system of regular housing inspection.[8] Complementary to this there was now active official encouragement to use the funds of regional insurance boards for non-profit housing from 1891 onwards, an initiative fully supported by Max Brandts through his position as director of the regional fund in Düsseldorf.[9] Towards the end of 1894, Berger-Thimme records that Brandts was already in the process of forming an organisation which would co-ordinate the activities of the non-profit housing groups and the regional insurance board; by December he had arranged a meeting of representatives of 27 housing associations, the local authorities and local industrialists in Düsseldorf.[10] By 1897 this loose grouping had been established as the Rheinischer Verein zur Förderung des Arbeiterwohnungswesens, with the express intention of advancing the programme that Brandts had set out in 1896, and undertaking a number of the tasks that he had envisaged being performed by his proposed General-kommission.

The purpose of the Verein was to co-ordinate the activities of the different organisations concerned with working-class housing and to act as a clearing house for information on advances in financing, administration and design of co-operative housing: 'the fostering of all non-profit activity directed at improving the housing of the working classes in the Rhineland and surrounding areas, through special publications, through the promotion of the foundation of new housing associations, and finally through representations to the State and communal authorities and other legislative bodies'.[11] To achieve these ends the Verein brought together representatives not only from non-profit housing associations but also from a range of government bodies, both regional and local, as well as representatives from industry. The committee of the Verein was composed principally of high government officials and industrialists and the Verein certainly enjoyed a considerable measure of government support through its membership; already in 1898 Oberpräsident Nasse, senior state official in the region, was recommending to the local *Regierungspräsidenten* of the region that the Verein should receive encouragement from official quarters.[12] No doubt, as Berger-Thimme argues, the aims of the Verein were essentially paternalistic, to educate the worker, to incorporate him into the existing order of society – intentions common to the non-profit housing movement as a whole – but it was able to do more: a measure of the Verein's achievement was the contribution made by the regional insurance boards to the funding of non-profit housing in the region.

The debate over government assistance

Support for housing along these lines aroused controversy and debate, both within the housing reform movement and outside. The issue of government intervention received considerable attention, for example, during the second enquiry by the VfSP into the housing question launched in 1899 by Professors Albrecht, Fuchs and Sombart.[13] Much of the enquiry was concerned with determining exactly what kind of support was being made available to non-profit housing in practice, but two papers, one by Brandts, 'Beschaffung der Geldmittel für die gemeinnützige Bautätkgkeit' and an opposing view presented by Adickes, 'Förderung des Baues kleiner Wohnungen durch die private Tätigkeit' do set out the basic principles of the case for and against government assistance as seen from within reforming circles.

For Brandts the overriding justification for government assistance to non-profit housing was the obvious failure of private enterprise. As in the English debate, he claimed that it was the inadequacy of private enterprise in providing housing at the bottom end of the market that led to the acute housing shortage. He contemptuously dismissed the claims of the Haus- und Grundbesitzer, the property lobby made at the annual general meeting of Centralverband in 1898, that there was no real housing shortage and drew attention to the failure of market forces to meet demand. If proper housing was essential to civilised life, then government should step in as it had done in the case of compulsory education. To Brandts the moral grounds for intervention were clear: 'Because of the reality of the housing shortage and because of the damaging effect of this on the community there unquestionably exists the need for government action to remedy the situation.'[14] In addition he also puts forward an economic case. First he argued that support for non-profit housing with money lent at below market rates was justifiable on the grounds that the return expected from housing of this form was lower. Second, he claimed that the only way to remedy the shortage was to stimulate the production of housing by reducing the costs of production through land, tax and planning policy and by ensuring adequate capital for building. The first of these two sets of measures he felt should benefit both private enterprise and non-profit housing, but, quoting Adolf Wagner, he maintained that to offer cheap capital to private enterprise would simply increase profits, whereas to offer money from the regional insurance funds at low rates of interest to non-profit housing, defined with suitable precision, would increase production of housing at costs that the working classes could afford.

In opposition to these arguments, Adickes warned of the dangers of State intervention. The starting point for his case was the inescapable fact that private enterprise would continue into the foreseeable future to build all but a very small amount of housing. In view of the limited number of employers who could afford to build for their employees and the shortage of those with sufficient ability and resources amongst the working classes to organise housing co-operatives, he argued that the contribution from these sources would inevitably remain insignificant. Government intervention in assisting the supply of housing was, he urged, to be viewed with the 'utmost caution'. It necessarily entailed a departure from the normal course of economic affairs: 'The artificial production of housing below the real market price must mean, if it is carried out with public funds, that in the final analysis one section of the ratepayers is supporting the building of housing for others. This kind of financial support, which lies quite outside the general framework of our economic way of life, creates a number of dangers.'[15] Housing produced on this basis might depress wages and lead to limitations on the worker's willingness to move in search of work. More seriously, if, by unfair competition, this method of building housing damaged or undermined the willingness, or the ability, of private enterprise to build it would inevitably result in an even greater housing shortage than ever. Adickes conceded that there might be occasional reasons for government subventions to non-profit housing. But to him the real task of government was to offer vitally needed assistance to create a healthy economic environment in which private enterprise and non-profit housing could both flourish. The most urgent programme that government should undertake was to control land prices and speculation along the lines demanded by Eberstadt and the VföG so that salubrious low-density housing could be built for all on cheap land in the suburbs.

Judging the attitudes of the majority of reformers from the response to these arguments at the VfSP's debate on housing in September 1901, when the question of government intervention was largely overshadowed by the controversy between Eberstadt. Phillipovich and Voigt over land values, it would appear that there was general support for the measures advanced by Brandts.[16] There seemed to be broad agreement that non-profit housing could never shoulder the whole of the burden of providing for the working-class and that non-profit housing and the housing built by employers were, as Beck argued, essential but subsidiary to the work of private enterprise; the non-profit sector therefore deserved support, even if it did operate at a slight economic advantage. However these policies were not acceptable to the representatives of the Haus- und Grundbesitzer. Government assistance to non-profit housing aroused first their suspicions, then outright hostility.

As the use of the regional insurance funds for housing expanded, so the opposition of the property lobby increased. By the mid-1890s there was widespread resentment at the use of the insurance funds and by 1897 the issue was regarded as sufficiently serious for it to be raised at the general conference of the Centralverband in Leipzig. At the next annual conference in Wiesbaden the following resolutions were approved:

1. The Centralverband does not recognise that, apart from isolated instances there exists a housing problem in our cities.
2. Support for housing co-operatives and societies from Reich, state or communal sources is to be renounced – as long as co-operatives are not demonstrably in a position to produce cheaper and better designs than private enterprise.
3. Support from public resources is required only where private enterprise cannot, because of exceptional circumstances, satisfy the demand for housing.
4. If, however, support is to be provided, then this must be offered to all those engaged in the construction of working-class housing to the standards determined by the State.[17]

In 1899, an amplified version of these resolutions was again adopted at the Centralverband's annual conference in Elberfeld.[18]

The standpoint from which the Haus- und Grundbesitzer attacked the work of the co-operatives and the 'unfair' support given to them from the regional insurance funds was set out in the extended but partisan study of the co-operative movement by Dr A. Grävell, commissioned by the Centralverband.[19] Grävell's attack was directed 'not at the co-operative movement as a whole, but at the system which requires support (from the State) and thus places the co-operatives in a favoured position in society – akin to that enjoyed by the old guilds – which they then exploit in unfair competition with private enterprise housing construction and home-ownership'.[20] To Grävell the notion of government action to provide anything more than the most rudimentary regulatory legislation was deeply offensive and tantamount to the policies of communism. 'The co-operatives favour the propagation of socialist theories, promote the embitterment of the class struggle and create, through the revolutionary elements that it spawns, a threat to Throne and Altar.'[21] For him, the whole field of housing, but particularly the supply of new housing, lay outside the competence of government: 'Housing provision is not the task of the State. Organisations engaged in the construction of housing are private in nature and their support should not be undertaken by the State.'[22]

This growing opposition of the propertied interests to the reformers' programme was one of the reasons for the increased interest in reforming circles in national legislation. The three-class voting system in Prussian municipal and state government ensured powerful support for property and the ability to oppose the programme of reform at these levels. But despite the strength of opposition at state level there are significant differences of attitude to these issues at regional and municipal levels. In the west where house-ownership was highest, the work of the housing co-operatives, especially those building for sale, might be welcomed by the representatives of the Haus- und Grundbesitzer as a means of extending the numbers of householders. But in the east, where home-ownership was very much lower, property interests strongly opposed any extension of the work of the co-operative housing movement which they feared would poach tenants, often those of the most desirable kind, from private enterprise. Regional differences of this type are reflected in the volume of lending by the different insurance boards to non-profit housing. As Beck's survey for the VfSP established, assistance to the non-profit sector was substantially greater in the west than in the east. But who could encourage municipal government to act where it did not wish to?

The hope that state government might compel recalcitrant municipalities into action was faint. The legislature, was naturally responsive to the views of property. In 1900 the Haus- und Grundbesitzer had petitioned the Abgeordnetehaus, calling for an end to 'the subvention of the co-operatives' and limits on the powers of non-profit housing to compete at an advantage with private enterprise. In the event the petition was passed over, ruled out of order because of a procedural technicality as a result of representations by the mayor of one of the Rhineland cities.[23] But the difficulties that frustrated the passage of Lex Adickes through the Prussian legislature were a good indication of the strength of the property lobby. Those like Brandts and others anxious to see an extension of government activity in housing, or at least to defend the advances that had been won, recognised that the only way to circumvent the strength of the Haus- und Grundbesitzer and the property lobby was to press for action at the level of the Reich. The need for some higher authority through which the reluctant municipalities and states might be goaded into action had long been recognised, even in the earlier debates over regulatory legislation.[24] By the late 1890s it was already clear to a number of those concerned with reform that if the programme supported by the variety of different associations was to succeed, it would have to be addressed to the Reich and the call for Reich legislation would have to be co-ordinated and orchestrated by a single body.

The organisation established to link together and strengthen the loosely knit campaign was the Verein Reichswohnungsgesetz (VRWG) founded in May 1898 in Frankfurt by a group closely associated with the Institut für Gemeinwohl and the periodical *Soziale Praxis* and placed under the direction of Karl von Mangoldt, the former secretary at the

Institute.[25] It had as its principal goal the mounting of a campaign for legislation along lines that brought together many of the demands by the reformers over the past decade:

1. Demolition of the worst dwellings and the clearance of the worst slums in our cities by means of housing inspections, housing surveys and compulsory purchase powers.
2. Reform of housing layout through new building ordinances and a new approach to planning.
3. Increased production of working-class housing by the local authorities, the co-operatives and by private enterprise: establishment of a 'Generalkommission für Wohnungswesen': provison of State funds for housing.
4. Cheap land for housing to be provided by the states and the local authorities: reform of the law relating to compulsory purchase of land.
5. Reform of urban and suburban transport system.
6. Reform of the rent contract.
7. Creation of special bodies to carry out the programme of housing reform: *Generalwohnungskommissionen*, building banks, formation of specially selected committees for the area administered by each *Generalkommission*, the establishment of a *Reichswohnungsamt*.[26]

While Mangoldt exaggerates the importance and the achievements of the Verein, its campaign for a single programme of reform and the organisation of the first Deutscher Wohnungskongress in 1904 established the VRWG as a valuable 'mouthpiece' for the housing reform movement; it was able to mobilise most of the best-known names in the housing reform movement to contribute to its publications. These varied both in quality and in length and included short pamplets such as Dr A. Liebknecht's *Reichshilfe für Errichtung kleiner Wohnungen* (1900) which called for financial assistance from government for non-profit housing, or Stübben's *Die Bedeutung der Bauordnungen und Bebauungspläne für das Wohnungswesen* (1902) which discussed ways in which planning procedures and building regulations could ensure better housing, as well as the massive 600-page study by Mangoldt, *Die städtische Bodenfrage* (1907).[27] Meanwhile the Jahrbücher and the Jahresberichte of the Verein provided a means of keeping in touch with and unifying a disparate and far-flung membership. Couched in sufficiently general terms, the aims of the Verein attracted a wide membership. But although there were frequent conflicts of opinion, the range of different interests was held together by the simplicity of the common goal: national legislation for better housing.

Changing attitudes of the SPD to the housing question

At the same time that the VRWG was launching its campaign for national legislation, support for a programme of not dissimilar proposals was emerging from the unexpected quarter of certain sections of the SPD. A number of social democrats, mainly at the level of local government, were already calling for the party to rethink its attitude to the housing problem. Particularly in the south, there were calls for the party to abandon Engels' analysis that had dominated party thinking on this subject since the 1870s and to agree a programme of housing reform applicable even in the context of the existing order of society.[28] These demands were prompted both by the new revisionist thinking and by the growing number of SPD councillors, particularly in the south (where the three class system did not militate against the election of socialists in local government elections) who wished to do, or at least wished to be seen to do, something to improve the housing conditions of those who elected them. But in addition to these electoral considerations there were also practical reasons. In the absence of a common policy the results, as Cohn explained, could be chaotic:

The necessity of this [need for a policy] is demonstrated by the fact that in one city, SPD members of the state government were voting millions of Marks to support a bankrupt co-operative for housing railway employees, while the city council was at the same time refusing to make municipal land available at advantageous rates, although this council itself contained members of the party and leading figures of the trades union movement.[29]

For those engaged in attempting to redirect the existing structure of the country towards socialism, the need for a common programme was vital.

These views were being pressed by the leaders of the SPD in municipalities in the south and a number of members on the revisionist wing of the party. But amongst the party establishment and in the north the orthodoxy that to support the non-profit sector was simply to strengthen the existing order of society still commanded widespread support.[30] As in the discussion of larger issues in the party there was also a division over the housing question between those, like the trade unions, who worked for improvements within the existing order, and those who believed that only fundamental change could bring lasting benefits. The question of housing had been touched on, as part of the discussion of *Kommunalpolitik* at the party conference at Hanover in 1899, and again at Mainz in 1900,[31] but the matter had not been brought out into the open and no national party resolutions on the subject had been approved.

Jäger reports with evident pleasure the disagreements that occurred at this time at SPD meetings where the housing question was discussed.[32] At the Versammlung der sozialdemokratischen Gemeindevertreter der Provinz Brandenburg, for example, there was loud confusion on the subject: the possibility of the municipality building housing for its own employees was supported by one faction, but denounced by another as a means of fettering the employee to the interests of his employer, whether private or municipal; for this latter faction the only acceptable course of action was for the city to build 'public utility' housing for all working families, as provided in the English legislation of 1890.

Despite these divisions within the party the local election programmes of social democrats in a number of cities were by 1900 already setting out a programme of housing reform. The programme published by Cohn for the SPD in Munich called for municipal housing offices, differential zoning, greater powers for the municipality in pursuit of its land policies,

and the building of public utility housing for the working classes. Nor
were these ideas restricted to the south. In Brandenburg, a broadly
similar programme was adopted by local representatives of the SPD
which included the following demands: the municipalisation of land,
the building of public utility housing for working families at cost rents;
the taxation of land at sale value, rather than the value in use; the
collection of housing statistics at regular intervals, the setting up of
municipal housing offices and the institution of a system of municipal
housing inspection.[33]

For those involved in local government elections and the rough and
tumble of local politics there was ample justification for these proposals.
But in the writings of the party's spokesmen on municipal and local
affairs, like Lindemann, Südekum and Hirsch on the revisionist wing
of the party,[34] the question of housing reform extended beyond the
putting together of a package of reforms that differed little from those
of the bourgeois parties. To them the success of any programme was
contingent on the reform of local government and the abolition of the
three-class system of local elections in Prussia. Hope of meeting these
preconditions may have appeared as remote as the advent of the
Zukunftsstaat, but from the turn of the century onwards the representatives of the SPD at both local and national level were nevertheless
willing to join the housing reformers in demanding legislation on the
housing question. Indeed by January 1901 the SPD faction in the
Reichstag was already thinking seriously of voting together with Jäger
and the Zentrum.[35]

The campaign for national legislation

At first sight it might appear a straightforward task to write a
comparative account of the campaign for national housing legislation
in England, Germany and France in terms of the acceptability of
government intervention. But on closer examination it is clear that the
issue is complicated by fundamental differences in the political systems
of the three countries. Thus what might in England appear to be a
relatively straightforward discussion on the acceptability, or not, of
central government intervention must, in Germany, be viewed against
the background of a federal system of government in which the different
states jealously guard their own rights and possess very different
systems of government. In constructing an account of the campaign in
Germany we must not only recognise, as in England, the different
interest groups such as those dealing in property, or land, and how they
operate at their different levels of government, but also assess the way
in which their influence is affected by differences in the form of
government between the individual German states.

Which different interest groups were directly involved in the campaign
for comprehensive housing legislation? Besides the housing reformers
there were, as we have seen, the overlapping but not necessarily
identical interests of property, the house building industry and those

involved in developing urban land, all of which were well represented in tne Prussian legislature. But there were other interests too. The representatives of the cities constituted another influential group. The *Bürgermeister* of some cities might be sympathetic to the cause of housing reform but this should not lead us to forget that the cities were naturally sensitive to proposals for legislation that would limit, or even hand back to the Reich or the state, powers, such as those the Prussian cities had acquired under the *Fluchtliniengesetz* of 1875. Housing legislation at Reich or state level was thus a potential threat to the independence of municipal government. Naturally too, there was opposition from the city representatives to measures urged by the housing reformers that threatened to increase the financial burdens of the cities; for example, the construction of working-class housing would draw in families who would contribute little in taxes while they might involve the local authority in expenditure on schools and other services which the better off could provide for themselves.

The campaign for national legislation also threatened the interests of the states. Legislation at Reich level was readily interpreted as a form of interference in issues which were regarded as the proper concern of the individual state. To Prussian conservatives it was unthinkable that the socialist deputies in the Reichstag should ever be in a position to demand action over rural housing conditions in East Prussia. There were also rivalries between states that stood in the path of national legislation. States such as Hesse and Hamburg had already by the turn of the century introduced legislation on housing. Were the provisions for the Reich to be modelled along these lines, in effect forcing on Prussia the arrangements of the lesser states, or were these states to abandon their own achievements to suit the Prussians? If, to escape this dilemma, the matter were left to the individual states, was there any guarantee that the Prussian legislature could be persuaded to act at all?

Finally there was the interest of government itself. Although these interests might combine against legislation, particularly at Reich level, there is evidence that a number of people in government circles did take a more positive view of housing reform. Early in 1890 the Kaiser had shown a keen interest in winning the loyalty of his working-class subjects by attempts to improve their conditions and by a policy of social reforms.[36] The decrees of February 1890 and the decision to convene the Internationale Arbeiterschutzkonferenz in May 1890 are the product of this enthusiasm. But although the Kaiser's interest remained short-lived, the more enduring support for social reform by Prussian civil servants like Freiherr von Berlepsch, Carl Heinrich von Boetticher or later Graf von Possadowsky, suggested that government might respond positively to calls for more direct action and might offer assistance in increasing the supply of new housing. Berlepsch, for example, Prussian Handelsminister from 1890 to 1896, was an upholder of a view of social reform that can be claimed to continue the conservative Christian tradition championed earlier by Huber and represented in the VfSP by

Adolf Wagner.[37] For Berlepsch the role of the State in social matters was to be a constructive one, a role that involved weighing and reconciling the demands of different interest groups for the greater good. During the 1890s Berlepsch was to show an active interest in social issues like unemployment, the employment contract and in housing too. In 1892 Berlepsch was instrumental in the founding of the CAW and both he and Boetticher had attended both days of the CAW conference on housing.

But by the mid-1890s hopes that this support in government circles might lead to real progress had been disappointed. After the early 1890s other issues such as the agrarian question and colonisation came to dominate government interest, and concern with the social question was relegated to the background. From 1894 onwards, reforming interests were further embattled by the tirade of violent propaganda from those like Carl Ferdinand Freiherr von Stumm-Halberg and his allies in the Zentralverband deutscher Industrieller who attacked social reform as pandering to the socialists and even denounced groups like the VfSP as being dominated by anarchists.[38] Berlepsch's departure from office in 1896 and his replacement by Possadowsky was seen, initially, as a major blow to reforming interests.

But after early 1899 and the rejection by the Reichstag of the *Zuchthausvorlage* which proposed prison sentences for those encouraging strike action or picketing and which had been supported by Stumm and his allies, Possadowsky experienced what reformers hailed as a 'Paul-like conversion'. He now showed himself to be as enthusiastic in his support for social reform as Berlepsch. By July 1899 he had set in hand revisions to the invalidity and old age insurance laws which, *inter alia*, were substantially to increase the availability of regional insurance funds for non-profit housing.[39] Thus, at least at the outset of the debate on housing legislation there were those in government circles who regarded the case for reform as an acceptable, even desirable, part of the government's response to the social problem.

To add yet another dimension, we must recognise that the best interests of these different groups also changed with time and the state of the economy. Reaction to government intervention and control during a boom might be very different from reaction to government assistance during a period of recession. The pressure for reform tended to be greater during periods of economic expansion because conditions were then worst. During a boom, as people flocked to the city, demand for housing naturally overtook supply, resulting in overcrowding, high rents and other consequences of a shortage of housing. Naturally there would be strong resistance from the property and house building lobbies to any form of legislative restraint on profits during this situation. But in periods when the housing market was stagnant the position might be reversed. Pressure for reform would now be less urgent; so too, would be the resistance to intervention. The regulation of sub-standard property might be welcomed as a means of reducing the glut of dwellings on the market; to the builder, the prospect of government assistance for non-profit housing might be keenly attractive.

How does the economic cycle affect the debate on housing legislation before 1914? The opening of the debate in the Reichstag by the reformers coincides with the sharp housing crisis of the turn of the century, but during the relatively prosperous years between 1903 and 1907 there seems to have been little willingness on the part of government to listen to the case for reform. However, by the start of the next debate after 1910, the housing market and particularly the property interests again faced real difficulties and interest in government action on housing was predictably greater. An illustration of this is the alliance made between the housing reformers and building interests in the call for government assistance and support for construction of low-cost housing made at the second German Housing Congress in 1911.

It was against this background and during a period of increasing housing shortage – in Berlin only 1% of all dwellings were empty in 1901, a more acute shortage than at any time since the housing crisis of the *Gründerzeit* – that the campaign for Reich legislation was presented to the Reichstag. The question had first been raised unsuccessfully in 1895, at a time when there was little government interest in the matter, by Professor Franz Hitze, secretary of the Verein Arbeiterwohl, and Dr Pichler, both of the Zentrum party, calling for an extension of the use of the regional insurance funds for working-class housing.[40] In November 1899 the question was again raised in the Reichstag by Pastor Bodelschwingh, on behalf of the Verein Arbeiterheim, and by Pfarrer Weber on behalf of the Gesamtverband der evangelischen Arbeitervereine in Deutschland.[41] Together they called for the implementation of proposals along the lines already publicised by Lechler and Schäffle. Yet despite the enthusiasm with which these proposals were received in the Reichstag by the Zentrum, the liberals and the socialists, the results of this initiative were again without positive results: it was agreed to defer consideration of the housing question by the Reichstag as a whole until the matter had been examined by a special committee.[42]

The indecisive debate on the issue anticipates many of the Reichstag's later difficulties with legislation on this subject. There appears to have been general agreement that something should be done to improve housing conditions; certainly nobody argued the case, made that year and the year before by the Haus- und Grundbesitzer, that there was no real housing problem.[43] But agreement on how to proceed foundered on the differences of opinion between those who were convinced that legislation should be established at the level of the Reich and those who wished to see the matter left to the states, or even to the local authorities. It was this issue which lay at the heart of the debate on housing legislation before 1914.

Those to the Right, including Gruner, the spokesman for the government,[44] favoured the latter view, basing their case on the impossibility of shaping legislation that would satisfy the range of local conditions, usages and climate to be found across the country, an argument already rejected by the VföG. A second line of defence was the argument presented by Gruner himself. Pointing to the positive achievements of local measures in areas like Düsseldorf, he warned that minimum Reich legislation would only serve to lame these local initiatives. At the time this argument may have acquired added plausibility in view of Miquel's assurances in the Prussian Abgeord-netenhaus to Hitze in June 1899 that the Prussian government had already been working for two years on the preparation of housing legislation.[45] Hitze, for example, appears to have been convinced of the Prussian government's sincerity and in November he supported the call for state action and challenged the efficacy of Reich-wide legislation.

Opposition to these views was voiced by liberals like Schrader and the SPD deputies who remained convinced of the need for Reich legislation to ensure action on the part of the states and cities. Schrader, for example, recognised the complexity of legislating for the country as a whole but called yet again for a committee to explore the question of national legislation further. This view, supported by the socialists, eventually carried the day and plans to form the committee were drawn up.

A year later nothing had happened; the committee had not even met. In the Prussian Landtag, however, things appeared to be slowly advancing. In the Royal speech at the opening of the new session of the Prussian legislature in January 1901, there were references to the intention to submit not only a new draft of Lex Adickes but also to prepare a draft of legislation 'to reduce the evident inadequacy (of housing) and especially to help, as far as possible, the housing needs of the lower income groups'.[46] But in the Reichstag there had been no advance. In late January three further requests to consider the question of housing were presented to the house.[47] The first sponsored by the National Liberals again demanded the implementation of the proposals along the lines of those of Lechler and Schäffle. The second sponsored by Albrecht and the SPD went further, demanding national housing legislation. The third presented by Schrader requested a national enquiry into housing conditions to determine how far some form of intervention might be necessary. Again no voice was raised against the need for action. Even the conservatives spoke in favour of some initia-tive. But again there was a clear division of opinion between those like the conservatives who urged state action and those like the SPD and the Freisinnige Vereinigung who demanded action by the Reich.[48] However, support for state measures was growing. Miquel who had championed the cause of national legislation in the 1880s, now, as Prussian Minister of Finance, took a more conservative line and pressed for state legislation. Speaking in June 1899 during a debate on the possibility of using the provisions of the Rentengutsgesetz to assist in the provision of housing, he called for action by the states and cities and denied the desirability of Reich involvement in housing:

Originally, before I became a minister, I was of the opinion that it would be possible to push through such legislation if it were restricted to specifying minimum standards; but since than I have become convinced that, particularly here in our federal German state, there exist great, almost insuperable difficulties to this course, at least for the present, and it will therefore be difficult to pass such legislation for the Empire as a whole... Circumstances vary so sharply between town and country, and between different parts of the country that it is a difficult enough enterprise to draw up even minimum standards which could apply across the whole country.[49]

Miquel's statement was bitterly attacked as a betrayal by the housing reformers and those associated with the Verein Reichswohnungsgesetz,[50] but it did give an unambiguous indication of the way in which government circles wished to treat the matter. As Possadowsky made clear in the debate in the Reichstag in 1901, Prussia intended to draw up her own legislation:

Although the Reichskanzler is wholly sympathetic to attempts which are directed at combating social evils in the field of housing, he is of the opinion that the question can only be successfully resolved administratively and constitutionally by means of legislation by the individual states. His Majesty's Prussian Government holds fast to this view, as was suggested in the King's Speech, and is resolutely determined to take the improvement of housing conditions in hand and to prepare comprehensive legislative proposals to this effect.[51]

To many, such as the property lobby and the conservatives, the attraction of considering the housing question in the Prussian legislature rather than the Reichstag was clear. Here the subject could be discussed without the worrying attention of the large group of SPD deputies in the Reichstag who would pursue sensitive issues such as the housing conditions in rural areas already raised by Dreesbach, an SPD deputy from Mannheim, in the November debate in the Reichstag.[52] In the Prussian Landtag the property lobby, the conservatives and the city interests would be able to exert a measure of control impossible in the Reichstag. To emphasise the commitment of the Prussian government to housing reform and to strengthen still further the hand of those pressing for state legislation on housing, Miquel drew attention to the pace at which preparations for a housing bill were proceeding in Prussia and the advanced state of negotiations between different government departments on questions like land policy and housing inspection.[53]

The Prussian Housing Bill of 1904

Despite all these assurances, progress was slow. It was not until 1903 that Freiherr von Rheinbaben, Finance Minister in Prussia, revealed in a debate on the use of government funds for small houses that a draft of the Prussian Housing Bill had been prepared for circulation to a number of representatives of the municipalities and the different provinces for consultation.[54] Although the full text was not published until July 1904, the principal elements of the draft were already being discussed in the press by June 1903 and by December Zweigert, *Oberbürgermeister* of Essen, was reviewing the draft bill at some length in a series of articles in *Zeitschrift für Wohnungswesen* (*ZfW*).[55]

The bill, divided into five articles,[56] provided in Article I for modifications to the *Fluchtliniensgesetz* of 1875 to enable the local authority, first, to control building lines to ensure more open space, especially for gardens, children's play spaces and other recreational activities, and, second, to ensure a reduction in the share of the street development costs for low-income housing. Article II provided for the introduction of density zoning through the building regulations as urged by the VföG. Article III established the principle of allowing a lower level of contribution, under the Kommunalabgabengesetz, to sewerage, gas and water charges for low-income housing. Article IV required the provision of minimum facilities, kitchen, WC and running water, in every new dwelling and the control, in cities with more than 10,000 inhabitants, of the use of existing housing, including servants quarters and the rooms used for lodgers. This was to be achieved by specifying the minimum air space per person and by requiring the provision of separate rooms for children over the age of ten or unmarried lodgers of different sexes. Finally, Article V provided for the establishment of a system of local housing offices which were to organise the inspection of housing and to ensure compliance with these provisions by advice and encouragement in the first instance, but by recourse to the 'police' powers of the authority if necessary.

In the preamble to the bill the government sought both to offer an interpretation of the proposals and to meet the criticisms that were anticipated from the cities and from property interests.[57] The strategy behind the bill was to avoid any form of direct intervention in the housing market, such as subsidising non-profit housing, as demanded by housing reform groups like Verein Reichswohnungsgesetz. Instead, the bill offered a series of incentives which were intended to be equally attractive to all those involved with low-income housing in both the non-profit and the private sectors.

The preamble made it clear that the state did recognise the need to ensure 'social and economic arrangements in housing that would satisfy the requirements of the public'.[58] But to achieve this the bill proposed regulatory measures on the one hand – inspection and limitations on overcrowding – and only the removal of economic restrictions on the building of low-income housing on the other, for example by reducing the development contribution. There was no mention of any direct financial assistance for low-income housing. The extent of government anxiety over the proposals can be seen in the confused attempts to forestall criticism from the different interest groups. As an illustration of these difficulties, Berger-Thimme cites the inept attempt by government to justify the proposals in the bill simultaneously in terms of social need, and, incompatibly, in terms of the profits and benefits to the house building and property interests.[59]

In the event, reaction to the draft was almost universally hostile both from the housing reformers and from their opponents. Naturally there was powerful opposition from the Haus- und Grundbesitzer. In March 1905, at the annual conference of the Verband deutscher Haus- und Grundbesitzervereine in Berlin, after conceding that there might be some justification for considering the problems of housing, the bill was dismissed as totally unacceptable. A critique of the bill from this point of view was published in a pamphlet by Dr Baumert, *Zum preussischen Wohnungsgesetzentwurf* (1905)[60] who rejected the proposed restraints on the activities of property and stridently attacked the idea of any form of subsidy for non-profit housing. Baumert also argued ingenuously that if subsidies were to go to non-profit housing, then private enterprise too should enjoy these advantages. To Baumert and the Haus- und Grund-besitzer, the principal cause of the housing question was the shortage of capital – a cause of mounting concern to private enterprise as money became more expensive in 1904/5 – and the only solution lay, not in tinkering with restrictive legislation, but in ensuring the availability of more capital.

Equally vigorous was the opposition to the bill by the *Bürgermeister* of a number of cities. Zweigert of Essen, who had taken part in the debates of housing in the VfSP and had contributed to the enquiry of 1900, attacked the draft as an undermining of the powers and the jurisdiction of the city authorities.[61] Repeating the well-rehearsed case that national, and even state-wide, legislation could not deal with the variety of circumstances to be encountered in practice, he pressed for local housing control through existing legislation such as the *Flucht-liniengesetz* and the *Kommunalabgabengesetz*. To Zweigert the bill was additionally offensive because it suggested, implicitly, that the city was controlled and managed only for the benefits of property and because it cast doubt on the sincerity of the cities' desire to improve housing conditions.

In government circles, too, there were reservations over the bill. Niethammer mentions the concern in the Treasury at the costs of administering the system of housing inspection proposed in the bill.[62] Other departments, for example agriculture, were also worried; enforce-ment of higher housing standards in rural areas, where housing conditions were generally far worse than in the cities, might lead to serious consequences for agriculture. At the most banal level, the Ministry of Defence, who supported housing reform as a means of improving the quality of recruits, were anxious about the extent to which limitations on overcrowding might affect the billeting of troops on field exercises.

Nor was the bill welcomed by the housing reformers. The draft, inevitably, fell short of the demands, many of them almost utopian, that the reformers were pressing and there was extended discussion of the wisdom of rejecting the bill as it then stood in the hope of getting more comprehensive provisions in a new version. Max Brandts spoke for many when he remarked bitterly that 'what is offered is not much and certainly not worthy of the grand title "A Law in Respect of the Improvement of Housing Conditions"'.[63] Nevertheless, he concluded that 'the best is the enemy of the good' and urged reformers to accept the bill as a starting point, arguing that, as with the old age and accident insurance legislation, it would be possible to modify and improve the proposals once a start had been made. Yet this view was not championed with much vigour. At a time when powerful support would have been needed to carry the bill, disagreement amongst the reformers robbed the government of even this source of support. It is hardly surprising in view of this generally hostile response to the bill from the cities, from property and land on the one hand, and the absence of positive support from reforming circles on the other, that the Prussian government should have judged it more prudent to let the matter rest, than to attempt to force the bill through.

Confusion amongst the reformers

Nowhere were the disagreements in reforming circles over the bill more evident than at the first Deutscher Wohnungskongress held in Frankfurt in October 1904.[64] Organised by Mangoldt and the Verein Reichswohnungsgesetz as a result of a proposal made at the International Housing Congress in Düsseldorf in 1902, it was clearly regarded by its organisers as an opportunity for discussing progress towards national housing legislation. The central issue of the programme was whether the housing reform movement should support the Prussian Housing Bill. There was a majority in favour of national rather than state legislation, but on this subject even the conference's organising committee was split.[65]

The opening of the conference went well and the size of the audience – well over 800 people – greatly exceeded the hopes of the organisers. But after the success of the first evening, the morning session started badly when the opening speaker, Professor Pohl, presented a paper which sought to show that housing conditions, far from deteriorating, were rapidly improving despite the absence of legislation. In place of the 'campaign speech' which many expected, Pohl's speech was regarded as undermining the whole purpose of the congress. From this lame beginning things went from bad to worse. The next speaker failed to catch the mood of the conference. He was then succeeded by the chairman of the Verband Deutscher Haus- und Grundbesitzer, Stadtrat Hartwig, who, with Justizrat Baumert, chairman of the Prussian Haus und Grundbesitzer Vereine, shouting encouragement from the floor, denounced the Verein's proposals as illegal and wholly unnecessary and endorsed the views of the unfortunate Pohl, now cast in the role of ally of the Haus- und Grundbesitzer.

By the afternoon, debate was again focussed on the original purpose of the conference, but there was clear evidence of sharp disagreements in the reformers' circles. As in the Reichstag, there was a division of opinion over what level of government should take responsibility for housing. To some, represented by Dr Sinzheimer, the unwillingness of the local authority, dominated by property interests, to take action could only be overcome by legislation at a higher level. Others, for example Oberbürgermeister Werner and Bürgermeister Körth, protested that the cities were being held back from a natural desire for reform by the reactionary attitudes of state government and called for greater freedom for the cities. But the true extent of these divisions was only revealed when Jäger called for the abandonment of the Verein's previous programme and for a campaign to support state legislation instead. Despite the defects of the Prussian bill, Jäger declared himself in its favour. This 'defection' by Jäger, with his long experience of dealing with housing issues in the Reichstag, came as a major blow to the hopes of those like Mangoldt who had been pressing for national legislation. The congress ended in disorder. Far from uniting the movement, the housing reformers were now more divided than ever and hopes for a united campaign for a national housing law were dashed.

In the housing reform camp, the debate over Reich or state legislation carried on long after the conference. Mangoldt and Zweigert, for example, engaged in a long and acrimonious correspondence on this issue in the *Zeitschrift für Wohnungswesen*.[66] By the end of the following year it was already clear to the leading figures of the housing reform movement that a common approach to legislation would have to be hammered out if anything concrete was to be achieved, a view that was probably strengthened by the mounting reluctance of the Prussian government to press the Prussian housing bill further. During 1904 the Verein Reichswohnungsgesetz had been reformed to give wider representation of the different groups involved in housing reform and had been renamed, more appropriately, Verein Wohnungsreform.[67] In its new form the Verein now sought to assemble representatives of the most important groups involved in housing reform to arrive at an agreed 'minimal programme of reform'.

In March 1906, 31 representatives of different reforming groups and a number of well-known figures in housing circles such as Eugen Jäger, Dr A. Liebknecht and Berthold, met at the first Deutsche Wohnungs-konferenz in an attempt to shape this common policy.[68] In contrast to the reformers' previous position, the starting point for the discussion was the recognition that although 'the far-reaching assistance of the Reich and the individual states' was regarded as necessary, the housing question was to be essentially a question for the local authority. Combined with this general statement was a series of specific recommendations demanding: the establishment of a system of housing inspection; review of the different forms of housing production and reform of the means of providing capital to encourage the local authorities and the regional insurance offices to do more to help low-income housing, especially in the non-profit sector; the initiation of a system of land control and planning measures at all levels of government to reduce land costs and to secure healthy forms of development; finally, the creation of an institution capable of overseeing and carrying through these reforms.

But despite the apparent harmony that prevailed at the conference, there were still clearly expressed doubts over the wisdom of regarding housing as a matter for the local authorities. These views were spelt out by Paul Lechler, the representative of the Evangelisch-Soziale Kongress, who argued that with a few notable exceptions local government had been wholly innocent of any attempts to tackle the housing problem, even for its own employees.[69] To Lechler the hope that the regional insurance offices could undertake a major role in housing provision was to allow other bodies such as the local authorities to escape their full obligations. Indeed the only proposal that he greeted with any warmth was the suggestion that a permanent Housing Commission be set up to co-ordinate and carry through housing reform, a proposal very similar to those that he himself had made twelve years before. The programme put forward at the conference was agreed. But the suspicion of the willingness of the local, and state, authorities to take action on these issues reflects the longstanding, and no doubt justified, anxiety of the reformers that the interest groups entrenched in state and municipal government would stifle attempts at reform. Whatever the political difficulties, the attraction of national legislation, or even of some national Housing Commission to coerce recalcitrant authorities, was a continual refrain in the reformers' debates.

At last, two years after the publication of the Prussian Housing Bill, the movement for housing reform had regained a fair measure of agreement and a new programme had been drawn up. Verein Wohnungsreform could claim with some justification to speak on behalf of the greater part of the movement. But by 1906 the opportunity of influencing government had passed, at least for the immediate future. The shortage of housing that Berlin and other cities had experienced between 1900 and 1903 had given way by 1905/7 to what was regarded by property interests as an excess of supply over demand. More important, government attention had been turned to more pressing matters; the housing question ceased to command public interest. As Jäger explained in 1912, the bill 'had disappeared under the weight of opposition of municipal government and in face of the implacable opposition of the land and financial speculators'.[70] It was not until the end of the decade that either the Reichstag or the Prussian legislature was to return to the issue.

Campaign for housing legislation 1912–14

In the Reichstag the issue of housing legislation was considered fitfully. Nothing resulted from the initiatives by Jäger and the Zentrum or the SPD to revive the issue in 1908 or again in 1910 and the decision to increase the interest rate for loans from the regional insurance funds for housing and to reduce the period of these loans, announced in May 1910, was a blow to the reformers' hopes that government would remain sympathetic to the housing reform cause. In 1911 their hopes were further dashed by the proposal to cut the level of support made available, since 1901, in the Reich budget for financial assistance in the construction of housing for lower-paid Reich employees.

However, one result of these proposals was to spur government supporters of housing reform into action. Niethammer shows that

Lewald, the civil servant responsible in the Reichsamt des Innern for 'housing policy' wrote in the autumn of 1911 to Wahnschaffe, the under-secretary charged by the Chancellor, Bethmann-Hollweg, with the formation of a non-socialist coalition for the election due the following year, suggesting that housing might well form an ideal issue with which to consolidate a new alignment of interests.[71] Rather than add yet more converts to socialism by cutting back on Reich support for housing, the government, he argued, should turn the housing question to its advantage: housing reform was not only viewed as an apolitical issue by the middle-class parties but action on this front might also serve to rally mass support. In the event these ideas were of little value in the election. But this initiative did result in a doubling of the allocation in the Budget for the housing of Reich employees from 2 to 4 million Marks and did lead to the formation of a special sub-committee of the Budget committee with 21 members to consider the question of housing along the lines since urged by Jäger and other housing reformers.[72]

In May 1912 the Reichstag again turned to the question of housing.[73] Three motions were to be considered: a petition from the Zentrum for a reversal of the decision taken in 1910 on the regional insurance funds, a demand from the SPD for national legislation on housing and a proposal from the Budget Committee to form a standing committee of the Reichstag to consider questions of housing. The ensuing debate covered again many of the issues already raised at the beginning of the decade. The government insisted that housing legislation had to be a matter for the individual states while the SPD and the more radical members of the Zentrum such as Jäger insisted with equal vehemence that only national legislation would compel states like Prussia to take action. Nevertheless by the end of the debate there was a clear majority in favour of the formation of the housing committee and it was agreed to select a committee without delay.

With Jäger as secretary, the committee set to work with a will.[74] Barely two months after its formation it put before the Reichstag proposals for a general framework for national legislation; these included proposals for minimum standards governing the use and occupancy of dwellings, housing inspection, the provision of capital and the extension of the leasehold system of land tenure for low-income housing. These measures were to be coupled with provisions to encourage individual states to ensure more effective land policies, extension plans, compulsory purchase powers for residential land and tax policies to encourage low-income housing. In May, when these proposals were adopted *unanimously* by the Reichstag, there was a general feeling of excitement. At last it appeared that progress was being made towards national housing legislation and number of suitably heroic speeches were made to note the 'historic hour'.[75]

But in November the government was stalling over its undertaking on housing legislation. In response to a question by Paul Göhre, asking whether the government intended to proceed on the basis of the vote taken in May, the house was simply referred to deliberations by the

Bundesrat on the competence of the Reichstag to determine such matters.[76] In the meantime preparations for the presentation of a Prussian housing bill had again been set in train, stimulated by the speed with which the Reichstag was moving on the issue. Niethammer emphasises the concern of Prussian civil servants to use the attraction of a Prussian housing bill, rather than legislation dictated by the Reichstag, as a means of cajoling the property interest in both state and municipal government into accepting housing legislation.[77] Acting as fast as possible to pre-empt the Reichstag initiative, the Prussian authorities hurriedly revised the proposals put forward in 1904 and in early February 1913 details of a new bill were published.

The publication of this revised bill only served to confirm the worst fears of many reformers that this was simply a stratagem to forestall national legislation and to secure a treatment of the issue by the Prussian legislature which would be sympathetic to the property lobby and where any radical measures would inevitably be emasculated. The debate in the Reichstag on 7 February reflects the frustration of the reformers hopes, as did the early discussion of the subject by the Housing Committee.[78] The government was represented by Dr Delbrück, Minister of the Interior, who was attacked for appearing to renege on the resolution passed by the Reichstag in the preceding year. But he defended his actions, first, on the grounds that the Bundesrat had ruled housing legislation of the form proposed in May as outside the competence of the Reichstag, and, second, on the grounds that he had already stated during the discussions of the sub-committee of the Housing Committee on 21 and 22 January 1913: 'I expressed my views against the regulation of this matter by Reichs legislation...I then declared that in the event that the states did not resolve to take action it must necessarily be the duty of the Reich to take control in this field.'[79] The initiative for housing reform had now been wrenched away from the Reichstag's Housing Committee and returned to the safety of the Prussian legislature.

The new bill, though modelled on that of 1904, was weaker. The same failings, from the reformers' point of view, were still present and a number of recommendations which had been included in 1904 had now been watered down or removed altogether.[80] Thus provisions granting the authorities the right to encourage the setting out of streets, or to grant a reduction in the development levy, were now set aside. So too were the provisions regarding housing inspection and the control of density through the building regulations. But the most significant modification was the removal of the provisions in the earlier draft for minimum standards of utilisation, which had been heavily attacked by the property lobby.

The response of the cities and the representatives of property was, predictably, more favourable. The capitulation of the authorities to the demands of the cities over the contents of Article I and to the demands of property over minimum standards of use, led to a more enthusiastic response from these quarters. But the housing reformers received the bill with even fainter enthusiasm that that shown for the earlier bill, although their frustrations were tempered by memories of the fate of the earlier draft. Certainly the view expressed by the *ZfW*, which seemed to be shared by most housing reformers, was that it was even weaker than the proposals put forward in 1904.[81] Nevertheless most judged it prudent to support the bill in the debate timetabled for the spring of 1914. Writing in the *ZfW*, Eugen Jäger regretted the abandonment of the progress that had been made towards national legislation and commented, ironically, that with the initiative now firmly in the hands of the individual states: 'the three-class voting system will now be given the chance to prove its sense of social responsibility'.[82] However, most reformers appear to have been convinced that the combination of interests in the Prussian legislature would weaken the bill still further.

As the housing reformers had feared, the debate in the Abgeordnetehaus and the subsequent committee stages further weakened the bill.[83] Although Sydow, Minister for Trade and Industry, introduced the bill for the government with a reminder of the need for Prussia to demonstrate to the Reichstag that there was no need for national legislation, and although the different interest groups expressed a welcome for the revised bill, the debate shows how each group sought to secure still further advantages. Thus members of the Fortschrittliche Volkspartei and National Liberals expressed concern over the extent to which the cities were to be deprived of their rights to self-determination. The Haus- und Grundbesitzer, who had already declared that the bill was loaded in favour of the tenant, stressed the limitations that it would impose on the construction of low-income housing. The Conservatives reiterated their anxieties over the damaging consequences of a 'thoughtless' application of the provisions of the bill to rural areas. Hirsch, the spokesman for the SPD, qualified his support for the bill by reminding the house that the housing problem could not be resolved within the existing order of society, but indicated that he was prepared to support the bill as a necessary first step towards any reform that would improve existing housing conditions.

After its first reading the bill was handed to a 21-man committee for detailed consideration.[84] A comparison of the composition of this committee with the Housing Committee of the Reichstag illustrates the very different balance of forces at the two levels of government: the Prussian committee contained six conservatives and one social democrat, while the Reichstag included six social democrats and two conservatives. During the first reading of the bill by the committee the conflict of interests became more pronounced. The protracted clashes between the spokesmen of the Haus- und Grundbesitzer and the representatives of the cities on the question of control of development was, Berger-Thimme argues, less an argument about housing reform than a confrontation between the two interest groups. That the issue should have been settled by a compromise that leaned in favour of property illustrates again the power of the property interest in the state government. During the committee stages the lone voice to press the housing reformers' case and to argue for a more radical approach to legislation was that of Flesch of Frankfurt. Starting from the conviction that the housing problem was not caused by a shortage of housing but by the imbalance between high rents and low wages, he pressed for the use of the funds proposed in the bill for 'ancillary facilities' such as play spaces and kindergartens, to subsidise housing and thus to reduce rents. But his arguments were hastily and decisively dismissed as being far too radical a form of intervention and one that would establish dangerous precedents for other fields.

By July the committee stages of the bill had been completed.[85] The committee urged the presentation of the diluted bill to the house together with recommendations that the house should consider means of making more capital available for low-income housing, ways of extending the leasehold system of land tenure and the introduction of a state-wide building code. As had been predicted by the housing reformers the result of the debate and the committee stages was to modify the bill to suit the interests of the groups entrenched behind the three-class system. The reformers had been able to make little impact on these groups; indeed, vested interests had shown themselves unwilling to make any concessions that would significantly limit their own advantages.

Furthermore, by allowing Prussia to take the initiative on housing legislation, the government had also condemned the Reichstag's housing committee to impotence. Despite the protests of a few members at the transfer of this responsibility, the committee had agreed to abandon its work on Reich legislation until the outcome of the Prussian bill was clear. In the meantime they turned to consider other issues which the Bundesrat had agreed as lying within the competence of the Reichstag.[86] From mid-1913 onwards the committee focussed largely on questions of extending the leasehold system, the production of housing statistics and thorough investigation of housing finance, in particular the use of regional insurance funds and the availability of capital for low-income housing. But here too its effectiveness was limited. Indeed its one real achievement was to have secured the passing of legislation (10 June 1914) to provide mortgages from Reich funds for housing for those employed in the service of the Reich.[87]

The second reading of the Prussian Housing Bill was timetabled for July 1915.[88] But this was overtaken by events beyond the scale of even the housing problem; it was not until 1918 that the Prussian government finally passed the housing law. How are we to interpret the inability of the German housing reformers to secure the kind of legislation that had been already passed in both England and France? The reformers' case, couched in terms of the moral duty of society, the threat to family life, or the dangers of civil disorder, did, as the Reichstag debates show, command attention. But it was not sufficient to overcome the combined forces of opposition: the sensitivities of the states to intervention by the Reich, the fears of the representatives of the cities to any limitation of municipal independence, or the opposition of the property lobby to any constraint on private enterprise housing. Set against the weight of these different interests, the attraction of exploiting housing reform as an important avenue of social conciliation, as a means of winning the working class over to the State and incorporating them in the existing order of society was not sufficient to assemble the political 'muscle' to force legislation through. Significantly it was only at a time of crisis for the house building industry after 1910, when active government support for the construction of working-class housing would have benefited private enterprise, that agreement on a Prussian housing bill, in its most reduced form, seemed possible.

The absence of legislation did not preclude the partial achievement of much of the reformers' programme, nor the development of the non-profit sector. But did not these very successes, however uneven, further weaken the campaign for legislation? To those opposed to a housing act it was attractive to argue that legislation might in some way stunt local initiative. More important, however, did the local achievements undermine the possibility of a larger common front to press for reform? Cities such as Frankfurt or Ulm showed what could be done, even within the constraints of the existing situation; individual employers like Krupp demonstrated that it was possible to arrive at an apparently successful accommodation with his own workforce. If all this was already possible, did it not further reduce the case for confronting the powerful interests of the cities, of property and of the states? For such reasons it is most important that we look beyond this meagre record of legislation in arriving at any judgement of what had been achieved before 1914.

Conclusion

The movement for housing reform in 1914 had come a long way since the late 1840s when the campaign had first been launched by a professor of Romance and Philology, a court architect and a few individuals. It had acquired a semi-official status. Housing reform was now the subject of huge conferences and congresses: the movement was backed by the propaganda activities of national campaign groups such as the Verein für Wohnungsreform. Members of government now shared the reformers' concerns and ministers attended the movement's meeting. But what achievements had this transformation made possible?

By 1914 the problem of housing was unavoidably a subject of concern to the middle classes to whom, previously, the living conditions of the worker and his family had been quite unknown. There was a great flood of publicity on the subject: books, pamphlets and public lectures. Much of this was repetitive, trivial or worthless. But, as in England, certain central themes formed a natural focus for the debate. In Germany the discussions of sanitarians, engineers, economists, planners and architects followed broadly the same pattern as in England, although in Germany the problem of land, highlighted by the campaign of the Bund deutscher Bodenreformer was regarded as an issue of more pressing urgency than in England. Moreover the timetable of the debate in Germany was, apart from the conspicuous absence of national legislation, surprisingly similar to that in England. In Germany too, it was the mid-1880s that saw a crucial change in attitudes to the housing problem. By the late 1880s, the issue was seen as an important part of the larger debate on the social problem. The improvement of the housing conditions of the working classes was too important a matter to be left to self-help or mere market forces. There was a recognition of the limitations of the ideal of 'self-help' and co-operation in housing. As reformers acquired a more realistic understanding of the shortage of housing in so many cities and of the very limited income of the typical workers' household, they were willing to explore new approaches to the problem. Albrecht notes this change of emphasis: 'While it is clear that the housing question touches upon important issues of public health, there can be no doubt that it is primarily an economic question.' Flesch's maxim, 'Die Wohnfrage ist eine Lohnfrage' (literally: the housing question is a question of wages) is a measure of how far the discussion of housing had advanced. To men like Miquel government regulation was necessary; here was a chance to improve the lot of the worker, offering an opportunity to combat the damaging effects of the anti-socialist legislation.

What had brought about this change in attitudes from which stemmed so many later developments? Schmoller had warned the propertied classes of the need to act if they were to avoid in German cities a repetition of the scenes of terror that Paris had witnessed during the Commune. This was a stern warning, but was it the product of a genuine fear of revolution, or was it a part of the rhetoric necessary to win support for reform? No doubt in Germany, with the largest socialist party in Europe still active despite its proscription, the fear of revolution must have been a spur to the imagination of those who in their complacency had never paused to consider the consequences of poor housing.

But this alone cannot account for the change in attitudes. To the majority of those within the movement, housing reform was a moral imperative, a natural expression of ideas of duty and caritas. German reformers may not, like the veteran French housing reformer Jules Siegfried, have attempted to determine from their own personal experiences the minimum diet necessary for 'physical efficiency', but to men like Albrecht the reform of housing conditions was an obligation that lay on the whole of society. For the reformers it was not a concession wrung by fear of socialism, although this might be attractive as an argument with others. They argued, like the earlier generations of reformers, that poor housing could lead to the decay of the family, to prostitution, to alcoholism, to criminality. But their view of duty extended beyond that of the 1850s. They recognised that improvement could not just be left to the individual. Government action was needed, legislation was necessary to regulate housing conditions and this would have to be sufficiently powerful to overcome the opposition of those with vested interests in the existing state of affairs. The case for reform could also be made in more positive terms. The advantages of a healthy, well-housed and contented workforce were not lost on industrialists like Krupp. Housing reform could be justified in economic terms as well.

That these measures served to strengthen the existing order of society goes without saying. To the housing reformers, inadequate housing was a failure of society that degraded the worker and risked alienating him from the society in which they believed he too should share the benefits of progress. The purpose of reform was to ensure that the worker could secure a healthy and reasonably priced dwelling for himself and his family. He could not expect this as of right. But government should regulate society so that the worker could by himself obtain a home if he chose to do so. Indeed housing reformers argued that government should not only regulate but even, through the regional insurance funds, help the worker to help himself.

How far had the housing reformers been successful in achieving these aims by 1914? In terms of the number of dwellings built, the achievements of the movement, working through the non-profit housing sector, had been pitiful. In Berlin the number of non-profit dwellings built by 1914 was less than a typical year's production by private enterprise. Judged in these terms alone, it would be safe to dismiss the reformers, as had Engels, as harmless cranks and utopian optimists.

But this would be to underestimate what had been achieved by 1914. True, the reformers had fought for national legislation and had lost. There is no legislation in Germany like that of the Loi Siegfried in France or the 1890 Housing of the Working Classes Act in England, but in some states and in cities up and down the country considerable progress had been made. In the field of public health, in the design and construction of working-class housing, in the regulation of the use and the supply of land for residential development, there had been important advances; in some fields Germany was now regarded as an innovator by England and France. In an important respect the housing reformers had even encouraged government to go beyond mere regulation. However limited the achievement by 1914, a non-profit sector had been established during the 1890s and had obtained very substantial capital assistance from funds controlled by government at advantageous rates of interest. The rate of growth of this non-profit housing sector was comparable with that of the work of the local authorities such as the LCC under the provisions of Part III of the 1890 Housing of the Working Classes Act.

To judge these achievements, limited and unevenly distributed as they are, only in terms of the restricted time scale that ends in 1914, is to deny the central continuity of both attitudes and institutions that spans the war. The great municipal housing programmes of the period of post-inflationary prosperity between 1925 and 1930 owed a great deal to the pre-war movement for housing reform. The widely publicised housing in Frankfurt not only owed much of its architectural inspiration to the ideas of the reformers before 1914 but much of its institutional form to the pre-war movement as well. May insisted on the house and its garden, rather than the flat, as the ideal form of housing, and built, using the forms of the 'neues Bauen', the kind of low-density housing on the outskirts of Frankfurt that had been so eagerly championed before the war. The Römerstadt estate and the developments built at Praunheim, Bockenheim and other sites around the outskirts of the city were not only built on land that the city had assembled as a result of the municipal *Bodenpolitik* pursued by Adickes, but was also built by the very same non-profit societies that had been operating before the war. The work of societies such as the Aktien-baugesellschaft für kleine Wohnungen, founded long before the war, carried right on through into the 1930s, even though the source of finance was now the allocation from the *Hauszinssteuer* – the tax on existing property – rather than the regional insurance funds. Frankfurt was atypical in the scale of its pre-war non-profit sector, but what happened in Frankfurt was also to be found elsewhere. Although the war brought important changes in the whole field of housing, we can see even in cities like Berlin a continuity of approach that links the pre- and post-war years; even the Berliner gemeinnützige Baugesellschaft was still operating through into the 1930s. Against this longer time scale, the achievements of the pre-war housing reformers do appear more substantial. Indeed in Germany, as in England, post-war housing policy starts from the foundations laid by the pre-war movement.

Judged by their achievements up to August 1914, the housing reformers had fallen short of the goals they had set themselves. Before 1914 the lack of national housing legislation left the benefits of housing reform unevenly distributed. In many cities, particularly those in Prussia where they were secure behind the bastion of the three-class election system, property interests successfully defied the reformers' attempts to improve housing conditions and to encourage the non-profit housing sector. For every Frankfurt or Ulm, there were tens, if not hundreds, of cities where nothing had been done before the war.

How does this record of housing reform compare with that in France? To German eyes, the movement in France started with certain natural advantages. Even before the German movement had really started, the reformers in France could point to achievements of note, whatever their effect in practice. By 1850 the French had already passed national legislation on hygiene and housing which was backed with all the power of central government in Paris. Haussmann's work on the replanning and cleansing of Paris was admired throughout Europe as the triumph of modern planning; had not the Emperor Napoleon III himself urged forward the building of 'model' dwellings as an example of how he wished to see the workers housed in his capital? Starting with these apparent advantages, what did the movement for housing reform achieve in France?

Part Two

◇◇

The movement for housing reform in France 1840–1914

Recognition of the Housing
Problem

13

◇◇◇

The context of the Housing Problem

In France, as in Germany, the movement for housing reform grew out of initiatives to resolve the problems of quality and quantity evident in the housing of working families in urban areas. But if the focus of reform was similar, it was set in a contrasting background in the growth of the two countries. In the middle of the nineteenth century the overall population of France and the area to be unified as the German Empire in 1871 was similar, each being about 35 million. Within this total, the population classified as urban in Germany was only slightly higher than in France: about 10 million, as opposed to 8.5 million. But by the outbreak of the First World War, these populations had evolved very differently. The urban population in Germany had increased by almost 29 million, the vast majority of this growth occurring after unification. In contrast, the urban population in France had grown by less than 9 million.[1]

The contrast between the two countries is emphasised when these figures are related to the growth of the population as a whole. A declining birth rate in France, particularly marked after the 1880s, meant that the population increased by only just over 4 million in the period being considered. In Germany, the increase was 30 million, again concentrated in the period after unification. While urban growth thus proceeded broadly in parallel with the population growth in Germany, in France it tended to be at the expense of the rural population.

The contrast in urban growth was therefore reflected in the relative importance of the urban and rural populations in the two countries. In Germany the urban population grew in importance from representing about 30% of the total population in the mid-nineteenth century, to 60% in 1911; but this shift was accomplished without substantially altering the size of the rural population in absolute terms. In France, on the other hand, the urban population remained less important than the rural population, moving only from 25% to 44%; but in spite of this, the rural population had diminished noticeably by 1911.[2]

These general figures say nothing of the pressure on the housing market in specific towns. The critical moments of urban growth tended to be concentrated into short bursts which created severe problems. Thus the 'housing problem' which existed in the inability of the housing market in individual towns to respond to the demand placed on it, was present in France as in Germany, despite the different picture of urban growth overall. But that different picture did mean that the housing problem in a specific town had a different relationship to the population as a whole.

Thus, in Germany the housing reformers were attempting to control and order the development of housing in cities which were growing on top of a rapidly expanding population. Their counterparts in France were faced with cities whose growth was acting as a drain on the country's population, drawing people in from rural areas at a faster rate than the natural growth of the population. It was therefore natural that during the critical period of the 1880s, when the housing reform movement was to be formalised into a national organisation in France, discussion of housing reform should centre around the Société d'Economie Sociale, a society whose founder had advocated the strengthening of the traditional rural structure of France. This aim was being undermined as cities compensated for their low natural rate of growth by drawing in migrants from rural areas.

While the French reformers did turn to the problem of housing in cities, they did not develop the close focus on the urban housing market, and particularly the land market, which reformers in Germany were to do. The overwhelming fact of urban growth caused the Germans to take up these issues, approaching the housing question from within the city; in contrast the French can be said to have approached the question from outside.

A second significant difference between the two countries also affected the way in which the housing problem was tackled. Throughout the period, France was a highly centralised country, dominated by Paris; successive changes of constitution did not alter this basic characteristic. In contrast, at the start of the period Germany was not even a unified country, and when it was brought together it was as a federal structure. German cities thus had a tradition of independence, and greater powers for independent action than their French counterparts which were looked over constantly from Paris. This relative weakness of the municipality in France is reflected in two ways in the efforts of the housing reformers. First, it left the municipalities in a weak position with respect to private interests, rendering early efforts to control standards of housing ineffective. Second, it left the municipalities in a weak position if they wished to implement active policies to help the construction of housing, whether in providing land for builders, or in building themselves. A further effect of municipal weakness was that cities took little initiative in resolving housing problems. Individuals or organisations within provincial towns might take action – the Société Industrielle in Mulhouse in the 1850s, or the Caisses d'Epargne in Marseilles and Lyons in the 1880s for example. But this action did not evoke a response from the public authorities in the towns concerned. For such initiatives to widen their effect through public action they had to wait until their significance was felt in Paris. Moreover, even if legislation introducing the possibility of public action were to be passed in the capital, this was still no guarantee that it would be taken up by provincial cities.

Against the contrasting characteristics of population growth and municipal independence, the French and German reformers followed similar concerns and investigated similar solutions. In both countries, the example offered by England was a frequent stimulant to action. This study of housing reform in France will follow thematically the same pattern as the study on Germany. In the first section, the context of late nineteenth-century housing reform will be examined in the debate which first focussed on housing in the middle of the century, and in the housing market in Paris. Paris was central to the housing reform movement for three main reasons. First, it presented the problems associated with inadequate housing in urban areas in a particularly forceful manner, being by a considerable margin the largest city in France. Second, as the heart of a centralised country, it focussed the societies, exhibitions and congresses which considered the question of housing. Third, when the problems of declining birth rate and rural depopulation started to attract particular attention in the 1880s, the size and dominance of Paris made the city the main offender in draining the population from the countryside.

In the second section, the major channels through which housing reform was evolved and implemented are examined. From the earliest debate on housing, the subject was dominated by men whose first concern was with social reform rather than with a narrower technical interest. These reformers defined the ideal form of workers' housing in the early 1850s; their ideal was maintained by their successors, who saw it as a means of defending society against radical change. This social emphasis provided the background against which the more technical aspects of housing reform were evolved. This can be seen in the efforts to resolve the questions of hygiene, land and planning and of the architectural design of housing. The issues of hygiene and land inevitably raised the question of the role of the public authorities, and in each case there were particular obstacles to effective action. In the case of hygiene, the strength of property interests hampered efforts to improve housing conditions. With respect to land and planning, the weakness of municipal authorities hindered any constructive action.

Consideration of the role of architects stresses the degree to which housing reform was dominated by the social reformers. In the absence of interest by architects in the design of cheap housing in the 1850s, it was the social reformers who defined the ideal form of housing which reform was intended to achieve, and architects only gradually became involved in cheap housing as the scale and complexity of projects grew towards the end of the century.

The dominance of the social reformers is also reflected in the attempts to increase the construction of new dwellings, which are considered in the third section. The working population which the housing reformers were trying to house was largely created by the development of industry in France, and the relationship between social reform and industry is indicated by the housing which stood as an ideal for the reformers; this originated in a discussion at the Société Industrielle in Mulhouse, an organisation of local industrialists which had acquired a reputation as one of the foremost pioneers of social reform in France.

Industry had an ambiguous relation to the housing problem. Where a factory was situated in an isolated area, away from existing towns, the employer was obliged to provide housing; some of these developments established a model for housing in qualitative terms, even if the paternalism of the employer was not always welcome. On the other hand, where industry grew up alongside an existing town, with a pool of surplus labour, it had no need to provide housing; in these circumstances the expansion of industry, and the resulting attraction of new labour, led to the particular housing problems of urban industrial areas. The Mulhouse housing overlapped these two situations: originating as a measure by industrialists to house workers for their factories, it was established as a limited dividend company which provided the model for the development of later housing societies operating alongside the speculative housing market in urban areas. Only in the 1880s did an alternative means of providing housing through the co-operation of the workers themselves begin to emerge.

These different forms of housing production failed to create a noticeable impact on the housing market, and from the 1880s initiatives to increase the quantity of cheap housing were focussed on the social reform organisation in Paris, the Société d'Economie Sociale. Out of discussion in the 1880s emerged a society specifically to encourage the construction of cheap housing, the Société Française des Habitations à Bon Marché (HBM), formed in 1889. This society promoted the first legislation to provide public aid for housing construction, passed in 1894.

The question of the relationship between public intervention and private interests, which this law raised with respect to housing construction, was central to the evolution of housing reform. It was at the heart of efforts to improve the standard of existing housing, and to increase the quantity of new housing. Before 1850 the housing market was the preserve of private enterprise; the public authorities had some control over the height of buildings, and types of construction, but little control over conditions within houses. By 1918 the public authorities had a role to play in the market in three areas: as a control on private enterprise, as an aid to private enterprise, and as actors in their own right. The emergence of this role structured the evolution of housing reform, and can be briefly summarised in relation to existing and new housing.

The existing housing stock before 1850 was in the hands of the private market; this established standards of size, and servicing, and levels of rent. The creation of a public role began with the introduction in 1850 of legislation to control the hygienic standards of privately rented dwellings; this did not go so far as to establish minimum standards of servicing or of size. The law was restricted to one of control; only in 1902 were the public authorities permitted to intervene as actors, when they were authorised to execute improvement works if recalcitrant landlords refused. This increase of public power preceded a more significant extension, in the form of a slum clearance policy. During the reconstruction of Paris and other urban centres notably in the 1850s, some unhealthy housing was demolished, but this was a by-product of the plans rather than a primary aim. It was not until the early 1900s that serious consideration was given to the possibility of allowing public authorities to act directly to clear slums, by expropriation and demolition.

With respect to the financial aspects of existing housing, the public authorities kept an even lower profile. As a standard measure, intervention was restricted to the public assistance available to paupers, which could include a rent allowance. Under the exceptional circumstances of the 1870 war, a temporary intervention was made to apply a moratorium on rents. The principle of direct rent control was only admitted as another exceptional measure, introduced during the First World War. In this case, however, the temporary intervention was less easy to withdraw, and rent control continued after the war.

If the private sector was the dominant force in the management of the existing housing stock before the First World War, so too it was the main agent in the construction of new housing. As a control on private action, public intervention was limited throughout the nineteenth century, and had more to do with the exterior of dwellings, as a by-product of street regulations, than with the standards of construction, servicing and size. Only in 1902 was the principle of basic standards requiring a certificate of approval introduced.

As an aid to private enterprise, public intervention was envisaged as an exceptional measure in the mid-nineteenth century. Subsidies allowed in 1848 and 1852 were only intended to prime the private sector, which would then continue on its own. Intervention of a permanent nature was not introduced until 1894, by the cheap housing law which the housing reformers promoted. The public aid provided by this law was purely financial, limited to tax reliefs, and loans to societies building cheap housing, although it was extended in 1906 to include the acquisition of shares in housing societies, and the provision of land.

The principle of allowing public authorities to intervene directly as actors, in competition with private enterprise, was still a contentious issue at the end of the period. It was admitted in 1912, but only under conditions which aimed to establish the public housing offices as independent agencies, acting on the same terms as their private counterparts.

This process of public intervention in relation to existing housing and new construction should not be taken as a gradual advance towards the resolution of the housing problem. That problem existed in 1850, and it still existed, if in somewhat different terms, in 1914. Rather, the process operated as a holding operation, aiming to keep in check those parts of the housing problem which might lead the housing market to break down, and thus represent a threat to society as a whole. It would be unfair to claim that the housing reformers had no desire to make society better; but it is clear that their first objective was to stop it, in their view, from getting worse.

The Housing Question in urban areas: a problem recognised

By the middle of the nineteenth century, France possessed several well-developed urban centres. As early as 1801, the population of Paris was over 547,000, making it the second largest city in Europe after London. At the same date France's three major provincial cities, Marseilles, Lyons and Bordeaux, were all larger than any of the provincial cities in England. But as England experienced the rapid growth of urban areas under the influence of industrialisation in the early nineteenth century, the major English manufacturing towns rapidly overtook the provincial cities of France.[3]

In the growth of her urban centres France was thus to lag behind England from the early nineteenth century and behind Germany and England in the later part of the century; however, the cities established by the beginning of the century were to retain their importance within France. A total of eight cities had populations of more than 50,000 by 1801. These cities were tending to grow faster than the population of the country as a whole, and urban growth increased in the 1830s to reach a peak in the 1850s and early 1860s. By that time, Bordeaux, Toulouse and Marseilles as France's major ports, and Lille and Lyons as the major urban centres within the northern and central areas of France, had all grown to between two and three times their 1801 population, while Paris, at 1.8 million, was over three times its 1801 size.[4]

These established cities were joined by some industrial centres whose rate of growth approached that of the industrial cities of England. Thus Saint-Etienne and Roubaix, both with populations below 20,000 in 1801, grew by almost six times, and over nine times respectively. Mulhouse, described by one writer in the 1840s as the 'French Manchester', had grown by 1866 to almost ten times its size at the end of the eighteenth century.[5]

It was the living and working conditions of workers in these established and new urban centres which were to lead to a recognition of the importance of housing in terms of social stability and public health. Crime and poverty, which could be tolerated or ignored on a small scale, presented a danger when concentrated in expanding towns. At times of epidemic and of economic depression, the poor represented a real threat to the remainder of society: through the spread of disease from the squalor of poor quarters, or the spread of dissent among the occupants of those quarters.

Attention focussed initially on the public health aspects of housing. The work of some doctors in the early nineteenth century drew attention

Table 1 *Population of France, and of major French cities, 1801–86*

	1801	1836	1866	1886
France	27,350,000	33,541,000	38,067,000	38,219,000
Paris	547,756	899,313	1,825,274[1]	2,344,550
Marseilles	111,130	146,239	300,131	376,143
Lyons	109,500	150,814	323,954[1]	401,930
Bordeaux	90,992	98,705	194,241	240,582
Lille	54,756	72,005	154,749[1]	188,272
Toulouse	50,171	77,372	126,936	147,717
Nantes	73,879	75,895	111,956	127,482
Rouen	87,000	92,083	100,671	107,163
Roubaix	8,000	—	65,091	100,299
St Etienne	16,259	41,534	96,620	117,875
Mulhouse	6,000[2]	16,932[3]	58,773	—

1. These figures include the effect of annexations of new areas of land to these cities during the 1850s.
2. Figure for 1798.
3. Figure for 1838.
Sources: E. Levasseur, *La population française,* vol. 2, p. 345; Société Industrielle de Mulhouse, *Histoire documentaire de Mulhouse,* vol. 1, p. 32; G. Dupeux, *French Society 1789–1970,* p. 37.

to the problems of hygiene in various towns. Their studies were reinforced by the investigations of the Conseils de Salubrité established after 1802. The first of these Conseils was set up in Paris, and by 1848 there were 65 in existence, mainly in urban and industrial areas.[6] From 1822 the local Conseils were joined by a central organisation, the Conseil Supérieur de Santé. The evidence of the studies by the Conseils was reinforced by the epidemics which punctuated the nineteenth century. Thriving in slum areas, disease had no respect for wealth or status, and epidemics served to focus concern. Thus a writer on housing reform in the 1880s was to note that 'in Paris, at the approach of cholera towards the end of 1831, the hygiene of housing became for the first time an object of attention'.[7]

In response to the threat of cholera in 1831, Commissions Sanitaires were set up in every quarter of Paris under a central Commission de Salubrité. Surveys of housing carried out by these Commissions were to make clear the correlation between bad housing conditions and the spread of disease. 'Wherever an impoverished population exists crowded into dirty, small dwellings, there the epidemic has multiplied its victims.'[8] The role of housing conditions was taken seriously enough for a special commission to be set up. Its three members were to consider the question of hygiene in relation to the construction of houses in Paris, and to the improvement of existing dwellings and lodging houses.

The special commission's report, presented in early 1832, proposed controls on the height of building, on the size of light-wells (which should, the commission urged, be open on at least one side), on water supply and sewage, and on the ventilation and size of habitable rooms.[9] These were clearly proposals for the long term, rather than the immediate crisis and they suffered the fate of many reforms drawn up in time of crisis. Once the crisis was passed, they seemed unnecessarily complicated, and difficult to implement, and were soon set aside. However, demands similar to those made by the commission were to become increasingly common during the second half of the century, and were to be met in part by the achievements of sanitary and architectural reform.

Although the 1832 special commission's proposals were not taken up, the 1830s and 1840s did see greater attention being paid to the problems of the working classes and their relationship to society as a whole. During the years following the cholera epidemic, Dr L. R. Villermé, a member of the central Commission de Salubrité in 1832, pursued detailed research on the living and working conditions of workers in various industries in France. His study, published in 1840,[10] provided the most comprehensive survey of workers' conditions to date. Earlier reports by doctors and Conseils de Salubrité had provided evidence of individual towns or areas, but Villermé's study brought together detailed information on a comparative basis. His work was rightly respected, and the facts gathered by him provided fuel for many later writers.

Villermé drew attention to the appalling housing conditions which he found in some towns. In Mulhouse, he saw 'miserable dwellings, where two families slept, one in each corner, on straw thrown on to the tiles and held in by two planks'.[11] In Lille, he described the cellar dwellings for whose occupants he noted that the day started an hour later, and night came an hour earlier than for other people. In examining such housing, Villermé was concerned not merely with the physical health, but also with the moral well-being of the workers. He discussed housing, along with length of the working day, child labour, wages and other factors, assessing their effect on the worker and his family. But while his description of housing in various towns confirmed the unhealthy conditions in which many workers lived, Villermé did not consider the improvement of housing as a direct means of ameliorating workers' conditions. Schooling, savings banks, limitation on the working day and on the age of children employed – such innovations as these were discussed by Villermé as valid reforms. Housing was considered to be a result, rather than a cause, of social problems, even if its role in assisting the spread of disease had already been accepted.

A study published in the same year as Villermé's, by H. A. Frégier,[12] did make a more direct link between the dwelling, and the moral standing of its occupants. As a senior official in the Prefecture of Police in Paris, Frégier had a working knowledge of the population about whom he was writing. In his discussion of housing, Frégier drew attention to the double threat of bad housing, to health and to morality. Thus overcrowding was 'a cause of insalubrity at the same time as it offends morality'.[13] Having identified housing as a possible cause of social ills, Frégier was led to see it as their possible solution. Significantly, he placed his discussion of housing in the section on 'Measures against the invasion of vice', and he called on the 'benevolent' capital of philanthropy to increase the construction of suitable housing for workers. Such action would have the advantages 'of diminishing the causes of public insalubrity, and...of offering to hard working, honest workers the means of obtaining a dwelling in keeping with their needs, which will stir in them the taste for the home and for domestic peace, so favourable to moral welfare'.[14]

If the home was to provide the setting for moral improvement, it was the family which would bring that improvement about. Frégier argued that 'the direct care, and...the development of individual morality belongs to the father of the family and to the minister of religion; but principally to the former who, in this respect, seems to hold in his hands not only the destiny of the members of his family, but also that of society as a whole'.[15]

In Frégier's study the overlapping concern for the physical and moral effects of inadequate housing, which was to dominate the evolution of housing reform is already apparent. So too is the belief that by helping working families to find good housing not only would their health be protected, but society as a whole would be strengthened through the securing of its moral base, the family. In these terms, action to improve housing conditions could be presented as the concern of society as a whole.

To see how the concern for housing was taken up, it is important to place the work of Villermé and Frégier in its context, as their studies contributed to a more informed discussion of social problems in the 1840s. The years after 1840 saw a change in the consideration of social problems which Louis Chevalier has noted in relation to the discussion of crime and poverty. Earlier writers could argue that only a minority of the poor – the 'deserving' poor such as the sick or elderly – required the assistance of society. The poverty of the majority was seen in the same terms as crime; these poor should avoid the pitfalls of destitution by their own efforts. But as Chevalier observes: 'the successive surveys after 1840 brought a real revelation. Misery was no longer a marginal fact; it was central. It was no longer innocuous...it became large, a public nuisance and a danger. In short, it existed.'[16]

The acknowledgement that destitution, and above all urban destitution, existed, and was derived from the economic basis of society rather than the failings of individuals, made the problems of the poor into problems of society as a whole. The manageable minority of the 'deserving' poor became a threatening mass of urban poor. In the field of housing, this was clearly of considerable consequence. The 'deserving' poor could be helped by charity, and by the construction of old people's homes, hospices or orphanages. The new concept of the urban poor embraced ordinary families and introduced a scale which could neither be ignored, nor dealt with by special institutions. The housing of the urban poor was a problem which society as a whole must confront.

During the 1840s several groups within society did confront this problem. In the main these were conservative groups, led to take an interest in housing as an extension of their concern to resolve the social questions which threatened to destabilise the social order. Three such groups made a particular contribution to the development of interest in housing: the Académie des Sciences Morales et Politiques, the Société Industrielle de Mulhouse, and the Société d'Economie Charitable. But, alongside these defenders of the social order, a more radical group also contributed to the discussion of housing; for housing was a central element in the proposals of the utopian socialists, and particularly the followers of Charles Fourier, to restructure society.

The Académie des Sciences Morales et Politiques had originally been established after the French Revolution, in 1795, but was suppressed less than ten years later by Napoleon. It was re-established in 1832, under the monarchy of Louis-Philippe; during his reign the Académie was to act as a focus for the discussion of social issues.

Dr Villermé was a founder member of the Académie when it was re-established, and his research in the 1830s was carried out on behalf of the Académie. Frégier's book was also related to the Académie's work, being awarded the prize offered for a study of the 'dangerous classes' of a large city. With the endorsement of the Académie, the views of Villermé and Frégier could not be dismissed as those of eccentrics, still less those of revolutionaries.

While carrying out his study in the 1830s, Villermé had drawn on a variety of organisations throughout France to gather information. Among these organisations was the Société Industrielle in Mulhouse, which had become a particularly active centre for the discussion of social questions. Founded in 1825, the Society was dominated by the Protestant industrial aristocracy of the town. The powerful combination of Protestant morality and a firm belief in the role of industry at the heart of society led the Mulhouse industrialists to develop a wide range of social institutions on behalf of their workers. The effect of such patronage was not without benefit to the industrialists themselves; but what is significant in the present context is not the motives of the industrialists so much as their interest in identifying the problems inherent in industrial society. Thus in 1838 the society offered a prize for a study of the relationship between industry and society. As the discussion of the studies submitted led to some disagreement over the facts concerning living and working conditions in Mulhouse, the society responded by requesting one of its members, Dr Achille Penot, to carry out a statistical study of the town. The result was a detailed report of over 250 pages, which was published in a special double issue of the society's bulletin, in 1843.[17]

The Mulhouse industrialists were to turn their attention particularly to housing in the early 1850s, but they heard a paper by one of their members, discussing workers' housing in England and France as early as 1845.[18] At this time the question of housing was also being taken up in Catholic charitable circles in Paris. R. H. Guerrand has analysed the importance of the group centred on Armand de Melun in this respect.[19] Workers' housing was the subject of an article in one of the first issues of the review founded by de Melun in 1845, *Les Annales de la Charité*. The Société d'Economie Charitable, formed two years later by de Melun, provided a new focus for discussion of social issues by the upper classes, and included the respected Villermé among its members.

The backgrounds of these three organisations – intellectual, industrial, charitable – were very different. But each contributed to the process of building up an awareness of the social problems created by industrial society. This process was more advanced by the mid-nineteenth century in France than in Germany. The political centralisation of France, and the more developed state of its economy in comparison to Germany at this date made possible the comparative study of different industrial areas. In this respect Villermé's research was perhaps the most outstanding achievement. But the organisations which have briefly been examined stimulated a wide range of study.

The Académie des Sciences Morales et Politiques, the Société Industrielle de Mulhouse and the Société d'Economie Charitable all grouped individuals who were among the 'establishment' of the 1840s; while their interest in social questions might place them on the side of reform, they were in no sense concerned to overthrow the existing social order. In contrast, the utopian socialists offered a new vision of society, which was reflected in their proposals for new forms of housing.

The most coherent and influential of these proposals had been developed by Charles Fourier in the 1820s. In contrast to the elevated social position of the members of the socially conscious groups already discussed, Fourier was a commercial traveller and clerk.[20] Rejecting the existing city, he proposed the creation of self-contained communities of about 1600 people. To house these communities, Fourier devised his *phalanstère*. This grouped the dwellings for the community into a single building which also contained all of the communal facilities for its occupants; circulation through the building was by means of a covered, glazed gallery. The *phalanstère* provided a powerful image, and was a proposal which had to be acknowledged – even if often rejected – by the housing reformers of the second half of the century (fig. 1).

In the 1840s, Fourier's wider political ideas gained considerable currency; his more eccentric notions were quietly dropped by his followers, but the concept of the *phalanstère* retained its central position. From 1843 the *phalanstériens* produced a daily paper, under the direction of Victor Considérant, the senior figure of the movement after Fourier's death. While their political views set them against the advocates of more cautious reform, the *phalanstériens* interest in housing did help to reinforce the recognition of the 'housing question' in the 1840s.

A key role in this respect was occupied by the architect César Daly. A friend of Considérant, Daly was involved in the late 1830s in drawing up the plans for a proposed *phalanstère* for 400 children, to be built at Condé-sur-Vesgres.[21] This project did not proceed, and it was as a publicist rather than as a practising architect that Daly was to make his

The *phalanstère* of Charles Fourier, interpreted by Victor Considérant

name. In 1840 he founded the *Revue Générale de l'Architecture et des Travaux Publics*, and rapidly established it as one of the most influential architectural journals in France; the *Revue* was to maintain an interest in questions of hygiene, and in buildings whose importance was social, not simply aesthetic. These buildings included housing for workers, and in 1846 Daly contributed a series of articles on this subject, including illustrations of model housing schemes recently built in England.

The Housing Question: The first solutions

During the 1840s the question of housing was thus raised as a part of the discussion of social issues. This recognition of the importance of housing paved the way for a wider debate on the question in the aftermath of the revolution which replaced Louis-Philippe's monarchy by a Republic, in February 1848. Over the next four years the issue of public responsibility for the housing conditions of the poor was to be viewed from a variety of angles. The effect of this in practice was limited, and no coherent movement for housing reform emerged. However, the debate during this period is important, as it touched on themes which were to recur in the development of housing reform. To identify these themes, in the rapidly changing political atmosphere after 1848, three phases will be considered: the early months of the Republic, when socialist ideas gained considerable currency, the re-establishment of order after June 1848, and the creation of a new Empire by Louis-Napoleon, after his *coup d'état* of 1851. In each of these phases the question of housing was on the agenda of public discussion.

The socialist experiment in the months after February 1848 was too turbulent and too short-lived for a policy towards housing to be established. Nonetheless, it is possible to see the potential which this experiment offered. These were the months in which workers' associations flourished; a workers' commission was set up in the Luxembourg Palace to consider issues affecting the working class, and the national workshops were created to provide work for the unemployed. César Daly saw the opportunity which the national workshops provided to implement socially desirable projects, and he addressed a proposal for the construction of housing to the Luxembourg Commission; this housing was to take up the image of communal housing established by Fourier, providing flats related to facilities such as reading rooms, crèches and schools.[22] The principle of State-financed housing of this form was also taken up by Considérant, who had been elected to the Constituent Assembly of the new Republic; however, by the time he presented his proposal in April 1849, the Republic had moved away from such direct notions of public action.[23]

In June 1848, rioting in Paris was fiercely suppressed by the provisional government. Influence had shifted among the leaders of the Republic, and the alliance between some of those leaders and the Paris Left was now replaced by a desire to re-establish order and renew economic confidence. In relation to housing, the socialist notion of public construction receded as attempts were made to stimulate private investment. This was a central measure in the policies of the new leaders. The building industry was a major employer of labour, and its renewal would help reduce the problems of unemployment in Paris;[24] moreover, the industry occupied an important position in encouraging the general recovery of the economy. Thus in July a series of tax reliefs on new construction were introduced, and a credit organisation – the Sous-Comptoir des Entrepreneurs – established to provide loans for building. However, the greater attention being paid to the provision of workers' housing was reflected in one measure also introduced in July, which offered a 6% subsidy to contractors building housing for workers in Paris.

Politically, the Republic continued to evolve and change, but in terms of housing it is possible to see the re-establishment of order after June as paving the way for a discussion which was to culminate in the passage of legislation during 1850. This discussion was to confirm the rejection of socialist solutions to the housing question, while responding to the concern over housing conditions which had emerged during the 1840s.

The replacement of the radical ideals of the socialists by a more moderate approach to reform is indicated by the fact that the Académie des Sciences Morales et Politiques was requested to assist in the process of 're-establishing the profoundly troubled moral order of our country'.[25] The Académie asked one of its members, Adolphe Blanqui, to visit those towns which had suffered the most severe rioting in June; the report which he presented at the end of 1848 acknowledged the need for action, but insisted that it must respect the existing social order. It is worth pausing briefly in the consideration of this turbulent year to examine Blanqui's position, as it contains elements which were to be characteristic of the housing reform movement as it later emerged.

Blanqui took care to separate the 'social order' from political change. 'How can one prevent the people', he asked, 'from thinking that one can change overnight the eternal laws which rule over the social order, when a mere handful of determined men can overthrow a constitution in a few hours?' The social order had its own logic, independent of man's attempts to change it. In holding this view, Blanqui placed himself firmly against socialist doctrines. Ironically, Blanqui's own brother, Auguste, had been one of the leaders of such doctrines in the early part of 1848. Victor Hugo describes a stormy meeting at that time at which Auguste offered the head of his brother; Adolphe was more restrained in his report, where he categorised socialist doctrines as having in common 'only the same sentiment of hatred against society'.[26]

In ascribing an internal logic to the social order, Blanqui argued that progress must obey that logic. Blanqui's comments on destitution indicate the ambiguity inherent in such a view. On the one hand he could argue that 'it must be shown through the sincere and striking exposition of the true state of things, that if there exists in France real destitution, this is inseparable from human weakness'. On the other hand, he claimed that destitution 'is everywhere softened by the progress of customs and institutions', and he acknowledged that in certain cases those customs and institutions needed direct intervention to encourage them.[27] The existence of this ambiguity is central to an understanding of later initiatives in housing reform. Those reformers who accepted the constraints of working within the existing social order had to decide whether a given problem derived from the current state of the social order, as reflected in human inadequacy, and could thus only be removed through the natural evolution of the social order, or whether it derived from society's management of the customs and institutions, within the social order, in which case society could take action.

In 1848, Blanqui placed the problem of workers' housing conditions in the second category. In concluding his report he demanded 'in the first place, special legislation on housing, whose horrifying insalubrity is the major cause of this untimely mortality and of this indescribable immorality which decimate and debase the population of some of our large towns'.[28] Legislation on housing conditions had already been advocated in the 1840s as a counterpart to the discussion on housing, and with the widening of discussion after 1848 the demand for legislation gained strength. It was particularly reinforced by the approach of a new epidemic of cholera towards the end of 1848. In response to this threat, the structure of hygiene councils throughout the country was reorganised, while in Paris, instructions were issued with the aim of maintaining hygiene standards in dwellings.

The proposal for general legislation to control housing conditions was placed before the Assembly in July 1849. R. H. Guerrand has drawn attention to the roots of this proposal in the social Catholic group centred on the Société d'Economie Charitable.[29] But, as finally passed in 1850, the law was not the achievement of a single pressure group. Rather, it was a logical response to the understanding of the importance of housing to social reform, within the moderate reforming position adopted by figures such as Blanqui. The 1850 law thus provides the opportunity to see how that general position was translated into a specific response to the problems of housing.

In this respect it is instructive to consider the way in which the law resolved two questions: first, whether public intervention was to imply an active role, or simply a passive role; second, how the balance between private and public interests was to be resolved.

The first question was posed directly by the original bill presented in 1849. This envisaged a system of control over the conditions in existing housing, but it also included an article which would have given local authorities the power to levy a special tax of two centimes 'to encourage the construction of small dwellings presenting the necessary conditions of hygiene and salubrity'.[30] Although this article received some support during discussion of the bill, it was eventually rejected by an Assembly which accepted deputy Raudot's assertion that 'official charity kills private charity'.[31] Public intervention was to be limited to the passive role of control; the active role of constructing housing was to remain with the private sector, as the economic measures introduced in July 1848 had already suggested.

But even if intervention in the form of control was accepted, the second question remained; in executing their controlling role, how far could the public authorities encroach on personal liberty? The 1850 law acknowledged the principle that society should protect tenants from unhealthy conditions deriving from the action, or lack of action, of the proprietor; but it left the public authorities very little power to provide this protection. The procedure for forcing a proprietor to make improvements was cumbersome, with frequent opportunities for appeal, while the penalties which could be imposed on intransigent proprietors were negligible; nor were the authorities granted the power to execute works at the proprietor's expense, if he consistently refused to carry out improvements. As a result, the principle acknowledged by the law was severely limited by the detailed definition of the relationship between public and private interests.

If the first few months of the Republic in 1848 had allowed César Daly to envisage a programme of publicly financed housing, the succeeding phase of the Republic had defined what was in effect a minimal role for the public authorities. The phase which followed this, after Louis-Napoleon's *coup d'état* in December 1851 was to mark an increase in that role, although from a different viewpoint to that of early 1848. In accordance with his belief that the State should provide the incentive to enable private enterprise to develop, Louis-Napoleon introduced a variety of initiatives which were to have an impact on housing.

Louis-Napoleon's personal patronage of housing initiatives had actually begun soon after his election as President of the Republic in December 1848. In the following year he joined other members of the Parisian upper classes to finance a housing society in the city.[32] Louis-Napoleon had spent part of his years of exile in England, and was aware of the lessons which that country could already offer in relation to workers' housing. Thus in November 1849 he sent a commission to England to study the examples of workers' housing there. In 1850 the study *The Dwellings of the Labouring Classes*, by the English architect Henry Roberts, appeared in France, translated at Louis-Napoleon's request; as this study was only presented to the Royal Institute of British Architects in 1850, it is clear that Louis-Napoleon was well briefed on the state of the English debate on housing.

It was soon after staging his *coup d'état* at the end of 1851 that Louis-Napoleon extended these personal initiatives. In January 1852, an official announcement declared that 10 million francs from the wealth of the Orléans family, deposed in 1848, would be devoted to 'improving the dwellings of workers in large manufacturing towns'.[33] This measure, together with the allocation of another 10 million francs from the same source, to provide help for the *sociétés de secours mutuels* was an astute political move. Taking money from the wealth of the old royal family, Louis-Napoleon could not be accused of misusing public funds. On the other hand, the uses to which the money was put were carefully chosen to gain Louis-Napoleon popular support among the workers – support which was to be essential to his plan to secure his position by an appeal to the people through a plebiscite.

Whatever its origins in the political manoeuvring of Louis-Napoleon, the 10 million francs was presented as a means of encouraging private investors to finance cheap housing. This aim appeared most clearly in a competition announced in May 1852, to find designs for three model housing projects in Paris; these were to be built with 3 million francs from the 10 million francs allocated in January. The conditions for the competition stipulated that the designs should be for cheap and healthy dwellings, but that they should give an adequate return to the owner. This latter condition was particularly important, as the designs were intended to 'serve as a model to private enterprise'.[34] It is in this respect, as an incentive to the private sector rather than as a commitment by the State to provide housing for workers that the 10 million franc subsidy should be interpreted. In the event, its impact was very limited, with only about 4 million francs being taken up for housing.[35]

Between 1848 and 1852, then, a series of initiatives relating to housing were discussed. The 'housing question' had been recognised, but had the solution? From the negligible impact which the debate in these years had in practice, it is clear that it had not. Consider the attitude to construction defined in the three phases discussed. The experiment with socialism raised the possibility of public construction, but this possibility disappeared as the experiment collapsed. The Republican Assembly of 1850 rejected any notion of public construction, while Louis-Napoleon provided an exceptional subsidy which had more impact as a gesture of propaganda than as a stimulant to private builders. These three attitudes reflect the political forces influential at the time, and owed little to any analysis of the means of production of housing, or the economics of housing. The housing problem had been recognised, but not analysed.

Turning to the question of conditions in existing housing, at first sight there is a more tangible achievement: in the law of 1850. But the deference which the law paid to the sacrosanct notion of property was to render it almost ineffective. Moreover, relatively few councils were to make use of the law, which was facultative rather than statutory. The intentions of the original authors of the bill, encompassing construction and control, had been ambitious. When filtered through an Assembly which opposed public construction, and local councils which lacked the high vision of the socially concerned circles in Paris, there was little left.

Nonetheless, the debate around 1850 was important as a reference point for later reformers. It offered both a minimum and a maximum programme of reform. The minimum programme was that defined by Blanqui and the 1850 law: respect for the existing social order, rejection of public construction, but an acceptance of the principle that society should exercise control over conditions in rented property. The maximum programme implied the restructuring of society which had been attempted after February, bringing with it the concept of the public provision of housing related to communal facilities. The reform movement of the later nineteenth century was to start from the former, while the latter stood as an alternative against which moderate reform had to define itself.

The debate around 1850 must be seen then, not as the beginning of a continuous period of housing reform, but as a presentation of the issues, a recognition that a housing problem existed. The real nature of that problem could only be defined as reformers built up a greater understanding of the forces operating on housing, in terms of the growth of urban areas, and the economics of the housing market. That understanding was to develop from their experience in dealing with the realities of housing. Where Villermé and Blanqui had simply been and looked at inadequate housing, the reformers of the later nineteenth century were to be more directly involved, whether in providing the sewers for housing, or in running a housing society.

14

◇-◇

The housing market: Paris

While the political developments around 1850 had done little to transform the housing conditions of workers, the economic development which France was to experience after 1852, during the Empire of Napoleon III, was to have a marked effect. An increase in the number of workers employed in industry and the development of urban areas were to be reflected in the evolution of the housing market in those areas. The prevailing philosophy of the Empire did not single out workers' housing for special attention, but held that workers, together with the other classes of society, would necessarily benefit from the general prosperity engendered by economic growth. By the end of the Empire in 1871, it was clear that this optimistic view had not been fulfilled, and reformers in the later nineteenth century were to take a more critical look at the operation of the housing market.

The evolution of the housing market is thus an essential background to the evolution of reform. This background can be illuminated by a consideration of the housing market in Paris between 1850 and 1914. While Paris, the dominant city of France, was not 'typical' in its development, it did provide reformers with the evidence on the provision of workers' housing and of the problems inherent in the housing market which they were to use in defining their approach to reform.

The area occupied by the city of Paris in 1914 housed 1.27 million people in 1851; this area included the city, still contained within the tax wall of the *fermiers généraux*, and the ring of suburban communes between this wall and the city's fortifications. The communes beyond the fortifications, which completed the department of the Seine, were still largely untouched by the city, and had a population of only 145,000. By 1911 the city limits had been extended to absorb the communes within the fortifications, and this area now housed 2.88 million; by the same date, the communes beyond the fortifications had been invaded by the suburban growth of the city, and now housed 1.26 million people.[1]

The characteristics of this population growth followed the development of employment in the capital. During the Second Empire the traditional structure of artisan employment was joined by manufacturing industry related to the artisan economy. S. Magri notes that the labour for this new industry was drawn from two sources: the old artisan sector within Paris, and seasonal immigration by workers from provincial towns; this seasonal immigration was to decrease in the 1880s, as the workers tended to settle permanently in Paris. From about the same time, the development of heavier industries in the city's suburbs became increasingly important; these industries, requiring less skilled labour, tended to attract agricultural workers from rural areas. With the industry of the city increasingly concentrated in the suburban areas, the city itself was to see a rise in the tertiary sector during the early twentieth century, as employment in banks and insurance offices developed.[2]

In each of these stages in the development of employment, Paris relied heavily on immigration to provide its labour force. The natural growth of the city's population was low throughout the period, and from the 1880s it was almost negligible. Immigration naturally put considerable strain on the housing market, as movement to the city tended to be un-even, according to the availability of work. The city itself witnessed two periods of particularly high immigration, coinciding with the periods of economic development at the start of the Second Empire, and in the late 1870s and early 1880s. Between 1851 and 1856 the population of the city (based on its post-1860 area) increased by over 20%, and in the next five years by over 10%; between 1876 and 1881 the population grew by 14%. These figures stand out in the general growth from 1850 to 1914, which tended to lie between 3% and 8% over the five-year periods between censuses. After the last major influx in the late 1870s and early 1880s, immigration towards Paris was increasingly absorbed by the suburbs, as the population of the city itself stabilised towards its maximum, reached in the early 1920s.[3]

The building industry in the Paris of 1850 was scarcely equipped to meet the demands which were soon to be placed on the housing market. Property presented a fragmented picture in the city, the average ownership of houses by landlords being only two properties. Builders operated on a small scale, tending to restrict their activity to one building at a time, and they lacked a structure of credit supply which would have allowed more extended activity.[4] The deficiencies of the industry had been recognised in the Second Republic, which had established the Sous-Comptoir des Entrepreneurs to provide building credit in 1848. But it was under the Second Empire that the structure for a more dynamic building industry was to be firmly established.

In 1852 a decree authorised the setting up of the Crédit Foncier. This was originally intended to provide credit for the rural population, replacing the traditional method of usury. But in practice it supplied money for urban construction projects, particularly those in Paris. The Crédit Foncier and the Sous-Comptoir des Entrepreneurs worked closely together, being formally linked in 1860, and provided a system of credit on land and buildings which was to play a major part in the development of Paris during the second half of the century. The Sous-Comptoir lent money against the security of a site value, and was thus able to help small firms and individual builders. The Crédit Foncier made advances on the security of completed buildings, and particularly provided finance for the large contractors and development companies which were to be established after 1850.

The most famous of these new companies was the Compagnie des Immeubles de l'Hotel de la Rue de Rivoli, set up by the Péreire brothers in 1854. This company developed the arcaded buildings along a full quarter mile of the Rue de Rivoli, while under the changed name of the Compagnie Immobilière de Paris, it developed buildings in other areas, including the Avenue des Champs Elysées, and the area around the new opera house.[5] The Péreire brothers also proposed a considerable investment in the construction of workers' housing, to take advantage of the subsidy announced in 1852. They did build some housing of this type, but on a very much reduced scale, and their main involvement remained in the higher end of the housing market.

Given the large scale of building operation undertaken by some development companies, certain contractors took on a considerable workforce. Joseph Thome, who undertook the construction of the Champs Elysées district, employed up to 700 men. But this new scale of development did not totally replace the earlier pattern of small-scale builders and landlords. In 1847 there had been 10 workmen for every building entrepreneur in Paris; in 1860, when the transformation of the city was well under way, this figure had only increased to 13. Similarly, the individual developer was still active in promoting much new building up to 1914.[6]

The restructuring of the building industry provided the basis for high levels of construction in Paris during the Second Empire. The public works directed by Napoleon III and Georges Haussmann, Prefect of the Seine department, created the opportunities for profitable investment by private enterprise, although there was a temporary slump in construction in the late 1850s. The end of the Empire was to see lower construction levels, which remained depressed in the aftermath of the Franco-Prussian War of 1871. However, construction again increased in the late 1870s and early 1880s as the economy expanded. This phase of high construction levels ended in a sudden depression in the early 1880s. C. Grison sees this depression as marking the end of the dynamic evolution of the Paris housing market. After this period, building was in increasing competition with other investments, and construction tended to stabilise and decline towards the early twentieth century. Only in 1910 did the signs of a new recovery appear, and this was to be cut short by the outbreak of war.[7]

In crude terms, it can be noted that the periods of high construction activity coincide with the periods of high immigration into Paris. But it remains to be seen whether the housing market was thereby expanded to meet fully the demands placed on it, or whether its expansion favoured certain sections of the community at the expense of others. Was the bias shown by the Péreire brothers towards the upper end of the market a typical feature of the Paris housing market? To answer this question it is necessary to look in more detail at the housing offered by the market.

The evolution of the housing market

The Second Empire opened with a period of distortion in the housing market, due to the large number of demolitions as the reconstruction of Paris was commenced. In the early 1850s, the number of houses in the city actually declined, at a period when high immigration was increasing the population to be housed. The results of these conflicting tendencies can be seen in the small number of vacant dwellings, which reached a low point in 1856, and in the increase in the population of the *garnis* (lodging houses) in the centre of the city. The *garnis* are a particularly useful guide to the state of the housing market for workers, as they reflect a demand for housing unsatisfied by the supply of cheap flats. They were a common form of housing for migrant workers, particularly those who were only in Paris for a few months of the year; but in the early 1850s, they also provided a refuge for Parisian working families made homeless by the demolitions.

The distortion of the housing market during the early 1850s was also reflected in a rapid increase in rents, which exceeded the general rise in prices in this period. The overall rise for rents in Paris has been estimated at 42% between 1852 and 1862, compared with only 9% in the succeeding period from 1862 to 1876. This lower rate of increase after 1862 is indicative of a greater balance in the housing market as new construction provided a net gain over demolitions and, in general terms, the rise in rents in the 1860s was to follow the evolution of prices. Moreover, the 1866 census enabled Haussmann to demonstrate that the increase in the city's population over the previous five years had been met by a corresponding increase in the number of dwellings available.[8]

But this general balance achieved in the 1860s masked two facts. First, if new building now matched the growth of the population, it was not adequate to make up for the imbalance in the 1850s. Thus in the 5th arrondissement the number of inhabitants living in *garnis*, which had risen in the 1850s, was to remain stable in the 1860s; the *garni* became the typical form of housing in certain streets in the area.[9] Second, the pattern of new construction did not match the pattern of the population. Between 1860 and 1863 just over 71,000 new dwellings came on to the market. Of these, 55% fell into the category of 'cheap' rents of up to 500 fr.; but in the same period, this category of housing accounted for 89% of the existing housing stock.[10] Thus, while the overall production of housing did match the population growth in the early 1860s, the new housing was still not meeting the demand for cheaper rents. In contrast, the supply of more expensive flats exceeded demand, leading to an increase in the number of vacancies in the mid-1860s, and a crisis in the building industry.

The location of the new housing also made it unavailable to certain sections of the working population, even if they could afford the rents. The cheaper housing tended to be built in the outer arrondissements of the city, annexed in 1860, where land was cheaper and more readily available than in the centre. While this housing was well located for workers in those industries which were developing in these areas, it was too far from the centre for workers whose employment depended on their living close to the sources of employment in the city centre.

The pattern of workers' housing in the capital thus showed two predominant characteristics during the Second Empire. In the city centre, the housing available to workers was reduced, being replaced by more expensive flats; those workers who needed to remain near the centre for employment reasons were thus forced to share accommodation, or move into *garnis*. On the outskirts of the city some new housing with cheap rents was provided, but its construction did not keep pace with the growth of the working population.

Reports written by the workers' delegates to the 1867 Exposition suggest that it was the increase in the cost of housing, rather than the standard of housing, which was the first concern of occupants. Those reports which commented on housing drew attention to the rise in rents in existing property, but had little to say about the conditions provided in such property. Statistics of overcrowding which would illuminate those conditions do not exist for this period. However, it is clear that overcrowding existed as a problem even before the reconstruction of the city. In its first report, published in 1852, the Commission des Logements Insalubres, set up to implement the 1850 law on housing hygiene, drew attention to the existence of overcrowding in dwellings which the commissioners had visited. In succeeding reports, the Commission repeated the evidence that overcrowding was one of the prime causes of unhealthy conditions.[11] But overcrowding was not a problem which the Commission could resolve; it derived from the workings of the housing market, and it is clear that the evolution of the housing market in the 1850s and 1860s tended to reinforce the problem of overcrowding rather than to remove it.

The war of 1870 and the economic depression of the years which followed served to reduce the pressure on the Paris housing market. But in the construction boom which accompanied the new wave of immigration in the late 1870s and early 1880s, it is possible to see the same bias in the evolution of the housing market as had existed during the Second Empire. Arthur Raffalovich refers to figures which show a percentage rise in the number of the cheapest dwellings at 8% between 1879 and 1884; in the same period the number of dwellings for the *classe moyenne* increased by 15–20%, while *logements de luxe* increased by 30–40%.[12] Over a slightly longer period of 1880 to 1889, C. Grison estimates that dwellings with rents below 500 fr. accounted for 65% of the net increase in the housing market; however, at this period they still represented a higher figure of 75% in the existing stock of housing.[13] Thus new construction was continuing to favour dwellings at the upper end of the market, to the detriment of cheap housing. As in the Second Empire, the imbalance between the housing offered by the market and the needs of a city subject to a high rate of immigration was reflected in a rise in the population of the *garnis* during the late 1870s and early 1880s.[14]

The crisis which ended the construction boom in the early 1880s marked the beginning of the more sluggish phase in the building industry which was to characterise the 1890s and early 1900s. This was also a period in which the pressure of immigration on the Paris housing market was less marked, and the overall increase in the housing stock of the city was to keep pace with the growth of its population. There is also some indication that in the 1890s the market became more adjusted to that population. Thus the years from 1889 to 1901 were the one period after 1850 when the number of cheap flats, with rents below 500 fr. per year, increased as a proportion of the housing stock.[15] Meanwhile, the population of the *garnis* had dropped from the level which it had reached in the mid-1880s. But these signs should be treated with some caution. C. Grison notes that the increase in the proportion of cheap flats was partly the result of a drop in the level of rents in the middle range of flats, bringing some of them into the 500 fr. category; as will be seen, this reduction in rents was not to be shared by the flats at the cheaper end of the market. Similarly, the fall in the population of the *garnis* may reflect not so much the assimilation of its occupants into the regular housing market, as the fact that workers who had come to Paris to find work in the early 1880s had left the city again as the availability of jobs declined.

The pattern of construction between 1890 and 1910 confirms the tendency for new building to fail to maintain the balance of rents in the existing housing stock, the tendency which had characterised the earlier, dynamic period of building. Between 1891 and 1911, dwellings with rents below 500 fr. represented 83% of the dwellings demolished but only 62% of those being built.[16] Even more significant than this relative decline in the proportion of cheap flats is the fact that in the early 1900s certain rental categories started to decline in absolute terms. Thus from 1905 more dwellings with rents below 200 fr. were demolished than were built, while in certain years after 1907 this reduction affected flats with rents below 300 fr.[17]

This insufficient production of cheap dwellings was reflected in rising rents in existing property. C. Grison has noted that in the 1870s and 1880s 'bourgeois' rents increased at a faster rate then working-class rents. However, when the higher rents tended to stabilise after 1889, cheaper rents continued to rise. This rise was modest in comparison to the increase during the Second Empire, and it affected the working family's budget as it came at a time when other aspects of the cost of living were falling in price.[18]

At the end of the period under consideration, as the brief boom in construction began after 1910, a familiar picture emerged. As in previous booms, it was towards bourgeois housing that investors turned. The number of vacant dwellings, notably among cheaper rent flats, fell, while the population of the *garnis* increased. At the same time, rents in existing property experienced a particularly sharp rise. This derived partly from the fact that proprietors had delayed rent increases until after the survey of property rent values in 1909–10, in order to obtain a lower tax assessment; one estimate places the rise between 1910 and 1914 as high as 10%.[19]

The housing problem

From this consideration of the housing market between 1850 and 1914, two related characteristics stand out: the underproduction of cheap flats in comparison to their importance in the existing housing stock, and continually rising rents in workers' flats. To place these characteristics in perspective, it is necessary to establish whether they created a problem for the working population, or whether they simply reflected an increased purchasing power which allowed workers to afford the more expensive new flats, or the increased cost of old flats.

In the most general terms, the average rent paid by working families tended to rise more rapidly than salaries, and tended to occupy a larger proportion of the family's budget. Gaillard has estimated that rents in workers' dwellings rose by 38% during the Second Empire, while salaries rose by only 30–33%. The rise in rents during the later part of the century was less marked, but it came at a time when workers' salaries were not increasing. With respect to the importance of these rents in the expenditure of the family, figures suggest a rise from about 12% of a working family's budget in the early 1850s, to 19% in the early 1900s.[20]

These general figures indicate a growing burden of rent payments during the period. But how readily could a working family accept this burden? A study presented by Arthur Raffalovich in 1887 makes it possible to establish the relationship between working families and the housing market in more detail. Studying the housing available to working families in the 1880s, Raffalovich found that a working family would have to pay from 84 fr. to 204 fr. annually for a single room, and from 240 fr. to 300 fr. for two rooms. Three rooms, the smallest number which allowed separate rooms for both sexes of children and for parents, were nowhere lower than 300 fr. per year. This rent made them an 'extremely rare luxury among the working class', for few working families could afford so much. Raffalovich quoted one budget for a family of four, with a rent of 300 fr. in a total annual expenditure of just over 2,000 fr. Allowing for days off for sickness or unemployment, this required a wage of 6–7 fr. for a day's work to make ends meet. Raffalovich quoted another estimate, indicating that a wage of 7–10 fr. was necessary for a worker with young children, allowing a rent of 240 fr. A wage of 7 or 8 fr. would thus enable a worker to afford a two-room flat, and he might just afford a three-room flat. But by no means all workers earned this wage.

Raffalovich identified four categories of worker in Paris. The élite, including jewellers and mapmakers, who accounted for about 10% of the working population, could command 20 fr. to 30 fr. per day, allowing them a choice of accommodation. The majority of the working population were grouped more equally in the three remaining categories. Skilled workmen, such as joiners and plumbers, could earn 8 fr. or more for a day's work; labourers, navvies and carters earned between 3 fr. 50 c. and 5 fr., while ragmen, street sellers and casual labourers rarely earned more than 2 fr. 50 c. As Raffalovich concluded, the élite could evidently afford 300 fr, but, of the majority of workers, only the skilled labourers were in a position to pay rents between 240 fr. and 300 fr.[21]

Raffalovich's findings indicate that the existence of flats with rents of 300 fr. and below was crucial to the working population of Paris. This is confirmed by the continuing importance of this category in the city's housing stock. In 1911 there were three arrondissements in the city where the average rent of the overall housing stock was below 300 fr.; in these same arrondissements, more than 90% of the dwellings had rents of 500 fr. or less. In these areas cheap housing thus dominated the housing stock, while in the city as a whole housing with rents of 300 fr. or below still represented over one third of the housing available.[22] This was a substantial proportion, but it consisted of an ageing stock of housing, which was neither being renewed nor expanded to maintain its relative importance. The limited production of cheap flats by the construction industry, leading in the early 1900s to an absolute reduction in the availability of the cheapest housing, affected directly that part of the market on which the working population depended.

Clearly, then, the evolution of the housing market between 1850 and 1914 did create a problem for the city's working population, as the housing available to them reduced in its relative importance within the housing market, and increased in price. This problem persisted because the need for housing as expressed by the growth of the working population could not be translated into a solvent demand, which would have attracted investment into housing. Raffalovich's study shows that many workers could simply not afford the cost of flats offered by the market. To reconcile their need for housing with their ability to pay, they were forced either to reduce their 'consumption' of housing by occupying overcrowded flats of tiny dimensions or moving into a *garni*; or to leave the housing market altogether, building a shack from salvaged materials in one of the squatter areas on the outskirts of the city.

If demand for cheap housing could have been expressed by an increase in the number of working families able to afford 300 fr., investment might have been attracted to provide workers' flats of reasonable standard. But as Raffalovich showed, the number of such families was limited. Moreover, the problems associated with building and managing cheaper flats tended to deter investment. Factors such as the taxes on building, which were proportionately higher in relation to the construction cost of cheap housing than of more expensive housing, and the need to be sure of the continuing security of a building against money borrowed for its construction, made bourgeois flats more attractive than cheap flats. Workers' flats were seen to involve a particular element of risk, as families might be unable to meet their rent payment, or might simply move out before the rent was due. The problem of extracting rent from working-class tenants was exaggerated by contemporaries, but it acted to deter investors. If they could achieve a similar return on a more secure basis by building housing for the middle classes, there was little incentive to invest in cheaper housing.

The ideal of the well-managed block of flats, economically but soundly built, providing spacious dwellings for hard-working families who paid their rent regularly was an exception in the housing market. The ideal could be realised, and was to be so under the guidance of the housing reformers. But the relatively low return of such ventures, coupled with the care that had to be put into management restricted their interest to philanthropic groups, and did not convince private investors whose interest was financial to turn to such housing.

The failure of the housing market to meet the needs of the city's growing population could be seen in the slums of densely built blocks. The cost of land meant that those investors who did build cheap housing favoured large developments where they could increase the use of the site by building alleys and courts leading back from the street. This form of development also had the advantage that the buildings within the site escaped some of the regulations and costs to which buildings along the public street were subject.

The notorious Cité Jeanne d'Arc illustrated how, in the speculative housing market, new construction could simply reproduce the inadequate and unhealthy conditions of the slums in the city's older housing stock. Completed in 1872, the Cité consisted of ten blocks of a uniform height of 17.5 m; it housed 2,000 people, crowded on to less than half a hectare of land. There was not a single drain within the buildings for waste water, which gathered in pools in the alleys between the buildings. The closets were dirty, and some had no door; the filters for solid waste overflowed in the basement, and affected the stairs. Most of the flats were served by dark corridors; inside the flats, insects harboured in peeling wallpaper, while floors were covered with a layer of dirt. Waste water and rubbish collected in the courts, where they were thrown from flat windows. Some of these windows were broken, others would not open; flats on the fifth and sixth floors had damp ceilings, due to penetrating rainwater.[23]

A contrast in form, though not in standards, can be seen in the developments of temporary shacks, on the outskirts of the city. One such site developed in the 1850s was taken on a lease of 12 years. For this relatively short period, the leaseholder had no interest in providing facilities beyond the barest essentials. No capital was devoted to the construction of roads or services; huts were knocked together from salvaged materials, and their only servicing was a cabin providing a closet in the garden, with a pit dug as a cesspool. Refuse gathered in the yard, while rain and waste water collected in stagnant pools.[24]

It was the emotive reaction to conditions such as these which had stirred interest in housing in the 1840s. The work of the Commission des Logements Insalubres confirmed that slum conditions were a permanent feature of the Paris housing market. But it was only at the end of the century that statistics were collected to define the housing problem in more concrete terms. The factor used to quantify the problem was overcrowding, a factor which demonstrated the imbalance between the city's population and its housing market. From 1891, statistics for overcrowding were regularly included in the census information, so that it is possible to see the implications of that imbalance more precisely from this date. The census of 1891 established the scale for measuring overcrowding: dwellings whose occupants had less than half a room each were considered 'overpopulated'; those where there was at least half a room, but less than one room per person were 'insufficient'; one room per person was classified as 'satisfactory', while more than one room was 'large' or 'very large'.[25] The first two categories were those in which improvement was considered necessary. In 1891, 49% of the population living in 'ordinary' dwellings – *garnis* not included – fell into these categories. The percentage rose to over 50% in 1896 and 1901, falling to 43·26% in 1911. This reduction was countered by the increase in the city's population, so that the actual total of people living in 'overpopulated' or 'insufficient' dwellings was still greater in 1911 than in 1891.

Within this general category of inadequate housing, the worst conditions of overcrowding occupied a significant place. The 1891 census revealed that 14% of the city's population was living in the 'overpopulated' conditions of more than two persons per room. This was over 300,000 persons, and more than 100,000 of these were families of three or four living in one single room. Fourteen families were living in the most extreme conditions of overcrowding, with ten or more people in a single room. The 1896 and 1901 censuses showed the same proportion of the population, 14%, in 'overpopulated' dwellings. The figures from the 1901 census also demonstrated that large families in poor areas suffered most from overcrowding. Among families with four children, the percentage living in 'overpopulated' dwellings increased from 27% in *quartiers aisés*, to 44% in poor quarters, and 48% in very poor quarters; for families of six children, the percentages increased to 67% in poor quarters and 71% in the very poor areas.[26]

However the worst conditions of overcrowding did show an improvement in the early years of the twentieth century. In 1911 only 8.3% of the population, about 230,000 people, were living in 'overpopulated' dwellings. C. Grison attributes this improvement at least partly to demographic factors – the proportion of large households of 6 or more people was reducing, while that of small families of 2 or 3 was, correspondingly, increasing, a tendency particularly marked since 1896.[27] The change was certainly not the start of a continuing improvement, as the population living in 'overpopulated' dwellings remained at about 9% in the 1920s.

The overcrowding of dwellings in Paris was paralleled by the high density of population in the city as a whole. Both of these characteristics particularly affected the working population. The higher incidence of overcrowding among families in poor areas has been noted; similarly the density of population varied from 76 persons per hectare in the wealthy area of Auteuil, to 800 in Bonne Nouvelle and 1,000 in Arts et Métiers. But there was no link of cause and effect between high density and overcrowding. This fact was emphasised by the development of the suburban area of Paris, as it started to absorb the immigration towards the city from the 1890s. Despite very much lower densities than the city, the degree of overcrowding was similar to that in the city. The 1911 census revealed a total of 45.5% of the population of the Seine department living in 'overpopulated' and 'insufficient' dwellings, while the 'overpopulated' category alone accounted for 7.6%.[28]

The existence of overcrowding in the suburbs stressed the fact that the causes leading to overcrowding were economic in origin, and were not determined by the form of urban development. The inadequacy of housing conditions in the suburbs was to be the subject of particular concern after the First World War, as the suburban population grew without any corresponding development of infrastructure or services. Some observers had drawn attention to the beginning of this problem just before the war, but in the period of 1850 to 1914 it was above all the dense and overcrowded housing market of the city which concerned the reformers. If the suburbs attracted their attention, it was more because of the idealised image they offered of low-density housing bathed in sun than because of the realities of suburban life.

It was against the background, then, of a housing problem derived from the imbalance between the housing market and the working population of the city that the reformers worked to improve housing conditions. The strands of reform which were to be developed in the second half of the nineteenth century, addressing the most detailed questions of waste disposal and the most general questions of urban development, were to attack some of the symptoms of the housing problem, But it was only when reformers acknowledged the imbalance in the housing market that they were able to evolve a coherent approach to the construction of housing, thus attempting to modify the housing market. That acknowledgement can be situated in the 1880s, and its impact will be considered in the third section of Part Two. But before considering the role of the reformers within the housing market, in the construction of housing, their activity in related strands of reform will be examined. For the reformers would have preferred to stay away from the housing market, affecting it only indirectly by offering models for imitation, or controls on its worst excesses.

The programme for reform

15

◇◇◇

The reformers' ideal

The housing debate of the late 1840s had allowed a range of possible solutions to the housing problem to be examined, leading to the moderate position adopted in the law of 1850. This debate about the principles of action in relation to housing, and the role of the public authorities, was accompanied by a more specific debate, in which the form that workers' housing should take was considered. As in the case of the debate over principles, a moderate consensus emerged in the 1850s. This consensus established the individual house, set in its garden and owned by its occupant as the ideal form of housing. It was an ideal which was to be maintained by reformers consistently throughout the later development of the housing reform movement. But it was an ideal which coexisted with an alternative form of housing, the block of workers' flats.

The question of workers' flats revealed a dilemma in the housing reform movement. The economic and practical arguments in favour of flats as opposed to houses were often strong, even overwhelming, in urban areas. But the moderate view of reform which identified the individual house as an ideal saw the grouping of large numbers of workers together as socially undesirable; it also saw the link between socialist thought and communal housing projects. Thus, in promoting the construction of flats as a means of increasing the stock of cheap housing available to working families, the moderate reformers feared that they might simply be reinforcing social values which they rejected. The reformers thus had to define the construction of flats in terms which they found acceptable before they could, albeit reluctantly, advocate this solution.

Flats for workers

The reformers' dilemma in relation to the question of flats focussed in the early 1850s on a block constructed in Paris, the Cité Napoléon. The creation of this block was one of the few cases where the discussion of housing in the late 1840s was paralleled by a practical achievement. In early 1849, a Société des Cités Ouvrières de Paris was formed, with the object of building blocks of flats for workers in each arrondissement of the city. In fact, it only built a single development, in the Rue

Cité Napoléon, rue Rochechouart, 1851. Arch. M.-G. Veuqnv

3 The glass-roofed access
stairs and galleries in the
centre of the main block of
the Cité Napoléon

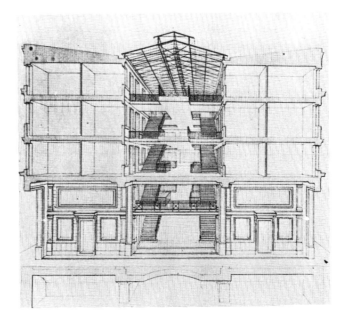

Rochechouart, which provided 194 flats housing about 500 people. The rents, which one contemporary observer considered average for the area, ranged from 130 fr. to 170 fr. per year for a flat of one or two rooms with a small kitchen.[1]

The Société des Cités Ouvrières reflected the moderation which rejected the radicalism of the early months of 1848. Its founder, M. Chabert, rallied eminent figures to support the society, including the President of the Republic, Louis-Napoleon and Benjamin Delessert, founder of the savings bank movement in France. Chabert specifically

4 View of the access stairs and galleries as they still exist today

presented his proposals as a defence against socialist ideas.[2] However, the building which emerged as the Cité Napoléon was not seen as fulfilling this aim.

In its design, and in its level of communal facilities, the Cité Napoléon demonstrated the importance of the housing model promoted by the Fourierists. The architect Gabriel Veugny grouped the flats in the main block on either side of a central gallery; the stairs and balconies giving access to the flats were covered by a glazed roof (figs 2, 3 and 4). This was an ingenious device which allowed Veugny to plan 'double-aspect' flats, with windows into the gallery as well as to the street or courtyard; but it also recalled the *phalanstère*, with its flats linked by a glazed gallery. Moreover, the facilities offered by the blocks included a crèche, laundry, baths and a doctor's surgery offering free medical consultation; the building thus went beyond the basic provision of a shelter from the elements. Despite the aims of its founder, the Cité Napoléon could be welcomed by Victor Meunier in *Démocratie*

Pacifique, the paper founded by the Fourierist Victor Considérant; he foresaw that the occupants of the building would be introduced to the benefits of association, and then to socialism.[3]

Faced with the ambiguities of the Cité Napoléon, the moderate reformers rejected it. Villermé criticised the building in a paper on *cités ouvrières*, delivered to the Académie des Sciences Morales et Politiques in 1850. His objections were rooted in his interpretation of the social implications of this form of housing. He feared that the grouping of many families together would threaten moral standards; 'the bad inhabitants will constantly exert a troublesome influence on the good'. He went on to stress that this problem was not simply one which affected the occupants of the building; he asked whether grouping workers, and isolating them from the rest of society 'might not strengthen their jealousy against those whom they call rich, and to whom they attribute so many imaginary wrongs'.[4]

Villermé pointed to the social problems which he believed were inherent in housing like the Cité Napoléon. In the discussion after Villermé's paper, Adolphe Blanqui made the link between such housing and the socialist initiatives of 1848, arguing that workers would abandon the *cités ouvrières*, as they had, he claimed, already turned away from the workers' associations.

Villermé and Blanqui thus opposed the construction of housing on the model of the Cité Napoléon. But to justify their opposition they felt the need of arguments which would reinforce their social and political views. After all, they were opposing a form of housing which, it could be convincingly argued, offered the best way of rapidly easing the housing problem; moreover, they were opposing a form of housing which they were never likely to inhabit themselves, on behalf of a class of society to which they would never belong. It was therefore to the people who did inhabit this housing that the reformers turned for support. Blanqui declared that workers referred to *cités ouvrières* 'by the name of convent, barracks, hospital, and they protest with pride against such housing'.[5] It was this opposition from the workers themselves which convinced Blanqui that they would abandon the *cités ouvrières*.

In his survey of the working population of France, published in 1854, Armand Audiganne supported the case put forward by Blanqui. He found widespread dislike of blocks such as the Cité Napoléon, due to 'the severe and inflexible rule' which governed the occupants.[6] The degree to which such arguments are a true reflection of workers' opinions, as opposed to a reflection of what the reformers wished to believe is difficult to assess. But the identification of the rules enforced in blocks as a source of complaint suggests that the dislike which the reformers claimed to find was not necessarily against the form of housing as such.

The control to which inhabitants were subject – such as the shutting of the main gates at night, or the discouragement of gathering in groups – was introduced to forestall the dangers which Villermé had identified. The reformers used the understandable objection to such regulation as evidence that workers themselves disliked dense blocks of flats; but the very existence of the regulations indicates that the reaction against the blocks stemmed initially from those who did not have to live in them, rather than from those who did.

The practical counterpart to the housing debate around 1850 had failed to establish a workable model for the construction of flats for workers. This failure derived from the ambiguity evident in the case of the Cité Napoléon. The building resulted from the overlapping of aspects of moderate social reform with aspects of radical socialist thinking. The regulation imposed on the occupants of the Cité Napoléon can be seen as an attempt to control the socialist model of housing, to make it acceptable to the moderate reformers and to the private investors they hoped would provide finance for housing construction. The attempt succeeded in satisfying neither the occupants, nor the reformers.

Given this failure to establish an integrated model for workers' flats, the two elements which had coexisted so uncomfortably in the Cité Napoléon were subsequently to evolve independently. The *phalanstère* continued to provide the inspiration for housing proposals in the second half of the century. At the same time the moderate housing reformers, still suspicious of the *phalanstère*, developed a more acceptable model.

The majority of the projects based on the *phalanstère* were to remain on paper, from Considérant's proposals to the Assembly in 1849 to proposals to build blocks on the site of the Paris fortifications in the 1880s. At one point it appeared that the Ecole Sociétaire, which grouped the followers of Fourier, might help to finance the *phalanstère* for children at Condé-sur-Vesgres when this proposal was renewed in the early 1850s. However, when the exiled Considérant moved to America, effort was shifted towards financing a *phalanstérien* colony there.[7]

Another proposal developed in the later 1850s was intended to make the *phalanstère* model more acceptable to capitalist investors. The title of Victor Calland's project, *Le Palais de Famille*, first presented in 1855, indicates his aim to achieve a balance between the advantages offered by a communal form of development, in the construction of a 'palace', with the family, central to the values of moderate reform. Thus Calland was able to present his project with some approval to the Société d'Economie Charitable in 1862. Nonetheless, he failed to gain the financial support necessary to realise his project.[8]

However, Fourier's ideas did form the inspiration for one major project which became a reality, in the Familistère at Guise. J. B. A. Godin, who founded the Familistère, was a worker who had set up his own firm in 1846, manufacturing cast iron stoves. The firm prospered, and in 1859 Godin was able to finance a major programme of construction next to the factory. The Familistère was built to house the workers in Godin's factory. As such, it did not realise the self-sufficient community which Fourier had proposed; but it was firmly based on principles of association and co-operation, and its design was an interpretation of the *phalanstère*. Communal facilities ranged from a swimming pool and theatre to a restaurant and school. The housing itself emphasised the importance of the community, with four storeys of flats arranged off

5 Godin's Familistère; the three interlinked blocks of dwellings, with the crèche connected to the central block, and other communal facilities on the opposite side of the court

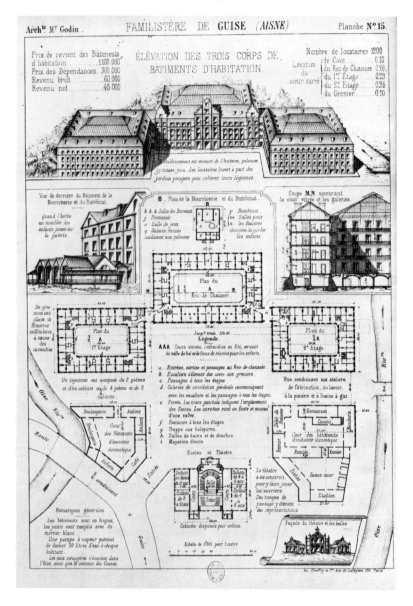

galleries around a glazed court; the flats thus overlooked the court, which from time to time functioned as a meeting place for the factory workers. The main part of the Familistère consisted of three blocks of this form, linked together at their corners (fig. 5). Management was in the hands of the inhabitants and in 1880 Godin handed over ownership of the Familistère and of the factory as a whole to a workers' co-operative.[9]

The Familistère inevitably evoked an ambiguous response from the moderate reformers. They could not deny that it provided healthy flats, with a lower death rate than the neighbouring town. But they were unwilling to welcome it as a model. This ambiguity was reflected at the

6 Housing on the Avenue Daumesnil, financed by Napoleon III at the time of the 1867 Exposition; the flats are grouped as separate 'houses', with a stair opening from the street giving access to a single flat at each landing.

1867 Exposition Universelle, in the housing exhibition which was to endorse the ideal of the owner-occupied house, and to present an alternative model for workers' flats. The Familistère, which conformed to neither of these categories, was not exhibited; but the contribution of Godin to the study of housing could not be denied and he was awarded a silver medal.

The alternative model for workers' flats which had been evolved by 1867 was described by the engineer C. Détain, writing in the *Revue Générale de l'Architecture*. Looking back to the experiments of the 1850s he noted that

the construction of *cités ouvrières* of this kind, of which the Cité Napoléon...is the model, has been completely abandoned, and today, in Paris, new buildings which carry this name are no more than groups of buildings linked along the side of the road like ordinary bourgeois houses.[10]

The key to this change was the shift from gallery-access flats, with a single entrance to the block, to flats grouped around staircases, with direct access to each stair from the street. The change was given symbolic emphasis by the patronage of Napoleon III. In 1849 he had supported and even given his name to the now rejected type of *cité ouvrière*. On the occasion of the 1867 Exposition he financed two groups of housing, both of which adopted the new 'bourgeois' form (fig. 6).

Détain's use of the term 'bourgeois' indicates why this new form of housing was more acceptable to the reformers than the Cité Napoléon. The socialist implications of that building, with its communal facilities, and the social threat seen in grouping so many workers in one building would be avoided by building housing with only a small number of flats. The workers would be assimilated into the structure of the rest of the city – the bourgeois structure – rather than set apart in their own environment.

This new form for workers' flats responded to the social and political concerns which had been evident in discussion of blocks in the 1850s.

The 1867 Exposition also helped to reduce concern that hygiene conditions in blocks of workers' flats might be difficult to maintain, and that illnesses might be passed between families living so close together. The examples of English housing societies which were exhibited in Paris in 1867 demonstrated that workers' flats could be designed and maintained in hygienic conditions.

The model for workers' flats which Détain identified in 1867 was to form a basis on which the reformers could work. The emotive discussion of the 1850s was now replaced by a more reasoned discussion, focussed on the hygienic design of flats. The ideological divide between the two models which had evolved independently since the 1850s persisted, and as late as the 1880s, the Familistère still gave rise to fierce opposition from some housing reformers.[11] But when the first International Congress of Cheap Housing was held in Paris in 1889, the alternative model of 'bourgeois' flats was firmly established as a valid form, which the reformers could endorse.

Houses for families

The 1850s had offered the reformers a model for workers' flats which they were to reject, and replace with a model which they found more acceptable. In contrast, the same period saw the construction of a group of individual houses which was to be acclaimed as an ideal by successive generations of reformers. The development, designed by the engineer Emile Muller, was built in Mulhouse, by the Société des Cités Ouvrières set up in the town under the lead of Jean Dollfus. Dollfus was a member of the Protestant industrial aristocracy of Mulhouse, running one of the major cotton mills in the area, and he was a respected member of the town's Société Industrielle. It was after a discussion of workers' housing at the Société that Dollfus and eleven other local industrialists decided in 1853 to found the Société des Cités Ouvrières.

The development which the Société went on to build contained 800 dwellings by 1867, covering 20 hectares and housing about 5,500 people.[12] The inhabitants of this small town enjoyed a range of communal facilities, including baths, a swimming pool, laundry, schools, shops, a library and free medical consultations. These facilities rivalled those of the Familistère, but the housing at Mulhouse was based on a fundamentally different premise; this enshrined the individual within the family, not in the community as a whole. The development at Mulhouse consisted almost exclusively of individual dwellings with their own garden. The use of the individual house was not simply a response to the availability of land at Mulhouse, but was part of a specific programme of housing and social reform. That programme was put forward in the report to the Mulhouse Société Industrielle in 1852.

The attention of the society had been drawn to the question of workers' housing in 1851, when the industrialist Jean Zuber presented the society with a copy of Henry Roberts' *The Dwellings of the Labouring Classes*,[13] and with details of the model dwellings erected at the 1851

7 The original section of the *cité ouvrière* at Mulhouse, with the town of Mulhouse in the background

8 A row of the most typical form of housing in the Mulhouse *cité ouvrière*, houses in groups of four, each with their own separate entrance and garden

9 Details of a typical group
of four houses as presented
by Muller and Cacheux in
*Les habitations ouvrières en
tous pays, situation en 1878,
avenir* (1879)

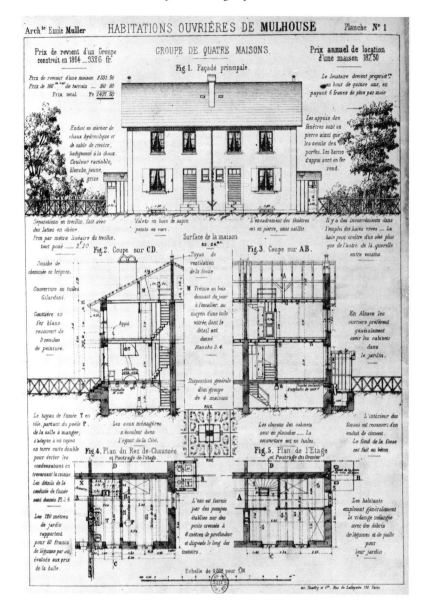

Exhibition in London. Zuber, who had already built a few houses for
the workers at his paper factory in Mulhouse, had attended the Exhibition, and returned to Mulhouse inspired by English efforts to provide
workers' housing. The Society's Comité d'Economie Sociale took up
Zuber's enthusiasm; after gathering details from various individuals
and firms which owned, or had built, housing for their workers, the
committee produced a report which Dr Achille Penot presented in June
1852.[14] Penot identified two possible solutions to the provision of
workers' housing: the large block of flats and separate houses. He
acknowledged the cheaper costs of construction and land for large

buildings, but drew attention to 'the only too frequent occasions for recrimination and disputes', and to 'how much morals suffer in this too intimate neighbourhood'. Taking these considerations into account 'the committee has unanimously rejected the principle...[T]he grouping of a large number of families, gathered into the same block must be avoided as far as is possible'. These conclusions were entirely natural given the general criticism of large blocks in the 1850s. The committee therefore considered that 'individual dwellings are much preferable'.[15]

In conclusion, Penot discussed the effect of housing on its occupants. The relationship between bad housing conditions and immorality, which Blanqui had emphasised in 1848, is countered here by a positive relationship between good housing and morality. It is this positive relationship which was to lie behind the housing reformers' enthusiastic approval of the individual house.

The convenience and cleanliness of a dwelling have a greater influence than one might initially suppose on the morality and well-being of a family. A man who finds when he gets home only a miserable slum, dirty and untidy, where he breathes nauseous and unhealthy air will find no pleasure there and will abandon it to spend much of his spare time at the *cabaret*. And so he will become a stranger to his own home, and will fall into habits of pernicious extravagance which his family will feel all too directly, and which will lead almost inevitably to destitution. If, on the other hand, we can offer these men clean and pleasant dwellings; if we give each man a small garden in which he can occupy himself happily and productively, and where, in anticipating his modest harvest, he will learn to appreciate the true value of that natural instinct of property which Providence has sown in us, will we not have solved in a satisfactory manner one of the most pressing problems of social economy? Will we not have contributed to a tightening of the sacred bonds of the family? Will we not have rendered a true service to the class of our workers, so worthy of our concern, and to society itself?[16]

Property and the family were particularly important to Penot, and to later housing reformers, since they represented stability. The worker described in the first part of the passage had no ties. His dwelling was not a home, with possessions and memories, and his family was disintegrating around him. He had no incentive to better himself, and every incentive to forget his problems at the *cabaret*. He also had nothing to lose if the existing social order was destroyed, or at least rocked, as had been apparent in 1848. On the other hand, Penot believed that the occupant of a house and garden, surrounded by his furniture and family, with vegetables in the garden (which would not be ready before next summer) had an incentive to improve his home, weed his garden, and to protect his possessions. The house and garden would given him a standard of living which neither the slum, nor dense urban blocks like the Cité Napoléon, could provide.

The housing built by the Société Mulhousienne des Cités Ouvrières went one stage further than Penot. Occupants could pay annuities towards the capital cost of the dwelling, instead of simple rent, so the worker could actually become the owner of his dwelling. The house thus became a system of *prévoyance*, of self-help by the worker, along with savings banks and sickness insurance schemes. While the notion of *prévoyance* provided protection for the worker, by building up reserves on which he could draw in an emergency, it also increased the workers' links with the existing institutions of society, and thus his interest in the continuation of society.

But the protection of owning one's own home, saving towards old age, or insurance against sickness were not within reach of the poorest worker. To buy the cheapest house in the Mulhouse *cité ouvrière* in 1853, the worker must have a down payment of 300 fr., and pay 240 fr. per year for 15 years. One writer concluded that it was mainly workers from the country, who already owned a plot of land which they could sell to raise the capital, who benefited from the *cité ouvrière*; others had taken out a loan or been granted an advance by their employer.[17] In either case, the down payment, and the regular instalments required, put the Mulhouse *cité* outside the reach of workers with irregular, low paid work. But it would be wrong to assume that the programme of housing reform described by Penot, and realised by Dollfus and Muller, was intended to reach every worker. It was intended to help the worker who was prepared to help himself. There would always, Villermé had observed, be a residuum of the very poor who could afford only a miserable slum.[18]

It was this selectiveness of reform which led Friedrich Engels to comment, in his series of articles on *The Housing Question* in 1872, that 'capital does not desire to abolish the housing shortage even if it could'.[19] Engels specifically criticised the type of housing which industrialists such as Dollfus built; he quoted a passage from the Spanish newspaper *La Emancipacion*, which argued that 'M. Dollfus and his colleagues sought to stifle all revolutionary spirit in their workers by selling them small dwellings...and at the same time to chain the workers by this property to the factory in which they work.'[20] Engels' critique under-lines the housing reformers' support for housing on the model of Mulhouse. The desire to reduce the housing shortage, while not perhaps as totally absent as Engels suggests, was outweighed by the desire to ensure social stability. The latter was not best achieved by a general improvement in housing, but by enabling members of the working-class élite to own their house and garden, turning them into *petits bourgeois*; the amorphous working class could thus be divided, and its élite won over to the support of the existing social order.

Those aspects of the Mulhouse housing which Engels criticised, were precisely the aspects which its supporters emphasised. Jules Simon, who was to become the honorary president of the Société Française des HBM on its foundation, wrote enthusiastically about Mulhouse in his classic study of working women, *L'ouvrière*, in 1861. He believed that the status of proprietor was 'the sanction and fulfilment of liberty'. The 'paternal home' was much more than a house; 'those who inhabit it and own it no longer feel themselves to be strangers in the midst of society'. Simon also shared the firm belief in family life evident in

Penot's report, and he discussed the housing at Mulhouse in the section of his book entitled 'Salvation through the Family'. The joint forces of property and family came together at Mulhouse; the father 'is doubly at home, in the midst of his family, in his house, in their common house'.[21]

Property ownership on the model pioneered at Mulhouse thus had a particular moral and social value for the housing reformers. Jules Siegfried, a central figure in the housing reform movement for over forty years from the 1870s asked in his study of pauperism,

Who can fail to see to what extent the hope of becoming a proprietor makes a man more hard working, more thrifty, more regular in his habits...
    If we wish to make at the same time happy, contented people, and true conservatives; if we want to combat at the same time pauperism and socialist errors; if we wish to increase guarantees of order, morality, of political and social moderation, then let us create *Cités Ouvrières!*[22]

Emile Cheysson, another senior housing reformer, expressed the value of the home not only in political, but also in spiritual terms. To Cheysson, the family was the 'true molecule of human societies', it was essential that it possessed 'a solid base, a material support'. This base was to be provided by the house;

it is the house which has seen ancestors die and offspring born; it is the house which forms the outer unity of the family and which preserves its traditions as a sacred trust, with the remembrance of joys and sorrows, of dark days and of happy days; it is the house which acts as a link between successive generations, between yesterday and today, and which plays a part in making, out of ephemeral elements forged end to end, that almost undefined succession of the family which survives in itself, makes good its losses, is born again out of its ashes and defies time.
    Considered from this point of view, the house takes on an importance which goes beyond the satisfaction of a purely material need, and rises to the level of a necessity which is at the same time moral and social.[23]

This was perhaps the most extreme statement of the moral significance of the workers' home, but throughout the second half of the century, the individual house, and the example of Mulhouse, are referred to repeatedly for their social importance. In his history of the working classes, published in 1867, Emile Levasseur remarked that 'to make proprietors, that is to say to attach to the soil a poor, semi-nomadic population... is surely the most effective means yet imagined of helping the development of morality among the working class'.[24] The architect Emile Trélat made a similar comment in his paper on workers' housing to the International Hygiene Congress held in Paris in 1878.[25] The importance of the Mulhouse housing in reinforcing this case is indicated by the fact that both Levasseur and Trélat – and also Siegfried in his study of pauperism – quoted at length the key passage from Penot's 1852 report.

Arthur Raffalovich took up the role of property when discussing Mulhouse in his study of workers' housing published in 1887. 'From the social point of view, the acquisition of a house, the accession to property, becomes a guarantee or order, and fixes the worker and his family more firmly to the workplace to which he has attached himself.'[26] Confident in the rightness of the Mulhouse solution, Raffalovich categorically defines its advantages in precisely those terms which Engels used to condemn it. Housing like that at Mulhouse was to provide the means of assimilating workers into the existing structure of society with as little disruption as possible; the social revolution based on class struggle led by the proletariat would thus be defused in advance. Housing, in the terms used by Raffalovich and other reformers, was a central element in pre-empting this revolution.

The *solution mulhousienne*, offering the possibility of workers owning a house set in its garden, represented the ideal of housing reformers throughout the second half of the nineteenth century. At the 1867 Exposition the model established at Mulhouse was acknowledged by the award of a gold medal. At the same exhibition, this ideal was joined by the 'bourgeois' model for workers' flats which the reformers could accept. But this model did not challenge the supremacy of the individual house. More than 20 years later, at the first International Congress of Cheap Housing in 1889, the choice between the two models was still a foregone conclusion. 'Between individual houses and collective blocks, whether one is considering them from the point of view of hygiene, or the point of view of morality, hesitation is not permitted, the choice should be in no doubt.'[27]

16

◇◇

Social reform

The achievement of the Société Mulhousienne represented an ideal wider than housing reform alone. In *L'ouvrière*, Jules Simon referred to the possibility of workers becoming the owners of 'a house and a patch of earth', and declared that 'if this project were realised, it would contain, so to speak, all reforms in a single one'.[1] Jules Siegfried echoed Simon's view when he stated his belief that 'among all the social or philanthropic works created during this century', housing on the model of Mulhouse offered 'without doubt the most positive and most certain results'.[2] The technical aspects of housing reform were to be pursued within this context of housing as a central element of social reform. When the Société Française des HBM was founded in 1889 it included doctors, architects and other experts, but the new society was led by men whose involvement in housing reform was inseparable from their interest in the wider questions relating to the development of society. The relationship between housing and social reform, and the reformers' reaction to the extremes of *laissez-faire* capitalism and revolutionary socialism, provide the background from which legislation to aid the construction of cheap housing was to emerge.

At its foundation, the Société des HBM was to be headed by Jules Simon and Jules Siegfried, as honorary president and acting president respectively. Both men were politically active, inspired by the need to resolve social questions. Simon, aged 75 in 1889, had been involved in politics since 1848, and was a convinced Republican. He refused to take the oath of allegiance to Napoleon III's Empire, thereby losing his position lecturing in history and philosophy at the Ecole Normale. In 1863 he was elected to the Corps Legislatif as a member of the liberal opposition to the Empire; when Napoleon III fell, and a new Republic was declared, Simon was one of its first ministers, and was closely involved in securing the foundations of the Republic in the 1870s. Adherence to the ideal of the Republic was more than simply a political statement. To Simon, and to Siegfried, the Republic stood as the only structure within which society could evolve for the benefit of all its members. They held to this ideal against the authoritarian structures which they saw offered on the one hand by the Empire or the restoration of the monarchy, and on the other hand by the extreme socialists and communists.

10 Jean Dollfus,
1800–1887; founder of the
cité ouvrière at Mulhouse

11 Jules Simon,
1814–1896; honorary
president of the Société
Française des HBM at its
foundation in 1889

12 Jules Siegfried,
1837–1922; founder of
housing societies in Le Havre
and Bolbec, first president of
the Société Française des
HBM, and promoter of the
first French legislation on
cheap housing in 1894

13 Georges Picot,
1838–1909; founding
vice-president of the Société
Française des HBM, and
successor of Jules Siegfried as
president in 1892

14 Emile Cheysson,
1836–1910; active in the
widest range of moderate
social reform, founding
vice-president of the Société
Française des HBM

15 Charles Robert,
1827–1899; advocate of
profit-sharing and
co-operation, founding
treasurer of the Société
Française des HBM

The view of society which found expression in Simon's Republicanism was paralleled by his growing interest in social questions in the 1860s. After a study tour through the manufacturing areas of north and east France, he wrote his book on working women, *L'ouvrière*. Within a year of its publication, in 1861, the book had gone into a second edition. An encounter with Jean Dollfus was of particular significance, and during 1861 Simon gave a series of lectures on the *cité ouvrière* of Mulhouse. In the mid-1860s, Simon was one of the leading advocates of a less restrictive attitude to co-operation and association among workers.[3]

Simon's combination of social and political concerns was a source of inspiration to Jules Siegfried in the 1870s. A generation younger than Simon, Siegfried was 52 when he presided over the foundation of the Société Française des HBM. Siegfried was born, like Jean Dollfus, into a Protestant family in the cotton industry of Mulhouse. In 1862, he and his brother Jacques, set up a new company importing cotton in Le Havre. Jules immediately set off for Bombay, where he set up an agency, and it was only in 1866 that he settled in Le Havre. By that time he had amassed a considerable fortune, benefiting from the boom years in Indian cotton during the American Civil War.

In France, Siegfried soon became involved in political and social matters. In 1868 he donated 100,000 fr. for the foundation of a workers' club in his home town, Mulhouse. After the defeat of 1870, Mulhouse was annexed by Germany, and Siegfried settled permanently in Le Havre. In 1871 he founded a housing society in the town, while in 1874 he helped to set up the Cercle Franklin, a workers' club. The address on the occasion of the opening of this club in 1876 was given by Siegfried's mentor, Jules Simon. In the following year Siegfried published his study of pauperism, *La misère*, and in 1878 he established a second housing society, in Bolbec, near Le Havre. During this period Siegfried was also active in local politics, being deputy mayor from 1870, and becoming mayor himself in 1878. He held this post until 1886, when he stood down to devote himself to his new role, as a deputy elected to parliament in 1885.[4]

Like Simon, Siegfried was a committed Republican. But where Simon had to struggle to establish the Republic, Siegfried joined a parliament in which the Republic was an accepted fact. By the 1880s the varied tendencies covered by the term Republican were becoming more apparent, as the radicals of the Left started to attack the moderate Republicans who held sway. Siegfried did not ally himself to any parliamentary faction. His son, André, notes that Siegfried's social preoccupations, and his support for a lay State, tended to place him on the Left. However, he also describes his father as a '*conservateur*', vehemently opposed to extremism. He remarks 'that dogmatism was a stranger to him and that, if he had convictions, he did not have, strictly speaking, political principles: I see in him the complete pragmatist, the perfect *opportuniste*.'[5]

Although the political climate of the 1880s was very different from that of the 1840s, Siegfried's pragmatism echoes the view of social reform outlined by Blanqui in 1848. Both men instinctively inclined towards the politics of *laissez-faire*, and the conservation of the social order. The natural development of that order, stimulated by individual initiative was to provide the basis for improving the welfare of all members of society. But Blanqui and Siegfried both recognised that the excesses of pure *laissez-faire* policies must be judiciously tempered. Thus both men were to support limited government intervention in the field of housing; but the softening of *laissez-faire* did not express itself solely in law. Siegfried, and other leading housing reformers were active in the 1880s in the movement for profit sharing between employers and workers, and in the co-operative movement. Their view of such initiatives was essentially moderate, envisaging them as an extension rather than a replacement of existing relationships between workers and employers. The internal logic of the reformers' position, accepting the existing structure of society as a given fact which could only gradually be altered, made any more radical view unacceptable. Nonetheless, in working for progress in these areas, the reformers parted company with the more doctrinaire proponents of *laissez-faire* policies. Neither wholly for the capitalist order of society, nor wholly against it, the reformers worked through private organisations and through government, to direct society towards a rather elusive goal of improvement in the material condition of all its members.

Siegfried's colleagues at the head of the Société Française des HBM, the two vice-presidents, were Georges Picot and Emile Cheysson. Like Siegfried they were in their early fifties in 1889. Picot had studied law, and was for a time a senior official in the Ministère de la Justice; he also made a name for himself as a historian. In the 1880s, he tried unsuccessfully to enter parliament as a Republican candidate. Central to his political views was a fierce opposition to socialism; to combat what he saw as its evil, Picot advocated the creation of a party on the lines of the English conservative party, and he emphasised the value of the patronage of the upper classes. Emile Cheysson had trained as an engineer and in this capacity he worked in the team organising the 1867 Exposition Universelle. During this time Cheysson worked closely with the director of the Exposition, Frédéric Le Play. Cheysson came to share Le Play's social concerns, and was to be a leading member of the Société d'Economie Sociale, which Le Play had founded in 1856. During this period working on the Exposition, Cheysson met Eugène Schneider, director of the large metal works at Le Creusot, who asked Cheysson to go to Le Creusot as a director of the firm, a post which he filled from 1871 to 1874; Cheysson was thus able to witness the company's system of industrial patronage, which included housing and other forms of assistance. Returning to Paris, Cheysson became involved in teaching courses of social economy during the 1880s, and, like Picot, he became increasingly involved in the movement for housing reform.[6]

Siegfried, Picot and Cheysson were joined on the board of the Société Française des HBM by the 62-year-old Charles Robert. Like several of the housing reformers, Robert had been born in Mulhouse.[7] During the

Empire, Robert was a senior civil servant, but after 1870 he started a new career, as director of a large insurance company. As early as 1854 Robert had visited the *cité ouvrière* at Mulhouse to prepare an official report for the Ministère de l'Intérieur. During the 1860s he became interested in social questions; like Cheysson, he was involved in the 1867 Exposition, being appointed *rapporteur* of Groupe 10. It was this section which Le Play introduced to include initiatives of social importance, among them examples of workers' housing.[8]

When these four men came together at the head of the Société des HBM in 1889, their paths had already overlapped, and were to continue to do so. In the field of profit sharing, Robert had founded a study society in 1879, in which Siegfried was also involved. Robert, and to a lesser extent Siegfried and Cheysson, were active in the co-operative movement in the 1880s and 1890s. Cheysson and Picot both sat on the committee of the Office Central des Oeuvres Charitables; founded in 1890, the Office aimed to 'make the exercise of charity more effective' by collecting information and publicising the extent of 'pauperism and works destined to alleviate it'.[9] Cheysson and Siegfried both served on the Conseil Supérieur d'Assistance Publique, the central government advisory body on social welfare; in 1904 they were among the founding vice-presidents of the Alliance d'Hygiène Sociale. This new organisation set itself against a range of social ills, proposing 'to fight against tuberculosis, alcoholism, child mortality, etc., by the improvement of housing and of nutrition, the development of mutuality, the action of the Musée Social, education societies, etc.'[10] The Musée Social, to which the Alliance was linked, was another organisation in which these four leaders of reform were prominent. The aim of the organisation, founded in 1894, was to make publicly available information on 'social institutions and organisations which have as their object and result the improvement of the material and moral situation of workers'.[11]

A common theme in these varied activities was provided by an interest in social economy. This study had been pioneered by Le Play, whose method consisted of a detailed examination of the relationship between the different elements of society, and of family life in particular. Emile Levasseur, himself a member of the Société d'Economie Sociale, described one of the key elements in the economic system favoured by Le Play as 'the constitution of a family home, having its foundation in property'.[12] In this emphasis on the family and its home, the study of social economy reinforced the housing reformers' ideal of the single family house; at the same time it linked that ideal to the wider context of moderate social reform advocated by members of the Société d'Economie Sociale.[13]

The Société d'Economie Sociale also provided a link between the reformers of the 1840s and their successors. The society's first president was no less a figure than Dr Villermé; Armand de Melun was on the committee and he served as president in the early 1860s. The next generation of reformers were represented by 1865, when Emile Cheysson joined the society. Cheysson was to be the most active of the housing reformers involved in the society, serving as its president three times.

But many of the other leading housing reformers, including Siegfried, Picot and Robert, were members of the Société d'Economie Sociale or of one of its related organisations.[14]

The range of social organisations in which the leaders of the Société des HBM were active emphasises that housing was just one part of the movement for reform which stretched from temperance to tuberculosis. But as Siegfried and Simon had made clear, housing was one of the major elements in that movement. Different methods of providing improved housing were confronted in the second half of the century, ranging from charity to communism. Within this range, the moderate position of the housing reformers, tempering individual initiative with patronage by the upper classes and industrialists, with association and co-operation, and with limited intervention by government, was to dominate until shortly before the First World War.

Charity and the poor

For the most basic level of assistance, the poorest members of society could turn to private or public charity. Private charitable organisations provided food and clothing, and the larger societies were involved in a variety of other activities. One of the main societies, the Société de Saint Vincent de Paul, was founded in 1833 to visit the poor and sick, and to distribute alms. However, it extended its work to range from soup kitchens to holiday camps. In 1846 the society formed a rent bank in Paris for working families and paupers where they could save towards their rent, and gain a bonus, of around 15%, on the money deposited.[15] The regular structure of public charity was based on the Bureaux de Bienfaisance, which provided assistance in money, in kind, or in work. By 1912 the Bureau de Bienfaisance in Paris was distributing up to 300,000 fr. annually to families with at least five children, in the form of allowances of around 30 fr. for the quarterly rent payment. A further 555,000 fr. was available to provide monthly allowances for single mothers. Alongside this work by the Bureau, the Prefecture of Police had a credit of 20,000 fr. to help paupers, preferably those with families, who were about to be evicted.[16]

While public and private charity both confronted the problem of housing, the solutions introduced tended to lead away from charity. Money distributed as rent allowance was not easily controlled. Emile Cacheux, a housing reformer who drew attention to the economic pressures on working-class tenants in the 1880s, observed this in one of his tenants who received money from the Bureau de Bienfaisance, and yet made frequent visits to the theatre, and was regularly absent from work.[17] Moreover, the money tended to reinforce the existing housing market, and might simply help a family to remain in an inadequate flat, paying an inflated rent. Rent allowances remained as the last defence of charity against bad housing. But they emphasised the need for control over the housing itself, whether through subletting existing dwellings, or constructing new buildings.

As early as 1880, the Bureau de Bienfaisance in Lille had extended its work to finance the construction of flats. Only paupers registered with the Bureau, or families who could prove that their income would not pay market rents were admitted.[18] But by charging low rents, the Bureau only returned 1% on its capital, which was a serious drawback in the eyes of the housing reformers. While cash given to a family to buy bread or pay the rent could be justified as an exceptional subsidy to help the destitute, the management and construction of housing was a permanent commitment. As such, the reformers believed that it should be a commercial, rather than a charitable, operation. When some charitable foundations started investing in housing on a large scale at the end of the nineteenth century, it was as a commercial proposition, anticipating a small but positive return. Similarly, when the central body of public charity in Paris, the Assistance Publique, started to build housing in the early 1900s, it was on this limited commercial basis.

While the traditional forms of private and public charity continued to aid those who could not aspire to the relative luxury of flats built by cheap housing societies, they attacked the effects more than the roots of poverty. T. Zeldin has commented of the Société de Saint Vincent de Paul that 'the attitude of the almost exclusively middle-class members of this society was paternalistic and traditional. They were not concerned with curing the causes of poverty'.[19] Poverty continued to be regarded, even by some housing reformers, as being at least partly the fault of the poor themselves. In his study published in 1887, Arthur Raffalovich noted that 'poverty may be the result of circumstance, or derive from bad habits, intemperance, laziness'. Although he saw poverty as being one of the factors contributing to bad housing, it was not a problem that subsidies could solve. 'Against extreme poverty there is no remedy: pauperism is incurable.'[20]

The logic of this was that the poor must be educated to live with their existing circumstances. This hard moral line was justified with the argument that by singling them out for help, society would 'corrupt the pauper classes'.[21] Raffalovich gave an example of what he saw as corruption in his comments on the housing built by the Bureau de Bienfaisance in Lille. Apparently the free medical service provided by the Bureau was abused by tenants. Quinquina wine supplied for medicinal purposes was used by some families for Sunday celebrations, while castor oil found its way into oil lamps, and on to the workers' shoes.[22] Raffalovich's disapproval of providing too much for the workers was echoed by Dr Jules Rochard, who commented that one could not force on working families which were not sober and hard working 'a well-being of which they are not worthy'. Unfortunately, as Rochard also observed, 'it is harder to change the habits of the unfortunate than to build them houses'.[23]

The dilemma of charity was summed up by Emile Levasseur, in his *Histoire des classes ouvrières*: 'Society must maintain its course of action between two equally dangerous perils: that of incurring the reproach of indifference and cruelty, and that of encouraging laziness and improvidence, through blind generosity.'[24] One answer to this lay in working towards the prevention rather than the relief of suffering. It was this concern to prevent the workers' fall into destitution which led the leaders of the Société Française des HBM, to their wide-ranging involvement in social organisations. But the pre-eminent position which Simon and Siegfried gave to housing reform derived in part from the fact that housing could avoid the perils identified by Levasseur. The work of the housing societies could provide dwellings, for some workers at least, without the stigma of charity, as the societies had a sound commercial basis. Moreover, the reformers anticipated that their ideal would resolve Rochard's problem. The habits of the unfortunate would be changed by the very fact of building them houses, provided of course that they were the right sort of houses.

In these respects housing could indeed be seen as the pinnacle of social reform. But as well as being a pinnacle to the reformers, it must have seemed so also to the poor, as it helped only the élite of the working class directly. As a consequence of their wider views of social reform, the housing reformers left the 'residuum' to fend for itself, to become 'the inevitable prey' of landlords and proprietors. Raffalovich borrowed the term 'residuum' from the English, accepting that one could not reach it directly. Instead, 'one must work by successive layers', freeing the better housing in the private market by enabling the élite workers to move into 'model' dwellings. While charity remained to help the 'residuum', the reformers focussed their attention on those who showed a willingness to help themselves.[25]

Self-help: saving and co-operation

To finance housing for the better-off workers, the housing reformers initially appealed to the patronage of the upper classes. The two housing schemes of the 1850s, the Cité Napoléon and the Mulhouse development, offered examples of this form of finance. The societies which built these schemes offered an alternative to purely speculative housing, but in order to avoid what were seen as the dangers of pure charity, the reformers did not abandon speculation entirely. Cheysson advocated that the upper classes involve themselves in speculation 'seasoning it with patriotism and philanthropy'.[26] Picot noted that 'any operation, be it inspired by philanthropy, is condemned to sterility if it does not take a reasonable interest from the capital involved'.[27]

The lack of reasonable interest was the one drawback with housing provided for workers directly by their employers. In his report on housing exhibited at the Exposition Universelle of 1889, Picot looked in vain for employers making a genuine commercial profit. But industrial housing was seen as a valid stepping stone to the full ideal of action by the worker himself:

We will start with the rudimentary method, of free temporary concession by the employer, to end with construction by the worker according to his tastes, the most perfect form that he can hope for.

First we will see the worker as a sort of child, under the paternal guardianship of the employer; we will follow the stages of his emancipation, to arrive at the time when he feels liberated by saving, that is, by his cumulative work.[28]

The notion of saving was of great significance to the reformers. It was their answer to the image of the improvident worker, abandoning his family to spend his wages in the *cabaret*, forcing his wife on to the streets, and his children to fend for themselves. To the reformers, the *cabaret*, where the worker could drink his wages away, and where he might meet undesirable, even socialist, troublemakers, epitomised the failure of the working man to take the care for the future which they felt he should have. 'One comes out almost always with an empty pocket, and a mind obsessed by unhealthy ideas.'[29] Against this, saving offered a means of ordering one's present life, and of preparing for an uncertain future. Jules Simon expressed this view of the potential of saving, declaring that with the worker's 'first deposit, the *cabaret* is already half vanquished'.[30] The reformers presented this potential not simply as helping the worker, but also as securing the stability of society by giving the worker a stake in that society. Dr Penot expressed this during the revolutionary year of 1848, claiming that 'the habit of saving and of work renders men better members of their family, and citizens more attached to their country'.[31]

Working families could save through the Caisses d'Epargne which developed after the first Caisse was founded by Benjamin Delessert in 1818.[32] Under the Second Empire the Caisses were officially encouraged, and the number of branches tripled in the 1860s. About half of the savers were from the working classes, but the Caisses did not become a mass movement: by 1870 only 5.5% of the population had savings in a Caisse.[33] In parallel with the Caisses, friendly societies – *sociétés de secours mutuels* – also developed from the early part of the century. In return for regular subscription, the societies would provide help during sickness, and some would cover the cost of burials; orderly budgeting was thus combined with the notions of *prévoyance* – of foresight and concern for the future – and of *mutualité* – the co-operation of workers themselves to provide mutual aid. Like the Caisses, these societies were encouraged during the Empire. When the Emperor allocated 10 million francs to workers' housing in 1852, he made the same sum available to friendly societies, though the societies receiving aid had to be approved, and were strictly controlled. Both Caisses d'Epargne and friendly societies were supplemented by private savings and insurance schemes organised by some industrialists for their workers. But while the social reformers continued to stress their value, both to the worker and to society as a whole, they remained minority movements. Jules Simon recognised this failure to achieve the scale necessary to make any real progress when he noted that Caisses d'Epargne were 'excellent for encouraging the taste of saving, and largely powerless in bringing that taste into existence'. He identified the problem as that of providing the worker with a means of saving with passion.[34]

The means envisaged by Simon was the acquisition of property. Just as the social economists' study of the family provided the theoretical basis for the housing reformers to enshrine the family in its individual house, so the more general concern of social reformers with saving and *prévoyance* lent support to the vision of the owner-occupied house. Not only did Simon consider the fact of being a proprietor to be of social value, but the actual process of becoming a proprietor, through the regular budgeting which that implied, was also of considerable value. It had all the advantages of saving as a mechanism of social reform, while having the added bonus that the results could be enjoyed immediately. Furthermore, as Jules Siegfried pointed out, the acquisition of a house acted as a form of insurance and pension; for if the worker had paid off his home by the time he retired, his expenses during retirement would be considerably reduced.[35]

These were benefits to the worker himself, but saving appealed to social reformers for a further reason. They were unwilling to advocate means of reform, some of which involved financial commitment from the wealthier members of society, if they felt that the worker would simply take advantage of the assistance offered. The worker must satisfy the reformers that he would make an appropriate effort to better himself; for in Simon's opinion, 'no one has the power to save the worker from pauperism, if it is not the worker himself'.[36] Saving provided evidence of this effort towards self-help.

While the acquisition of property marked a significant stage in the workers' improvement by self-help, the initial capital of societies such as the Mulhouse society was still provided by the upper classes of society. The logical next step was for the workers themselves to establish their own capital, through co-operative societies. In his paper on housing delivered at the 1886 hygiene exhibition in Paris, Emile Cheysson called for the creation of construction co-operatives in France, to fulfil a role similar to the building societies in England.[37] Although Cheysson had little confidence in the idea being taken up by workers in France, interest in the co-operative movement was growing. The previous year had seen the first National Congress of Consumer Co-operatives; this led to the foundation of a central organisation, the Fédération Coopérative, subsequently renamed the Union Coopérative. At the second co-operative congress, held three months after Cheysson delivered his paper in 1886, the opening speaker, Charles Gide, gave a rallying address which was to establish a line of development for the movement.

Drawing on the work of Charles Fourier and also of the Rochdale Pioneers, the consumer co-operative group founded in England in the 1840s, Gide set the French co-operative movement in opposition to the laws of *laissez-faire* economists. But while opposing the wage system and capitalist profit, the Union Coopérative of the 1880s did not support revolutionary socialism. Gide's speech was interpreted as a call for a 'reformist' co-operative party, and as the expression of 'a will for battle against political socialism, against workers' organisations of revolutionary inspiration'.[38]

To either side of the view of co-operation outlined by Gide, the movement still contained a wide range of opinion. The more radical co-operatives envisaged a closer relationship with socialist groups; in 1895 they broke away from the Union to form their own organisation, a division which was only healed in 1912. On the other hand, some supporters of co-operation saw it as a means of introducing workers to the benefits offered by a capitalist society. While the radical co-operators looked back to the workers' associations of 1848 and to Rochdale for inspiration, the moderates took up a view which linked back to the interest in co-operation during the latter years of the Empire; it was this view which was to characterise the housing reformers' interest in co-operation.

In the early 1860s, a group of Orléanists and moderate Republicans had grouped around the businessman Casimir Périer to advance the cause of co-operatives. Casimir Périer was careful to distinguish between association as a stabilising force, uniting different ranks in society, and association as a threat to society, in the form of communism. He saw co-operation as the condemnation of communism, and 'against the errors and perils of socialism, the most certain and most noble of remedies'.[39] In these terms, co-operation linked up with the idea of saving, as a healthy moral force which enabled the worker to improve himself by his own efforts, and those of his fellow workers. Léon Say, one of the advocates of co-operation in the 1860s expressed this view of co-operative societies as 'perfected savings banks, in which the funds are employed by and for the depositor'.[40]

Jean Gaumont, supporter and historian of the co-operative movement, accused these bourgeois supporters of co-operation in the 1860s of wishing to rally to their cause

employees, temperate and thrifty workers, by the lure of provident societies, institutions of mutual aid, of domestic economy, of cheap credit, thanks to which a small aristocracy of workers and artisans would be constituted, on which they could count to maintain the large mass of wage earners, *their wage earners*, in the situation, convenient for employers and their interests, of cheap labour.[41]

Gaumont saw the same limited view in some of the men who revived interest in co-operation in the 1880s. He referred to 'certain representatives of political economy who tend towards social interest, Catholics or Protestants, endeavouring to temper their rigid materialism with a little sympathy for the working classes'.[42] Gaumont criticises this view of co-operation from the standpoint of the autonomous co-operative movement which Charles Gide guided into existence, following a path between *laissez-faire* policies and revolutionary movements.

The creation of an aristocracy of workers and artisans, which Gaumont criticises, would not have been considered unreasonable to the housing reformers, although they might not have accepted his comment on the implication of such an aristocracy. Rather than perpetuating a system of cheap labour they saw the reforms they campaigned for as percolating through to the poorer classes, by the process of 'levelling up'. In accordance with their gradual view of social progress they advocated reforms which would not overturn society. They saw co-operatives in the field of housing primarily as a means of raising capital from the efforts of the workers who would become tenants or proprietors. It was thus natural that they should envisage such co-operatives as extensions of institutions for saving and credit.

One of the leaders of the credit co-operatives, Eugène Rostand, was also an active housing reformer. A poet and man of letters, Rostand became increasingly interested in questions of social economy in the mid-1880s. In addition to founding the *banque populaire* in Marseilles, he was president of the Caisse d'Epargne des Bouches du Rhône from 1886, and established more than twenty other savings institutions. In the Centre Fédératif de Crédit Populaire he provided a focus for study and propaganda. To Rostand, savings banks and credit co-operatives were ideal sources of finance for the construction of housing. He championed the use of savings bank funds to provide capital for housing societies, and advocated the creation of credit co-operatives and construction co-operatives to enable workers to finance housing themselves.[43] In each case, housing was envisaged as a tangible result of workers' savings, whether through a savings bank, or a co-operative.

Like Picot, Rostand was among the members of the Société Française des HBM who spoke out most strongly against State intervention in the field of construction. He saw the resolution of housing and social problems through co-operation in its widest sense: the working together of all members of society. This would operate at two levels. First, in direct association between workers themselves. Second, in the association of the rich and poor classes through patronage. The co-operation of workers was thus not to threaten the leading role still played in society by the upper classes. Echoing the beliefs of his fellow reformers, Rostand declared that social questions could only be resolved through 'thrift and moral conduct on the one hand, patronage on the other; in a word, the reciprocal and beneficial support of human beings'.[44]

Socialism

For reformers such as Rostand, housing reform offered the possibility of blurring the distinction between classes. To advocates of more radical reform, housing performed the opposite role. Emphasising the exploitation of tenants by landlords, anarchists and socialists worked towards a division and conflict between classes. Just as the moderate reformers used housing to try to win over some of the workers to their view of a stable society, so radical reformers and revolutionaries used housing to convince workers of the need for a change in the relationship between classes. Although revolutionary attitudes achieved little directly in the field of housing, they did form a continuous undercurrent to the housing reformers' work, as R. H. Guerrand has demonstrated.[45]

The reform of property had been advocated by Proudhon in 1851. He proposed that ownership of property should pass to the municipal administration; accommodation would be let at cost price to its occupants. In a series of 14 brochures by various authors published in the late 1850s and early 1860s, Guerrand notes that the majority advocate measures to 'socialise' property for the community, and intervention by government to regulate relations between tenants and landlords. The authors of these brochures were not workers, nor slum dwellers themselves, and Guerrand sees them as evidence of a current which he describes as 'the small change of the various schools of utopian socialism'.[46]

At the time of the 1867 Exposition Universelle, workers' delegations prepared reports which gave workers an opportunity to express themselves directly. Several reports drew attention to the problems of housing, and the rise in rents.[47] Workers were not free during the Empire to promote radical solutions, but, with the downfall of the regime in 1870, popular clubs and newspapers proliferated. During the siege of Paris and the Commune the question of rents was much discussed. The Government of National Defence introduced tribunals which could grant a delay in the payment of rent. For the besieged city of Paris, the Government granted a moratorium of three months on rent due in October 1870, extended by another three months in January 1871. By the time the next rent payment was due in April, the Commune was in power in the city. Guerrand has observed that the leaders of the Commune did not promote a fundamental change in the tenant landlord system. 'None of the members of the Commune was capable of viewing the relationship of tenants and proprietors in a truly revolutionary perspective.'[48] Far from the expropriation of property, the most radical proposal to resolve the rent problem was simply exemption from rent payments – a solution which a commission set up by the mayors of Paris before the Commune had already contemplated.

The resurgence of the workers' movement in the 1880s led to the revolutionary perspective which was lacking in the Commune. The anarchists were vocal in attacking the rights of proprietors, and advocating expropriation. While working towards the revolution which would bring this about, they gave practical help to tenants. The Ligue des Antipropriétaires, active in the late 1880s, assisted tenants in moving themselves and their furniture out of a flat before the arrival of the bailiff. Anarchist groups and their newspapers were disbanded by the *lois scélérates* which followed the anarchist campaign of 1892–4. Nonetheless, their activities were an indication of 'social tensions which seriously begin to worry the men of "order"'.[49] As such, they helped convince the men of order of the need for social legislation.

While the anarchists were taking direct action, the socialist parties were defining their attitude to housing more theoretically. The newspaper *L'Egalité*, which was published from 1877, indicated the difference in the assumptions of the socialists and the conservative social reformers. An item in 1878 struck at the very foundations of conservative reform, aiming to show 'that the three great conservative principles of existing society (religion, property, family) are the sources or rather the causes of all the monstrosities which afflict humanity'.[50] *L'Egalité* had been founded by Jules Guesde, a supporter of the Commune in 1871, who had left France to avoid a prison term imposed for his activity. He returned to France in 1876, and was to become the main advocate of Marxist theory in France. Guesde and his followers promoted a collectivist policy, demanding the expropriation of private property, and opposed the construction of housing by the communes in competition with private enterprise. In the intermediate stage before expropriation, they advocated reductions in rent.

Guesde argued that tenants would only be saved from the clutches of landlords by the return of all dwellings to the community; the process of expropriation of capitalist property would necessarily be revolutionary. The socialist congress held in 1882 led to a split between the Guesdists, and the more moderate proponents of a municipal socialism. These *possibilistes*, led by Dr Paul Brousse, evolved the theory of 'public services'; according to this, capitalist structures would be transformed into public corporations not in one revolutionary blow, but as their economic development made them ready.

The *possibilistes* saw their first task as winning power at municipal level. When one of their number, Jules Joffrin, was elected to the Paris council in 1882, he was the first socialist to gain a seat on the council since the commune; by 1887 the group had nine council members.[51] Among the public services which the commune would run for its population was the housing service, and Joffrin advocated the construction of housing by the city of Paris. The interventionist position which the *possibilistes* adopted was also evident in proposals made by other radical councillors in the early 1880s, calling for expropriation of land, and public construction. In the Chambre des Députés this interventionist position was reflected in the views of Tony Révillon; together with a group of radical deputies, he advocated the use of land owned by the city of Paris for the construction of housing, either by leasing the land to private builders, or through direct construction by the city.[52] There was thus a sizeable minority advocating some form of public action both at communal and State level in the early 1880s, but the opponents of such action were still the majority. Discussion by the Paris council and the State led to a moderate proposal for cheap loans, but even on this the parties involved could not agree. As in the 1850s, construction was left in the hands of private enterprise.[53]

The action of the socialists achieved little practical result at this time, whether in the reformism of the *possibilistes* or the revolutionary activity of the anarchists. Guerrand sees the fundamental reason for this as 'the real distress of the working population at this time and in its complete inferiority before the representatives of the propertied classes'.[54] It was only in 1893 that the socialists entered the Chambre des Députés as a significant force. But their activities both within the Chambre and outside were enough to cause the propertied classes some unease. Thus the Paris administration, and the government, had felt obliged to consider the proposals of the socialists in the 1880s, even if they finally took no action.

Some conservatives reacted to the threat of socialism with a declaration of war. Georges Picot published a pamphlet in 1885 entitled *La lutte contre le socialisme révolutionnaire.* Arthur Raffalovich, another housing reformer who was vehemently opposed to socialist views, condemned the Paris council in the 1880s for being 'sullied by socialist ideas'.[55] Other reformers took a more subtle approach to the threat of socialism. Jules Siegfried was no more a supporter of extremism than Georges Picot; but in his pragmatic way, Siegfried was prepared to see that social reform and socialism shared the ideal of improving the workers' conditions, even if the methods proposed were separated by an ideological gap. At the opening meeting of the Société Française des HBM in 1889, Siegfried attempted to bridge that gap, declaring that 'we are not indulging in charity, we are involved in enlightened philanthropy, or, to use a more modern expression, socialism, but *practical socialism*'.[56]

'Practical socialism'

Siegfried's equation of enlightened philanthropy with socialism expresses an aspiration towards unified action; it reflects his personal rejection of extremes, of either Right or Left. The term 'practical socialism' was more than a mere rhetorical catch-phrase, and in Siegfried's own career in municipal and national government, its implications are apparent. At Le Havre, as deputy mayor and mayor in the 1870s and early 1880s, Siegfried guided the municipality towards an active role. He oversaw the construction of new schools, and the organisation of the lay teaching staff. He took a close interest in the design and construction of the Pasteur hospital, and established the first municipal hygiene office in France, centralising decisions on public health in a single organisation. His concern with hygiene led Siegfried to consider the environmental problems related to the servicing and growth of Le Havre. The eminent sanitary engineer Alfred Durand-Claye was asked to advise on questions of sewer systems in 1885; when he left office in 1886, Siegfried had overseen the preparation of proposals for a waterborne sewer system, plans for a series of new streets in the town, and outline plans for the layout of development in the suburbs. Such planning was farsighted, but so active a role on the part of the municipality did not meet with universal approval in the 1880s. Siegfried's successor as mayor did not pursue the sanitation scheme, while property interests in the town secured the suppression of the hygiene office.[57]

In the Chambre des Députés, Siegfried campaigned for increased powers for municipalities to control their own evolution. In 1886 he deposited a bill which would have obliged towns to introduce and enforce basic public health regulations, and would have increased their powers in relation to the inspection and demolition of unhealthy housing. This bill was not considered by parliament, but it contributed to the campaign for revision of the 1850 housing law, which was finally to bear fruit in 1902. During the early 1900s Siegfried maintained his interest in municipal power, being involved in the campaign to revise expropriation legislation in order to enable municipalities to clear slum areas, and in efforts to encourage municipalities to draw up town development and extension plans. Both of these campaigns succeeded in introducing legislation to the statute books, in 1915 and 1919 respectively. In relation to housing, Siegfried left the law which bears his name, the Loi Siegfried of 1894. This law appealed to private enterprise to build housing – Siegfried saw no role for the municipality in the construction of housing. But in parallel with his interest in the extension of municipal powers over expropriation and urban growth in the early 1900s, he was involved in the extension of the municipality's role as an assistant to private enterprise in 1906. In his activity as a deputy, Siegfried thus worked to give municipalities the power to extend the practical socialism which he had begun to introduce in Le Havre.

The housing reformers were not a uniform group, sharing identical views and ideals. Arthur Raffalovich could castigate a fellow reformer Emile Cacheux for 'allowing himself to be swept along on the fatal slope of State socialism'.[58] But within the variety of individual views, Siegfried's pragmatism provides a unifying thread. In his activity in Le Havre, and in parliament, Siegfried started to define a role for the public authorities which would support the work of private initiative, without inhibiting or supplanting it. His policy of 'practical socialism' may lack the rigour of liberal economics or socialist collectivism. But it has a logic which shows reform to be more than simply a rearguard action in the face of the threat from the Left. That threat was undoubtedly an element which increased the pressure for change. But the slow evolution of the social order which Blanqui described provided its own logic for reform.

This logic also provided its own limitations, envisaging reform as a process which must go at the pace of the social order. Since the reformers were self-appointed as interpreters of this pace, they could hide behind their logic as a reason for introducing inadequate, tardy reforms. Nonetheless, the housing reformers of the Société Française des HBM did initially take a lead, advocating measures which parliament or investors were not always disposed to approve. It was only in 1912 that they lost the initiative in housing legislation, as the radicals and socialists took up the question in earnest. In the law of that year it is possible to see the views of the Société Française des HBM acting as a brake on the more radical proposals set before parliament. Having stood in 1894 ahead of a majority which they convinced of the need for reform, by 1912 the reformers were among the majority which needed convincing.

17

◇◇

Housing and hygiene

Armed with the housing law of 1850, the French entered the second half of the nineteenth century apparently better prepared than their German neighbours to tackle the problems of insanitary housing. But the restrictions imposed in the final text of the law indicated a degree of resistance to its measures which was to be confirmed in its ineffectiveness in all but a few areas. The framework for the improvement in housing conditions was initially to come not from legislation to control existing property, but through efforts to improve the hygiene of the city as a whole.

But here, too, improvement was not immediate. The outstanding achievement of the second half of the nineteenth century in the field of works to improve public health was the reconstruction of urban centres, accompanied by the improvement of water supply and sewer systems during the Second Empire. But while this helped the city as a whole, improvement was not automatically reflected in the interior of dwellings. The ability of the bourgeoisie to pay increased rents in return for improved standards meant that more expensive housing was able to benefit from the sanitary equipment available in the later nineteenth century. But working families could offer no such financial incentive towards improvement. With the occupants of cheap housing more concerned about the level of their rent than the standard of their dwelling, and public activity focussed on large-scale public works, the question of the relationship of individual dwellings to the public services received little attention during the Empire. Thus in resolving the crucial question of waste disposal, and whether the unhealthy system of cesspits and night-soil in dense cities could be suppressed, the French lagged behind their neighbours. The issue only came under detailed consideration in the 1880s, while it had been examined in Germany from the early 1870s and in London before the middle of the nineteenth century. This was a central issue, as the improvement of water supply, essential to higher standards of hygiene, depended on an adequate system of disposal. It was only when this issue had been settled that it was possible for the improvement of urban hygiene through public works to be paralleled by realistic measures to extend control of conditions in existing housing, and of the standard of new construction.

342

The campaign to revise the 1850 law to introduce these measures thus
only started to have an impact in the 1880s, leading slowly to a greater
definition of public standards.

The Second Empire: public and private rights

The public works of the Second Empire in Paris have been well
documented, and will not be considered in detail here.[1] Rather, the more
general question of why such works were limited in their effect on
existing housing conditions will be considered by looking at the
regulations governing existing and new building. As in the field of public
works, it is Paris which offers the most material, but the implications
are not limited to that city. For despite the existence of a system of
regulation, particularly for new construction, which was among the
most advanced in the urban centres of Europe, the gap between urban
renewal and the individual dwelling remained.

The relationship between public and private rights in existing property
can be seen in a series of *ordonnances* and instructions passed in Paris
in the late 1840s and early 1850s. These were published in the context
of concern over cholera, a new outbreak of which struck France in
1848–9. As in 1831–2, the threat of cholera led to a reorganisation of
hygiene services. At a national level, the central Conseil Supérieur de
Santé was superseded by the Comité Consultatif d'Hygiène Public in
1848, while local Conseils d'Hygiène et de Salubrité were established
in the main town of every arrondissement in France. In Paris, Commissions Sanitaires similar to those of 1831 were renewed in each
arrondissement, but it was not until 1851 that the hygiene structure
of the city was placed on a more permanent base. Commissions
d'Hygiène et de Salubrité were now formed in every arrondissement,
and also in the suburban arrondissements of Saint Denis and Sceaux;
these Commissions were grouped under the Conseil d'Hygiène et de
Salubrité du Département de la Seine, which itself took over from the
old Conseil de Salubrité dating from 1802.

As cholera approached Paris towards the end of 1848, advice on the
maintenance of hygiene standards in housing was published by the
Conseil de Salubrité and the Prefect of Police. A more general *ordonnance*
was issued by the police in 1853; appearing just as the reconstruction
of Paris was commencing, the *ordonnance* was explicit that 'it would not
be enough to have established, at great expense, a vast system of sewers
and water distribution for the cleansing of streets; to have, by creating
numerous new streets, eased the circulation of air in the various
quarters of the town, if similar measures, no less important for public
health, were not extended to every house, and more particularly to those
occupied by the working population'.[2]

Despite this acknowledgement that a link must be forged between
public works and the dwelling, the public powers to enforce such a link
were limited. This derived partly from a division of responsibilities in

relation to public health. The Prefect of the Seine was responsible for large public works such as sewers and water supply, while it was the Prefect of Police who had authority over conditions of salubrity within public buildings and housing. The split between public works and the dwelling thus existed administratively as well as physically. Moreover, the authority of the police was strictly limited in relation to housing. The Prefect had the power to enforce measures only in the common parts of buildings. This enabled him to have some control over the disposal of rubbish, drainage of waste, shared privies and the cleaning of courtyards. But the individual dwelling was beyond his jurisdiction. An attempt to rationalise the divided administration of public health was made in 1859, when certain responsibilities – including the cleansing of sewers and cesspits – were transferred from the Police to the Prefect of the Seine. However, the restriction of authority to the common parts of housing was not altered.[3]

The possibility of bringing about improvement of conditions within the dwelling rested with the Commission des Logements Insalubres. created under the 1850 housing law. The general bias of the final version of this law, leaving public authority relatively weak against private right, has been noted. In the specific operation of the Commissions this was reflected in the fact that they could only act upon a request to inspect a property. They had no power to carry out a regular system of inspection – even an optional inspection which a proprietor or tenant might refuse. They remained unable to build up anything more than a partial picture of housing conditions, and unable to initiate a co-ordinated programme of improvement.

Within this restricted role, the Paris Commission was one of the few consistently active Commissions in France. By the 1860s it was dealing with well over 1000 cases per year; the 30-man Commission was meeting once a week, under the chairmanship of the Prefect of the Seine. The Commission's prescriptions generally related to cleaning measures within houses, but in the 1860s the Commission extended its view of insalubrity to include that which resulted from a lack of water. In certain cases it exercised its authority under the 1850 law to order landlords to provide water for cleaning purposes. This was a step towards closing the gap between public works and the dwelling, but it was a small step. The Commission asserted this authority in only 211 cases out of the 33,167 cases it had considered up to 1869. Moreover, the Commission's report of 1866 tended to reinforce the gap again, noting that the increase in the number of public fountains made the enforcement of a water supply to houses unnecessary in many cases.[4]

The structure and control over conditions in existing housing thus provided no programme which would have extended the benefits of the city's public works to the existing housing stock. The services provided to cheap housing remained sparse. The nearest water was generally a tap in the courtyard, or the public fountain in the street. Waste water could be drained into the street sewer, but solid waste was collected in a cesspit which was periodically emptied. The system of cesspits gave proprietors an incentive to oppose the introduction of water to their houses, for the more water was used, the sooner they would have to meet the cost of having the cesspit emptied.[5]

While the control of existing housing did little to improve conditions, the control over new buildings allowed unhealthy conditions to be reproduced as the city grew. The Commission des Logements Insalubres drew attention in its 1866 report to the fact that it had had to visit a large number of recently completed dwellings. Defective construction continued in spite of amendment of the building regulations during the Second Empire.

The principle of public control over building in Paris had been established by regulations introduced in 1783 and 1784. These regulated the height of new buildings, relating it to the width of the street, and to construction methods; but they said nothing about the interior conditions of the buildings. A decree law passed in 1852 gave Paris, and other towns, the right to introduce regulations in the interests of public safety and health, and to require approval of plans before construction. In practice, however, the definition of *salubrité* was too vague to lead to useful control.

When the Paris building regulations were amended in 1859, the principle of relating building height to street width was confirmed. More significantly in terms of interior conditions, the regulations extended height control to buildings facing on to courtyards within the block, and introduced a minimum internal room height of 2·6 m. These changes sought to prevent some of the worst excesses of speculative building which had become apparent as construction expanded in the 1850s. The regulations also reduced the overall maximum height of construction permissible. Given the generous width of many of the streets created in the 1850s and 1860s this reduction was seen as an unnecessary restriction on the freedom of builders, and in 1864 the old maximum of 20 m, permitted by the 1783 regulations, was restored. Shortly after the end of the Empire, the 1864 regulations were confirmed by a decree in 1872; this decree also extended the regulations by introducing minimum sizes of light-wells or courts within the building blocks[6] (fig. 16).

The Paris building regulations in this period thus established a coherent system governing the creation of the urban environment, whose strength is still evident in Paris today. But the impact of the regulations within buildings was limited. Within the framework which defined the volume of building possible in relation to the size of the street, the only measures which affected the interior were the control of room heights after 1859, and the control over courtyards introduced in 1859 and 1872.

Within the system of control of existing or new construction defined during the Second Empire, the individual dwelling thus remained almost untouched. Approached on one side by the construction of sewers and water mains, and the control of drains, privies and cesspits, and on the other side by generalised control of the shape and volume of building,

16 The building envelope
defined by the Paris
regulations of 1783/4 and
1859, and subsequently
modified in 1884 and 1902

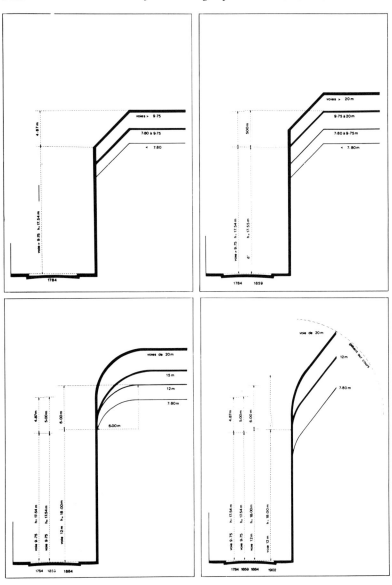

the individual dwelling was defined as the private realm between these areas of public action. There was still no means of closing the gap between the improvement of services by public works, and the use of those services in new and existing dwellings.

The Third Republic: the widening of debate

While the public works of the Second Empire had stopped at the threshold of working-class dwellings, they had improved the hygiene of the city as a whole. The overall death rate in Paris had fallen in the 1850s and 1860s, and outbreaks of cholera in 1854 and 1865 were less serious than earlier epidemics.[7] But the siege of Paris in 1870 indicated how rapidly a dense city with a large population could become unhealthy if not properly serviced and supplied.[8] With the demise of the Empire, which had given such dominant direction to urban development, the question of hygiene and the city was to be the subject of increasing public discussion in the 1870s. When the Exposition Internationale et Speciale d'Economie Domestique opened in 1872, it included a complete section devoted to the 'Hygiene of housing and of the city: ventilation, drainage, cesspits, sewers, etc.'[9] The *Revue Générale de l'Architecture* applauded this initiative; while noting the greater attention paid to the questions of public hygiene in England, the *Revue* observed that in France they were now 'more than ever the order of the day'.[10]

The discussion of urban hygiene was given a firmer base through the greater availability of statistical evidence, and the formation of professional societies. In Paris, a municipal statistics department had been set up in 1865, and this made possible the collection of mortality statistics for the whole city. The 1876 census enabled one statistician to demonstrate the correlation between poor areas of the city and high death rates, confirming the fact arrived at empirically by earlier housing reformers.[11]

In the following year two national organisations which were to provide a forum for the discussion of hygiene were formed in Paris: the Société Française d'Hygiène, and the Société de Médecine Publique et d'Hygiène Professionelle; these were followed in the next few years by smaller local societies in some provincial towns. At the same time the Paris Commission des Logements Insalubres was increasingly acting as a pressure group, drawing on the experience of its members in studying specific cases to sustain a more general discussion of hygiene conditions and control.[12] This widening of debate within France was reinforced by international discussion, focussed on the International Congress of Hygiene. From 1876 this congress held a regular series of meetings, at which housing and hygiene were frequent subjects for discussion.

Discussion of housing at the hygiene congresses indicates the extent to which the experience of urban sanitary reform lent weight to the housing reformer's ideal of the individual house and garden. The problems of air, light, water and sewage were emphasised by the density of occupation in urban housing; they could be avoided, or solved much more simply, with individual dwellings. As an ideal, this solution was established at the first two congresses, in Brussels in 1876, and Paris in 1878.[13] But while this ideal avoided the problems which sanitary reform attempted to solve, urban areas still existed, and they still required a solution.

One of the major papers to the hygiene congress on conditions in existing housing, was delivered in 1878 by Dr du Mesnil, one of the most active reformers to emerge from the Paris Commission des Logements Insalubres. The discussion following his paper identified two areas of concern which were of particular relevance to sanitary reform in France. Dr Marjolin, a senior Paris surgeon, regretted the 'non-execution of the 1850 law'.[14] His comment was backed up by Dr Ulysse Trélat, also a surgeon in Paris, and brother of the architect, Emile Trélat; he was outspoken in challenging the rights of property which had impeded the implementation of the law. 'It is essential', he declared, 'that when a dwelling has been recognised as unhealthy, it be destroyed or transformed without regard to the right of property. The right of healthiness is superior, because property is transient and unhealthiness is eternal, unless one destroys it.'[15] On a more specific level, Alfred Durand-Claye, chief engineer in the city sanitation service in Paris, drew attention to the problem of privies, which 'are the plague of dwellings. Where does the great drawback of the system come from: it is the lack of cleanliness; and, in my opinion, that derives from the complete absence of water in the majority of blocks of workers' dwellings.'[16] At the end of the discussion, resolutions were passed by the congress urging the revision of the 1850 law, and the introduction of regulations to make compulsory the provision of water in every house.

The 1880s were to see the development of a campaign to revise the 1850 law, although this was not to bear fruit for twenty years. The questions of privies and water supply were also to continue to concern hygienists, and in this case the discussion of the 1880s was to establish an important principle, defining the relationship between the individual dwelling, and the infrastructure of urban services; this prepared the way for an extension of the sewer and water systems in Paris and other cities in the 1890s.

This discussion was opened in 1879, when Jean Alphand, director of public works in Paris, put forward a programme of sewer and water improvement. Reflecting the concern of hygienists, this programme proposed the suppression of cesspits; all drainage would be connected direct to the sewer, with a filter to retain solid waste. Alphand stressed the basic requirement for water; 'without the abundant distribution of water, it would be impossible to ensure the cleansing of conveniences... if the complete sluicing of the sewers was not assured, in all seasons... the drainage of waste into the sewers would become dangerous precisely in that season when putrid miasmas are most dangerous.'[17]

As the Paris council considered Alphand's proposals, in the summer of 1880, a persistent easterly wind reinforced the need for action, blowing foul smelling vapours over certain parts of Paris. These vapours came not from the sewers, but from the factories for treating waste on the edge of the city. A ministerial commission set up to consider the problem accepted that the system of cesspits, whose contents provided the raw material for the sewage factories, should be suppressed. But the commission opposed the conclusion of some engineers that all waste should be discharged directly into the existing single sewer. Instead, it proposed that a separate system of sealed metal pipes should be provided to carry the waste from conveniences to treatment factories situated outside the built up area of Paris.[18]

The key issue of the relationship between the dwelling and the city's services was now firmly on the agenda. During the early 1880s, the relative merits of the separate sewer system, and the single-sewer *tout-à-l'égout* proposal received widespread discussion. The Société de Médecine Publique considered the question in 1882, as did the Association Française pour l'Avancement des Sciences at its 1883 Congress in Rouen. At an international level, the 1882 Hygiene Congress in Geneva devoted considerable time to the discussion of different types of sewer system.[19]

The debate over sewers was inevitably linked to the method of sewage treatment. Since 1869 the city of Paris had been experimenting with natural filtration at a sewage farm in Gennevilliers. However, this only treated the liquid waste which had previously been discharged into the river Seine; waste from cesspits was still taken as night-soil to the chemical treatment factories which created the odours of 1880. By that date, the sewage farm had proved successful, both hygienically and financially, and supporters of the *tout-à-l'égout* argued that it could satisfactorily purify water containing all sewage, whether from kitchens or conveniences.

Among the main contributors to the debate was the engineer Alfred Durand-Claye. After qualifying at the top of his year at the Ecole des Ponts et Chaussées in 1866, he had joined the sanitation service of the city of Paris. One of his first tasks was to prepare the project for the Gennevilliers sewage farm, and he quickly gained a high reputation in matters of urban hygiene. In 1875 he acted as consultant to the city of Budapest; in the 1880s several towns in France and abroad turned to him for advice, among them Le Havre, where Jules Siegfried had been elected mayor. Visits to foreign towns, notably to Danzig, Berlin and Breslau in 1881, convinced Durand-Claye of the need to suppress completely the use of cesspits. Similarly visits to London confirmed his view that it was hygienic to discharge all waste into the mains sewer, provided this was well washed by water.[20]

In October 1882, Durand-Claye was appointed secretary of the Commission Technique de l'Assainissement, set up by the Paris council to study sewage disposal. The Commission was made up largely of doctors and engineers; there were also three architects and two members of the Commission des Logements Insalubres. The conclusions of the Commission, covering the entire scale of the problem from the individual dwelling to the city as a whole, were published in July 1883. In relation to the dwelling, its conclusions were quite definite. Every dwelling should have its own convenience, supplied with at least ten litres of water per person each day, and fitted with a trap seal to the downpipe. The convenience could be outside the dwelling, but it should be on the same floor. The Commission stressed the need to suppress cesspits, and considered that filtering devices were an imperfect solution. But there was no unanimity on the kind of sewer and treatment which should be employed. After lengthy discussion during four sessions, the Commission finally approved the *tout-à-l'égout* system championed by Durand-Claye, by a majority of 21 to 7, with 2 abstentions.[21]

The example of foreign cities, and particularly London, had played

17 A section through an apartment block, showing the application of the *tout-à-l'égout* system; illustrated by Emile Cacheux in the supplement to his joint study with Emile Muller, published in the early 1900s

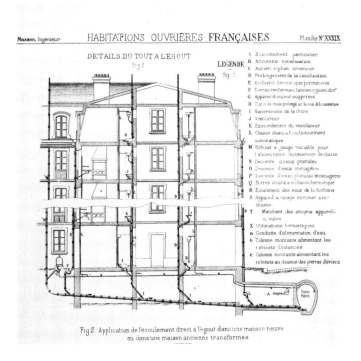

HABITATIONS OUVRIÈRES FRANÇAISES   Planche N°XXXIX

Masson Ingenieur

DETAILS DU TOUT A L'EGOUT

LEGENDE

A Branchement particulier
B Ancienne canalisation
C Ancien siphon déversoir
D Prolongement de la canalisation
E Occlusion hermétique permanente
F Cuveau renfermant l'ancien appareil dont'
G Appareil diviseur supprimé
H Tuyau de chute prolongé au dessus de la couverture
I Raccordement de la chûte
J Ventilateur
K Raccordement du ventilateur
L Chasse d'eau à fonctionnement automatique
M Robinet a jauge variable pour l'alimentation du réservoir de chasse
N Descente d'eaux pluviales
O Descente d'eaux ménagères
P Descente d'eaux pluviales et ménagères
Q Entrée d'eaux à occlusion hermétique
R Écoulement des eaux de la fontaine
S Appareil a usage commun avec chasse
T Maintient des anciens appareils à valve
X Obturations hermétiques
a Conduite d'alimentation d'eau
b Colonne montante alimentant les robinets d'immeuble
c Colonne montante alimentant les robinets au dessus des pierres déviers

Fig.8 Application de l'écoulement direct a l'égout dans une maison neuve ou dans une maison ancienne transformée

an important part in the Commission's deliberations. Visits were made to Brussels, Amsterdam and London; it was the study of workers' housing in London which indicated the desirability of having one convenience per dwelling. Similarly, foreign cities could provide statistics showing the improvement in the mortality rate after introducing sewage disposal systems with direct discharge of all waste. London had employed this method for over 60 years, and both Brussels and Berlin now used it. The Commission's report was approved by the Paris council; however, implementation depended on the extension to the water and sewer system which Alphand had proposed in 1879. The council had approved Alphand's proposals in 1880, but they had not received the necessary authorisation from parliament. It was only in 1893 that the city was able to float a loan in order to extend the water and sewage disposal systems; the following year, proprietors were obliged by law to connect their properties directly to the mains sewer. Proprietors showed no hurry to meet this obligation, so that the problems of sewage disposal were not resolved overnight. Nonetheless, the Commission Technique had defined the means by which the problem was to be tackled (fig. 17).

The problem of slums

The 1882 Commission had addressed directly the gap which existed between urban improvement and the individual dwelling. It proposed the technical means of closing that gap, but left unresolved the question of inadequate control over new and existing buildings, which allowed the gap to persist. In Paris, the Prefect of the Seine had adopted a set of recommendations relating to new construction, prepared by the Commission des Logements Insalubres in 1880; but in the absence of any inspection procedure, the recommendations were of little effect.[22] The inadequacy of existing control procedures led to demands for stricter controls over new and existing dwellings in the 1880s. These demands were reinforced by advances in the study of disease which enabled the reformers to define more accurately the problems which they were trying to resolve.

Discussion of urban hygiene in the middle of the century had been centred on the epidemic diseases, notably cholera. When cholera broke out for the second time, in 1848–9, the prevailing theories of disease were dominated by the anti-contagionist view that disease was derived from local causes, particularly the various manifestations of dirt. The case for public works in the form of sewers and water supply was reinforced by this view, which held that disease would be kept in check by the general cleansing of the environment.[23] Although the 1850 housing law acknowledged that the conditions within dwellings affected the health of occupants, the emphasis was more on the visible causes of insalubrity, rather than the less tangible causes, such as lack of sunlight or overcrowding. In this, the law paralleled the general cleansing programme which was realised through public works.

By the 1880s it was becoming clear that the dominance of this programme in sanitary improvement needed to be reviewed. While public works had helped to reduce general mortality levels in Paris in the 1850s and 1860s, those levels had risen again in the late 1870s. Mortality rates in working-class areas were consistently higher than in wealthier areas, and certain diseases, such as smallpox, were effectively becoming localised in particular areas of the city. The rise of the germ theory of the disease contributed to this review of sanitary improvement policies; it re-emphasised the importance of the individual dwelling, which did not automatically benefit from the general improvement derived from public works. At the end of the 1880s this more informed consideration of sanitary improvement was reflected in the creation of a municipal disinfection service in Paris, while proposals were also being considered for the treatment of patients with infectious diseases outside the city altogether.[24]

The role of the dwelling was further emphasised by the increasing importance of respiratory diseases in mortality statistics, as epidemic diseases where checked. Attention focussed particularly on tuberculosis, whose virus was isolated in 1882. If the issue of housing hygiene in the 1840s had been related above all to the threat of cholera, from the 1880s – and particularly in the early 1900s – it was to be seen in relation to tuberculosis. The study of this disease showed that it was encouraged not so much by superficial insalubrity, as by more funda-mental aspects of the housing problem, notably overcrowding, and lack of direct sunlight.[25] These issues thus came under closer study in the 1880s.

At the 1887 International Hygiene Congress, a doctor from Lyons, Dr E. Clement, presented a set of guidelines for the orientation of streets, for building heights and room arrangements; these were based on Clement's conclusion that 'the height of buildings and the width of streets must be calculated in order to permit the access of *direct rays of light* to the base of the ground floor'.[26] The revision of the Paris building regulations in 1884 reflected this growing interest in light, extending control over the size of courts and light wells. But such minor changes to the regulations were not sufficient to open up the form of urban development, and they did not ensure adequate penetration of light and air.[27] Moreover, the control of new building did nothing to improve the situation in old housing. This led Emile Trélat to the extreme proposal which he put forward at the 1887 hygiene congress, that the upper floors of certain tall buildings should be expropriated and demolished.[28]

While this idea was hardly likely to be taken seriously, it did emphasise the fact that inadequacies of some existing housing could only be eradicated by demolition. This had been acknowledged by the 1850 law, but the law had left unresolved the procedure for expropriation, and rehousing of tenants. As a result, no policy of slum clearance could be pursued. The Commission des Logements Insalubres in Paris started to move towards such a policy in 1882, when it proposed that the city should finance temporary accommodation for people evicted from condemned property. This would have realised the initial intention of the proposers of the 1850 law; but it got no greater welcome than their text, being rejected by the Prefect of the Seine.[29]

While the responsibility for existing housing conditions was not yet to be extended to include that of rehousing, the system of control in Paris was improved in the 1880s and 1890s. The rise in the population living in *garnis* in the late 1870s led the police to introduce new regulations for this form of housing in 1878 and 1883. The latter regulations introduced a corps of permanent inspectors, but their duties remained restricted to the *garnis*, and appear to have had little effect.[30] Reorganisation of the city's hygiene services in the 1890s was to have a greater impact, creating two new bodies responsible for housing. In 1892 the Commission d'Assainissement et de Salubrité de l'Habitation was set up under Dr A. J. Martin. In the following year the control and investigation of housing conditions was strengthened by the formation of the Bureau de l'Assainissement de l'Habitation. This was itself divided into two sections, an administrative section, carrying out the duties of the Commissions des Logements Insalubres under the 1850 law, and a technical section charged with preparing a survey of housing throughout the city.[31]

The technical section extended the study of housing conditions into much greater detail than had previously been possible, by establishing a comprehensive record of unhealthy houses in the city, the *Casier Sanitaire*. Now that the general objective of cleansing the environment had given way to a more specific acknowledgement of the relationships between disease and housing, such a record was a vital tool in defining improvement policies: 'before declaring war on unhealthy dwellings, it is important to know with certainty each of the causes of unhealthiness, to know on which illnesses these causes have direct repercussions, in order to make the remedy suitable to the evil it must combat'.[32]

The *Casier Sanitaire* consisted of files recording details of each dwelling in Paris in which a death occurred due to transmissible disease. The record was continuously updated to include improvements or alterations to the house, and its sanitary arrangements, and to add any further deaths. The initial survey took until 1900 to produce, by which time a wealth of detailed information was available. 'One can say that each house is followed day by day, and that it possesses its own daily sanitary journal'[33] (fig. 18).

By the time this initial survey was complete, the long campaign to revise the 1850 housing law had almost achieved its object. Since the start of the campaign in the late 1870s, at least eight specific proposals had been put forward by a variety of hygiene organisations, and four bills had been presented to parliament, in 1881, 1886, 1887 and 1891. It was this final bill which formed the basis of the law which eventually emerged in 1902.[34]

Although the Paris Commission des Logements Insalubres had raised the issue of the relationship between the control of housing conditions and the construction of housing, the proposals for revision focussed on the established aspect of the law, that of control. The 1891 bill brought together the two aspects of control: existing buildings and new construction. A permanent inspection service of paid staff would be introduced for existing buildings, while new buildings would be subject to inspection before occupation was authorised. A. L. Shapiro has noted that the hygienists' aim was to transfer the executive power in implementing control from the political bodies – the municipal council and administrative courts which held the power under the 1850 law – to professional bodies backed up by the authority and funds to act.

This aim was not to be satisfied in the 1902 law. The law did extend the control over new and existing building, but the control remained in the political hands of the mayor and council. The formation of Commissions Sanitaires, which were to supersede the Commissions des Logements Insalubres within the context of general hygiene issues, was made compulsory; but the Commissions did not have executive power, and the law allowed for no paid inspectors, either for existing buildings or new construction.

While the enforcement of control still remained weaker than the hygienists desired, it had been strengthened in comparison to 1850. In relation to new building, the mayor and council of every commune had the duty to establish 'the regulations destined to ensure the salubrity of houses...notably the regulations relative to the supply of drinking water and the evacuation of waste matter'.[35] Moreover, the standards which these prescriptions enforced had evolved since 1850. The Conseil Supérieur d'Hygiène Publique drew up a model set of regulations for new building, which brought together the controls on the building envelope imposed by earlier regulations and the control of sanitary provision. Thus the height of houses in relation to the street, and the size of courts and light-wells were specified; minimum height and area for habitable rooms were stated, together with a minimum area of window for ventilation and light. In relation to sanitation, an obligation was imposed to provide water to every dwelling, where a public supply existed. Every dwelling of two rooms or more must also have its own convenience.[36]

In relation to existing housing, the new law strengthened control by making the procedure for dealing with unhealthy housing cases less cumbersome, and allowing councils the right to execute improvement works at the proprietor's expense if the proprietor refused to do so. The law also retained the right of councils to expropriate buildings which posed a threat to public health. However, it did not revise the procedure for expropriation, which remained governed by legislation designed for the implementation of large public works programmes such as railways and street construction; the expense and complexity of this procedure was still inappropriate to the task of identifying and clearing slums.[37]

It was the high mortality from tuberculosis revealed in the early 1900s which provided the impetus for the revision of expropriation legislation, and the clearance of slums. The information gathered by 1900 in the *Casier Sanitaire* in Paris demonstrated clearly that tuberculosis persisted in certain locations despite all attempts at improvement. A special study of dwellings affected by tuberculosis was carried out by the *Casier Sanitaire* in 1904, and in the following year the Prefect of the Seine formed a committee to study the relationship between dwellings and tuberculosis. These detailed local studies were paralleled on a wider scale. In 1904, Paris was host to the first International Congress of House Cleansing and Hygiene; the following year the International Tuberculosis Congress was held in the city. Discussion of tuberculosis emphasised the importance of sunlight in preventing the disease, and in new blocks of flats built at this time, the influence of this discussion is clear. But for old buildings, with their tiny light-wells and overshadowed courts, demolition seemed the only solution.

By the end of the first decade of the new century, six tubercular zones had been identified in Paris. A campaign led by Councillor Ambroise Rendu had secured the allocation of 15 million francs to clear the zones in the public works programme approved in 1909;[38] a parallel campaign had led to 15 million francs also being allocated to loans to housing societies, to encourage construction to replace the demolished slums. Alongside these campaigns, efforts were being made to provide the necessary machinery to make clearance possible, by revising expropriation legislation. The central problem under existing law was that of compensation. This was based on the income derived by the owner from his property, and took no account of the condition of the property. This was reasonable enough when the cause of expropriation was the construction of a railway or street, when the properties to be demolished were selected by the dictates of the public project. But it was anomalous

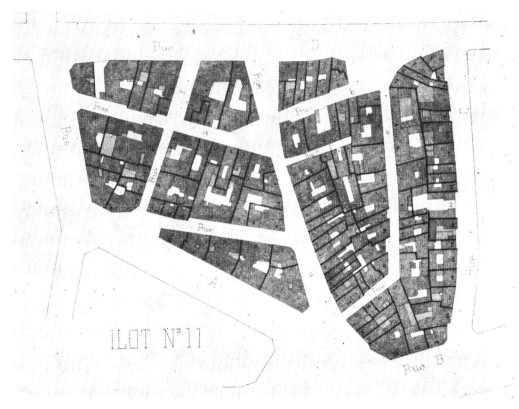

ILOT N° 11

18 An area of housing in central Paris, identified by the Casier Sanitaire in the early 1900s as a zone with a particularly high death rate due to tuberculosis

when the reason for expropriation was the inadequacy of the property itself. The return from a building did not reflect the condition of the building, as the return could be increased by saving money on maintenance, or overcrowding the flats. Compensation for an unhealthy building could thus equal that paid for houses in good condition; unscrupulous landlords could actually increase the compensation by introducing more tenants before the return was assessed, thus increasing overcrowding. The principle that compensation for slums should reflect the state of the building, long established in England, was contained in a proposal for legislation presented by Jules Siegfried in 1904.

Legislation based on Siegfried's proposal finally came into effect in 1915. This law stated that compensation would be based on the market value of the building, allowing for the expense required to render the building healthy. In extreme cases, compensation could be set at the land value alone. The new law also removed another problem in clearing slum areas. Interpretation of the earlier legislation required that every house to be expropriated must be proved unhealthy. Houses in a slum area which themselves had no intrinsic causes of unhealthiness could therefore not be expropriated. The new law specifically permitted the expropriation of slum areas as a whole, unprejudiced by the existence of a few individually healthy houses. This law related to expropriation for reasons of public health only; but in the face of post-war reconstruction, the general expropriation law was revised in 1918. This further eased the expropriation of large areas by introducing the concept of 'zone expropriation', allowing expropriation of land required for satisfactory realisation of a project, even if it was not contained within the perimeter of the proposed plans. By 1918, then, municipalities had considerably improved terms of compensation and powers of acquisition in order to carry out the clearance of large slum areas.

Slum clearance was the final element in the programme of sanitary reform which had evolved since the middle of the nineteenth century. The legislation passed since 1850 gradually incorporated the principles voiced by sanitary reformers at congresses and committees. These principles had constantly to battle against the principle of property: for of necessity, sanitary reform involved the control of private property, and the imposition of regulations on proprietors. The law of 1894 making compulsory the connection of all properties in Paris to the sewer was actively opposed by the Chambre Syndicale des Propriétaires Immobilières de la Ville de Paris,[39] and as late as 1925 one third of the houses in the city still failed to comply with the law. But despite the time which it inevitably took for the reformers' ideals to be even partially implemented, the public standards upheld by law did develop through the reformers' efforts. By the early twentieth century, the principles of control of old and new building had been established, together with the basic standards which control should enforce.

18

◇◇◇

Housing and urban growth

The discussion of housing and hygiene tended to focus on the urban areas, where the failure to achieve basic standards was most apparent. But in the earliest consideration of housing in the late 1840s and early 1850s, reformers had expressed their opposition to dense urban housing in favour of the individual house. While the achievements of sanitary reform helped to make the urban block of flats more acceptable to the reformers, the experience of efforts to introduce sanitary improvement served to emphasise the apparently simpler resolution of hygiene problems in the case of the individual house.

This ideal of the individual house inevitably raised the wider question of the layout of towns. In response to the demand for housing in urban centres, builders developed their land to its maximum potential. In Paris, the maximum heights specified by the building regulations became a norm for construction, while courts and light-wells were kept to a minimum. The potential of any site was reflected in its value as land, and this in turn determined the development of the site. The individual houses at Mulhouse were built on land costing 1 fr./m²; such low-density development could never have been economic on the site of its contemporary in Paris, the Cité Napoléon, which cost about 75 fr./m².

The response of housing reformers to this problem was not so much to attack the high cost of urban land, as to look to areas where cheap land still existed, on the outskirts of towns. The development of new suburban areas would, it was argued, make practical the ideal of the individual house; it would also contribute to the improvement of unhealthy urban housing. Maurice Daly, son of César Daly, summed up this overall concept of planned urban development in an article in the *Revue Générale de l'Architecture* in 1883:

Offer workers larger dwellings outside Paris, where land is cheaper and therefore rents will be lower, and excessive agglomeration, the first cause of unhealthiness in Paris, will be avoided; and so that this system is practical, provide them with rapid, cheap means of communication to their place of work; they will then leave unhealthy dwellings of their own accord. Given this solution, one would not delay in helping the demolition of the unhealthy and miserable houses still standing in Paris, and their replacement with new buildings, constructed in more hygienic conditions.[1]

Although some proposals, such as Fourier's *phalanstère*, had already questioned existing forms of urban development, it was only in the 1870s and 1880s that the discussion of development came to parallel that of housing reform, as the individual house was extended into the suburban ideal outlined by Daly. Initially the reformers saw the key to realising this ideal as the provision of public transport systems to make suburban land more accessible. It was not until the end of the century, when this process could be seen to result in a simple extension of dense urban forms, or in the creation of sprawling areas of cottages which produced their own problems of hygiene, that the reformers began to tackle the question of controlling development through municipal land policies and planning.

Forms of development

The development which exemplified the reformers' ideal of the individual house, at Mulhouse, also provided a model for low-density development. The *cité ouvrière* was built on the outer edge of Mulhouse, between the town and the industrial area, and it was to a considerable degree self-sufficient in its generous provision of public services. By building on the edge of the town, where land was both cheaper and more readily available than within the existing town, an open, low-density environment could be achieved. For such a solution to be generally adopted, its implication on the planning of towns must be acknowledged. This first development in the relatively small town of Mulhouse could succeed without the support of public transport. In larger towns, transport would be crucial, for new development must always be able to expand far enough from the town and its industry to find cheap plentiful land.

The development of Le Vésinet, outside Paris, illustrated the possibilities offered by transport facilities. The hunting forest of Le Vésinet had an important feature in that the Paris–St Germain railway ran through it. This made possible the development of a new community, only thirty minutes by rail from the business district of Paris. Developed from 1858, Le Vésinet demonstrated that new means of transport would allow people to live in a town of gardens and parks, while working in Paris.[2] At present such delights were the prerogative of the rich families who could afford to build themselves a house in so exclusive a development. But Le Vésinet represented an ideal which the housing reformers were to promote on a more modest scale for the working population.

If Mulhouse and Le Vésinet showed the form that suburban development might take, the growth of Paris during the Second Empire emphasised that urban expansion did not conform to such ideals without some kind of encouragement or control. As the city expanded into the suburban area which was annexed in 1859, two types of development characterised its growth. First, before the construction of permanent buildings, shacks and huts were built, in some areas from salvaged materials. In providing low-density housing on the edge of the

19 'La Fosse aux Lions', an area of shacks in the 13th arrondissement, shown in 1863

city, these huts might seem to realise the ideal aimed at by the reformers. But they were temporary buildings, and both their form of construction and their sanitary arrangements left much to be desired. Opinion was divided as to whether they created 'new harbours of insalubrity', or whether 'these dwellings, as a result of being more spread out, and having better ventilation, are in a condition which largely mitigates the problems inherent in their inadequate construction'.[3] In either case, the huts were clearly not the ideal sought, nor were they the result of a planned extension of the city (fig. 19).

Of longer-term consequence were the permanent buildings which replaced these huts. As the city grew out into the annexed area, underdeveloped sites became increasingly attractive for the construction

20 Passage Auvry, in the 19th arrondissement; the more permanent constructions and paved streets which replaced areas such as the 'Fosse aux Lions' themselves gave way to new housing forms eventually – the Passage Auvry was demolished and replaced by a development of cheap flats after the First World War.

of new houses. As no local planning policy had been established, the new building continued the density of construction of the city centre, filling the building envelope defined by the regulations. Moreover, large plots were developed, with private roads and cul-de-sacs linking together blocks of building. It was some of these new buildings which came under the scrutiny of the Commission des Logements Insalubres within only a few years of completion[4] (fig. 20).

The growth of Paris thus fell between two stools, neither providing enough healthy housing for workers within the city centre, nor achieving the lower densities which might have been possible if the development of the annexed land had been planned more closely in conjunction with the public transport system. Despite the reorganisation of the omnibus companies into the Compagnie Générale des Omnibus in 1854, and the extension of routes into the annexed area after 1860, services remained inadequate in many areas of the city, both centrally and in the outskirts.

However, in the 1870s the city's transport system was improved by the extension of the tram network. The trams proved not only more efficient than the horse-drawn omnibuses, but they also started to open up the suburbs. The initial tram network provided a circular line around the city, run by the Compagnie Générale des Omnibus, and ten routes radiating into the suburbs, run by two new companies; this network was to be extended in the later 1870s, both in the city and in the suburban areas. Parallel to this actual improvement in transport, the possibility of constructing a metropolitan railway was discussed in the city and departmental councils in the early 1870s.[5]

Given the potential which these developments in Paris indicated, the housing reformers started to examine seriously the idea of suburban development. Speaking at the International Hygiene Congress in Paris in 1878, Dr du Mesnil was confident that the problem of the provision of new housing was almost solved, due to the increase in public transport. M. Fischer, an industrialist from Soissons, confirmed du Mesnil's view, commenting that 'means of communication which have become so simple, in the last few years, by the means of railways and tramways, radiating in all directions around large manufacturing towns, make it possible for a good number of workers to house themselves cheaply, over considerable distances.'[6] A rather less positive view was put by Alexandre Boulanger. He advised against peripheral housing developments in Paris, although in principle he favoured the individual house. He considered the time taken by travelling, and the separation of the worker from his family, negated the advantage of such development.[7]

While Boulanger's remarks gave some perspective to the more optimistic views, the advocates of suburban development provided a growing lobby. Maurice Daly's comments in the *Revue Générale de l'Architecture* in 1883 have already been quoted. In 1886, in his paper delivered at the urban hygiene exhibition in Paris, Emile Cheysson drew attention to the fresh air and cheap land in the suburb. He referred to the London suburbs, where efficient transport had encouraged a much greater extension than Paris. Cheysson argued that the proposed Métro system, still under discussion in Paris, would soon allow 'the construction of numerous individual dwellings in the suburb, linked to the centre by cheap transport'.[8]

The control of development

The reformers' view of the dangers of too high a density of building, and the contrasting advantages of low-density suburban development was well established by the end of the century. But just as little had been done to discourage the former, so there was little encouragement to the latter. In contrast to the detailed discussion of land reform in Germany, which led to some control of urban development, French reformers argued that the extension of cities as their transport systems grew would automatically bring about the low-density development they championed.

The lesser emphasis placed on land reform in France derived in part from the fact that France, with an urban population growing much more slowly than that in Germany after 1870, did not experience the acute land speculation which accompanied rapid urban growth in

Germany.[9] Nonetheless, from the 1880s there was increasing discussion in France of the role which municipal authorities could take in relation to the supply and control of land. While this did not amount to a movement of land reform comparable to that in Germany, it does indicate a gradual understanding of the role of land, both in relation to housing and to the growth of the city.

In the early 1880s, various proposals to promote the construction of cheap housing were considered by the Paris council. Several of these were based on making new areas of land available for construction, including the land currently occupied by the city's fortifications. The dismantling of the fortifications was to offer a unique opportunity for the city to plan and control the development of a large area of land, encircling the whole city. The proposals made in the 1880s were, however, only the first of many before the use of the land was finally settled.[10] The only practical result of the discussion in the council emphasised the difficulty of controlling the activity of private builders. It was agreed that the city should make land available to builders, for the construction of cheap housing, and in 1885 sites were offered on leases of 75 years. However, builders were discouraged by the conditions imposed by the city, and the sites were not taken up.[11]

Although this experiment was not a success, the French became increasingly aware of the achievements of German towns in the field of land reform, through discussion at international congresses in the 1890s. From 1897, the International Congress of Cheap Housing regularly considered the question of municipal action in relation to land, both to encourage the construction of cheap housing, and to control the growth of towns. In the 1900s, French reformers began to urge cities to implement a municipal land policy of their own, based on foreign examples.

The foundation for any such policy was the constitution of a reserve of land, held by the municipality to prevent speculation. After the 1902 housing congress in Düsseldorf, two French delegates, the housing reformer Emile Cacheux and the leader of the campaign to introduce a slum clearance policy in Paris, councillor Ambroise Rendu, drew conclusions which they repeated on their return from the London congress in 1907: 'French towns should follow the example given abroad, that is methodically to enlarge their reserves of land for construction.'[12] This view was enthusiastically taken up by the architect, A. A. Rey, winner of the competition held in 1905 by the Fondation Rothschild for the design of a block of flats in Paris. At the 1907 International Hygiene Congress, held in Berlin, he presented an important resolution which was adopted by the Congress:

The Congress is of the opinion that the heart of the question of cheap housing rests in the question of land. It is of the highest importance, in order to combat the effects of speculation on urban land, that the municipalities, whose first interest is to safeguard public health, have a significant holding of cheap land.[13]

However, the creation of municipal land reserves required an active role which French towns were ill-prepared to play. French reformers were not unaware of this problem. In a paper presented at a planning exhibition held in Nancy in 1913, Georges Hottenger contrasted German and French municipalities. He attributed the success of German municipalities to the relative autonomy of cities, a characteristic shared with England. In contrast, the conception of the centralised State in France left towns dominated by the State and less able to act autonomously in response to local needs. In a study on the development of Nice, also published in 1913, Robert de Souza supported the principle of municipal land reserves; but he contrasted the German towns, which had the support of the Lex Adickes, with French towns, straitjacketed by local government legislation.[14]

French towns thus failed to prevent speculation by acquiring land in advance of carrying out the works which would raise its value. They failed either to establish a reserve of land freed from the pressures of the private market, or to take advantage of the increase in values on behalf of the community. In the absence of any attempt to pre-empt individual speculation, there were demands to tax the increase in value gained by the proprietors. Legislation passed in 1807 had envisaged this, but the law was unsatisfactory and hardly used. The Paris council tried unsuccessfully to implement the law in the early 1900s and in 1912 the socialist group in the Chambre des Députés tabled a resolution demanding the application of the law. But it was in the context of revised expropriation powers that new legislation was finally introduced.

Since the French towns had very small reserves of land in relation to their German counterparts, strong expropriation legislation was particularly important. Only through expropriation could municipalities initiate a realistic policy of acquisition. Parallel to efforts to improve the legislation governing the expropriation of unhealthy dwellings, there was thus a need to revise the general law of 1841, which governed expropriation for public projects. According to Georges Risler, speaking at the 1913 exhibition in Nancy, the law 'hardly functions except for the benefit of proprietors and to the detriment of towns, and makes all large operations almost impossible for them'.[15] Reporting on the 1913 International Housing Congress in the Hague, Georges Hottenger noted general support for expropriation powers strong enough to allow towns to buy land for their development plans without bankrupting themselves, and also to buy land not directly required, but which would increase in value as a result of the municipality's work. In this respect, Hottenger observed 'the deplorable inadequacy of present legislation' in France, compared to some foreign countries.[16]

In fact the measures described by Hottenger did form the basis of the new expropriation legislation passed in 1918, which introduced the principle of zone expropriation. The law also allowed expropriation of property which, due to its proximity to the municipal development, would increase in value by more than 15%. In theory this made it possible for municipalities to pre-empt private speculation. In practice, the process of expropriation remained extremely cumbersome, and required further revision during the inter-war period. However, the

1918 law demonstrates a response, in the face of the task of post-war reconstruction, to some of the principles of land policy which the French reformers had taken up in the 1900s.

An essential counterpart to the acquisition of land reserves by the municipality was the control of their development and this cause was also taken up by the reformers. In their comments after the 1907 housing congress, Cacheux and Rendu stated that, having established a stock of building land, municipalities should 'encourage the cons-truction of new quarters in which they would prevent the creation of slums, by obliging builders to follow special building regulations for each region'.[17] A. A. Rey, in his paper to the International Hygiene Congress in the same year, urged that speculation in the land in the future be prevented by leasing the land, rather than selling it, to builders.

Another means of controlling development, also taken up by the French reformers in the early 1900s, was the Garden City, proposed by the English reformer Ebenezer Howard. In this case, ownership of land and the construction of buildings were entrusted to two separate co-operatives. These could control the initial form of the development on behalf of the community, and could also prevent its subsequent deterioration. Maurice Dufourmantelle, a senior member of the Société Française des HBM, noted this long-term advantage of Howard's proposal; by separating ownership of land and buildings 'it shelters the development from those alterations which are inevitable when land and house are assigned to individual ownership. By the same token, it bars the way to the possibility of speculation.'[18]

However, Dufourmantelle noted the overriding obstacle in the way of any system of land control which separated ownership of land and house either by simple leasehold, or by co-operative ownership. The French mentality was 'little prepared to conceive of the possession of a house separate from ownership of the land, and...perhaps even the laws lend themselves badly to the application of this idea'.[19] The alternative of selling land with special building regulations to control its development had been successfully used at Le Vésinet. But at Mulhouse, conditions imposed in the contract of sale of the houses, had been insufficient to prevent some deterioration due to speculative alteration and sale of properties. As a middle way which the French might adopt, Dufourmantelle advocated the system used in Germany, whereby the original land owner reserved the right to buy back both house and land when its occupant wished to sell. This system was used in the development built by a co-operative housing society at Draveil, south of Paris, from 1909. The society sold its land for individual members to build on, laying down in some detail the principles of design to which members must conform. The right of re-acquisition was based on fixing the value of the land permanently at its original cost of 2 fr./m²; individual speculation on the land was thereby made impossible. However, members were allowed to benefit from any improvements or alterations which they made to their home, as these were taken into account in assessing the value of the house.[20]

Draveil was one of the models considered by J. Dépinay, secretary of the public housing office formed in the Seine department, during the First World War. Following the model of German municipalities, the office acquired sizeable land reserves. It was planned to sell some of this land to private builders and societies who would develop the land in conformity with plans prepared by the office. In a report in 1919 Dépinay set out to define 'the legal guarantees to be obtained from eventual purchasers...to maintain the developments in their initial form, and to paralyse any speculation'. He concluded on the need for an arrangement giving the office first option on any properties subsequently offered for sale.[21] But while legal contortions could protect individual developments in this way, they were very much a second best to the breadth of control possible through the municipal land policies which the French reformers so admired in some German cities.

The planning of development

Without any history of municipal land ownership, or policy of acquisition to establish reserves, and with no form of zoning regulations to apply positive control to urban development, French towns could have no coherent land policy to direct their growth. One of the individuals most active in drawing attention to this fact was Henri Sellier, a socialist councillor on the Conseil Général de la Seine; as director of the public housing office of the Seine department, Sellier was to define a planning policy in the suburban housing developments built by the office after the First World War. In a report to the Conseil Général in 1914, in which he recommended the creation of the public housing office, Sellier argued that the housing and hygiene problems facing Paris were 'due to the absence of a land policy in the Paris urban area'. He referred to the numerous conferences which 'have underlined the necessity of applying in our urban areas the principle of the *Bodenpolitik* of German towns'.[22]

Sellier acknowledged that the full realisation of a land policy required changes in legislation. Still, he stressed that municipalities could achieve some progress by the careful use of land which they did own. But even this modest principle was by no means generally accepted. In Paris, the municipality had recently sold off part of the major urban open space at the Champ de Mars, and this land was being built up by private developers. This decision was opposed by some environmental groups, which had put forward alternative proposals.[23] The use of publicly owned land was now on the agenda, but it was the larger question of the development of the fortifications which turned it into an issue of public discussion and even political campaign.

The Paris fortifications, owned by the State, occupied a strip of about 150 m width, over 400 hectares in area. Outside the fortifications was a second strip, of about 250 m width; this land was privately owned, but in order to provide a clear firing zone around the fortifications, it was subject to restrictions which forbade any construction.[24] In fact the authorities had tolerated the building of houses, but because of their ambiguous status, these were little more than temporary shacks, with inadequate sanitation. With the demolition of the fortifications, this area, the *zone*, would be freed of its restriction. It was generally agreed that the city should expropriate the *zone*, although there was debate as to whether the compensation should be assessed while the restrictions were in force, or on the market value of the land once they were removed.

Georges Cahen noted that it was in the early 1900s that the development of the fortifications ceased to be mainly the concern of financial and military circles, and became a matter of wider interest. 'Will the project have the effect of transforming a long reservoir of air into a thick wall of stone?'[25] By 1908, the fortifications were an important issue during the council elections. The project which the council prepared proposed separate development of the fortifications and the *zone*. The fortifications would be demolished, roads and services installed, and the land be sold for construction. The *zone* was to be expropriated, and reserved exclusively for parks and sportsgrounds.

The council proposals accepted the vested interest of property in the city; Councillor Dausset presented them as designed to avoid the depreciation of real estate which would result from the construction of a large quantity of new housing. The interests of hygienists, who urged that the fortification and *zone* be used to provide much-needed parks and open space for the city, were thus reinforced by the politically more powerful interests of real estate. The Ligue des Espaces Libres, one of several organisations active in discussion of the fate of the fortifications, indicates the overlap of those interests, as the secretary of the Ligue was also secretary general of the organisation of proprietors in Paris, the Chambre des Propriétaires. The Ligue's manifesto clearly expressed the determination to protect property by preserving undeveloped land. 'The conversion of the *zone* into open space must be considered as a true defence against property speculation and against particularly dangerous competition[26] (fig. 21).

The proposals of the Ligue des Espaces Libres were criticised by Eugène Hénard, who wondered why the Ligue did not follow its own logic by proposing legislation to prohibit all new building within 10 km of Paris.[27] Hénard, an architect working for the City of Paris, had himself made a proposal for the development of the fortifications in 1903. This was one of a series of studies on the transformation of Paris, which Hénard published in the early 1900s. These studies made an important contribution to the debate over urban development, and established Hénard as a leading figure in the debate. From 1908 he gained a powerful base of support, when the Musée Social took up his ideas in relation to the development of the fortifications, and to the more general need for urban growth to be coherently directed.[28]

The Musée Social provided a context in which the issues of planning which the fortifications raised were seen against the background of housing reform; the land released by the fortifications would provide not just open space, but also sites for cheap housing. The question of

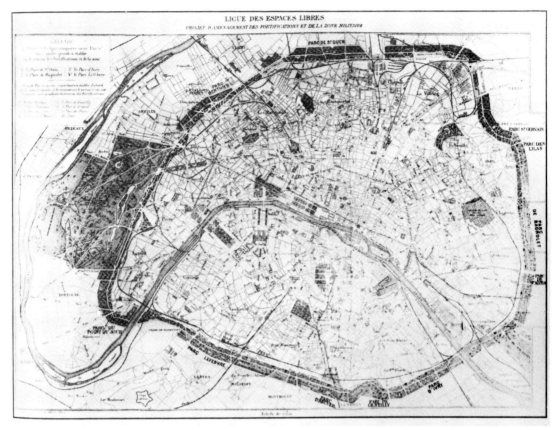

21 Development of the Paris
fortifications: the proposals
of the Ligue des Espaces
Libres

the fortifications was considered by a new section formed within the
Musée Social in 1908, the Section d'Hygiène Urbaine et Rurale. This
section was to study matters affecting the family life of workers, ranging
from housing to food. But its membership emphasised the widest scale
of this study, as it brought together 'the most influential and most
knowledgeable men in France on urbanistic questions'.[29] These included
Hénard, Georges Benoît-Lévy, student of the Garden City, Louis Bonnier
a senior architect in the city of Paris, and men who united housing
reform with the general issues of planning: Jules Siegfried, Georges
Risler, Ambroise Rendu and A.A. Rey. The new section developed
Hénard's fortification proposal, and in 1909 it was presented to the city
council, together with a supporting document prepared by Hénard and
Siegfried.

The Musée Social proposal differed from those of Dausset and the
Ligue in allowing more land for housing, and by being less rigid in its
treatment of the fortification and the *zone*. Instead of setting up a barrier
of open land between the dense city and its suburbs, the plan aimed to
integrate the two areas. Sports areas were to be provided within the
fortification land, while nine major parks would straddle both fortifications and *zone*; a regular distribution of open space was thus ensured

22 Development of the Paris
fortifications: the proposals
of Eugène Hénard

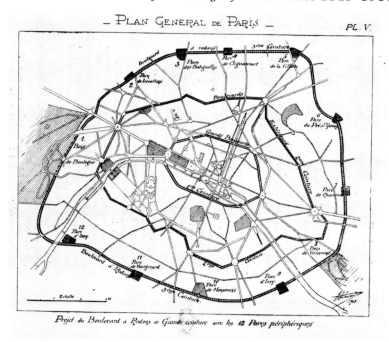

_ Plan Général de Paris _   *PL. V.*

Projet du Boulevard à Redans de Grande ceinture avec les 12 Parcs périphériques

in both strips of land. Having set up this structure of parks and
sportsgrounds, the Musée Social plan proposed a major formal boulevard
on the fortification land. The plan reduced the difficult problem of what
level of compensation to set for the expropriation of the *zone* by only
requiring the acquisition of part of the land, for the nine parks and for
new streets. The majority of the *zone* was to remain in private hands,
and its development be legally permitted (fig. 22).

If development by private enterprise were to provide the sort of
housing the reformers desired, then strict control was necessary.
Considering the development of the fortification land, Emile Cacheux
urged in 1908 that the city sell the land after clearing the fortification
structures, and impose conditions on the sale; these would be worded
to ensure the construction 'in the west part of the city of beautiful
mansions surrounded by magnificent gardens, and in the east, groups
of cottages with gardens as one finds so often in Germany and
England'.[30] The reformers were also naturally anxious to use the land
to further the work of the cheap housing societies. The national
congress of the societies in 1911 called on the State to contribute
'directly, by the supply of land, particularly at the time of the declassifi-
cation of the Paris fortifications, to the development of cheap housing
societies'.[31]

The plan finally adopted by the council (fig. 23), and formalised by
law in 1919, accepted the principle of the Dausset plan; building was
to be restricted to the fortification land, although the interest of the
housing reformers was acknowledged by the reservation of one quarter
of this land for cheap housing. But what was the planning framework

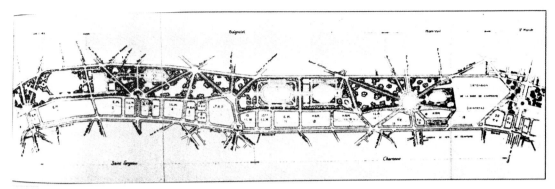

23 Official plan for the development of part of the Paris fortifications, in the 20th arrondissement, 1924; this plan shows the reservation of the inner strip of land for housing, much of it HBM or ILM (Immeuble à Loyer Modéré) in this area, with a proposal for parkland beyond.

within which this plan was to be implemented? Alongside the discussion of the specific problem of the Paris fortifications, the need for such a framework was also being forcefully argued by the reformers.

In the early 1900s, the equation of city planning with large-scale public street works, which the Third Republic had inherited from Haussmann, began to give way to a more complete study of the structure and growth of cities. Two individuals each made a notable contribution to this process: the architect Tony Garnier, in his proposals for 'an industrial city', and Eugène Hénard, in his studies on the transformation of Paris. Garnier's project was exhibited in 1901 and 1904, but it only appeared in published form in 1917; Hénard's studies made a more immediate contribution to the debate in the early 1900s, appearing in eight parts between 1903 and 1909.[32]

The Section d'Hygiène Urbaine et Rurale in the Musée Social formed a natural forum for the discussion of these general planning ideas. At the very first meeting of the Section, in 1908, Jules Siegfried had stressed the need for towns to draw up extension plans; later that year Siegfried was signatory to a bill relating to the fortifications which included a proposal that a planning committee be established for the Paris region to draw up an extension plan for the city and its suburb. This proposal did not proceed, but in 1909 another bill put forward the principle that all towns with a population of over 10,000 people should draw up extension plans. Charles Beauquier presented this bill which expressed the interest of several groups in the concept of planning – the Section d'Hygiène Urbaine et Rurale, the Association des Cités-Jardins led by Benoît-Lévy, and the group of countryside preservationists led by Beauquier himself.[33]

The Section d'Hygiène Urbaine et Rurale continued to publicise the foreign planning initiatives which impressed the reformers, particularly the land policies of German municipalities and the Garden City in England; it was among members of the Section that the first French organisation devoted exclusively to the study of planning, the Société Française des Architectes-Urbanistes was formed in 1913. The achievement of foreign countries in the field of planning was also made known through the pioneering Town Planning Conference held in London in

1910, and the congress and exhibition held in Ghent in 1913. Robert de Souza had compared the French exhibits in London unfavourably with the German display, but by 1913 the French were able to mount their own exhibition of La Cité Moderne in Nancy. In the following year Lyons held an international planning exhibition.

With this growth in publicity devoted to the virtues of planning, some municipalities were stirred to take action. In 1911, the Prefect of the Seine set up the Comité d'Extension de Paris, whose leading figures were the architect Louis Bonnier and Marcel Poëte, a historian of the growth of Paris who was to play an important part in initiating the teaching of *urbanisme*. In 1912, the mayor of Lyons, Edouard Herriot, set up a Commission du Plan de l'Extension et de l'Embellissement de Lyon, whose members included Tony Garnier. In the following year, the Conseil Général de la Seine approved a proposal by Henri Sellier, to establish a Commission des Habitations Ouvrières et du Plan d'Extension.

Alongside these local initiatives, the campaign to introduce national planning legislation was maintained. In 1912 a bill prepared by the Section d'Hygiène Urbaine et Rurale was presented to the deputies by Jules Siegfried. This proposal was considered by a parliamentary commission along with two others: Beauquier's bill of 1909, and a bill proposed by Amadée Chenal in 1913, relating to the drawing up of road and open space plans. The text which was eventually passed in 1919 incorporated the principles of planning for future growth which the Section d'Hygiène Urbaine et Rurale had advocated, obliging all towns of more than 10,000 inhabitants to draw up a development plan.[34]

The need for such plans had been emphasised by the destruction of French towns during the First World War. While the war continued, the Société Française des Architectes-Urbanistes and the Société Française des HBM both initiated studies on the planning of reconstruction. Competitions for reconstruction proposals were held, and an organisation formed under the title of La Renaissance des Cités; in Paris, an exhibition of La Cité Reconstituée was held in 1916. The war years also saw the first steps taken in establishing courses for the teaching of planning, and in 1919 an international competition for the planning of Paris and its region was held.[35]

But while the war quickened the appreciation of the value of planning, the practical achievement was almost non-existent. The Paris plan remained on the drawing board, and Paris was without a regional plan until the 1930s. Similarly, even twenty years after the planning law was passed, less than one quarter of the towns which should have approved plans had begun to prepare them. This failure is hardly surprising since the administrative machinery necessary to implement planning policy did not yet exist. On the one hand the municipalities did not have the trained officials to draw up plans. On the other hand, the planning law left unresolved the issue of municipal control over land, on which any town plan depended. With little or no land reserves, an unsophisticated system of building regulations, and a still complex procedure of expropriation, municipalities were not in a position to rebuild towns on radically new principles.

The *Cité-Jardin*: a symbol of planning

If the concept of planning had little effect on the development of urban areas as a whole during the inter-war years, it could more readily be applied to the construction of areas of housing by private societies and public offices. At the scale of the housing development rather than the city as a whole, planning was symbolised by the idea of the Garden City. The formal aspects of this idea, particularly as evolved in England by Parker and Unwin, architects of the first Garden City at Letchworth, provided a basis for the design and layout of groups of housing, while the organisational aspects of Howard's proposal gave a context which related the housing to the community as a whole. The full implications of Howard's concept, in the creation of new communities, were hardly taken up in France; but the concept provided a powerful image, and the term *cité-jardin* a useful shorthand, which stressed the need to see housing in relation to its wider environment.

The Garden City received its earliest publicity in France through the Musée Social. In 1903 the Musée sponsored Georges Benoît-Lévy on a trip to England, during which he visited Bourneville and Port Sunlight, as well as studying Howard's ideas. Those ideas were of interest to members of the Musée Social in part for their basis in co-operative principles; the promotion of co-operation had been a particular concern of the Musée since its foundation, and when Benoît-Lévy's study of the Garden City was published in 1904, it contained an introduction by the president of the French consumer co-operatives, Charles Gide. Gide saw the Garden City as a natural extension of co-operative principles;[36] but the concept was to be more important for its planning implications. It was adopted by the housing reformers as a natural extension of their ideal of low-density suburban housing. In this form, debased in the purist terms of the English Garden City movement but nonetheless influential for that, the Garden City entered the armoury of French housing reform.

The importance of the Garden City to the housing reformers was indicated by the vice-president of the Société Française des HBM, Maurice Dufourmantelle. Addressing the National Congress of Housing Societies in Lyons in 1914, he declared that 'the Garden City...seems to us an institution in which the different efforts to which the problem of modern housing has given rise, combine and reach harmony. It is the synthesis and culmination of those efforts.'[37]

The Garden City was to provide the inspiration for housing built by public offices and co-operatives, and also by industrialists and large companies after the First World War. The most notable achievement in this context was the programme of garden suburbs built around Paris

24 The satellite communities
constructed by the Office
Public des HBM du
Département de la Seine after
the First World War

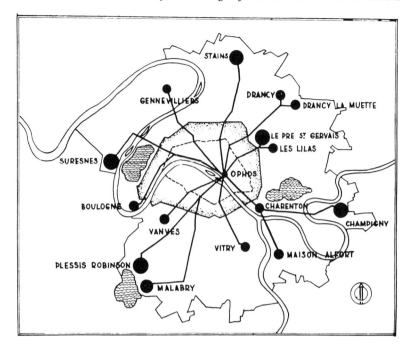

25 Part of the project for the
cité-jardin at Les Lilas; the
early projects of the Office
drew both on the French
tradition of the individual
house and on the
architectural and planning
theories of the English
architect Raymond Unwin.

by the Office Public des HBM du Département de la Seine, directed by Henri Sellier. Sellier looked to the Garden City both for his overall planning policy, in forming satellite communities outside the city, and initially for the design of the housing, which applied the lessons of Raymond Unwin. In 1918 the housing office formally adopted a subtitle, 'Les Cités-Jardins du Grand Paris'[38] (figs. 24 and 25).

Through the Garden City, the lessons of land reform and planning were thus fed back into the housing reform movement. The campaign in favour of planning had failed to establish a structure which would control urban growth after the First World War. But some of the implications of that campaign were to be realised at a smaller scale in housing developments such as those inspired by Henri Sellier. While Paris and other cities continued to grow without any planned structure, the cheap housing organisations stated the possibility of a more ordered alternative.

19

◇◆◇

Architectural reform

In the revolutionary atmosphere of 1848, César Daly saw architecture as 'the great instrument of modern reforms'. Architects would play a central role in the evolution of new institutions for the poorest classes, from housing to credit organisations.[1] As editor of the *Revue Générale de l'Architecture*, Daly had already started to give encouragement to such views. But the optimism of 1848 was hard to turn into reality. Daly failed to win a seat in the Assembly when he stood in the elections of April 1848. And while the architectural profession had endorsed him as their candidate, architects by no means fulfilled the role which Daly foresaw. In the field of cheap housing, individual architects might be commissioned to prepare plans for a block of flats, or a group of cottages. But few architects became involved in the continued study of housing. The individuals who were most closely concerned with housing reform tended to be outside, or on the fringe of, the architectural profession.

While few architects were among the leaders of housing reform, some were involved in the interpretation of the physical implications of the new attitudes to housing after the 1840s. The most direct way in which they were confronted by the problems of existing housing was through membership of official commissions. From 1838 architects, and also engineers, were appointed to the Conseil de Salubrité du Département de la Seine,[2] but it was in the 1850s that their presence was more generally felt. From 1850 the profession was represented on the central hygiene committee for the whole country, the Comité Consultatif d'Hygiène Publique et de Salubrité. In Paris, the Commissions d'Hygiène et de Salubrité set up after the reorganisation of the city's hygiene services in 1851 each included an architect.[3] The law on housing hygiene in 1850 particularly focussed attention on housing conditions; individual architects were appointed to the Commissions des Logements Insalubres, and the Societé Centrale des Architectes set up a special commission to consider the questions raised by the law.

The conclusions of the architects' commission were recorded in a report written by Adolphe Lance in 1850.[4] The report summarised the reasons for concern over housing conditions, acknowledging the evidence of Blanqui, and described the conditions witnessed by members of the commision in housing visited in Paris. Lance went on to examine the causes of insalubrity in housing, drawing attention to those factors

374

which particularly concerned architects in the construction of housing. Different methods of sewage disposal were described, and Lance stressed the importance of 'ventilation, that science which has become indispensable to the architect'. The report also suggested reforms beyond the scope of the architect's work, stemming from the interrelationship between the individual house and the city as a whole. It advocated regulations to encourage 'a reduction in the height of houses', proposed 'the widening of streets' and urged an increase in the number of public squares and gardens.[5]

Those architects who did take a specific interest in housing reflect the varying concerns evident in the late 1840s and, particularly, the contrasting strands of moderate reform and of radical socialism. The architect who instigated the creation of the housing commission within the Société Centrale des Architectes, Nicolas Philippe Harou-Romain, was an active supporter of moderate reform; as a member of the Société d' Economie Charitable, he had already contributed to the discussion of housing reform in that society in the late 1840s. Writing in the society's journal, *Les Annales de la Charité*, in 1849, he discussed the current interest in the construction of *cités ouvrières*. In this article, Harou-Romain showed a clear recognition of the ambiguity of projects like the Cité Napoléon, drawing attention to the confusion as to whether they represented 'brotherly charity' or socialism. Harou-Romain himself argued that the designs for blocks of workers' flats were closer to socialism than to charity, and he emphasised the social problems which he believed to be inherent in such housing.[6]

In an article published in the following year, Harou-Romain put forward a proposal for discouraging the density of building in urban centres; he thus responded to the social concerns which he had outlined in his earlier article, and to the environmental concerns relating to the city which had been expressed by the architects' commission. In Harou-Romain's proposal, taxation on buildings would be redistributed to penalise tall buildings and excessive coverage of the site. He anticipated that this system of taxation would encourage the horizontal rather than the vertical growth of the city, making possible the ideal of the individual house set in its own garden.[7] In trying to attack the housing problem at its root, in the land use and development factors giving rise to high densities in urban areas, Harou-Romain saw more clearly than many of his contemporaries that the problem would not be solved by isolated gestures of philanthropy or subsidy. The attempt to encourage housing reform by controlling development was to be taken up in the later nineteenth century by the German land reformers; but Harou-Romain's approach found little following in the Paris of the 1840s, where recent proposals to amend the regulations controlling building had been set aside by a city administration which, the architect Charles Gourlier claimed, considered that 'one would risk displeasing the electorate of proprietors'.[8]

Harou-Romain applied his particular professional abilities to the reforming ideals espoused by the Société d'Economie Charitable. But his interest in reform also had a wider architectural context, which can be seen in his work in the field of prison design. Harou-Romain took this interest over from his father, who as architect of the department of Calvados had designed a new prison at Beaulieu, near Caen; this design was based on the innovatory principles of a radiating plan, with individual cells. Harou-Romain followed his father as departmental architect, and as architect for the prison, and he continued to study the design of prisons using the cellular system. This led in 1840 to a request from the Minister of the Interior that Harou-Romain collaborate in the preparation of official guidelines for prison design.[9]

The housing commission of the Société Centrale des Architectes was presided over by Charles Rohault de Fleury; like Harou-Romain, he was the son of an architect, and he continued an interest in reform which his father had already developed. Hubert Rohault de Fleury, winner of the *grand prix* for architecture in 1800, and later a member of the influential Conseil des Bâtiments Civils, had represented the architectural profession on the special commission set up in 1832 to consider the question of hygiene in relation to housing construction in Paris; he was responsible for drawing up the commission's report, with its proposals for control to be applied to building forms and standards in the city. Ten years later he was a member of the commission set up by the Conseil des Bâtiments Civils to draw up new building regulations, but these had no greater impact in practice than the 1832 proposals. Charles Rohault de Fleury was to take up his father's interest in the control of building, and presided over a commission of the Société Centrale des Architectes in the early 1860s to prepare a manual of building legislation. But in the late 1840s it was towards housing that his attention was turned.

The 1832 report prepared by Rohault de Fleury's father became topical again as cholera returned, and it was one of the documents from which the architects' housing commission started in 1850. Well aware of the problems of housing hygiene considered by his father, Rohault de Fleury had already made a proposal in 1848, that sanitary commissions be set up in each quarter of Paris, to study housing conditions. This proposal had been partly realised in the law of 1850. Rohault de Fleury also proposed that subsidies be provided towards the construction of workers' housing, but in this he was already moving away from the ideal of moderate reform, which saw construction as the province of private initiative.[10]

The question of housing subsidies raised issues which went beyond the minimum controlling programme of the 1850 law, to envisage the possibility of a public role in construction. Similarly the design of housing could not remain within the limits of the moderate reformers' individual house ideal, and inevitably encountered the ambiguity of purpose noted by Harou-Romain. Housing built in 1847 for customs workers in Le Havre by the city architect Brunet-Desbaines was exhibited at the Paris salon in 1849; accommodating 1,300 people in a plan of three-storey buildings, with communal facilities including a school, restaurant, and medical dispensary, it could be seen as a healthy development of workers' family housing, or as a step towards a more communal form of housing.[11] More clearly 'socialist' in inspiration was the project for a *cité de l'union* by the architect Théodore Charpentier. This was prepared in 1849 for the publicist H. Dameth, who was a member of the Fourierist Ecole Sociétaire.[12] But while in political terms this project for a development of communal housing was directly opposed to Harou-Romain's ideal of the horizontal extension of cities with individual houses and gardens, in architectural terms Charpentier shared some of the interests of Harou-Romain and Rohault de Fleury. Thus Charpentier had contributed to the discussion of urban hygiene stimulated by the cholera epidemic of 1832, and to the research of new prison design based on cellular plans in the 1830s.[13]

A commitment to the radical ideals of the Fourierist or socialist groups led some architects to more direct political activity in the late 1840s. Joseph Delbrouck was active in the co-operative movement after 1848; he was particularly involved in the formation of a union of 83 workers' associations in 1849, to provide interest-free loans, and assistance to the elderly and sick among its members. In the restrictive atmosphere existing with respect to workers' associations by 1850, the union's administrators, among them Delbrouck, were arrested in May of that year; Delbrouck himself served a fifteen-month prison sentence. Parallel to this political activity, Delbrouck presented several projects for social buildings at the annual Paris salon. In 1849 he exhibited a project for workers' housing; in 1851 he submitted a housing project which included a school, meeting rooms and other facilities, while in 1852 he showed a 'Bourse pour les travailleurs'.[14]

1848 also saw César Daly launch his confident appeal to architects to lead the new reforms, and saw him make his unsuccessful attempt to become a deputy. At a more practical level in relation to housing, he made his proposal for the construction of communal housing to the Luxembourg Commission, while it was in the early 1850s that he tried unsuccessfully to renew the construction of the *phalanstère* at Condé-sur-Vesgres.

But with Delbrouck and Daly we are already on the fringe of the architectural profession – Delbrouck, imprisoned for 'revolutionary activity', later to take part in the Paris Commune, Daly, successful as a journalist of architecture more than as an architect. Nearer the heart of the profession, as members of the Société Centrale des Architectes, and with official positions as departmental architect of Calvados, and as architect to the Paris Museum of Natural History respectively, Harou-Romain and Rohault de Fleury were more reserved in their views. While their involvement in housing reform indicates that their profession did respond to the current interest in housing, they remained within the path of moderate reform as it was already being established by the social reformers.

This pattern of involvement can be seen in one of the most senior architects, in terms of the architectural profession, to contribute to the discussion of housing reform in the 1850s. As one of the inspectors on the Conseil des Bâtiments Civils, Charles Gourlier was an influential member of the profession. This council was responsible for supervising public building projects, and also advised on more general aspects of urban development. Gourlier himself sat with Rohault de Fleury senior on the 1842 commission to propose new building regulations – the proposals which Gourlier considered were blocked by excessive deference to property interests. The interest in workers' housing in the years around 1850 was reflected in the council's work, as several projects for *cités ouvrières* were submitted for consideration.[15]

Gourlier himself took up the question of workers' housing in the early 1850s. At the request of the Ministers of the Interior and of Commerce, he visited London in 1851 to report on the Great Exhibition, and on the development of London. Gourlier's reports considered aspects such as sewers, housing and street regulations. On his return to Paris he prepared a report on the development of that city, focussing on the same issues. In his section on housing in Paris he described at some length the Cité Napoléon, as a representative of the first generation of *cités ouvrières*; he considered it as a satisfactory first experiment although, like Villermé and Harou-Romain, he had reservations about bringing together so many people in one block.[16]

Gourlier paralleled his analysis of urban housing with a practical study of housing design; he prepared a series of plans for blocks of flats, and also for associated facilities such as public baths and schools. Gourlier exhibited this study at the 1853 Salon; he also submitted it for, and gained an award in, the competition for housing designs opened by the government in 1852.[17]

Gourlier's activity indicates that workers' housing was not considered to be a problem of no interest to the architectural profession. But nor was it a problem to which the profession had immediate answers. When he reviewed the 1853 Salon, Adolphe Lance, author of the report of the architects' housing commission, welcomed Gourlier's practical approach. But he noted that the standard of Gourlier's dwelling, with a convenience and water supply in each flat, was unrealistically high.[18] Gourlier would have seen such accommodation in some of the model housing schemes in London, but it was far in advance of French designs such as the Cité Napoléon. But if the profession had no immediate answers, it is possible to see a variety of ways in which the study of workers' housing, and of related building types, was encouraged in the 1850s and 1860s.

One method was the competition. The most notable competition in this period – notable for its origins rather than its results – was the 1852 competition launched by Louis Napoleon. The competition brought no radical proposals for housing design, but it did confirm the status of workers' housing as an architectural problem to be resolved. This status was strikingly defined in the introduction to the French translation of Henry Roberts' *The Dwellings of the Labouring Classes*, published two years before the competition. R. H. Guerrand has drawn attention to the passage in which the author contrasts the high architecture of the Rome scholars with more mundane matters:

It is a great honour to be judged worthy to go to Rome; it is to one's merit when one returns, to bring the plans of some palace destined to ornament our cities; but he who finds or propagates the art of keeping out the humidity which renders unhealthy so large a number of the dwellings of our urban and rural workers, he will have earned the respect of the nation.[19]

Humidity in buildings had actually been the subject of a competition held by the Société d'Encouragement pour l'Industrie Nationale in the 1840s. It was won by Léon Vaudoyer, who thus managed to bring together the two aspects of architecture defined in the introduction to Roberts' book, as he had won the Rome scholarship in 1826. In 1854 the city of Marseilles held a competition for a design for a laundry, which was won by Gourlier. In the late 1860s, the idea of the competition was again taken up in relation to housing in the towns of Saint Quentin, Amiens and Lille.[20]

A second method by which the study of building types was encouraged was through official councils, and the publishing of model plans. The Conseil des Bâtiments Civils provided a permanent source of guidance, and its involvement in workers' housing in the early 1850s has already been noted. Guidance in relation to specific building types was also provided by government ministries and commissions, in the manner of the guidelines for prison design drawn up by Harou-Romain. The design of public baths and laundries, an important counterpart to housing with limited servicing, was the subject of study by a government commission in 1849. The commission examined the system of baths and laundries in England, and prepared a series of plans of English examples; these were distributed to Prefectures and local chambers of commerce as a model for projects carried out with the aid of subsidies, made available by a law in 1851. Another facility related to housing developments, the kindergarten, was the subject of model plans issued by the Ministère de l'Instruction Publique in 1862, while at the same time the ministry also took an initiative to improve the standard of school designs; five architects were asked to prepare plans, from which a selection of model plans would be made. In the same year, the Ministère de l'Intérieur set up a commission to study the construction of hospitals, and to prepare model plans.[21]

Alongside this official encouragement to the study of building design, architectural magazines provided information and comment. The *Encyclopédie d'Architecture*, under the editorship of Adolphe Lance from 1852 to 1862, provided detailed coverage of government action on housing hygiene, public baths, and the model plans discussed above. The *Nouvelles Annales de la Construction*, directed by C. A. Opperman, illustrated workers' housing built in Germany, as well as the *cité ouvrière* at Mulhouse in 1856. The following year the magazine requested its readers to send in for publication, details of work they had done on cheap housing. The response to this request gave the magazine little material to publish, but in the 1860s a few articles on workers' housing in France and abroad did appear.[22] The *Revue Générale de l'Architecture*, which had taken up the question of workers' housing under Daly's guidance, in the 1840s, continued its interest in housing and other buildings of social importance. Between 1849 and 1851, it published a series of articles on the design of schools and crèches; in 1859 it started a series on kindergartens. Its most exhaustive study of housing came between 1866 and 1870, in the series of articles by C. Détain, discussing in detail the housing exhibited in 1867.

Exhibitions provided another form of encouragement to the study of housing. Several projects for workers' housing had been exhibited at the annual Salon around 1850, as a counterpart to the debate of housing at that period. In 1855 the first of a series of large Expositions Universelles was held; this included some exhibits related to housing, among them Gourlier's studies. But it was in the next Exposition, in 1867, that workers' housing was given a major place. Under the guidance of the Exposition director, Le Play, an entire group in the Exposition was devoted to social initiatives. Within this group a number of workers' houses were constructed full size, while models and plans illustrated numerous designs from France, England, Prussia, Belgium and Austria.

The 1867 Exposition confirmed the consensus of reform opinion in favour of the individual house, while providing examples of urban flats which the reformers could accept. Both of these housing types could be seen, full size, in the Exposition. But despite the evident relevance of the Exposition to architects, the profession did not take a leading role in its organisation. The organising committee of thirteen included only one architect. The other members were industrialists, doctors, engineers and government officials, or had links with social and charitable institutions. Ironically, architects had the same representation as that other group of individuals intimately concerned in the question of workers' housing, but rarely accorded a leading role: the committee included one workers' representative.[23]

If the competitions, commissions, journals and exhibitions were not sufficient to attract more than a minority of the architectural profession to take an interest in housing, perhaps a more radical change was needed. Such a change was proposed in the mid-1860s, when a new architectural school was set up in Paris. While the purpose of the school was not specifically related to housing, many of its founders and supporters were closely involved in housing reform – notably Emile Muller, one of the three administrators of the school and designer of the *cité ouvrière* at Mulhouse. Equally, the founder of the school, Emile Trélat, for whom architecture was a second career, was to become active in the cause of housing reform in the 1870s and 1880s.

The Ecole Centrale d'Architecture

Architectural education in nineteenth-century France was dominated by the Ecole des Beaux Arts, with its system of competitions, and studio apprenticeship. Construction was taught at the school, but the main emphasis was on design, culminating in the entries for the Prix de Rome. Quality of design was the goal, and more practical questions derived from the application of scientific understanding took second place. Yet it was such application, in the form of improved servicing, cheaper construction, or hygienic design, which was most essential to housing reform.

A trend towards functionalism in design, in projects for workers' housing and other social buildings encouraged by the Imperial government, was noted by César Daly in 1860. He observed that 'since 1852, questions of style have ceased to occupy the central place in the preoccupations of the architect. The activity of national projects, the need to produce in quantity, at speed, has given the practical questions of our profession a preponderance over all others. Utility prevails today over all other considerations.'[24] Reaction to such a situation took two forms. Supporters of the Ecole des Beaux Arts tried to safeguard what they saw as their main contribution, the art of architecture. But others argued that this contribution depended on a mastery of the utilitarian aspects of design, and attempted to bring to architecture the benefits of the engineer's functional training.

Among those who accepted and encouraged the functional basis of architecture was Emile Trélat. Born in 1821, he trained as an engineer at the Ecole Centrale des Arts et Manufactures, and directed a ceramics factory before turning to architecture. He became a pupil of Louis Visconti, but did not pass through the Ecole des Beaux Arts. When Trélat started to teach a course on construction at the Conservatoire des Arts et Métiers in 1854, his combination of architectural and technical concerns was apparent; it was Trélat, wrote the architect Anatole de Baudot, 'who first introduced the scientific element to a course of construction designed specifically for architectural studies'.[25]

Alongside this combination of professional concerns, Trélat held firmly Republican views, and developed a particular interest in questions of hygiene. Both of these characteristics link Trélat closely to his father, Ulysse Trélat. Ulysse was a doctor in Paris (as too was Emile's brother, also named Ulysse) and was elected deputy in 1848. His political activity dated back to the 1830s when he had served a prison term of three years for his involvement in dissident secret societies. Subsequently he gained a reputation as a doctor treating the poor in Paris, and this activity as much as his radical views ensured him a place in the Constituent Assembly elected in April 1848. The President of this Assembly, Pierre Buchez, was an old colleague of Ulysse Trélat's from the revolutionary Carbanaro movement, and the two men had published a study of hygiene together in 1825. Under Buchez, Ulysse was appointed Minister of Public Works – a post which gave him responsibility for the *ateliers nationaux* set up in this early phase of the new Republic. His tenure was short, and he left the post after less than six weeks, shortly before the closure of the *ateliers nationaux* and the repression of June 1848.[26]

Emile Trélat inherited his father's Republican views and was himself to serve as a deputy in the 1890s. More immediately, he was forced to give up a job working on plans for the Louvre in 1852 because he refused to take an oath of loyalty to the newly declared Emperor. Similarly, Emile was to make a particular study of hygiene in relation to architecture, and as early as 1849 he was appointed to the commission set up to consider the design of public baths and laundries. These varying aspects of Trélat's background were to come together in his proposal to found a new school of architecture – in the search for an alternative to the existing structure of architectural education, in the application of scientific study to architecture, and in the consideration of the relationship between hygiene and architecture.

The Ecole Centrale d'Architecture opened its doors to students in November 1865. In the school's prospectus, Trélat pointed out that, of all the liberal professions, architecture alone did not have a formally organised education. He acknowledged that the Ecole des Beaux Arts was a source of excellence, stimulating the élite. But he argued that neither the Ecole des Beaux Arts, nor the related system of apprenticeship in architectural studies, satisfactorily educated students in the range of skills and knowledge which they required. His intention in the Ecole Centrale d'Architecture was to establish a full time course, lasting three years, based on lectures, drawing studies, and project designs. This would provide the basic grounding required for the profession of architecture. 'For the studio, undemanding and impoverished, [the school] substitutes taxing and interesting tuition.'[27]

Trélat was careful to conclude his brochure by emphasising that the new school would not damage existing interests, and that the Ecole des Beaux Arts would keep 'the dominant position which belongs to it'.[28] But Trélat's moderate words did not disguise the fact that the new school came into being as a direct opposition to the Ecole des Beaux Arts. In 1863 and 1864 the architect Viollet-le-Duc had been involved in controversial attempts to reform the education offered by the Ecole des Beaux Arts and, resigning from the school in the face of fierce opposition, he planned the creation of a new institution. Trélat, who had known Viollet-le-Duc since childhood, and had worked with him in the office of the architect Achille Leclère, was invited to head this new school. Viollet-le-Duc himself helped with the organisation, and was one of its directors, but he took no part in the teaching. Trélat's prospectus emphasised the positive characteristics of the new school to play down the antagonism towards the Ecole des Beaux Arts; but the Ecole Centrale d'Architecture did not open with the goodwill of the architectural establishment.[29]

While seeking architectural independence the new school also sought independence from the State, which ran the Ecole des Beaux Arts. In this it followed the lead of the Ecole Centrale des Arts et Manufactures, which had been set up in 1829 to break the monopoly of the State-run Ecole Polytechnique in the training of engineers. It was financed by private subscription, and trained 'civil engineers, factory directors and heads of industry.'[30] The statutes of the new architectural school explicitly acknowledged the debt to the older school; the Ecole Centrale d'Architecture was intended to 'train architects, as the Ecole Centrale des Arts et Manufactures trains civil engineers'.[31]

Emulating its model, the Ecole Centrale d'Architecture gained the support of the liberal bourgeoisie; many of the shareholders were themselves engineers or industrialists, and of 114 initial subscribers, only twelve were architects. As the *Revue Générale de l'Architecture* pointed out it was 'engineers who seem to be the initiators not architects'.[32] Several of these initiators also had more than a passing interest in workers' housing. Emile Muller and Jean Dollfus, creators of the Mulhouse *cité ouvrière*, were both founder shareholders. So too were J. B. A. Godin, whose Familistère was partly occupied by 1865, and Menier, who had recently built a new chemical factory at Saint Denis; in 1874 the Menier firm was to commence a workers' village adjacent to its chocolate factory in Noisiel. Jules Siegfried became a shareholder in 1868, and the Paris engineer, Durand-Claye, was also associated with the school. Charles Robert, then a senior official in the Ministère de l'Instruction Publique, was among the guests at the school's opening assemblies during the late 1860s.[33]

If the supporters of the Ecole represented the interests of industry as much as those of architecture, they also indicate the school's links with the currents of thought of the mid-century. Alongside the staunchly liberal, moderate reformers, Siegfried, Dollfus and Robert were figures such as Emile Péreire and Michel Chevalier, advocates of the Saint Simonist philosophy of industrial growth as a creator of general welfare, and Godin, follower of that more radical proponent of change, Fourier. François Coignet, another Fourierist sympathiser, was also among the founders of the school; Théodore Lachez with whom Coignet collaborated in the construction of an experimental concrete house in 1853, and who was a contributor to the *Revue Générale de l'Architecture* in the 1840s, was among the teachers at the school. Also on the staff was Joseph Delbrouck, veteran of the ideals of the early phase of the 1848 republic. Trélat himself, of course, was familiar with those ideals through his father, who joined the founding shareholders of the school. If it would be wrong to attribute any strong political direction to the school, it is clear that it had the support of a wide range of opinion, from moderate reform to socialism.[34]

In the tuition of the school, the importance accorded to the practical abilities of the engineer is apparent. The three adminstrators of the school – Trélat, Muller and C. Dupont – all had engineering training. Of fifteen course teachers appointed when the *Revue Générale de l'Architecture* reported on the school, only three were architects: Trélat, Lachez and Delbrouck. Trélat's assistant in teaching the theory of architecture course was the young architect Anatole de Baudot, who had been a pupil of Viollet-le-Duc; later, in the 1890s, de Baudot was to pioneer the use of reinforced concrete. The courses offered by the school included the theory and history of architecture, but also placed great emphasis on scientific studies as physics, chemistry, geology and construction.

One of the main innovations of the school was the importance accorded to studies of hygiene. The first year included a complete course on the subject, taught by Trélat's brother, the surgeon Dr Ulysse Trélat. In the second and third years Emile Muller taught a course on physics applied to architecture which covered the servicing and sanitation of buildings.[35] Trélat considered an understanding of practical questions such as these essential if architecture were not to fall under the supremacy of the engineer. The skills of the engineer had led him to 'invade a large part of the domain of the architect'.[36] Trélat wished architects to acquire the knowledge necessary to regain this domain not in order to produce a purely functionalist architecture, but in order that the architect could continue to exercise his main skill: the artistic design of buildings.

In addition to the scientific basis which it introduced to the teaching of architecture, the tuition at the Ecole Centrale de l'Architecture aimed to give the architect an awareness of his social responsibility. The second and third years included a course in political economy which summarised the characteristics of production, labour and capital, concluding optimistically with 'the apparent antagonism of interests disappearing as light is spread, bringing about a general harmony'.[37] This vague optimism was expressed in more concrete terms by Henry Cole, director of the South Kensington Museum in London (forerunner of the Victoria & Albert Museum). When Cole presided at the opening session of the school in 1867 he declared that

Architecture, in our day, is not studied in cloisters to raise up cathedrals, fortresses for nobles, or numerous palaces for kings. It must, throughout the whole world, provide for the needs of a civilised democracy, and can only progress by means of common sense directed by science and inspired by art.[38]

Such ideals were difficult to translate into architectural form. By 1868 the school could be judged on the evidence of a complete cycle of its three-year course. But the projects displayed at the end of the year drew criticism even from within the school. Anatole de Baudot attributed the disappointing content of the projects to the teaching. He supported the intention of the school; but it had failed to provide the sense of direction which he saw lying

in the true appreciation of the philosophy of the programmes, of their material requirements, of the needs which they indicate, linked to the knowledge of the characteristics of materials, of their logical use, and of the forms which they are capable of adopting.[39]

De Baudot's comments show a clear understanding of the importance of a theoretical base, linking social and practical factors. Without this base, the gap between the intention of the programmes and the students' designs could not be closed.

This gap was evident in submissions for the final exam in 1869, when the programme was a Working Men's Club.[40] The introduction to the programme was eloquent in its equation of social environment with architectural form.

The Architect who observes his age must not let the programme of the Working Men's Club pass without being struck by the context in which it arises, the causes which give birth to it, the influences which it possesses. In all this there is a unity of powerful circumstances, which provide on these well-interpreted foundations an architectural bearing which is of the most sound and highest order.[41]

Unfortunately, the 'architectural bearing' which the author of the programme anticipated would be derived from the social significance of the Working Men's Club did not materialise. The designs of the students were competent, but no more competent than students at the Ecole des Beaux Arts might have produced, and offering no radical alternative in design or construction. Some of the designs were exhibited at the 1870 Salon, together with other projects by students at the school. They were greeted with disdain by the architectural profession, receiving critical reviews in the *Moniteur des Architectes* and the *Revue Générale de l'Architecture*. Charles Garnier, celebrated architect of the Opéra, attacked the school in the journal *XIXe Siècle*, commencing a vigorous correspondence between himself and Trélat.[42]

Such attacks were to be expected from an architectural press which was generally suspicious of the new school, and from a profession which saw the traditional values of architectural education and practice under threat. But it is undeniable that the school failed to live up to its ideals. The scientific and social context of architecture which its courses emphasised were not assimilated into a coherent philosophy of design. De Baudot's doubts about the teaching provided by the school led him to resign in 1868, when Viollet-le-Duc also severed his links with the school; their criticism focussed on the fact that Trélat, and his associate Chipiez, were promoting a theory of design based more on symbolism than on function and structure.[43]

The internal and external difficulties which the school faced were compounded by financial problems. These led the school to seek aid from the State, and to introduce an important concession. In his opening address in 1879, Trélat announced that the diploma of the school would now entitle students to go on to pursue their training in a studio at the Ecole des Beaux Arts. While he defended the education of the school as being entirely satisfactory from a professional point of view, he acknowledged that it did not provide the refinement of artistic education which the Ecole des Beaux Arts could give. But Trélat also justified the change by reference to the lack of acceptance of the school among the 'official world of architects', admitting that the school's diploma did not assist its holders' careers in the same way as a training through the Ecole des Beaux Arts.[44] These changes marked the end of the school as the independent alternative to the Ecole des Beaux Arts which it was intended to form: and it was now little more than a preparatory course for the Ecole.

The history of the Ecole Centrale d'Architecture is of significance to a discussion of housing reform on two levels. First, the background of many of these who brought it into being, and financed it, demonstrates a concern for the physical environment among men whose first interest was not architecture or design. Industrialists such as Dollfus and Siegfried came to appreciate the significance of the physical environment through the particular importance it had for social reform. The progression of thought from the social problems of morality and hygiene to a solution through building a new environment is at the heart of the housing reform movement. If that progression can be seen in the individuals who supported the Ecole Centrale, it is emphasised by the second level of the school's significance. The limited support which the school received from the architectural profession, and its eventual absorption back into the profession underlines the single direction of the progression noted above. While social concern could lead to interest in the design of buildings, a training in design did not necessarily lead architects to see their skill, as Daly had, as 'the great instrument of modern reforms'.

Moreover, the leaders of the school had found the task of forging a new approach to architecture based on social and scientific ideals harder than they anticipated, and had retreated into the easier architectural waters of symbolism. The definition of that new approach was only finally to come about as housing reform passed from the phase of debate to that of practice: as architects established their role through working directly for housing societies.

Emile Muller and Emile Cacheux

In the process of moving housing reform from debate to practice in the 1870s and 1880s, two figures stand out: Emile Muller and Emile Cacheux. Muller's reputation was initially based on the *cité ouvrière* at Mulhouse, built in the 1850s. But he went on to make a detailed study of housing design, collaborating with his former pupil Emile Cacheux. When the results of their study were published in 1879 they were acclaimed by one reviewer as 'the most useful and most complete of the works which have yet appeared, concerning workers' housing'.[45]

Muller was born in Altkirch, to the south of Mulhouse, in 1823. After building his first group of houses in 1846, he extended his knowledge 'by a laborious study of all books written on this subject, by working trips to the countries which had preceded us in the field'.[46] The construction of the first houses at the Mulhouse *cité ouvrière* in 1853 led Muller into further housing projects. At Guebwiller he designed a small group of houses for the Bourcart firm; in Paris he designed another small development of houses similar to those at Mulhouse, although this was not executed in accordance with Muller's plans.

Muller used the experience he had already gained as the basis for his

first study of workers' housing, published in 1856. French literature on
the construction of workers' housing at this date was still sparse, and
the reviewer in the *Nouvelles Annales de la Construction* welcomed this
book which 'has filled a gap which has existed for many years in the
bibliography of construction'.[47] Muller's intention was to 'publish
genuine working drawings, to give to all persons who wish to build a
practical, sure basis, sanctioned by experience'.[48] In addition to detailed
drawings, the book included costs, methods of finance, and rent or sale
arrangements. The study also considered public baths and laundries,
and food provision societies. It was completed by some observations on
hygiene by Dr A. Clavel.[49]

Muller pursued his concern with housing alongside activity as an
industrialist and a teacher. The year after starting the Mulhouse
housing, he opened a successful factory in Ivry, near Paris. The factory
made ceramic products, and exhibited the first machine-made roofing
tiles at the Exposition of 1855. In the early 1870s the factory supplied
the glazed infill bricks for the renowned iron-framed factory built by the
Menier company at Noisiel. The reputation of Muller's products was
such that in 1882, the National Congress of Architects made an official
visit to the factory. As a teacher, Muller already had experience before
he helped to found the Ecole Centrale d'Architecture in 1865. By this
date he was on the staff of the Ecole Centrale des Arts et Manufactures,
running a course in which he introduced the question of workers'
housing.

Among Muller's pupils at the Ecole Centrale des Arts et Manufactures
was Emile Cacheux, who graduated in 1869. Cacheux had been born
in Mulhouse in 1844, and after qualifying as an engineer, he returned
there to direct a chemical products factory. He soon returned to Paris,
where he married the daughter of a public works contractor. As a result
of his marriage, Cacheux came into possession of about fifteen properties
in the city, housing some 500 families. His experience as a landlord
confronted Cacheux with the inadequacy of workers' housing conditions.
'On visiting my blocks of flats, I was distressed to see the deplorable state
of the dwellings which were teeming with my tenants. Wishing to
remedy the situation, I visited similar dwellings, and I was very surprised
to find in them the same conditions.'[50] Cacheux's response was twofold.
He contacted his former teacher, Emile Muller, initiating their fruitful
partnership of research and publication; and he started building houses
himself. He financed several small groups of individual houses on the
outskirts of Paris, which the occupants were able to acquire by monthly
payments, on the model pioneered at Mulhouse. Between the early
1870s and 1900, Cacheux built over 300 such dwellings (fig. 26).

When Cacheux contacted him, Muller was himself working on a
scheme for a housing development in Paris. Cacheux joined Muller in
working on the project, which had been initiated by Jean Dollfus. The
housing was never built, but Muller and Cacheux published the material
they had gathered on workers' housing in 1879, as *Les habitations ouvrières en tous pays*. Like Muller's study of 1856, the heart of the book was in

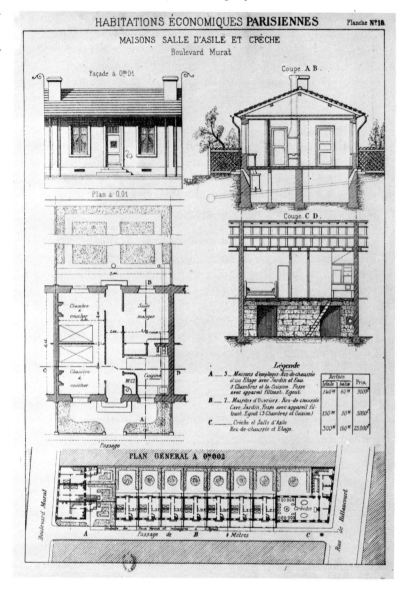

26 A typical group of housing as built by Emile Cacheux; this group was built on the western edge of the city, on the Boulevard Murat, and provided a crèche as well as housing.

its copious illustration volume. This included detail drawings of housing built in France and Europe;[51] there were also several designs prepared by Muller and Cacheux. The text argued the case for action in relation to workers' housing, and examined the practical problems from the choice of a site and materials for construction, to the type of housing. The different means of promoting the construction of housing were also considered, and a whole section was devoted to a study of building societies, including sample statutes and contracts. Muller and Cacheux's study was awarded a gold medal at the 1878 Exposition, and it became established as a standard work. In 1889 it was published in a revised edition, in which 'architects and engineers will find their textbook';[52]

this edition was given a 1,000 fr. award by the Académie des Sciences Morales et Politiques. In the early 1900s Cacheux published a supplement to the book, including further illustrations of house types.

After the original publication of the book in 1879 Cacheux was involved in an abortive attempt to establish a housing society in Paris, and in a successful one at Passy Auteuil, in west Paris;[53] he also pursued his own programme of house construction. However, he continued to feed this practical experience back into publicity promoting the construction of cheap housing. The organisations which he addressed in the late 1870s and early 1880s included the Association Française pour l'Avancement des Sciences, the Société des Ingénieurs Civils, the Société d'Encouragement pour l'Industrie Nationale and the Société d'Economie Sociale. To a steady flow of papers and articles, Cacheux added two more weighty works. In 1882 he published *Le philanthrope pratique*, a study of workers' housing, which included plans. This was the first part of a series under that title, but no further parts appeared. Instead, Cacheux published a single volume entitled *L'économiste pratique*, in 1885. This consisted of four parts, the first of which was on housing. It included the established combination of detailed drawings, sample statutes and discussion of the form of housing societies. But in *L'économiste pratique* Cacheux extended this method to consider the buildings and organisations required for a range of social facilities, as the book's sub-title indicated:

Construction and organisation of Crèches, Nurseries, Schools, Workers' dwellings and Employees' houses, Hostels for single men, Cheap Kitchens, Baths, Laundries, Popular Clubs, Child Clinics, Maternity Homes, Dispensaries, Hospitals, Hospices, Night Shelters, First Aid Posts. Structure, Statutes and Regulations of Institutions of *prévoyance* and charity.

Cacheux exhibited *L'économiste pratique* at the 1889 Exposition, together with articles and brochures, plans of his housing developments, and the second edition of *Les habitations ouvrières*. He was awarded a gold medal for this considerable range of propaganda in favour of workers' housing. He was also involved in the 1889 Exposition professionally since he was the engineer in charge of constructing the full-size housing exhibits. After the Exposition, he published yet another volume on housing, which illustrated many of the housing developments exhibited.[54]

Through books, articles, lectures and construction, the engineers Muller and Cacheux dominated the study of housing design in the 1880s. The attitude of housing reformers to the architectural profession remained mixed at this time. Félix Mangini, who founded a major housing society in Lyons in the 1880s, considered the first economy in designing cheap housing as that of dispensing with an architect. However, Mangini was director of a construction company which provided the design and building expertise for the new society, so his rejection of architects was not entirely without self-interest. A contrasting view was expressed by M. Satre, also from Lyons; he considered that 'an excellent and conscientious architect is indispensable'.[55] But as

Muller and Cacheux had found, close study of the practical problems involved in constructing cheap housing was an essential first step, and this was not a step which architects generally included in their training. One of Cacheux's objections to the construction of housing by the city of Paris was the lack of experience of its architectural staff. 'The city architects are too good as builders, and too enamoured of their art to build houses similar to those which are built for workers by persons who concern themselves with this type of building.'[56] However, by the time Cacheux wrote this in the 1880s, a growing number of architects were gaining experience designing cheap housing as the number of housing societies increased.

Housing construction and design: the architecture of reform

When the Ecole Centrale d'Architecture held its opening assembly in November 1865, the architect Stanislas Ferrand was among those present. Over the next few years, Ferrand was to make a study of economic construction methods, with the aims of resolving the economic problems which architecture had failed to answer: cheap rents, and the democratisation of property. He exhibited his solution at the 1867 Exposition, gaining a silver medal. Ferrand's proposal (see fig. 27) consisted of a structural system of iron columns and beams supporting shallow brick vaults. Exterior infill walls were two skins of hollow blocks, with a cavity open to the cellar below and attic above; Ferrand argued that the air flow in the cavity would help keep the dwelling warm in winter and cool in summer. The column and infill construction was to be exposed, and the architectural expression would thus 'result naturally from the materials employed and their architectonic forms'.[57] Ferrand claimed that his system would save money by reducing the amount of material used for construction; by reducing wall thicknesses, there would also be an economy in the area of land required.

Ferrand's structure was applicable to individual houses and to multi-storey blocks. For the 1867 Exposition he constructed a two-storey house; together with Jules Simon he founded a co-operative society to build houses based on this prototype.[58] The society did build one development, but the system did not prove more economic than traditional construction. Iron was already widely used in public buildings, but in the small storey heights and spans of domestic architecture, the economy of material was not significant enough to lead to the widespread use of iron frame structures.

At a larger scale, the potential of iron-framed construction formed the basis for the engineer H. J. Borie's visionary concept of *aérodomes*, first proposed in 1865. Borie envisaged the reorganisation of dense city areas with ten-storey buildings which allowed him to open up the urban structure to light and air. Borie's proposal remained unbuilt.[59] At a more mundane level, an iron frame was used in 1878 as the structure for a block of flats in Paris; but neither this, nor Ferrand's system for individual houses, was the basis for the development of cheap housing.

Maison de la Société Coopérative immobilière

par Mr STANISLAS FERRAND, archᵀᴱ

Elevation.

Coupe CD.

Coupe AB.

Rez-de-Chaussée.

Caves

1er Etage

27 Stanislas Ferrand's proposal for an iron-framed house, exhibited at the 1867 Exposition in Paris

The group of four houses exhibited alongside Ferrand's house in 1867, designed by Emile Muller for the Mulhouse Société des Cités Ouvrières, was more typical in its construction. The exterior walls were rendered masonry and the interior partitions plastered brickwork; floor and roof structures were in timber, with clay tiles in the kitchen, timber floor boards elsewhere, and interlocking roof tiles. Although the houses had a cellar, an asphalt damp proof course was installed. A chimney was provided to the kitchen range, but there were no other fireplaces. The closest discharged into a cesspit, while rain water and kitchen drainage ran along a stone channel to the street gutter. Water was supplied from a pump on the street (see fig. 9).

In the 1880s Emile Cacheux experimented with concrete construction for a terrace of houses, a technique also used ten years later by a society founded at Oullins, near Lyons. However, this form of construction does not appear to have been any more successful for individual houses than Ferrand's iron structure. The general acceptance of traditional methods for workers' housing is emphasised by the village built by the Menier company at Noisiel. While the adjacent factory used an innovatory iron frame structure, the housing was as traditional as that at Mulhouse (figs. 28 and 29).

When the Mulhouse housing was started, a back-to-back arrangement was used for some of the houses. While this was soon abandoned at Mulhouse, Muller and Cacheux developed it in the 1870s in some of their unbuilt plans for housing in Paris. But it was Muller's plan for a group of four houses which became widely known as the 'Mulhouse

28 The Menier chocolate factory at Noisiel, designed by Jules Saulnier, 1871–2; the building is noteworthy for its pioneering use of an iron frame.

plan'. Clustered around a party wall forming a cross on plan, the arrangement was economical, although it was not ideal from the point of view of orientation. *La Semaine des Constructeurs* pointed out in 1886 that one house was deprived of sun, while its opposite received very little shade.[60] Despite this, the plan was used for many years, and as late as 1905 it was still being used by the mining company in Dourges.

The ideal realised at Mulhouse retained its potency throughout the latter half of the nineteenth century. But the alternative, the urban block of flats, went through considerable development. The three blocks constructed for the 1867 Exposition already showed a reaction against the Cité Napoléon plan, towards more 'bourgeois' housing (fig. 30). In each case a staircase, entered off the street, served the flats on each floor: eight flats in the Cité du Champ de Mars, two in the Maison des Ouvriers, and a single flat in the housing on the Avenue Daumesnil. Every flat had its own closet, although at the Cité Daumesnil this was outside the flat, on the landing. In the Cité du Champ de Mars water was only supplied to the courtyard, but in the other two developments it was taken to each flat.

The Cité du Champ de Mars was traditionally built with structural walls of rendered masonry and brick. The use of iron was limited to the beams of the floor structure; the roof was timber, with zinc covering. Floors were paved in the kitchens, and boarded elsewhere. The Maison des Ouvriers was also built in traditional construction, although the committee of workers which supervised it preferred exposed brickwork for its qualities of hygiene and solidity. In contrast, the Cité Daumesnil employed an English system of concrete structural walls, devised by Joseph Tull. Like Ferrand's iron structure, this system claimed the advantage of reduced wall thickness in comparison to brick or stone; the *Revue Générale de l'Architecture* also referred to the assertion of the

29 Part of the housing built next to the Menier factory from 1874; the housing is reminiscent of the Mulhouse housing of twenty years earlier in its use of traditional building techniques.

English sanitarian Edwin Chadwick that concrete was more resistant to water absorption than brickwork. The system was certainly structurally satisfactory, and supported an extra storey constructed after the Exposition.[61]

The use of concrete offered more potential in the construction of large blocks than individual houses. When Félix Mangini founded his housing society in Lyons in 1885, lightweight concrete using clinker had been commonly used in the area for over twenty years. Mangini made use of the material for the construction of a large programme of economical blocks of flats. A typical five-storey block had a structure of concrete walls built off a stone base. The floors were also concrete, poured over shallow brick arches supported on iron beams. The floor finish over the concrete was generally timber; the underside of the brick vaults was simply plastered and the profile left exposed. The construction system proved successful, and when Alfred Dubois studied it for the Société Française des HBM in 1896, he advocated its general use in order to reduce construction costs.[62]

In 1889, when workers' housing again figured prominently in the Exposition Universelle in Paris several architects were recognised by awards for their activity in workers' housing. Two architects in particular had made an important contribution to the design of urban flats: Edouard Lecoeur who received a silver medal, and Wilbrod Chabrol, who received a gold medal. Lecoeur was employed by a housing society formed in Rouen in 1885, to design a block of flats in the city. After a visit to England, armed with letters of introduction to housing societies from Georges Picot, he finalised the design which was built (see fig. 31). This design used the staircase access established by the blocks exhibited in 1867, with each stair generally serving three flats. However, the building was constructed around a court to give a larger open area

30 Housing built for the
Exposition Universelle held in
Paris in 1867

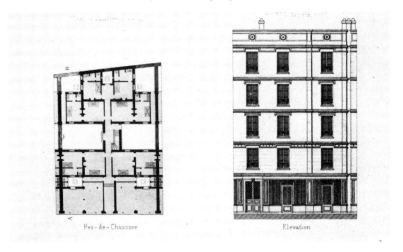

a.   The Cité du Champ de Mars, financed by Napoleon III, and designed by
     E. Lacroix

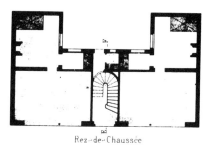

b.   The Maison des Ouvriers, built under the guidance of a committee of workers

c.   The Cité Daumesnil, built on the Avenue Daumesnil, financed by Napoleon
     III, who is also reputed to have provided the plan for these flats (see also fig.
     6)

31 The group
'Alsace-Lorraine', built by
the architect Edouard
Lecoeur for the Société des
Petits Logements de Rouen in
1885

than the Cité du Champ de Mars, which was of comparable scale. A water supply was taken into the building, but for economic reasons was only extended to a tap on each landing. The closets were also on the landing, and were initially planned to discharge into cess-pits; however, during construction the city council voted to accept the principle of the *tout-à-l'égout*, and the closets were altered to link directly to the mains. The construction of the five-storey block was of structural brickwork although iron was used for the stairs. The hygiene standard of the building was demonstrated by its average death rate during the late 1880s and early 1890s: this was only 12.27 per thousand whereas in Rouen as a whole it was 33.88.[63]

Chabrol had achieved the eminence of being a Rome scholar, but this did not prevent him from designing a successful block of workers' flats for the Société Philanthropique in Paris in 1888. This building in the Rue Jeanne d'Arc grouped five flats on each floor around the access stair. Shops on the ground floor were surmounted by seven floors of flats. The flats were of a high standard, with gas and water to each flat, and closets linked to mains drainage. Construction was load-bearing brick, with iron floor structure. Emile Cacheux criticised the layout of the flats because through ventilation was impossible. However the planning of the site maximised sun and air to all flats, by maintaining almost two-thirds of the plot as an open court[64] (fig. 32).

Among the other architects to receive a medal at the 1889 Exposition was Alphonse Gosset. Since the late 1860s Gosset had been involved in initiatives to build workers' housing in Reims. His experience also led to his appointment as one of the architects on the organising committee of the first International Congress of Cheap Housing, held in Paris to coincide with the Exposition. As in 1867, architects were outnumbered in the field of cheap housing – there were only three architects on this committee of 25. But the events of 1889 do show architects beginning to take a more active role. Thus Gosset was joined on the organising committee by the president of the Société Nationale des Architectes, Bourdeix, and by the architect who was most closely involved with housing reform at this date, Emile Trélat.[65]

Trélat's concern with hygiene had led him to take an active interest in housing reform since the late 1870s. In 1878 he gave a major report on housing, 'Cités ouvrières, maisons ouvrières', to the International Hygiene Congress; in this he contrasted the two archetypes of housing reform, the Cité Napoléon and the housing in Mulhouse, to the considerable advantage of the latter.[66] He spoke on the same subject to the National Congress of Architects, also held in Paris in 1878. Trélat served as president of the Société de Médecine Publique et d'Hygiène Professionelle in 1880, while in 1882 he was appointed to the Commission Technique set up to consider the sewer systems in Paris; in the debate over which system to adopt Trélat strongly supported the *tout-à-l'égout* advocated by the engineer Durand-Claye. Trélat was also active in preparing papers for three of the international hygiene congresses in the 1880s: in 1882 he discussed the effect of the

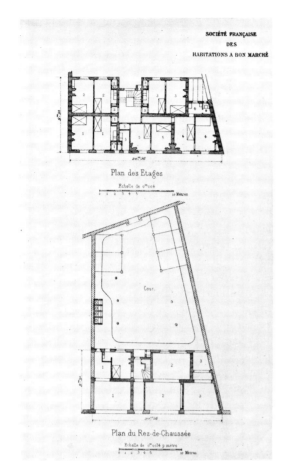

permeability of walls to air on the interior environment; in 1884 he considered principles of heating and ventilation; in 1887 he turned to the importance of sunlight in buildings.[67] The year before this last congress, in 1886, Trélat had been among the exhibitors at the Exposition d'Hygiène Urbaine held in Paris. He showed plans and details of housing, hospitals and schools, illustrating methods of providing fresh air, heating, and direct light, and of disposing of waste. Associated with the exhibition, Trélat gave a lecture on ventilation and heating, and he also initiated a visit to the exhibition by the National Congress of Architects.[68]

By 1889 Trélat was thus an authoritative contributor to the discussion of housing hygiene. When the Société Française des HBM was founded after the housing congress of that year, Trélat was one of the few architects to sit on its administrative council. Two years later, Trélat was elected to the Chambre des Députés, where he concerned himself particularly with questions of art and public health. When Siegfried presented his housing bill in 1892, Trélat was among the signatories to the proposal; he also sat on the parliamentary commission which

32 The first block of cheap flats built by the Société Philanthropique in Paris, in the Rue Jeanne d'Arc, designed by the architect Wilbrod Chabrol, in 1888

examined the bill, eventually guiding it into law in 1894. The following year, Trélat was among the appointments to the Conseil Supérieur des HBM which the 1894 law introduced.

The administrative council of the Société Français des HBM also included Chabrol, architect for the Société Philanthropique, and Charles Lucas. Like Chabrol, Lucas had studied architecture at the Ecole des Beaux Arts, and took a particular interest in the social aspect of architecture, designing several schools in Paris. At the 1878 Exposition, he gave a public lecture on housing, in which he outlined his view of the ideal form of workers' housing. He identified several of the characteristic strains of housing reform, favouring the construction of suburban housing based on a public transport system, extolling the virtues of the individual house as realised at Mulhouse, and accepting the moral role which the reformers attributed to the house and to property. His audience warmly greeted Lucas' assertion that 'the house which will have been sanctified by a life of work and respectability should one day become the property of him who will thus have well earned it, and attach him by an indestructable link, the strongest of all, to the soil of the Fatherland.'[69] Lucas was to develop close links with England at a time when the example of cheap flats built in England was particularly important in France. Both the development in Rouen, by Lecoeur, and that in Paris by Chabrol were specifically indebted to English models. Lucas became an active corresponding member of the Royal Institute of British Architects, and his death in 1905 was mourned as the loss of the Institute's 'fastest and most loyal friend abroad'.[70] Within France, Lucas encouraged the diffusion of information on housing in England, France and other countries, through his collaboration on *La Construction Moderne*, a journal started in 1885, and particularly in his study of housing in France and abroad, published in connection with the architectural and housing congresses held in Paris in 1900.[71]

1900 marked the first year in which housing reform was officially debated at the International Congress of Architects. At the request of the British delegation, 'cheap housing in all countries' was placed on the programme. Charles Lucas was on the organising committee for the Congress, and he was asked to open the session on housing. He was joined on the organising committee by Emile Trélat, while the senior members of the Société Française des HBM, Jules Siegfried and Georges Picot, were among the Congress patrons. Lucas was to have introduced Owen Fleming, architect of the Boundary Street housing recently built by the London County Council.[72] In the event, Fleming was unable to attend, and Lucas called on Edouard Lecoeur to describe the housing he had designed in Rouen in 1885. The ensuing discussion did not go into great technical detail, and concentrated on the well-worn question of the individual house and the urban block of flats. No resolutions were voted by the Congress, but Emile Trélat forcefully stated the accepted view of the housing reformers on these two options. 'It is evident. We must wish for the first solution, but put up with the second.'[73]

During the early 1900s, the second solution evolved from the basic model established by Chabrol in his flats for the Société Philanthropique. New structural possibilities were opened up by the introduction of the reinforced concrete frame, first used for the construction of a block of flats in 1900, by François Hennebique; three years later, Auguste Perret's flats in the Rue Franklin also used a concrete frame. Neither of these blocks was intended to be workers' housing; but in 1903, contemporary with the Perret flats, Henri Sauvage and his partner Charles Sarazin constructed a block of flats in the Rue Trétaigne, for the Société des Logements Hygiéniques et à Bon Marché. This society had been founded in 1903, to build housing within the context of the 1894 housing legislation. In the Rue Trétaigne building, Sauvage and Sarazin left the structural frame clearly visible on the façade (fig. 33); the infill was brick, although it was originally to have included ceramic tile, a material favoured in the early 1900s for its hygienic qualities. The building was completed by a roof garden, although this was later replaced by a mansard roof.[74]

The Société des Logements Hygiéniques et à Bon Marché provided Sauvage with a sequence of commissions, totalling six blocks of flats between 1903 and 1909. The Rue Trétaigne was the most striking in its revelation of its structure, and the later buildings have simpler brick façades. However, Sauvage took advantage of the relaxation of the building regulations in 1902, which gave greater freedom to use bow windows. The flats display a variety of triangular and facetted bays which contrast with the severity of Chabrol of Lecoeur's brick façades. Sauvage also gave great prominence to the eaves, using deep overhangs from pitched roofs (fig. 34).

The desire to break up the architectural mass of urban flats evident in Sauvage's façades was paralleled in proposals to open up the interior of the built volume, to let light and air into the centre of the building. In the year that the Rue Trétaigne was built, Eugène Hénard published his project for a boulevard around the Paris fortifications.[75] This included designs for housing which employed at large scale a technique which Perret used in his Rue Franklin flats. In the Rue Franklin, Perret minimised the internal light-well, and increased the façade of the small building by setting back its central portion. Experiments of this type, like Sauvage's use of the bay window, had been encouraged by the new building regulations of 1902, which allowed a reduction in the size of interior courts in return for the opening up of the main façade. Hénard applied the same principle as Perret by setting back his flats around large courts which were open to the street; he accepted light-wells for the service rooms, but his arrangement ensured that living rooms were on elevations overlooking open space.

Hénard's proposal was not built; but the principle of opening up the interior of the city block was taken up in housing projects of the early 1900s. This period saw an increase in the scale of construction by housing organisations, both financially and physically, led by the philanthropic foundations. Foremost among these in developing the

33 The flats built by Sauvage and Sarazin in Rue Trétaigne in Paris, for the Société des Logements Hygiéniques et à Bon Marché, in 1903; the concrete structural frame of the building is clearly visible on the front elevation.

design of workers' flats were the Groupe des Maisons Ouvrières, founded in 1900, and the Fondation Rothschild, formed in 1904. In their work, the 'bourgeois' model of workers' flats which had dominated since the late 1860s, and been confirmed in the work of the Société Philanthropique, was modified to create an autonomous model for cheap housing developments.[76]

The Société Philanthropique had built blocks of up to 55 flats, which were of small enough scale for the majority of flats to be served from a stair opening directly off the street. The most complex of its early blocks was the Rue d'Hautpoul, in which flats were arranged in three parallel blocks across the site, the first two linked by a shared staircase opening on to the street, the third separated by a small court and served by its own stair. This model was similar to the typical speculative form, in which a deep site was developed with parallel blocks separated by courts, though in the case of the Société Philanthropique flats the court was of a more generous size. This model was also used by the Groupe des Maisons Ouvrières for its first development, in the Rue Jeanne d'Arc in 1900. In this case three parallel blocks alternated with open courts linked by archways through the buildings.

This adoption of a speculative model by housing organisations was

34 An example of Sauvage's
elaboration of bays and
eaves, on the flats built in
Rue Sévero in Paris in 1905

dictated by the nature of the site: a deep site with a relatively narrow street frontage enforcing construction parallel, rather than at right angles, to the street. But in subsequent developments the Groupe des Maisons Ouvrières broke free of this model. Developments in the Rue Ernest Lefèvre, in 1905, and the Avenue Daumesnil, in 1908, provided nearly 200 flats each as opposed to the 80 at the Rue Jeanne d'Arc, and were constructed as complete quadrangles of building enclosing large courtyards.

This change had the effect of shifting the emphasis from the street to the court, which was the true centre of the developments. Entrance to the flats was no longer from stairs opening off the street, nor from the passageway linking rear courts, but was from the central court itself. A single major entrance past a concierge's lodge led from the street to the court, from which stairs gave access to the individual flats (fig. 35).

In one respect, the workers' flat had come full circle. From the large self-contained development of the Cité Napoléon with its single access from the street, via the smaller developments based on the model of bourgeois flats, the increase in the scale of construction in the early 1900s brought a return to the self-contained development. But this evolution was not a simple return to the Cité Napoléon model (see figs 2–4), which still retained its overtones of social threat. If the scale and the grouping of flats around an internal court reproduces the form of the Cité Napoléon, the disposition of the flats applied the 'bourgeois' model within the court. Thus in place of the glass-roofed access galleries within the main block of the Cité Napoléon, the Groupe des Maisons Ouvrières built a series of stairs giving access to only two or three flats per landing. This arrangement reinforced the independence of each individual dwelling, a fundamental principle to the housing reformers, within the larger scale of the development.

The housing built by the Groupe des Maisons Ouvrières represented a compromise by the reformers between the economic logic of constructing cheap urban flats, and their own insistence on the social value of the dwelling as an independent entity. If the form of the housing recalled early experiments, the distinction in the reformers' mind was clear. In an analysis of 'comfort in popular housing', published in 1904, a work which summarised the reformers' programme for urban flats, Emile Cheysson stated: 'I have just used the term: collective house; but I did not refer to barracks. For if we are forced by the necessities of space and the cost of land to bring together many families under one roof, it does not follow that we must resign ourselves to a model which is justifiably condemned by public opinion, and to which no one thinks of returning today.'[77]

Having determined that the independence of the flats would prevent the repetition of the unacceptable aspects of the Cité Napoléon, the reformers felt able to assimilate further elements from that housing type, notably the shared facilities which a large development could support. Cheysson advocated the introduction of laundries, restaurants, co-operative societies for food, sickness insurance societies, and even

35 Housing on the Avenue Daumesnil in Paris, designed by Labussière, and built by the Groupe des Maisons Ouvrières in 1908; an archway opening from the street leads to a central court, which gives access to the stairs to the individual flats.

meeting rooms and libraries. Cheysson acknowledged his concern that such institutions might bring about 'a sort of *phalanstérien* communism':[78] but the elaboration of their moderate view of co-operation in the 1880s and 1890s gave the reformers a position from which they could accept, and control, the introduction of communal facilities. If the spectre of the 'barracks' was still in the reformers' minds, they now felt confident enough to allow the occupants of a block of flats to meet each other.

The programme outlined by Cheysson was largely realised in the housing built by the Fondation Rothschild. The competition held by this foundation in 1905 served to establish the model of workers' flats in which the architectural device of opening up the block to light and air, the use of staircase as opposed to corridor access, and the integration of communal facilities, combined to create a particular type of housing, independent of bourgeois housing and of speculative cheap housing alike.

The Fondation Rothschild was founded to work 'for the improvement of conditions of workers' material existence'[79] by buying or constructing cheap housing in Paris. In addition to six members of the Rothschild family, the committee of the Fondation included the senior housing reformers Jules Siegfried, Georges Picot and Emile Cheysson. The competition for the design of housing on a site in east Paris attracted 127 entries. The entries were anonymous, and 25 were selected for the second stage. The reviewer in *La Construction Moderne* observed that these submissions fell into three broad categories: 'closed quadrilateral', 'separated blocks' and 'arrangement in a folded line'.[80] The most extreme project, in the last category, had been noted for its originality in the first stage. The accommodation was organised in two zig-zag lines,

36 Tony Garnier's entry to
the Fondation Rothschild
housing competition in
1905; Garnier broke
radically away from the
street, to create a series of
open courts.

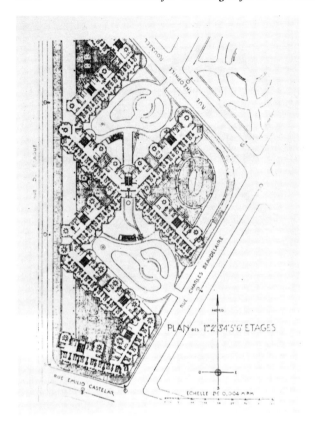

36 Tony Garnier's entry to the Fondation Rothschild housing competition in 1905; Garnier broke radically away from the street, to create a series of open courts.

crossing at the centre of the site. This organised the flats around six courts, all of which were open to the street (fig. 36).

This project was by Tony Garnier; it did not win the competition, but Christophe Pawlowski has noted that ideas from it were taken up by several other competitors in their second stage submissions.[81] The eventual winner was A. A. Rey, a pupil of Jules André. His plan presented an almost continuous line of building on the site boundary at ground level; but above he broke the building up to create three courts open to the street. Rey planned the courts to maximise ventilation through the scheme, while protecting it from the west and north winds. In addition to the open courts allowing in sun and air, he arranged the staircases as links between groups of flats; by leaving the stairs partially open, ventilation could be continuous through the courts and the building itself. The same concern for ventilation led Rey to propose 3 m ceiling heights, with windows stretching from 100 mm above the floor to ceiling level. At roof level, Rey proposed a roof garden with facilities for drying clothes (figs. 37, 38 and 39).

The Fondation did not construct Rey's plan in its competition form, but asked a group of the prizewinners to collaborate on the final design, opened in 1909. This retained the basic layout of Rey's plan, although the degree of openness between the courts and the street was reduced.

37 The elevation of A. A. Rey's winning entry in the Fondation Rothschild competition

The development provided 321 flats, and 36 workshops; communal facilities included baths, a crèche, a service for looking after older children outside school hours if their parents were not at home, a dispensary, courses for adults, and a kitchen which provided meals to be taken back to tenants' flats to eat. The building also had an innovatory system of waste chutes on each landing, and introduced electric lighting.[82]

The principle of open courts on which the Fondation Rothschild housing was based was taken up in other housing developments in the early 1900s.[83] But it was not the only way to open a building up to air and light. A. A. Rey himself envisaged an alternative architectural device, which he referred to in an article in the *Town Planning Review* in 1914. 'The magic formula of health, "more air and more light", which has been adopted by our day, is found to be fully satisfied by this method of construction by receding stages.'[84] This was a technique which had already been used in a block of bourgeois flats on the Rue Vavin in Paris, built by Henri Sauvage in 1912; the vertical street façade was replaced by a series of terraces stepping back from the street, opening both the street and the building to greater light. Sauvage did not use this form of construction in the cheap flats which he built for the Société des Logements Hygiéniques et à Bon Marché in the early 1900s; but after the First World War he was commissioned by the City of Paris to build a block of cheap housing in the Rue des Amiraux. In this block, Sauvage combined the use of terraces with the introduction of communal facilities to create an integrated building form, in which the flats step back from the street line to enclose a skylit swimming pool (fig. 40).

If Sauvage's housing was a successful architectural resolution of a particular brief, it did not establish itself as a general model for the integration of housing with communal facilities; the swimming pool of the Rue des Amiraux was perfectly adapted to the rooflit space within the centre of the block, but the number of facilities so adapted was limited. Rather, it was the simpler building form of the Fondation Rothschild model, in which communal facilities were built into the lower floors of the building, or left as completely independent pavilions, which

38 The plan of Rey's scheme, showing the way in which he arranged the flats around courts open to the street

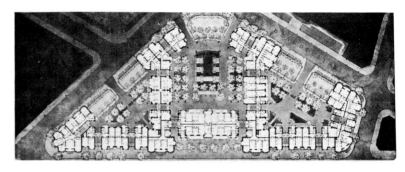

39 Rey's diagrams of wind circulation through the courts and open stairs of the building

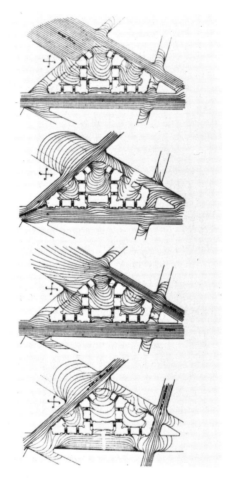

provided the model for later housing. This was confirmed in 1912, when the city of Paris introduced a programme of direct public housing construction to complement the work of the large foundations. The competition held by the city in 1912, to find the designs for its first two blocks, confirmed the principles of design established in the Rothschild competition seven years earlier. The competition jury observed that the entries contained certain ideas 'which it seems will have to constitute

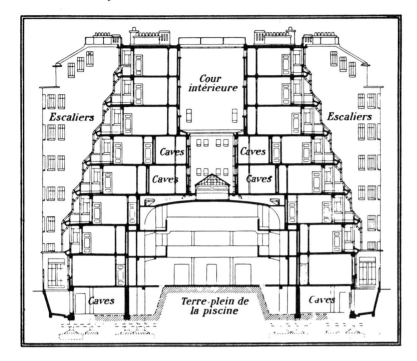

Cour
intérieure

Escaliers

Escaliers

Caves

Caves

Caves

Caves

Caves

Terre-plein de
la piscine

Caves

40 Housing in the Rue des
Amiraux, Paris, built by
Henri Sauvage for the City of
Paris in 1922; the flats step
back over an internal roof-lit
swimming pool.

from now on the directing principles of the construction of cheap housing...Thus the majority of the competitors and, furthermore, all those placed by the jury, readily apply the principle of the open court.'[85]

The housing programme of the city of Paris was thus to be the natural continuation of the work of the Groupe des Maisons Ouvrières and of the Fondation Rothschild. The 1912 competition was organised by Labussière, architect for the Groupe des Maisons Ouvrières, and the competition brief took up the two types of flat which the Groupe had favoured. The Emile Zola site was to be developed with flats containing separate kitchen and dining room, with a variable number of bedrooms. In distinction to the 'normal' type, the Henri Becque housing was to consist of a more basic type, in which a single 'salle commune' functioned as kitchen, dining, living and bedroom, with bedrooms opening from it; the maximum rent of this type was to be only 275 fr. per year[86] (fig. 41).

In addition to reinforcing the model for cheap urban housing, the Paris competition of 1912, together with a second competition in 1913, and the housing programme to which these competitions gave rise, created the opportunity to form a body of 'housing architects'. When the city's public housing office, initially established in 1914, started actively to implement a programme of construction after the war, it appointed a group of salaried architects to work on housing projects. Of the five architects initially appointed, two were prizewinners in the pre-war competitions, while the other three had all worked for the Fondation Rothschild.[87]

41 The winning schemes in
the competition for the
design of cheap housing held
by the City of Paris in 1913

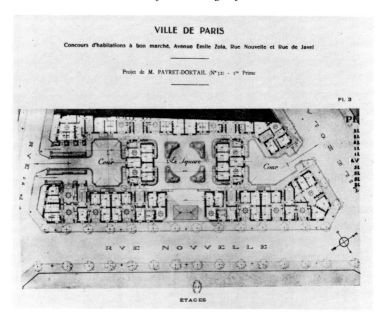

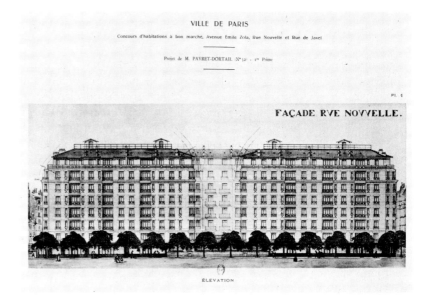

a. Two views of Avenue Emile Zola, project by Payret-Dortail

Meanwhile, in the city's suburbs, Henri Sellier was starting to
elaborate his policy of satellite communities based on the Garden City.
Faced with the problem of selecting architects for public projects, he
decided to accept the expertise already found by the Paris competitions.
Each of the winning architects or teams for the six sites which had been
the subject of the competitions, was asked to work for the Seine public
housing office on projects outside Paris.

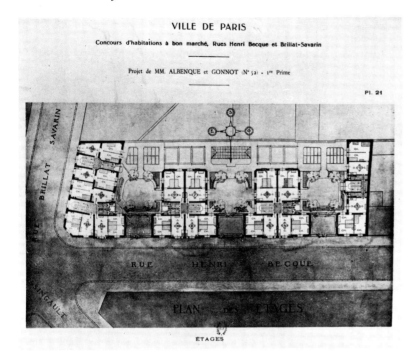

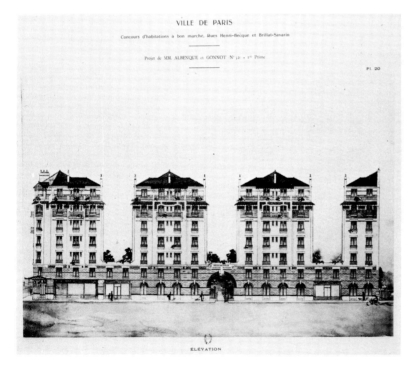

b. Two views of Rue Henri Becque, project by Albenque and Gonnot

The architectural teams created by the City of Paris, and the Seine public housing office, brought together architects who were to spend a large part of their careers in the study and construction of housing. Some private housing societies, such as the Société des Logements Economiques et à Bon Marché, had been able to employ one architect on a series of buildings; but it was the public housing offices which had the resources and continuity of workload to set up a permanent organisation directed to the construction of housing. With the advent of the large housing societies and the public housing offices in the early 1900s, the nature of housing design was thus gradually transformed. Muller and Cacheux had established themselves as experts in this field through a combination of philanthropic concern and technical ability. Now the concern and ability took on a professional character as architects accepted their role as the practitioners of housing reform.

Reform and the provision of new housing

20

❖◇❖

The reformers and the housing market

It is simple to obtain the plans for healthy, comfortable houses from an architect, but it is less easy to persuade investors to make them a reality.[1]

This fact, stated here by Emile Cacheux in 1880, was at the heart of the 'housing problem'. The strands of reform discussed in the previous section all made a significant contribution to the evolution of housing reform, but that contribution could only be partial so long as the housing market failed to provide a sufficient number of suitable dwellings. The housing debate which took place around 1850 had left the construction of housing as the responsibility of the private sector, but as has been seen, the housing market in Paris consistently failed to renew the stock of cheap housing in the city. Providing a decreasing proportion of that stock, cheap dwellings with an annual rent of 500 fr. or below were characterised by overcrowded conditions and rising rents. The families which occupied these dwellings were not able to provide the solvent demand which would have encouraged investors to expand this section of the market.

If reformers were to alter this situation, they must acknowledge the problems inherent in the housing market. In this respect, the late 1870s and 1880s were a key period, as reformers identified the gap between the economic rent of housing on the private market and the ability of many working families to pay. The need to study the reasons for the failure of the housing market was emphasised by the demographic characteristics of this period. The years after 1876 saw an exceptionally high rate of migration from rural areas to urban centres throughout France. This created a pressure on urban housing markets which brought to the fore the problems facing workers trying to find housing. At the same time the country's declining birth rate was seen as being related to housing conditions. 'We marry less than before, and above all we no longer have enough children: there, in two words, is our national affliction.' Thus Emile Cheysson raised the problem in 1880, at a meeting of the Société d'Economie Sociale devoted to the question of housing.[2] If workers could be offered healthy dwellings, large enough to have a family, they would be encouraged to have children, and those children would have a better chance of growing into healthy adults.

Allied in this way to the strength of the French population, the question of housing took on a new importance. The action taken in the

413

1850s had as its aim to prevent bad housing conditions developing to the extent that they posed a threat to society as a whole, either through the spread of epidemics, or through social unrest. By the 1880s bad housing conditions were seen as threatening society in a more insidious manner, by inhibiting the natural growth of healthy citizens. The problem could no longer be dismissed as one of superficial lack of hygiene. It was a fundamental problem derived from the relationship between working families and the dwellings available to them. That relationship found its expression in the housing market and it was therefore to the market that the reformers turned, and in particular to the specific workings of the housing market in Paris.

The work of the Paris Commission des Logements Insalubres provided an important source of information on the physical characteristics of the Paris housing stock. Dr du Mesnil was able to draw attention to the consequences of the reconstruction of Paris during the Second Empire, when he spoke at the 1878 International Hygiene Congress, held in the city. Du Mesnil observed that

in rapidly creating large streets, through populous quarters, first the over-crowding in all the adjacent streets was increased, then on both sides of the new street, vast new blocks have been erected...the numerous inhabitants of the demolished dwellings, obliged to find a shelter immediately, have crowded, whatever the cost, either as we said above, into the adjacent streets, or sometimes into huts built by their occupants, with salvaged materials, in the disordered areas of the zone which Paris has recently annexed.[3]

The economic factors which lay behind this picture were filled in more slowly. But the study which Emile Muller and Emile Cacheux made in the late 1870s enabled them to indicate the basic problem within the housing market. Drawing on their own experience of building, and on a survey which they carried out of the budgets of a random sample of working families in Paris, they were able to compare the two sides of the housing market. Allowing a net return of 5% to the proprietor, a figure which represented an average return on property at the period, they arrived at an annual rent between 344 fr. and 388 fr. for a newly constructed flat of three rooms and kitchen. But this figure was well above the typical range of rents which they found in their survey, centring on 200 fr. to 250 fr.[4]

Optimistically, Cacheux and Muller dwelt on the fact that their survey also revealed that a minority of families had a high enough income to support a higher rent, and also to set aside some money as savings. They considered that these families were able to afford the annual payment of 470 fr. necessary to buy an individual house in Paris. They were therefore able to maintain the reformers' ideal, even for Paris, and Cacheux was to go on to realise that ideal on a small scale in his construction of cottages for sale to working families.

But even Cacheux had to accept the limitation of this ideal. Speaking to the Société d'Economie Sociale in 1880 he noted that only 4% of the families in the survey were in a position to buy a house. The inability of the majority of the workers to afford the rent of a three-room flat was reflected in the overcrowding which Cacheux noted in the vast majority of the dwellings he visited. Recognising the economic pressure which was bringing this situation about, Cacheux had already approached the government in 1878, with a proposal for State loans at cheap rates of interest, to allow a reduction in the rents charged to tenants.[5] Cacheux was to renew this proposal in 1882, by which time the boom in the construction industry had made the housing market a topic of discussion in the press, and had added weight to Cacheux's arguments.

As early as 1879, *L'Economiste Français*, the journal of the defenders of the private market, had drawn attention to the problems associated with the current increase in construction and population in Paris. 'Previously, the worker often had difficulty in paying his rent; now he has difficulty in finding somewhere to live.'[6] The editor of the journal, Paul Leroy-Beaulieu, took up the question of urban growth and speculation, warning against ill-considered developments based on money borrowed at high rates of interest. This article was prompted by the recent formation of several development companies. Two and a half years later, Leroy-Beaulieu was able to comment on the housing which these companies had built.[7] Leroy-Beaulieu noted that, while the main increase in the population of the city had been caused by the influx of workers, the majority of the housing built had been at the expensive end of the market. Anticipating a slump in construction, as the rents of expensive property dropped due to overproduction, he urged investors to turn towards cheaper housing, where production was notably lacking. Leroy-Beaulieu traced the reluctance of investors to finance cheap housing to the problems associated with managing such housing. It was easier to build flats for four or five tenants, let on leases of up to twelve years, with a security of rent payment, than to build for forty or fifty families, with leases of three months, and with the possibility of non-payment and consequently eviction proceedings against tenants.

Leroy-Beaulieu's intervention in the debate over the housing market throws the reformers' position into clearer focus, defining it against the position adopted by the supporters of the classic free market. Leroy-Beaulieu had to acknowledge the fact to which Cacheux had also drawn attention, that new construction in Paris was failing to provide the cheap dwellings which were evidently needed. But, faithful to the freedom of the market, he could not accept that this failure would be resolved by taking special measures in relation to a particular sector of the market. His proposals were of a general nature, affecting the housing market as a whole by means of credit facilities and tax changes. These proposals were intended to avert the danger which he saw in the position of some housing reformers, urging the creation of a 'privileged' category in the housing market. This position had been outlined in Leroy-Beaulieu's own journal the week before the first of his articles on housing construction in April 1882, by Emile Cacheux. Noting the discrepancy between the rents of new flats, and the ability of working families to pay, Cacheux restated his suggestion for low interest loans, to be provided by the public authorities to builders conforming to certain conditions relating to rent levels and housing standards.[8]

From a common starting point, then, two solutions emerged. Both Leroy-Beaulieu and Cacheux acknowledged that the housing market of the early 1880s was failing to provide suitable new housing. But while Leroy-Beaulieu insisted that this situation must be corrected by maintaining the integrity of the housing market as a whole, taking action only in relation to that whole, Cacheux was effectively admitting the possibility that the 'housing market' was not one, but several. If this possibility was accepted, it was conceivable that action could be taken with respect to the housing market for workers, without touching the market for more expensive housing.

The distinction between these two solutions was critical to the development of housing reform. For the reformers were not fundamentally opposed to the principle of the market economy, and thus needed to find a way of justifying action, while not threatening that economy. By distinguishing between the market for cheap housing and that for expensive housing, and by arguing that private investors showed no interest in the cheap housing market, reformers could advocate a degree of intervention in the cheap housing market, without abandoning their commitment to the market economy as a whole.

The difference of opinion between reformers such as Cacheux and economists like Leroy-Beaulieu was thus not one of fundamental principles, but more of how those principles should be interpreted. Emile Cacheux's own preference for the unaided operation of the market economy is indicated by the fact that by early 1883, when he observed an increase in the number of cheap flats being offered by developers in the outer arrondissements of Paris, he withdrew his proposal for low-interest loans. Moreover, throughout the discussion of the housing market, both Leroy-Beaulieu and Cacheux were active in founding a limited dividend housing society in Paris to build houses for sale to working families.[9] Both men saw such societies as offering a model to private investors, demonstrating that particular forms of housing were economically viable.

But the limited dividend housing societies were to take on a greater importance than that of being simple models. In moving away from his proposal for low-interest loans, Cacheux had given a second reason for his change of opinion. This derived from his study of the effect of the 1852 housing subsidy of 10 million francs. Cacheux concluded that the limited use made of this money derived from the conditions which were necessarily placed on builders, to ensure that the subsidy provided suitable housing.[10] It is certainly true that the most remarkable developments built with the aid of a subsidy after 1852 were based on philanthropic motivation, and were not dependent on the subsidy for their existence. On the other hand, some of the speculative developers tempted towards cheap housing by the offer of a subsidy either considerably reduced their initial projects, or decided to forego the subsidy altogether in order to develop a more commercially profitable scheme.[11] The 1852 subsidy showed that the number of societies whose aims were in accordance with those of the subsidies was limited, while the power of the subsidies to convince speculators to invest in housing was also limited.

It was in this respect that the limited dividend company was to take on an increasingly important role. Cacheux's flirtation with and rejection of State loans in the early 1880s can be seen as a recognition of the fact that the housing market for workers had failed, but that the machinery to create a 'substitution market' did not exist. Hence his relief when he believed that private developers were resolving the problem by taking up the construction of cheap housing. The development of limited dividend companies in the 1880s was to alter this picture. As the number of such companies grew, and particularly as a handful of important companies were formed in several urban centres in the 1880s, the basis of a 'substitution market' was to be brought into being. The existence of these companies orientated towards the construction of flats or houses for workers, meant that a market was established which was able to accept the constraints which inevitably accompanied the creation of special sources of finance, or special tax concessions.

Despite Cacheux's optimism in 1883, the need to regard the provision of workers' housing as a distinct part of the housing market was reinforced by the evolution of the market in the later 1880s. Raffalovich's study, published in 1887, drew together information which confirmed the discrepancy between the economic rent of new housing, and the capacity of workers to pay. Similarly, when he prepared his study on workers' housing for the international jury at the 1889 Exposition Universelle in Paris, Georges Picot noted the particular problems associated with the market for workers' housing. Picot was no enemy of the market economy; but when discussing the system of letting and management of workers' flats he was prepared to admit that 'from the congestion of towns is born, as one sees, a quite immoral but lucrative industry, hardly threatened by competition, and making weigh on the worker a tyranny which he revenges by nourishing in his heart a hatred against all proprietors'.[12] Picot had to acknowledge that the 'normal' mechanism of the market in resolving imbalance between supply and demand was not able to function in relation to workers' housing; investors had little interest in spending large sums of capital to build new housing when the shortage of housing was resolved by levels of overcrowding which enabled working families to meet the increasing costs of rents.

The reformers' approach to the construction of new housing was thus to follow two lines from the 1880s. Having identified the housing market for workers as a distinct market, with its own problems, they promoted the formation of housing societies whose prime object was to construct a particular type of housing, rather than to make the highest possible commercial profit. The roots of this housing society movement can be seen in the development of industrial housing, a category which could be entirely independent of any general housing market, and of the limited dividend and co-operative societies which started to occupy the sector of the housing market which private investors were reluctant to fill. Parallel to this development of the organisations to build cheap housing, the reformers worked to set up a structure to provide finance for these organisations. This structure developed from the discussion of the housing market in the early 1880s, and was established by housing legislation in 1894. This law confirmed the existence of a distinct market for cheap dwellings, defined in the law under the term *habitations à bon marché*.

21

◇◇◇

Housing for industry

One important type of housing existed independent of the private market; this was the housing provided by some employers for their own workforce. The benefit which an employer anticipated in constructing housing was not primarily the return which the houses yielded on capital invested. Employers were thus in many cases able to provide housing which fulfilled the housing reformers' aspirations, without making it too expensive for their workers to afford. However, the financial basis of the housing, and the low return which employers accepted, indicated the unattractiveness of such housing to the investors of the private market.

The initial incentive to an employer to build housing was often the necessity of attracting workers to an area in which housing was scarce. This was particularly the case with industries based in rural areas close to natural resources. Thus in the village of Montceau-les-Mines housing was built by the Compagnie des Mines de Blanzy 'to attract and settle mining workers, whose recruitment is difficult in the surrounding region'.[1] Beyond this basic incentive, the construction of housing formed part of the wider scope of industrial patronage. Measures such as the provision of cheap bread, or a free medical service combined social responsibility with economic good sense; the workers' health and welfare benefited, but the employer in turn benefited from a fitter workforce. Other forms of patronage, such as pensions schemes, helped the worker in his old age. But they also increased his dependence on his employer, and made him less likely to move to another job, since he would be unable to take his pension with him. Depending on one's point of view, such patronage could be considered 'a social obligation, or a good economic transaction'.[2]

Housing formed a natural part of this system. Like a free medical service, hygienic housing helped to ensure the worker's good health. Like a pension scheme, a comfortable house rented cheaply from the employer encouraged the worker to remain. These advantages outweighed the low return, and in some cases direct subsidy, which housing involved. The employer could simply regard expenditure on housing as 'part of the outgoings on tools and labour'.[3] Like those outgoings, it ensured a satisfactory return to the employer, indirectly if not directly.

Examples of housing built by employers for industrial workers can be found before the end of the eighteenth century. In Le Creusot, housing was built for workers at the Fonderie Royale established there in the 1780s, and at the turn of the century the Fonderie was housing all of its employees. But it was particularly in conjunction with the growth of industry from the 1830s that the construction of housing was taken up on a larger scale by employers. Le Creusot itself developed more rapidly from this time, after the foundry was taken over by the Schneider family in 1836. It was at this period also that the development of Montceau-les-Mines began. In Alsace, the Mulhouse industrialist André Koechlin and the Hartmann Company were both building housing in the 1830s. Jean Zuber, whose communication to the Mulhouse Société Industrielle in 1851 stimulated the discussion which led to the foundation of the Société des Cités Ouvrières had built a few houses adjacent to his paper factory in Mulhouse in the 1840s. In northern France, the Compagnie des Mines d'Anzin already owned over 1,000 dwellings by the end of the 1840s.[4]

Initially some employers experimented with different types of housing. The Compagnie de Blanzy started by constructing four large blocks, each containing more than 150 flats before turning to individual houses. The Schneider family took over several blocks of flats built before they acquired the foundry; they added two large blocks in the 1840s, providing more than 200 dwellings altogether, in buildings of four storeys. By 1852 they owned a total of 18 blocks, housing 662 families.[5] André Koechlin's housing in the 1830s included three-storey houses with a flat on each floor, while the Hartmann company built a block of five-storey flats providing two-room flats for its workers. However, after the variety of housing tried in the 1830s and 1840s, most employers shared the conclusion of the Compagnie de Blanzy, that individual houses were preferable to large blocks. This view was a reflection of the discussion of housing in the 1850s. The role of housing in creating social stability, evolved by the housing reformers, was related as much to the need to ensure a steady workforce for industry, as to the desire to improve physical and moral conditions in urban areas. Indeed, it was an industrialist from the cotton factories of Mulhouse, rather than a philanthropist from Paris, who sponsored the development which enshrined the reformers' idealised version of the individual house.

A survey of patronage at the time of the 1867 Exposition in Paris confirmed that the individual house was well established in the provision of housing by employers.[6] Some employers did provide accommodation in large blocks, but these were generally dormitories for single workmen or women. The majority of the housing, and particularly the family housing, was in the form of small houses with gardens. The most notable exception was the Familistère constructed by J. B. A. Godin in Guise (see fig. 5), which tried to provide a genuine alternative, both to the forms of housing provided by other employers and to the dependence of the occupants on their employer.

The Familistère provided healthy dwellings of reasonable size and standard; in this, Godin's aims were those of other industrialists building housing, or of the housing reformers. But the social ideal on which the building was based, and the physical form adopted to implement the ideal, were not generally shared. If the reformers accepted the value of co-operation, it was as a complement, rather than as a replacement, of existing relations between employers and workers. If they tolerated blocks of flats, it was in the 'bourgeois' form of dwellings off a staircase, not the 'Social Palace' of dwellings grouped as a community.

The employers who became involved in the construction of more traditional forms of housing shared with Godin the belief that housing was itself a means of enabling workers to achieve a new position in society. But their disagreement came over exactly what that new position would be. In adopting the individual house, employers were generally endorsing the moderate views of the housing reformers, in defence of a gradual improvement of the status quo. Georges Picot was to see this process culminating as workers left the guardianship of the employer to reach a state of emancipation by rising to the hallowed status of proprietor.

Houses for sale; houses for rent

The Salon of 1869 included drawings of housing designed for the Compagnie des Mines d'Aniche in the mining area of North France. This company constructed two groups of houses, which employees could buy at cost price. A deposit of a quarter of the cost was required, and the remainder was paid off, with no interest, at 20 fr. per month. To help workers save for their deposit, the company could arrange for a proportion of the workers' salary to be paid every fortnight into the Caisse d'Epargne in Aniche. Other companies provided housing on similar terms. The Manufacture de Peugeot Jackson in Doubs sold dwellings at their cost price of 2,950 fr. in monthly instalments. In Moselle, the Compagnie des Cristalleries de St Louis sold its houses in instalments over ten or more years; this company also provided a garden of 500 m² at no extra cost.[7]

In these cases, the company was effectively performing the function of a housing society: providing the capital for construction which was reimbursed by the worker over a number of years. Unlike a private society, though, the company was making little or no interest on its capital. However, some companies chose to set up independent housing societies to finance construction; the pioneering society at Mulhouse was initiated in this way. As a general society, not tied to any specific company, it was operated as a private housing society, and its main influence was as a model for later societies working within the private market. But the structure of the society was equally suitable to organisation by an employer for his own workforce. This possibility was followed up in several towns in the industrial area around Mulhouse.

In Beaucourt, the clockmaking firm of Japy Frères started building houses financed directly by the firm in 1862; but in 1864 the company established a housing society to build detached houses for sale. The society's capital of 100,000 fr. was made up of shares of 100 fr.; in contrast to the expensive shares of the Mulhouse society, which at 5,000 fr. each were taken up by wealthy industrialists, these modest shares could be bought by 'a large number of simple workers, foremen, employees and tradesmen in the area'.[8] The workers's repayment covered the basic cost of the house, and 5% interest on the capital; on this basis, the society financed the construction of 97 houses during its first year of operation.[9]

In Guebwiller, to the north of Mulhouse, the spinning mill of Bourcart et Fils had begun building houses to let in 1854, using designs by Emile Muller. From 1860, construction adjacent to these houses, and on a second site, was continued by a housing society, in which Bourcart were shareholders. By 1865, the society had built 90 houses to supplement the 49 built by the company directly. In Colmar, Antoine Herzog provided the majority of the capital for a housing society founded in 1866. With a capital of 1 million francs, the society had built 90 houses by 1867, with another 90 planned. The societies in Beaucourt, Guebwiller and Colmar were all located close to the pioneer society of Mulhouse. But industrialists further afield also followed the example of Mulhouse. Near Lille, in northern France, the Scrive brothers formed a society in 1853 to finance housing for workers in their factory. At the time of the Exposition Universelle held in 1867, at least two other companies, one in Doubs and one in Eure, were in the process of setting up societies to sell houses on the model of the Mulhouse society.[10]

Another method by which employers helped their workers to become owners of their house was by means of mortgage loans. The Compagnie de Blanzy acquired 200 hectares at Bois Roulot to develop in this way. The company divided the land into plots and laid out roads; miners and workers could buy land at cost price by repayments over ten years. The company provided loans, also repayable over ten years, to enable workers to have their own house built. In this way Picot's ideal of the worker building his own house to his own taste was realised for some at least. By 1866 this little community consisted of 99 houses. The company charged no interest on the loans, although if a worker left the company before paying off the loan, he was obliged to repay the interest.[11] The Peugeot company in Doubs also offered loans, but unlike the Blanzy company, it charged 5% interest. By 1867, 38 loans averaging just less than 2,000 fr. each had been granted to workers to build houses for themselves.[12] At this date, the Peugeot company employed 800 workers, and Blanzy 3,500. Picot's ideal was thus only enjoyed by a minority, even within these companies.

Both Peugeot and Blanzy were outsized by the Schneider organisation, which dominated the growth of Le Creusot. At this factory alone it employed 8,500 people in 1867, and the town which had grown up around the factory housed 25,000 people. Schneider, and also Blanzy, built some housing for rent for their workers – by the end of the century they had both built more than 1,000 houses. But Schneider concentrated

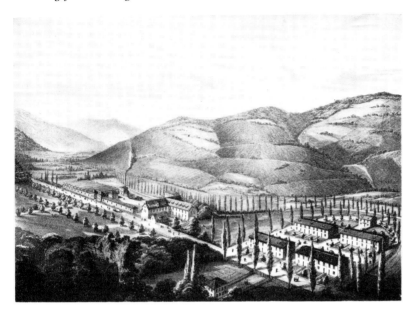

42 The initial development of housing next to the Bourcart et Fils mill in Guebwiller; this housing was built from designs by Emile Muller in 1854.

particularly on providing loans for construction, doing so from the earliest days of the company in the 1830s. By 1889 it had granted over 2,300 loans, totalling more than 3 million francs; at the turn of the century the total stood at 4.5 million francs, the majority of which had been repaid by the borrowers who were then fully fledged as property owners.[13]

The fact that capital employed to build housing for sale was ultimately repaid was a major advantage to the employer. The money did not remain tied up in property, as it did with rented accommodation, particularly if the rents were subsidised. Schneider's 4.5 million francs worth of housing loans were thus financed at any one time by a figure of only a few hundred thousand francs. But this advantage to the employer was paid for by the worker. For while employers could afford to subsidise heavily the rents of housing on which they retained the basic security of its capital value, they were less prepared to subsidise houses for sale to the same extent, as this would involve actual capital loss. The subsidies which were granted on houses for sale might take the form of a reduction or complete suppression of interest, as at Aniche or Blanzy. Alternatively, if interest were charged, a direct subsidy in the form of land or development costs might be made: at Beaucourt, Pierre Japy donated the land. In either case, though, the basic capital cost of the house, whether built by the company, or by the worker through a loan, remained to be repaid in total.

The housing at Guebwiller and Beaucourt illustrates the typical cost of owner occupation to the worker, and the standard of accommodation which he could buy. At Guebwiller, the cost of buying a house in the mid-1860s ranged from 20 fr. to 30 fr. per month over 15 years, after an initial down payment of one tenth of the cost. At Beaucourt, the expense of detached housing was offset by the economy of single-storey

43 Typical house built for workers at the Japy factory in Beaucourt; a single-storey house, with the possibility of additional rooms in the attic space

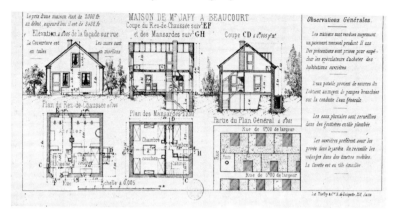

construction. Moreover, buyers did not have to pay for the land. In the 1860s, the four-roomed houses could thus be bought, without down payment, for 21 fr. 55 c. per month over 11 years; a down payment of 300 fr. reduced this to only 18 fr. 55 c. The accommodation provided in these houses was similar, with three rooms and a kitchen. At Guebwiller these were planned on two floors in an arrangement of wide frontage back-to-back houses; at Beaucourt they were all on a single level. In both cases there was a small cellar, and the attic was accessible; the houses generally had an internal closet, upstairs at Guebwiller, and off the kitchen at Beaucourt. The houses did not have an individual water supply, but at Beaucourt some occupants took advantage of the products they were making, installing Japy pumps to take water to their sink (figs. 42 and 43).

From the employer's point of view, the sale of houses had certain disadvantages in comparison with renting. Once sold, the house passed out of the employer's control; occupants could not be moved out if they ceased to work for the company, and, if they chose, they could sell the property to a third party, quite unconnected with the company. Georges Picot noted that at Anzin the 'thrifty worker' had in some cases been replaced, as houses were turned into *cabarets*.[14] In contrast, by retaining ownership, the employer had a monopoly of control over the housing stock. The letting of houses could be restricted to workers in the factory; even if a retired worker was allowed to remain in a rented house, the employer knew that the house would ultimately revert to the firm's housing stock. Housing could also be used to exercise control over the workers themselves. Thus some employers offered their workers an incentive to good behaviour and regular work by the prospect of reduced rents after a number of years service. Occupants were encouraged to look after their house by prizes awarded for the best-kept home, or the best-decorated façade. Subsidised rents were an incentive to workers to remain in his employment rather than move elsewhere. They were also less of a financial commitment than they might appear, for in the enclosed market of employer housing, the wage levels could be fixed to reflect the level of rents. As an extension of the tools of the factory, a stock of housing could be used as a positive asset by the employer.

The survey of patronage at the time of the 1867 Exposition showed the majority of respondents who were involved in housing to be providing housing for rent; furthermore, a majority of those who did help their workers to acquire dwellings, also provided rented housing. The type of housing for rent, or provided free of charge, ranged from detached houses with their own gardens to accommodation in a dormitory block. Within this range it was naturally the independent houses which came closest to the housing reformers' ideal. While the housing exhibits at the Exposition included blocks of flats for urban housing, it was examples of individual houses which dominated the contributions from industrial concerns. These examples show how employers, set apart from the private housing market, were able to provide spacious, hygienic housing at rents which their workers could afford.

The Compagnie de Blanzy exhibited a pair of semi-detached houses which each provided 39 m² of habitable space, in four rooms; the roof space gave a further 25 m². Construction and land totalled 2,200 fr. per dwelling, and so the rent of 4 fr. 50 c. per month returned only 2.5% gross. This would barely cover charges and repairs, so that the company can have made little or no net profit on its capital. The Société des Mines de Carmaux exhibited a similar house, though in terraced form; two rooms on the ground floor gave a basic habitable area of 31 m², which could be increased by using the roof space; outside, each house had a pigsty. The rent for the house was 4 fr. 20 c. per month, giving a gross return on construction capital of 2.5%, as at Blanzy. However, this return was not always realised at Carmaux, as the company allowed its most deserving workers to live rent free, and gave rent reductions to the families who kept their home cleanest.[15]

The Compagnie des Mines d'Anzin exhibited three dwellings in 1867, which had slightly higher space standards. A two-room, single-storey house provided 42 m²; two-storey houses, grouped either as back-to-backs or in a terrace, gave four rooms with a total area of over 50 m². The rents for these houses were 6 fr. or 6 fr. 50 c. per month, which returned about 4% gross. The company's earlier housing, which had been in the form of detached houses, returned rather less with rents of 5 fr. to 6 fr. giving only 2.5% gross.[16]

The design of the terraced house at Anzin allowed for an alternative arrangement, by placing the stair in a lobby against the exterior wall: if required, the house could also be occupied as two units. This principle was used for one of the houses exhibited by the Schneider company, although in this case the separation into two dwellings was permanent, as the stair to the upper dwelling was external. The dwellings were built as a block of four units, two on each floor. Each flat had two rooms, giving a habitable area of 42 m². Costing just over 2,000 fr. per flat for construction and land, the flats were let for 8 fr. 30 c. per month. Schneider also exhibited a single-storey terraced house, which the company now preferred to the flats. It had two rooms, with a habitable area of 39 m². The cost of this house was similar to the cost of the flats, at 1,900 fr., and it was let at the same rent. On these two types of

44 A house built by the
Compagnie des Mines
d'Anzin, representative of the
housing type established for
industrial housing by the late
1860s

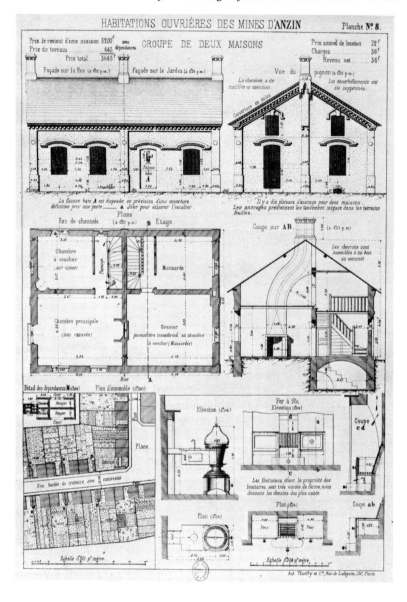

housing, Schneider were therefore making about 5% gross, which should have left a small return after expenses and repairs. As at Carmaux, though, some tenants had reduced rents: at half cost for 700 deserving workers, and free of charge for office workers and foremen.[17]

With the exception of the flats at Le Creusot all of these houses follow similar principles in design (see, e.g., fig. 44). In each case there is a small cellar, two rooms on the ground floor, and two further rooms, or a more or less habitable roof space above. The ground-floor rooms are arranged to give one large room, a *salle commune*. This has a fireplace for cooking, and heating the house; acting as a general living room during the day, it would also be used for sleeping at night. The size of this room varied from 19 m² or 23 m² at Anzin, and 20 m² at Carmaux, to 25 m² at

Blanzy and Le Creusot. The remaining small room on the ground floor and the upper rooms were simple bedrooms, so that these houses generally provided at least the three rooms which the reformers advocated for family housing. The closet was usually outside the house; the kitchen might have a drain for waste water, but a water supply was not taken to individual houses.

In contrast to these houses, those built for sale in Alsace provided a kitchen separate from the living room. The latter was thus rather smaller than in the examples above: 18 m² at Guebwiller, 15 m² to 17 m² at Mulhouse, and only 11 m² at Beaucourt. This difference relates to regional preferences rather than the fact that these houses were for sale. The main contrast between the rented houses and those for sale was simply one of cost to the occupants. The single-storey houses at Beaucourt, costing just over 2,000 fr., were of comparable capital cost to several of the rented houses exhibited in 1867. But where the rented houses cost only 4 fr. to 10 fr. per month, the Beaucourt house cost around 20 fr. The housing for sale reflected the constraints of the private market, in which capital must be recovered and interest paid. In contrast, the rented house was intrinsically related to the company for which its tenants worked; as such it was free of any direct link to the private market.

The basic pattern of the individual houses built by employers had been established by the time of the 1867 Exposition. But the planning of the settlements in which the houses were grouped was as important to the success of the housing as the detail design. The larger developments, such as Le Creusot or Montceau-les-Mines, grew into towns in their own right, providing all the facilities required by a community. But initially these facilities might need to be encouraged by the employer, and in small developments this was not always done. The *corons*, stark rows of houses set down adjacent to pits in the mining areas, provided little incentive for a community to establish itself.[18] The Anzin company tried to overcome this by building its houses in groups of 60 to 80. Each group had a bakehouse, well, crèche and some other facilities.[19] But still such small groups, sometimes set some way from the nearest town, were not large enough to grow into towns themselves.

The development of 500 houses built by the Menier factory at Noisiel, near Paris, from 1874, was planned as a self-contained community which would avoid the problems of isolated clusters of houses. The houses were arranged in a rectilinear street pattern running from a central square. Around this square were grouped a school, restaurant and shops. The village also included a bakery, town hall, fire station, post office, and old people's home. In terms of its facilities, the village was not unlike the Familistère at Guise. But its organisation was as different as its physical form. The Menier family retained ownership of the houses and facilities they had provided; the company – and the Menier family in particular – remained the generous benefactors and did not imitate Godin in allowing the workers to run, or to own, their village[20] (fig. 45).

The rectilinear planning of the Noisiel village was typical of the

45 The Menier workers'
village, built from 1874 on a
strictly rectilinear street
pattern, typical of industrial
housing developments at that
time

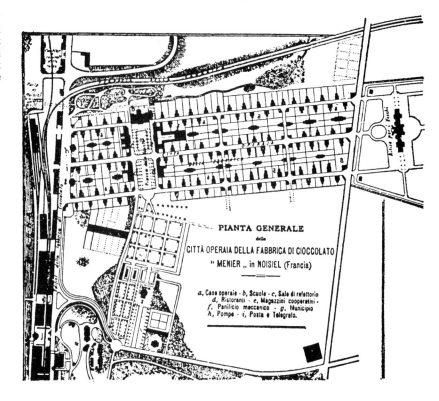

PIANTA GENERALE
della
CITTÀ OPERAIA DELLA FABBRICA DI CIOCCOLATO
" MENIER ,, in NOISIEL (Francia)

a, Case operaie · *b*, Scuola · *c*, Sale di refettorio
d, Ristoranti · *e*, Magazzini cooperativi ·
f, Panificio meccanico · *g*, Municipio
h, Pompe · *i*, Posta e Telegrafo.

nineteenth-century industrial housing developments. But in the early
1900s, it was industrial housing which first reflected, if only superficially,
the new ideas in planning emanating from England. The Compagnie des
Mines de Dourges, in north France, started by building housing similar
to that at Mulhouse or Noisiel. But in 1907 and 1908 it constructed
what was claimed as the 'first Garden City in France'.[21] For a group of
74 houses this was an exaggerated claim. Nonetheless, the inauguration
of the group in 1909 indicates the importance of this development to
the reformers, as it was organised by the Association des Cités-Jardins
de France, and the Section d'Hygiène Urbaine et Rurale of the Musée
Social, and was presided over by Jules Siegfried. The arrangement of
curving, tree-lined streets of the new development, in addition to giving
'a most aesthetic appearance', had 'the major hygienic advantage of
increasing the circulation of air, and the fortunate moral effect of
ensuring complete independence of the working families'[22] (fig. 46).

In being acclaimed by the Garden City movement in France, the
Dourges housing played a part in the later spread of new planning ideas.
After the First World War, the informal layout and picturesque houses
were imitated in other industrial villages. But what is more striking in
retrospect is the fact that the new appearance of industrial housing left
its principles unchanged. The housing may be less repetitive, but the
message of the Garden City as a system for constructing a self-sufficient
community was not applied to these developments. They remained

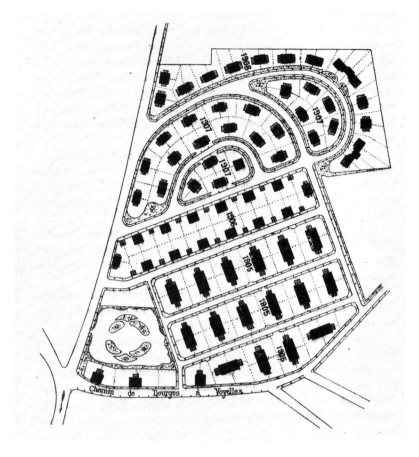

46 Changing patterns: housing built by the Compagnie des Mines de Dourges, based on a rectilinear layout of streets in the areas laid out in 1905 and 1906, but on a radically different disposition of curved streets and irregular house plots from 1907 in response to the planning ideas related to the Garden City movement

employer housing in the sense established during the nineteenth century.

A self-contained world

The quality of housing built by employers was acknowledged at the Expositions Universelles in 1867 and 1889. In 1867, the industries awarded medals or honourable mentions included Japy Frères, Schneider et Cie, and the mining companies in Anzin and Blanzy. In 1889, Schneider, Anzin and Blanzy reappeared among the medal winners, and were joined, among other industries, by Menier Frères. The housing provided by industrialists runs as a continuous counterpart to the efforts of the housing reformers. In one area in north France, 18 out of a total of 23 mining companies were building houses by 1875; at that date they had together provided 7,000 houses, accommodating 31,500 people. At Blanzy, the mining company had built almost 1,000 dwellings by 1891. The railway companies were also active in construction, and by the 1890s the Chemin de Fer du Nord had invested 1.7 million francs in housing. By the turn of the century the Anzin mining company alone had built over 2,800 houses; at Le Creusot, Schneider had built more than 1,300 houses, and made loans for at least another 3,000.

A study of the Somme prepared in the early 1900s revealed the existence of 2,000 dwellings attached to the textile factories in the department. The value of these was estimated at 6 million francs, representing between 15% and 30% of the capital value of buildings and plant owned by these firms. A survey of mining companies gave the total value of the housing built by these companies between 1850 and 1907 as 124 million francs. This had provided almost 40,000 houses; the survey indicated a considerable increase in construction in the 1890s and 1900s, when half of these houses were built.[23]

To the housing reformers, both the quality and the quantity of housing built by industrialists were worthy of imitation. But they realised that the financial basis of most of the housing placed it outside their efforts to sponsor cheap housing in the private market. In his report on housing at the 1889 Exposition, Georges Picot remarked that 'the employer who builds cottages and lets them to his workers makes them concessions which constitute a supplement to salaries'. He acknowledged that perhaps 20,000 families were housed by employers in 1889. But he also remarked: 'Let one of [the employers] discover the secret of raising the profit between capital and rent and through the natural play of forces, within a few years, two hundred thousand working families will possess a house and a small garden.'[24]

While he had reservations about the financing of housing by employers, Picot had no objections to the principle of industrial patronage. But to the socialists, industrial housing was a particular object of condemnation. Henri Turot, a Paris councillor who advocated action by the city to encourage the construction of housing in the early 1900s, commented on industrial housing in a report in 1905. He stated that 'The worker should not, in our opinion, be the tenant of his employer, nor co-owner with him of the house (as occurs in sale by instalments). In both cases the domination of the employer over the worker is established in too close a manner.'[25]

Between these opposing views, the construction of housing by employers continued in its own, almost self-contained world. The housing which the reformers admired and the socialists abhorred was never applicable as a general solution to urban housing problems. As Emile Cheysson remarked, 'while, in the country, the employer is forced to resolve the question of cheap housing, he has no interest in the question within towns, abandoning his workers as prey to speculation and suffering'.[26] The industrialist had little incentive to turn his efforts to the housing of workers in urban areas, since those areas attracted a steady stream of migrant workers. Nor was the paternalist nature of industrial housing directly applicable to the more stringent economic constraints and more pressing demands of quantity and density in urban areas. Industrial housing was closely tailored to the particular industry and to the working population that was to inhabit it. To solve the problems of urban housing, a more flexible system was needed, providing a general supply of housing which could compete in price with private enterprise, while improving its quality. It was towards establishing such a system through housing societies that the housing reformers turned their efforts.

22

◇◇◇

Housing societies

In his report on workers' housing at the 1889 Exposition Universelle, Georges Picot observed that 'to achieve the reform of housing, the moralist and the financier must march invincibly united'.[1] This uneasy unity was sought by housing reformers in the constitution of housing societies, in which social ideals were allied to a limited return on capital invested. It was vital to the reformers that they should get the balance right: too much social idealism and too little profit would turn the construction of houses into a charitable operation, while the reverse would lead to speculative development as in the private market. Emile Cheysson identified this balance in the work of the cheap housing organisations in England, which 'intended to derive a reasonable interest from their funds, low enough to remove any idea of pure speculation, high enough, however, to attract capital and to take out of the operation that character of charity which would have considerably limited its vitality, while at the same time wounding the dignity of those whose recovery one was seeking'.[2]

In France, the first limited dividend housing societies were formed in the 1850s, but their main development began in the late 1860s. At that time, interest in workers' housing was increased by the 1867 Exposition, while the relaxation of company law in the same year made the creation of limited liability companies considerably simpler. The total number of housing societies remained relatively small, but those that were set up helped prepare the way for the formal organisation of cheap housing societies under the 1894 legislation.

Alongside the evolution of the cheap housing societies there were individual initiatives by philanthropists and charitable foundations. Unlike the societies, which relied on investment in their shares to raise capital, philanthropic individuals or foundations established their basic capital by a single donation. This made the task of financing initial development much simpler, but if it was the intention to continue by reinvesting the basic capital, or contracting loans, then philanthropic ventures were subject to the same financial constraints as housing societies. Both societies and philanthropic organisations thus aimed to achieve a gross return of 4% to 6%, which would cover administrative costs, taxes and maintenance, and still leave a small net return on the capital.

432

The housing subsidy of 1852

The subsidy of 1852 effectively freed the aided housing from the demands of the private market. Some philanthropic organisations – most notably the Société des Cités Ouvrières in Paris, and the Société Mulhousienne des Cités Ouvrières – took advantage of the subsidy anticipating a low return in their attempt to keep rents to a minimum. But the subsidy also attracted some speculative investors, including the Péreire brothers; for even if the return on the overall capital cost of the housing were low, the subsidy could make the venture acceptably profitable. Thus a subsidised group of twenty houses in the Boulevard d'Enfer in Paris gave a net return of less than 4%; however, as the subsidy had met one third of the construction cost, the developer, M. Cazaux, enjoyed a rather high return on the capital which he had personally invested, at a figure of 6% net. While not exceptional, this was a reasonable return on a private investment.[3]

The subsidy provided the opportunity for some experimentation with new forms of housing. M. Seiler, a Paris timber merchant, successfully constructed, dismantled, and rebuilt a group of demountable houses. At the urban scale, the Puteaux brothers proposed to build a boulevard around Paris, linking 14 new villages outside the city; although apparently approved for subsidy, this proposal was not executed. Emile Muller was involved in a proposal to transfer the concept of housing established in Mulhouse to Paris. He drew up plans for a site on the edge of the city's pre-1860 limits, between the Rue de Reuilly and the Rue de Picpus. The intention was to construct 110 houses, using the Mulhouse plan of four grouped houses each with its own garden; communal facilities were to include baths and laundry. Occupants would be able simply to rent their house, or to buy it by paying annuities over 15 years. The project was approved for subsidy, but it was not in fact constructed; the developer opted to increase the speculative value of the development by building larger houses, with two floors, to be let as flats, over workshops.[4]

At the larger scale of multi-storey flats, the subsidised Cité Napoléon was innovatory in design, with its central band of stairs and gallery access covered by a glazed roof (see figs. 3 and 4). But the subsidised flats built by speculative developers in Paris were generally more conservative in their acceptance of the standard forms of the city, with staircases giving access to two to four flats per landing.[5] These flats typically provided two rooms and a kitchen. By the standards of reformers in the 1880s, such accommodation was criticised as it did not allow separate rooms for children of each sex and parents. The economical planning also led to some rooms which were less than ideal: Emile Cacheux particularly noted a bedroom in a block of several storeys, which was lit only from a light-well of 4 m². However, Cacheux also pointed out that the overall size of the flats, typically 27 m², did conform to the standard set out by the Conseil d'Hygiéne in the 1850s. The arrangement of a closet within many of the flats was itself a generous level of provision.[6]

47 The 'Puteaux' housing
type, with variants of the
same type by other
developers

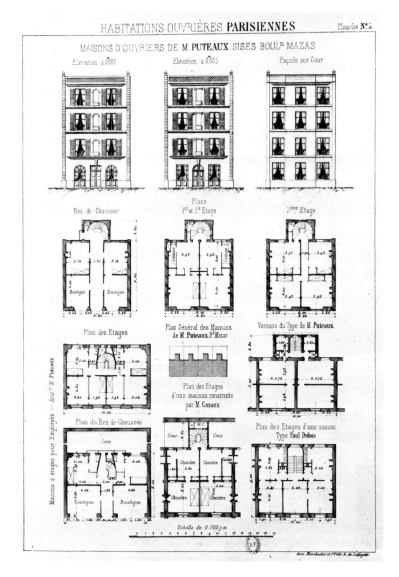

47 The 'Puteaux' housing type, with variants of the same type by other developers

This type of housing was exemplified in the project by Lucien
Puteaux. His plan for a block of flats was the premiated project in the
competition for housing designs held in 1852. A four-storey block
provided shops on the ground floor, with a stair at the rear giving access
to two dwellings on the first floor, and two on the second floor; the third
floor contained rooms for single men. The flats on the first and second
floors were made up of two rooms with a small kitchen, providing a floor
area of about 30 m²; the closet for these flats, as for the single rooms
on the third floor, was situated on the landing. Houses of this type were
built by Puteaux with the aid of the subsidy; Puteaux himself refers to
a total of 30 such blocks built in Paris, on the Boulevard Diderot, and
in the area just outside the city's pre-1860 limits, at Grenelle and
Batignolles[7] (fig. 47).

The Puteaux housing appears to have been the only built example to result from the entries to the 1852 competition. The judges of the competition also acknowledged Gourlier's studies, but these were not implemented directly. Another claimant to the 1852 prize was Emile Muller: according to Muller and Cacheux, the Conseil Général des Bâtiments Civils judged in 1860 that Emile Muller be retrospectively awarded the prize; however, by this time apparently, the prize money no longer existed.[8]

Shortly after the announcement of the 10 million franc subsidy in 1852, the government tried to extend its impact, negotiating with two groups of investors who proposed large-scale developments. One group was headed by the Péreire brothers, who agreed to build lodging houses and flats worth 4.5 million francs. A second group, headed by Baron de Heeckeren, and William Kennard of London, undertook to build housing costing just over 4 million francs.[9] Both groups did finance some housing with government subsidies, but with mixed success. The Péreire brothers built a four-storey block of 148 dwellings with a single room and kitchen at La Chapelle, and another four-storey block, in this case providing 192 beds for single men, at Batignolles. The latter experiment responded to the shortage of accommodation for single workers attracted to Paris in search of work in the early 1850s; but it was not a success. The standard of accommodation was basic, with dormitories of 50 cells separated by low partitions. Puteaux claimed that the building was never occupied by more than 10 tenants at a time; the Péreire brothers eventually converted the block into bourgeois flats.[10]

The society founded by de Heeckeren and Kennard also constructed a block of single rooms, and it acquired the Cité Napoléon when the Société des Cités Ouvrières went into liquidation in the early 1850s.[11] But neither de Heeckeren and Kennard nor the Péreire brothers built on the scale of their original intentions. Emile Cacheux states that the total of subsidies accorded to builders in Paris was 1.2 million francs; at one third of the construction cost, this would give an overall figure of only 3.6 million francs invested in subsidised housing in the city.[12]

The breakdown of the 1852 subsidy given by Cacheux and Muller shows that, in France as a whole, only 2.13 million francs of the total of 10 million francs was distributed to private developers and housing societies. The 1.2 million francs made available in Paris thus represented the lion's share of this money. Paris also benefited from a further 2 million francs of the total, which was used directly by the State to finance a group of flats on the Boulevard Diderot. The subsidies taken up in provincial towns helped to finance lodging houses in Marseilles, and an old people's home in Reims, as well as the Mulhouse *cité ouvrière*; other projects were planned in Rouen and in Lille, where the society set up by the Scrive brothers to build housing for their workers was granted a subsidy.[13]

The 5.87 million francs not taken up by developers or housing societies, nor used directly by the State for the Boulevard Diderot housing, were diverted from the original intent that the subsidies be used to improve housing conditions. However, they did help some of those whose health suffered from the housing conditions in the capital, being used to finance the sanatoria at Vincennes and Le Vésinet, on the edge of Paris.

In 1854, the Minister of the Interior, F. de Persigny, presented a report to the Emperor outlining the use of the 10 million franc subsidy. His report left little doubt as to which subsidised development offered the most positive model; of the towns where workers' housing had been built up to that date 'Mulhouse is the one which has conformed in the most complete manner to the views of the Administration'[14] (see figs. 7–9). This early acclamation was to be continually reinforced by later housing reformers.

The statutes of the Société Mulhousienne des Cités Ouvrières established the two principles which the society came to embody: the restriction of the shareholders' dividend to a maximum of 4%; and the possibility of occupants buying their house by small payments stretched over a period of years. The society's founding capital of 300,000 fr., over half of which was subscribed by Jean Dollfus, was supplemented by the subsidy of 300,000 fr. from the government; the subsidy was used to pay for general works such as street paving and sewers, and for some of the communal facilities. The society started by building three types of house. The cheapest were two-storey back-to-backs, costing 1,850 fr., but because of the problems of ensuring adequate light and ventilation this design was soon abandoned. The most expensive houses were two-storey terraced houses, costing about 3,000 fr., while the typical Mulhouse plan of four grouped dwellings initially cost 2,500 fr. to 2,800 fr. These houses could all be rented for an annual sum which the society's statutes limited to a maximum of 8% of the construction costs. However the majority were let with an assurance of sale, becoming the property of the occupant after about 14 years.[15]

To acquire the house, the occupant made a down payment of 250 fr. to 300 fr. to cover the costs of the contract of sale. This contract was not actually executed until the house was fully paid for, after about 14 years. However, the initial payment was important to the reformers, who saw it as evidence of the buyer's commitment, and his ability to manage his budget. On occupying the house, the buyer made monthly payments into a credit account, gaining interest at 5%. The credit account would be used annually to pay off part of the capital cost of the house, together with interest of 5% which was added to the outstanding sum annually. For a house costing 3,000 fr. the monthly repayment was 25 fr., and the capital was paid off after 13 years and 5 months. To rent the same house, the tenant would pay 18 fr. per month. Over the total repayment period, the owner of a house had paid 4,326 fr. 80 c., while the tenant had paid 2,898 fr. – the owner had thus paid less than 1,500 fr. more in order to acquire his house.

Certain conditions were imposed on the houses for sale. The occupant must maintain the garden in good order, and was not permitted to build over it. After his house was finally paid for, and had become his property, the owner was not allowed to sell the house, or to sublet it, for a period of ten years without the permission of the society. These controls were intended to maintain the initial form of the housing, preventing speculation through subletting at high rents, or the construction of large extensions. However, once the period of control had elapsed, some owners took advantage of their freedom to increase the height of the house, or to extend it into the garden; 270 houses had been altered in this way by the 1880s. Moreover, the restriction on subletting was not rigorously imposed, as some occupants took in lodgers to help cover their repayments. An inspection during the cholera outbreak of 1884 revealed one house containing six families, a total of 42 people. The danger that occupants would misuse their property led some reformers in the 1880s to have reservations on the wisdom of helping them to ownership. But the ideal remained, and reformers such as Georges Picot accepted that the freedom to enjoy inevitably implied the freedom to abuse.[16]

One hundred houses were built in the first year of the society's existence. To finance continued development before the initial capital was repaid, the society contracted a loan to cover half of the construction cost of each house. At first the society borrowed from the Crédit Foncier, paying 5.49% for the loan. When this rate was increased, the society looked elsewhere, benefiting from the personal guarantee of Jean Dollfus. By 1867 the balance of repayments to the society by occupants exceeded the costs of share and loan interest. The society was then theoretically in a position to build 50 or 60 new houses annually, without recourse to further loans. The average annual construction rate since the society's foundation had been about 60 houses up to 1867, when 800 had been built. Although this rate was not in fact maintained, more than 300 houses were added by 1888, giving a total of 1,124 houses.

The terraced houses, costing 25 fr. per month in the 1850s, proved too expensive for ordinary workers, and were occupied mainly by foremen. The houses grouped in fours, which could be bought for 18 fr. to 20 fr. in the 1850s became the most common form of housing for workers in the *cité ouvrière*. It was this type of house which was exhibited at the 1867 Exposition in Paris, alongside the examples built by industrial employers. The original design for the grouped houses had provided two rooms and a kitchen on the ground floor; stairs led down to a cellar, and up to three bedrooms. The number of rooms in these houses proved generous and some occupants sublet one of the rooms. Later houses were therefore made slightly smaller, with only one room and kitchen on the ground floor, and two rooms above; in some of these houses, the closet was relegated to the garden. The houses had a habitable floor area of 56 m², as against the 63 m² of the earlier houses, a reduction which helped to keep down the cost; payments for the houses built in the 1860s had nonetheless increased in relation to the earlier, larger houses, being 25 fr. per month. A single-storey version of the grouped houses was also built, giving about 35 m² of habitable space. This allowed two rooms in addition to the kitchen on the ground floor. The roof space above was accessible, and could be made habitable. At 20 fr. per month to buy in the 1860s, the cost of the single-storey house was comparable to the industrial housing for sale at Beaucourt.

If the Mulhouse development was a model in terms of the 1852 subsidy when the government report was prepared in 1854, it was a model in slightly different terms in 1867. The subsidy had attracted a few speculative investors in the 1850s because it enabled them to maintain their return, while charging relatively low rents. But the subsidy was an exceptional measure. When it was no longer available, investors had to choose whether to accept a lower return or charge higher rents if they wished to continue building the same type of housing. If financial gain were the main objective, an investor would naturally choose the latter course. The investors in the Société Mulhousienne had chosen the former, and the continued activity of the society in 1867 demonstrated that their aims could be realised. The society had achieved a modest, but positive, return, while building houses which could be bought for 20 fr. to 25 fr. per month. If this did not make the houses accessible to all workers, it undoubtedly helped a large number of the relatively well-paid workers, in secure jobs, to acquire their own property. In making possible the reformers' ideal, the structure of Mulhouse society was as much a model for later developments as the housing itself.

The followers of Mulhouse

The system pioneered at Mulhouse was followed up by some industrialists during the 1860s, but does not appear to have been taken up by private housing societies until the end of that decade. The economic prosperity inaugurated by the Second Empire to some extent pushed discussion of workers' housing into the background in the late 1850s and early 1860s. Thus, when an invitation for exhibits to be displayed in the housing section of the forthcoming Exposition was published in 1866, the *Revue Générale de l'Architecture* was prompted to observe that it had 'reawakened interest in a question which the high level of current salaries, and the general activity of business have allowed to be too much forgotten'.[17]

The houses exhibited in 1867 indicate the relative maturity of industrial housing in comparison to the housing society movement. Of six French companies awarded medals or an honourable mention, four were already actively building houses by the mid-1850s. Three housing societies were awarded medals, but of these only the Mulhouse society dated back to the 1850s. The other two societies were both founded to coincide with the Exposition, and were products of the renewed interest in co-operatives in the mid-1860s. As such, they were isolated examples which were not immediately followed up.[18] The model of the Mulhouse society, however, was taken up in various towns in the late 1860s and 1870s.

The reawakening of interest in housing is indicated by three competitions held in 1866 and 1867. In Saint Quentin, the local Société
Académique initiated a comparative study of different types of housing;
the winning paper discussed examples in France, England, Germany and
Belgium.[19] In contrast to this academic interest, competitions in Amiens
and Lille were intended to find designs for housing to be built. In Amiens
the competition was organised by the Société Anonyme des Maisons
Ouvrières which had been founded in 1866. The society went on to build
84 houses by 1889, for sale to occupants on the pattern established at
Mulhouse; the society limited the dividend paid on shares to 5% and
buyers paid from 20 fr. to 30 fr. per month.[20]

In Lille, a Compagnie Immobilière was projected in 1865, but it only
came into existence in 1867, when it organised the competition for
house designs. The company was formed with considerable official
support. Several members of the local council were among the founders,
and the council agreed to guarantee the 5% dividend on the company
shares for 50 years; furthermore, the Emperor granted 100,000 fr. to
the new company, supplementing the share capital of 600,000 fr. The
company built houses for rent or for sale, using repaid capital to finance
further construction. Thus by 1882 it had built housing to a value of
1.1 million francs, providing more than 300 houses without issuing
further shares, or contracting loans. The cheapest single-storey houses
could be bought for 21 fr. per month over 14 years. Most of the houses
built by the company were of this type, and were bought by their
occupants; however, the company also built larger houses costing up
to 70 fr. per month. These were far beyond the reach of working
families, but the cheaper houses were taken by families which included
cotton and buildings workers, as well as the better paid tax and railway
employees[21] (fig. 48).

Dunkirk joined the growing band of provincial towns showing an
interest in workers' housing, with a competition for the design of a *cité
ouvrière* in 1868. In Reims a group of houses were built by the housing
society which the architect A. Gosset helped to found in 1869. Houses
in the typical Mulhouse arrangement of four dwellings could be bought
for 25 fr. per month over 16 years. After building the initial houses the
society does not appear to have proceeded. However, the following year,
1870, saw the foundation of a co-operative society in the town, which
was to be one of the few successful co-operatives formed before the late
1880s; this society will be considered in more detail in the discussion
of co-operatives in the following chapter.[22]

The Franco–Prussian war of 1870 brought the downfall of the
Empire, and the emergence of a new Republic. It also deprived France
of Alsace and Lorraine. The Société Mulhousienne des Cités Ouvrières,
though still acclaimed by the French housing reformers, had to appear
in the German section of studies such as that by Raffalovich in the
1880s. To some citizens of Mulhouse, and to the town's Ecole de
Commerce, Le Havre became a new home, in company with Jules
Siegfried and others who were already established there. As if to

48 Housing built by the
Compagnie Immobilière de
Lille from 1867

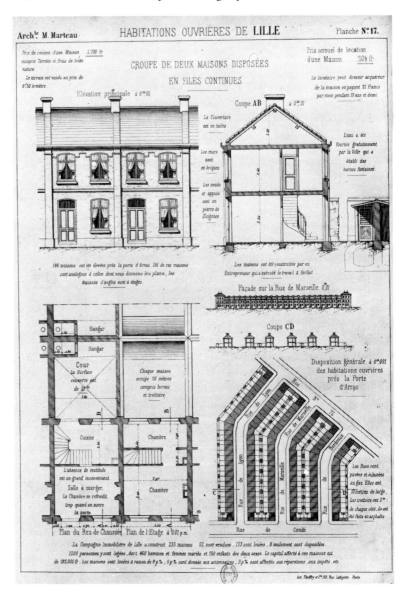

symbolise the continuity of the initiative begun in Mulhouse, it was in
1871 that Siegfried founded the Société Havraise des Cités Ouvrières.

The founder members of the society, who included several Mulhou-
siens, subscribed 200,000 fr. capital in shares of 500 fr. Siegfried was
already prominent in local politics, and the council in Le Havre agreed
to assist his society by a subsidy of 25,000 fr. The society's dividend
was limited to 4%; to keep their monthly payments to a minimum,
buyers could stretch the repayment period up to 20 years. After a down
payment of 300 fr., a house of two storeys, with two rooms on each
floor, could be bought for 20 fr. per month in the early 1870s. Like the
Mulhouse society the Société Havraise imposed restrictions on its

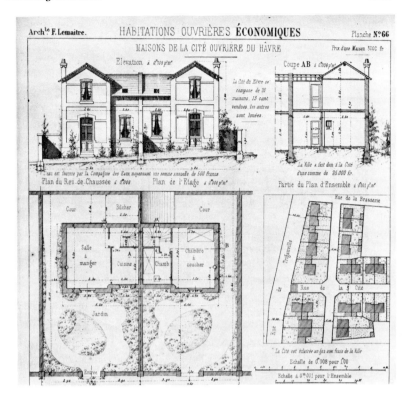

49 Housing built by the Société des Cités Ouvrières in Le Havre, founded by Jules Siegfried in 1871

buyers, controlling additions to the houses, and the subletting or sale of houses. The possibility of occupants subletting was used as an argument against making the houses too large. By 1889, the society had financed 117 dwellings, of which 70 were already fully paid for[23] (fig. 49).

Further societies on the model of Mulhouse were set up in Nancy in 1872 and Bolbec in 1877. Founded, like the nearby society in Le Havre, by Jules Siegfried, the Bolbec society remained small, building less than 40 houses by the turn of the century. The Société Immobilière in Nancy had built 55 houses by the mid-1880s, but stopped building because the economic crisis of those years reduced demand for its houses; moreover, the cost of land and labour at that time would have reduced the society's return to only 2.5 %.[24]

The problems encountered by the Nancy society were those faced by all societies trying to build housing cheap enough for workers to buy. Raffalovich quotes a correspondent from Nancy who noted that the cost of executing the contract of sale, and the range of taxes from the door and window tax to the sewer tax, were a major obstacle to acquisition by workers. He observed that the houses built by the Nancy society 'were not intended for the *poor*'.[25] This comment could stand for any of the followers of Mulhouse, but it did not devalue the model in the eyes of the reformers. The fact that their houses were too expensive to help the poor directly did not cause them to seek a more radical solution. Instead, they justified their work in the terms which F. Mallet, director of the Société Havraise des Cités Ouvrières, used in a letter describing the society's work, published in the first issue of the Bulletin of the Société Française des HBM in 1890: 'the occupants of our 117 houses have vacated 117 of the better worker's dwellings, and we have thus indirectly contributed to improving the situation of another 117 families...'[26]

If the Mulhouse ideal achieved some success in provincial towns during the late 1860s and 1870s, it was rather harder to transfer the model to Paris. The problems facing the Nancy society were there exacerbated by the high costs of land and construction. This is evident in the case of the housing development which came closest to the Mulhouse ideal in Paris during the Empire, financed by the philanthropist Mme Jouffroy Renault. This development was started in 1865, and by 1867, when the design was exhibited at the Exposition, 36 out of the proposed total of 90 houses had been completed. Situated on a long narrow site near the large number of factories and workshops in Clichy and Asnières, the houses were built in two terraces, against the boundary wall to either side; they faced on to a small garden and street between the terraces. The smallest house had a single room on the ground floor, with the kitchen range to one side, and an alcove for the bed; upstairs were a single room with an alcove, and the closet. The largest house had two rooms on each floor, and a generous cellar. The houses could be paid for over a period of 15 years, the smallest house costing 32 fr. per month, and the largest 43 fr.; these payments allowed a return of $5\frac{1}{2}\%$ gross. The conditions of sale included control over alterations and subletting, and required occupants to look after the tree planted in every garden. The conditions also insisted that the worker's wife be regarded as joint owner of the property, to give her an equal interest in its maintenance and improvement.[27] (fig. 50).

At the 1867 Exposition, Mme Jouffroy Renault shared the honour accorded to the Société Mulhousienne. Both were awarded gold medals in the housing section; no other gold medals were awarded, and the only higher honour was the Grand Prix given to the Emperor. But if Mme Jouffroy Renault and the Société Mulhousienne both realised the reformers' ideals, the contrast between their housing emphasises the economic problem involved in building cheap housing for sale in the capital. In terms of accommodation, the larger houses in Clichy were similar to the two-storey houses in the grouped houses at Mulhouse. Both have a kitchen and one other room on the ground floor, and two rooms upstairs; neither has a water supply to the house. At Clichy there is an internal closet, while at Mulhouse it is outside; on the other hand, the built area at Clichy is rather smaller: 30.25 m² as opposed to 35.3 m² at Mulhouse. This contrast is even greater in the garden, which is only 16.5 m² at Clichy, as against 120 m² in Mulhouse. The attempt to keep down the cost at Clichy which these areas indicate is also evident in the grouping of the dwellings. Built against the party wall, they are effectively back-to-backs, although the closets

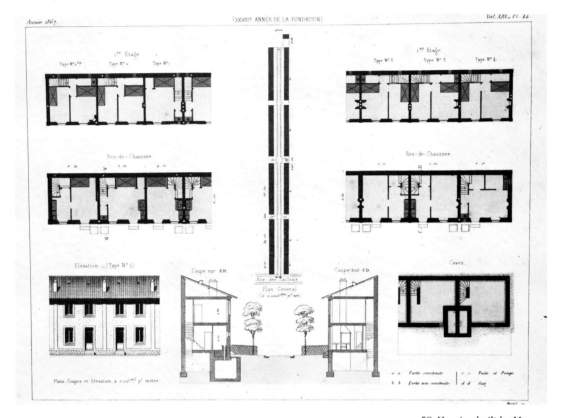

50 Housing built by Mme Jouffroy Renault in Clichy, just to the north of the city limits of Paris, from 1865

had borrowed light over neighbouring property. The grouping of four houses at Mulhouse was not ideal from the point of view of orientation and ventilation, but the dual façade of each dwelling provided better conditions than the Clichy houses.

Being on the outskirts of Paris, the land at Clichy was cheaper than in central Paris, costing 9 fr./m²; moreover, by developing the site as a narrow cul-de-sac, the cost of street works was kept to a minimum. But despite the economies in the form of the houses and of the development, the Clichy housing was considerably more expensive than that at Mulhouse. In the mid-1860s, the basic construction cost was 4,100 fr. at Clichy, 2,518 fr. at Mulhouse; land costs were 600 fr. for the small plot in Clichy, 207 fr. for the more generous site in Mulhouse. The cost of fees, street paving, drains, water supply and other common expenses came to 800 fr. at Clichy, and 382 fr. at Mulhouse. Thus, while the Mulhouse house could still be bought by monthly payments of 25 fr. over 15 years, the Clichy houses cost 43 fr.

The contrast between industrial salaries in the provinces and Paris was itself considerable,[28] so that the Clichy and the Mulhouse houses would both be within the reach of the secure, highly paid workers in the vicinity. Indeed, at Clichy it was the more expensive houses which were particularly sought after. But when he discussed the housing exhibited at the 1867 Exposition, Détain asked if a dwelling for 25 fr. per month was not often too expensive for workers in Paris. His answer was equivocal, but 20 years later Raffalovich was in no doubt that only a small proportion of workers in the city could afford to pay 25 fr. While discussion was focussed around the figure of 25 fr., Mme Jouffroy Renault's houses at 43 fr. were, like the housing of the Nancy society, not intended for the poor.

During the 1870s, Jean Dollfus and Emile Muller came together, in an abortive attempt to repeat the success of the Mulhouse housing, in Paris. At about the same time, Muller was joined by Emile Cacheux, whose experience of building housing in Paris left him quite clear as to why it was so hard to transfer the Mulhouse system to Paris. In addition to the greater cost of land and construction in Paris, he noted the considerable expense of complying with regulations on such matters as drains and cesspits. He particularly bemoaned the fact that 'the city now only accepts streets of 12 metres width, paved, with footpaths, lit by gas, and supplied with sewers'.[29]

Such standards were desirable, but while the costs of establishing the street were borne by the neighbouring properties, the charge was too great to allow the construction of individual workers' houses. This factor led Cacheux, like Mme Jouffroy Renault, to make use of deep plots with narrow frontages to minimise the cost of street construction. In such a development off the Boulevard Murat, built in 1876 (see fig. 26), Cacheux was able to offer houses for sale at 50 fr. per month. But according to his own calculations only 4% of the working population in Paris could afford such housing. This was housing for what Cacheux's critics described as 'the aristocracy of poverty'.[30]

Although it was expensive, the housing built by Mme Jouffroy Renault and by Cacheux did demonstrate that housing could be built in Paris on the model of Mulhouse. But this housing was financed by philanthropic individuals rather than by housing societies. The amount of capital which individuals could provide was inevitably limited, and Muller and Cacheux therefore tried to increase the capital available by founding a housing society which would attract investment. At the end of *Les habitations ouvrières en tous pays*, published in 1879, Muller and Cacheux included the statutes of a proposed society in Paris, the Société des Habitations Economiques. 120,000 fr. was actually raised by a group which included the familiar names of Dollfus, and the Siegfried brothers. However, the capital was inadequate to found a society similar to the Société Mulhousienne, which required a substantial initial capital in order to start building. In *Les habitations ouvrières* Muller and Cacheux had described in some detail the work of the English building societies, which resolved the problem of raising capital by acting as savings banks as well as financing construction. Despite Cacheux's enthusiasm for this system, the subscribers to the Paris society were unwilling to extend their capital by founding this form of society, and the project was abandoned.[31]

In 1882 Cacheux was involved in the foundation of a society in Paris which did finally realise 'the idea tried to such good effect in various places, notably in Alsace'. In that year, the Société Anonyme des Habitations Ouvrières de Passy Auteuil was set up to build houses for sale to 'moral and thrifty workers and minor employees'.[32] Among the shareholders were the economist Paul Leroy-Beaulieu and Emile Cheysson. Other shareholders included Alban Chaix, who in 1879 had collaborated with Charles Robert in founding the Société pour l'Etude Pratique de la Participation aux Bénéfices, and Jacques Zopff, who was president of one of the *banques populaires* found in Paris in the early 1880s. The first president of the Société de Passy Auteuil was Frédéric Dietz-Monnin, the vice-president of the Chambre de Commerce de la Seine. Dietz-Monnin had been born in Alsace, and was associated with the lock and clockmaking firm of Monnin Japy et Compagnie. The society thus grouped an eminent body of men, who had links with the initiatives for social reform in the late 1870s and early 1880s, and also with the roots of the society's work in Alsace. Those roots were acknowledged at the inaugural meeting of the society when the choice of honorary president fell on the pioneer of housing reform, Jean Dollfus.

To its practical aim of building houses, the society added one of propaganda; it was intended 'to serve as a model and to give its moral patronage to the formation of all other local and independent societies which may be constituted to the same end'.[33] The society's capital was fixed at 200,000 fr., and the annual dividend limited to a maximum of 4%. More than half of the shares were exchanged for land, including a site on which Emile Cacheux had already built ten houses. The plans for the development were the subject of a competition whose judges included the director of public works in Paris, Alphand, the housing reformers Emile Muller and Emile Trélat, and the engineer Auguste Choisy who had made a close study of systems of cheap, demountable housing. The plans submitted were put on public display in the town hall of the 16th Arrondissement, but the judges felt that none was suitable without considerable modification.

The society initially built 26 houses, but to pursue its work it supplemented its capital by borrowing money. This was done by issuing bonds on which interest of 4% was paid. Emile Cacheux noted the problems facing a society wishing to extend its work in this way. As the payments by the occupants of the houses were fixed on the basis of the 4% paid to shareholders, the society could not afford to pay a higher rate of interest when it issued bonds. This rate was not high enough to attract the money of small investors, so that the society would still find its work restricted by the difficulty of raising capital. In the 1880s the issue of extending the work of housing societies by establishing sources of credit which would accept a low rate of interest was to become central to discussion of housing reform.

The costs of street construction and services conforming to the Paris requirements, and the cost of construction in the city, ensured that the Passy Auteuil houses would not be inexpensive. Although the land exchanged for shares was granted at its cost price of 15 fr., rather than the 20–30 fr. it was currently worth, the total cost of the cheapest single-storey house was over 5,000 fr. A two-storey house with cellar, kitchen and living room, and three bedrooms upstairs cost up to

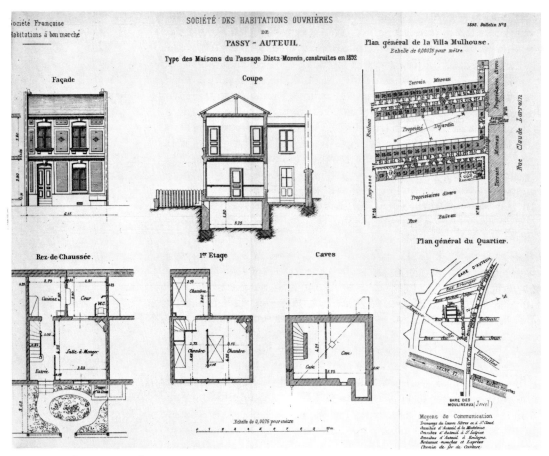

51 Société de Passy Auteuil,
plans of houses built in
1892; of particular interest
is the emphasis placed on the
transport links from the site
into the centre of Paris,
indicated on the general plan
of the quarter

10,000 fr. The closets were outside, but they had mains sewer connections in Doulton pipework; each house also had a gas and water supply,
so that the servicing of these houses was of a considerably higher
standard than those exhibited in 1867 (fig. 51). But the undoubted
quality of 'this little Alsatian Eden',[34] with its low mortality rate in
comparison to the surrounding arrondissement, was not cheap. The
two-storey houses cost about 50 fr. per month, allowing 20 years rather
than 15 for repayment. Not surprisingly, demand was greater for the
cheaper single-storey houses. Three rooms and a kitchen could be
bought for around 40 fr. per month – a figure which Cacheux claimed
was comparable with rents for an equivalent property on the private
market in that area. The cost of street works, which was partly borne
by the purchasers, also meant that the society was unable to realise the
full dividend of 4%, paying only 2% to 3%.[35]

The Société de Passy Auteuil was founded almost 30 years after its
model in Mulhouse. Since 1867 the method pioneered at Mulhouse had
been taken up in several provincial towns, and Emile Cheysson saw the
chief merit of the Société de Passy Auteuil in applying this method in
Paris. It demonstrated that 'even in Paris, where land and construction

are expensive, it was possible to lead workers and employees to ownership of their house'.[36] But if the housing reformers continued to defend this system, which they acknowledged could only directly help a minority of workers, they had to accept that they could no longer leave the poorer workers to wait for housing improvement to filter through to them. In a report on workers' housing delivered to the Société d'Encouragement pour l'Industrie Nationale in 1882, Charles Lavollée challenged the reformers' cherished aim. He requested

that we may be allowed to express our doubts on the system of individual houses, and on the system of the 'worker of Paris as proprietor'. What is practicable in Lille[37] and Mulhouse seems to us hardly practicable in Paris...Let us limit our ambition therefore to improving, for the worker, the condition of tenant, and let us reduce the problem by seeking quite simply the means of increasing the number of cheap dwellings for families, and lodging rooms for single workers.[38]

During the 1880s, the efforts of the reformers were to shift in the direction urged by Lavollée. The ideal of the owner-occupied individual house was not replaced; but a less emotive reaction to the social implications of blocks of workers' flats, and the progress in sanitation and design enabled the reformers of the 1880s to accept the form of housing which their predecessors in the 1850s had rejected.

Workers' flats

The experiments in constructing large-scale developments of workers' flats in the 1850s had been met with reservation by the reformers and, if the reformers are to be believed, by the inhabitants. The rejection of the Cité Napoléon, and the failure of the Péreire brothers' lodging rooms at Batignolles, was accompanied by the reacton towards small-scale housing which was not socially threatening; this reaction was typified in the acknowledgement of Puteaux's project in the 1852 competition. But if his houses were reassuring, they were not in scale with the housing shortage which the Cité Napoléon or the Péreires' lodging houses confronted; his 30 blocks created only 120 flats and 120 rooms in Paris.

The growth of Paris in the 1850s and 1860s was thus dominated by housing responding to speculative pressures, with developments such as the schemes subsidised after 1852 making only a small contribution. While some of these speculative developments were soon to come under the scrutiny of the Commission des Habitations Insalubres, others started to indicate the assimilation of workers' flats with bourgeois forms which was to characterise the flats acclaimed at the 1867 Exposition.

One of the largest of these developments was that financed by the Comte de Madre in east Paris. Borrowing money from the Crédit Foncier, he built a group of 88 houses, from which he was able to make a return of 6.5%. This development was almost a town in its own right, housing about 4,000 people. But the flats were broken up into small units with an average of twelve flats per house. The streets between the houses were open during the day, making the development a simple extension of the city. But the concerns which led to the strict regulation of the Cité Napoléon are evident in the fact that at night the streets were closed off, and entry to the development could only be made past a concierge's lodge.[39]

Other housing built in the 1860s already established the pattern to be adopted in 1867. C. Détain drew attention to two major developments, also in east Paris, in which flats were grouped around independent staircases opening off the street.[40] It was this model, demonstrated in the Cité du Champ de Mars, the Maison des Ouvriers, and the Cité Daumesnil built on the occasion of the 1867 Exposition (see fig. 30), which formed the point of departure for the construction of workers' flats when this question was taken up in earnest by the reformers in the 1880s.

Two of the societies which turned to the problem of urban flats in the 1880s made a particular contribution to the evolution of design of flats, acknowledged by the awards to their architects Lecoeur and Chabrol at the 1889 Exposition. Lecoeur built his block of 100 flats in Rouen for the Société des Petits Logements founded in 1885 (see fig. 31). Chabrol built the flats on the Rue Jeanne d'Arc in Paris, for the Société Philanthropique, an older charitable organisation which decided to devote a bequest in 1888 to the construction of workers' housing (see fig. 32).

In the case of each of these societies, the example of English housing societies was a source of inspiration, communicated through the person of Georges Picot. In his study *Un devoir social, et les logements d'ouvriers,* published in 1885, Picot described the work of five of the societies which he had recently visited in London, and in May 1885 Picot presented some of his observations to the annual meeting of the Société d'Economie Sociale. A report of this meeting caught the imagination of an industrialist in Rouen, and led to the foundation of the Société des Petits Logements. This society raised 460,000 fr. to build the flats designed by Lecoeur, but did not finance any further developments.[41]

When he gave 750,000 fr. to the Société Philanthropique in 1888, Michel Heine stipulated only that it should be used to 'lighten the burden of those who suffer and those who work', by making good 'some of the gaps in the public and private charity'.[42] It was at the suggestion of Georges Picot that the directors of the society decided to invest in the construction of housing, taking as a model the Peabody Foundation in London. Thus the income derived from the housing built with the initial capital was to be reinvested to allow further construction. This made possible the construction of four blocks of flats in Paris, providing almost 200 homes. Chabrol designed two further blocks after the Rue Jeanne d'Arc housing, while the fourth block was designed by the architect Cintrat.[43]

Both the Rouen society and the Société Philanthropique made a modest return from their investment. The Rouen society limited its dividend to 4%, but in fact only about 3% was paid, due to difficulty in letting the shop units at ground level. For the Société Philanthropique, figures from the late 1890s show a return of only 2.2% on the first block, but the next two blocks were returning just over 3%. The societies provided a variety of flat types. At Rouen, rents ranged from 7 fr. 50 c. per month for a single room, to 37 fr. 50 c. for the largest four-roomed flats. Rents in the Société Philanthropique flats ranged from 14 fr. to 31 fr.

The average of rents paid in the Rue Jeanne d'Arc block in the late 1890s was about 20 fr. per month. If this was still not within the reach of all Paris workers described by Raffalovich, it could be paid by many more families than the 40 fr. to 50 fr. of the Société de Passy Auteuil. The Rue Jeanne d'Arc flats showed how Lavollée's aim of multiplying the number of low-cost dwellings in Paris might be achieved, and the building was enthusiastically welcomed by the housing reformers. The laying of the foundation stone in June 1888 was the occasion for a gathering of eminent supporters of housing reform; Georges Picot himself placed the stone, watched by Jules Siegfried, Dr du Mesnil, Dr Rochard and Dr Marjolin, According to another housing reformer, Charles Lucas, the flats were widely regarded as 'the model of dwelling most appropriate to the Parisian worker'.[44]

Two other societies also started to build urban flats in the 1880s, in Lyons and Marseilles. In Lyons, Félix Mangini and his brother joined with the president of the local chamber of commerce, Edouard Aynard, to found the Société des Logements Economiques. From an initial capital of 300,000 fr. in 1885, the society grew rapidly, and in 1888 it was reconstituted as a *société anonyme* with a capital of 1 million francs. This high level of capital enabled the society to undertake a larger building programme than other societies. Using the economical construction and contracting facilities of the Mangini brothers, it completed 100 blocks of flats in 11 years, housing more than 1,000 families.[45] In Marseilles, the initiative in setting up a housing society was taken by Eugène Rostand, founder of the city's *banque populaire*, and president of its Caisse d'Epargne. In 1889 he established the Société Anonyme des Habitations Salubres et à Bon Marché with a capital of 250,000 fr. The society was less productive than the Lyons society, but by the end of the century it had built 19 blocks, containing more than 100 flats.[46] The rents in the Marseilles flats ranged from 12 fr. to 22 fr. per month; at Lyons, a three-room flat could be rented for as little as 15 fr. 50 c.

The activity of the Lyons and Marseilles societies reinforced the evidence of the Rouen society and the Société Philanthropique, that workers' flats could be built hygienically and economically, without making a loss. Other societies in provincial towns, and the Société de Passy Auteuil in Paris, had shown the potential for the construction of individual houses for a rather better paid class of workers. But what both types of society required were the resources with which to extend their work. It was in resolving this problem that the societies in Lyons and Marseilles were of particular interest, due to their relationship to their local Caisse d'Epargne.

The extension of the housing society movement

The accumulated total of savings deposited in Caisses d'Epargne throughout the country represented a sizeable potential source of investment. However, no use could be made of this potential, as the Caisses were obliged to place all deposits on account with the central Caisse des Dépôts et Consignations. The release of part of these deposits to provide investment for housing came under serious consideration in the early 1880s. But before any progress was achieved, the Caisses in Lyons and Marseilles had demonstrated the role which Caisses could play, by making use of their private reserves.

In Lyons, the Caisse initially lent the Société des Logements Economiques 150,000 fr. This was soon repaid, but in 1888 the Caisse invested 500,000 fr. in the society. This investment was later increased to 1 million francs, of which 950,000 fr. was repaid in 1902. The Caisse d'Epargne thus made a major contribution to the early success of the society. The 4% dividend due to shareholders was regularly paid, and the society's total capital rose from 1 million francs in 1888 to 5 million francs by 1900. This capital set the society apart from its contemporaries, and it was not until after 1905 that the Lyons society was joined by other societies with a capital of more than 1 million francs. By that date, the Caisse d'Epargne had withdrawn most of its money to invest in other housing projects, but its support in the 1880s and 1890s had been crucial.

In Marseilles, the Caisse invested rather less than its counterpart in Lyons, but in a wider range of projects. When Rostand established the Société des Habitations Salubres et à Bon Marché, the Caisse subscribed 20,000 fr. to the share capital; two years later it also invested in the shares of a new co-operative society, La Pierre du Foyer. But the Caisse invested its largest sums directly in housing construction and individual mortgage loans, without the intermediary of a housing society. By 1900, it had built 80 flats, and 25 houses using the 'Mulhouse plan'. At the same date, it had about 60,000 fr. owed to it by individuals who had borrowed to build their own house.

The contribution to these two Caisses indicated the potential for action, whether to assist housing societies, lend to individuals, or build directly. The Caisses did not anticipate a great profit from these investments. The Lyons Caisse enjoyed the 4% paid by the successful housing society, but the Marseilles Caisse accepted rather less: in 1897 it gained 2.2% on its investment in construction, and 3.5% on its mortgage loans. But in the context of the overall investment of the reserves of French Caisses, these figures were not unreasonable: in 1897 the average return was only 2.58%;[47] it was precisely because the Caisses were not aiming to make the highest commercial return on their investment that they offered so suitable a source of capital and credit for housing. In contrast, the interest rate of the Crédit Foncier remained between 4% and 5% throughout the 1880s and 1890s.[48] But tapping the source required some effort; the Marseilles Caisse had to obtain authorisation by two government decrees before it could start investing in housing. Similarly, the general use of the funds held by the Caisse des Dépôts et Consignations remained impossible. Nonetheless, the work of the Lyons and Marseilles Caisses demonstrated the potential if administrative barriers could be overcome.

While the French housing society movement had still achieved only negligible results in comparison with its English equivalent, it could be said to have at least come of age by 1889. At the Exposition Universelle held in Paris that year, the housing exhibits were no longer dominated by examples of industrial housing, as they had been in 1867. Alongside the companies which won gold medals in 1889 were housing societies which followed the lead of Mulhouse – in Le Havre and at Passy Auteuil – and those which had pioneered the construction of flats – the societies in Rouen and Lyons, the Société Philanthropique in Paris, and the Caisse d'Epargne in Marseilles. While the medals maintained a judicious balance between societies building houses, those building flats, and industrial companies, the highest awards acknowledged the continuing sources of inspiration for French housing reformers. Two Grand Prix were awarded to English exhibits: the Improved Industrial Dwellings Company, the largest of the model dwellings companies in London by the 1880s; and the Mansion House Council on the Dwellings of the Poor, a permanent council for the study of housing in London, established in 1883. The remaining Grand Prix was awarded to Alfred Engel, grandson of Jean Dollfus, the founder of the Société Mulhousienne; Dollfus himself had died two years earlier, in 1887.

In his report on the 1889 housing exhibition, Georges Picot noted that 'the Mulhouse housing type has become a model'.[49] But the limitations of this model had been recognised and the societies formed in the 1880s to build flats offered a new model for urban areas. Picot, who had himself played a significant role in establishing this new model, looked forward with enthusiasm to its future development alongside the example of Mulhouse:

Rouen, Lyons, Paris and Marseilles have taken initiatives which allow one to state that, in principle, the problem of workers' housing within inner towns is resolved in France. The Exhibition of Social Economy will have drawn attention to the assimilation to French methods of models conceived in England: the path is mapped out, all that is needed is to advance down it, encouraging imitation by all possible means.[50]

23

❖◇❖

Housing and co-operation

Until the 1890s, co-operation occupied a rather ambiguous position for the housing reformers. On the one hand, it was a natural extension of their views of social reform that workers should use their own savings to finance housing. On the other hand, co-operative action had the potential to challenge the capitalist order of society; while the reformers themselves saw the need to question certain aspects of the order, they were not prepared to follow co-operation too far in the challenge. Co-operation was thus assimilated into housing reform only gradually, in a process which ran parallel to the development of other aspects of co-operation, but in which the co-operative initiative was led from above, not below.

In the 1850s, workers' groups of all kinds had been kept under strict control by the Imperial régime. When the German V. A. Huber visited France and Belgium to study co-operation in the mid-1850s, he met little active response in France, and it was only in the 1860s that the Imperial government started to allow greater freedom to workers' groups. In 1862 a delegation of workers was assembled by the government, to visit the Universal Exhibition in London; the delegation's reports, published under Imperial patronage, called for rights of association similar to those enjoyed by English workers. Progress in this direction was made in 1864, when legislation removed the offence of combination, and gave limited rights to strike, although trade unions remained outlawed. At the same time, a renewed interest in co-operatives was tolerated, as the idea was taken up by some of the veterans of 1848, and some of the members of the Orléanist and liberal opposition to the Imperial régime.

The workers' associations which had flourished briefly in 1848 and 1849 were largely production co-operatives, but in the 1860s the leading role was to be taken by credit co-operatives. In 1863, the Société du Crédit au Travail was formed in Paris combining the roles of savings bank and friendly society with that of a credit bank for other co-operatives. The society's founder, J. P. Beluze, was a joiner who had been an active supporter of the utopian socialist Etienne Cabet since 1846; but in 1863 he stopped working towards the creation of new, ideal communities, and turned to the more immediate potential of co-operation within the existing community. A year after founding the Crédit au Travail, he formed a consumer co-operative in Paris, based on the principles of the Rochdale Pioneers. The founders of this co-operative also included two members of the Association des Maçons, its director Cohadon, and the architect Delbrouck. This association, originally formed in 1834, was one of the few which survived under the Empire, and actually flourished due to the building work in Paris.

In men such as Delbrouck and Beluze, the co-operative movement had a direct link to the leaders of association, and the doctrines of socialism, of the late 1840s. But the new interest in co-operation also attracted members of the liberal financial and political circles. The subscribers of the crédit au Travail included Casimir Périer, owner of the Anzin mines, and Auguste Cochin, director of the Orléans railway company. The same range could be seen in the shareholders of *L'Association*, a periodical founded in 1864. Followers of Fourier, Cabet, and other socialist thinkers found themselves alongside industrialists and economists. This combination, while symbolising the inclusive ideal of co-operation, could not mask the essential difference between the two groups. The editorial committee of *L'Association*, which included Beluze and Cohadon, took a more radical view of co-operation than the converts among the 'grande bourgeoisie'. Gustave Chaudey, himself a member of the editorial committee, identified the difference in approach; he distinguished between the philanthropic view of the Orléanists and the opposition Republicans in parliament, who saw co-operation as requiring protection and aid from above, and the view of the co-operators of *L'Association*, who believed in the complete autonomy and independence of the co-operative movement.[1]

When Chaudey made this distinction in 1865, the 'philanthropic' group had just deposited a proposal for legislation to aid co-operatives. The fifteen signatories to the proposal included three former Orléanist deputies: Casimir Périer, Comte d'Haussonville, and Vicomte de Melun; two directors of railway companies: Cochin and Léon Say; and the opposition deputy, Jules Simon. These men had contributed to the spread of interest in co-operatives since 1863. Casimir Périer had published his study on co-operatives in 1864, and the following year he founded a consumer co-operative for the workers at the Anzin mines. Also in 1864, Simon, Say and d'Haussonville were involved in founding a credit bank initiated by Léon Walras. Like the Crédit au Travail founded by Beluze, the new Caisse d'Escompte des Associations Populaires was set up to provide loans to co-operatives. However, it was indicative of the difference in attitude of the founders of the two banks that the Caisse was not itself a co-operative. While the Crédit au Travail gained much of its capital from the small investments of co-operative members, the Caisse was founded on capital from the wealthy classes.

In 1865, Jules Simon travelled to England to study the co-operative movement; during this trip he accompanied the Comte de Paris, the Orléanist pretender to the throne of France, on a vist to the Rochdale Pioneers. Despite studying this society, which co-operators in the 1880s were to claim as a radical model, Simon and the other signatories to the proposal for legislation retained their conservative view of co-operation;

as Casimir Périer expressed it in 1864, co-operation was a defence against socialism, while Say stressed the value of co-operatives as an extension of saving. Like Chaudey, they were clear of the distinction of this view from the independent development envisaged by more radical co-operators.

Housing co-operatives 1867–70

The Imperial government responded to the legislative changes proposed by the 'philanthropic' co-operators, and to two other proposals, by presenting its own projected law in 1865; at the end of the year it set up a commission to study co-operatives. In 1867 these initiatives culminated in the passage of the company law which simplified the procedure for founding limited liability companies of joint stock or co-operative form. Imperial tolerance of co-operation extended to direct patronage in a few cases, and among those which benefited in this way was a housing co-operative founded in Paris. This co-operative was also one of the first to take advantage of the new company law, being established within a month of the passage of the law.

The Société Coopérative Immobilière des Ouvriers was founded as a result of the Exposition held in Paris in 1867. One of the exhibits in the housing section was the Maison des Ouvriers (see fig. 30b), whose design and construction were supervised by a committee of workers. Not that these were typical workers. The committee was led by the tinsmith Chabaud, who had been president of the 1862 workers' delegation to London, and was the workers' representative on the admissions jury for the housing exhibited in 1867. The design approved by the committee was built as part of the exhibition, at the cost of the Emperor. The building provided six flats in a block of three storeys. The ground-floor flats were shop units with a room behind; those above had a dining room, kitchen and two bedrooms. The habitable area of the upper flats was 35 m², and they could be rented for 25 fr. per month.

The workers' committee hoped to be able to build similar blocks throughout Paris by establishing a workers' co-operative. In the event, the exhibition design was not repeated, but a co-operative was formed to take advantage of an offer by the Emperor. In addition to the workers' committee housing, Napoleon III had financed the group of dwellings, built with the concrete construction system of Joseph Tull, in the Avenue Daumesnil (see figs. 6 and 30c). He agreed to hand over these dwellings to a co-operative which was founded by members of the workers' committee in August 1867. The buildings which the Société Coopérative Immobilière des Ouvriers took over consisted of 41 three-storey houses, which had a flat on each floor. The flats had a habitable area of 36 m², providing two rooms and a kitchen. The economic rent of the flats at 8% of their cost, would have been 28 fr. per month; however, Muller and Cacheux noted a rent of only 17 fr. in *Les habitations ouvrières*, which suggests that the co-operative may have taken advantage of the fact that it was given the buildings, to charge a reduced rent.

In addition to the capital represented by the Avenue Daumesnil housing, the Société Coopérative Immobilière des Ouvriers raised an initial capital of 100,000 fr. This was made up of shares of 100 fr., which could be paid up in monthly instalments of 5 fr. One fully paid-up share gave a member the right to a flat. To supplement its basic capital, the co-operative was able immediately to contract a loan from the Crédit Foncier on the security of the Avenue Daumesnil housing. With this money, the co-operative financed construction on two further sites. At Grenelle it built four-storey blocks, with two flats to each landing. At Belleville, four blocks of this type were built, and also 16 two-storey units; some of these were arranged with a flat on each floor, others as single houses, which were sold by instalment payments. By 1889, the co-operative owned housing representing an investment of 880,000 fr. which was yielding a net return to the members of just over $3\%^2$ (fig. 52).

Founded under the patronage of the Emperor, the Société Coopérative Immobilière des Ouvriers was clearly a product of the 'philanthropic' interest in co-operation. So too was the similarly named Société Coopérative Immobilière, which was also formed in 1867. This co-operative was headed by Jules Simon, Léon Walras, and the architect Stanislas Ferrand. The society's founders noted that the principles of co-operation had been little used to finance housing, due to the length of time it took to establish sufficient capital from the small savings of co-operative members. They proposed to overcome this by taking advantage of the ability of some members to pay off the capital for their house more rapidly than others. Thus the capital could be subscribed immediately, or over any period up to 30 years. During the early years, when subscriptions would be at their highest, the society would devote its own capital to building. It would then take out a mortgage loan on the security of the houses built and the later subscriptions from members would be used to repay the loan. It was estimated that if one third of the members paid off the capital cost of their house in 10 years, another third in 20 years, and the final third in the full 30 years, it would be possible to finance the housing for each group within four years, seven years, and ten years respectively.

At the 1867 Exposition, the co-operative exhibited the iron-framed house which Ferrand had designed (see fig. 27). The ground floor provided an entrance, giving on to the stair and closet, and a single *salle commune*; upstairs there were two bedrooms. The space standards of this house, planned for sites in or near Paris, were lower than those of the industrial housing exhibited in 1867, The *salle commune* in particular was less than 13 m², compared to the 19 m² to 25 m² of the industrial examples. On the other hand the services, with an interior closet and a water supply, were superior in the Paris house. Based on a construction cost of 3,000 fr., the house exhibited in 1867 could be bought for 25 fr. per month over 30 years.

The society's aim was to build individual houses and flats within Paris, and also outside the city, 'wherever land is cheap and where workers

52 Housing built by the Société Coopérative Immobilière des Ouvriers at Belleville and at Grenelle; this plate also shows the alterations made by the society to the Cité Daumesnil (plans and elevation at top right of plate).

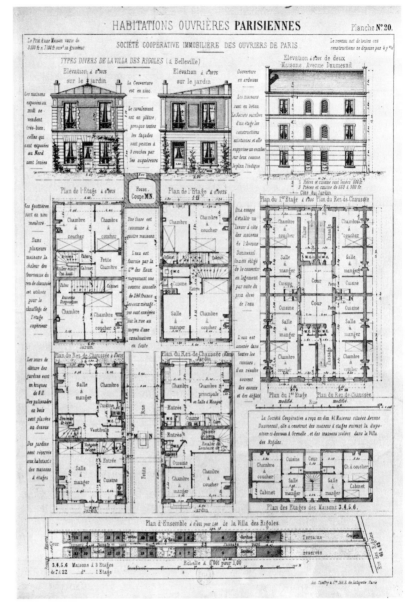

will find an economic cost of living, healthy air, and transport facilities'.[3] After the Exposition it started building a group of up to 30 houses at Colombes. This village was a quarter of an hour from Paris on the Argenteuil line. However, the ideal of forming a co-operative of workers was not realised. Of the 2,000 enquiries received during the 1867 Exposition, less than ten came from workers. Moreover, the cost of the houses planned for Colombes varied between 5,000 fr. and 15,000 fr.[4]

The workers' committee, and the co-operative founded by Simon were both awarded medals at the 1867 Exposition. But if their achievement was recognised by those involved in workers' housing, it was not universally acclaimed. The co-operative formed by the workers' committee, and Simon's co-operative both relied on the patronage of the upper classes; for this reason they were suspect to supporters of an independent co-operative movement. Thus the workers' commission which visited and discussed the 1867 Exposition did not share Chabaud's enthusiasm for the co-operative he helped found, nor for the generosity of the Emperor.[5]

A co-operative founded in the following year at the instigation of the Association des Maçons avoided this reliance on the 'philanthropic' co-operators, but it too received criticism. It was accused of being an association of capital, rather than of men, an assertion which the proposal for an 8% dividend did little to dispel. In the event, the co-operative appears only to have built a single block of flats.[6] Of this group of co-operatives formed in the late 1860s, only the Société des Ouvriers achieved any scale of activity; but with its exceptional origins in the benevolence of the Emperor, it did not indicate a path which others could easily follow.

A society which gave a clearer indication of the potential of a co-operative housing society was founded a few years later in Reims. The Union Foncière was established in 1870, but, because of the intervention of the war, it did not start its operations until 1873. Founded by 172 employees and workers, subscribing 4,497 fr., the Union had 786 members by 1888; 400,000 fr. were currently invested in the co-operative. The Union operated as a savings bank, and it was consciously designed to be accessible to workers, whether they required housing or not. The entry fee was 3 fr., and the minimum annual deposit was 25 fr. This would yield 5%; and the Union was prepared to collect savings from members' homes, even deposits of as little as one franc. Moreover, the Union provided an emergency fund to aid members who were genuinely unable to meet their annual deposit.

The Union used its funds to build new housing in the suburbs of Reims, and also rehabilitated existing properties in the city. By 1881 it had built 48 houses with gardens, which could be bought by members for 30 fr. to 39 fr. per month, over 20 years. In 1883, the 5% paid to depositors was reduced to 4%, but the Union remained active. By 1888 it had bought or built 74 houses and made loans to twenty members.[7]

The success of the Union Foncière illustrates the potential, but also the dilemma in applying co-operative principles to housing. Unlike a consumer co-operative, which at the most basic level could start working on a capital of only a few francs, a housing co-operative had to establish a considerable capital to finance construction. Simon and Walras hoped to reduce this problem by grouping well-paid employees and artisans with simple workers, so that the comparative wealth of the former would provide initial capital rapidly. But the source of capital was still restricted to the individuals buying houses. The Reims society tried to widen its sources by welcoming savers, whether they wanted to buy a house or not, but in so doing it inevitably acquired the characteristics more of a saving bank than of a radical co-operative.

Furthermore, the co-operative could not miraculously alter the laws of economics which resulted in the cost of 30 fr. or more per month for its houses. Housing co-operatives were thus forced away from the ideal of an autonomous association, to a form which either relied on the patronage of the wealthy, or which simply extended the conservative reformers' ideal of savings. In either case the workers who could afford to buy a house through a co-operative, like those buying through a limited dividend society, were an élite group.

Housing and co-operation

The Société Coopérative Immobiliére des Ouvriers and the Union Foncière both survived to appear in the housing exhibited at the 1889 Exposition. At that date these examples had still found little response in France, but in other countries co-operatives had made a greater contribution to the housing reform movement. In his report on the housing exhibition in 1889, Georges Picot referred to two precedents for co-operative action by workers, discussing the English building societies, and the housing societies founded in Italy in the 1880s.[8]

The early English building societies, formed as terminating societies, had encountered the basic problem of the co-operative, in the time taken to establish capital. This problem was overcome by the permanent societies, which welcomed both savers and borrowers; provided the number of savers exceeded the number of borrowers by a sufficient margin, the society could finance housing continuously. In France the Union Foncière had adopted this principle of linking saving and borrowing, a fact which led Emile Cacheux to describe it as 'the first French society based on the building societies'.[9]

Emile Cacheux did much to publicise the potential of building societies, but the Union Foncière was not typical of the way in which co-operation was to be applied to housing in France. The English societies had grown as an independent movement, alongside the friendly societies. The French co-operatives were to have more in common with their German counterparts, which developed from the credit co-operatives pioneered by Schulze-Delitzsch. These did not exclusively provide credit for housing, but the principle of small individual savings forming the capital for loans was clearly applicable to housing. The presence of leading figures in the French credit co-operative movement, notably Eugène Rostand, at the head of housing reform, indicates the close relationship between the two movements in France.

The 1860s had seen a growth of credit co-operatives in France, in the wake of Beluze's Crédit au Travail; but the majority of these had disappeared by 1871. However, in the 1870s the approach advocated by Schulze-Delitzsch was publicised in France, to some effect. In 1874 some of Schulze-Delitzsch's work appeared in translation in France; four years later one of his associates sent a report to the Congrès des Institutions de Prévoyance held in Paris, describing the development of credit co-operatives and popular banks in Germany. Direct contact with

Schulze-Delitzsch and his followers was difficult in the aftermath of 1870, and it was through the Italian economist Vigano that his ideas were most directly spread in France. In 1875 Vigano published his *Banques Populaires* in Paris, and in the same year founded a *banque populaire* in Cannes. The following year he visited France and gave lectures in several towns, explaining Schulze-Delitzsch's system of credit.[10]

In Italy, it was the popular bank in Milan, along with the savings bank of the town, which made possible the foundation of the Milan housing society in 1879. This marked the beginning of the rapid development during the 1880s, which Picot described in his report. In France, the spread of credit co-operatives was only really organised in the Mediterranean region of the country, where the first Congrès des Banques Populaires was held at Marseilles in 1889. It was only after this date that the implications of credit co-operatives for housing were studied in France, and the most successful co-operative housing society formed in the 1870s and 1880s remained an isolated example.

The Société Immobilière d'Orléans, founded in 1879, emphasises the ambiguous position of co-operative housing societies between the co-operative and housing reform movements. Although it was founded by 'two workers, having no capital', it relied on 'the aid of several disinterested men'.[11] The society's capital was subscribed by small savings. But the society's subtitle shows more attachment to the conservative ideals of social reform than to an autonomous co-operative movement; it aimed 'to develop the spirit of thrift by facilitating accession to property'. Indeed Georges Picot considered the society in the section of his 1889 report devoted not to co-operatives, but to commercial and philanthropic societies.

As an extension of the housing reform movement rather than the development of autonomous co-operatives, the Orléans co-operative was not unsuccessful. Paying 5% on capital subscribed, it had a total paid-up capital of 400,000 fr. by 1887; this had made possible expenditure of 2.2 million francs, financing 215 houses. The difference between capital and expenditure was covered by a combination of mortgage and loan arrangements. Buyers who had a down payment of about 500 fr., to cover the cost of land, could buy a two-storey house costing 4,000 fr. for 24 fr. per month, or a 6,000 fr. house for 35 fr. 50 c.; these repayments were made for a period of 25 years. If this procedure was little different from that adopted by the Mulhouse society, in one respect the Orléans society did differ. While the Mulhouse society and its successors generally disapproved of lodgers because they interfered with family life, the Orléans society realistically planned its houses on the assumption that the occupants would sublet to help meet their payments.[12]

From the mid-1880s, the cause of the autonomous co-operative movement was led by the consumer co-operatives, which held their first national congress in Paris in 1885. Under the leadership of Charles Gide and the co-operative group of the Ecole de Nîmes, the Union Coopérative was to move away from the orthodoxy of liberal economists. This also led to a distinction between the consumer co-operative movement, and the credit co-operatives which perpetuated the conservative view of co-operation as an extension of saving. Housing co-operatives shared this distinction from the autonomous co-operative movement; however, this did not occur immediately, and during the 1880s and 1890s the consumer and credit co-operatives shared common ground. Credit co-operatives were accepted at the 1885 congress in a consultative status, and by 1889 the links between the two types of co-operative were such that Eugène Rostand was one of the honorary presidents at the consumer co-operatives' congress.

The consumer co-operatives did not ignore the question of housing. The Société d'Economie Populaire, the centre of the Ecole de Nîmes, considered a report on the subject in 1887. The report envisaged four methods of financing housing; the first was for a commercial society on the model of Mulhouse, the remainder financed housing through a consumer co-operative.[13] This principle of a consumer co-operative helping to finance housing was taken up by the Union des Agents du PLM in Oullins, near Lyon. M. Marescot, who was one of the officials of the PLM railway company, returned from the 1889 Paris exhibition enthused by the housing he had seen there. He passed his enthusiasm on to the members of the union's consumer co-operative, and towards the end of 1890 a group of model houses was built to plans prepared by the architect M. Roucheton and approved by a committee of the workers. The houses were small, single-storey cottages, to be bought by their occupants. Although the consumer co-operative was closely involved in the initiation of this project, its history again stresses the difficulty a co-operative faced in establishing adequate capital; construction of the first group of 60 houses for sale could only be continued by means of 'an agreement with the capitalists of the area'.[14]

It was this problem which led Robert Steinmetz, a leading figure in the consumer co-operatives, to argue that workers' housing co-operatives were impractical, due to the slender resources of workers. As a socialist, Steinmetz's vision of co-operative action was more radical than that of the 'philanthropic' co-operators; not surprisingly, when Steinmetz's comments were challenged, it was by a representative of the 'philanthropic' view. Steinmetz had expressed his views at the 1889 Congress of Consumer Co-operatives; at the congress in the following year, Eugène Rostand argued strongly in favour of housing co-operatives. Disputing the view that workers' resources were inadequate, Rostand pointed to one of the social reformers' favourite institutions, the Caisse d'Epargne; he also referred to the success of housing co-operatives abroad. He saw two main ways in which a housing co-operative could operate. First, as a savings bank which granted loans to enable members to build or buy a house – the type epitomised by the English building society. Second, as construction societies which built houses which were then sold or rented to members; it was this second type which was to form the basis of development for French housing co-operatives in the

1890s. In an emotional conclusion to his speech, Rostand called for a committee to be set up to found a housing co-operative in Marseilles. He publicised the offer by the city's Caisse d'Epargne, of which he was president, to buy 40 shares in the first housing co-operative to be founded in the city.[15]

The difference between Steinmetz and Rostand reflects the division in the supporters of co-operation since the 1860s; as in the 1860s, contrasting views existed side by side in the late 1880s and 1890s. During this period several housing reformers in addition to Rostand played a significant role in the co-operative movement. Jules Siegfried was elected president of the parliamentary commission which considered a proposal for legislation on co-operatives, put forward in 1888. This proposal formed a point of contact for co-operators of varying opinions, as it was considered and reconsidered through the early 1890s. It was finally rejected in 1896, and this failure to establish a unified structure contributed to the separation of the different types of co-operative. Also during this period, from 1889 to 1895, Charles Robert was secretary general of the consumer cooperatives' central committee, and he continued his interest when he resigned to take up the post of secretary general to the new Musée Social.

The Musée Social itself promoted the study of co-operation. In 1896 and 1897 it sponsored missions to Italy and Germany to investigate credit institutions; the German study was undertaken by Maurice Dufourmantelle who, like Rostand, was active in the work of credit co-operatives and of housing reform. In 1896 the Musée Social was host to the congresses both of the French consumer co-operatives, and of the International Co-operative Association; a French committee of the International Association was subsequently formed, whose members included Siegfried, Rostand and Robert.

The mid-1890s were the period of closest links between the credit movement and the consumer co-operatives. Jean Gaumont notes that credit co-operation 'took precedence over the emancipatory ideal of the Equitable Pioneers'.[16] The more radical co-operators opposed this trend, and in 1895 left the Union Coopérative, which grouped the consumer co-operatives, to form a group of socialist co-operatives. The unity of co-operatives was further weakened in the later 1890s, as consumer and credit co-operatives followed independent paths, with separate congresses. With the election of Charles Gide to the presidency of the Union Coopérative in 1902, the consumer co-operatives renewed their allegiance to the spirit of Rochdale, and it was under the guidance of Gide that the Union was thus able to reunite with the socialist co-operatives in 1912.

The housing reformers did not abandon their links with co-operation, and in 1912 Siegfried was the first president of a new parliamentary group set up to promote co-operatives. But the reformers were not part of the main stream in the development of an autonomous co-operative movement. Nor did that movement itself take up the question of housing on a scale which offered an alternative to the work of the housing reformers. As housing co-operatives became more common in the 1890s, they were thus more closely allied to the housing reform movement, and to the ideals which reformers had evolved since the 1850s, than to a radical form of co-operation.

Housing co-operatives in the 1890s

Rostand's appeal at the 1890 co-operative congress did not go unheard, and in 1891 La Pierre du Foyer was founded in Marseilles. The Société Française des HBM was consulted on the form of the new co-operative; its report, prepared by Emile Cheysson, provided the Société des HBM with the opportunity to formulate 'scientifically the principles which should form the basis for co-operative construction societies, a type flourishing abroad, and unfortunately unknown in France.'[17] Cheysson established the financial system for a worker to buy a house valued at 3,000 fr. Estimating the amount a worker could devote to rent as 150 fr. to 200 fr. per year, to which could be added annual savings of 50 fr. to 100 fr., he argued that the worker could afford 250 fr. to 300 fr. per year – 21 fr. to 25 fr. per month – to buy his house. To do this with a co-operative society, the worker must initially save 300 fr.; this could be done with the society, by subscribing six shares at 50 fr. When fully paid up, these shares would be exchanged for 60 shares, each of which was paid up to the extent of one tenth by the initial saving. These shares would be paid up by regular instalments, augmented by the interest accruing to paid-up capital. Once the shares were fully paid up they would be exchanged for the ownership of the dwelling. While the shares were being paid up, the occupant would pay rent to service the capital, at 4%, and to cover charges, at 2%. The total cost of acquiring a house would thus be 21 fr. per month over 25 years, or 24 fr. over 19 years.[18]

To the occupant of the house, this system was little different in financial terms to paying rent to a *société anonyme* to cover the shareholders' dividend, charges, and an annuity to refund the capital. However, the process of establishing capital inevitably tended to be slower for the co-operatives. La Pierre du Foyer had a subscribed capital of only 92,900 fr. in 1899, of which 57,219 fr. was paid up; in 1906 the subscribed capital had risen to 149,000 fr., but the paid up capital was still only 73,644 fr.[19] Although shares in housing co-operatives could be bought by members simply wishing to benefit from the interest, the early co-operatives did not attract savings on the scale which enabled the English building societies to operate.

The most successful of the societies in the 1890s, La Ruche Roubaisienne, was only able to ensure its success by the aid of 'a committee of commercial and industrial notables'.[20] When the society was founded in 1895, this committee made a loan of 250,000 fr. The society supplemented this by another loan, so that by 1899, when its paid-up capital was still only 37,500 fr., it had 170 houses under construction[21] (fig. 53). Charles Gide acknowledged that La Ruche Roubaisienne was one of the most important of the French housing co-operatives.

53 Terraced housing built by
the society La Ruche
Roubaisienne

However, he drew an unfavourable comparison with the English and
American building societies.

Naturally, like all construction societies, it has been obliged to request the
necessary advances from sources other than its applicant proprietors, but in
contrast to the English and American co-operative societies, its lenders remain
simple creditors, and do not become shareholder-members, and this, from the
co-operative point of view, constitutes a serious inferiority.[22]

Gide's comments were made as author of the official report on the social
economy section of the 1900 Exposition in Paris. In this report Gide saw
a role for the consumer co-operatives in the provision of housing, which
he noted was 'one of the articles of the Rochdale programme'.[23] Such
co-operatives could invest surplus capital derived from their operation
in construction, to provide housing for their members. But Gide saw the
major contribution of co-operation to housing in the form of the English
and American building societies, which he regarded as 'the solution of
the future'.[24]

The solution which actually emerged was the development of societies
similar to La Ruche Roubaisienne rather than the building societies. The
French co-operatives did not mobilise the capital of small savers in the
manner of the English societies, and tended to rely on a very small
capital and high borrowing. They also remained small in scale; in 1905
La Ruche Roubaisienne was still the most productive of the co-operatives
founded since 1890, although it had still only built 170 dwellings. But
the co-operatives had increased considerably in number, and by 1905
there were more co-operative housing societies than *sociétés anonymes*.
Based on a lower capital than the *sociétés anonymes*, and with higher
borrowing in proportion to their capital, the co-operatives emphasised
the need for substantial credit sources for housing. Like the *sociétés
anonymes*, the co-operatives were reinforced after 1905 by the creation
of a few societies based on more substantial capital, of 1 million francs

or more. But, despite this development, the majority of co-operatives remained limited in their work before the First World War.

In terms of the number of societies at least, the development of housing co-operatives consisted no longer of isolated examples, but of a continuous growth after 1890. In this they shared the impetus given to all housing societies by the foundation of the Société Française des HBM in 1889, and the legislation passed in 1894. The co-operatives were now fully assimilated into the housing reform movement, and they even became the main inheritors of the ideal of the owner-occupied individual house. By 1906 houses for sale formed the vast majority of the output of the co-operative societies. In taking over the ideal, the co-operatives increased the number of families which could benefit from the status of proprietor, but they could not alter the category of family which obtained the benefit. By involving buyers more directly in the process of acquiring a house, the co-operatives may have given an incentive to some families who would not otherwise have sought their own home. But operating in the same market as the Société Mulhousienne and its successors, the co-operatives could not radically transform the supply of housing to the poor.

24

◇◇◇

The Société Française des Habitations à Bon Marché and housing legislation

The exhibition of workers' housing in 1867, and the housing societies formed in the following years had kept alive the question of housing reform. But the discussion of urban flats, and of co-operative housing in the 1880s took place against a background of sharpened awareness of the housing question. During the early 1880s, housing became the focus of debate as it had been in the late 1840s. As in those years, concern was stimulated by fears for public health, and for the stability of the social order. But unlike the debate in the 1840s, which subsided in the early 1850s, discussion in the 1880s led to the creation of a permanent forum and a continuity of action in relation to housing.

With respect to public health, concern derived initially not from an epidemic, as in 1848, but from the rapid growth of Paris. The population of the city had fallen as a result of the war of 1870, and the Commune which followed; during the early 1870s, when France suffered not only the after-effects of the war, but also the widespread economic depression of those years, the population of Paris grew, but at a considerably slower rate than it had during the 1850s. However, in the late 1870s, economic recovery, and the Exposition Universelle held in 1878, combined to increase the attraction of Paris as a source of work. This resulted in the high rate of immigration, and the rapid growth of the city's population in the late 1870s and early 1880s, which were to focus public attention on housing conditions. At the same time the housing reformers' concern with urban housing was reinforced by their growing concern with the low rate of population growth in the country as a whole.

The consequences of a rapid influx, particularly of labourers seeking work, were quickly taken up by the medical reformers. It was the increase in the population of *garnis* which led the Commission des Logements Insalubres to press for the introduction of controls in 1878. The problems of slum housing in general were publicised by doctors such as du Mesnil and Marjolin, at the Hygiene Congress in 1878, at the Académie de Médecine, and the Académie des Sciences Morales et Politiques in early 1880s. This publicity was intended to gain support for the proposals for revision of the 1850 law on housing hygiene, which first came seriously under discussion at this time. Parallel to these attempts to improve the condition of older property, revision of the regulations governing new building was considered, leading to the still rather inadequate regulations of 1884. At a more general level, the growth of the city, and the consequent increase in demand on public services, gave rise to the proposals for a new programme of public works, and the considerations of the hygiene and technical commissions in the early 1880s. Given this range of concern already focussed on public health, the outbreak of typhoid in 1882 was hardly necessary to evoke interest.

While the issue of public health gave ample reason for professional and bourgeois reformers to attempt to improve the housing conditions of the poor, it was supplemented by unease in relation to the social order. From the late 1870s the workers' movement was re-established under the lead of figures such as Jules Guesde, promoting socialist demands for expropriation of property, or municipal intervention. As the socialists turned their attention to housing, so the concept of housing reform as a moderating social force was taken up with renewed interest. This potential of housing reform as a counter to socialist ideas made it particularly relevant to the social aims of the Société d'Economie Sociale, and during the 1880s the reform movement gained a considerable impetus from the society. Commenting on the housing question in the society's periodical, *La Réforme Sociale*, in 1882, A. Fougerousse stressed the need to oppose revolutionary theories by direct action, not simply by words.[1] Three years later, Georges Picot gave a similar message of urgency when he spoke on housing at the society's annual conference. He saw housing reform as one of the social duties (*devoirs socials*) which the upper classes must fulfil, if they were to retain the initiative in running society. And they must fulfil it without delay: 'If we wait, it will be too late, and we will no longer have the merit of having acted in our full liberty. It will be the tide of the common man which will have reached us, and curbed our will.'[2] This fear that they would lose their position in the vanguard of society, a fear that embraced not only revolutionary socialism but also the quieter progress of State socialism, was to be a powerful incentive to the housing reformers.

The housing debate

The housing market in Paris in the late 1870s and early 1880s responded to the economic buoyancy of these years, but failed to provide accommodation matched to the city's population. The rapid growth of that population placed the cheaper housing available to working families under particular pressure. As early as 1879, the problem of rising rents was brought up in the Paris council by spokesmen for the working areas of the 13th and 20th Arrondissements; another indication of the pressure on the cheap housing market was the rise in the population of the *garnis*. Alongside these general characteristics of the housing problem, the cases of more acute hardship attracted public attention. In the winter of 1880 the plight of a group of more than 150 people, expelled from a house in La Villette, and forced to wander the streets for two days, burning their furniture to keep warm, led to a flood of contributions after it was reported in the press.[3]

Socialist groups naturally took up the issues which were raised by the problems in the housing market, and the early 1880s witnessed a series of proposals which received enough support to stimulate Fougerousse's call for pre-empting action by the reformers. The socialists centred on Jules Guesde organised a petition in 1882, demanding a reduction of 50% in all rents of 400 fr. and below. The more moderate *possibilistes* of the Union Fédérative du Centre favoured municipal construction of housing, and also proposed a tax on property left vacant for more than one month. The discussion of such measures did not remain limited to the meetings of the socialist groups. Guesde's rent petition was presented to the Chambre des Députés, while councillor Joffrin placed the *possibiliste* programme before the Paris council in August 1882.

The rent petition and Joffrin's proposals joined a series of other initiatives in the Chambre des Députés and the Paris council in 1882 and early 1883. In the Chamber, Tony Révillon headed the group of radical deputies who advocated the use of public land for housing, and who demanded the creation of a commission to study the question of rents. In the council, propositions ranged from Councillor Manier's suggestion that the city should expropriate all buildings within its boundaries, a suggestion originally put forward in 1880 and renewed in 1883, to proposals for the introduction of tax exemptions for builders of low rent dwellings.[4]

The expropriation of the city, and municipal construction were to remain outside the housing reformers' view of public action. But in response to proposals in the early 1880s, the reformers did start to examine the ways in which the public authorities might assist the work of housing societies. Emile Cacheux identified a series of related proposals, which were to be central to the housing reformers' campaign in the later 1880s. He urged that the city of Paris should use land which it owned in outlying areas, notably the fortifications, establishing the basic structure of streets and services before selling sites for housing; it should ease access to these areas by improving the system of cheap transport.[5] Such proposals were within the range of ideas raised in the Paris council. The possibility both of using communal land and of constructing housing on the fortifications was brought up by councillors in relation to the consideration of workers' housing; at a more general level, the construction of the metropolitan railway again came under discussion after the passage of legislation relating to local lines in 1880. These proposals were to remain on the council agenda for many years, and neither the use of the fortifications, nor the metropolitan railway was to come to fruition before the turn of the century. However, the perspective of this tardy progress, ultimately disappointing in terms of housing reform, should not be allowed to cloud the image of the 1880s. At that time the fortifications and the Métro together opened the real possibility of implementing the ideal of dispersed, low-density housing in the Paris suburb.

This ideal was within the main stream of housing reform, the natural development of the individual house ideal. But in the proposals which he made in the early 1880s, Cacheux gave consideration to measures which went beyond the limits of moderate reform. Thus he suggested that the city of Paris should provide the gas and water supply free of charge to workers' housing, and even admitted the possibility that the city might expropriate undeveloped land which private owners were holding in anticipation of an increased value.[6] These proposals derived not from any theoretical socialist principles, but from Cacheux's own direct experience; he knew the difficulty involved in finding land on which to build his housing, and the cost of providing the services to his houses. In his proposals, Cacheux was following the pragmatic path of 'practical socialism' characteristic of Jules Siegfried, refusing to withhold ideas simply because they echoed those of the socialists. Not all reformers saw his work in this light, however, as Arthur Raffalovich's accusation that Cacheux was indulging in State socialism indicates.[7]

Cacheux's work shows that, at its limits, the path of housing reform could share common ground with the moderate socialists. Equally, Cacheux's activity in the early 1880s indicates that, on the other side of the path, housing reform involved a dialogue with the supporters of *laissez-faire* economics. It was in 1882 that Cacheux renewed his 1878 proposal for low-interest loans financed by the State, before withdrawing it in the following year as private enterprise apparently rose to the challenge of building cheap housing.

Just as the revolutionary socialists centred on Guesde saw no role for housing reform, arguing that it was a palliative to divert the attention of the working classes from the need for more complete change, so at its limit the doctrine of *laissez-faire* had no place for housing reform. Discussing the question of rents in *L'Economiste Français* in September 1882, Arthur Mangin attributed a large part of the problem, reasonably enough, to the rapid growth of the city's population. However, he went on to argue that the construction of large quantities of cheap housing would only make matters worse by creating further incentive for workers to flood in to the city. He saw no 'correct and legitimate' method of provoking a reduction in rents – subsidised housing or controlled rents being naturally anathema. Totally ignoring the living conditions of those people already in Paris, graphically described by du Mesnil and others, Mangin questioned whether a reduction in rents was actually desirable. 'Cost is the moderating influence on consumption. The high cost of rents is a brake on the excessive immigration of provincials to Paris; it is perhaps useful to maintain the brake.'[8]

But other economists were prepared to enter into a dialogue with the housing reformers, acknowledging that there were problems within the housing market which it might be possible to resolve. The exchange between Cacheux and Leroy-Beaulieu, editor of *L'Economiste Français*, has been discussed earlier, indicating the existence of shared principles, but of differences over how those principles should be applied. The resulting debate provided a more vigorous context for economic discussion than had previously existed. Individual societies from Mulhouse to Le Havre had tackled the problems of raising capital, but no general solution had arisen from these specific, and local, initiatives. But now serious thought was being given to the problem at a more general level, in a search for a system of housing finance which would allow the work of housing societies and development companies to expand.

In this search, Leroy-Beaulieu was an early supporter of the use of the funds of the Caisses d'Epargne. He drew attention to the potential of the Caisses in 1882 – before the Caisses in Lyons and Marseilles had begun to invest in housing – in reply to Cacheux's proposal for State-funded loans at low interest.[9] The money held by the Caisses, lodged with the central Caisse des Dépôts et Consignations, had risen rapidly during the 1870s; as Leroy-Beaulieu wrote, the total stood at almost 2,000 million francs, and it rose to 2,500 million by 1886.[10] Leroy-Beaulieu proposed that one tenth of the sum deposited with the Caisses be devoted to housing, making 200 million francs available in loans over a period of five or six years.

Leroy-Beaulieu's advocacy of the use of the Caisses d'Epargne to finance housing is significant. For the Caisses offered a source of loans which was not subject to the degree of political debate still surrounding any attempt to involve the budget of the State or of the municipality directly. In effect, through the Caisse des Dépôts the State was simply returning for private investment money which had been privately saved (as opposed to publicly taxed), but with the advantage that, having been centrally pooled in the Caisse des Dépôts, there was a substantial sum available from a single source. As Leroy-Beaulieu's position demonstrates, it was a proposal which could be supported even within *laissez-faire* circles. This pragmatic advantage was parallelled in the reformers' eyes by the fact that, in increasing the supply of housing, the money saved by working families and employees in the Caisses d'Epargne would be being recycled to their benefit. The use of these funds was thus a natural extension of the reformers' interest in saving.

The housing debate which unfolded in 1882 had brought a range of conflicting proposals to the fore. The process of putting some order into the debate began in 1883, with the consideration of housing by a series of official commissions, and proposals from the council and from the government. At the end of January, the Prefect of the Seine set up an administrative commission which brought together representatives from the city council, and from outside groups interested in housing reform. Several active housing reformers sat on the commission, including Cheysson, du Mesnil, Muller and Trélat; among the four vice-presidents were Alphand, whose technical commission was currently considering the sewer system in Paris, and Dietz-Monnin, president of the Société de Passy Auteuil, and recently elected to the Senate. The administrative commission was divided into three sub-committees, which considered questions of hygiene, land and transport, and finance respectively.[11]

Shortly after this commission was set up, the Paris council received the report of its finance commission, which had been asked to consider the various proposals submitted to the council relating to the use of the fortifications, and to measures to reduce rents. The commission showed a marked reluctance to involve municipal finances in housing, opposing both the direct construction of housing and the reservation of communal land for cheap housing. Its most positive proposal was that the city build a small group of model dwellings as an example to private enterprise. Apart from this, the commission simply looked to the Prefect's commission to solve the problem, asking the administration to prepare a project which would result in the construction of 30,000 dwellings in 1884 and 1885.[12]

Meanwhile, the government was also examining ways of encouraging housing construction; it announced in March that a proposal would be presented to the deputies immediately after the Easter recess. Drawn up by the Ministers of the Interior, and of Finance, and the director of the Crédit Foncier, this proposal aimed to make money available for cheap housing through the Crédit Foncier, and to allow certain tax exemptions for workers' housing. The proposal was in two parts, relating to France as a whole, and to Paris specifically.[13]

In April, the Paris council set up a special housing commission to consider the government proposal; the proposal was also studied by the Prefect's administrative commission. After several months of being revised and passed between the commissions, the council and the government, a definitive proposal was finally examined by the Paris council in February 1884, when the council also debated other proposals related to housing. The council held firmly back from the direct action which had been discussed over the previous two years: councillors voted to reject the partnership with the Crédit Foncier, to reject tax exemptions for builders of cheap housing, and to reject the municipal construction of housing.[14]

The partnership with the Crédit Foncier foundered partly because of political factors unrelated to housing. A. L. Shapiro has drawn attention to the tension within the Paris council between supporters of the State's authority, and the 'autonomists' who wished to strengthen the authority of the municipality. An agreement bringing together the State and the city, as the Crédit Foncier agreement would have done, could not avoid this tension. At another level, the memory of Haussman's unorthodox financial methods, leaving the city with debts which were still being paid off, made councillors cautious about engaging the city's money, particularly with the Crédit Foncier, which had been Haussman's financial partner.[15]

The only positive actions accepted by the Paris council in February 1884 were that the city should build a group of four model houses, and that it should lease communal land to builders of cheap housing. Yet even these modest decisions yielded no results in practice. Plans were prepared for the model houses, and sites found, but the council never discussed the project to approve its execution. The attempt to make land available got slightly further, and in 1885 the first site in the Rue Tolbiac was offered. However, it was not taken up, and the issue of using communal land in this way was quietly shelved. The abortive experiment had encountered the problems which the 1852 subsidy had revealed;

the conditions imposed on builders reduced their return to a level at which it was not worth their taking advantage of the assistance. An estimate by a group of architects working for the city of Paris showed that the return would be less than 4%.[16]

The history of the proposals made in the early 1800s, from expropriating the city of Paris to maintaining the high level of rents, makes dispiriting reading. The intensified level of debate, and the rosy vision offered by the proposal for the Métro and clearance of the fortifications give rise to expectation of rather more than the series of crude attempts to encourage the construction of housing. And yet the debate was crucial as a trial run through the possibility of State or municipal action; the comparison with 1850 is instructive. Then, as in the 1880s, debate was galvanised by the threat of revolutionary doctrines. But whereas in 1850 the threat was from physical revolt in the city, which had already been suppressed in June 1848, in the 1880s the threat was within the council chamber, within parliament. The failure of the proposals of the early 1880s indicates that the threat was not yet strong enough to force real action; but as Picot made clear in 1885, the progress of democracy remained as an urgent incentive to action.

The debate of the early 1880s was also significant in raising certain issues which were to remain important. The principle on which the government proposal was based, that of a special credit source for cheap housing, combined with tax reliefs, was to reappear ten years later in the proposal for legislation presented by Jules Siegfried. As a potential contributor to this credit source, the funds of the Caisses d'Epargne came under repeated discussion. Siegfried's proposal was to take up the idea of using the funds deposited centrally with the Caisse des Dépôts, but individual action by Caisses was also considered. From 1886, a special delegation set up by the congress of Caisses d'Epargne examined the desirability of freedom of investment by Caisses; at the 1890 congress, Eugène Rostand argued strongly in favour of freedom of control over part of the savings deposited with a Caisse. By that time the Caisses in Lyons and Marseilles offered a clear demonstration of the potential of such freedom to housing reform. Rostand's view did not prevail in 1890, but five years later it was partially realised when new legislation on Caisses allowed them to contribute to the working of housing societies. Rather slower in taking effect were two other proposals which remained under discussion after 1880: the clearance of the Paris fortifications and the revision of the 1850 housing law.

The debate of the early 1880s initially raised more questions than it resolved, and this is perhaps the fundamental reason for the failure to transfer debate into effective action. Within the range of proposals made to the Paris council, none predominated. Socialists were divided between the Guesdists, opposed to municipal construction, and the *possibilistes* who favoured it; opponents of socialism did not agree on the extent to which the State should act. Within this disarray, one line did gradually being to emerge, centred on the Société d'Economie Sociale. When Georges Picot stressed the urgency of action to members of the society in 1885, he also emphasised the need for a pragmatism which would avoid theoretical solutions. 'We must not listen to the State socialists, nor to those who believe in the indefinite effectiveness of competition left to itself.'[17] Around this pragmatic position, the housing reformers were able to develop proposals which gained enough support to push through the turmoil of the 1880s into law in the 1890s.

Social economy and the Société Française des HBM

The Société d'Economie Sociale sought the resolution of social questions in the middle path between the extremes identified by Picot. When a workers' congress was held in Paris in 1876, the society invited a representative to speak about the congress; the society's reply, prepared by Emile Cheysson, consciously attempted to seek the common ground between the workers' movement, and the efforts of reformers to improve workers' conditions. Housing was among the topics discussed by Cheysson, and in the 1880s the subject was to be regularly considered in its own right by the society.

In 1880, members of the society heard a paper by Emile Cacheux, while at the first conference organised by the society, in 1882, Cheysson gave a report on housing. By that date, the society had a practical example to consider: in the Société de Passy Auteuil, which Cheysson had helped found; the conference visited the housing there in 1882 and in 1883, while in 1884 it visited housing built by Emile Cacheux. Meanwhile the Unions de la Paix Sociale, the more dispersed organisation of correspondents studying questions of social economy which Le Play had established in the 1870s, also considered housing. The programme for the Unions published in 1881 urged members to work towards the creation of building societies, based on those in England, the construction of housing by employers, and of suburban housing linked to public transport. The message did not go unheard. Members of the Unions were actively involved in each of the four societies which tackled the problem of urban flats in the later 1880s, in Rouen, Lyons, Marseilles and Paris.

By accepting a limited return on capital invested, these societies fulfilled Picot and Cheysson's belief in a path which mediated between socialism and *laissez-faire* – though it was undeniably rather closer to the latter than the former. In order to spread the limited achievement of such societies, the social economists turned to their favourite means of action: the survey. In 1886 Cheysson described the surveys of housing conditions carried out in England in 1885 and Belgium in 1886. The following year the Société d'Economie Sociale initiated its own survey, designed to investigate conditions and initiatives to improve them. Over the next few years the social economists' journal, *La Réforme Sociale*, included surveys from Lille, Nantes, Nancy and Bordeaux. But while they tried to encourage private initiatives in the form of surveys and housing societies, the members of the Société d'Economie Sociale and the Unions de la Paix Sociale also began to define a role for the State, and municipal administration.

At its most basic level this role was stated by Arthur Raffalovich in a form which had been established in 1850: the State and municipalities should 'make war on unhealthy dwellings', but they should not provide subsidised housing. But the ground was no longer as clear as in 1850, as the debate in the early 1880s had shown. In his paper to the urban hygiene exhibition in Paris, in 1886, Emile Cheysson elaborated on the distinction noted by Raffalovich. Cheysson personally argued that the State should provide reduced-interest loans or fiscal advantages to housing societies; recognising that these policies would not have universal support, he went on to list less contentious forms of action. By improving public transport the State could help to increase the supply of cheap land available for housing; by organising a national survey the State could identify the true nature and extent of the housing problem; finally, as an employer, the State was fully entitled to set an example to industrial employers by financing housing for its own workers.[18]

Dr Jules Rochard, who had sat with Cheysson on the housing survey commission set up by the Société d'Economie Sociale, also urged the State to set up a national survey, and to finance housing as an employer. But, in an article on housing in the *Revue des Deux Mondes* in 1888, he outlined a more active role for local municipalities. Noting the expense which Emile Cacheux had encountered in providing the roads and servicing to his housing in Paris, Rochard argued that the city should meet the cost of public service installations, and that it should lay out public streets before the construction of housing. He also saw a duty for the municipality to arrange adequate public transport to housing built on the edge of the city. While these activities gave the municipality a considerable role in creating the public infrastructure, Rochard was adamant that municipalities should not substitute themselves for private construction companies by building housing on their own account.[19]

In his authoritative report to the International Jury of the 1889 Exposition Universelle in Paris, Georges Picot drew together these attitudes to public authorities. Considering the role of the State, he defined four lines of action which required legislative intervention. First, the initiation of a survey. Second, encouragement to construction by a reduction in interest rates. Picot noted that most housing societies could not afford the 4.85% to 5% which loans were then costing, but he ruled out preferential rates for cheap housing because of the danger of creating a privileged category of citizen; he thus urged a general reduction in interest rates for all loans, and drew attention to the funds of the Caisses d'Epargne as a source of credit which could be opened to cheap housing. Third, reform of the inheritance laws which required equal distribution of goods between the surviving family when the head of a family died. In this, Picot took up an issue which had long concerned the social economists, as equal distribution often involved the sale – and thus loss – of the family home, on which Le Play and his followers placed so much stress. Finally, the revision of the 1850 law controlling unhealthy dwellings. With respect to municipalities, Picot, like Rochard, acknowledged their duty to provide roads and public services. He also accepted that they had a right to inspect the plans of housing developments for approval before construction. But this was the extreme limit of intervention; in conclusion, he reiterated the principle on which his comments were based: 'Not only does [direct] official aid stultify initiative, but it also corrupts the worker by making him think that the public authorities can undertake to provide his housing, which they would be incapable of doing without ruin.'[20]

While there was still room for differences of opinion – as over the question of whether loans should be at market rates or at special rates of interest – the views of these reformers indicate a broad consensus emerging by the later 1880s. It was the Exposition in 1889, for which Picot wrote his report on housing, that was to concentrate support behind the consensus established by the social economists. The Exposition took up the interest in social questions which Le Play had introduced in 1867, but which had been less apparent in the intervening Exposition of 1878. R. H. Guerrand has noted that the term Economie Sociale gained a sort of official sanction in 1889, and became fashionable in philanthropic circles.[21] Jules Siegfried, who had been involved with Charles Robert and Emile Cheysson in the preparation for the Exposition since 1887, emerged as a leading figure, acting as vice-president to the organising committee of the Groupe d'Economie Sociale as a whole, and president of the workers' housing section. While not formally connected to the school of social economy at this date, Siegfried shared many of the aspirations of the social economists, and above all their pragmatism. During the 1890s Siegfried did become affiliated to the Unions de la Paix Sociale, and joined with long-standing members of the Société d'Economie Sociale in founding the Musée Social. Siegfried was thus particularly well suited to fulfil the role of figurehead to the housing reform movement, as he provided a link between the social economists and the Chambre des Députés.

The doctors, engineers, architects and social reformers who had developed an interest in housing reform were naturally aware of each other's work, and in several cases had already collaborated. But the events of 1889 brought many of them together, not in a specific housing society or project, but with a view to the general consideration of housing. In the organising committee of the workers' housing section of the Exposition, Siegfried was joined by Georges Picot as vice-president, and by Emile Muller, Emile Trélat, Dr du Mesnil, and even J. B. A. Godin, as ordinary members. A second committee was set up to organise the International Housing Congress, the first event of its kind, planned for June 1889. This committee was also led by Siegfried and Picot, along with two further vice-presidents, Emile Muller and Dietz-Monnin. The committee secretaries were Arthur Raffalovich, who had published his study of housing in France and abroad in 1887, and Antony Rouillet, a lawyer who had made a particular study of legislation on cheap housing; the committee treasurer was the indefatigable Emile Cacheux. Of the eighteen ordinary members of the committee, the majority were active in the provision of workers' housing, either through societies or industry. Among the industrialists were Guary, the director of the Anzin mines, and Gaston Menier. The housing societies in Reims, Rouen, Le Havre, Amiens and Lyons were represented, while Emile Cheysson and Eugène Rostand combined activity in housing societies with a wider role in social reform. The architects provided a smaller group, in the form of Bourdeix, Gosset and Trélat, while Dr du Mesnil sat as the only doctor on the committee.[22]

The housing exhibited in 1889 gave prominence to the variety of types which had emerged in France: industrial housing with its roots in the 1830s; Mulhouse, and its imitators after 1867; the urban societies building flats since 1885. Only the co-operative movement, still without a clear sense of direction in relation to housing, was sparsely represented. The housing congress was open to international visitors to the Exposition, but its contributors presented the French case for housing reform. Picot spoke on housing from the moral point of view, Raffalovich on economics, Rouillet on legislation; Muller and du Mesnil prepared the paper on construction and hygiene, although Muller was too ill by mid-1889 actually to attend the congress.

The resolutions voted by the congress endorsed the French position and touched on the issues which had been raised during the 1880s. Private enterprise was acclaimed as the mechanism for housing reform, and public intervention in either construction or rent control was rejected; the extent of intervention was limited to the questions of transport, hygiene and fiscal control. With respect to resources for housing, the congress placed its main hope in the Caisses d'Epargne, urging that the Caisses should be given the freedom to invest part of the savings of depositors in housing. As regards the form of housing, the congress maintained the ideal of the individual house wherever it was practical.[23]

The congress also passed a resolution which proposed the creation of national societies to publicise and encourage the work of housing reform. Before the end of the year a French society had been formed in execution of this resolution: the Société Française des Habitations à Bon Marché (HBM). The inaugural meeting of the society, held on 2 February 1890, confirmed the familiar principles on which the French housing reform movement was based. Jules Siegfried referred to the origins of the movement in Mulhouse and drew attention to the spread of the approach pioneered there. Georges Picot similarly referred to Mulhouse, but he also looked to the work of the housing societies in London as examples for the society to promote. Dr Rochard followed by considering hygiene in housing; he acknowledged the preference shown by both Siegfried and Picot for the individual house, but admitted that this was only available to the élite of the working class. Rochard stressed that 'barracks' like the Cité Napoléon must be avoided, but supported the view which Muller and du Mesnil had already put forward at the housing congress: that properly designed blocks of flats could offer satisfactory guarantees of hygiene. It remained only for the veteran 75-year-old Jules Simon to bring the gathering at the Hotel Continental to a resounding burst of applause with his bracing conclusion: 'In a word, gentlemen, without dwellings there can be no family – without family there can be no morals – without morals there can be no man – without men there can be no nation!'[24]

As the elder statesman of social reform, Simon took the post of honorary president of the new society. The active leaders were a generation younger than Simon: Siegfried as president, Cheysson and Picot as vice-presidents, and Charles Robert as treasurer; the board was completed by Antony Rouillet as its secretary. Siegfried led the society until 1892, the year in which he presented the society's proposal for legislation to the Chambre des Députés; he was succeeded by Picot, who held the position until his death in 1909. Many of the members on the organising committees for the exhibition and congress in 1889 joined the new society, alongside other figures who had been drawn into housing reform in the 1870s and 1880s. Cacheux, Rostand and Raffalovich took their places alongside the doctors A. J. Martin, Rochard and du Mesnil. Durand-Claye had died in 1888, but his widow joined the society, as did the head of the Paris Bureau des Logements Insalubres, G. Jourdan. The architect Emile Trélat found himself in the company of Chabrol, Lucas, and the architect of Rostand's Marseilles society, Charles d'Albert. The opponent of architects, Félix Mangini, was among the founder members, as were the financier Léon Say, and the industrialists Menier and Peugeot. Three honorary members were nominated by the society. These were Dietz-Monnin, of the Société de Passy Auteuil; Dr Marjolin, champion of child welfare and advocate of the reform of the 1850 housing legislation; and Auguste Dollfus, president of the society which had contributed to the early development of housing reform, the Société Industrielle de Mulhouse.

The role of the new Société Française des HBM was to be primarily one of propaganda. Specifically debarring the society from making or contracting loans, or becoming involved in the construction of housing, the statutes declared that the society would encourage the construction of cheap housing, the improvement of existing dwellings, and, particularly, the means to enable employees, artisans and workers to become owners of their dwellings. The society adopted the title *habitations à bon marché*, as opposed to the title *habitations ouvrières* which had been commonly used to describe the type of housing which the reformers aspired to build. This change of terminology had been made in relation to the housing congress of 1889, at the suggestion of Dietz-Monnin. His own society at Passy Auteuil used the term *habitations ouvrières*, but as early as 1881 one writer had commented that, as the society was more relevant to *petits employés* than to *ouvriers*, the description *habitations à bon marché* would be more appropriate.[25] The change was thus not a detail of semantics, but acknowledged that the main effort of the housing reform movement was of benefit to employees, and artisans, and not primarily to the majority of workers.

The society's role as a propagandist was centred on its quarterly bulletin. The early issues discussed foreign legislation on housing, and the society's own proposal for legislation in France. They also gave details of the work of housing societies, including the Société Havraise and the Société Philanthropique in France, the Metropolitan Association and Peabody Trust in London, and the Berliner Baugenossenschaft in Germany. In 1891 the bulletin included sample statutes for housing societies, and Cheysson's report on housing co-operatives. Meanwhile, the society was involved in the foundation of a new housing society in Saint-Denis, north of Paris. A competition was held under the auspices of the Société Française des HBM in 1890, attracting 48 entries; all of these entries were put on display in the Hôtel de Ville in Paris, where they created considerable interest, and were visited by the President of the Republic, Sadi Carnot. The winning scheme, designed by Georges Guyon (see fig. 54), was naturally important to the reformers, as it effectively represented their own aspirations. Guyon rose to the brief, which requested a range of dwelling types, by developing most of the site with 21 individual houses, but he also included three blocks of flats, providing 20 dwellings. These four-storey blocks grouped flats around staircase access, avoiding shared corridors; each flat had its own WC and water supply. The housing thus represented in built form the current thinking on cheap housing, which the Société des HBM was publicising in its bulletin.[26]

The aims of the Société des HBM included the improvement of existing dwellings, and the society quickly set up a commission to consider this subject; the commission added its voice to the demands for revision of the 1850 housing law, and of the law on expropriation. The society also initiated a competition for studies of cheap housing in local areas. In this field of surveying the existing situation, the society was happy to request the aid of the State, and in 1893 the time for such a request was ripe. Since December 1892 the government had been led by Alexandre Ribot, a founder member of the Société des HBM; in January 1893 he appointed Jules Siegfried to the Ministère du Commerce et de l'Industrie, and it was this ministry which the society intended to request to undertake a survey. A pilot study in the 13th Arrondissement of Paris was undertaken by Dr du Mesnil and Dr Mangenot, a member of the local Conseil d'Hygiène. Unfortunately, the rapid turnover of French governments took its toll, and in April 1893 Ribot fell from power.

If this attempt to introduce a government survey yielded no fruit, the Société des HBM had come into being at a time when statistical information on housing was becoming more available. The details of overcrowding in Paris, derived from the 1891 census, were published in 1894, the year in which the *Casier Sanitaire* was started. Alfred de Foville's study of housing types had been commenced in 1890, and in the same year Ribot, then foreign minister, instigated a study of foreign workers' conditions. Within France, a major study of charitable institutions in each department was commenced in 1890 by the Office Central des Oeuvres Charitables, under a commission headed by Emile Cheysson. The Musée Social provided another focus of information after 1894, and

54 Georges Guyon's winning project in the competition for a housing development in Saint Denis, held under the auspices of the Société Française des HBM in 1890. House types A, B and C were two-storey individual houses, while types D, E, F and G were four-storey blocks of flats.

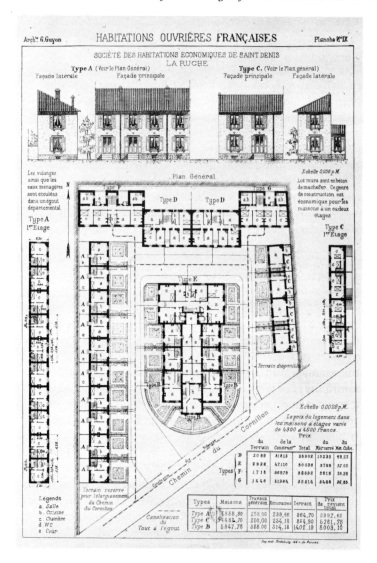

so the Société des HBM was working within a range of organisations gathering and disseminating information on housing and social issues. But despite the importance they placed on the survey as a means of action, the housing reformers were not prepared to sit waiting for information throughout the 1890s. The 1880s had allowed them to develop a clear enough picture of the nature of the housing problem for them to submit their own proposals for national legislation in 1892.

The Siegfried Law 1894

The legislative proposal drawn up within the Société Française des HBM was presented to the Chambre des Députés by Jules Siegfried on 5 March 1892. In its broad outline, the proposal brought together some of the ideas discussed in the 1880s: tax exemptions for cheap dwellings and housing societies, and the release of credit through the Caisse des Dépôts et Consignations and charitable organisations. But if these innovations had already been well discussed in France, the example of neighbouring countries was none the less important. Belgium had passed housing legislation in 1889, England in 1890, and Austria–Hungary in 1892. Siegfried discussed these laws in the preamble to the proposal of the Société des HBM, and included the full texts as an appendix. The Belgian example was particularly relevant to the French reformers, and Siegfried and Cheysson visited Brussels in 1891. Like the French proposal, the Belgian law was based on tax advantages and the provision of a credit source – in this case the Caisse Nationale d'Epargne et de Retraite. The Belgian law also introduced local housing committees to encourage and co-ordinate initiatives throughout the country, a system which the French took up in their proposal.

In contrast, the English law went too far for Siegfried and his colleagues, introducing public intervention beyond the consensus which French reformers had reached in the late 1880s. Referring to Part 3 of the English Act of 1890, which enabled the London County Council to commence its pioneering series of housing developments, Siegfried asked 'Would we not be right in saying that the law of 18 August 1890 has entered very deeply into the path of State socialism?' However, whether the example was one to follow or to avoid, the lead taken by foreign countries was enough to stir a patriotic enthusiasm in Siegfried, sharpened by his own belief in the superiority of the Republican system. He stressed that 'Republican France should not lag behind the monarchies which surround us, she above all who has always defended with such ardour the interests of the lowly and the underprivileged.'[27]

Siegfried's bill was speedily approved by the deputies, but fared less well in the Senate. The right wing saw the bill as a massive intervention by the State, leaving little room for private initiative. Particular worries were expressed over the involvement of the Caisse des Dépôts; the director of the Caisse was himself reluctant to invest his resources in housing, fearing that this would reduce the ability of the Caisse to meet a sudden rush of withdrawals from the Caisses d'Epargne. The Caisse de Dépôts was finally reconciled to its role, but with an ill grace which was to be reflected in its unenthusiastic implementation of the law.

As eventually passed in 1894 – a swift passage in comparison to the time it was taking to revise the 1850 law – the law applied to housing built by or for persons owning no property, and 'notably to workers or employees living principally from their work or their salary'. Submitted in 1892 as a law relating to *habitations ouvrières*, the law went through the same change in terminology as the 1889 housing congress, emerging with the less demanding title of *habitations à bon marché*. Dwellings taking advantage of the law must not exceed a certain rent: this varied from 132 fr. per year in the smallest communes, to 440 fr. in cities of over 200,000 population, and 550 fr. in Paris. Dwellings conforming to these restrictions enjoyed limited tax reliefs, as did societies building such dwellings; to prevent speculative companies taking advantage of the law, societies must agree to limit their dividend – to a figure set at 4% in the regulations relating to implementation of the law. Two aspects of the law were introduced to reduce the problems associated with home-ownership. Thus arrangements for temporary life insurance were made available, providing cover which would meet outstanding payments for a house if the breadwinner died before payment was complete. Similarly the law amended inheritance procedures, to allow a period of five to ten years during which the division of the property could be delayed. Both of these measures reflect the social economists' emphasis on the bond between a family and its home, which must be protected from a sudden break.

The major credit source offered by the 1894 law was through the Caisse des Dépôts. However, certain public charitable organisations (Bureaux de Bienfaisance, almshouses, hospitals and the Assistance Publique in Paris) were also permitted to use part of their reserves to finance housing. Caisses d'Epargne were not included, as separate legislation was under discussion; this resulted in 1895 in authorisation for the Caisses to invest not the money deposited by savers, but a proportion of their independent reserves, in cheap housing. In addition to providing loans to housing societies, the charitable organisations and the Caisses d'Epargne were also authorised to build housing on their own account.

To supervise implementation of the measures introduced in 1894 and 1895, and to extend the propaganda role of the Société des HBM to the local level, the law authorised the creation of Comités des HBM. Like the central Société des HBM, the Comités could organise competitions, award prizes, carry out surveys, and encourage private initiatives to build cheap housing. Above the Comité, a government advisory body was introduced, attached to the Ministère du Commerce et de l'Industrie. This Conseil Supérieur des HBM was to receive annual reports from the local Comités, and act as a central monitoring organisation.

While the Senators of the Right saw the law as excessive in its intervention, and the defenders of *laissez-faire* such as Leroy-Beaulieu saw it as contrary to the principle of equality of all before legislation and taxation,[28] the 1894 law was in reality only a modest intervention in the housing market. Private enterprise was unchallenged as the mechanism of housing reform, and Siegfried was careful to present his proposals as producing the maximum effect with the minimum disturbance. 'Gentlemen,' he commenced in his initial proposal to the deputies, 'among the number of truly effective measures which while respecting the essential bases of society, can bring a marked improvement in the conditions of workers, it is fitting to cite in the first place the construction of healthy and economical houses.'[29] Had Siegfried and his fellow reformers found the miraculous potion which would cure society's ills without unpleasant side effects or were they simply administering a placebo?

The 1894 law did lead to an increase in the number of new housing societies; in doing so it accelerated a trend apparent since the 1880s. A list of active housing societies published by the Société Française des HBM in 1895 showed only one society dating from the 1850s: the Mulhouse society; between 1867 and 1889 14 societies were formed, most of them during the 1880s, as a practical counterpart to the housing debate. The foundation of the Société Française des HBM further increased the rate of foundations, with 16 new societies by the end of 1894. Setting aside the Mulhouse society, now in Germany, the list thus showed a total of 30 societies active in 1894.[30] The law passed in that year divided the subsequent development of societies into two streams: those which received approval of their statutes in order to benefit from the company tax reliefs in the law, and those which remained independent. The majority of new societies formed after 1894 adopted approved status, but not all of the earlier societies did so. Some, such as the Société des Logements Economiques in Lyons, which provided a cheap restaurant service as well as housing, or the Union Foncière co-operative in Reims, were too wide-ranging in their activities to fit the company structure envisaged by the law. The most significant single group which remained independent was the foundations, such as the Société Philanthropique which was to be joined by several larger foundations after 1894.

Of the 30 housing societies listed by the Société Française des HBM in 1895, 15 were subsequently approved as official societies under the 1894 law. By the end of 1899, a total of 34 active societies had received approval for their statutes – nine of the societies listed in 1895, and 25 formed since the passage of the 1894 law. Approval of statutes by the Conseil Supérieur des HBM was by no means automatic. The Conseil found that a substantial number of societies failed to achieve the solid base necessary to start operating, and at least one society approved before 1900 had been dissolved almost as soon as it was approved. Notwithstanding the problems associated with expanding the reform movement from a small group of societies animated by committed individuals, to a more widespread network of financially sound companies, the number of societies did start to increase. By the end of 1905, over 150 societies had applied for approval, and 120 had been approved. This growth was soon dominated by the co-operatives. In 1899, the *sociétés anonymes* were still in the majority, with a total of 22 against 12 co-operatives; by 1905 the position was reversed, with 50 *sociétés anonymes* and 70 co-operatives. But while the reformers could gain some comfort from this expansion, the societies were mostly operating on a very small scale. The co-operatives in particular were hampered by a low level of capital, only partially paid up; and while the co-operatives and, to a lesser extent, the *sociétés anonymes*, supplemented their capital by borrowing, the sources of credit opened in 1894 and 1895 fell far short of the aid which they could have provided.[31]

The major disappointment of the 1894 law had been foreshadowed during its passage through the Senate. The Caisse des Dépôts et Consignations showed no intention of encouraging the use of the 15

55 Graphs showing the evolution of investment in housing by approved housing societies, foundations, and savings banks. Statistics taken from the annual reports of the Conseil Supérieur des Habitations à Bon Marché, and from Paul Strauss' report to the Sénat, *Documents Parlementaires*, Sénat (1912), No. 352. The figures relate to the position at 31 December of each year. (For discussion of the figures between 1906 and 1911, see Chapter 26.)

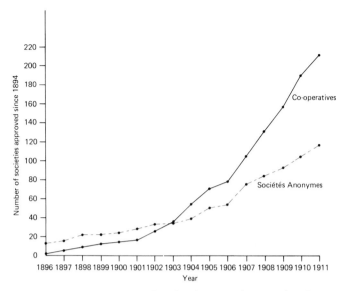

1 Housing societies approved under the 1894 housing legislation

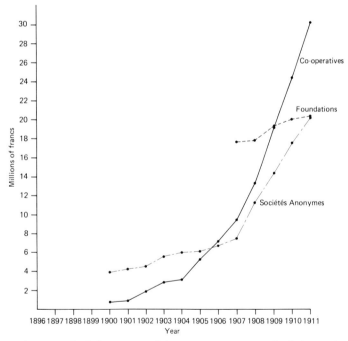

2 The capital of the approved housing societies, and of the major housing foundations in Paris (the Groupe des Maisons Ouvrières, the Fondation Rothschild and the Fondation Weill). The figures for the *sociétés anonymes* are adjusted to exclude the Groupe des Maisons Ouvrières – initially founded as a *société anonyme*, but subsequently transformed into a foundation; the Société de Crédit des Habitations à Bon Marché has also been excluded from the *société anonyme* figures, as it acted as a simple intermediary between the Caisse des Dépôts et Consignations and housing societies (see graph 3a).

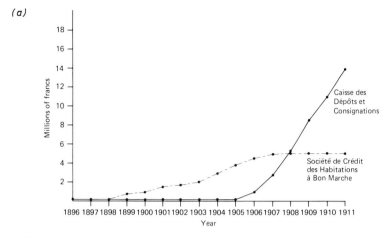

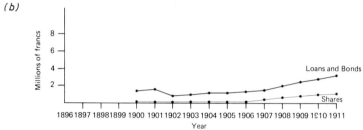

3 Sources of finance for housing societies: (a) Total of loans granted to approved housing societies by the Caisse des Dépôts et Consignations, independently, and through the intermediary of the Société de Crédit des Habitations à Bon Marché. (b) Outstanding current investment by the Caisses d'Epargne in approved housing societies, by loans and bonds, and by investment in shares.

million francs which the law authorised it to lend to housing societies. By 1898 only a single loan, of 150,000 fr., had been granted. In that year Jules Siegfried tried to overcome this stalemate by creating a credit society as an intermediary between the Caisse and borrowers. Borrowing from the Caisse at 2%, the credit society loaned to housing societies at 3%. Under this system, credit did start to flow into housing. By the end of 1905, the credit society had agreed 75 loans, committing almost all of the 5 million francs it was authorised to lend. Not all of these loans had yet been taken up, so that the actual total investment was 3.83 million francs (see fig. 55, graph 3a). Repayments had reduced the outstanding investment to 3.48 million francs – a figure still far short of the potential indicated in 1894.

The Caisses d'Epargne similarly fell short of the potential, which by late 1905 would have allowed them to invest more than 36 million francs in housing. By the end of 1905, only 14 Caisses had invested in housing societies, providing a total investment of 2.4 million francs up to that date, of which 1.12 million francs was outstanding as the current investment (see fig. 55, graph 3b). Even these figures are hardly

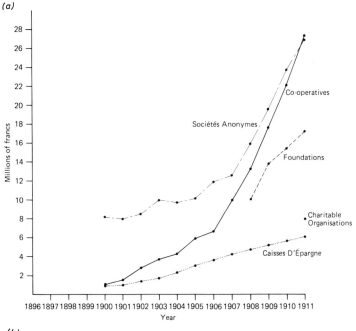

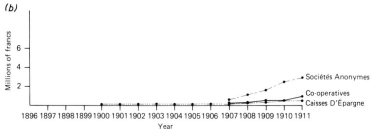

4 Investment in construction: (a) Current investment in construction and land by approved housing societies, the major Paris foundations, Caisses d'Epargne, and charitable organisations (the latter dominated by the Assistance Publique in Paris). (b) Current investment in mortgage loans to individuals by approved housing societies, and Caisses d'Epargne.

representative, as they included the investments by the Caisses in Lyons and Marseilles which predated the law of 1895 on the Caisses d'Epargne. That law permitted Caisses to provide loans to housing societies, but the earlier activity of the Marseilles Caisse had gone beyond this to include contribution to share capital, and mortgage loans to individuals. Thus the 1.12 million franc current investment can be broken down into 1.05 million francs in housing society bonds and loans to housing societies, as envisaged by the legislation, 24,160 fr. in shares, and 55,474 fr. in mortgage loans. But it was the Lyons Caisse in particular which dominated the investment of Caisses before 1905, with its 1 million franc contribution to the local housing society. If the Lyons and Marseilles Caisses are omitted, a more accurate estimate of the effect of the 1894 and 1895 laws can be set at a total investment of 1.1 million francs, and a current investment of just under 1 million francs. But even this meagure contribution appeared generous in comparison to the work of the charitable institutions. Up to 1905, apparently only two organisations acted at all. In Saint Amand, the local hospice lent 50,000 fr. to a housing co-operative, while in Paris the Assistance Publique had made loans to two housing societies, totalling 275,000 fr.

The inadequacy of the credit system introduced in 1894 and 1895 was made apparent by contrast with Belgium, where the law of 1889 had released more than 50 million francs by 1905. The French reformers could not hide their disappointment, as Georges Picot acknowledged at the general assembly of the Société Française des HBM in 1905. 'A small country with a population six times less than ours', he complained, 'has accomplished a task ten times as great'.[32]

This low supply of credit, coupled with the low capital resources of the housing societies, was reflected in the output of the societies. Figures published by the Ministère du Commerce show the total of construction by approved societies up to 1902 ranging from 87 to 266 dwellings per year.[33] The largest of the societies in terms of building were still making a very limited contribution when compared to the output of many English housing societies, and within France, to independent societies such as that in Lyons. Even the largest co-operative, identified by Charles Gide in 1900, La Ruche Roubaisienne, had built only 170 houses by the end of 1905. The main *société anonyme*, active since 1889, was the society founded by Rostand in Marseilles, but this had still only built about 200 dwellings by 1905.

La Ruche Roubaisienne was typical of the co-operatives in building houses rather than flats. Houses represented more than 85% of the dwellings built by co-operatives up to the end of 1905, and over 80% of these houses were for sale rather than rent. While the co-operatives thus adopted the reformers' ideal, the *sociétés anonymes* reflected the increasing interest in urban flats since the 1880s. The oldest of the approved societies building flats dated back only to 1885 – the Société des Petits Logements de Rouen. However, by 1906 flats represented more than one third of the output of the *sociétés anonymes*; the remaining dwellings were divided almost equally between houses for sale and houses for rent.

The figures of the Conseil Supérieur des HBM for the year ending in December 1905 make it possible to assess the financial contribution of the approved societies to housing construction at this date (see fig. 55, graphs 2 and 4a). Of the 120 societies which had received approval, 98 had already completed a years' activity – 42 *sociétés anonymes*, and 56 co-operatives. The capital on which these societies were based totalled 6 million francs for the *sociétés anonymes*, and 5.31 million francs for the co-operatives; this capital had been augmented by borrowing to the extent of 3 million francs by the *sociétés anonymes* and almost 4 million francs by the co-operatives. With this finance, the societies had investments in land and building which stood at 10 million francs for the *sociétés anonymes*, and almost 6 million francs for the co-operatives. The report of the Conseil Supérieur des HBM does not indicate the quantity of housing built by the societies; but in statistics relating to 96 societies, Alfred Dubois gives a total of about 3,400 dwellings constructed by the end of 1905. This total is small enough in itself, but for some of the societies it included housing dating back before 1894; however, the majority, at least 2,750, were built under the housing legislation introduced in that year.[34]

A smaller contribution was made by the Caisses d'Epargne and the charitable institutions. The Caisses found the prospect of building housing themselves, a process over which they had direct control, preferable to lending money to independent societies. Thus, by the end of 1905, 28 Caisses had built housing, a total investment of 3.31 million francs, of which 3.06 million francs was the outstanding current investment (see fig. 55, graph 4a). But this represented only about 480 dwellings added to the housing stock of France. The main single builder was the Caisse in Marseilles, which had gained special permission to build cheap housing in 1889; by the end of 1905 it had built more than 100 dwellings. The charitable institutions made even less use of the rights extended to them in 1894. In his report on housing legislation to the Chambre des Députés in 1912, parliamentary *rapporteur* Laurent Bonnevay noted only one institution which had built housing before 1906 – the Bureau de Bienfaisance in Nancy, whose investment of 100,000 fr. provided 20 dwellings.

By virtue of their official status, the approved societies are well documented; but in assessing the impact of the housing reformers' work, the societies which remained independent must also be considered. The dwellings which they built qualified as HBM, enjoyed tax reliefs under the law, and thus contributed to the stock of housing built under the law. Moreover, the independent societies included some of the most productive. The Société des Logements Economiques in Lyons had built 1,600 flats, costing more than 5 million francs by the end of 1905. With its paid-up capital of 5 million francs, the Lyons society was still the only society whose scale of finance and construction approached that of the large English societies. But in Paris, philanthropic foundations founded in the early 1900s were commencing operation on a similar scale. The example of the Société Philanthropique was followed by the Groupe des Maisons Ouvrières. Founded initially as a commercial society in 1899, the Groupe received endowments which led to its reorganisation as a philanthropic foundation in 1906. By the end of the year it had housing worth 4.4 million francs under construction. The previous year, 1904, had seen the creation of the Fondation Rothschild based on an endowment of 10 million francs. In addition to the site on the Rue de Prague, the subject of the influential competition in 1905, the Fondation had plans for two smaller sites under consideration.

It is not possible to arrive at a definite total for the number of dwellings built by the independent housing societies. However, from the tables prepared by Alfred Dubois for the Société Française des HBM, it is possible to say that 15 societies had built a total of at least 3,800 dwellings by the end of 1905. This is, if anything, an underestimate, as Dubois himself acknowledged that his lists were not exhaustive. However, insofar as those societies which were known to the reformers in the Société des HBM were included, it is reasonable to regard this figure as representative of the movement which those reformers were leading.

Adding this assessment of the achievement of the independent societies, to the houses built by approved societies, Caisses d'Epargne, and charitable institutions, a total of around 7,700 dwellings had been built by 1906. Since this represented the activity of some societies dating back nearly 40 years, to 1867, and covered the whole of France, it is clear that the housing society movement had a negligible impact on the housing market. An idea of how the work of the societies related to the need for housing can be gained by looking at the Paris region. With the reservations already expressed on the completeness of the data on independent societies, it can be stated that about 2,000 of the dwellings were built in Paris, or in its immediate suburbs. The most notable omission from this figure from the housing reformers' point of view would be the housing financed by Emile Cacheux, a total of more than 300 by 1906. Yet, accepting this figure as necessarily approximate, there remains an immense gulf between an achievement in the order of 2,000 dwellings spanning up to 40 years, and the need for housing as revealed in the censuses of 1891 and 1901. These had shown more than 300,000 people living in overcrowded conditions in the city. At the turn of the century, the Société de Statistique de Paris had estimated the number of new dwellings required in the city at 50,321.[35] With an average annual increase of 7,000 dwellings in the city's housing stock in the 1890s, and almost 10,000 in the 1900s, the contribution of the housing societies clearly did not threaten the private market; but equally clearly, the societies had still hardly begun the task of curing the unhealthy state of the market for workers' dwellings.

25

◇◇◇

The evolution of housing legislation 1: 'Free action is superior and sufficient'

The 1894 law had failed to extend the impetus of housing reform from the core of reformers centred on the Société Française des HBM into a national movement. It is true that by 1906 housing societies had been formed in many towns, no longer simply the major cities and provincial towns. But the creation of one housing society in a town, particularly given the small scale of most societies, hardly represented a dramatic awakening to the problems of cheap housing. The number of towns which witnessed a more concerted effort, with two or more societies registered under the law remained small – less than 20 – by the end of 1905. Even cities such as Lyons and Marseilles, pioneers in the 1880s, showed little inclination to follow their own lead: Lyons had only four active societies (excluding the independent Société des Logements Economiques), and Marseilles three. Paris remained the heart of the movement, with more than twenty active societies by 1906, and with the additional benefit of the large independent foundations.

This failure to break through the limited scale of a reform movement to become a real force was reflected in the formation of the local Comités des HBM. The reformers hoped that these would spread the word throughout France, stirring worthy citizens to rise to the challenge of the 'social duty', which Picot had identified. However, the interest of local councils was limited. In 1895 the Ministère du Commerce sent a circular to Prefects, urging them to consider with the departmental council the value of setting up a Comité. Only 14 councils chose to act. By 1899 there were still only 88 Comités, set up in 50 departments; almost half the departments were without a Comité, and of the 88 Comités which did exist, only 21 provided useful information to the Conseil Supérieur des HBM. In the absence of a widespread network of active Comités, a survey of local housing conditions which was commenced in 1895 could still not provide the overall picture which the reformers were anxious to establish.[1]

The annual reports prepared by the Conseil Supérieur des HBM ensured that the reformers were aware of the slow progress of their movement, and revision of the 1894 law came under serious discussion in the early 1900s. Public attention had been focussed on housing again by the Exposition held in Paris in 1900. As in 1889, the Exposition included a Groupe d'Economie Sociale, whose president for 1900 was

488

Jules Siegfried. Together with Georges Picot, Siegfried headed the organising committees of the housing exhibits within the Groupe d'Economie Sociale, and of the International Housing Congress to be held during the Exposition. Since the first meeting in Paris in 1889, this congress had become established by further meetings in Antwerp, Bordeaux and Brussels. In 1900, it returned to Paris where the question of cheap housing was also on the agenda at the International Congress of Architects and the International Congress of Hygiene.

In the first detailed session they had devoted to cheap housing, the architects did little more than rehearse the arguments for and against the individual house, and the block of flats. The hygiene congress, with a much longer history of discussion on housing, covered a variety of points. It called once again for the revision of the 1850 housing legislation, and delegates heard a paper on existing housing conditions as analysed by the *Casier Sanitaire* in Paris. The detailed design of housing was considered in the guide presented by H. Pucey, while Emile Trélat examined the wider implications of hygienic design for street layout and building mass. The housing congress was naturally able to concentrate more closely on detailed aspects of cheap housing, ranging from the question of helping tenants to buy furniture, to the extension of the housing law to benefit gardens as well as dwellings. However, there remained questions of basic principle on which the delegates to the congress were by no means unanimous; these related to the intervention of the public authorities, an issue which Eugène Rostand discussed in the final paper to the congress.

In the conclusion to his paper, Rostand outlined the areas in which the public authorites could act. To the usual categories, from public transport to fiscal aid, he was prepared to add the possibility of municipalities providing loans, or buying shares in private housing societies. If these were extreme measures for the French, they were not for some of the other delegates to the congress. In England, the 1890 law allowed municipalities to build on their own account; the potential of this innovation had been illustrated at the International Housing Congress in 1897, when London County Council architect Owen Fleming discussed the Boundary Street Estate. In Germany, a lead was set by Ulm, which started building houses for sale in the early 1890s. These initiatives were still the exception rather than the rule. But the growing acceptability of such initiatives was indicated by the degree of opposition which Rostand faced when he presented his final resolution. This placed a limit on the extent of public action, declaring that it 'should come as an aid to private initiative, without substituting itself, and without making public authorities the privileged competitors of free action'.[2]

Rostand's resolution was only passed by a small majority, after heated argument. As R. H. Guerrand has observed 'the fine unanimity of 1889 was shattered'.[3] After 1900, private initiative was referred to by some foreign congress delegates as 'the French method'.[4] The French were thus aware that they were standing out against the more advanced opinion in foreign reforming circles. They were also aware that the 1894 law had achieved very little. How, then, could the French reformers maintain their faith in the private sector?

One means of doing so was to stress not the achievement of the private sector, but the dangers inherent in impairing its independence. In an article reviewing the current state of housing reform, which appeared in the Bulletin de la Société Française des HBM shortly before the 1900 congress, Rostand put forward this argument. He stated that 'if the community, acting through the public budget of the State or the commune, makes a direct intervention, it will only succeed in falsifying the natural play of goods at the expense of tax-payers, in creating problems for itself, in paralysing the spontaneous contribution of individuals and of association; in construction, and even more in management, it will be unequal to the task. Free action is superior and sufficient.'[5] If one shared Rostand's belief that direct intervention would lead to worse results than the existing economic system, then it became considerably easier to justify the workings of that existing system.

However, Rostand himself was confident enough to describe free action not merely in relative terms as 'superior', but more categorically as 'sufficient'. In the context of housing reform, 'sufficient' had a particular meaning, as the private sector had manifestly not provided a sufficient number of dwellings to house all families in hygienic conditions. The key to Rostand's faith emerges in the conclusion to his article, when he leaves his fellow reformers with a rallying call: 'Let us not fear to do too little at a time: it is little by little, one step after another, that progress is made, and every improved dwelling created is equivalent, perhaps, to a family saved.'[6]

Rostand's emphasis on the smallest scale of housing is reasonable in itself. But this focus was not balanced by a willingness to come to terms with the scale of the housing problem. On the contrary, in acclaiming the value of the reformers' work, however small its contribution, Rostand was diverting attention away from the failure of their work to have any real impact on the housing market. Until they resolved that failure, the reformers could do little to help the 300,000 people in Paris living in overcrowded conditions. Rostand could only see free action as sufficient by ignoring the problems of the 300,000, and focussing myopically on a single family.

Rostand was still constrained by the view of reform evident in Blanqui's attitudes fifty years earlier. To both men, reform must strike a balance between social change, and the 'eternal laws' governing the social order; as long as the upper-class reformers retained their dominance in the face of the 'inevitable progress of democracy',[7] the eternal laws could be invoked to oppose radical change and defend even the slowest rate of progress. To Rostand, the achievement of free action could thus be 'sufficient', even if it was hardly so to the occupants of slums in Paris. If reform was to be made sufficient for them as well, then the reformers would have to accept two principles which they had hitherto rejected. First, the principle that society did have the ability to guide its own development in a direct manner, without hiding behind ill-defined eternal laws, or the intangible unseen hand of capitalism. Second, the principle that housing was a service to which all members of society had a right, not an exclusive commodity produced by an unwritten contract between the upper classes, fulfilling their 'social duty', and the moral and thrifty working man.

The French housing reformers centred on the Société Française des HBM could not endorse these principles. But while they refused to envisage the radical change which would have taken the initiative in directing society out of their hands, they did accept the need for a measured reaction which would help to secure their own position. Fougerousse and Picot had expressed this in the 1880s when urging the upper classes to act. While the ideal form of action, in the reformers' view, remained where Rostand firmly placed it, in the private sector, the reformers acknowledged that public action was a necessary support in some areas. Blanqui had argued this in 1848; the next generation of reformers adopted a similar position in 1894, in the law which, as Leroy-Beaulieu made clear, marked a step away from the purest logic of *laissez-faire*. Now, in the later 1890s and early 1900s some reformers proceeded to argue the case for further public action. Thus at the International Housing Congress in 1897 Dr du Mesnil criticised the inadequacy of the French housing reform movement, which he saw as having progressed little since 1852. In contrast to Rostand, du Mesnil was prepared to admit that 'private enterprise is truly insufficient', and therefore that 'the intervention of the public powers is sometimes decisive'.[8] Other reformers were beginning to define the areas in which they believed such action was desirable: Trélat argued for controls to limit the volume of building on a given site, Cacheux for the acquisition of land reserves by municipalities, and Siegfried for greater powers of expropriation. Public support for the private sector was also acceptable, even to Rostand, who advocated municipal intervention to the extent of buying shares in housing societies, and granting them loans. But if these proposals would have given municipalities considerable scope for action, that action was to be fundamentally one of controlling and encouraging the private sector; the public sector was not to threaten private action by taking any direct initiative in the production of housing.

The consideration of these proposals in housing reform circles reflected a wider discussion of the role of the municipality in the early 1900s. At the heart of the discussion was the concept of 'municipal socialism', a concept which was illustrated by the work of some of the large British municipalities. While conservative opinion limited its progress, municipal enterprise in Britain was advanced in comparison to France, and stimulated discussion there. When Emile Cheysson introduced a discussion of this topic at the Société d'Economie Politique in 1904, he described England as 'the promised land of *municipalisme*'.[9] But, not surprisingly, this society of defenders of private enterprise rejected the ideas of the municipality as entrepreneur. This view accorded with that of the Société Française des HBM in relation to housing; it restricted the activity of the municipality to a secondary role, supporting rather than replacing private action.

But this view was opposed in the early 1900s by a growing support for more direct action by the municipality. In relation to housing this can be seen in the deliberations of the Paris council, which set up a special commission in 1903 to consider the question of housing. This commission originated in a proposal made by the socialist councillor Henri Turot, along with other councillors who included the leader of the *possibilistes*, Paul Brousse. In May 1903, Turot proposed that the council ask the city administration to consider making land owned by the city available to housing societies; he also requested that the council establish a commission to study the question. This request was approved, and in July the 16 councillors who put forward their names for membership were formally appointed by the council.[10]

Through socialists such as Turot, who was to be nominated as president of the commission, the principle of municipal construction was brought before the council. Among the other councillors who asked to sit on the commission there were firm opponents of this principle, notably Ambroise Rendu. While Rendu was to press for municipal action in clearing slum areas, he remained opposed to direct municipal action in construction. He continued this opposition throughout the discussion of housing in the council; but, significantly, when the housing commission was renewed by election in June 1904, Rendu failed to secure his place.[11]

While the commission was deliberating, the council considered various proposals which were related to housing. At the end of 1903, councillors approved the suggestion that the city's share of the profit derived from the sale of part of the Champ de Mars should be used to finance cheap housing, and that the State be asked to employ its share in the same way. In 1904, councillors also approved a proposal by Henri Turot to pursue the application of the 1807 legislation taxing the unearned increment in land values, and that half of the proceeds from this be reserved to finance cheap housing.[12]

The acceptance of these proposals demonstrates the willingness of the council to take seriously the issue of housing, but the measures remained unimplemented in practice. At the same time, Turot was preparing the ground for the discussion of the delicate issue of who should build the cheap housing which the council was anxious to promote. The first principle to establish was that the city should make its land available for construction. In December 1903, Turot specified certain sites which, he proposed, should be reserved 'for the construction of cheap workers' housing'; but he was careful to leave vague the issue of how the housing would be built, an issue to be 'subsequently determined'.[13]

During 1904 the housing commission considered ways in which the city could act in collaboration with private enterprise; discussions were opened with the Fondation Rothschild to take advantage of the fact, as

Turot put it, that 'the Fondation Rothschild has a great deal of money; the city has a great deal of land'.[14] In December the council approved the transfer to the Fondation of three sites, among them the site for the housing competition opened in 1905. In more general terms, the council approved a report by the housing commission, listing over 200 sites which might be used for housing, and considering the conditions under which they could be sold to private societies and builders.[15]

While he supported the policy of partnership, Turot's presentation of the Fondation Rothschild agreement suggested that the commission would not be content to remain so constrained. Speaking on behalf of the commission, Turot noted that the present state of legislation made it difficult for the city to take the initiative in the construction of houses, even on its own land. It was for this reason that the commission had entered into discussion with private enterprise; but as Turot remarked, the transfer of public land was only 'the first step on the path of constructing cheap dwellings'.[16]

The further steps on this path were set out in the housing commission's main report, presented to the council by Turot in April 1905.[17] The report made various proposals which remained within the framework established by existing national legislation. These related to action by the Caisses d'Epargne and the Caisse des Dépôts; to the construction of *garnis*; to the tax reliefs available to cheap housing; to the possibility of construction by the Assistance Publique in Paris; and to the definition of guidelines for builders of cheap housing. But the report also went beyond this level of action, to put forward the principle of direct municipal construction. The council commission urged the rapid adoption of revised housing legislation, currently under consideration in parliament, and proposed that in the new law, 'direct construction by municipalities be formally authorised'. In relation to Paris, the commission proposed that the council ask the city administration to consider contracting a loan of 50 million francs, to finance housing construction by the city.

When the commission report was discussed, the erstwhile commission member Ambroise Rendu was outspoken in attacking the principle of public construction. While he could accept many of the commission's proposals in support of private enterprise, he insisted that 'I will not associate myself to the project for the municipalisation of cheap housing advocated by Henri Turot. I will fight with the utmost energy this highly dangerous socialist proposal.'[18]

Rendu's energy proved insufficient to overturn Turot's proposals, because Turot was content to let those proposals remain at the level of principle, rather than pressing for immediate action. Turot stressed that the proposed authorisation of municipal construction was intended simply to establish the principle of this form of construction, and that it did not raise the question of an actual programme of construction by the city. This question was, however, raised by the proposal that the city be asked to study a loan to finance housing. Here, Turot had to introduce a minor but significant change as a result of a discussion with the Prefect of the Seine, before the report was discussed in the council. The clause relating to this loan in the April report was worded 'The administration is invited to study without delay the terms of a loan of 50 million francs destined for the construction of cheap housing on land owned by the City.' As presented to the council in debate, it began 'The administration is instructed to study the possibility and the terms of a loan...'[19] If the administration was thus more directly obliged to consider the loan, the introduction of the word 'possibility' made it clear that, once again, it was a principle that was to be examined. Even if the administration had confirmed that a loan was possible, the council was in no sense committing itself to a housing programme based on such a loan.

With Turot's assurance to Rendu, and the modification of the clause relating to the loan, these aspects of the commission's report were approved by the council in November 1905. The council was thus effectively requesting the *right* to introduce a programme of direct construction: the legal right to be defined in national legislation, and the right to engage the city's finances through a loan. But in each case the actual issue of whether the council wished to exercise these rights was carefully left to one side, to be considered once the principles were established.

In the event, the council was not immediately granted the rights which it requested. The national housing legislation was not to introduce the formal authorisation of municipal construction, and the city administration was in no rush to examine the possibility of a loan. As in the 1880s, the Paris council gave voice to housing proposals which neither the central government nor the city administration under the Prefect were yet willing to endorse. Yet the debate in 1905 was significant, as the council did accept the principle of direct construction; when the possibility of acting on this principle was seriously taken up by the council six years later, discussion was to focus on the means rather than the principle of carrying out a housing programme.

The revision of housing legislation: 1906, 1908

Not surprisingly, the housing reformers in the Société Française des HBM opposed the views expressed in the housing commission's report in 1905. In a letter to *L'Economiste Français*, the society's president, Georges Picot, challenged Turot's assessment of the achievement of private enterprise.[20] But if Picot was ready, as always, to defend private enterprise against socialist criticism, he and his fellow reformers were aware that the achievement of housing societies under the 1894 law had remained limited. The reformers were thus already involved in the discussion of revisions to the 1894 law, discussion which led to the passage of new legislation in 1906. This law firmly rejected the proposal of the Paris council that municipal construction be authorised, and defined the maximum role which the reformers were prepared to grant to municipalities.

The discussion of revision to the housing legislation formed part of the debate over *municipalisme* in the early 1900s, endorsing the role of control and support of private enterprise which was being defined in other areas related to housing. Thus the new public health law of 1902 increased the responsibility of communes in inspecting new building, while in Paris the supporters of slum clearance led by Ambroise Rendu were starting to convince the council of the need for a coherent policy of demolition. At the same time, the opening of the Paris Métro in 1900, and the debate over the use of the fortifications, raised the possibility of a municipal policy to encourage particular forms of development.

The initiative in revision of the housing legislation was taken by Paul Strauss; like Siegfried, Strauss provided a link between the Société Française des HBM and parliament. As a councillor in Paris, elected in 1883 when the question of housing was preoccupying the council, he had taken a particular interest in social issues; in 1897 he was elected to the Senate, where he maintained his interest, later serving as Minister of Hygiene in the 1920s. Strauss gained authority as a spokesman on housing reform as president of the Comité des HBM du Département de la Seine, one of the few active Comités set up after 1894.[21] It was in this capacity that in 1901, Strauss addressed a letter to the head of the government, Waldeck Rousseau, requesting him to consider what powers could be allowed to communes to aid the construction of housing.

No action was taken immediately but in 1903 the Combes government set up an inter-ministerial commission to consider the question raised by Strauss. The governments headed by Waldeck Rousseau and Combes were more inclined to the Left than their predecessors, being based on the support of radicals and socialists in the Bloc des Gauches; Strauss himself was among the radical group in the Senate.[22] But they could not ignore the moderate views of the centre, on which they also relied for support. Thus while municipal intervention in housing as a principle applicable nationally came under serious discussion for the first time, the proposals were to remain within the moderate limits which were acceptable to the housing reformers. The reformers were represented on the six-man inter-ministerial commission by Strauss and Jules Siegfried; when they were presented in 1904, the proposals of the commission went no further than the conservative Rostand in his 1900 article, allowing municipal action through loans, shareholding, and the provision of land.

The commission's report was passed to a Senate commission headed by Strauss to consider; this commission also examined two further sets of amendments to the 1894 law, presented by Strauss in 1902 and 1904. During its deliberations, the Senate commission consulted both the Société Française des HBM and the Conseil Supérieur des HBM. Strauss was himself a member of both of these organisations, and he particularly acknowledged the collaboration of Siegfried, Picot, Cheysson and Jules Challamel. After these consultations, the Senate commission presented its proposals in March 1905, and these formed the basis for the law finally passed in April 1906.

In the introduction to these proposals, the government made it clear that they remained within the limits of intervention permitted in foreign countries and within the limits set by the International Housing Congress. The introduction made reference to municipal action in Germany, England and Italy, and quoted in full the resolution on public intervention passed by the 1900 Housing Congress. But the commission made no mention of the controversy which surrounded this resolution, and played down the fact that the proposed law remained not merely within, but still fell considerably short of, the degree of intervention countenanced in some countries. Thus the powers available to English local authorities since 1890 were covered in only six short lines. Paul Strauss was more forthright in his report for the Senate, giving details of the dwellings being built or planned by the London County Council to house 96,000 people; this represented a total investment of 125 million francs. As Strauss remarked with a degree of understatement, 'in France we are far from these results'.[23] However, there was no question of allowing such powers to French towns. The government commission had only accepted the intervention of the public authorities after 'making all the necessary guarantees to secure the management of their budgets against imprudence, at the same time as to eliminate all unjustified competition against the normal construction enterprises'.[24] The spirit of Rostand's resolution of 1900 was indeed still intact.

The 1906 law permitted communes and departments to assist housing societies by granting loans, acquiring bonds, or by subscribing shares. Authorities could also cede land or buildings to societies, at a price not less than half of the market value. Finally, they could guarantee the dividend of societies up to 3%, during the first ten years of a society's existence. Controls were placed on this action, both on the authorities and on the societies. The question of shareholding was particularly delicate, as it involved the authority in the risks and the management of societies. To avoid an unexpected call on the public budget, all shares must be fully paid up on acquisition; similarly, to prevent an authority forming wholly owned societies as a form of disguised public enterprise, the maximum shareholding was fixed at two thirds of the registered capital. The commission had reassured the critics of public intervention by insisting that 'unjustified competition' would be avoided; to ensure this, societies receiving aid were not permitted to sell dwellings for less than their cost price, nor rent them for a return of less than 4%.

The powers granted to communes and departments introduced a new element into housing legislation. The remaining sections of the 1906 law simply extended the provisions of the 1894 law. The Comités des HBM, whose creation was left to local authorities under the 1894 law, were now made mandatory in every department. At the same time their powers were increased in two respects. They were made responsible for inspecting the dwellings eligible for tax relief under the law, and for issuing a *certificat de salubrité*; previously, the standard of dwellings had only been subject to the approval of the tax authority, hardly expert in matters of hygiene. The scope of the committees' work was also extended to cover a wide range of social questions, similar to the work done by their counterparts in Belgium. The renamed Comités de Patronage des HBM et de la Prévoyance Sociale now became a centre for the study of 'the allied problems of saving, of mutual aid, of workers' insurance, of old-age pensions, of economic housing, of workers' gardens, of public baths'.[25] This assimilation of general social questions into a structure set up for housing indicates the leading role which housing had come to play in social reform – fulfilling the central role which Simon and Siegfried had accorded to it more than a quarter of a century earlier.

The tax reliefs offered by the housing law were increased in 1906; however, Strauss regretted that the Senate commission could not fully satisfy the housing reformers in this respect, as the Treasury was unwilling to concede more tax income than it must. More substantial changes were introduced to the credit arrangements governed by the law. The Caisses d'Epargne and charitable institutions were allowed to buy shares in housing societies under the same conditions as local authorities. Furthermore, the Caisses were permitted to grant individual mortgage loans, making general a right which the Marseilles Caisse had pioneered. The role of the Caisse des Dépôts et Consignations remained unchanged, as the Senate commission was satisfied by the assurances of the director of the Caisse that he was studying ways of easing the procedure for granting loans. Aware of the unfavourable comparisons drawn between the contribution of his Caisse, and the central Caisse d'Epargne in Belgium, he promised to consider methods similar to those used in Belgium. The Caisse did introduce a new policy, granting the first in a series of direct loans to housing societies shortly before the 1906 law was finally approved.

In response to a request from the Conseil Supérieur des Caisses d'Epargne, the final version of the 1906 law allowed Caisses to invest not only in housing, but also in public baths and workers' gardens. Interest in the question of workers' gardens had been stimulated in 1903 by an international congress in Paris devoted solely to that subject. Taking up a resolution passed by the Conseil Supérieur des HBM, Paul Strauss also included a general clause on gardens in his 1904 proposal. This extended the provisions of housing law to benefit gardens as well as dwellings, and was incorporated in the final text of the new law.

The 1906 law thus extended both the aid offered by the 1894 law and the work for which that aid could be used. But it left unchanged one aspect of the law which concerned the reformers. 'The study of statistics shows that it is only in urban agglomerations or in the neighbourhood of industrial centres that it has been possible, up to the present, to put into effect the law of 1894.'[26] This conclusion was stated in a proposal for new legislation, presented by Alexandre Ribot and Jules Siegfried a few months after the 1906 law was passed. Their reservations about the effect of the 1894 law were not simply geographical, but lay in the implication behind the concentration on urban and industrial areas. 'It must be recognised: it is only an élite of employees and workers which the construction and credit societies can, in the present situation, assist. The cost of the houses built by the societies places them out of reach of workers whose salary is not high, and in particular of the large mass of rural workers.'[27]

Prior to the passage of the 1894 law, rural housing had not been a major concern of the housing reformers. The idealisation of rural life which was central to the school of social economy, and the concentration of the housing problem in urban areas, led the reformers to focus their efforts on urban housing. In his report to the international jury of the 1889 Exposition, Georges Picot somewhat complacently remarked that 'in other countries, attention is rightly paid to the means of improving the housing of rural workers. In France, the initiative of our strong rural stock has resolved the problem: their ardent attachment to the earth, their affection for the family home has provided for everything.'[28]

However, the closer study of rural housing towards the end of the century was to turn the reformers' attention towards this area. The *Encyclopédie d'hygiène et de médecine publique*, directed by Dr Jules Rochard, a founder member of the Société Française des HBM, devoted over 100 pages to rural housing. A general study of housing types throughout France was undertaken in the early 1890s by Alfred de Foville, while in 1898 the Société Française d'Hygiène opened a competition for a paper on rural housing. In both 1898 and 1900, the French contribution to the International Hygiene Congresses included studies recommending rules for improving and ensuring the hygiene of rural housing.[29] The housing reformers responded to this growing interest, and in 1897 Jules Siegfried tabled a proposal to extend the advantages of the 1894 law to properties of up to 5 hectares. Discussed in parliament in the following two years, the proposal came to nothing. But rural housing was established as an issue whose importance was to increase as concern grew over the low growth rate of the French population.

As early as 1877 the Société d'Economie Sociale had heard a report by one of its members on the decline in the population growth rate. The persistence of the low birth rate led to the creation in 1897 of an association specifically to promote population increase.[30] In relation to housing, this continuing concern over population helped to shift the housing reformers' attention from urban areas, to include rural areas as well. In the 1880s, the reformers could see their aim as the creation of housing which would stabilise the workforce in urban and industrial areas, creating a greater self-sufficiency in the population of such areas through the reinforcement of the family unit. But housing could inevitably make only a partial contribution to this aim, whose realisation would have depended on a more radical restructuring of the system of industrial employment. Members of the Société d'Economie Sociale worked towards such a restructuring within their moderate terms of reference, promoting such measures as greater stability in the employment market. But the continuing demands of industry, and the low rate of population growth, meant that the reformers were unable to create a self-sufficiency within the population of urban areas.

This fact was evident in the migration of workers from rural areas, attracted by the work opportunities which the urban workforce was insufficient to fill. The reformers now came to see a need to complement their action within urban areas by measures to promote housing in rural areas, hoping to minimise the drift to the city by offering better conditions in the country. Thus, in presenting their proposal for legislation in 1906, Ribot and Siegfried were explicit in their hope that the law would slow down 'as far as possible, the movement which leads workers to desert the countryside'.[31] They had identified the need for a system of aid and credit to allow rural workers to buy a plot of land in advance of building a house, as a first step towards establishing a property. Once this step was achieved, the worker could go on to the further commitment of building a house.

The proposal submitted by Ribot and Siegfried was the basis of the law 'relating to small property and cheap houses' passed in 1908. This introduced a system of mortgage loans, through which an individual could borrow up to 80% of the cost of a site; he could borrow on the same terms towards the cost of constructing a house on the site. Finance for this system was to come not from the already established HBM sources, but from the central Caisse Nationale des Retraites pour la Vieillesse. The State opened a credit of up to 100 million francs, which the Caisse could make available at 2% to local credit societies – Sociétés de Crédit Immobilier. The difference between this interest rate and the current rate charged by the Caisse was to be borne by the State. Having borrowed at 2%, the credit societies were to provide mortgage loans to individuals, at a maximum interest of 3.5%. A link to the 1906 housing law was forged by allowing the credit societies to lend to housing societies as well as to individuals, but only for projects falling within the scope of the 1908 law; similarly the Caisses d'Epargne were allowed to reduce their interest rate to 2% for borrowers who qualified under the 1908 law.

The 1908 law differed in one major respect from the initial proposal of 1906. That proposal had derived from concern that the limited resources of rural workers prevented them from taking advantage of the 1894 law. In the original text this concern was followed to its logical conclusion, in the provision that the interest on mortgage repayments be reduced for families with at least two children younger than 16, and whose total annual income was less than 1,500 fr.; the cost of this would be met by the State or the local authority. The Finance Ministry objected to this proposal because of the added burden it would place on the budget; the parliamentary commission drafting the law also had reservations, believing that the clause would not have unanimous support in parliament. As a result, Ribot withdrew the clause. However, he had drawn attention to a problem which was to preoccupy the reformers increasingly in the next few years, in relation to both rural and urban areas.

Although introduced as a measure to aid rural housing, the 1908 law differed most from the 1906 law in working through credit societies rather than construction societies. The 1894 law had in fact anticipated that part of the finance which it provided would pass through credit societies to individuals. However, by 1906 only three such societies had been formed, and they had made only 41 loans, totalling less than 200,000 fr.[32] The majority of societies formed under the 1894 law were construction societies building dwellings for rent or sale. The procedure for buying one of these dwellings which the Société Française des HBM promoted, and which the law envisaged, left the ownership of the dwelling with the society until the final payment by the buyer.[33] The 1906 law did not alter this procedure, but it did extend the principle of lending direct to individuals by allowing the Caisses d'Epargne to do so. The principle was further extended by the 1908 law, which operated exclusively through credit societies. Although these could lend to construction societies operating under the 1906 law, the main borrowers were intended to be individuals. The individual would thus be the agent of construction rather than a society, and as the loan was based on a mortgage on his property he could become the legal owner immediately; for this reason, life insurance was compulsory for borrowers under the 1908 law, while it was only optional for individuals buying from a society under the 1894/1906 law.[34] The process of becoming a proprietor was therefore rather different under the two laws, reflecting the different nature of the credit arrangements. However the laws clearly complemented one another, and gave the private sector an opportunity to fulfil Rostand's faith by improving on its performance since 1894.

The effect of the revised legislation (see fig. 55)

Comparison of the investment by credit sources up to the end of 1905 with investment up to the end of 1911 does show a marked increase. The Caisse des Dépôts et Consignations fulfilled its director's promise, making direct loans which increased the total lent through the Société de Crédit up to 1905 by almost five times. These loans were granted at interest rates of 3% to 3.25%; most of the money being taken by co-operatives. The Caisses d'Epargne also responded, with more than 100 investing in housing by 1911. As in 1905, direct investment in construction exceeded the amount devoted to loans to housing societies; however the aid to housing societies was increased by 14 Caisses which made use of the right to buy shares, while 17 had joined Marseilles in providing individual mortgages. The crucial role which a Caisse could play in encouraging local initiative was illustrated by the Caisse in Lyons. This subscribed half the capital to found a Société de Crédit Immobilier under the 1908 law, and two thirds of the capital of the Société des Habitations Economiques de Lyon-Vaise; in the latter case, the Caisse also agreed to lend the society the difference between its share capital and the estimated cost of its first building. At the end of 1911 the Lyons Caisse had invested more than 800,000 fr. in loans, shares and direct construction, the largest investment of any Caisse, while the Caisses in Marseilles and Paris had each invested almost as much. Thus, although many more Caisses had invested in 1911 than in 1905, their overall investment remained dominated by a handful of major investors. More than 5 million francs, almost half of the total investment, was accounted for by only ten Caisses.[35]

The charitable institutions were also dominated, in this case by a single investor. The Assistance Publique in Paris, which had granted two loans by 1905, increased its lending to a figure of 2.24 million francs by 1911. The Assistance Publique also responded to the 1905 report of the Paris council's housing commission, which had urged the organisation to make use of its right to finance its own housing programme under the 1894 legislation; by the end of 1911 it had housing worth 7.7 million francs under construction. Twenty-one other organisations had also invested in housing by that date, mainly in direct construction, but even when combined their investment was dwarfed by that of the Assistance Publique.

The contribution of the credit sources after 1906 did thus show a marked increase in comparison to the earlier period. By the end of 1911 the Caisse des Dépôts had lent about one third of the sum it was authorised to lend. The investment by Caisses d'Epargne naturally varied according to the will of the directors of each Caisse, but in some cases the total invested was approaching the limit set by the housing legislation. This limit itself varied according to the size of the Caisse – from the 800,000 fr. invested in Lyons, to the 16 houses which the Caisse in Hesdin was able to build. But if the investment from the sources established in 1894 increased after 1906, the aid provided by communes and departments proved more disappointing.

In a summary of the contribution of the local authorities up to 1911, in his report to the Senate in 1912, Paul Strauss identified only five authorities which had made loans to or bought shares in housing societies, providing a grand total of 45,000 fr. Another five authorities had agreed to guarantee dividend payments, while seven had ceded land to housing societies. The most active authority was in Paris, although this restricted its role to the supply of land; between 1908 and 1911, 26 sites had been taken up by housing societies.

If the major innovation of the 1906 law produced only a limited effect, the 1908 law was similarly slow in yielding fruit. Two societies were set up under the guidance of the instigators of the law: by Ribot in Arras, and Siegfried in Le Havre. But subsequent development was slow, partly as a result of the condition that societies have a capital of at least 200,000 fr. By the end of 1910, only five societies had been formed, and less than 1 million francs advanced. At the beginning of the following year, Ribot and Siegfried again took the initiative, using the reserves of the now inactive Société de Crédit formed as an intermediary between the Caisse des Dépôts and housing societies, to establish the Société Centrale de Crédit Immobilier in Paris. After this, the movement expanded more rapidly, with a total of 11 societies which had received approval by the end of the year, and a total of 2.7 million francs had been advanced to the societies by the Caisse Nationale des Retraites pour la Vieillesse.

The majority of the credit provided through housing legislation up to 1912 continued to be channelled through the housing societies; in parallel with the increase in credit available after 1906 the number of societies also increased more quickly. Thus by the end of 1911, 326 societies had received approval for their statutes: an increase of 206 in six years, compared to 86 in the six years before 1906. Co-operatives continued to dominate the new societies, accounting for 210 of the 326 societies. By 1911 eight societies were operating with a capital of 1 million francs or more. While societies of this scale could make a significant contribution to the local housing market, as the Lyons Société des Logements Economiques had shown, they were isolated peaks in the sea of much smaller societies. The 50.45 million franc capital of the 276 societies which had completed a full year's exercise by the end of 1911 still represented an average capital of less than 200,000 fr. per society.

The 276 societies had 54.24 million francs currently invested in land and construction by the end of 1911. Since 1906, some of the societies had also fulfilled the role which the 1894 law had envisaged, by making loans to individuals as well as investing directly in building; at the end of 1911, outstanding loans totalled 3.84 million francs. At the same date, the savings banks had 6.06 million francs invested in land and construction, and 550,000 fr. in individual loans; while the charitable institutions (dominated by the Assistance Publique in Paris), had 8.88 million francs invested in building. This total of 73.57 million francs represents the overall effect of procedures governed by the 1894 and 1906 housing laws in channelling investment into housing. As in the period before 1906, however, the societies operating within the law were complemented by significant independent organisations. Between 1906 and 1911, these were dominated by three major foundations in Paris: the Groupe des Maisons Ouvrières, the Fondation Rothschild, and the Fondation des Habitations Economiques des Employés de la Banque, du Commerce et de l'Industrie, established in 1905. By the end of 1911, the capital on which these foundations were based totalled 21.75 million francs, while their investment in building stood at 17.18 million francs.

In addition to functioning as a channel for credit and investment, the housing legislation also provided tax reliefs as an incentive to builders of cheap housing. The reformers complained regularly of the parsimony of these reliefs; neither the 1894 nor the 1906 laws gave as generous relief as the reformers advocated, and the taxation authorities were also less than generous in their interpretation of the law. As a result, the benefit in monetary terms was extremely limited: the value of exemptions in 1905 was 150,000 fr. and in 1911 500,000 fr. In his annual report on behalf of the Conseil Supérieur des HBM, Emile Cheysson and his successor in drafting the report, Georges Risler, regularly contrasted this aid to housing with the amount provided for friendly societies (*mutualité*), for which 8 million francs were set aside in the 1904 budget.

But while the tax reliefs were financially hardly significant, they do provide an indication of the extent to which housing reform spread beyond its core in the housing societies and foundations. Thus in 1907, the total of relief accorded to approved societies, Caisses d'Epargne, charitable institutions and foundations was matched by a roughly equal amount to 'private individuals'. The reports on tax relief give no detail within this category, but it would have included proprietors taking advantage of the tax reliefs when developing sites for housing, philanthropic individuals who financed cheap housing, and individual workers or employees who were able to finance their own home. The tax relief figures emphasise the fact that 'cheap housing' was not the exclusive domain of the housing reformers.

The reformers were in effect operating at two levels through the housing legislation. First, through the housing societies and credit sources, they were actually increasing the flow of capital into the construction of housing. Second, through the tax reliefs, they were able to exert some influence over the use of capital from other sources by granting relief on dwellings which conformed to the standards established for cheap housing. In so doing, they were not necessarily increasing the quantity of capital devoted to housing, as in many cases a proprietor or an individual would have built without the meagre benefit of the relief. But, in offering tax relief, the reformers were trying to exert some control over the housing built by private investment, and to bring more of that housing into the category of HBM.

This trend is more apparent after 1906, when the increased tax reliefs did attract an increasing number of speculative builders. From a negligible proportion in 1907, their share of the tax relief increased to over one quarter by 1911; the category of 'private individuals' remained at around 50%, while the proportion accounted for by the approved organisations and the major independent foundations fell to around a quarter. While this change suggests some success for the reformers in breaking through to the private market, it was not unqualified. In some cases the private builders were able to take advantage of the law without providing the type of housing envisaged by the reformers; the existence of loopholes in the law was apparent enough by 1912 for amendments to be introduced to close them.

If the tax reliefs provided a link between the reformers' work and the private market, the main task of increasing the supply of capital for new housing remained focussed on the housing societies and foundations. By 1911 the combined investment in construction by approved societies, savings banks, charitable organisations and foundations stood at almost 100 million francs. This was a dramatic contrast with the position six years earlier. But it still lagged behind comparable achievement in neighbouring countries. In Belgium, so much smaller than France, the Caisse Nationale d'Epargne on its own had provided a similar total. In England, the plans of a single building agency, the London County Council, exceeded this figure. In Germany, the regional pensions and insurance boards had made 172 million Marks available for housing by 1906, rising rapidly to 1,400 million Marks in 1916.[36]

In his annual report for the Conseil Supérieur des HBM in 1911,

Georges Risler exhibited an ambiguous attitude towards the French achievement. Commenting on the facts he had presented, he admitted that the French had only created 'a few healthy islands in the midst of an extensive mass of slums whose existence is a veritable shame for our time'. But, buoyed up by his faith in private enterprise and in his homeland,[37] Risler went on to acclaim the French housing laws as 'better than those of the other European countries – it is easy to see this at the international congresses'. As to why these superior laws had not produced the same results as the laws in other countries, Risler could only fall lamely back on the claim that 'they are not sufficiently well known by those who are called to take advantage of them'.[38] Risler still clung to the view which had been put forward since the 1850s, that private enterprise would succeed if only it was shown the way.

26

◇◇

The evolution of housing legislation 2: 'Unbiased rivalry'

As Risler declared his faith in French legislation in the spring of 1911, concern over housing conditions was once again evolving into a sense of crisis. The high costs of living in general had led to working-class agitation in Paris in 1910, and this was to spread to other areas in 1911.[1] Rents were one of the central elements in the cost of living, and in July 1911 the high level of rents was brought before the deputies by two *interpellations*. One, questioning the government on 'the rise in housing rents', was tabled by the socialist Lucien Voilin. While it is not surprising to find the socialists taking up the question of rents, the other *interpellation* indicates that concern was not restricted to the socialists; thus four socialists were joined by three moderate or right of centre deputies in asking 'what measures the government plans to take to remedy the consequences of the crisis of rents'.[2] The representatives of housing reform in parliament also expressed their concern; on the same day that the two *interpellations* were presented to the deputies, a third was presented in the Senate by Alexandre Ribot and Paul Strauss. The sense of crisis produced by exceptional circumstances called for exceptional measures, as Paul Strauss was to acknowledge in addressing the Senate during 1912. The output of private housing societies was, he insisted, adequate 'during a normal period'; but the present situation was no longer normal.[3] Strauss was politically inclined to accept a greater degree of public intervention than fellow housing reformers such as Risler or Siegfried; yet even they had to accept the logic of Strauss' argument, that action more productive than that so far provided by housing legislation was required.

The background to the sense of crisis apparent by mid-1911 was, as in 1848 and the 1880s, dominated by Paris. However, the reformers' efforts to build up a more general picture of housing conditions had yielded some fruit since 1906. Responding to pressure from the Conseil Supérieur des HBM, the authorities had included a section in the 1906 census to provide information on housing conditions in all towns of 50,000 or more inhabitants. The results of this survey demonstrated clearly that the problem of unhealthy and overcrowded housing was not restricted to Paris. While Paris continued to provide them with their most detailed information, the reformers could argue that the conditions revealed there were repeated throughout the country.

Paris received the lion's share of investment through the cheap housing organisations; about half of the 50 million franc capital invested in approved societies was held by societies working in or around Paris, while the foundations added another 17 million francs. Despite this considerable capital, and the increasing rate of construction by these organisations after 1906, the output of cheap dwellings was falling rather than rising. As has been noted in the discussion of the Paris housing market, this was most strikingly seen in the reduction in the proportion of the housing stock represented by dwellings with rents of 300 fr. and below, and in the absolute decline in this category in some years after 1907. But against this inadequate construction of cheap dwellings, the census of 1911 offered a more optimistic picture. The total number of people living in cramped conditions had decreased since 1901, and there had been a marked shift: the reduction was greater in the 'overpopulated' category than in the 'insufficient' group. While this suggests a degree of success for the reformers' theory of 'levelling up', to which the work of the large Parisian housing societies and foundations had contributed, it also suggests that the problem of overcrowding was becoming focussed on a hard core whose improvement was to be particularly difficult. This is confirmed by the subsequent statistics for the post-war years, which show no further reduction in the percentage of the population living in overcrowded dwellings. While the 1911 census showed evidence of improvement for some, the problems facing the low-paid workers, and particularly those with large families, were increasing. The low level of new construction led to a reduction in the number of vacant dwellings in the city, affecting the cheaper dwellings more than the expensive.[4] Unable to pay the rent of the dwellings which were being built, unable to find a vacant flat with a cheaper rent, some families literally fell out of the housing market. In 1911, as in 1880, public attention was drawn by the dismal picture of homeless families wandering the streets of Paris.

The factors preventing the construction of suitable housing were not new; the cost of materials, land and labour were such that economic rents were too high for many families. Material costs had dropped slightly in the first five years of the new century, but this was more than matched by subsequent increases. The Société des Habitations Economiques de la Seine, which had built for 65 fr. per m² at the end of the nineteenth century, was paying more than 100 fr. by 1909; similarly the Société des Logements Economiques pour Familles Nombreuses saw its costs rise from 77 fr. per m² in 1904, to 100 fr. by 1909.[5] The consequences of such costs were expressed by F. Fourcade, drawing on his experience as president of Le Progrès, one of the largest approved housing societies in Paris. In a report written on behalf of the Société Française des HBM in November 1911, he stated categorically that 'the majority of large families cannot, from their own resources, pay for the dwelling which they really need, even in so-called "cheap" housing'.[6] The Société des Logements Economiques pour Familles Nombreuses had reached the same conclusion, and approved a proposal to grant rent rebates to families with four or more children.[7]

Fourcade's statistics demonstrated that the cheap housing societies, even when aided by the housing legislation, were powerless to meet the real need for housing which large families could afford. The problem of large families was one aspect of the exceptional situation observed by Strauss, and was to prompt the most direct intervention by the public authorities which the new laws of 1912 were to permit. But at a more general level, the situation was made exceptional by a rapid increase in rents after 1910. Alongside the effect of building costs on new property, an increase in existing rents was stimulated by the survey of property rent values carried out in 1909 and 1910. Publishing the results of this survey, the tax administration acknowledged that many proprietors had delayed raising the rent on their property until the survey was complete, leading to a compensating rush of rent increases in 1910 and 1911.

High rents and the problems facing large families were reflected in increased tension between tenants and landlords. During 1911 and 1912 popular demonstrations were organised in Paris by a tenants' group, the Syndicat des Locataires Ouvriers et Employés. Led by Georges Cochon, the Syndicat arranged protests against eviction, and helped families to move if they could not meet their rent. In one case, the Syndicat transposed an evicted family in Puteaux, complete with its furniture, to the local town hall. Cochon himself was evicted, after what almost amounted to a police siege around his flat.[8] Although the Syndicat was short-lived, its activities helped to draw attention to the plight of the poor in Paris – while reminding the upper classes of the danger that discontent would lead to disorder.

The reformers might have taken heart from the fall in overcrowding revealed by the 1911 census, and from the increase in new building in Paris in the years just before the First World War. But neither of these factors, which could have been used to defend private enterprise, was apparent in 1911. When he presented his report on the proposal for new housing legislation, in March of the following year, Bonnevay drew a picture of persistent overcrowding in Paris, affecting the same proportion of the city's population in 1901 as in 1891; he used the results of the 1906 census to illustrate overcrowded and unhealthy housing in other towns. Referring to the Paris housing market, he described the falling rate of construction up to 1910, the reduction in vacant dwellings, and the increase in rents revealed by surveys taken during 1911. Bonnevay stressed that 'one could not render too great a homage' to private initiative, 'the creator of so many generous works', but he acknowledged that 'from now on, it is essential to make up its deficiencies'.[9]

The means of making up those deficiencies had come under further consideration in the Paris council and the city administration since 1906. In 1907 Turot renewed the question of a loan to finance housing. The council approved a request to the Prefect of the Seine to study the conditions that would be attached to a loan of 10 million francs for this purpose, although without specifying whether the money would be used directly by the city, or distributed to private societies. In the following year Turot again brought up the question, pointing out the lack of response from the Prefect either to the 1907 request, or to the earlier request of 1905. After this discussion, the council approved Turot's motion that the Prefect be invited to consider a loan of 50 million francs to finance housing, the loan to be secured against the rents received.[10] With this invitation the council went beyond possibilities and principles, making clear its desire actually to commence a programme of construction.

The council's invitation drew a counter-proposal from the Prefect, which would have provided a total of 15 million francs. Not only was this considerably less than the council requested, but it was to be used to grant loans to housing societies, and not for direct construction by the city. In the following year, this proposal was incorporated in the public works programme of 900 million francs which the city was authorised to undertake. In this programme, new construction was directly linked to slum clearance, acknowledging the interrelated nature of the two operations. Thus 30 million francs was made available for 'Measures against tuberculosis – Demolition of unhealthy housing – Loans to cheap housing societies'.[11]

This link helped to justify the city's intervention, which could be seen as simply helping to reinstate demolished housing, rather than stepping directly into the housing market; moreover, in working through private societies, the city would be acting within the role established by the 1906 law. But in relating slum clearance and construction, the programme failed to provide adequate finance for either operation; as a further disadvantage of being tied to slum clearance, new construction shared the delay in implementation while expropriation legislation was being revised. As a result some councillors continued to press for an independent housing programme. The socialist councillor Frédéric Brunet, an advocate of the reforming socialism pioneered by Paul Brousse, and signatory of Turot's 1908 council motion, urged in May 1911 that the city borrow no less than 200 million francs to finance housing. His proposal was considered by the council's housing commission whose conclusions were presented by Henri Rousselle in July. Rousselle had been one of the initial members of the housing commission in 1903, and, like Brunet, had been a signatory to the 1908 motion. He took up the proposal for a loan, though he suggested a figure of 100 million francs; he also supported the policy, which the city was already pursuing, of making sites available to cheap housing societies, and renewed the idea of an architectural competition to find designs for the sites.

Brunet had proposed that the city should act directly in constructing and managing the housing to be financed by the proposed loan. Rousselle, however, avoided making a categorical statement as to how the money borrowed by the city should be spent. He put the options of direct construction by the city, or of assistance to private societies to the council to consider, while calling on the leaders of housing societies to give their own reaction. This moderate line was acceptable even to Ambroise Rendu, who had been re-elected to the housing commission, and who endorsed Rousselle's conclusions.[12]

In his report for 1911 to the Conseil Supérieur des HBM, Georges

Risler indicated what the reaction of the housing society leaders had been. The Société Française des HBM, and the directors of cheap housing societies 'have pronounced themselves opposed to the system of construction and of management, whether direct or through indirect procedures, by the State or by municipalities'.[13]

The French reformers had not shifted from the position defined by Rostand in 1900. At the International Housing Congress held in Vienna in 1910, Maurice Dufourmantelle, a senior member of the Société Française des HBM, had 'accepted communal intervention manifesting itself as the assistant of private initiative...but rejected the participation of municipalities by the direct construction of housing'. As in 1900, the French were out of step with other congress delegates, and Dufourmantelle had to admit that there was considerable support for what he called 'the radical thesis of complete intervention of municipalities in the construction of working-class housing'.[14]

The reformers recognised that, if they were to prevent the radical thesis from being adopted in France, they must strengthen the alternative provided by private initiative. At the instigation of Ribot, Strauss and Siegfried, the directors of housing societies and foundations in Paris met for a series of sessions in which they prepared a common approach. Their proposal was that the city make sites for housing available, and lend a total of 50 million francs to finance construction by the private societies. In response to the particular problems of large families, at least half of the housing would be reserved for families with three or more children; it was also suggested that the city should directly subsidise the rents of families who could not afford the economic rent.

A more general set of proposals for aid to housing societies in Paris was drawn up by the Comité de Patronage de la Seine in conjunction with the Paris council. This did little more than repeat the options already open to municipalities through the 1906 law. The proposals were circulated for comment, and the Société Française des HBM gave its response in November 1911, in the report prepared by F. Fourcade. Although the proposals related only to forms of aid for housing societies, Fourcade could not resist the mandatory rejection of direct public intervention which he regarded as 'ill omened from every point of view'. Fourcade considered that the city could help most productively by providing cheap land and cheap loans; he estimated that such measures could permit up to 15% reduction in rents. Even these measures, however, were 'insufficient to reach large families earning average salaries'. Fourcade therefore described two courses of action recommended by the Société Française des HBM. First, municipalities could provide cheap loans or subsidies to societies which would rent existing blocks of flats and sublet them to large families; this procedure had the advantage of making a large number of dwellings available rapidly, without the time delay and the high level of capital involved in new construction. Second, the city should directly subsidise societies providing housing for families with more than five children, whose daily income was 8 francs or less.[15]

In advocating special subsidies to help large families the consortium of housing societies and the Société Française des HBM went beyond the forms of public aid outlined by Rostand in 1900. The subsidies would be aid of a different order to that allowed since 1906: on the one hand they would involve a direct charge on the public budget, on the other hand they would create a 'privileged' group of citizens within the general category of those eligible for HBM. Ribot had drawn attention to this group in 1906, while Fourcade's statistics of 1912 illustrated the particular problem of housing large families. The problem itself was not new – Raffalovich had indicated its existence in the 1880s; but at that time concern was only just beginning to be focussed on France's low birth rate. However, the persistence of the low birth rate, and the growing strength of Germany's population, provided a context in which a subsidy for large families was seen as a measure to increase the number of strong, healthy children born to French mothers; fear that the measure would attack the independence of private enterprise was less potent than the desire to defend the nation.

In early 1912, the Société Française des HBM produced another report, responding to the proposals made in the Paris council by Brunet and Rousselle. The report was written by Georges Risler, a reformer who had followed in Cheysson's footsteps, acting as director of the Société de Passy Auteuil, and taking over the task of preparing the main annual report of the Conseil Supérieur des HBM after Cheysson's death in 1910. Risler drew on the detailed analysis of construction costs, rents and family budgets which Fourcade had undertaken, to emphasise the inability of large families to pay economic rents. Risler thus repeated the proposal for direct subsidies to reduce the rent of large families. With respect to the wider issue of the financing of housing, Risler welcomed the idea of a major public loan, but, like Fourcade, he rejected public construction. According to Risler, the public authorities were less efficient than private enterprise, and would therefore build fewer dwellings for a given sum of money. This inefficiency would be compounded in the management of dwellings. Risler referred to the Foyer Schaerbeckois in Brussels, which had been financed by the local commune; bad management had led to losses, and as a result, rents had been raised above the average for the area. Risler also feared that electoral influences would interfere with management. The rents of housing built by the city of Milan had, he claimed, been reduced because of electoral pressure; in consequence, the income from the housing was no longer sufficient to cover the cost of interest payments on the construction capital.

Risler quoted several other similar cases, and noted that his examples could easily be multiplied. But he quoted no example of successful housing developments carried out by local authorities; the most notable omission in this respect was the housing built by the London County Council. If the principle of public housing were to be convincingly rejected, then housing which had been widely acclaimed could not simply be ignored. Risler's failure to mention successful public housing, let alone to argue his case against it, indicates that the reformers opposition was based more on doctrine than on critical analysis.

Whatever their personal opinions, the reformers were aware that the supporters of public intervention were gaining strength, and that their views must be accommodated. The compromise which Risler put forward on behalf of the Société Française des HBM was the partnership of public and private enterprise in a *régie intéressée*. Risler noted that this partnership was already possible under the 1906 law; by acquiring shares in private societies, a local authority could effectively establish a *régie intéressée*.[16]

The most striking aspect of the measures put forward by the housing reformers in 1911 and 1912 is that they only go beyond the 1906 law in the proposal to subsidise housing for large families. All of the other forms of action by local authorities were already entirely possible under the 1906 law. The reformers had reached the limit of their conception of the respective roles of public and private enterprise. At the annual assembly of the Société Française des HBM in March 1912, after a year in which housing had evolved from a problem into a crisis, Jules Siegfried could offer no radical solutions. Echoing the reformers' proposals of thirty years earlier, he saw a significant role for the local authorities in providing public transport, in opening up new areas of land for housing, and in constructing roads and public services. But municipal action similar to that in England or Germany was out of the question. In France 'housing societies, under a system of *régie intéressée* to be established, would be entrusted with the task of building with funds lent by towns at reduced interest, and of managing the new buildings'.[17] The reformers had reached a position of stalemate, acknowledging that the assistance of local authorities was essential if housing societies were to extend their work, yet unable to envisage that assistance in an effective form.

Housing: a shared responsibility

Two weeks after Siegfried addressed the Société Française des HBM, Bonnevay presented his proposal for revised housing legislation to the deputies. Bonnevay's report came after nine months during which time the question of housing had been repeatedly brought before the Chamber. The report provided a delicately balanced compromise, defusing the issues which had threatened to make housing into a source of confrontation. The stage had been set by the *interpellations* presented in response to the crisis of rents in July 1911. The government agreed to hold a debate, but requested time to gather information. This was granted, and in September the government initiated a survey of housing in ten European countries, as well as Russia and America. The survey covered methods of encouraging the construction of workers' housing, average rents, the number of rooms these rents could buy, and the number of inhabitants per room.[18] In November, the government gave its response to the housing crisis by presenting proposals to revise the 1906 housing law. On the issue of public intervention, the government adopted the solution favoured by the housing reformers: *régie intéressée*. It also acknowledged the importance of housing for large families, by allowing a reduction in rents charged in the housing built by *régie intéressée*.

In December 1911, two proposals were tabled by the socialist group in the Chamber. One would have introduced rent controls while the other sought to prevent confiscation of furniture of tenants who defaulted in their rent. These measures were a direct attempt to limit the rights of proprietors, and protect those of tenants. They were reinforced in January 1912 by a further *interpellation*, presented by Paul Aubriot. This followed the eviction of Cochon, leader of the Syndicat des Locataires, who was one of Aubriot's constituents, although Aubriot's question was of more general relevance; he requested information 'on the measures which the government means to take to protect poor tenants with large families against the unreasonable demands of proprietors'.[19] Three days after this question, another project originating from the socialist group was tabled. Marcel Sembat, one of the socialists' leading spokesmen, who had entered parliament along with the first substantial group of socialists in 1893, proposed that municipalities be allowed to intervene directly, building housing on their own account. Sembat had tried to have this proposal adopted as an amendment during discussion of the 1911 budget. The budget *rapporteur*, Henry Chéron, did not accept it as an amendment, but when Sembat submitted it separately in 1912, Chéron supported him as a joint proposer. Chéron's support is particularly significant, as he was not himself a socialist, but a radical Republican; he had held a series of government posts from 1906 to 1910. Support for the principle of direct construction could not be dismissed as coming only from the extreme left wing.

The socialists' proposals introduced the prospect of fierce political argument, particularly if they could increase their support from the radicals. To try to avoid this, Charles Dumont headed a group of deputies who put forward a resolution declaring that

The Chamber invites the Government to ensure the urgent vote of legislative dispositions modifying the law of 1906 on workers' housing, and permitting communes to borrow with a view to the construction of cheap, healthy dwellings, with particular advantages for large families.[20]

Dumont, himself a radical, saw the need for greater intervention by local authorities, but realised that direct construction would not gain universal support. He therefore advocated municipal construction through an intermediary – possibly by authorising the Comités de Patronage to build. Dumont consciously attempted to forestall any conflict on political theory; he appealed to the notion of *solidarité*, which stressed the mutual obligations of all parts of society and whose theorist, Léon Bourgeois, was currently the minister responsible for the housing legislation.

A fortnight after Dumont's resolution was adopted, the unity of will which he evoked was put to the test, when the debate on the *interpellations* to the government was finally held, on 23 February 1912.

In fact, only the two *interpellations* presented by socialist deputies Voilin and Aubriot were discussed. The debate thus became a set piece in which the socialists forcefully expressed their views.[21] The main speaker was Aubriot, who noted the unanimity of the Chamber in wishing to resolve the housing crisis. He favoured the direct intervention of municipalities in construction, but stressed that it would take some time to build housing in sufficient quantity to affect the housing market and reduce rents. During that time, rents would continue to rise, and more families would be thrown on to the streets. Aubriot attacked the 'truly exorbitant privileges'[22] enjoyed by property interests, and opposed Dumont's view that the current crisis had arisen because the laws of economics were no longer working. Aubriot argued that it had developed precisely because those laws were functioning and producing their natural results in a capitalist régime.

To counter these natural results, Aubriot presented a series of proposals. He urged approval of the projects already submitted to introduce rent controls, and protect tenants' possessions. He declared his own intention to introduce legislation which would prevent landlords from discriminating against large families. Publicly subsidised rent banks should be established in every commune. In the light of the role played by the police in the eviction of Georges Cochon, Aubriot demanded that the Prefect of Police should not substitute his authority for that of the courts. In relation to new construction, Aubriot noted that a source of capital could be provided by enforcing the law of 1807, taxing unearned increase in property values.

Lucien Voilin followed Aubriot, and supported his proposals. But Voilin was anxious not to cut the socialists off from the rest of the Chamber. He concentrated on the need to improve the existing housing laws, and stressed that the socialists did not wish to threaten the principles of those laws. Discussing the Ribot law of 1908, which enshrined the concept of private property in the owner-occupied house, Voilin commented that

Perhaps some of you have seen in the making of this law a means of combating socialism. In that case, you have shown that you know little. If you knew how far we are from being adversaries of that modest property holding, which no one can exploit, and which can exploit no one, you would not say that this accession to property is contrary to our ideas.[23]

This attitude to property, and particularly rural property, had been accepted by the socialists since the 1890s; at that time the Guesdists had provoked Engels' disapproval by declaring that they would support peasant proprietors in the possession of their land. This was electorally advantageous, if not doctrinally pure; in restating the position in 1912, Voilin left the way open to *solidarité* on certain issues, even if Aubriot's proposals could not expect such wide support.

The first reply to Aubriot and Voilin came from Jules Siegfried. He did not comment on the specific proposals made by the socialists; instead, he reviewed the history and achievements of housing reform, starting, characteristically, with the foundation of the Mulhouse housing

society. He described and defended the system of housing finance
channelled through private societies, which the laws of 1894 and 1906
had set up.

The task of reconciling the position taken by Siegfried with that of
the socialists fell to Bonnevay, as *rapporteur* of the commission considering the proposals to amend housing legislation. Bonnevay recognised
that the current crisis demanded a response which the private societies
had been unable to provide, but he could not accept the premises on
which the socialists operated. Picking his way carefully, he declared

> if I do not share the opinion of our colleague M. Aubriot who, earlier, declared
> that housing was a public service...I believe that there are times in the evolution
> of a people, of cities, when the development and organisation of housing must
> be assured by active intervention of the public authorities.... Therefore, leaving
> aside the theoretical question, placing myself in the presence of the facts, of
> experience, I seek not only to develop further the efforts of private initiative,
> but to find other solutions which can complete those efforts.[24]

The 'other solutions' which Bonnevay outlined centred on the introduction of housing offices, which would be 'autonomous public estab-
lishments'; he did not describe these in detail, but announced that the
commission would shortly be presenting its report, elaborating this
solution.

At the end of the debate, the Chamber was presented with two
resolutions. Eleven socialists, led by Aubriot and Voilin, outlined the
specific reforms advocated by Aubriot. A more moderate text was put
forward by a group of deputies led by Siegfried; they expressed
confidence in the government, renewed the resolution voted on Dumont's
instigation two weeks earlier, and confirmed that legislation on housing
and on expropriation would shortly be put before the Chamber. Aubriot
was under some pressure to withdraw his resolution, but he insisted that
the Siegfried text did not fully meet the issues he had raised; both
resolutions were therefore put to the vote. Socialist deputies were joined
by a few of the left-wing radicals, but Aubriot's resolution was still
heavily defeated, by 448 votes to 87. The Chamber then accepted
Siegfried's resolution, and the debate closed.

The *interpellation* debate confirmed that, while the Chamber did not
have the united will sought by Dumont, there was certainly a will shared
by the majority. Aubriot had gone against the moderate line advocated
by Dumont, and made a specifically political speech; with uncompro-
mising criticism both of proprietors and of the economic system from
which they benefited. His demands inevitably polarised the Chamber;
with their implication of direct intervention in the rent market they
received little support beyond the extreme Left. The common will of the
Chamber was clearly not to be sought on this path. And yet both Left
and Right acknowledged the need to implement new legislation rapidly
in the face of the housing crisis; if this were to be achieved, then political
division between the advocates of private and public enterprise, as was
evident in the speeches of Siegfried and Aubriot, must be avoided.
Bonnevay had given a preview of how his commission intended to tackle

this problem, and in late March he presented his formal report to the Chamber.[25]

Bonnevay's report set the background to the commission's proposal by summarising the achievement of the existing French laws, outlining the legislation in force in neighbouring countries, and drawing on the available statistics to define the particular nature of the current housing crisis in France. While the proposed legislation revised most aspects of the existing housing laws, its heart was in the relationship which it defined between private and public enterprise. Bonnevay attributed the failure of the system of public assistance introduced in 1906 to the double constraint placed on the public authorities – subject to official scrutiny by the Government, and to the particular demands of private enterprise. 'Considered by the law as incapable of action of their own, they have found themselves little inclined to help the actions of others with their own funds.'[26] The commission had considered the two options presented by the government and by Sembat: *régie intéressée* and direct intervention. *Régie intéressée* was rejected because it would inevitably force the public authority to share the aim of financial gain pursued by its private partner. 'This is no longer housing provided for the working classes at cost price as is desirable, but housing provided at a price burdened by commercial profit.'[27] On the other hand, the commission rejected the unlimited right of communes to build and manage housing; it particularly opposed public management, as this would turn elected councillors into landlords. The rejection of both of these options reflected the commission's concern to avoid a political fight. Bonnevay stressed the danger of 'lively and lengthy controversy, partisans and opponents of "municipalisation" being unable to miss this occasion to open a resounding battle'; he went on to observe that the cost of such a battle would be met by 'the unfortunates who suffer the shortage of dwellings and the rise in rents'.[28]

Bonnevay presented his proposal for public offices of cheap housing quite openly as a measure to overcome this danger. The public office, he pointed out to deputies, 'could be accepted by the partisans of municipal administration, who would see it as an embryo autonomous administration, and by the adversaries of municipal administration, who would consider it as a public foundation, sheltered from political interference'.[29] The public offices were modelled on the housing institutes set up by some Italian municipalities. Administrative independence was to be ensured by the tripartite structure of the board; one third of the members selected by the Prefect, chosen from experts in hygiene, construction and management; one third elected by the local council; and, to mediate between these groups, one third elected by local groups concerned with housing, including the Comité de Patronage, approved housing societies and Caisses d'Epargne. While the offices were thus protected from political domination, they must equally be prevented from competing unfairly with private enterprise if Bonnevay were to retain the support of the advocates of private enterprise. To achieve what he termed a 'parallelism' between the public offices and private societies, the offices were subject to the same conditions governing the letting of dwellings, with minimum and maximum rents, as were applied to the private societies benefiting from public aid.

The proposal for public offices went beyond the *régie intéressée* favoured by the Société Française des HBM. But the independence of the offices, and the principle of 'parallelism' helped to reassure the reformers. Although the public offices would compete with private societies, they were not to be the 'privileged competitors' which Rostand had feared in 1900. Bonnevay himself used the term 'unbiased rivalry'[30] to describe the relationship between public offices and private societies. However, in one respect the commission did accord privileged powers to the local authorities. Communes were to be permitted to build housing directly, provided that the housing was intended for large families, and provided that the buildings were handed over to the public office on completion, so that the commune did not become involved in management. When this proposal was discussed in the Chamber, Bonnevay argued that no one should oppose it. 'Individuals cannot complain of the competition provided by communes which were building housing for large families. We have seen, alas, that private property has not always known how to welcome them.'[31]

Large families were also to be helped by reduced rents. In housing built by public offices, or by private societies aided by the local authority, the minimum rent was fixed at a lower level for large families than for ordinary families.[32] To preserve equality between the public and private sector, the authorities could grant direct subsidies to private societies, to be used to reduce the rent of large families.

The remainder of the commission's proposals retained the existing structure of the 1906 law, introducing improvements in detail. Thus the limit set on the amount which the credit sources governed by the law could invest in housing was raised to allow the Caisses d'Epargne which had reached their limit, to extend their work. Certain controls were proposed to prevent abuse of the law, including a clause restricting the use of the term *habitation à bon marché* in future to approved housing societies. The link between the 1908 law and the 1906 law was strengthened by the commission's proposals. The 1908 law had itself been amended in February 1912 to ease the formation of credit societies, a change which led to a considerable increase in the number of societies during 1912. The commission also responded to the new interest in the planning of urban development, easing arrangements for the financing of large-scale projects by co-operatives, and including the creation of *cités-jardins* among the objectives of the new public housing offices.

Bonnevay presented the commission's proposal to the Chamber, emphasising the commission's desire to achieve 'a work of conciliation, and to secure for it the unanimous adherence of Parliament'.[33] In this, the commission was largely successful; a few amendments on points of detail were accepted during discussion, but proposals which threatened to delay the passage of the law were generally either withdrawn, or passed to parliamentary commissions for consideration. Deputies of the

Left did succeed in amending the organisation of the public housing offices to include a trades union representative on the board. But they did not threaten the passage of the law by attempting to introduce the measures advocated by Aubriot to govern landlord–tenant relationships. Neither they, nor the supporters of the private sector, raised any objection to the principle of the public offices as autonomous housing organisations. Neither Right nor Left could afford to be seen to delay a law whose intention was accepted as being in the public interest. After debate in the Chamber on 4 and 11 July, deputies gave the commission's work their unanimous support. In the Senate, the approved text was presented in a report by Paul Strauss. The Senators considered the text on 10 and 12 December, and approved it with no amendments.

The commission's proposal, helped by Bonnevay's skilful presentation, could be approved by the supporters both of *régie intéressée* and of direct intervention without either having to abandon their personal convictions. The traditional advocates of private enterprise in the Société Française des HBM were thus prepared to endorse the new law. Jules Siegfried, who had defended the principle of *régie intéressée* at the society's assembly in March, did not speak or vote against the public offices in July. Alexandre Ribot, who introduced the debate on the law in the Senate, did not hide his personal opposition to direct action by municipalities, nor his regret that the proposal of *régie intéressée* had been so quickly discarded by the commission; however, Ribot, who had collaborated in the preparation of the commission's proposals, recognised that the law responded 'to a pressing need in public opinion, and in the vital necessities of the country'. He expressed the supremacy of this need over personal convictions, when he declared that 'I give my vote... while reserving certain personal views, because I believe there is an absolute urgency'.[34]

A housing programme for Paris

While Bonnevay's commission was considering the question of housing in terms of national legislation, the Paris council's housing commission was addressing the particular requirements of the city. Henri Rousselle presented the commission's report to the council on 23 March 1912, a few days before Bonnevay submitted his report in parliament. Rousselle adopted the same tactics as Bonnevay, emphasising the joint role of private and public initiative. In general terms, Rousselle called for the assistance offered to private enterprise by the 1906 law to be made less restrictive. But like their parliamentary counterparts, the members of the council commission accepted that the work of private enterprise must be complemented by public action.

In his report, Rousselle discussed three methods of involving the public authorities in the construction of housing. The commission shared the parliamentary commission's rejection of partnership between private societies and public authorities in a *régie intéressée*. Rousselle supported the creation of public offices, but he arged that they would take too long to set up, to provide the rapid response which the housing crisis in Paris demanded. As an interim measure until the offices were functioning, Rousselle supported the view that the city should enter directly into the housing construction market. He thus presented the commission's proposal that the city contract a loan of 200 million francs, to enable the city itself to construct cheap housing.[35]

Rousselle's proposals were approved by the council and were passed on to the government, which prepared a bill to authorise the city to contract the loan. By the time the proposals were finalised, in July 1912, Bonnevay had submitted his report on general housing legislation. The Paris law permitted the city to commence a housing programme in advance of the passage of the general law, but it went no further than that law in the degree of intervention allowed. Direct construction by local authorities was envisaged by Bonnevay, provided most of the housing was reserved for large families, and if management of the dwellings was handed over to a private housing society, or the local public housing office. The housing built with the Paris loan was to conform to these conditions. Opposition to the law from the advocates of private enterprise was thus forestalled, as it was in the general law, by restricting direct action to housing for a special group, which had particular needs, and a particular importance to the health of the nation. The interests of private enterprise were further accommodated by the reservation of 50 million francs out of the 200 million franc loan, to be used by private housing societies.

If the Paris law avoided offending private interests, it did nonetheless present the principle of public finances entering the housing market. The housing was intended to be self-financing, but the law authorised the city to meet any deficit from the public budget. This principle was attacked by the right-wing deputy Joseph Denais when the law was debated in parliament; Denais also objected to the fact that the housing for large families was not required to yield its full economic return, and thus involved an element of public assistance. Other opponents of public intervention were less doctrinaire. Thus Guillaume Chastenet, speaking in the Senate, stated the familiar fear that if the city were to act in competition with private capital, then capital would shift away from cheap housing in favour of more expensive dwellings. But Chastenet was prepared to suppress this fear in relation to large families, arguing that all of the housing built by the city, and not just the majority, should be for this special category within the housing market.

Both Denais and Chastenet made their comments in the general discussion preceding the reading of the individual articles of the law. They were making affirmations of principle rather than a determined effort to alter the law. The majority of members of both Chambers were prepared to grant this special programme to Paris to allow the city to take action before the general housing law came into effect. The sense of urgency is evident in the presentation of the proposals before the parliamentary recess in July 1912. Approved by the Paris council on

5 July, they were presented in parliament on 9 July; the parliamentary commission considered the proposals, but time was too short before the recess to allow publication of its report prior to discussion. The report was thus read to the deputies on 11 July; the deputies approved the text that day, before going on to their final debate on the general housing law. The following day the text was approved by the Senators in their last session before the recess. The law received its final approval one year to the day since the presentation of the three *interpellations* on the Paris housing situation.[36]

The city started its housing programme by opening the architectural competition for two sites in the outer arrondissements of the city. The winning projects, incorporating the advances made in the design of urban flats during the early 1900s, were announced at the beginning of 1913 (see fig. 41). By the end of the year the proposals for these two sites had been finalised and approved, together with projects for a further nine sites; in December the city was in a position to take up the first part of the loan authorised in 1912. During 1913 the city had also pursued a policy of acquiring new sites in the outer arrondissements, and had opened a second competition for the design of four groups of housing. The projects for these groups were approved in June 1914, while a third competition for housing on another four sites was opened; during the year, construction work started on six of the projects approved in 1913. Meanwhile, the details for granting loans to private housing societies were set out, and a first group of loans to seven societies, totalling just over 4 million francs, was authorised.

Alongside this programme, which originated in the Paris law of 1912, the first steps were taken in establishing the public housing offices authorised by the general housing law. Within the city of Paris, an office was set up in early 1914, under the presidency of Paul Strauss. In the department of the Seine, containing the suburban area of Paris, the council approved a decision in favour of forming a departmental housing office. However, before this or the Paris office could achieve any progress war had broken out. The only tangible result of public intervention in Paris was the six sites on which construction had started; on only one of these sites had building reached as far as the first floor.

Looking forward: slums and garden suburbs

The housing programmes in Paris and its suburbs, cut short in 1914, were to be resumed after the war. The relationship of those programmes to the overall development of the city is indicative of the extent to which the ideals of housing reform had been taken up in practice. The housing programmes themselves addressed the issues which the reformers had raised, from the design and servicing of the individual dwelling, to its relationship with the city; they created an alternative to the housing built by speculators and developers. But at the same time as they were demonstrating the possibility of an alternative, the rapid growth of the city's suburbs was leading to the creation of new areas of shoddily built housing, with inadequate servicing.

The housing reformers had recognised the need to control urban growth if housing conditions were to be generally improved, and they had provided a powerful group arguing for the introduction of planning controls in the early 1900s. But they had taken up this issue later than their German or English counterparts; and while they could claim a technical success in the passage of the 1919 planning law, this came too late to establish the framework of planning control which would withstand the influx of population to Paris in the 1920s. Without this framework, creating the urban structure within which housing would take its place, the public health regulations of 1902 were insufficient to ensure the hygiene of individual dwellings.

Thus, despite the work of the housing reformers, Paris was to witness the development after the war of considerable areas of suburban slums, where in some cases mortality rates were as high as in the city centre slums. In the worst of these *lotissements*, the landowners who subdivided their land to provide individual sites for construction, failed to make any provision for proper roads, public services, communal facilities, or open space. Parisians attracted out of the city centre by the seductive image of a suburban cottage and garden, and migrants moving to the city from the country, were not always in a position to finance construction immediately after they had bought a site. The makeshift huts of wood and plaster which some families built only added to the physical and social problems which the uncontrolled development of the land engendered.[37]

The process of *lotissement* did not create such conditions everywhere. In many cases landowners laid out their property with some care, and provided the sites for houses which realised the housing reformers' ideal of the well-built cottage set in its own garden. Some of the *lotisseurs* even made use of the language of the reformers to promote their development. MM. Gabillon and Boutillon advertised their development at Petit Groslay as a *cité-jardin*, and in a publicity brochure they contrasted life in such an environment with life in an urban slum. But the 'country dwellings and bourgeois houses'[38] which Gabillon and Boutillon hoped to see in their *cité-jardin* were beyond the means of the families who took up the sites on less desirable *lotissements*.

The inadequate *lotissements* were widespread enough to lead to a political campaign for their improvement in the 1920s. Legislation was passed in 1924 and 1928, and between 1928 and 1932 there was a major programme to construct roads and sewers, to provide water and eventually electricity and gas.[39] This programme brought the worst *lotissements* up to the standard of housing for which the reformers had campaigned. But the fact that the programme was necessary emphasises that the building and planning controls to which the reformers had contributed in the laws of 1902 and 1919 depended on the willingness and ability of the local administration to implement them; these characteristics were inevitably more difficult to establish than legislative principles. The *lotissements* were the product of the delay between the establishing of those principles, and of the machinery to implement them. This delay led to the irony of the creation of large new areas of slums with rates of overcrowding and tuberculosis comparable to those in the slums of central Paris, at just the time when the campaign to clear those existing slums had been won, and their demolition begun.

The public housing programmes which offered an alternative to the chaotic development of the *lotissements* took up the housing models which the reformers had defined. In Paris, the city's Office Public des HBM developed the form of urban flats built around open courts, while in the suburbs, the departmental office started from the individual house and garden.

The majority of the housing built by the city office was situated on the old fortifications, whose fate had finally been resolved after 30 years of debate. Here too, the absence of a planning framework so evident in the *lotissements* led to a compromised development. Cacheux's proposal that special building regulations be applied to the land was not taken up, and as a result the dense urban form of Paris was extended into much of the newly available land. The city housing office faced the dilemma of whether to build on the land reserved for cheap housing at high density, in order to house the maximum number of people, or to build more open housing at lower density, with correspondingly fewer dwellings made available.

In London, the housing department had overcome this dilemma by gaining the right to build housing outside the area of the city, enabling it to build the cottage estates in suburban London. But in Paris, the administrative split between the city and its suburbs remained. The land offered by the fortifications provided the city housing office with the only major source of land within the city limits, and the office was thus obliged to maximise the use of this land. The servicing and planning of the flats which it built were of high standard; but the principle of the open court could not overcome the effect of the dense development of seven- or eight-storey blocks, which created densities of up to 1,700 persons per hectare.

The advantages of seeing the development of housing within an overall planning policy for the city and its region were apparent in the work of the departmental housing office directed by Henri Sellier. The garden suburbs created after the war brought together, in the most coherent form in France, the full range of the housing reformers' work, exploring improved methods of construction and design of housing while at the same time offering a model of how the city might grow. They demonstrated in practice the ideals which the reformers had developed, and provided the basis for the critical assessment and subsequent evolution of those ideals.

The housing programmes in and around Paris represent the practical achievement of housing reform; it was only after the First World War that such programmes, whether built by public offices or private housing societies, established a scale of housing production which made a significant contribution to the housing market, and still that achievement was limited, as the *lotissements* illustrate. But the programmes were the natural continuation of the process begun by the pre-war reformers. In this respect the pre-war movement can be seen to have evolved in two major periods, pivoting around the critical years of the 1880s.

Before 1880, the reform movement was dominated by the élitist ideal of the individual house. This ideal fulfilled the reformers' aim of securing social stability by improving the situation of the élite of the working class. The fact that the majority of the working class fell outside the scope of this ideal was disguised by the argument that these poorer workers would benefit through the process of 'levelling up'.

This model of housing reform was thrown into question in the 1880s by two factors. On the one hand the study of the housing market threatened the principle of 'levelling up', by demonstrating the basic gap between the cost of even the cheapest improved accommodation and the ability of many workers to pay. On the other hand, the recognition of the particular problem of population growth in France led the reformers to see improved housing not simply as a measure of social stability, but also as a means of increasing the strength of the nation through the encouragement given to healthy families. If the latter provided a reason to extend reform, the former emphasised the need to find new means to do so.

Thus, while the old élitist model remained as an ideal, it was joined by the new model of the urban flat: it was from the mid-1880s that the societies aiming to build such housing developed, offering accommodation which would be available to a wider group than would the individual cottage. At the same time the reformers started to work to expand the housing society movement, seeking sources of finance which would allow the housing societies to move in to the sector of the housing market left vacant by speculative builders.

This new phase of reform also saw the movement become a political lobby of some importance, supporting the campaigns to introduce new public health legislation, planning legislation, and the legislation which was designed to encourage the development of the housing society movement.

It was this new phase which established the basis for the achievement of housing reform after the war, while also determining the limitation of those achievements. But this process was not limited to France alone. A consideration of the legacy of the housing reform movement raises issues which were common to both France and Germany, as well as to other European countries. That legacy, which is symbolised in the garden suburbs around Paris, a counterpart to the garden suburbs around Frankfurt, can now be considered in more general terms which unite the French and German housing reform movements.

Conclusion to Parts One and Two: from workers' housing to social housing

Looking out across the housing estates which proclaim the values of the New Architecture in the suburbs of Frankfurt and Paris, it is easy to forget how much the work of Henri Sellier or Ernst May owes to the pre-war movement for housing reform. Yet, ultimately, many of the ideas realised in these developments, like so much of the achievement in the field of housing between the wars, can be traced back to the ideas of Huber, Blanqui and the early days of the housing reform movement in the 1840s. In our studies of housing reform in Germany and France we have emphasised the continuation into the post-war period of a number of the central issues considered by the pre-war reformers. The inter-war developments were remarkable in terms both of their design and of the quality of housing built; in Germany and France, together with many other European countries, the inter-war years saw the construction of housing for the less affluent by housing societies and public agencies in a quantity far exceeding any pre-war achievement. This housing and the architectural and planning principles on which it was based, was to form the foundation for later housing in both France and Germany; indeed it was these developments which marked the beginning of the 'social housing' programmes which continue to make up such an important part of housing today.

It was the desire to understand these inter-war developments and their origins which formed one of the most important points of departure for our studies. The housing built in the suburbs of Frankfurt and Paris was not conceived overnight in the minds of politicians, administrators and architects; this achievement necessarily depended on the legacy of the years before 1914. What, then, was the legacy which the pre-war housing movement bequeathed to its post-war successors? How did it provide the foundations on which the idea of 'social housing' has subsequently been built?

The period from the late 1840s to the outbreak of the war saw the evolution of the 'housing question' from the concern of a committed minority to a political issue of national importance. In 1840 the inadequacy of housing conditions of the poor in Germany and France was still largely unacknowledged by any but a handful of doctors; the notion of a new approach to the provision of housing still the preserve of a few political visionaries. Public control over conditions in existing housing was non-existent, while the degree of control over new building was related more to the prevention of fire, or, exceptionally, the creation of grand streets as a setting for the life of monarchs and the ruling classes, than to any desire to control or improve the standard of housing for the many.

However, by 1914 the position was very different. Much of the programme of reform that we have outlined had been introduced or was under serious discussion: measures to monitor and control conditions in existing housing, to control the construction of new housing and, ultimately, to bring order to the growth of the city, had been implemented in England, France and Germany. Meanwhile the financing and construction of cheap housing was no longer undertaken exclusively by private enterprise: housing societies, assisted by the special sources of finance available by 1914, had established an independent housing market, a non-profit or 'substitution' market to provide housing for those with low incomes. As this 'substitution' market grew, architects, sanitarians and others were able to explore new forms of housing for both cottage and tenement, freed from the absolute constraint of maximising profit for private enterprise.

By 1914, then, the housing question was a public issue which could no longer be brushed aside in the formulation of public policy; housing the working classes was by now the domain of a number of specialised organisations who lobbied governments, campaigned for improvement, and, in some cases, actually engaged in financing and constructing cheap housing. That public perception of the housing problem and its dangers had changed so dramatically during the period from 1840–1914 is a measure of the achievement of the housing reformers.

The emergence of an orthodoxy of reform

The fact that the public were so readily persuaded to accept the terms in which the reformers approached the housing question as the 'natural' approach, must not blind us to the different stages and the changes in direction involved in establishing what, by 1914, had come to be seen as the prevalent orthodoxy. Interest in the housing question raised by Huber and Blanqui in the 1840s had almost subsided by the 1860s. In France, for example, housing legislation had been passed in 1850, a testimony to the level of interest in the question, but was then left unenforced. Public discussion of housing subsided and the Société des Cités Ouvrières in Paris proved no more successful than the BgB in Berlin. Only the housing society in Mulhouse, formed during this early period, continued quietly to function, situated fittingly on the French/German border, but its lessons were not to be widely taken up until the 1870s.

But in Germany, France and England, the 1880s mark a threshold in the development of the movement for housing reform. From the 1880s onwards the range of the debate widens, the pace of involvement quickens. It was in the years during the widespread economic depression that followed the buoyancy of the 1870s that reformers in France and Germany began to relate the housing problem to its roots in the economics of housing. This process was not restricted to Germany and France. The most striking instance of the effort to gain a greater understanding of the housing problem was the setting up in 1884 in England of the Royal Commission on the Housing of the Working Classes.

More general studies of the industrial crisis were inaugurated in France in 1884, and in Belgium in 1886; although the commissions appointed considered the widest range of factors affecting the well-being of workers, they inevitably turned their attention to housing. It was the example of English and Belgian studies in particular which led the French Société d'Economie Sociale to sponsor a survey of housing conditions and proposals for their improvement in 1886, while in the same year in Frankfurt the Verein für Sozialpolitik published and debated the results of the investigations which it had launched the previous year. It was studies like these which impelled the reformers to advance beyond a concern with the symptoms of the housing problem, and to examine the basic question of the relationship between the costs of housing and the resources of the working-class family.

The 1880s also saw the formalisation of the loose contacts between individuals in different countries in a series of international housing congresses and conferences. Here is further evidence of the continuity of debate during the 1890s and early 1900s, and of the essential similarities that existed between the debate in different countries. The ten International Housing Congresses span the period from 1889 to 1913 and mark the culmination of housing reform, confirming the existence of common problems in various countries and the underlying similarity of the means to tackle these problems.

It was only natural that this debate should have been conducted in terms which reflected the values and interests of the reformers, and it is the establishment of an orthodoxy of housing reform that is the reformers' most direct legacy to their post-war successors. By 1914 they had already determined the form in which the housing question was to be discussed. Indeed as the volume of information on the housing question increased, so, it appears, the range of solutions narrowed. There is a striking contrast between the limited information available on housing in 1840, with few centres of discussion, and the wealth of statistical information and the national, even international, conferences at which it was discussed by 1914. Yet, this new-found wealth of information did not lead to the opening up of new approaches. In both France and Germany the housing reform movement was, by 1914, firmly based in the conventional political and economic wisdom of the period, tempered only by a refusal on the reformers' part to accept, at least in housing, the most damaging consequences of this established view. In Germany the increasingly narrow focus of the movement can be clearly seen in the campaign mounted by the Vereinreichswohnungs-gesetz to agree a unified but limited programme of reform as a basis for action on housing by the State, while in France the Société Française des HBM defended the programme defined in the legislation of 1894 and 1906.

As the range of debate was limited to fewer solutions, the success of these solutions and the terms in which they were judged became yet more important. In the late 1840s the programme of reform that gave rise to the Cité Napoléon was highly ambiguous – was it a defence against socialism, or was it a step towards socialism? To resolve such problems the reformers attempted to define the social implications which they believed were inherent in certain housing types as a series of generally valid laws.

These laws were developed by the reformers into the ideal view of housing which came to dominate their thinking in both France and Germany. We have seen how the workers' home was presented as more than a mere shelter, as the heart of the family, the hearth, where the family could build up its reserves of moral, physical and financial strength. In the reformers' eyes the home was closely linked with the concept of thrift and saving, with the status of proprietor, with the responsibility of the working man to help himself, and also with the corresponding responsibility of the propertied classes to discharge their social duty towards the workers who proved themselves worthy.

In these terms the reformers created an abstract ideal, linking housing reform to their own social intentions and values. It was this link which attracted the reformers to go beyond the limited goal of improving hygienic conditions in existing housing, to redefine the ideal of the worker's dwelling in physical terms. The closest physical counterpart to the reformers' social ideals was the individual house, the worker's cottage, and this model dominated housing reform in both France and Germany throughout the period from 1850 to 1914. The process of reconciling these same social ideals with the block of flats was less straightforward, raising more directly than the individual house, the problems of an urban society. The model for this kind of housing was only gradually developed, building on the slow advances in practice. However, by the 1880s, the reformers could point to specific examples of improved tenements that were fit to be set alongside the individual house.

It was this redefinition of the workers' house, summarised in the complementary models of the individual house and the urban flat, which endowed the reformers' social ideals with such power. These abstract ideals were made visible in the buildings – buildings which, the reformers believed, would contribute directly to the realisation of the larger social programme of reform.

The orthodox ideal and its realisation through the non-profit market

The reformers' social ideals, and the physical models which embodied them, represented the orthodoxy of housing reform. It was this view which the reformers proclaimed by encouraging discussion of the housing question, but the discussion in which these ideas were developed was principally within the limited circle of the reformers themselves. As the movement for reform became established, the transfer from theory into practice inevitably involved the reformers in the realities and compromises of politics and economics. In both Germany and France the limited number of houses built by the reformers serves to emphasise the gap between theory and practice. Nonetheless, by 1914 much had been achieved. The balance between public and private interests in public health and planning, now defined by mandatory legislation and local regulations, and the creation of a non-profit housing sector meant that the pre-war reformers were able to bequeath to the next generation a tradition of both the theory and the practice of housing reform.

It is during the 1880s that the housing reformers for the first time consider the housing question, both in theory and in practice, not in isolation but as part of the larger problem of rapid urban growth and change. The growing interest in the economics of housing at this time was paralleled by a new awareness in France and Germany of the problems created by the far-reaching changes in the characteristics and the distribution of population. In both countries the rapid expansion of the urban population and the size of cities created new tensions and exacerbated existing difficulties; in France, in particular, these develop-ments were further complicated by the wider problems of low overall population growth and a sharp decline in the rural population. Against this background, reformers in both France and Germany were forced to look more closely at two related issues which lay at the heart of the housing question: on the one hand, they had to promote the construction of cheap housing, but on the other, they had to do this while controlling the inadequacies of the existing pattern of urban growth.

During the 1890s measures to control the growth of the city are greatly extended. The reformers go beyond controlling conditions within the individual dwelling and now see the dwelling as a part of the city as a whole. The campaign for sanitary reform is now reinforced by those calling for land reform policies and for wider planning powers. We have emphasised the contribution of the German land reformers; in France, too, the views of the urban reformers begin to be important from the 1880s onwards: they champion the case for suburban development as an alternative to building yet more housing in the dense urban centre, and call for the necessary framework of regulation to ensure rapid construction of cheap housing in the suburbs.

These calls for new means of directing urban growth widened the scope of discussion but added little that was fundamentally new. But in the debate on the means of providing new housing, the emergence of a viable non-profit market during the early 1890s in both France and Germany represented a radical change of direction. Before the 1890s there had of course been housing societies paying limited dividends and housing built by workers' co-operatives; these had tested the principles of providing cheap housing outside the speculative market, but they had been no more than isolated initiatives. Only where employers constructed housing for their workforce was a substantial quantity of housing built outside the private enterprise market and, as we have seen, the circumstances in which such housing was built meant that it had no effect on the urban housing market. Only in the 1890s did the number of new societies founded in urban areas increase to the point at which a non-profit or substitution housing market became a practicable possibility.

Thus by the turn of the century it was possible to see in the evolution of both the theory and the practice of housing reform the consolidation of certain key advances which were to determine the nature of the legacy left to the post-war generation of housing reformers. But how was this legacy transferred? Central to this process was the idealisation of the worker's home and the development of the non-profit sector which was to build it.

The very concept of 'workers' housing', or, in its less specific form, 'cheap housing' was effectively the creation of the housing reformers. If most workers had always lived in houses, and cheap houses had always existed, it was the housing reformers who identified this category of housing as one which needed special attention. But in going beyond this identification of a category, to elaborate a social and physical ideal, they created a concept which was a powerful tool for reform. The threat of disease and unrest spreading from unhealthy working-class areas was used by reformers to frighten their listeners to action; but against this threat, the vision of the happy, healthy family seated contentedly in their garden provided a more positive incentive.

This vision was the creation of reformers whose interest was to stabilise the existing social order, to offer the worker enough of an improvement in his condition to dissuade him from striking or rioting. But the ideal created by these reformers achieved a certain degree of autonomy; we have seen how by the turn of the century the movement of housing reform had gained the support of some socialists who were prepared to work for gradual reform rather than revolutionary change. The classic vision of the house bathed in sun in its garden was even used by the French trades union, the Confédération Générale du Travail (CGT), in a series of leaflets campaigning for the five-day week in 1913.

In these terms the idealisation of the workers' house established a form of social contract. As initially put forward by the reformers, the contract was distinctly one-sided. Industrialists and the upper classes offered to help to finance housing for workers, but it was to be housing of a form defined by the upper classes, and the workers were to prove that they were worthy of the privilege. The reformers also established the means to implement this contract, in the form of the limited dividend company financed by the patronage of the wealthy.

However, as the housing reform movement evolved, the terms of the contract gradually changed. This can be seen most significantly in the sources of finance available to construct cheap housing, provided through the substitution market which evolved in the 1880s. The housing societies operating in these years still relied heavily on the patronage of the wealthy classes; even those few co-operatives which

Camarade, en réclamant la **Semaine anglaise, tu prouveras**
à tes exploiteurs qu'en **plus des** heures de sommeil, **tu veux**
pour ta dignité d'homme, ta part de liberté.

1 Leaflet from a publicity campaign by the Confédération Générale du Travail (CGT) in 1913, in favour of the five-day working week; the individual house bathed in sunlight is the visual counterpart of the 'dignity' and 'liberty' claimed in the text – a connection which is symptomatic of the continuity of thought from the time of Jean Dollfus in the 1850s.

were formed were in many cases dependent on such patronage. But the existence of these housing societies, together with the well-defined models for the form of housing which they were to build, whether houses or flats, served to demonstrate the feasibility of constructing housing independent of the speculative market. The investors who put money into the Société des Cités Ouvrières de Paris, or the Berliner Gemeinnützige Baugesellschaft in the late 1840s were venturing into the dark. They knew neither whether they would achieve any return on their money, nor whether the housing they financed would realise their social aims. By 1890 the investor could be more sure of the results. The housing reformers had defined the type of housing to be built in terms which did not threaten the social order; they had established a form of housing society which made a modest return, while not threatening the existing economic order.

It was against this background that the housing reformers in both Germany and France were able successfully to promote legislation in the 1890s, to shift the financing of housing societies from private patronage towards 'public' sources. In Germany, the Invalidity and Old Age Insurance Act of 1890 made finance from the insurance fund available to housing societies; four years later the Siegfried Law in France provided societies there with a source of finance from the Caisse des Dépôts et Consignations.

This change in finance effectively changed the terms of the social contract promoted by the housing reformers. If the patronage of the upper classes remained an important factor in the founding of many housing societies, those societies were now able to extend their work by calling on money which was independent of the notions of charity or philanthropy. The money pooled in the German insurance fund or the French Caisse de Dépôts et Consignations was money derived from the contributions or savings of an admittedly small percentage of the population. But in moving from reliance on the generosity of individuals to public funds established for social purpose, the financing of housing was placed on a more impersonal basis, as the business of society as a whole rather than of a handful of philanthropists. The new sources of housing finance thus allowed a considerable extension of the housing society movement in Germany and France, in terms of both the number of societies formed and of the quantity of housing built. Equally, in creating a more impersonal basis for housing reform, it helped to consolidate the support for reform. While the possession of a home was seen to depend on the generosity of the upper classes its appeal was inevitably limited as the reformers themselves had acknowledged. But if the possession of a home was achieved through the forms of social finance established in the 1890s, this could be presented as an honourable contract between worker and society. The concept of a substitution market which developed after the 1880s thus gained the same degree of acceptance among liberal reformers and moderate socialists as the idealisation of the workers' home. To either side of this spectrum, the principles of housing reform were still rejected – whether by the ardent defenders of private enterprise, who objected to any interference in the free market, or by the socialists working towards the Zukunftstadt, who saw reform as a compromise which would delay their goal. But the framework of reform established by the end of the century was able to rely on support from those groups whose aim was to achieve reform within the existing structure of society.

It was this consensus of support and the framework of reform which were to make possible the social housing programmes started after the First World War. Inevitably the war left its mark on the housing question. It saw the end of the free rent market which the liberal reformers had tried to defend. If the rents in non-profit housing built with loans through the housing legislation of the 1890s had been set to cover costs rather than to secure a profit, the rents of the greater part of the housing market had remained uncontrolled; the reformers hoped that the example set by the housing societies in charging cheap rents would influence speculative builders to follow suit. In the particular circumstances of the war, with family incomes disrupted, rent moratoria and controls were quickly introduced in both France and Germany. After four years of operation, these controls could not be removed overnight with the end of the war. The market for working-class housing after 1918 was thus, of political and economic necessity, a controlled market.

The housing situation after the war also served to emphasise the contradiction on which the nineteenth-century reformers' policies had been based. From the earliest discussion of housing reform in the 1840s, reformers clung to the belief that, if it could be convincingly demonstrated that healthy housing could be built, and let for low rents, then private enterprise would start to build such housing. This belief was never fulfilled, a fact which the reformers effectively admitted in the 1880s; in working towards the creation of a non-profit housing market, and in attempting to secure special sources of finance for that market, the reformers were acknowledging that cheap housing had to be constructed independently of the free market. But the reformers' attitude to this substitution market remained ambiguous. While they accepted that it was the only way to ensure the construction of the type of housing they wished to see, they were anxious that it should not threaten the ability of private enterprise to construct housing. Ultimately, their desire to increase the output of cheap housing societies was in direct conflict with their hope that, ideally, the free market would take up the construction of cheap housing.

This contradiction lies at the root of the disappointing achievement of housing reform in practice; the nineteenth-century reformers were simply unable to resolve the dilemma between their recognition of economic realities, and their underlying economic preconceptions. In the aftermath of the First World War, this contradiction became critical. The problems derived from the absence of investment in housing during the war, and the destruction of large quantities of housing, particularly in northern France, were compounded by the inability of the private market to respond to the need for construction. The uncertain financial climate in the immediate post-war years, and the reduction of rental income due to the continuation of rent controls ensured that little private money was available for investment in housing. In these circumstances, the substitution market created by the housing reformers offered a practical alternative; but for it to rise to the challenge, the ambiguity of the reformers' attitude had to be removed, and sufficient finance provided to allow the substitution market to operate on a large scale.

This necessity to expand the output of the substitution housing market was accompanied by a shift in the rhetoric of housing reform. The reformers before the war had felt able to excuse their limited achievement with the claim that 'every improved dwelling created is equivalent, perhaps, to a family saved'. After the war this attitude gave way increasingly to the claim that 'the nation has an absolute obligation to ensure for every family a healthy dwelling, at a rent corresponding to its ability to pay'.[1]

But behind this new rhetoric and the search for new forms of finance, the two central elements of pre-war housing reform retained their potency. The reformers' equation of environmental renewal with social renewal, and the specific models which they had evolved for the individual home and the urban flat formed the starting point for the social housing projects designed in the 1920s. The fact that the scale of housing construction in such projects was to be increased did not automatically cause the rejection of the individual house ideal; indeed, one of the incentives to the research of new forms of building design and construction was precisely to make this ideal more attainable. Similarly, the organisations which constructed this housing were to be those which the reformers had already established before the war. The extension of the housing society movement by the action of municipalities or by public housing offices had already been accepted before the war, within the structure of finance and housing types established since the 1880s for the housing societies. The fundamental change which allowed the framework of housing construction created by the reformers to realise its potential was thus not so much the intervention of public agencies for construction, as the introduction of major programmes of State finance.

These programmes cut straight through the ambiguity of the pre-war housing reformers in relation to the housing market. Their promoters argued that the free market had failed to provide suitable housing, and that the substitution market had not been able to operate on a scale to compensate for this failure. The economic situation after the war which delayed an immediate resumption of investment in the free market lent weight to the case that the substitution market should be given further support. Direct State intervention could be justified by varying shades of opinion – either by the traditional reforming logic that expenditure now would secure social stability in the future, or by the new logic that every family had a right to a home.

The case for State action was thus strong, and was not restricted to France and Germany. Great Britain, pioneer of housing reform, was quick to promise a programme of 'Homes fit for Heroes', and to provide the State subsidies to finance it. In France, the sources of finance established before the war were extended, and from 1921 the State took over the role of the Caisse des Dépôts et Consignations as the initiator of loans to cheap housing organisations. The principle of a major State investment in housing was accepted by the Chambre des Députés shortly after the war, but the programme was initially blocked by the more conservative Senate. It was thus only in 1928 that the level of investment in housing was increased through the Loucheur programme, introduced through legislation in that year. Large-scale investment was also delayed in Germany, but here the underlying reasons were predominantly economic. A programme of investment had to await the stabilisation of the country's economy in 1924, and the introduction of the *Hauszinssteuer* in the same year; a portion of the revenue from this tax which was levied on rents in housing built before 1914, provided the finance for the construction programmes of the following years.

Thus, in France, the socialist administrator of the public housing office in the Seine department, Henri Sellier, was able to build a series of suburban developments around the edge of Paris; while in Germany the social-democratic council in Frankfurt under Ludwig Landmann appointed the architect Ernst May to oversee the extension of the city through the creation of satellite communities. These two programmes illustrate the central themes of housing reform which gave the post-war reformers their starting point. In each case, the intention was to create developments of low-density housing in which working families would have the benefit of sun, air and greenery, and a home with exemplary standards of space and equipment, which would yet be within easy reach of the city centre by means of public transport. The specific ideal of the individual home and garden was the preferred form of housing, although in both Paris and Frankfurt this had to be adapted to meet

2 View across the Nidda Valley to the Römerstadt Siedlung (1927/8), Frankfurt am Main

3 The central square of the *cité-jardin* at Chatenay Malabry, in the Paris suburb

the constraints of cost. Thus the architects were involved both in researching into economic forms of construction in order to retain the ideal, and, at the same time, like their nineteenth-century predecessors, evolving designs for blocks of flats which would contain, as far as possible, the advantages of the individual house.

If the suburban developments in Paris and Frankfurt shared a common heritage from the housing reform movement, they were also the product of the differing emphasis of the movement in France and Germany. The Seine public housing office depended for its existence on the French housing legislation of 1912, which introduced a national framework of housing organisations; in contrast, the greater importance of local power in Germany is evident in the fact that it was the city of Frankfurt itself which continued its traditional role of independent action by initiating its housing programme. Similarly, in relation to the land used for construction the contrast between the French and German reform movements is clear. In Frankfurt, the land for suburban development was readily available, since the city had long established reserves of land. In Paris, on the other hand, the process of piecing together the sites for construction was much more difficult, as much of the land had to be bought from private owners. Although Henri Sellier was a firm advocate of land policies on the German model, he was having to operate in a country where such policies had no traditional basis.

The housing developments around Paris and Frankfurt are the visible outcome of the extension of finance for cheap housing after the war. The period of housing reform between 1850 and 1914 can be seen from this perspective as a period in which the problems associated with housing were recognised, in which practical solutions were proposed, but in which the resources necessary to implement those solutions were never adequately provided. This failure was inevitable given the reformers' view of their role as one of demonstration, to show others the way. What began to emerge during the 1880s was that private enterprise would not, indeed could not, follow, and that the role of reform must change from that of demonstration to that of execution. Before 1914 the reformers could never fully accept this change, and the contradiction of their position was evident in the limited achievement of reform in practice. It was a later generation who were to benefit from the organisation which the reformers had created, claiming the public finance necessary to make that organisation work. With the introduction of programmes of State finance, housing reform as demonstration finally gave way to housing reform as execution. The contract which had been written in the mid-nineteenth century, between the individual, generous philanthropist and the individual, worthy worker was now finally presented as a contract between society as a whole and the individual who was entitled to a home as a member of that society. It is this version of the contract which has formed the basis of subsequent housing policy, and of the construction no longer of workers' housing, nor even cheap housing, but of the more general commodity, social housing.

Abbreviations used for periodicals

PART ONE: GERMANY

DBZ	*Deutsche Bauzeitung*
SCAW	*Schriften der Centralstelle für Arbeiterwohlfahrtseinrichtung*
SDVfAW	*Schriften des deutschen Vereins für Armenpflege und Wohltätigkeit*
VföG	*Deutsche Vierteljahrschrift für öffentliche Gesundheitspflege*
VfVK	*Die Vierteljahrschrift für Volkswirtschaft und Kulturgeschichte*
ZfW	*Zeitschrift für Wohnungswesen*

PART TWO: FRANCE

ASMP	*Compte rendu des Séances et Travaux de l'Académie des Sciences Morales et Politiques*
BSES	*Bulletin de la Société d'Economie Sociale*
BSFHBM	*Bulletin de la Société Française des Habitations à Bon Marché* (note that the volumes for 1905 and 1906 are both numbered 16 and those for 1912 and 1913 are both 22)
BSIM	*Bulletin de la Société Industrielle de Mulhouse*
GAB	*Gazette des Architectes et du Bâtiment*
RGA	*Revue Générale de l'Architecture et des Travaux Publics*

Notes

Introduction

1 The recent literature on housing reform in England is extensive, see for example: E. Gauldie, *Cruel Habitations, a History of Working-Class Housing 1780–1918* (London, 1974); A. Sutcliffe (ed.), *Multi-Storey Living: The British Working-Class Experience* (London, 1974); M. Swenarton, *Homes Fit for Heroes, the Politics and Architecture of Early State Housing in Britain* (London, 1981); J. N. Tarn, *Five Per Cent Philanthropy, an Account of Housing in Urban Areas between 1840 and 1914* (Cambridge, 1973); A. S. Wohl, *The Eternal Slum, Housing and Social Policy in Victorian London* (London, 1977).
2 S. Smiles, *Thrift* (London, 1875).
3 W. Thompson, *Housing Handbook* (London, 1903), p. 9.
4 Karl Marx, *The Communist Manifesto* (London, 1847), ch. 3, section 2: Conservative and Bourgeois Socialism.

PART ONE: GERMANY

1 The emergence of the Housing Problem

1 J. Strang, *Germany in 1831* (London, 1836); and T. C. Banfield, *Industry of the Rhine*, vols. 1 and 2 (London, 1846–8).
2 J. H. Clapham, *The Economic Development of France and Germany 1815–1914*, 4th edn (Cambridge, 1968); M. Kitchin, *The Political Economy of Germany 1815–1914* (London, 1978); W. C. Henderson, *The Rise of German Industrial Power 1834–1914* (Berkeley, Cal., 1975).
3 W. Köllmann, *Bevölkerung in der industriellen Revolution* (Göttingen, 1974); J. Reulecke, *Die deutsche Stadt im Industriezeitalter, Beiträge zur modernen deutschen Stadtgeschichte* (Wuppertal, 1978); I. Thienel, *Städtewachstum im Industrialisierungsprozess des 19ten Jahrhunderts, das Berliner Beispiel* (Berlin, 1973).
4 A. F. Weber, *The Growth of Cities in the 19th Century, a Study in Statistics* (New York, 1899), pp. 80–94, especially tables 42 and 44.
5 C. Janke and D. Hilger (eds.), *Die Eigenthumslosen, der deutsche Pauperismus und die Emanzipationskrise in Darstellungen und Deutungen der zeitgenössischen Literatur* (Freiburg, 1965).
6 K. Weimann, 'Bevölkerungsentwicklung und Frühindustrialisierung in Berlin 1800–1850', in O. Busch (ed.), *Untersuchungen zur Geschichte der früheren Industrialisierung, vornehmlich im Wirtschaftsraum Berlin/Brandenburg* (Berlin 1971), pp. 151–90; E. Reich, *Der Wohnungsmarkt in Berlin 1840–1910* (Munich and Leipzig), 1912, p. 124.
7 Quoted in A. Voigt, 'Bodenbesitzverhältnisse, das Bau- und Wohnungswesen in Berlin und seinen Vororten', in C. J. Fuchs (ed.), *Neue Untersuchungen über*

die Wohnungsfrage in Deutschland und im Ausland (published as vols. 94 and 95 of the *Schriften des Vereins für Sozialpolitik*, Leipzig, 1901) vol. 1, section 1, pp. 152–260.

8 For a discussion of the early development of Berlin see W. Hegemann, *Das steinerne Berlin, die grösste Mietskasernestadt der Welt* (Berlin, 1930); and I. Thienel, 'Industrialisierung und Städtewachstum, die Wandel der Haupt-siedlungsformen in der Umgebung Berlins 1800–1850', in Busch, *Unter-suchungen*, pp. 106–49.

9 For a discussion of the developments around the Hamburger Tor see G. Liebchen 'Zu den Lebensbedingungen der unteren Schichten in Berlin des Vormärz', in Busch, *Untersuchungen*, pp. 270–314; and J. F. Geist and K. Kürvers, *Das Berliner Mietshaus 1740–1862* (Munich, 1980).

10 Voigt, 'Bodenbesitzverhältnisse', p. 153.

11 Thienel, 'Industrialisierung', pp. 117–18 and 122–5.

12 Hegemann, *Das steinerne Berlin*, p. 273.

13 Liebchen, 'Zu den Lebensbedingungen', p. 308.

14 ibid. pp. 310–12; and Reich, *Wohnungsmarkt*, p. 78–80; the conversion of Thaler to Marks is not straightforward: in Prussia the silver Thaler was equivalent, by the 1840s, to three Marks, but the conversion rate varied considerably between one state and another, despite the efforts of the Zollverein, cf. Clapham, *Economic Development*, p. 125.

15 See the report by the Magistrat. *Statistische Übersicht von der gestiegenen Bevölkerung in den Jahren 1815 bis 1828* (Berlin, 1829), quoted by Liebchen, 'Zu den Lebensbedingungen', p. 285.

16 For a discussion of the different types of lodger in Berlin see H. Lindemann 'Wohnungsstatistik' in Fuchs, *Neue Untersuchungen*, vol. 1, section 1, pp. 353–69 and Thienel, *Städtewachstum*, pp. 118–30 and 387–90.

17 Liebchen, 'Zu den Lebensbedingungen', p. 313.

18 ibid. pp. 310–11.

19 ibid.

20 ibid. pp. 299–307; for a more detailed description, including illustrations of the *Familienhäuser*, see Geist and Kürvers, *Berliner Mietshaus*.

21 B. von Arnim, *Dies Buch gehört dem König* (Berlin, 1843), p. 541.

22 The standard biography of Huber is R. Elvers. *Victor Aimé Huber, sein Werden und Wirken* (Bremen, 1874); the collection of Huber's writings edited by K. Munding, *Victor Aimé Hubers ausgewählte Schriften über Sozialreform und Genossenschaftswesen* (Berlin, 1894), is of little use in following Huber's interests in the housing question.

23 *Janus, Jahrbücher deutscher Gesinnung, Bildung und Tat*, edited by V. A. Huber, Berlin, 1845–8.

24 For a fuller discussion see W. C. Shanahan, *German Protestants Face the Social Question*, vol. 1 (Notre Dame, 1954), especially ch. 3 and 7; and T. S. Hammerow, *Restoration, Revolution, Reaction: Economics and Politics in Germany, 1815–1871* (Princeton, 1958).

25 For a discussion of Wichern and the position of the Innere Mission on the social question see V. A. Huber, *Innere Mission und Association, eine Denkschrift* (Berlin, 1853); and G. Brakelmann, *Kirche, soziale Frage und Sozialismus* (Gütersloh, 1977).

26 Elvers, *Huber*, p. 148; V. A. Huber, 'Eindrücke und Betrachtungen eines Reisenden: Manchester, das Proletariat', *Janus*, 1845, vol. 2, sections 23 and 24, pp. 641–78, 705–26.

27 Huber was impressed by the ideas of Blandford, but put off by his meeting with Ashley whose attitude to the housing question Huber found too negative. Elvers, *Huber*, p. 146–8.

28 For Liedke's contribution to the German co-operative tradition see H. Zeidler, *Geschichte des deutschen Genossenschaftswesen der Neuzeit* (Berlin, 1893).

29 V. A. Huber, *Selbsthilfe der arbeitenden Klassen durch Wirtschaftsvereine und innere Ansiedlung* (Berlin, 1848), new edn: C. J. Fuchs (ed.), published as vols. 21–3 of *Genossenschaftliche Kultur* (Berlin, 1916).
30 ibid. p. 16.
31 V. A. Huber, 'Über innere Colonisation', in *Janus*, 1846, vol. 1, Issues 7 and 8, pp. 193–222, 225–55.
32 Huber, *Selbsthilfe*, p. 16.
33 Hegemann, *Das steinerne Berlin*, p. 293, quotes Huber as saying: 'This aristocracy has still not learnt a thing, it must be flayed with scorpions and pounded to dust before it can comprehend the true meaning of Duty, Honour and Excellence.'
34 For a discussion of liberal attitudes to the social problem see D. G. Rohr, *The Origins of Social Liberalism in Germany* (Chicago, 1963); and L. Krieger, *The German Idea of Freedom* (Chicago, 1957).
35 Quoted in Rohr, *Social Liberalism*, p. 90.
36 An account of the founding of the Centralverein and its early history is given by A. Lette, 'Zur Geschichte der Bildung und Wirksamkeit des Central Vereins in Preussen für das Wohl der arbeitenden Klassen', in *Arbeiterfreund*, vol. 1, pp. 1–25.
37 *Mittheilungen des Centralvereins für das Wohl der arbeitenden Klassen*; Berlin, 1849–59 (Neue Folge, 1855–9); continued as *Zeitschrift des Central-Vereins in Preussen für das Wohl der arbeitenden Klassen*, Leipzig, 1859–61 and finally as *Der Arbeiterfreund, Zeitschrift für die Arbeiterfrage*, Berlin 1863–1914.
38 Quoted in Rohr, *Social Liberalism*, p. 139.
39 The committee investigating housing conditions 'in relation to sanitary control and non-profit housing associations' consisted of Sussmann (a factory owner from Berlin), Building Inspector Emmich, Dr Gaebler (a lawyer), and Dr Reimer (a medical doctor), see 'Nachrichten welche die Tätigkeit des Central-Vereins betreffen', *Mittheilungen des CVWaK*, 1850, Issues 7 and 8, p. 9.
40 J. Faucher, *Die Vereinigung von Sparkasse und Hypothekenbank und der Anschluss eines Häuserbauvereins als sozialökonomische Aufgabe unserer Zeit*, (Berlin, 1845).
41 E. Kalisch, 'Zur Geschichte des Berliner Lokalvereins für das Wohl der arbeitenden Klassen', in *Mittheilungen des CVWaK*, 1848, Issue 1, p. 85.
42 Huber, 'Innere Colonisation', p. 205; this was a point he emphasised from his first involvement with housing through into the 1860s.
43 There is extensive documentation of the BgB: *Concordia, Blätter der Berliner gemeinnützigen Baugesellschaft*, V. A. Huber (ed.), Berlin, 1848–50 (not to be confused with Huber's later occasional periodical of the same name), in the *Mittheilungen des CVWaK* and the *Arbeiterfreund* these include: C. W. Hoffmann, *Die Aufgabe einer Berliner gemeinnützigen Baugesellschaft* (Berlin, 1847); C. W. Hoffmann, 'Die Berliner gemeinnützige Baugesellschaft', in *Die Wohnungen der Arbeiter und Armen*, Heft 1 (Berlin, 1852); E. Gaebler, *Idee und Bedeutung der Berliner gemeinnützigen Baugesellschaft* (Berlin, 1848): Krokisius, *Die unter dem Protektorat Seiner Majestät des Kaisers und Königs Wilhelm II stehenden Berliner gemeinnützige Bau-gesellschaft und Alexandra-stiftung, 1847 bis Anfang 1908* (Berlin, 1908); *Geschichte der gemeinnützigen Wohnungswirtschaft in Berlin* (Berlin, 1957) (this was written shortly after the recovery of a number of early documents, long believed lost, containing details of shareholdings etc.); Geist and Kürves, *Berliner Mietshaus*, pp. 413–63.
44 Quoted in *Geschichte der gemeinnützigen Wohnungswirtschaft*, p. 22.
45 Hoffmann, 'Die Berliner gemeinnützige Baugesellschaft', p. 70.
46 *Geschichte der gemeinnützigen Wohnungswirtschaft*, p. 24.

47 ibid. p. 26.

48 The rents for dwellings in the BgB (25–45 Thaler for small dwellings, 40–60 Thaler for large dwellings and 30–40 Thaler for workshops) are given in 'Nachricht für diejenigen, welche eine Wohnung in den Genossenschaftshäusern zu mieten wünschen', in *Mittheilungen des CVWaK*, 1850, Issue 9, pp. 116–17, and in 'Über Zwecke, Mittel und Wirksamkeit der BgB', in *Mittheilungen des CVWaK*, 1850, Issue 7, p. 41. Comparable rents for the rest of the city are given in Reich, *Wohnungsmarkt*, pp. 126–8, tables 3 and 4.

49 See Kitchin, *Political Economy*, pp. 87–109; Hammerow, *Restoration*, pp. 199–237; J. Kuczynski, *Die Geschichte der Lage der Arbeiter unter dem Kapitalismus* (vols. 1–38, Berlin, 1961–79), vol. 2, 1962.

50 Hammerow, *Restoration*, pp. 208–10; Kuczynski, *Lage der Arbeiter*, vol. 2, ch. 2, especially p. 154.

51 Quoted in Shanahan, *German Protestants*, p. 255.

52 H. Schulze-Delitzsch, 'Kapitel zu einem deutschen Arbeiterkatechismus', quoted in E. Schraepler (ed.), *Quellen zur Geschichte der sozialen Frage in Deutschland*, vols. 1 and 2 (Berlin and Frankfurt, 1964), vol. 1, p. 182.

53 Reich, *Wohnungsmarkt*, p. 124.

54 ibid. pp. 126–7.

55 E. Knoblauch, 'Warum werden in Berlin nicht mehr Gebäude mit kleinen Wohnungen gebaut?', in *Mittheilungen des CVWaK*, vol. 1 (neue Folge), 1855, pp. 246–9.

56 W. Emmich, 'Betrachtungen über Ursache und Abhülfe des Mangels an kleinen und mittleren Wohnungen in Berlin, nebst Ermittelungen über die Anlagekosten und die Erträge-Verhältnisse von Grundstücken verschiedenen Anfangs, mit bürgerlicher Einrichtung', in *Mittheilungen des CVWaK*, vol. 1 (neue Folge), 1855, pp. 249–57.

2 The first debate on the Housing Problem

1 V. A. Huber, 'Die Wohnungsfrage: die Noth', in *Concordia, Beiträge zur Lösung der socialen Fragen* (Leipzig, 1861), vol. 2, p. 1.

2 For an account of Huber's trip of 1857 to France, Belgium (where he attended the Congrès International de Bienfaisance) and to England, see Elvers, *Huber*, pp. 329–35.

3 Huber, 'Wohnungsfrage: die Noth', p. 9.

4 Later published as V. A. Huber, *Die Wohnungsnoth der kleinen Leute in grossen Städten* (Leipzig, 1857).

5 E. Krieger, 'Über Kellerwohnungen in Berlin', *Mittheilungen des CVWaK*, vol. 2. (neue Folge) 1857, pp. 218–48.

6 W. Emmich, 'Vergleichende Bemerkungen über die Bestrebungen zur Verbesserung der Wohnungsverhältnise der arbeitenden Klassen in verschiedenen Ländern, namentlich England', in *Mittheilungen des CVWaK*, vol. 2 (neue Folge), 1859, pp. 145–9; and V. A. Huber, 'Die Wohnungsfrage in Frankreich und England' in *Mittheilungen des CVWaK*, vol. 2 (neue Folge), 1859, pp. 3–37; 1860, vol. 3, pp. 123–96.

7 W. Emmich, 'Betrachtungen über den Stand des Unternehmens der gemeinnützigen Baugesellschaft und über neuere Vorschläge zur Abhülfe der Wohnungsnoth in Berlin', in *Mittheilungen des CVWaK*, vol. 2 (neue Folge), 1859, pp. 195–201.

8 Huber refers ('Wohnungsfrage: die Noth', p. 10) to articles by Louis Pappenheim in the *Monatsschrift für Sanitätspolizei* in 1860; other journals such as the *Vierteljahrschrift für gerechtliche Medizin*, Berlin, also carried such articles; however, much of the evidence produced in the discussion of public

health and housing was drawn from English sources: E. Sax. *Wohnungszustände der arbeitenden Classen und ihre Reform* (Vienna, 1869), pp. 24–44,
quotes Edwin Chadwick, James Hole, Dr Southwood-Smith and the National
Association for the Promotion of Social Science as the principal sources on
this question.

9 Huber, 'Wohnungsfrage: die Noth', p. 8.

10 ibid. p. 13.

11 Huber, 'Wohnungsfrage: die Hülfe', in *Concordia...*, 1861, vol. 3, p. 15.

12 ibid. p. 47.

13 F. A. Lange, *Jedermann Hauseigenthümer* (Duisburg, 1865).

14 L. Parisius, 'Die auf dem Prinzip der Selbsthülfe beruhende Baugenossenschaft' in *Arbeiterfreund*, 3 (1865), pp. 262–99.

15 *Die Vierteljahrschrift für Volkswirtschaft und Kulturgeschichte (VfVK)*, Berlin,
1863–93; edited by J. Faucher from vols. 1–30, with editorial assistance
from K. Arndt, V. Böhmert, C. Braun, O. Michaelis and E. Wiss.

16 J. Prince-Smith, 'Die sogennante Arbeiterfrage', in *VfVK*, 4 (1866), p. 192.

17 A. Lette, 'Zur Geschichte', pp. 20–1.

18 'Siebenter Kongress deutscher Volkswirte', in *VfVK*, 2 (1864), p. 236.

19 ibid.

20 The committee consisted of Lette (chairman), Lange, Faucher, Huber and
Schmidt.

21 V. A. Huber, 'Über die geeignetsten Massregeln zur Abhülfe der Wohnungsnoth', in *Arbeiterfreund*, 3 (1865), p. 141.

22 In addition to the articles by Huber and Parisius already mentioned, the
Arbeiterfreund, 3 (1865), also contained the following articles: K. Brämer,
'Die nützlichen Baugenossenschaften in England'; R. Klette, 'Die Wohnungsfrage vom Standpunkt der Technik aus'; Ende and Boeckmann, 'Über
den Einfluss der Baupolizeivorschriften auf das Entstehen von Arbeiterwohnungen und deren gesunde und angemessene Gestaltung'. All these
articles were later published as *Die Wohnungsfrage mit besonderer Berücksichtigung auf die arbeitenden Klassen* (Berlin, 1865).

23 'Achter Kongress deutscher Volkswirte', in *VfVK*, 4 (1866), p. 196.

24 The committee's response to the material submitted the previous year and
its discussions were reported in 'Weitere Behandlungen der Wohnungsfrage
seitens des Centralvereins in Preussen für das Wohl der arbeitenden
Klassen', in *Arbeiterfreund*, 4 (1866), pp. 1–19.

25 ibid. p. 11.

26 ibid. p. 2.

27 'Neunter Kongress deutscher Volkswirte', in *VfVK*, (1867), p. 122.

28 ibid.

29 ibid. p. 130.

30 Sax, *Wohnungszustände*.

31 F. Engels, *Zur Wohnungsfrage*, 1872 (translated by C. P. Dutt as *The Housing
Question*, London, n.d.), p. 46.

32 ibid. p. 47.

33 ibid. p. 45.

34 ibid. p. 71.

35 S. Neumann, *Die Berliner Volkszählung vom 3 December 1861 im Auftrag
der städtischen Volks-Zahlung-Commission* (Berlin, 1863).

36 An article by M. Neefe, 'Hauptergebnisse der Wohnungsstatistik deutscher
Grossstädte', in *Die Wohnungsnoth der ärmeren Klassen in deutschen Grossstädten und Vorschlage zu deren Abhülfe* (published as vols, 30 and 31 of the
Schriften des Vereins für Sozialpolitik, Leipzig, 1886), pp. 161–91, vol. 1,
provides a brief survey of the historical background to the various housing
surveys carried out by the statistical offices of the different cities.

37 H. Senftleben, 'Die Bedeutung und der Fortschritt der Wohnungsfrage', in *Arbeiterfreund*, (1868), p. 396.
38 ibid.

3 Boom, depression and the second debate on the Housing Problem

1 For an account of the VfSP see F. Boese, 'Geschichte des Vereins für Sozialpolitik, 1872–1932', *Schriften des Vereins für Sozialpolitik*, vol. 88 (Berlin, 1939); for a more recent study see J. J. Sheehan, *The Career of Lujo Brentano; a Study of Liberalism and Social Reform in Imperial Germany* (Chicago, 1966), especially ch. 4.

2 G. Schmoller, 'Ein Mahnruf in der Wohnungsfrage', in *Jahrbuch für Gesetzgebung, Verwaltung und Volkswirtschaft im deutschen Reich*, (1887), p. 24.

3 H. Rosenberg, *Grosse Depression und Bismarckszeit* (Berlin, 1967), especially ch. 6.

4 Weber, *The Growth of Cities*, p. 82; for a more recent discussion see Köllmann, *Bevölkerung*.

5 For a discussion of the growth of Berlin during the nineteenth century see Thienel, *Städtewachstum*; E. Heinrich and F. Mielke (eds.), in *Berlin und seine Bauten*, pt 2 (Berlin, 1964), pp. 29–79; A. Zimm, *Die Entwicklung des Industriestandortes Berlin, Tendenzen der geographische Lokalisation bei den Berliner Industriezweigen von überörtlicher Bedeutung sowie die territoriale Stadtentwicklung bis 1945* (Berlin (East), 1959). For a discussion of the growth of the public transport network see D. Radicke 'Die Entwicklung des öffentlichen Personennahverkehrs in Berlin bis zur Grundung der BVG', in *Berlin und seine Bauten*, pt 10, vol. B (Berlin, 1979), pp. 1–11.

6 This point, regularly made by contemporaries, is discussed by G. Berthold, 'Die Wohnverhältnisse in Berlin, insbesondere die der ärmeren Klassen' in *Die Wohnungsnoth*, vol 2. p. 223.

7 Data on the proportion of empty dwellings are drawn from Reich, *Wohnungsmarkt* pp. 126–7; Reich also refers to the difficulties in interpreting official statistics caused by the inclusions of virtually uninhabitable dwellings, ibid. p. 92.

8 ibid. p. 92.

9 These data on rents are drawn from the summary of the *Mietssteuerkataster* or municipal tax records in Reich, *Wohnungsmarkt*, pp. 126–8, tables 3 and 4.

10 Data on dwelling size were presented in the form of the number of heatable rooms per dwelling; in Berlin the kitchen was counted as a heatable room, but in other cities this was not always the case, see Neefe, 'Hauptergebnisse p. 169, note 1.

11 This concern is evident from the early writings of Huber onwards, and is reflected in the wealth of information on lodgers of different types in the VfSP's housing survey; for a discussion of the various types of lodgers see Reich, *Wohnungsmarkt*, pp. 97, 123, 133 (table 12); Thienel, *Städtewachstum*, pp. 118–30, 387–90; and Berthold, 'Wohnverhältnisse', p. 206.

12 There is little material on the lodger's point of view, but see P. Göhre (trans. A. D. Carr), *Three Months in a Workshop, a Practical Study* (London, 1895); L. Niethammer, 'Wie wohnten die Arbeiter in Kaiserreich?', in *Archiv für Sozialgeschichte*, 16 (1976), pp. 127–48; J. Ehmer, 'Wohnen ohne eigene Wohnung', in L. Niethammer (ed.), *Wohnen im Wandel, Beiträge zur Geschichte des Alltags in der bürgerlichen Gesellschaft*, (Wuppertal, 1979), pp. 132–150 and, though for a different pattern of lodging, F. Brüggemeier, L. Niethammer, 'Schlafgänger, Schnappskasinos und schwerindustrielle Kolonie. Aspekte der Arbeiterwohnungsfrage im Ruhrgebiet vor dem ersten

Weltkrieg', in J. Reulecke, W. Weber (eds.), *Fabrik, Familie, Feierabend, Beiträge zur Sozialgeschichte des Alltags im Industriezeitalter* (Wuppertal, 1978), pp. 153–74.

13 See the household income and expenditure surveys carried out in Berlin before the First World War referred to in Chapter 8, note 32; the point is also confirmed by more recent studies, e.g., Ehmer, 'Wohnen ohne eigene Wohnung', p. 143.

14 This measure of density has the obvious disadvantage that it takes no account of plot size which, Rudolf Eberstadt (*Handbuch des Wohnungswesens und der Wohnungsfrage*, 2nd edn, Jena, 1910, pp. 59–67) argued, increase significantly during the later years of the nienteenth century.

15 Quoted in Schmoller, 'Mahnruf', p. 428.

16 The wealth of data available on housing conditions by the mid-1880s is clearly illustrated in the statistical section of the VfSP's survey, Neefe, 'Hauptergebnisse', pp. 162–4.

17 For a general discussion of social policy see K. E. Born, 'Sozialpolitsche Probleme und Bestrebungen von 1848 bis zur Bismarkschen Sozialgesetzgebung' in *Vierteljahrschrift für Sozial- und Wirtschaftsgeschichte*, 46 (1959), pp. 29–44; L. Heyde, *Abriss der Sozialpolitik* (Heidelberg, 1949); Rosenberg, *Grosse Depression*, pp. 192–227, 253–7.

18 The response of those associated with the CVWaK to Bismarck's policies is set out by V. Böhmert, 'Die soziale Frage im Reichstage und vor dem Reichskanzler', in *Arbeiterfreund*, (1876), pp. 1–15.

19 K. Brämer, 'Die Eisenacher Konferenz über die soziale Frage', in *Arbeiterfreund*, 10 (1872), p. 182.

20 G. Schmoller, 'Die soziale Frage und der preussische Staat', in *Zur Sozial- und Gewerbepolitik der Gegenwart* (Leipzig, 1890), pp. 37–63.

21 Brämer, 'Die Eisenacher Konferenz', pp. 207–10.

22 A. V. Desai, *Real Wages in Germany 1871–1913* (Oxford, 1968), p. 36, table 4.1.

23 ibid. pp. 35–7, especially table 4.1; and Kuczynski, *Lage der Arbeiter*, vol. 3, pt 2, ch. 2, pp. 297–8, 319–21, 340.

24 E. Engel, *Die moderne Wohnungsnoth; Signatur, Ursachen und Abhülfe* (Leipzig 1873).

25 In addition to the limited studies such as those of E. Reichardt (see note 27 below) and P. Hansen *Die Wohnungsverhältnisse in den grösseren Städten* (Heidelberg, 1883), there was some technical interest in housing: in Prussia both sanitarians and architects were closely involved in the debate over the *Fluchtliniengesetz* and had hopes that this might lead to an improvement in the standards of new housing.

26 'Die heutige Wohnungsfrage' and 'Zur Lösung der Wohnungsfrage' in *Arbeiterwohl, Organ des Verbandes katholischer Industrielle und Arbeiterfreunde*, F. Hitze (ed.) (Cologne), (1882) Heft 7, pp. 117–28, Heft 8, pp. 139–52.

27 E. Reichardt, *Die Grundzüge der Arbeiterwohnungsfrage mit besonderer Berücksichtigung der Unternehmungen, die Arbeiter zu Hauseigenthümern zu machen* (Berlin, 1885).

28 Miquel is a figure of some importance for the movement for housing reform both for his work with the VfSP and the Verein für öffentliche Gesundheitspflege (VföG), and his energetic support for initiatives to improve housing in Frankfurt; sadly, however, H. Herzfeld's study, *Johannes Miquel, sein Antheil am Ausbau des deutschen Reiches bis zur Jahrhundertwende*, 2 vols (Detmold, 1938), makes little explicit reference to this aspect of Miquel's work.

29 Herzfeld, *Miquel*, ch. 3, especially pp. 526–30.

30 See, for example: W. Ruprecht, *Die Wohnungen der arbeitenden Klassen in England* (Göttingen, 1884); A. Gumprecht, 'Die Arbeiterwohnungsfrage' in *Arbeiterfreund*, 25 (1887), pp. 8–11; P. Aschrott, 'Die Arbeiterwohnungsfrage in England' in *Die Wohnungsnoth*, pp. 93–146, especially p. 146.

31 The results of the enquiry were published as *Die Wohnungsnoth der ärmeren Klassen in deutschen Grossstädten und Vorschläge zu deren Abhülfe*, in *Schriften des Vereins für Sozialpolitik* (Leipzig, 1886), vols. 30 and 31; the discussion was published as *Verhandlungen der am 24 und 25 September 1886 am Frankfurt am Main abgehaltenen Generalversammlung des Vereins für Sozialpolitik*, in *Schriften des Vereins für Sozialpolitik* (Leipzig, 1887), vol. 33, pp. 5–139.

32 Schmoller, 'Mahnruf', pp. 428–9.

33 ibid. p. 429.

34 Neefe, 'Hauptergebnisse'.

35 ibid. p. 183, table 26.

36 ibid. p. 196, table 39.

37 ibid. pp. 172, 194, table 35; see also Flesch's discussion of the unfairness of the rent contract to the tenant and the need to revise the relationship between landlord and tenant in K. Flesch, 'Die Wohnungsverhältnisse in Frankfurt am Main', in *Die Wohnungsnoth*, pp. 75–88.

38 J. Miquel, 'Einleitung', in *Die Wohnungsnoth*, p. xi.

39 F. F. L. von Bodelschwingh, 'Die Wohnungsverhältnisse der ärmeren Klassen in deutschen Grossstädten', in *Verhandlungen*, pp. 61–76.

40 Schmoller, 'Mahnruf', pp. 429–30.

41 ibid. p. 427.

42 J. Miquel, *Verhandlungen*, p. 59.

4 The reformers' ideal

1 One of the earliest statements of the advantages of the cottage over the tenement block was made by Huber in just these terms; Huber, 'Eindrücke und Betrachtungen', p. 663.

2 J. N. Tarn, *Five Per Cent Philanthropy, an Account of Housing in Urban Areas between 1840 and 1914* (Cambridge, 1973), especially ch. 2.

3 The attractions of the English cottage were championed by Huber, Sax, Lette and other early housing reformers, but particularly by Julius Faucher in two articles: 'Die Bewegung für Wohnungsreform', in *VfVK*, 4 (1865), pp. 127–99; 5 (1866), pp. 86–151.

4 Emmich, 'Vergleichende Bemerkungen', pp. 148–9; Henry Roberts' book, *The Dwellings of the Labouring Classes* (London, 1850), was translated into German by C. Busse as *Wohnungen für die arbeitenden Classen* (Berlin, 1852).

5 The housing at Mulhouse was widely reported in Germany, see, for example, the *Mittheilungen des CVWaK* and Huber, 'Die Wohnungsfrage: die Hülfe', pp. 38–9. Interest in the scheme remained considerable well into the 1880s: Reichardt (*Arbeiterwohnungsfrage*, p. 37) was still referring to it as 'the most shining example of all enterprises to resolve the question of working-class housing'.

6 For a discussion of the housing provided by the mines and other employers in areas such as the Ruhr see O. Täglichsbeck, 'Die Beförderung der Ansiedlung von Arbeitern der Staatsberg-, Hütten- und Salzwerke durch Gewährung von Bauvorschüssen und Bauprämien seitens des preussischen Bergfiskus', in *Die Verbesserung der Wohnungen* published as vol. 1 of the *Schriften der Centralstelle für Arbeiterwohlfahrtseinrichtungen* (Berlin 1892) (see Chapter 6, n. 18), pp. 98–107; for a more recent discussion see

F. Bollerey and K. Hartmann, *Wohnen im Revier, 99 Beispiele aus Dortmund* (Dortmunder Architekturhefte No. 1) (Munich, 1975); and R. Günther, 'Arbeitersiedlungen im Ruhrgebiet', in E. Trier and W. Weyres (eds.), *Kunst des 19ten Jahrhunderts im Rheinland, Architektur*, vol. 2, (Düsseldorf, 1980).

7 For a discussion of the cottage tradition of housing in the Rhineland see R. Eberstadt, *Rheinische Wohnverhältnisse und ihre Bedeutung für das Wohnungswesen in Deutschland* (Jena, 1903); for a discussion of the housing forms in the Bremen areas see G. Albrecht, 'Das Bremer Haus, ein Sonderfall in der deutschen Baugeschichte um 1850', in Niethammer, *Wohnen im Wandel*, pp. 233–51.

8 These are illustrated in C. W. Hoffmann, *Die Wohnungen der Arbeiter und Armen* (Berlin, 1852); the link with Bremen was regarded as significant both because of the 'cottage' form of housing and because Huber's uncle (who lived in Bremen) had put up money for the development.

9 Huber, 'Innere Colonisation', p. 204.

10 The argument used here by Huber was frequently used in Germany as a means of securing support for housing reform; the most widely known version of this case must be Schmoller's 'Mahnruf in der Wohnungsfrage'. Naturally the same case was also made for social reform generally, see, for example, V. Böhmert, 'Materielle und ideale Losung der socialen Frage', in *Arbeiterfreund*, 24 (1886), pp. 20–8.

11 Huber, 'Innere Colonisation', p. 205.

12 ibid. p. 207.

13 W. Riehl, *Die Familie*, vol. 3 of *Naturgeschichte des Volkes als Grundlage einer deutschen Social-Politik* (Stuttgart and Augsburg), 1855, pp. 195–6.

14 ibid. p. 196.

15 E. Wiss, *Über die Wohnungsfrage* (Berlin, 1872), p. 13.

16 Parisius, 'Selbsthülfe', pp. 274–5.

17 Engels, *Zur Wohnungsfrage*, p. 11.

18 Sax, *Wohnungszustände*, p. 63.

19 Reichardt, *Arbeiterwohnungsfrage*, p. 21.

20 ibid.

21 Schmoller, 'Mahnruf', pp. 424–6.

22 The conferences of the Verein are reported in some detail in the Verein's journal, *Deutsche Vierteljahrschrift für öffentliche Gesundheitspflege*, (*VföG*) 1869–1922 (Braunschweig), published on behalf of Die Versammlung deutscher Naturförscher und Aerzte, which provides an invaluable summary of the current debate on sanitary affairs.

23 C. Gatliff, *Practical Suggestions on Improved Dwellings for the Industrious Classes* (London, 1854).

24 W. Strassmann and E. Von Haselberg, 'Anforderungen der öffentlichen Gesundheitspflege an die Baupolizei in Bezug auf die neue Stadtteile, Strassen und Häuser', *VföG*, 7 (1875), p. 56.

25 'Über die hygienischen Anforderungen an Neubauten zunächst in neuen Quartieren grösserer Städte', *VföG*, 8 (1876), pp. 97–138.

26 ibid. p. 109.

27 'Die unterschiedliche Behandlung der Bauordnungen für das Innere, die Aussenbezirke und die Umgebung von Städten', *VföG*, 26 (1894), pp. 13–47; and 'Die Notwendigkeit weiträumiger Bebauung bei Stadterweiterungen und die rechtlichen und technischen Mittel zu ihrer Ausführung', *VföG*, 27 (1895), pp. 101–30.

28 'Die unterschiedliche Behandlung', pp. 17–18.

29 The Margaretenhöhe estate is described at length in A. E. Brinckmann and B. Rath, *Die Margareten-Höhe bei Essen* (Darmstadt, 1913).

30 Schmoller, 'Mahnruf', p. 444.

31 Eberstadt, *Handbuch des Wohungswesens*, p. 240.

32 The Centralstelle was founded in 1891 and brought together those interested in social and housing reform in government and industry in the Berlin area; for a fuller discussion see Chapter 6, n. 17.

33 The Verein, founded in 1882, became interested in the problems of housing as a result of the VfSP's survey and debated the housing question at some length during the late 1880s. The debates, to which Fritz Kalle, Paul Aschrott and Karl Flesch (all already involved in the VfSP's and the VföG's discussion of housing) contributed, are summarised in 'Die Wohnungsfrage vom Standpunkt der Armenpflege' in *Schriften des deutschen Vereins für Armenpflege und Wohltätigkeit (SDVfAW)*, 6 (1888), pp. 67–120; 11 (1892), pp. i–xxiv, 1–57; 13 (1894), pp. 67–79, 146–57.

34 *SDVfAW*, 13, pp. 67–79, 147–9.

35 The work of the Verein, which was closely associated with the CVWaK, is reported in the *Arbeiterfreund*, for a further discussion of the work of the Verein see *Geschichte der gemeinnützigen Wohnungswirtschaft*, pp. 50–7.

36 F. Kalle, 'Das Wohnhaus der Arbeiter', *VföG*, 23 (1891), pp. 153–78.

37 H. Albrecht, 'Die Mitwirkung der Arbeitnehmer bei der Lösung der Wohnungsfrage', in *Die Verbesserung der Wohnungen*, p. 43.

38 T. Goecke, 'Das Berliner Arbeiter-Mietshaus, eine bautechnisch-soziale Studie', *Deutsche Bauzeitung (DBZ)*, 24 (1890), pp. 501–2; 508–10; 522–3.

39 ibid. p. 501.

40 This development attracted considerable attention: it is described by H. Albrecht in *Fünf Jahre praktisch-sozialer Tätigkeit, aus der Versuchsstation der Centralstelle der Arbeiter-Wohlfahrtseinrichtungen*, published as vol. 14 of the *Schriften der Centralstelle der Arbeiter-Wohlfartseinrichtungen (SCAW)* (Berlin, 1898); and by E. Roscher, 'Der Berliner Spar- und Bauverein und die Herausarbeitung grossstädtischer Mietshaustypen', in *Zeitschrift für Wohnungswesen (ZfW)*, 10: 8, pp. 109–15.

41 Albrecht, *Fünf Jahre praktisch-sozialer Tätigkeit*, pp. 24–39.

42 D. Jacobi, *Die gemeinnützige Bautätigkeit in Deutschland, ihre kulturelle Bedeutung und die Grenzen ihrer Wirksamkeit*, published as vol. 167 of *Staats- und sozialwissenschaftliche Forschungen*, G. Schmoller and M. Sering eds. (Munich and Leipzig, 1913), pp. 79–106.

43 Eberstadt, *Handbuch des Wohnungswesens*, p. 248.

44 C. J. Fuchs (ed.), *Die Wohnungs- und Siedlungsfrage nach dem Kriege* (Stuttgart, 1917); the book contains contributions by nearly all the established housing reformers of the time: Eberstadt, Kuczynski, Ermann, H. Wagner, Gretzschel, Mangoldt, Goecke, Schmohl, Albrecht, Lindemann, Vormbrock, Kampffmeyer, Damaschke and Martin Wagner.

5 Public health and housing reform

1 For a concise summary of the central issues at stake see A. J. Taylor, *Laissez-faire and State Intervention in 19th Century Britain*, Studies in Economic History (London, 1972), particularly ch. 6.

2 The divorce between the 'official' chronology of public health reform and the slow advance of reform in practice is reviewed in M. W. Flinn's introduction to *The Medical and Legal Aspects of Sanitary Reform*, new edn (Leicester, 1969).

3 This characterisation of reform is from *The Times* of August 1854, quoted Gauldie, *Cruel Habitations*, p. 131.

4 S. Neumann, closely involved with CVWaK, is known as a doctor keenly interested in the 'soziale Frage' and, later, for his work on the Berlin census; he was the author of the pamphlet *Die öffentliche Gesundheitspflege und das*

Eigenthum (Berlin, 1848), in which he vigorously demanded an interventionist approach to public health reform. Rudolf Virchow is best known for
his achievements in the field of medical science, but his political activity and
his work for sanitary reform deserve wider recognition, particularly his part
in the campaign for adequate water supply and drainage in Berlin. His
views of the late 1840s were expressed in the journal *Medicinische Reform*
(Berlin, 1848–9), which he edited with Lebuscher; for a more general
account of his achievements see E. Ackerknecht, *Rudolf Virchow: Doctor,
Statesman, Anthropologist* (Madison, 1953); for a summary of the development of the campaign for sanitary reform in Germany see A. Fischer,
Geschichte des deutschen Gesundheitswesens (Hildesheim, 1965); and
M. Neuberger and J. Pagel (eds.), *Handbuch der Geschichte der Medizin*
(3 vols., Jena, 1902–5).

5 'Die Kanalisation Danzigs', *VföG*, 1 (1869), pp. 168–212; 'Zur Kanalisation
   Danzigs', *VföG*, 4 (1872), pp. 628–40; and 'Danzig, seine Canalisation mit
   Rieselfeldern', *VföG*, 6 (1874), pp. 493–8.

6 'Die Kanalisation von Frankfurt am Main', *VföG*, 2 (1870), pp. 504–63;
   and G. Varrentrap, 'Über die neue Canalisation Frankfurts', *VföG*, 5 (1873),
   pp. 656–68.

7 R. Virchow, *Über die Kanalisation Berlins* (Berlin, 1868); the debate on
   sewerage in Berlin was extensively reported in the *VföG*: 3 (1871), p. 165;
   4 (1872), pp. 456–86, 641–51; 5 (1873), pp. 434–65; 6 (1874), pp.
   359–65.

8 'Die Massregeln zur Bekämpfung der Cholera', *VföG*, 27 (1895), pp.
   139–66.

9 Max von Pettenkofer, *Untersuchungen und Beobachtungen über die Verbreitungsart der Cholera* (Munich, 1855). Pettenkofer returned to the subject
   again in numerous articles in the *VföG* and other publications, and similar
   studies were undertaken by Delbick, Günther, Reichard, Pfeiler and even
   by Cuningham in England; Virchow, however, remained opposed to
   Grundwasser theories. For a relatively dispassionate discussion of the
   Grundwasser theory see K. B. Lehmann, 'Max von Pettenkofer und seine
   Verdienste um die wissenschaftliche und praktische Hygiene', *VföG*, 25
   (1893), pp. 361–85.

10 The *Sanitätspolizei* in Prussia already possessed powers, under the *Polizeiverordnung* of 12 February 1850, to close insanitary dwellings, see Krieger,
   'Über Kellerwohnungen'.

11 The new attitude is voiced in the circles around the CVWaK, see Krieger,
   'Über Kellerwohnungen'; Emmich, 'Betrachtungen über Ursache'; and
   Huber, 'Wohnungsfrage: die Noth'.

12 Huber, 'Wohnungsfrage: die Noth', p. 24.

13 Sax, *Wohnungszustände*, p. 24.

14 ibid. p. 41.

15 See, for example, K. Reclam, 'Die englische Gesetzgebung für Hygiene',
   VföG, 1 (1869), pp. 5–39.

16 Strassmann and von Haselberg, 'Anforderungen'.

17 For a discussion of the early evolution of the system of extension planning
   see G. Albers, *Entwicklungslinien im Städtebau: Ideen, Thesen, Aussagen
   1875–1945, Text und Interpretationen* (Düsseldorf, 1975), and A. Sutcliffe,
   Towards the Planned City (Oxford, 1981).

18 Hegemann, *Das steinerne Berlin*, pp. 313–30.

19 For summary of the building bulk regulations for Berlin see D. Frick,
   'Einfluss der Baugesetze und Bauordnungen auf das Stadtbild', and
   F. Monke, 'Einflüsse der Baugesetze und Bauordnungen auf das Wohnhaus',
   in *Berlin and seine Bauten*, pt 4, vol. A, Berlin 1970, pp. 41–57, 58–63.

20 This description, by Beta, a well-known Berlin journalist of the 1840s, is quoted in Strassmann and von Haselberg, 'Anforderungen', p. 53.
21 'Die hygienische Section auf der 45ten Versammlung deutscher Natur- forscher und Aerzte zu Leipzig', *VföG*, 4 (1872), pp. 596–614.
22 R. Baumeister, 'Thesen über Stadterweiterungen', *DBZ*, 8 (1874), p. 265, and pp. 337–9.
23 Strassmann and von Haselberg, 'Anforderungen'.
24 Eberstadt, *Handbuch des Wohnungswesens*, p. 215.
25 R. Baumeister, *Stadt-Erweiterungen in technischer, baupolizeilicher und wirt- schaftlicher Beziehung* (Berlin, 1876).
26 G. Varrentrap, 'Über die hygienischen Anforderungen an Neubauten zunächst in neuen Quartieren grösserer Städte', *VföG*, 8 (1876), pp. 97–138.
27 Strassmann and von Haselberg, 'Anforderungen', p. 54.
28 H. Schwabe, 'Einfluss der verschiedenen Wohnungen auf die Gesundheit ihrer Bewohner, soweit er sich statistisch nachweisen lässt', *VföG*, 7 (1875), pp. 70–7.
29 The list of recommendations also included provision to control the drying out of new housing before habitation; to ensure adequate ventilation and heating; to provide a kitchen having direct ventilation to the outside air for each dwelling; and to limited dampness and inadequate ventilation in roof and cellar dwellings.
30 R. Manega, *Die Anlage von Arbeiterwohnungen von wirtschaftlichem, sanitärem Standpunkte* (Weimar, 1871).
31 For example, K. Weissbach, *Wohnhäuser* (Stuttgart, 1902), published as pt 4, vol. 2 of J. Durm, H. Ende, E. Schmitt under H. Wagner (eds.), *Handbuch der Architektur* (32 vols., Darmstadt and Stuttgart, 1883–1907).
32 H. von Ziemssen and M. von Pettenkofer (eds.), *Handbuch der Hygiene und der Gewerbekrankheiten* (20 vols., Leipzig, 1882–1910).
33 T. Weyl, *Handbuch der Hygiene* (10 vols., Jena, 1896–1901).
34 Pettenkofer wrote popular articles in a variety of family journals, for example, in *Gartenlaube*, *Nord und Süd*, and *Deutsche Bücherei*; see E. Roth, 'Von Pettenkofer als populärer Schriftsteller', *VföG*, 25 (1893), pp. 386–96.
35 J. von Fodor, *Das gesunde Haus und die gesunde Wohnung* (Braunschweig, 1878).
36 H. Schülke, *Gesunde Wohnungen* (Berlin, 1880).
37 T. P. Teale, *Dangers to Health: a Pictorial Guide to Domestic Sanitary Defects* (London, 1879).
38 Sax, *Wohnungszustände*, p. 47.
39 M. von Pettenkofer, *Untersuchungen und Beobachtungen über die Verbrei- tungsart der Cholera* (Munich, 1855).
40 M. von Pettenkofer, *Über die Beziehung der Luft zu Kleidung, Wohnung und Boden* (Dresden, 1872).
41 Fodor, *Das Gesunde Haus*, p. 58.
42 Pettenkofer, *Beziehung der Luft*.
43 Ascher, 'Über die gesundheitlichen Nachteile des Bewohnens feuchter Wohnungen und deren Verhütung von sanitätspolizeilichen Standpunkte', *VföG*, 25 (1893), pp. 178–205.
44 Manega, *Arbeiterwohnungen*, p. 25.
45 Sanitarians had long been convinced of the importance of light, and particularly sunlight for health, but it was Trélat's work of the 1880s which showed that sunlight 'killed' germs and thus led to a new-found interest in securing sunlight in housing layouts, see E. Roth, 'Über Wohnungs- hygiene', *VföG*, 21 (1889), pp. 139–63, especially p. 152.

46 A. Vogt, 'Über die Richtung städtischer Strassen nach der Himmelsgegend und das Verhältnis ihrer Breite zur Häuserhöhe', *Zeitschrift für Biologie*, 15 (1879), pp. 317–47.

47 Lissauer, 'Über das Eindringen von Canalgasen in die Wohnräume', *VföG*, 13 (1881), pp. 341–68.

48 I. Soyka, 'Über Canalgase also Verbreiter epidemischer Krankheiten und über Richtung und Stärke des Luftzuges in den Seilen', *VföG*, 14 (1882), pp. 33–77.

49 For a discussion of the building regulations in Germany and their evolution during the nineteenth century see B. Schilling and J. Stübben, 'Die Bauordnung', in *Neue Untersuchungen*, vol. 1, pt 2, pp. 189–248; for a summary of the regulations in Berlin see Frick, 'Einfluss der Baugesetze' and Monke, 'Einflüsse der Baugesetze'.

50 'Neue Bauordnung für Berlin', *DBZ*, 5 (1871), pp. 297, 310, 313, 328, 329, 337, 345, 354.

51 R. Baumeister, *Normale Bauordnung, nebst Erläuterungen* (Wiesbaden, 1880).

52 There are frequent articles on the need for reform of the building regulations in the technical press, see, for example, *DBZ*, 14 (1880), p. 291; *DBZ*, 15 (1881), p. 415; *DBZ*, 18 (1884), p. 120, 289.

53 Adickes, for example, naturally conscious of the sensitivities of the cities, was very much aware of the problem and pressed for minimum requirements which would be acceptable across the whole country: see his contribution to the debate at the annual conferences at Frankfurt (1888) and Strasbourg (1889), see note 57.

54 'Stadterweiterung, insbesondere in hygienischer Beziehung', *VföG*, 18 (1886), pp. 9–39.

55 The provisions of the 1887 Bauordnung are summarised in Frick, 'Einfluss der Baugesetze'.

56 R. Baumeister, 'Die neue Berliner Baupolizeiordnung', *VföG*, 19 (1887), pp. 600–8.

57 'Massregeln zur Ereichung gesunden Wohnens', *VföG*, 21 (1889), pp. 9–41; 'Massregeln zur Ereichung gesunden Wohnens', *VföG*, 22 (1890), pp. 20–60.

58 ibid. pp. 58–60.

59 The recommendations made included, besides those already mentioned, a discussion of water supply, drainage, the control of fire and structural stability.

60 The question of court size was crucial to rethinking the design of the 'Block' and is considered at greater length in the next chapter; for details of the new provisions see Monke, 'Einflüsse der Baugesetze...auf das Wohnhaus'.

61 'Massregeln', vol. 22, pp. 58–60, especially section 2.

62 ibid. p. 35; for a general discussion of the ideas of zoning see F. Mancuso, *Le Vicende dello Zoning* (Milan, 1978), especially pt 1.

63 For a summary of the Frankfurt regulations see W. Nosbisch, *Wohnungswesen in Frankfurt am Main* (Frankfurt, 1930), pp. 64–9.

64 F. Adickes, 'Die unterschiedliche Behandlung der Bauordnungen für die Innere, die Aussengebiete und die Umgebung von Städten', *VföG*, 26 (1894), p. 19.

65 F. Adickes, 'Die Notwendigkeit weiträumiger Bebauung bei Stadterweiterungen und die Rechtlinien und technischen Mittel zu ihrer Ausführung', *VföG*, 27 (1895), pp. 101–30.

66 T. Goecke, 'Verkehrsstrasse und Wohnstrasse', *Preussische Jahrbücher*, 73 (1893), pp. 85–104.

67 R. Eberstadt, *Städtische Bodenfragen* (Berlin, 1894), see also Chapter 7 n. 34 and 35.

68 R. Baumeister, 'Bericht über die aus deutschen Städten eingegangen Mitt-heilungen, betr. Neuerungen auf dem Gebiete der Baupolizei', *VföG*, 28 (1896), pp. 9–12.
69 For example in Mannheim and Chemnitz, see A. Sutcliffe, *Towards the Planned City, Germany, Britain, the United States and France, 1780–1914* (Oxford, 1981), p. 38; see also Mancuso, *Le Vicende*, chs 2 and 3.
70 See for example F. W. Becker, MP, *Letters on the Cholera in Prussia* (London, 1832); E. Schmitz-Cliever, 'Die Anschauungen vom Wesen der Cholera bei den Aachener Epidemien 1832–1866', in *Sudhoffs Archiv für Geschichte der Medizin und Naturwissenschaft*, vol. 36 (Wiesbaden, 1943–53), pp. 261–76.
71 Dr Goldthammer, 'Über die Kost- und Logirhäuser für die ärmeren Volks-klassen', *Vierteljahrschrift für gerechtliche Medezin und öffentliche Sanitatswesen* (neue Folge), 28 (1878), pp. 296–333.
72 M. Pistor, 'Über die Anforderungen der Hygiene an Kost- und Logirhäuser', *VföG*, 12 (1880), pp. 55–102.
73 J. Stübben and E. Zweigert, 'Handhabung der gesundheitlichen Woh-nungspolizei', *VföG*, 21 (1882), pp. 57–107.
74 The Parisian regulations referred to are those of 1850, but Stübben was clearly aware of the attempts by Nadaud, Maze and Siegfried to secure more stringent measures, Stübben and Zweigert, 'Handhabung', p. 81.
75 These powers were already available in Prussia under the *Polizeiverordnung* of 12 February 1850.
76 Zweigert gives an optimistic account of the system of Wohnungsinpektion in practice in 'Die Beaufsichtigung der vorhandenen Wohnungen' in *Neue Untersuchungen*, vol. 1, pt 2, pp. 45–112; see also J. J. Reincke, 'Die Beaufsichtigung der vorhandenen Wohnungen (inkl. Sanierung oder Beseitigung ungesunder Quartiere)', in *Neue Untersuchungen*, vol. 1, pt 2, pp. 3–44; G. Gretzschel, 'Wohnungsaufsicht und Wohnungsordnung' in *Wohnungs- und Siedlungsfrage*, pp. 111–27.
77 The Prussian Housing Bills of 1904 and 1913 are discussed in more detail in Chapter 12; a clause-by-clause comparison of the two was published by Altenrath, 'Der Preussische Wohnungsgesetzentwurf' *Zeitschrift für Woh-nungswesen*, 11 (1912/13), pp. 137–48.
78 Gretzschel, 'Wohnungsaufsicht', pp. 113–16.
79 W. H. Dawson, *Municipal Life and Government in Germany* (London, 1914), p. 185.
80 ibid. pp. 185–6.
81 Sutcliffe, *Towards the Planned City*, p. 38.
82 'Wohnungsgesetzgebung', *Zeitschrift für Wohnungswesen*, 4 (1905), p. 160.

6 The design of working-class housing

1 Manega, *Arbeiterwohnungen*, p. 29.
2 See, for example, Emmich, 'Vergleichende Bemerkungen', and Roberts (trans. Busse), *Wohnungen für die arbeitenden Classen*.
3 For a discussion of the documentation of the BgB see Chapter 1, n. 43.
4 The development of the tradition of multi-storey housing in Berlin is discussed in Voigt, 'Bodenbesitzverhältnisse'; A. Gut, *Das Berliner Wohnhaus* (Berlin, 1917); A. Schinz, 'Das mehrgeschossige Mietshaus von 1896–1945', in *Berlin und seine Bauten*, 4, vol. B (Berlin 1974), pp. 1–20; Geist und Kürvers, *Berliner Mietskaserne*.
5 By comparison with the English literature, the treatment of the subject in German was thin; other publications during the 1860s and 1870s include articles in the *Arbeiterfreund*: H. Senftleben, 'Über gesundheitsgemässe Einrichtung ländlicher Arbeiterwohnungen', 3 (1865), pp. 171–86; Klette

'Wohnungsfrage'; Senftleben, 'Bedeutung und Fortschritt' (which includes an extended report on the housing displayed at the 1867 Paris Exhibition). There are occasional references to the design of workers' housing in the technical press, for example in *Die Baugewerbe* or in *Die Zeitschrift für Bauwesen*, but nothing to match the interest shown in English journals such as *The Builder*.

6 Examples of 'improved' tenement blocks built during the 1880s, including those mentioned here, are illustrated in K. Weissbach and W. Mackowsky, *Das Arbeiterwohnhaus* (Berlin, 1910), especially ch. 6.

7 See, for example, the range of housing illustrated in *Die Verbesserung der Wohnungen*.

8 For a discussion of the forms of workers' housing built by employers such as the mines see Täglichsbeck, 'Die Beförderung der Ansiedlung von Arbeitern'; Bollerey and Hartmann, *Wohnen im Revier*; and Günther, 'Arbeitersiedlungen'.

9 Thiele, 'Über die Kolonie Leienhausen', in *Die Verbesserung der Wohnungen*, pp. 122–37.

10 Harms, 'Über die Arbeiterkolonie zu Friedrichsort', in *Die Verbesserung der Wohnungen*, pp. 108–18.

11 H. Albrecht, 'Bericht über die Ausstellung von Plänen von Arbeiterwohnungen', in *Die Verbesserung der Wohnungen*, pp. 191–2; C. Nussbaum, 'Grundsätze für die Einrichtung von Arbeiterwohnungen', in *Die Verbesserung der Wohnungen*, p. 73.

12 Weissbach and Mackowsky, *Das Arbeiterwohnaus*, pp. 233–5.

13 The Krupp estates have been extensively documented, mostly in publications produced with the blessing of the firm, which are generally no more than well-illustrated hagiographies; they include: *Wohlfahrtseinrichtungen der Kruppschen Gussstahlfabrik zum besten ihrer Arbeiter un Beamten* (Essen, 1876; 3rd edn, 1902); *Die Entwicklung des Arbeiterwohnungswesens auf der Gussstahlfabrik von Friedrich Krupp zu Essen a.d. Ruhr* (Düsseldorf, 1902); D. Gussmann, 'Die Kruppschen Arbeiterwohnungen', in *Die Verbesserung der Wohnungen*, pp. 138–55; H. Hecker, *Der Kruppsche Kleinwohnungsbau*, (Wiesbaden, 1917). A more critical approach is offered in R. Günther, 'Krupp und Essen', M. Warnke (ed.), *Das Kunstwerk zwischen Wissenschaft und Weltanschauung* (Gütersloh, 1970), pp. 128–74.

14 Gussmann, 'Die Kruppschen Arbeiterwohnungen', p. 139.

15 See Chapters 10 and 11.

16 Accounts of the Berliner Architekten Verein's debates on working-class housing were published in *DBZ*, 25 (1891), pp. 123–8, 162–3, 170–2, 181–2, 200–1, 233–4, 241–3.

17 The Centralstelle für Arbeiterwohlfahrtseinrichtungen (CAW) was founded in 1891 with the blessing of those in government circles like Freiherr von Berlepsch, the Minister for Trade, to encourage industry to provide actively for the welfare of its employees. The directing committee in 1891 included Professor Heinrich Albrecht, Ernst Roscher, Heinrich Freese (who was closely involved with the campaign for land-reform), R. Freund (chairman of the Regional Insurance Fund for Invalidity and Old Age in Berlin), and had as its manager Julius Port who had earlier been actively involved in the Hannoversche Spar- und Bauverein; for further discussion of the Centralstelle see *Geschichte der gemeinnützigen Wohnungswirtschaft*, p. 50.

18 This report, *Die Verbesserung der Wohnungen* (Berlin, 1892), was the first volume in a series of occasional papers, *Schriften der Centralstelle für Arbeiterwohlfahrtseinrichtungen*, which are of great interest for the study of reformers' attitudes to the housing question.

19 'Kundgebung der Vereinigung Berliner Architekten betreffend die Mittel zur Lösung der Arbeiter-Wohnfrage für Berlin', *DBZ*, 25 (1891), pp. 233–4.

20 Schinz, 'Das mehrgeschossige Mietshaus'.
21 The larger block sizes and their effect on building form are discussed by Goecke in 'Das Berliner Arbeiter-Mietshaus', *DBZ*, 24 (1890), p. 522, and, for a non-professional audience, in 'Verkehrsstrasse und Wohnstrasse' and by Eberstadt, *Handbuch des Wohnungswesens*, pp. 59–67.
22 Goecke, 'Arbeiter-Mietshaus', pp. 501–2, 508–20, 522–3.
23 The discussion at the colloquia (together with some suggestion of those attending) is summarised in *DBZ*, 25 (1891), p. 162, and by H. Albrecht, 'Wohnungen für die Armen', *Deutsche Rundschau*, 65 (1890), pp. 265–78, 368–84.
24 *DBZ*, 25 (1891), p. 233, para. 6.
25 Messel's report on his work for the Verein zur Verbesserung kleiner Wohnungen was published in *DBZ*, 25 (1891), pp. 181–2.
26 *DBZ*, 25 (1891), p. 233.
27 These schemes were extensively documented; two of the most helpful articles are the report on the work of the Berliner Spar- und Bauverein published by the CAW: Albrecht, *Fünf Jahre praktisch-sozialer Tätigkeit*; and E. Roscher, 'Der Berliner Spar- und Bauverein und die Herausarbeitung grossstädtischer Mietshaustypen', *Zeitschrift für Wohnungswesen*, 10 (1911), pp. 109–15.
28 This project is discussed in H. Albrecht, *Das Arbeiterwohnhaus* (Berlin, 1896), pp. 34–5; in P. F. Aschrott, *25 Jahre gemeinnütziger Tätigkeit für Kleinwohnungen* (Berlin, 1913), pp. 13–14; and in *Geschichte der gemeinnützigen Wohnungswirtschaft*, pp. 52–4.
29 Advances elsewhere are summarised in C. Nussbaum, 'Bau und Einrichtung von Kleinwohnungen', *SCAW*, vol. 20 (Berlin, 1901), pp. 6–16; and in Weissbach and Mackowsky, *Arbeiterwohnhaus*, pp. 198–251.
30 Van Marken presented a paper on the housing built by the company of which he was director, 'Der "Agnetapark", Arbeitersiedlung der Niederländischen Presshefe- und Spiritusfabrik in Delft', in *Verbesserung der Wohnungen*, pp. 119–22.
31 Details of the competition and a number of the other schemes submitted are published in 'Kleine Wohngebäude für invalide Arbeiter in Essen', in *Deustsche Konkurrenzen*, 2: 6 (1893), pp. 1–32.
32 Hecker, *Kruppsche Kleinwohnungsbau*, pp. 9–15.
33 H. Muthesius, *Kleinhaus und Kleinsiedlung* (Munich, 1918), pp. 40–1.
34 'Kleine Wohngebäude für invalide Arbeiter', p. 1.
35 See for example, K. Henrici, 'Arbeiterwohnungen', *Der Städtebau*, 3 (1906), p. 71; however, the same ideas were taken up with equal interest by the *DBZ* (vol. 35, 1904, pp. 187, 198, 214, 243, 245) and the *Centralblatt für Bauverwaltung* (1900, pp. 578, 585, 598; 1906, p. 419; 1908, p. 78; 1909, pp. 250, 589).
36 The conference was organised in Hagen under the patronage of Karl Ernst Osthaus and broadly represents the views that were later to be championed by the Werkbund, one of the most important fora for the debate on design in Germany before 1914; the proceedings were published as *Die künstlerische Gestaltung des Arbeiter-Wohnhauses*, *SCAW*, vol. 29 (Berlin, 1906).
37 H. Muthesius, 'Die Entwicklung des künstlerischen Gedankens im Hausbau', in *Die künstlerische Gestaltung*, pp. 9–10. The importance of the English connection for German architecture and design is discussed at length in S. Muthesius, *Das englische Vorbild* (Munich, 1974), especially chs. 8–10.
38 Muthesius, 'Entwicklung des künstlerischen Gedankens', p. 11.
39 P. Schulze-Naumburg, 'Die Gestaltung des Arbeiterwohnhauses', in *Künstlerische Gestaltung*, pp. 29–47, and, by the same author, *Kulturarbeiten*, vol. 1, *Hausbau*, vol. 3, *Dörfer und Kolonien* (Munich, n.d.).
40 Schulze-Naumburg, 'Die Gestaltung des Arbeiterwohnhauses', p. 40.

41 K. Henrici, 'Arbeiterkolonien', in *Künstlerische Gestaltung*, pp. 59–70.

42 C. Sitte, *Der Städte-Bau nach seinem künstlerischen Grundsätzen* (Vienna, 1889).

43 The development of Sitte's ideas is discussed by G. R. and C. C. Collins in *Camillo Sitte and the Birth of Modern City Planning* (London, 1965).

44 See particularly R. Unwin, *Town Planning in Practice, an Introduction to the Art of Designing Cities and Suburbs* (London, 1909), and in Germany, see Muthesius, *Kleinhaus*, especially ch. 3.

45 Even in the early 1850s the layout of one or two projects for 'improved' workers' housing was related to orientation: see, for example, G. Schmoll, 'Die Arbeiterhäuser in der Breite in Basel (1854–1857)', in *Basler Zeitschrift für Geschichte und Altertumskunde*, 76 (1980), pp. 125–65. During the 1880s, interest in the effects of sunlight on germs, supported by the work of Trélat in France and Schönbein in Germany, led to greater emphasis on correct orientation in housing layout, as in Vogt's study 'Über die Richtung städtische Strassen'; but this interest is not reflected in Baumeister's *Stadterweiterungen* published in the mid-1870s.

46 C. Nussbaum, 'Grundsätze für die Einrichtung von Arbeiterwohnungen', in *Verbesserung der Wohnungen*, pp. 61–3; and, by the same author, *Bau und Einrichtung*, pp. 21–4.

47 This point of view is well represented by Muthesius in *Kleinhaus*, pp. 56–78, 155–7.

48 See Muthesius, *Kleinhaus*, pp. 137–46, 157–66; significantly this issue is not discussed by Nussbaum, although regional variations were probably greater in Germany than in England, see, for example, Chapter 4, n. 7.

49 The planning of the kitchen and its relation to the rest of the dwelling is discussed in a host of publications: Weissbach and Mackowsky, *Das Arbeiterwohnhaus*, pp. 23–6; Muthesius, *Kleinhaus*, pp. 65–80; Nussbaum, *Bau und Einrichtung*, pp. 32–8; L. Braun, *Frauenarbeit und Hauswirtschaft* (Berlin, 1901); for a more recent discussion, see G. Uhlig, *Kollektivmodell 'Einküchenhaus', Wohnreform und Architekture zwischen Frauenbewegung und Funktionalismus 1900–1933* (Giessen, 1981) and C. Nussbaum, 'Die Ausbildung der Küchen in kleinen Wohnungen', *Zeitschrift für Wohnungswesen*, 1 (1902), pp. 165–7, 178–9, 183–5.

50 Nussbaum, 'Ausbildung der Küchen', p. 165.

51 ibid. p. 166.

52 Muthesius, *Kleinhaus*, pp. 75–6.

53 Manega, *Arbeiterwohnungen*, pp. 58–9.

54 There was endless discussion of space standards for workers' housing, but see particularly: Nussbaum, *Bau und Einrichtung*, pp. 30–42; Weissbach and Mackowsky, *Arbeiterwohnhaus*, pp. 15, 18, 21, 23, 31, 198; Weissbach, *Wohnhäuser*, pp. 230–7; and Muthesius, *Kleinhaus*, pp. 39–64, 68, 81.

55 Roscher, 'Herausarbeitung grossstädtischer Mietshaustypen', pp. 114–15; Nussbaum, 'Ausbildung der Küchen', pp. 183–5.

56 *Berlin und seine Bauten*, pt 4, vol. B, pp. 145–6.

57 Muthesius, *Kleinhaus*, pp. 39–64.

58 The cost of 'improved' housing, as built, is often available but difficult to interpret in general terms because of the necessarily wide variations in cost due to different forms of construction, different locations and different dates of construction. Even when comparing housing of broadly similar type, similar form and built in the same year, there may still be wide variations in cost: for example, the housing built by Krupp at Alfredshof cost approximately 85 M per m² in 1895 prices, while the cost of similar housing built by the I. G. Farben at Höchst were as low as 45–50 M per m² again in 1895 prices.

Information on building costs from the around the mid-1880s can be assembled from the *Deutscher Baukalendar*. Costs from this source are used by Voigt, Ascher and others in the theoretical studies of land prices and rent levels discussed in Chapter 8, but contemporaries appear to have viewed the results with scepticism and held them to be of limited value, usable only for broad comparative purposes. Comparisons of cost over time are further complicated by the absence of a single index, but, using a number of proxy or component costs, attempts have been made (see A. V. Desai, *Real Wages in Germany 1871–1913*, Oxford, 1968, pp. 82–5) to construct an index of building costs running from 1871–1914.

Evidence on the relative cost of 'cottage' as opposed to 'tenement' housing is fragmentary. However, the construction costs per m² of floor space in tenements was not, generally, lower than in cottage housing, although rents were normally less in the former; indeed such flimsy evidence as does exist suggests that costs per m² for high-rise tenements were then (as they still are now) higher. This raises the question as to whether the higher overall costs of 'cottage' housing was not largely a product of higher space standards. Many firms built cottages for their skilled employees, foremen and overseers, with floor areas that range from 50–70 m² and sometimes higher. By contrast, in 'improved' tenements built in central areas at high densities, the area per dwelling is generally lower, often around 40 m²; it is this (despite higher construction costs) that make central area tenement housing cheaper, the higher costs of central area land being offset by the high level of site utilisation.

59 Roscher, 'Herausarbeitung grossstädtischer Mietshaustypen', pp. 110–11.

7 Housing reform and the Land Question

1 Huber, *Selbsthilfe*, pp. 32–5.
2 For a discussion of Hobrecht's plan see Hegemann, *Das steinerne Berlin*, pp. 295–330, and, more recently, D. Radicke, 'Die Berliner Bebauungsplan von 1862 und die Entwicklung des Weddings: zum Verhältnis von Obrigkeits-plannung zu privatem Grundeigentum', in G. Poeschken, D. Radicke and T. Heinisch (eds.) *Festschrift für Ernst Heinrich* (Berlin, 1974), pp. 56–74.
3 Both Emmy Reich's study, *Wohnungsmarkt*, and Paul Voigt's *Grundrente und Wohnungsfrage in Berlin und den Vororten* (Jena, 1901), provide invaluable summaries of the processes of development in Berlin and its financing.
4 Voigt, *Grundrente*, p. 114.
5 ibid. p. 115.
6 Faucher, 'Die Bewegung für Wohnungsreform', p. 196.
7 Reich, *Wohnungsmarkt*, p. 137, table 18.
8 Voigt, *Gundrente*, p. 115.
9 Voigt, *Grundrente*, pp. 118–19, provides a number of salacious details of the operating methods of the more dubious companies such as the Nordend Gesellschaft; see also Hegemann, *Das steinerne Berlin*, pp. 344–65.
10 This view of the development of residential land achieved widespread circulation through Eberstadt's *Handbuch des Wohnungswesens*.
11 J. Faucher, 'Über Häuserbauunternehmungen' in *VfVK*, 2 (1869), pp. 48–74.
12 ibid. p. 52.
13 Engel, *Moderne Wohnungsnoth*; Bruch first published his views in a series of articles in the *DBZ*, 4 (1870), and later as a pamphlet: E. Bruch, *Berlins bauliche Zukunft und Bebauungsplan* (Berlin, 1870). The critical response to Hobrecht's plan is discussed by Hegemann, *Das steinerne Berlin*, pp. 313–30, and by Albers, *Entwicklungslinien im Städtebau*, pp. 38–9, 61–5.

14 Engel, *Moderne Wohnungsnoth*, p. 3.
15 Baumeister, *Stadterweiterungen*, p. 90.
16 Engel, *Moderne Wohnungsnoth*.
17 Reich, *Wohnungsmarkt*, p. 137, table 18; p. 142, table 12a.
18 For an introductory account of the land reform movement see H. Freese, *Die Bodenreform, ihre Vergangenheit und ihre Zukunft* (Berlin, 1918); for a more recent, and more incisive account see D. Berger-Thimme, *Wohnungsfrage und Sozialstaat* (Frankfurt am Main, 1976).
19 A. Damaschke, *Die Bodenreform, Grundsätzliches und Geschichtliches* (Jena, 1902) and *Die Aufgaben der Gemeindepolitik* (Jena, 1902).
20 H. George, *Progress and Poverty* (New York, 1879).
21 Freese, *Bodenreform*, pp. 74–6.
22 *Progress and Poverty* was translated as *Fortschritt und Armut* by C. D. F. Gütschow (Berlin, 1881).
23 Berger-Thimme provides a very helpful indication of both the size and the type of membership of the Bund, *Wohnungsfrage*, pp. 71–170, see especially pp. 86–8 and p. 315.
24 M. Flürscheim, *Auf friedlichem Weg* (Braunschweig, 1884).
25 *Deutsch Land*, edited by M. Flürscheim, Berlin, 1887–9.
26 Flürscheim's new approach is set out in *Deutsch Land*, no. 6, August 1887, and no. 22, December 1888, and in his book *Der einzige Rettungsweg* (Dresden and Leipzig, 1890).
27 A. Wagner, *Grundlegung der politischen Ökonomie* (2 vols., Leipzig, 1894).
28 On the importance of Wagner within the BdB, see Berger-Thimme, *Wohnungsfrage*, pp. 80–2; Freese also places considerable emphasis on Wagner's contribution to the ideas of the BdB, *Die Bodenreform*, pp. 17–35.
29 Wagner, *Grundlegung*, vol. 2, pp. 426–517.
30 A. Wagner, 'Communalsteuerfrage', in *Verhandlungen der fünften General-Versammlung des Vereins für Sozialpolitik*, published as vol. 14 of the *Schriften des Vereins für Sozialpolitik* (Leipzig, 1878), pp. 5–26.
31 A. Damaschke, *Zur Geschichte der deutschen Bodenreformbewegung* (Berlin, 1906), p. 20.
32 The first edition was published in 1909, the final edition in 1922; all quotes are taken from the enlarged second edition of 1911; see also Chapter 31 n. 14.
33 The first essay, 'Berliner Communalreform', had already appeared in *Preussische Jahrbücher* as had the third, 'Die Besteurung der Bauplätze', the second essay, 'Grundsätze der städtischen Bodenpolitik' had been published in Schmoller's *Jahrbuch für Gesetzgebung. Verwaltung und Volkswirtschaft im deutschen Reich*; only the fourth essay, 'Von den Aufgaben der Verwaltung' was new.
34 Adickes refers enthusiastically to the book in his address to the VföG in 1893 at Würzburg, 'Unterschiedliche Behandlung', pp. 13–47, but for a highly critical response see A. Voigt and P. Geldner, *Kleinhaus und Mietskaserne, eine Untersuchung der Intensität der Bebauung vom wirtschaftlichen und hygienischen Standpunkte* (Berlin, 1905).
35 J. H. von Thünen, *Der isolierte Staat in bezug auf Landwirtschaft und National-ökonomie* (Hamburg, 1826).
36 Alfred Weber, *Über den Standort der Industrien* (Tübingen, 1909).
37 For an account of the development of the housing market from the 1890s to the First World War, see Chapter 9.
38 Voigt, *Grundrente*, p. 142.
39 ibid.
40 ibid. pp. 218–51.
41 ibid. pp. 163–75.

42 For a discussion of the provisions of the 1887 and 1892 Bauordnungen see Voigt, *Grundrente*, pp. 127–37, Monke, 'Einflüsse der Baugesetze' das Stadtbild', and Frick, 'Einfluss der Baugesetze'.

43 Voigt, *Grundrente*, pp. 137–40.

44 Reich, *Wohnungsmarkt*, p. 138, table 18.

45 Voight, *Grundrente*, pp. 205–13.

46 Eberstadt, *Handbuch des Wohnungswesens*, pp. 68–107.

47 ibid. p. 70.

48 ibid. p. 80.

49 ibid. pp. 110–11, 121–2.

50 ibid. pp. 109–10, 120; see also Voigt, *Grundrente*, p. 145 and Chapter 8 n. 3.

51 Reich *Wohnungsmarkt*, pp. 19–29.

52 R. von Mangoldt, *Die städtische Bodenfrage* (Göttingen, 1907).

53 ibid. pp. 316–59; Faucher had coined the term in his article 'Über Häuserbauunternehmungen'.

54 Voigt, 'Bodenbesitzverhältnisse' and Voigt and Geldner, *Kleinhaus und Mietskaserne*.

55 See, for example, *Jahrbuch für Gesetzgebung, Verwaltung und Volkswirtschaft im deutschen Reich*, 31 (1907), pp. 1339–67; 32 (1908), p. 676.

56 Voigt, 'Bodenbesitzverhältnisse', p. 239.

57 ibid. pp. 196–202; 254–60, table 3, column 8; see also A. Voigt, 'Die Bedeutung der Baukosten für die Wohnungspreise', in *Neue Untersuchungen*, vol. 1, pt 1, pp. 339–64.

58 Voigt, *Grundrente*, especially ch. 8; in Voigt's view, land values are, of course, not affected by building form, but are the result of the growth of the city as a whole.

59 As a result of the Eberstadt–Voigt debate there was extended discussion of the profits made by the land companies, see E. Wagon, *Die finanzielle Entwicklung der deutschen Aktiengesellschaft* (Jena, 1903), and A. Weber, *Über Bodenrente und Bodenspeculation* (Leipzig, 1904).

60 Eberstadt's views are well represented in Fuchs (ed.), *Wohnungs- und Siedlungsfrage*, which serves as an authoritative summary of the mainstream of housing reform thought just before the First World War.

61 *Jahrbuch für Bodenreform*, edited by A. Damaschke, Berlin, 1909–1942.

62 The literature on the Deutsche-Gartenstadtbewegung is extensive: H. Kampffmeyer, *Die deutsche Gartenstadtbewegung* (Berlin, 1911), provides a contemporary summary; for a more recent (but uneven) account see K. Hartmann, *Deutsche Gartenstadtbewegung, Kultur und Gesellschaftsreform* (Munich, 1976), which contains an extended bibliography.

63 See, for example, R. Petersen, *Aufgaben des grossstädtischen Verkehrs* (Berlin, 1980); Voigt and Gelder, *Kleinhaus und Mietkaserne*; Eberstadt, *Handbuch des Wohnungswesens*, pp. 327–35; R. Petersen, 'Die Verkehrsmittel', in Fuchs (ed.), *Wohnungs- und Siedlungsfrage*, pp. 231–44.

64 F. Adickes, 'Förderung des Baues kleiner Wohnungen durch die private Tätigkeit', in *Neue Untersuchungen*, vol. 2, pp. 275–302.

65 A useful summary of the expansion of the railway system and its consequences for housing is given by Voigt, *Grundrente*, pp. 159–88; see also Radicke, 'Entwicklung des öffentlichen Personennahverkehrs'.

66 For a discussion of the changing pattern of industrial location in Berlin and the consequences for housing see Zimm, 'Die Entwicklung des Industriestandortes'.

67 Radicke, 'Entwicklung des öffentlichen Personennahverkehrs', pp. 10–11.

68 See, for example, Adickes, 'Die Notwendigkeit weiträumiger Bebauung...', pp. 108–10, 112.

69 Damaschke, *Bodenreform*, p. 89.
70 For a discussion of the application of the system of 'stepped' density regulations in practice, see Schilling and Stübben, 'Bauordnung', and Mancuso, *Zoning*, especially pp. 115–220.
71 A convenient (but not very penetrating) summary of the provisions of the *Kommunalabgabengesetz* of 1893 is provided by Dawson, *Municipal Life*, pp. 369–72, 386–402; the subject was investigated at some length by the Verein für Sozialpolitik and its findings, *Gemeindefinanzen*, published as vols. 126 and 127 of the *Schriften des Vereins für Sozialpolitik* (Leipzig, 1910); see particularly W. Boldt, 'Das Interesse als Grundlage der Besteurung', in *Einzelfragen der Finanzpolitik der Gemeinden, Gemeindefinanzen*, vol. 2, pt 1, pp. 85–138; and O. Landsberg, 'Die Entwicklung des Gemeindeabgaben-wesens in den preussischen Städten unter der Herrschaft des Kommunal-abgabengesetzes mit besonderer Berücksichtigung der östlichen Provinzen', in *Einzelfragen*, pp. 1–42.
72 For a critical appraisal see Berger-Thimme, *Wohnungsfrage*, pp. 101–7.
73 Dawson, *Municipal Life*, pp. 394–5.
74 Damaschke, *Bodenreform*, pp. 113–15.
75 But see also Berger-Thimme, *Wohnungsfrage*, pp. 92–6.
76 H. von Wagner, *Die Tätigkeit der Stadt Ulm a. D. auf dem Gebiet der Wohnungsfürsorge* (Ulm, 1903).
77 W. Bangert, *Baupolitik und Stadtgestaltung in Frankfurt am Main: ein Beitrag zur Entwicklungsgeschichte des deutschen Städtebaues in den letzten 100 Jahren* (Würzburg, 1936); see also Berger-Thimme, *Wohnungsfrage*, pp. 213–20.
78 Dawson, *Municipal Life*, pp. 394–402.
79 Berger-Thimme, *Wohnungsfrage*, pp. 102–6.
80 Eberstadt, *Handbuch des Wohnungswesens*, pp. 323–6.
81 Sembritzki, 'Die Besteurung', in *Wohnungs- und Siedlungsfrage*, pp. 128–35.
82 Dawson, *Municipal Life*, pp. 419–34; much of Dawson's statistical information is drawn from the *Statistisches Jahrbuch deutscher Städte*, but for a general discussion of this subject see Landsberg, 'Entwicklung des Gemeindeabgabenwesens', especially pp. 11–17.
83 Voigt, 'Bodenbesitzverhältnisse', pp. 151–3.
84 Dawson, *Municipal Life*, p. 129.
85 ibid. p. 137.
86 Eberstadt summarises the legal background to the leasing of land in Germany in *Handbuch des Wohnungswesens*, pp. 312–16.
87 Berger-Thimme, *Wohnungsfrage*, p. 97.
88 ibid., pp. 97–100.
89 Wagner, *Tätigkeit der Stadt Ulm*, pp. 13–15, 50–3.
90 For a discussion of the importance of these powers, see J. Stübben, *Der Städtebau* (Darmstadt, 1890), published as the 9th half-volume of Durm (ed.) *Handbuch der Architektur*, especially section 3, pp. 270–315.
91 J. Stübben, 'Der Stadterweiterungsplan und seine Durchführung', in *Neue Untersuchungen*, vol. 1, section 2, pp. 155–67.
92 There is no satisfactory biography of Franz Adickes; however, his achievements in planning are covered (though perfunctorily) by Bangert, *Stadtgestaltung in Frankfurt*; the debate over Lex Adickes is covered by Berger-Thimme, *Wohnungsfrage*, pp. 213–19.
93 Dawson, *Municipal Life*, p. 126.
94 *Geschichte der gemeinnützigen Wohnungswirtschaft*, p. 61.
95 ibid. p. 62; see also *Der Städtebau*, 6 (1909), pp. 24–5.
96 *Geschichte der gemeinnützigen Wohnungswirtschaft*, p. 62.
97 Dawson, *Municipal Life*, pp. 124–9.
98 N. Bullock, 'Housing in Frankfurt and the "neue Wohnkultur", 1925–1931', *Architectural Review*, 163 (1978), pp. 333–42.

8 Housing by private enterprise

1 Reich, *Wohnungsmarkt*, p. 1.

2 Voigt, 'Bodenbesitzverhältnisse', pp. 254–60.

3 The municipal fire insurance office provided a valuation of a building for mortgage purposes. As both Eberstadt and Paul Voigt pointed out (Chapter 7, n. 51) this system was open to abuse, particularly by private fire offices coupled with insurance companies who provided high valuations (thus securing high insurance premia) to increase the size of the mortgage that could be raised on the property. The basis of the calculations of the replacement value of older property, and the drawbacks of this method are discussed by Voigt in 'Bodenbesitzverhältnisse', pp. 198–200.

4 S. Ascher, *Die Wohnungsmieten in Berlin von 1880–1910*, Bodenpolitische Zeitfragen, Heft 7 (Berlin, 1914), pp. 26–8; H. Höpker, *Denkschrift über die Verluste der Bauhandwerker und Baulieferanten bei Neubauten in Gross-Berlin in den Jahren 1909–1911* (Berlin, 1914), p. 87; G. Haberland, *Der Einfluss des Privatkapitals auf die bauliche Entwicklung Gross-Berlins* (Berlin, 1913), p. 41.

5 Voigt, 'Die Bedeutung der Baukosten', pp. 340–64, table 1.

6 Reich, *Wohnungsmarkt*, p. 19.

7 ibid. p. 21.

8 M. Rusch, 'Die private Bautätigkeit', in *Wohnungs- und Siedlungsfrage*, p. 253.

9 It was widely recognised that workers in the building industry were exploited by their employers, and that they suffered harshly from the uncertainty of the trade; one of the elements of the *Bodenreformers'* programme was reform of the terms of employment in the industry. Legislation to do this was passed (1 June 1909), but, with the progressive collapse of the industry in 1910, its provisions were not enforced.

10 Reich, *Wohnungsmarkt*, pp. 26–9, 149–50; Ascher, *Wohnungsmieten*, pp. 42–5, 49–51.

11 Desai, *Real Wages*, pp. 82–3.

12 Ascher, *Wohnungsmieten*, pp. 42–5, and table 7.

13 ibid. pp. 19–25.

14 Desai, *Real Wages*, pp. 82–3.

15 Höpker, *Denkschrift*, pp. 100–101.

16 Voigt, 'Bodenbesitzverhältnisse', pp. 254–6, table 3.

17 Reich, *Wohnungsmarkt*, pp. 30–1.

18 ibid. p. 35.

19 The attraction for the small landlord of managing property is well illustrated by Haberland: it was customarily assumed that rent would cover mortgage repayments and other costs such as taxes and repairs, together with a 5% profit on the original capital investment and $1–1\frac{1}{2}\%$ interest on the total value of the property to cover the costs of administration and rent collection. In Haberland's example (quoted in Reich, *Wohnungsmarkt*, p. 33) the landlord purchases the building for 300,000 M investing only 30,000 M and paying only 6,000 M in fees, legal charges and taxes. According to then current usage, he would have expected to make 5% on his capital and costs (i.e. on 36,000 M) as well as a further 1% on the value of the building for administration; together this would yield a return of 4,800 M, to many a handsome income for so little work and such a small initial investment of personal capital.

20 Reich, *Wohnungsmarkt*, p. 138, table 17.

21 There is an extended contemporary literature on the question of capital for the house building industry. Reich lists nearly 50 titles on this subject alone; frequently cited are R. Eberstadt, *Der deutsche Kapitalmarkt* (Leipzig, 1901),

and Paul Voigt's study, *Hypothekenbanken und Beleihungsgrenzen* (Berlin, 1899); a brief summary of the supply of capital is also provided in Desai, *Real Wages*, ch. 7.

22 ibid. p. 74.

23 The differences in interest rates for different types of property and different areas within the city are discussed by Reich, *Wohnungsmarkt*, p. 47, and by Ascher, *Wohnungsmieten*, pp. 47–9.

24 Voigt, *Grundrente*, ch. 7, but especially pp. 205–13.

25 Reich, *Wohnungsmarkt*, pp. 109–18.

26 See Thienel, *Städtewachstum*.

27 This was obvious from both Reich's book, *Wohnungsmarkt*, and Höpker's study, *Denkschrift*.

28 The choice of city districts was based on the census data for 1910, 'Die verheirateten und die nicht verheirateten Selbsttätige nach Berufsgruppen, sozialer Stellung und Geschlecht in Standesamtsbezirken', *Statistisches Jahrbuch der Stadt Berlin*, Berlin, 1916, vol. 33, pp. 32–47. Concentrating on seven major occupational categories (VII Metalworking; VIII Engineering; XIV Woodworking; XVI Clothing; XVIII Building; XXI Trade), the five districts were chosen as those having over 40% of those described as 'Gesellen, Gehilfen, Lehrlinge und andere Hilfspersonen mit und ohne gewerbliche Ausbildung'; other occupational categories were ignored as being too insignificant to affect the choice of district.

   The choice of working-class suburbs was based on census data for 1900, 'Volkszählungs-Ergebnisse: Bevölkerung nach Beruf'. *Stat. J. Berlin*, vol. 27. p. 38. Here the definition of 'Arbeiter' includes both those described as general labourer or 'Arbeiter ohne nähere Angabe' and 'Handel und Gewerbe, niedere Abhängige' or junior assistants in trade and crafts; the four districts were chosen as those having over 60% of the total work force in these categories.

29 City districts (see fig. 41) Va and Vb (Luisenstadt jenseits des Kanals, westlich und östlich) have similar types of employment: metalworking and wood-based trades predominate, but commerce and building also provide employment for about 6% of the workforce. Districts VIIa and VIIb (Stralauer Viertel, östlich und westlich) both share a similar emphasis on wood-based trades, building, and, particularly in VIIa, commerce. In the Rosenthaler Vorstadt, district Xb, the metalworking industry, with its relatively high wages have been replaced by the turn of the century by the building industry as the largest employer. In Gesundbrunnen, district XIIa, one of the newer suburbs that expanded so rapidly during the 1880s and 1890s, metalworking is the largest single employer, followed by building and engineering.

   In the three suburban districts in the south-east the pattern of employment is broadly similar: in Lichtenberg, 'general commerce', clothing, transport and engineering predominate, in neighbouring Weissensee the distribution is similar, and in Rixdorf employment is similar but with a higher proportion of the workforce in the building industry. However, Reinickendorf, to the north of the city, has a different pattern of employment with engineering far outreaching all other forms of employment.

30 Voigt, 'Bodenbesitzverhältnisse', pp. 222–3; Voigt, *Grundrente*, pp. 201–5; and Eberstadt, *Handbuch des Wohnungswesens*, p. 137.

31 Reich, *Wohnungsmarkt*, pp. 110–11, 117–18, 132, table 11.

32 According to Schwabe's law, the lower the income, the higher the proportion paid in rent; the law was first formulated by Schwabe in 1868: H. Schwabe, *Berliner Gemeinde-Kalender und städtisches Jahrbuch* (Berlin, 1868); for a fuller discussion see R. Kuczynski, 'Miete und Einkommen', *Wohnungs- und Siedlungsfrage*, pp. 29–33.

33 A brief introduction to the income and expenditure surveys carried out over a number of years by the Statistisches Amt is given in *Stat. J. Berlin*, vol. 27, pp. 269, the results are summarised in *Stat. J. Berlin*, Vol. 27, pp. 270–1, and vol. 28, pp. 200–4.

34 Ascher, *Wohnungsmieten*, pp. 88–99; he also discusses, though very briefly, similar studies in Cologne, Basel and Hanover.

35 See Eberstadt, *Handbuch des Wohnungswesens*, pp. 149–54.

36 Kuczynski, 'Miete und Einkommen', pp. 29–33.

37 Schmoller, 'Mahnruf', pp. 8–9.

38 ibid. p. 13.

9 Housing by the employer

1 H. Albrecht, 'Bau von kleinen Wohnungen durch Arbeitgeber, Stiftungen, gemeinnützige Baugesellschaften und Vereine, Baugenossenschaften und in eigner Regie der Gemeinden', in *Neue Untersuchungen*, vol. 2, pt 1, pp. 1–88; F. Kalle, 'Die Fürsorge der Arbeitgeber für die Wohnungen ihrer Arbeiter', in *Die Verbesserung der Wohnungen*, pp. 1–28; E. Jäger, *Die Wohnungsfrage* (Berlin, 1902); G. Schmohl, 'Die Arbeitgeber', in *Wohnungs- und Siedlungsfrage*, pp. 263–77.

2 Täglichsbeck, 'Die Beförderung der Ansiedlung von Arbeitern', pp. 98–107.

3 Huber, 'Über die geeignetsten Massregeln', p. 166, and Sax, *Wohnungszustände*, pp. 105–25.

4 Sax, *Wohnungszustände*, p. 108.

5 'Achter Kongress deutscher Volkswirte', p. 188.

6 See, for example, Bollerey and Hartmann, *Wohnen im Revier*, or Günther, 'Arbeitersiedlungen im Ruhrgebiet'.

7 Albrecht, 'Bau von kleinen Wohnungen', p. 17.

8 Thienel, *Städtewachstum*, pp. 191–2.

9 Reichardt, *Arbeiterwohnungsfrage*, p. 31.

10 Täglichsbeck, 'Die Beförderung der Ansiedlung von Arbeitern', pp. 101–2.

11 Reichardt, *Arbeiterwohnungsfrage*, p. 30.

12 Miquel, 'Einleitung', p. xix.

13 Schmoller, 'Mahnruf', p. 14.

14 F. Brandts, 'Die Wohnungsfrage', in *Arbeiterwohl*, 8 (1888): 11 and 12, p. 239.

15 See Chapter 6, n. 17; not surprisingly the committee was dominated by employers.

16 Kalle, 'Fürsorge der Arbeitgeber', p. 1.

17 Gussmann, 'Die Kruppschen Arbeiterwohnungen', p. 147.

18 For a discussion of the regulations governing the tenancies in workers' housing see A. Günther, 'Die Wohlfahrtseinrichtungen der Arbeitgeber in Deutschland', in *Die Wohlfahrtseinrichtungen der Arbeitgeber in Deutschland und Frankreich*, published as vol. 114 of the *Schriften des Vereins für Sozialpolitik* (Leipzig, 1905) pp. 29–50.

19 Albrecht, 'Bau von kleinen Wohnungen', pp. 11–24.

20 J. Marcuse, 'Beiträge zur Arbeiterwohnungsfrage in Deutschland', in *VföG*, 31 (1899), pp. 371–83.

21 For a summary see Jäger, *Wohnungsfrage*, pp. 250–65; for a more detailed discussion see 'Die Wohnungsfürsorge im Reiche und in den Bundesstaaten', in *Stenographische Berichte des deutschen Reichstages*, Session 1903–1904, Appendices, vol. 4, no. 4.

22 'Wohnungsfürsorge im Reiche', pp. 9–24.

23 ibid., pp. 49–53.

24 This figure is based on the optimistic assumption that the average cost of

a dwelling was 4,250 M; in practice costs ran from 4,000–5,000 M and varied sharply from region to region (see Chapter 6, n. 58).

25 'Wohnungsfürsorge im Reiche' contains a section on the Reich and each of the states; Rusch, 'Die Förderung der Kleinwohnungsproduktion durch Reich, Staat und Gemeinden', in *Wohnungs- und Siedlungsfrage*, pp. 312–19; and H. Lindemann, 'Die öffentliche Produktion (Reich, Staat, Gemeinde)', in *Wohnungs- und Siedlungsfrage*, pp. 297–311.

26 'Wohnungsfürsorge im Reiche', pp. 109–44.

27 Albrecht, 'Bau von kleinen Wohnungen', p. 11; the cities are: Essen, Aachen, Altona, Cassel, Darmstadt, Dresden, Hanau and Heidelberg. For a general discussion of housing built by the cities for their own employees, see Lindemann, 'Öffentliche Produktion', pp. 304–11, and Rusch, 'Klein-wohnungsproduktion', pp. 317–19.

28 'Wohnungsfürsorge im Reiche', p. 78.

29 There is a considerable body of literature on the housing work of the city; see, for example, E. Cahn, *Die gemeinnützige Bautätigkeit in Frankfurt am Main*, Frankfurt, 1915; Nosbisch, *Wohnungswesen*; and H. Kramer, 'Die Anfänge des sozialen Wohnungsbaus in Frankfurt am Main, 1860–1914', in *Archiv für Frankfurts Geschichte und Kunst*, vol. 56 (Frankfurt am Main, 1978).

30 Kalle, 'Fürsorge der Arbeitgeber', p. 1.

31 Eberstadt, *Handbuch des Wohnungswesens*, p. 366.

32 Kalle, 'Fürsorge der Arbeitgeber', pp. 1–2.

33 ibid. p. 3.

34 Krupp, for example, offered the services of his surveyor's department, Gussmann. 'Die Krupp'schen Arbeiterwohnungen', p. 151.

35 Täglichsbeck, 'Die Beförderung der Ansiedlung von Arbeitern', pp. 105–7.

36 Gussmann, 'Die Krupp'schen Arbeiterwohnungen', p. 149.

37 Schmohl, 'Die Arbeitgeber', pp. 271–2.

38 ibid. p. 272.

39 Günther, 'Wohlfahrtseinrichtungen'.

40 Gussmann, 'Die Krupp'schen Arbeiterwohnungen', pp. 148–9.

41 Günther, 'Wohlfahrtseinrichtungen'.

42 Gussmann, 'Die Krupp'schen Arbeiterwohnungen', p. 147.

43 K. Flesch, 'Die Wohnungsfrage vom Standpunkt der Armenpflege', *Schriften des deutschen Vereins für Armenpflege und Wohltätigkeit*, vol. 6 (1888) pp. 121–64; and K. Flesch and Birndorfer, 'Das Mietrecht in Deutschland', in *Neue Untersuchungen*, vol. 1, pt 2, pp. 271–333.

44 Albrecht, 'Bau von kleinen Wohnungen', p. 23.

45 ibid. p. 1.

10 Non-profit housing before 1890

1 Albrecht, 'Bau von kleinen Wohnungen'; the same view is taken by Jacobi, *Die gemeinnützige Bautätigkeit*.

2 For example: Emmich, 'Vergleichende Bemerkungen'; and Huber, 'Die Wohnungsfrage in Frankreich und England'.

3 See for example, Parisius, 'Die auf dem Prinzip der Selbsthülfe', Brämer, 'Baugenossenschaften in England', and Faucher, 'Über Häuserbauunternehmungen'.

4 For a general account of the development of the co-operative housing movement in Germany see H. Crüger, *Einführung in das deutsche Genossen-schaftswesen* (Berlin, 1907); W. Vossberg, *Die deutsche Baugenossenschafts-bewegung* (Jena, 1906); Zeidler, *Geschichte des deutschen Genos-senshaftswesens*; and H. Faust, *Geschichte der Genossenschaftsbewegung*,

Urpsrung und Weg der Genossenschaften im deutschen Sprachraum (Frankfurt am Main, 1977).

5 'Achter Kongress deutscher Volkswirte', p. 205
6 Huber, 'Wohnungsfrage: die Hülfe', pp. 15–22, 41–2, 46–8.
7 Huber, 'Über die geeignetsten Massregeln', pp. 164–7, 170–2.
8 Brämer reported the existence of societies in the following cities and towns: Berlin, Bremen, Halle, Stettin, Lüdenscheid, Heilbronn, Pforzheim, Stuttgart, Frankfurt am Main, Hagen, Nürnberg, Dresden, Chemnitz, Konigsberg, Görlitz, Hamburg, Munich, Mannheim, Wiesbaden, but concluded that only 11 of these societies were still active.
9 The work of the FgB was widely publicised, see: G. Varrentrap, *Zur Gründung einer gemeinnützigen Baugenossenschaft in Frankfurt am Main* (Frankfurt, 1860); G. Varrentrap, 'Häuser der gemeinnützigen Baugesellschaft zunächst in Frankfurt am Main', *VföG*, 6 (1874), pp. 393–401; Cahn, *Gemeinnützige Bautätigkeit*, pp. 22–5; and Kramer, 'Anfänge des sozialen Wohnungsbaus', pp. 132–8.
10 Varrentrap, 'Häuser der gemeinnützigen Baugesellschaften'.
11 For a summary of non-profit housing in Frankfurt, see Cahn, *Gemeinnützige Bautätigkeit*; and Kramer, 'Anfänge des sozialen Wohnungsbaus'.
12 Albrecht, 'Bau von kleinen Wohnungen', pp. 62–8.
13 ibid. pp. 62–8; see also *Geschichte der gemeinnützigen Wohnungswirtschaft*.
14 G. S. Liedke, *Hebung der Not der arbeitenden Klassen durch Selbsthilfe* (Berlin, 1845), and Huber, *Selbsthilfe*; Liedke was involved in banking and charitable works, set up a 'savings shop' near the Hamburger Tor, and was one of the founder members of the BgB.
15 Crüger, *Das deutsche Genossenschaftswesen*, pp. 37–52.
16 ibid., pp. 37–40; 71–4.
17 F. H. Schulze-Delitzsch, *Vorschuss-Vereine als Volks-banken, Praktische Anweisung zu deren Gründung und Errichtung* (Leipzig, 1855), 7th edition, Berlin, 1904.
18 ibid. p. 25.
19 Crüger, *Das deutsche Genossenschaftswesen*, pp. 46–8.
20 ibid., pp. 55–8.
21 For a summary of the evolution of the English building society movement, see E. J. Cleary, *The Building Society Movement* (London, 1965), particularly chs. 1–4.
22 Sax, *Wohnungszustände*, p. 170.
23 Brämer, 'Baugenossenschaften in England', pp. 233–40, and Parisius, 'Die auf dem Prinzip der Selbsthilfe' cover both co-operatives (Hamburg) and limited divided societies (Berliner gemeinnützige Baugesellschaft).
24 The KdV passed resolutions in support of the co-operative housing movement at its annual conferences in 1864, 1865 and 1866; in 1865 the VdA and the VdEW passed similar resolutions.
25 Jacobi, *Gemeinnützige Bautätigkeit*, p. 39.
26 T. J. Jones, *Every Man his Own Landlord, or How to Buy a House with its Own Rent* (London, 1863).
27 Vossberg, *Deutsche Baugenossenschaftsbewegung*.
28 Parisius, 'Die auf dem Prinzip der Selbsthülfe', pp. 309–12; for a more recent account see H. J. Nörnberg and D. Schubert, *Massenwohnungsbau in Hamburg* (Berlin, 1975), pp. 49–53.
29 Parisius, 'Die auf dem Prinzip der Selbsthülfe', p. 277.
30 For a discussion of the background to the changes in legislation in the 1860s see Crüger, *Das deutsche Genossenschaftswesen*, pp. 65–71, 128–36.
31 Reichardt, *Arbeiterwohnungsfrage*, pp. 65–6.
32 Parisius, 'Die auf dem Prinzip der Selbsthülfe', pp. 312–13.

33 *Geschichte der gemeinnützigen Wohnungswirtschaft,* p. 39.
34 P. C. Hansen 'Der Arbeiterbauverein in Flensberg', *Arbeiterfreund,* 16 (1878), pp. 289–99; and P. C. Hansen, *Die Wohnungsverhältnisse in den grösseren Städten* (Heidelberg, 1883).
35 P. C. Hansen, 'Das Dänische Arbeiterwohnungswesen', *VfVK,* 17 (1879): no. 2, pp. 112–48.
36 Jacobi, *Gemeinnützige Bautätigkeit,* pp. 38–43.
37 P. Schmidt, 'Der Spar- und Bauverein zu Hannover als Muster für die Lösung der Klein-wohnungsfrage in den Grossstädten', *Arbeiterfreund,* 30 (1892) pp. 34–46.
38 *Geschichte der gemeinnützigen Wohnungswirtschaft,* pp. 47–50.
39 P. Nathan, *Die Wohnungsfrage und die Bestrebungen der Berliner Baugenossenschaft* (Berlin, 1890).
40 Reichardt, *Arbeiterwohnungsfrage,* pp. 70–2.
41 Jäger, *Die Wohnungsfrage,* p. 269.
42 Miquel, 'Einleitung', p. xiv; 'Verhandlung' *Schriften des Vereins für Sozialpolitik,* 33 (1887), pp. 11–12.
43 Schmoller, 'Mahnruf', p. 20.
44 ibid. p. 16.
45 The Verein was one of the societies that tried to apply the ideas of Octavia Hill in Germany (similar attempts were made in Aachen and Dresden); its work is discussed in more detail in the next chapter.
46 The Verein's proposals for housing were discussed at length at the annual conferences in 1888, 1889 and 1890; see P. F. Aschrott, 'Einrichtung und Verwaltung grosser Arbeiter-Mietshäuser in Berlin', in *Schriften des deutschen Vereins für Armenpflege und Wohltätigkeit,* 11 (1890), pp. 5–27.
47 F. Brandts, 'Die Wohnungsfrage' pp. 233–43.
48 *Geschichte der gemeinnützigen Wohnungswirtschaft,* pp. 47–59.

11 Non-profit housing after 1890

1 For a discussion of the background to the Act and its place in the development of social policy see W. H. Dawson, *Social Insurance in Germany, 1883–1911* (London, 1912), and, more generally, K. E. Born, *Staat und Sozialpolitik seit Bismarcks Sturz* (Wiesbaden, 1957).
2 *Stenographische Berichte...Reichstages,* Session 1888/89, vol. 3, pp. 1617–27.
3 See, for example, Nathan, *Die Wohnungsfrage.*
4 A number of high-ranking civil servants, such as Berlepsch and Bötticher, were clearly sympathetic to the cause of social reform, Born, *Staat und Sozialpolitik,* pp. 84–134; both Berlepsch and Bötticher attended the CAW conference on employers' housing in 1890, *Die Verbesserung der Wohnungen,* p. 95.
5 Berger-Thimme, *Wohnungsfrage,* p. 61.
6 Jäger, *Die Wohnungsfrage,* pp. 322–4; for a more general discussion see A. Liebrecht, *Reichshilfe für Errichtung kleiner Wohnungen* (Göttingen, 1900) (vol. 2 of the publications of the Deutscher Verin für Wohnungsreform).
7 'Bericht über den ersten Verhandlungstag', *Verbesserung der Wohnungen,* pp. 159–60.
8 The terms on which the different regional funds lent to different categories of organisation is set out in 'Wohnungsfürsorge im Reiche', pp. 25–45.
9 The work of the ABG is well covered in *25 Jahre gemeinnützigen Wohnungsbaus Jubiläumsbericht der ABG, 1890 bis 1915* (Frankfurt am Main, 1915); see also Kramer, 'Anfänge des Sozialenwohnungsbaus', pp. 148–57.
10 The annual meetings of the Verein were reported in the *Arbeiterfreund* from

1886 onwards; see also P. F. Aschrott, *25 Jahre gemeinnützige Tätigkeit für Kleinwohnungen, Festschrift zum 25 jährigen Bestehen des Vereins zur Verbesserung der kleinen Wohnungen in Berlin* (Berlin, 1913).

11 Aschrott, 'Einrichtung und Verwaltung'.
12 The alliance between the two groups is reported in H. Albrecht, *Die Wohnungsnot in den Grossstädten und die Mittel zu ihrer Abhülfe* (Munich, 1891), pp. 75–6.
13 See Chapter 6, n. 28.
14 Rents for dwellings in the non-profit sector are reported regularly in *Stat. J. Berlin*; the rents for 1905 are drawn from *Stat. J. Berlin*, vol. 30 (1907), pt 3, p. 116; comparative rents for the open market are discussed in Chapter 8.
15 Albrecht, 'Bau von kleinen Wohnungen', pp. 62–85.
16 ibid. this figure is the sum of columns 5 and 15. For a summary of the achievement by 'Organised Private Effort' in London, see E. Dewsnup, *The Housing Problem in England, its Statistics, Legislation and Policy* (Manchester, 1907), p. 167.
17 Cahn, *Die gemeinnützige Bautätigkeit*, pp. 10, 17.
18 *State. J. Berlin*, vol. 32 (1913), pt 3, p. 319.
19 Jacobi, *Die gemeinnützige Bautätigkeit*, pp. 96–11, 116–24.
20 Crüger, *Das deutsche Genossenschaftswesen*, pp. 136–77.
21 Albrecht, 'Bau von kleinen Wohnungen', pp. 62–85.
22 H. Albrecht, 'Die gemeinnützige Produktion', in *Wohnungs- und Siedlungsfrage*, pp. 278–96.
23 Nathan, *Die Wohnungsfrage*.
24 Albrecht, 'Bau von kleinen Wohnungen', pp. 62–85.
25 Albrecht, 'Gemeinnützige Produktion', pp. 286–7.
26 Albrecht, *Fünf Jahre praktisch-sozialer Tätigkeit*.
27 *State. J. Berlin*, vol. 30 (1907), pt 3, p. 116.
28 The rise of the Beamtenwohnungsvereine is discussed in general terms in Vossberg, *Deutsche Baugenossenschaftsbewegung*; for developments in Berlin, see *Geschichte der gemeinnützigen Wohnungswirtschaft*, pp. 68–77.
29 Albrecht, 'Bau von kleinen Wohnungen', pp. 62–85.
30 Albrecht, 'Geimeinnützige Produktion', p. 287.
31 *Geschichte der gemeinnützigen Wohnungswirtschaft*, pp. 68–77.
32 *Stat. J. Berlin*, vol. 30 (1907), pt 3, p. 116.
33 Schmoller, 'Mahnruf', pp. 15–16.
34 Albrecht, 'Bau von kleinen Wohnungen', p. 85.
35 Cahn, *Die gemeinnützige Bautatigkeit*, p. 18.
36 *State. J. Berlin*, vol. 30 (1907), pt 3, p. 116.
37 Albrecht, *Fünf Jahre praktisch-sozialer Tätigkeit*.
38 Jacobi, *Die gemeinnützige Bautätigkeit*, pp. 52–67.
39 ibid. p. 62.
40 These figures for the non-profit sector up to 1900 are based on Albrecht, 'Bau von kleinen Wohnungen', pp. 62–85.
41 Figures for non-profit housing up to 1917 are based on Albrecht, 'Gemeinnützige Produktion', pp. 286–7.
42 ibid. pp. 285–7.
43 ibid.
44 These figures should be treated with some caution because they do not include capital lent by Reich, state or municipal governments: these figures are based on Jacobi, *Die gemeinnützige Bautätigkeit*, pp. 144–5, table 6, column 3.
45 Jäger, *Die Wohnungsfrage*, pp. 322–7.
46 ibid. p. 284; see also Berger-Thimme, *Wohnungsfrage*, p. 305, n. 35.
47 For a discussion of the interest levels, amortisation rates and other details

of loans for non-profit housing from the regional insurance funds see 'Wohnungsfürsorge im Reiche', pp. 25–45.

48 ibid. pp. 25–9.

49 Rusch, 'Die Förderung der Kleinwohnungsproduktion', p. 313.

50 M. Brandts, 'Aufgaben und Organisation der Wohnungsfürsorge insbesondere in den Städten', *Arbeiterwohl*, 16 (1896), pp. 272–7.

51 For a discussion of the work of the Rheinischer Verein see Berger-Thimme, *Wohnungsfrage*, pp. 55–69.

52 *Geschichte der gemeinnützigen Wohnungswirtschaft*, pp. 63–4, 235, n. 26.

53 This point emerges clearly from Jacobi's study of the co-operative movement and was certainly reflected in the attitude of the Rheinischer Verein, see Berger-Thimme, *Wohnungsfrage*, p. 307, n. 54.

54 By 1903, the Reich had allocated 10 million Marks (of which only 8.2 million Marks had actually been loaned; by contrast, the regional insurance funds had loaned 109.5 million Marks, 'Wohnungsfürsorge im Reiche...,' pp. 9–29; by 1914, only 54 million Marks had been lent as *Reichsfürsorgefonds*, while 482.8 million Marks had already been lent by the regional insurance funds, Rusch, 'Die Förderung der Kleinwohnungsproduktion', pp. 312–13.

55 'Wohnungsfürsorge im Reiche', pp. 18–24, and Rusch, 'Die Förderung der der Kleinwohnungsproduktion', p. 312.

56 ibid. p. 312.

57 See the relevant sections on each state in 'Wohnungsfürsorge im Reiche'.

58 'Wohnungsfürsorge im Reiche', pp. 75–6, 167–77.

59 O. Beck, 'Förderung der gemeinnützigen Bautätigkeit durch die Gemeinden', in *Neue Untersuchungen*, vol. 2, pp. 172–272.

60 Cahn, *Die gemeinnützige Bautätigkeit*, especially pp. 47–53; the details of the leasehold agreement between the city and the ABG are reproduced in the *Jubiläumsbericht der ABG*, pp. 31–2.

61 Kramer, 'Anfänge des sozialen Wohnungsbaus', p. 175.

62 Adickes argues fiercely against direct subsidies of any form for non-profit housing, see F. Adickes, 'Förderung des Baues kleiner Wohnungen durch die private Tätigkeit', in *Neue Untersuchungen*, vol. 2, pp. 275–302.

63 In his discussion of each non-profit organisation, Cahn gives the details of the rates at which capital was borrowed by each organisation, *Die gemeinnützige Bautätigkeit*, pp. 20, 22–38.

64 ibid. pp. 20–21.

65 Albrecht, 'Bau von kleinen Wohnungen', pp. 46–9.

66 To Adickes, for example; Adickes set out his views on the extent of the cities' social responsibilities in an interesting speech to the Deutscher Städtetag later published as *Die sozialen Aufgaben der deutschen Städten*, Leipzig, 1903.

67 Dawson provides a brief summary of the extent of municipal enterprise in Germany in *Municipal Life*, pp. 208–59. He bases his account on the investigation of the Verein für Sozialpolitik, *Gemeindebetriebe*, published as vols. 128–9 of the *Schriften des Vereins für Sozialpolitik* (Leipzig, 1906).

68 Lindemann, 'Die öffentliche Produktion', pp. 304–6.

69 Wagner, *Tätigkeit der Stadt Ulm*.

70 Lindemann, 'Die öffentliche Produktion', pp. 320–1.

71 The extent to which housing conditions in the large eastern cities and in Berlin were worse than in the cities of the west like Cologne and Frankfurt can be seen in the comparative tables of Lindemann's articles for the Verein für Sozialpolitik, 'Wohnungsstatistik'.

72 *Geschichte der gemeinnützigen Wohnungswirtschaft*, pp. 36–50.

73 Jäger, *Die Wohnungsfrage*, p. 236, publishes a most revealing table (drawn from data published in the *Statistisches Jahrbuch deutscher Städte*) giving this data for 25 Prussian cities.

74 *Stat. J. Berlin*, vol. 26 (1903), pt 3 pp. 116–17.

75 *Geschichte der gemeinnützigen Wohnungswirtschaft*, pp. 65–77.

76 *State. J. Berlin*, vol. 28 (1904), pt 3, pp. 165–6: this does not include the dwellings of the Beamtenwohnungsverein.

77 ibid. vol. 30, pt 3, pp. 115–16; this figure includes 789 dwellings built by the Berliner Baugenossenschaft (see *Stat. J. Berlin*, vol. 29 (1905), pt 3, p. 122), confusingly, the society's returns were again included independently in the annual report from 1912 onwards.

78 *Stat. J. Berlin*, vol. 33 (1916), pt 3, pp. 318–19.

79 *Geschichte der gemeinnützigen Wohnungswirtschaft*, pp. 71–4.

80 *Stat. J. Berlin*, vol. 33 (1916), Ergänzungen, p. 1082.

81 Jacobi, *Die gemeinnützige Bautätigkeit*, pp. 47–52, 146–7, table 7.

82 Albrecht, 'Die gemeinnützige Produktion', p. 288.

83 A. Grävell, *Die Baugenossenschaftsfrage. Ein Bericht über die Ausbreitung der gemeinnützigen Bautätigkeit durch Baugenossenschaften, Aktienbaugesellschaften, Bauvereine, usw. in Deutschland während der letzten 12 Jahren* (Berlin, 1901), quoted in Berger-Thimme, *Wohnungsfrage*, p. 60.

12 The campaign for national housing legislation 1890–1914

1 A. E. Schäffle and P. Lechler, *Nationale Wohnungsreform* (Berlin, 1892), and, by the same authors, *Der erste Schritt zur nationalen Wohnungsreform* (Berlin, 1893).

2 Jäger, *Wohnungsfrage*, p. 176.

3 Brandts, 'Aufgaben und Organisation der Wohnungsfürsorge'; these proposals were later published as *Aufgaben von Gemeinde und Staat in der Wohnungsfrage* (Cologne, 1897).

4 The provisions of this act and details of its application are set out in 'Wohnungsfürsorge im Reiche', pp. 49–53.

5 M. Brandts, Beschaffung der Geldmittel für die gemeinnützige Bauthätigkeit, in *Neue Untersuchungen*, vol. 2, pt 1, pp. 89–178.

6 J. Latscha and W. Teudt, *Nationale Ansiedlung und Wohnungsreform* (Frankfurt am Main, 1899), published with the backing of the Innere Mission.

7 Jäger, *Wohnungsfrage*, pp. 186–8.

8 For a summary of the regulations in the Düsseldorf area see 'Wohnungsfürsorge im Reiche', pp. 61, 71, 153–4.

9 Brandts work at Düsseldorf was the subject of widespread discussion by housing reformers at the time and is described in his 'Beschaffung der Geldmittel', and in Berger-Thimme, *Wohnungsfrage*, pp. 55–70. For a more general discussion of the work of the insurance boards see 'Wohnungsfürsorge im Reiche', pp. 25–45; Leibrecht, *Reichshilfe*; and, particularly for the relationship between insurance boards and regional housing associations, H. Vormbrock, 'Die Landes- und Provinzial-Vereine für Kleinwohnungswesen', in *Wohnungs- und Siedlungsfrage*, pp. 320–8.

10 Berger-Thimme, *Wohnungsfrage*, pp. 62–3.

11 ibid. p. 62.

12 ibid. p. 63.

13 Opposing views on this subject were expressed most clearly in two papers: Beck, 'Förderung der gemeinnützigen Bautätigkeit' and Adickes, 'Förderung des Baues kleiner Wohnungen'.

14 Brandts, 'Beschaffung der Geldmittel', p. 97.

15 Adickes, 'Förderung des Baues kleiner Wohnungen', p. 276.

16 'Verhandlungen des Vereins für Sozialpolitik über die Wohnungsfrage', *Schriften des Vereins für Sozialpolitik*, vol. 98 (Leipzig, 1902), pp. 15–118.

17 'Die Stellung des Verbandes der 'Haus- und städtischen Grundbesitzvereine'

zur Arbeiterwohnungsfürsorge', *Arbeiterwohl*, 18 (1898), pp. 289–91; see also Brandts, 'Beschaffung der Geldmittel', pp. 90–2, and *Geschichte der gemeinnützigen Wohnungswirtschaft*, pp. 78–81.

18 *Geschichte der gemeinnützigen Wohnungswirtschaft*, p. 90.
19 Grävell, *Die Baugenossenschaftsfrage*.
20 ibid. p. 111.
21 ibid. p. 196.
22 ibid. p. 21.
23 Brandts, 'Beschaffung der Geldmittel', p. 92.
24 This point had been strongly emphasized by Baumeister during the campaign for national building regulations and in the debates on the question of minimal regulations for housing in the VföG, see Chapter 5.
25 The work of the Verein Reichswohnungsgesetz is described with enthusiastic detail in *30 Jahre Wohnungsreform 1898–1928; Denkschrift aus Anlass des dreissigjährigen Bestehens herausgegeben vom Deutschen Verin für Wohnungs-reform EV* (Berlin, 1928); for a more critical appraisal see Berger-Thimme, *Wohnungsfrage*, pp. 39–54.
26 *30 Jahre Wohnungsreform*, p. 9.
27 In addition, the Verein published pamphlets on the rent contract, Stier-Somlo, *Unser Mietrechtsverhältnis und seine Reform* (1900), on housing reform and transport, C. Heiss, *Wohnungsreform und Lokalverkehr* (1903), and on the inspection of housing, H. v. Goltz, *Die Wohnungsinspektion und ihre Ausges-taltung durch das Reich* (1900).
28 Typical of this view was that expressed by L. Cohn in *Die Wohnungsfrage und die Sozialdemokratie, ein Kapitel sozialdemokratischer Gemeindepolitik* (Munich, 1900).
29 ibid. p. 65.
30 Jäger, *Wohnungsfrage*, pp. 168–70.
31 *Protokolle über die Verhandlungen des Parteitages der sozialdemokratisden Partei Deutschlands zu Hannover, 1899: Protokolle über die Verhandlungen des Parteitages der Sozialdemokratischen Partei Deutschlands zu Mainz 1900*.
32 Jäger, *Wohnungsfrage*, pp. 171–2.
33 ibid. p. 173.
34 For a discussion of the stance of the party on the housing question see Berger-Thimme, *Wohnungsfrage*, pp. 133–46, 329, n.t 13: Südekum was party spokesman on *Kommunalpolitik* (the housing problem was treated as an aspect of this larger field), Lindemann is known as the author (under the psuedonym C. Hugo) of *Die deutsche Städteverwaltung: Volkshygiene, Städtebau, Wohnungswesen* (Stuttgart, 1901), Hirsch was a member of the Prussian lower house and a councillor in Charlottenburg.
35 See the changing balance of interests during the debate on 23 and 30 January 1901, *Stenographische Berichte…Reichstages*, Session 1900–1903, Verhandlungen, vol. 1, pp. 821–45, 1005–16; as early as November 1899 Wurm and others in the SPD faction in the Reichstag were voting with Schrader for the housing commission: *Stenographische Berichte…Reichstages*, Session 1898/1900, Verhandlungen, vol. 4, p. 2780.
36 Born, *Staat und Sozialpolitik*, pp. 7–30.
37 ibid. pp. 120–4; see also L. Heyde, *Abriss der Sozialpolitik* (Leipzig, 1931), especially ch. 3.
38 ibid., p. 57.
39 Brandts, 'Beschaffung der Geldmittel', p. 119.
40 *Stenographische Berichte…Reichstages*, Session 1894/5, Verhandlungen, vol. 2, p. 991.
41 *Stenographische Berichte…Reichstages* Session 1898/1900, Verhandlungen. vol. 4, pp. 2772–82.

42 *Stenographische Berichte…Reichstages*, Session 1898/1900, Verhandlungen, vol. 4, p. 2782.

43 See the resolution passed at the annual conference of 1898 in Wiesbaden, Brandts, 'Beschaffung der Geldmittel', p. 90.

44 *Stenographische Berichte…Reichstages*, Session 1898/1900, Verhandlungen, vol. 4, pp. 2780–1.

45 *Stenographische Berichte über die Verhandlungen der beiden Häuser des Landtages* (*Haus der Abgeordneten*), Session 1898/1900, vol 4, p. 2481.

46 Berger-Thimme, *Wohnungsfrage*, p. 221.

47 *Stenographische Berichte…Reichstages*, Session 1900/1902, Verhandlungen vol. 1, pp. 821–45; vol. 2, pp. 1005–16.

48 The Conservatives such as Richthofen-Lambsdorf and Stockmann pressed for state legislation; the SPD and the Centre demanded national legislation.

49 *Stenographische Berichte…Landtages* (*Haus der Abgeordneten*), Session 1898/1900, vol. 4, pp. 2481–2.

50 Jäger, *Wohnungsfrage*, pp. 190–2.

51 *Stenographische Berichte…Reichstages*, Session 1900/1902, Verhandlungen vol. 1, p. 832.

52 *Stenographische Berichte…Reichstages*, Session 1898/1900, Verhandlungen vol. 4, pp. 2779–80.

53 Jäger, *Wohnungsfrage*, p. 190.

54 Berger-Thimme, *Wohnungsfrage*, p. 221.

55 Zweigert, 'Der Entwurf eines Gesetzes zur Verbesserung der Wohnverhältnisse für die Preussische Monarchie', *Zeitschrift für Wohnungswesen* (*ZfW*), 2 (1903/4), pp. 57–61, 169–74, 297–307.

56 For the text of the bill see J. Altenrath, 'Der preussische Wohnungsgesetzentwurf', *ZfW*, 11 (1912/13), pp. 138–45.

57 Berger-Thimme, *Wohnungsfrage*, pp. 224–6.

58 ibid. p. 225.

59 ibid. pp. 222–6.

60 Baumert, *Zum preussischen Wohnungsgesetzentwurf* (Berlin, 1905).

61 Zweigert, 'Der Entwurf'.

62 L. Niethammer, 'Ein langer Marsch durch die Institutionen. Zur Vorgeschichte des preussischen Wohnungsgesetzes von 1918' in *Wohnen im Wandel*, pp. 375–6.

63 M. Brandts, 'Einige Bemerkungen zu den Entwurf des Gesetzes zur Verbesserung der Wohnverhältnisse', *ZfW*, 2 (1903/4), pp. 297–308.

64 The proceedings of the Congress are reported in detail in K. von Mangoldt, 'Der deutsche Verein für Wohnungsreform 1898–1920', in *30 Jahre Wohnungsreform*, pp. 20–2; less partisan accounts were published in the *ZfW*, 3 (1904/5), pp. 189–92 and *Arbeiterfreund* 42 (1904), pp. 362–3.

65 Hansen, 'Der erste allgemeine deutsche Wohnungskongress zu Frankfurt am Main', *Arbeiterfreund*, 42 (1904), pp. 362–3.

66 Zweigert, 'Der Entwurf', pp. 57–61, and K. von Mangoldt, 'Herr Oberbürgermeister Zweigert und der Verein Reichswohngesetz', *ZfW*, 2 (1903/4), pp. 149–52.

67 Mangoldt, 'Der deutsche Verein für Wohnungsreform', pp. 23–5.

68 Lechler provides a helpful summary of the Conference in 'Deutsche Wohnungskonferenz' in *ZfW*, 3 (1904/5), pp. 188–92.

69 ibid. p. 190.

70 *Stenographische Berichte…Reichstages*, Session 1912–14, Verhandlungen, vol. 284, p. 979.

71 Niethammer, 'Ein langer Marsch', pp. 376–8.

72 *Stenographische Berichte…Reichstages*, Session 1912–14, Verhandlungen, vol. 284, p. 984; this new committee consisted of Jäger (as Secretary) and

4 other Zentrum delegates, 7 SPD, 2 NL, 3 FVP, 1 Conservative and 3 others, see Verhandlungen Vol. 285, 1912, p. 2255.

73 *Stenographische Berichte...Reichstages*, Session 1912–14, Verhandlungen, vol. 285, pp. 255–8; the committee's report was ready by 21 May.

74 *Verhandlungen: Anlagen*, vol. 299, Aktenstücke 508, p. 644.

75 *Stenographische Berichte...Reichstages*, Session 1912–14, Verhandlungen, vol. 285, p. 2257.

76 *Stenographsiche Berichte...Reichstages*, Session 1912–14, Verhandlungen, vol. 286, p. 2398.

77 Niethammer, 'Ein langer Marsch', pp. 375–7.

78 *Stenographische Berichte...Reichstages*, Session 1912–1914, Verhandlungen, vol. 287, pp. 3551–76.

79 ibid. p. 3557.

80 The text of the second bill, together with that of the first, was printed, with a commentary by Altenrath in *ZfW*, 11 (1912/13), pp. 137–47.

81 See for example, E. Jäger, 'Zur Beurteilung des preussischen Wohnungsgesetzentwurfs', *ZfW*, 11 (1912/13), pp. 169–71.

82 ibid. p. 171.

83 For a discussion of the debate and the committee stages see Berger-Thimme, *Wohnungsfrage*, pp. 236–42.

84 The committee, which first met on 21 January 1914, and which had finished its deliberations by July, was made up of 6 Conservatives, 3 Free Conservatives, 4 National Liberals, 2 Progressive Liberals, 5 Centre Party representatives and 1 representative from the SPD; the only member of the committee to uphold the values of the reformers in a radical manner was K. Flesch from Frankfurt; see Berger-Thimme, *Wohnungsfrage*, pp. 239–42.

85 The progress of the bill was reported blow by blow in *ZfW*: 'Die erste Lesung des preussischen Wohnungsgesetzentwurf', *ZfW*, 11 (1912/13), pp. 145–8.

86 The work of the Reichstag committee, and its composition, is described in J. Altenrath, 'Die Reichs-Enquete über den städtischen Immobilarkredit', *ZfW*, 12 (1913/14), pp. 121–8.

87 *Stenographische Berichte...Reichstages*, Session 1912–14, Verhandlungen, vol. 302, Aktenstücke 1020, pp. 1631–5.

88 J. Altenrath, 'Der preussische Wohnungsgesetzentwurf nach den Kommissionsbeschlüssen zweiter Lesung', *ZfW*, 12 (1913/14), pp. 335–9.

PART TWO: FRANCE

13 The context of the Housing Problem

1 The urban population in France was artificially reduced by the annexation of Alsace-Lorraine by Germany after the Franco-Prussian War of 1870; but as the total population, urban and rural, of these areas was only 1.5 million at this time, the reduction was a minor contribution to the fundamentally slower rate of urban growth in France in comparison to Germany. J. H. Clapham, *The Economic Development of France and Germany 1815–1914*, 4th edn (Cambridge, University Press, 1968), pp. 159, 278–9. G. Dupeux, *French Society 1789–1970*, trans. P. Wait (London, Methuen & Co. Ltd; New York, Barnes & Noble, 1976), p. 37.

2 A. Sutcliffe, *Towards the Planned City*, Comparative Studies in Social and Economic History, 3 (Oxford, Basil Blackwell, 1981), p. 136.

3 J. and M. Lough, *An Introduction to Nineteenth Century France* (London, Longman, 1978) pp. 26–7; Sutcliffe, *Towards*, p. 127.

4   E. Levasseur, *La population française* (3 vols., Paris, A. Rousseau, 1889–92), vol. 2, p. 345–8; Dupeux, *French Society*, pp. 13–15.

5   Clapham, *Economic Development*, pp. 53–4; Société Industrielle de Mulhouse, *Histoire documentaire de l'industrie de Mulhouse et de ses environs au XIXe siècle* (2 vols., Mulhouse, Veuve Bader et Cie., 1902), vol. 1, p. 32; E. Buret, *De la misère des classes laborieuses en Angleterre et en France* (2 vols., Paris, Paulin libraire, 1840), vol. 2, p. 343.

6   R. H. Guerrand, *Les origines du logement social en France*, Collection 'L'évolution de la vie sociale' (Paris, Les Editions Ouvrières, 1967), p. 68.

7   A. Raffalovich, *Le logement de l'ouvrier et du pauvre. Etats-Unis, Grande Bretagne, France, Allemagne, Belgique* (Paris, Guillaumin et Cie., 1887), p. 214.

8   *Rapport sur la marche et les effets du choléra-morbus dans Paris et les communes rurales du département de la Seine* (Paris, Imprimerie Royale, 1834), quoted in Guerrand, *Origines*, p. 33.

9   C. Gourlier, *Des voies publiques et habitations particulières à Paris* (Paris, Librairie d'architecture de B. Bance, 1852), pp. 41–2.

10 Dr L. R. Villermé, *Tableau de l'état physique et moral des ouvriers dans les manufactures de coton, de laine et de soie* (2 vols., Paris, Jules Renouard et Cie, 1840).

11 Villermé, *Tableau*, vol. 1, p. 27.

12 H. A. Frégier, *Des classes dangereuses de la population dans les grandes villes et des moyens de les rendre meilleures* (2 vols., Paris, J. B. Baillière, 1840).

13 Frégier, *Classes dangereuses*, vol. 2, p. 128.

14 Ibid., pp. 126–7.

15 Ibid., Vol. 1, p. 6.

16 L. Chevalier, *Classes laborieuses et classes dangereuses à Paris pendant la première moitié du XIXe siècle* (Paris, Plon, 1958), quotation taken from English translation: *Labouring classes and dangerous classes in Paris during the first half of the nineteenth century*, trans. F. Jellinek, (London, Routledge and Kegan Paul, 1973), p. 139.

17 Dr A. Penot, 'Recherches statistiques sur Mulhouse', *BSIM*, XVI (1842–3), pp. 263–532.

18 *BSIM*, XIX (1845–6), pp. 117, 194.

19 Guerrand, *Origines*, pp. 63–82.

20 T. Zeldin, *France 1848–1945* (2 vols., Oxford, Clarendon Press, 1973, 1977), vol. 1, p. 439. For discussion of Fourier's housing proposals, see Guerrand, *Origines*, pp. 141–6; L. Benevolo, *The Origins of Modern Town Planning*, trans. J. Landry (London, Routledge and Kegan Paul, 1967), pp. 56–64.

21 I. Frazer 'La vie secrète de César Daly' in H. Lipstadt and H. Mendelsohn (eds.), *Architecte et ingénieur dans la presse: polémique, débat, conflit* (Paris, CORDA, IERAU, 1980), p. 251.

22 H. Lipstadt, 'César Daly: Revolutionary Architect?', *Architectural Design*, 48, No. 11–12 (1978), p. 22.

23 Guerrand, *Origines*, p. 149.

24 The national workshops set up in the earlier phase of the Republic had been closed down in June 1848, an act which was one of the catalysts to the rioting of the June Days.

25 J. A. Blanqui, 'Rapport sur la situation des classes ouvrières en 1848', *ASMP*, XIV (1848), p. 317.

26 M. Agulhon, *1848 ou l'apprentissage de la république 1848–1852*, Nouvelle Histoire de la France Contemporaine, 8 (Paris, Editions du Seuil, 1973), p. 49; Blanqui, *ASMP*, XIV (1848), pp. 318, 326.

27 Blanqui, *ASMP*, XIV (1848), p. 320.

28 Blanqui, *ASMP*, XV (1849), p. 312.
29 Guerrand, *Origines*, pp. 65–74.
30 'Proposition de M. de Melun (Nord) sur l'assainissement et l'interdiction des logements insalubres', *Annales de la Charité*, V (1849), p. 445.
31 Quoted in Guerrand, *Origines*, p. 72.
32 This society, the Société des Cités Ouvrières de Paris, is discussed in more detail in Chapter 15, 'The reformers' ideal'.
33 *Moniteur Universel*, 23 January 1852, p. 119.
34 *Moniteur Universel*, 13 May 1842, p. 727. Interest in English initiatives in workers' housing may have been joined by the emulation of a Belgian initiative in relation to the competition; in 1849 the Belgian Ministry of the Interior had held a competition for housing designs, a competition of which the French were certainly aware. See Dr L. R. Villermé in *ASMP*, XVII (1850), p. 225.
35 The use of the 10 million francs is considered in Chapter 22, 'Housing societies'.

14 The housing market: Paris

1 Dupeux, *French Society*, p. 40.
2 S. Magri, *Politique du logement et besoins en main d'oeuvre* (Paris, Centre de Sociologie Urbaine, 1972), pp. 55–81; S. Magri, 'Politique du logement de l'état: exigences du capital et lutte des classes', *International Journal of Urban and Regional Research*, 1(1977), pp. 309–10.
3 Dupeux, *French Society*, p. 40.
4 A. Sutcliffe, *The Autumn of Central Paris. The Defeat of Town Planning 1850–1970*, Studies in Urban History, 1 (London, Edward Arnold, 1970), p. 116.
5 D. H. Pinkney, *Napoleon III and the Rebuilding of Paris* (Princeton, NJ, Princeton University Press, 1958), pp. 90–1.
6 G. P. Palmade, *French Capitalism in the Nineteenth Century*, trans. G. M. Holmes (Newton Abbot, David and Charles, 1972), pp. 168, 241; Sutcliffe, *Autumn*, p. 255.
7 C. Grison, 'L'évolution du marché du logement dans l'agglomération parisienne du milieu du XIXe siècle à nos jours', Thèse pour le Doctorat de Sciences Economiques, Faculté de Droit, Université de Paris (unpublished thesis, 1956).
8 Ibid, p. 74; J. Bastié, 'Capital immobilier et marché immobilier parisiens', *Annales de Géographie*, No. 373 (1960), p. 237. 'Mémoire presenté par le Préfet de la Seine', *GAB*, IV 1866), P. 346.
9 J. Gaillard, *Paris, la ville 1852–1870* (Paris, Editions Honoré Champion, 1977), p. 213.
10 Grison, 'L'évolution', p. 71; the figure of 71,000 was the total of dwellings built, rather than the net increase in the housing stock allowing for the number of dwellings demolished.
11 Guerrand, *Origines*, pp. 92–4; A. L. Shapiro, 'Working class housing and public health in Paris, 1850–1902', Brown University, USA (unpublished thesis, 1980), p. 96.
12 Raffalovich, *Logement*, p. 265.
13 Grison, 'L'évolution', p. 82.
14 Magri, *Politique du logement*, p. 89; Conseil Municipal de Paris, *Rapports et Documents* (1883), No. 8, p. 14. These sources differ in the absolute figures given for the population of the *garnis*, but both confirm the increase during this period.
15 Grison, 'L'évolution', p. 94.

16 J. Bouvier (ed.), *L'ère industrielle et la société d'aujourd'hui (siècle 1880–1980)*, Histoire Economique et Sociale de la France, 4, 1 (Paris, Presses Universitaires de France, 1979), p. 494.

17 Grison, p. 105; Conseil Municipal de Paris, *Rapports et Documents* (1912), No. 31, p. 5. The years in which the number of flats with rents below 300 fr. was reduced were 1907, 1909 and 1911; 1911 also saw a reduction in the number of flats with rents below 400 fr.

18 Grison, 'L'évolution', pp. 81–2, 99–100.

19 J. Bastié, *La croissance de la banlieue parisienne* (Paris, Presses Universitaires de France, 1964), p. 189.

20 Gaillard, p. 132; Bastié, *Annales de Geographie*, No. 373 (1960), p. 237; Magri, *International Journal of Urban and Regional Research*, 1 (1977), p. 311.

21 Raffalovich, *Logement*, pp. 274–80.

22 G. Cahen, *Le logement dans les villes; la crise parisienne* (Paris, F. Alcan, 1913), p. 7; P. Meuriot, 'Le livre foncier de Paris, 1911', *Journal de la Société de Statistique de Paris*, LIV (1913), pp. 391, 395, 397.

23 Dr O. du Mesnil, *L'hygiène à Paris. L'habitation du pauvre* (Paris, J. B. Baillière et fils, 1890), pp. 99–117.

24 A. Chevallier, 'De la nécéssité de bâtir des maisons pour loger les classes moyennes (les ouvriers); de la possibilité de faire des constructions, en retirant un intérêt raisonnable de son argent', *Annales d'Hygiène Publique et de Médecine Légale* 2nd series, VIII (1857), pp. 108–9.

25 The definition of 'room' included the kitchen, and store rooms if these were large enough to take a bed, but excluded corridors and toilets.

26 Dr J. Bertillon, *Essai de statistique comparée du surpeuplement des habitations à Paris et dans les grandes capitales européenes* (Paris, Chaix, 1894); H. Sellier, *La crise du logement et l'intervention publique en matière d'habitation populaire dans l'agglomération parisienne* (Paris, Editions de l'Office Public d'Habitations à Bon Marché du Département de la Seine, 1921), pp. 118–19; Cahen, *Logement dans les villes*, p. 29; Magri, *Politique du logement*, pp. 86–7.

27 Grison, 'L'évolution', pp. 105–6; Magri, *Politique du logement*, p. 88.

28 Cahen, *Logement dans les villes*, pp. 29–30; Magri, *Politique du logement*, p. 100.

15 The reformers' ideal

1 C. Détain, 'Un mot sur la question des habitations ouvrières à Paris, à propos de l'Exposition Universelle de 1867', *RGA*, XXIV (1866), col. 224; A. Audiganne, *Les populations ouvrières et les industries en France dans le mouvement social du XIXe siecle* (2 vols., Paris, Capelle, 1854), vol. 2, pp. 307–9; Gourlier, *Des voies publiques*, pp. 27–31.

2 Guerrand, *Origines*, p. 78.

3 Ibid., p. 79.

4 Dr L. R. Villermé, 'Communication sur les cités ouvrières', *ASMP*, XVII (1850), pp. 230–1.

5 Ibid., p. 240.

6 Audiganne, *Populations ouvrières*, vol. 2, p. 310.

7 Frazer, 'Vie secrète', p. 259.

8 Guerrand, *Origines*, pp. 153–60.

9 J. B. A. Godin, *Solutions sociales* (Paris, A. le Chevalier, 1871); Guerrand, *Origines*, pp. 160–7; Benevolo, *Origins*, pp. 65–75; T. G. Beddall, 'Godin's Familistère', *Architectural Design*, 46 (1976), pp. 423–7. Beddall notes that the occupants of the Familistère moved into the building by choice, and came to represent an élite among the factory workers; even in this development, with its high social ideals, the beneficiaries were a privileged group.

10 Détain, *RGA*, XXIV (1866), col. 223. Détain's initial article in 1866, 'Un mot sur la question des habitations ouvrières à Paris, à propos de l'Exposition Universelle de 1867' was followed by a substantial series on the Exposition, appearing between 1867 and 1870–1, under the title 'Exposition Universelle de 1867. Habitations ouvrières'.

11 See Dr J. Rochard, 'L'hygiène en 1889', *Revue des Deux Mondes*, XCVI (1889), p. 69; or E. Cheysson's comments at a meeting of the Société d'Economie Sociale, in *Bulletin de la Société d'Economie Sociale*, VII (1880–1), p. 137.

12 Détain, *RGA*, XXV (1867), col. 232.

13 This copy was in English, but the society's library also had a copy of the French translation of Roberts' book.

14 Dr A. Penot, 'Projet d'habitations pour les classes ouvrières; rapport presenté au nom du comité d'économie sociale', *BSIM*, XXIV (1852), pp. 129–41.

15 Ibid., pp. 135–6.

16 Ibid., pp. 140–1.

17 See Raffalovich, *Logement*, p. 454.

18 Villermé, *ASMP*, XVII (1850), p. 238.

19 F. Engels, 'Die Wohnungsfrage', *Volksstaat* (1872–3); quotation taken from English translation, *The Housing Question*, edited by C. P. Dutt (London, Martin Lawrence, 1935), p. 63.

20 Engels, 'Wohnungsfrage', p. 35.

21 J. Simon, *L'ouvrière* (Paris, Hachette, 1861), pp. 336, 351–2.

22 J. Siegfried, *La misère. Son histoire, ses causes, ses remèdes* (Le Havre, J. Poinsignon, 1877), pp. 211–12.

23 E. Cheysson, *La question des habitations ouvrières en France et à l'étranger* (Paris, G. Masson, Editeur, 1886), p. 6.

24 E. Levasseur, *Histoire des classes ouvrières en France depuis 1789 jusqu'à nos jours* (2 vols., Paris, Hachette, 1867), vol. 2, p. 415.

25 E. Trélat, 'Cités ouvrières, maisons ouvrières', *Congrès International d'Hygiène 1878* (2 vols., Paris, Imprimerie Nationale, 1880), vol. 1, p. 542.

26 Raffalovich, *Logement*, p. 449.

27 E. Muller and Dr O. du Mesnil, 'Des habitations à bon marché au point de vue de la construction et de la salubrité', *Annales d'Hygiène Publique et de Médecine Légale*, 3rd series, XXII (1899), p. 152.

16 Social reform

1 Simon, *L'ouvrière*, p. 336.

2 Siegfried, *La misère*, p. 211.

3 For biographical details of Simon, see the obituary notice read to the annual assembly of the Académie des Sciences Morales et Politiques in 1896, by fellow housing reformer G. Picot, *Notice historique sur la vie et les travaux de Jules Simon* (Paris, Firmin-Didot et Cie, 1896); and L. Sèche, *Jules Simon. Sa vie et son oeuvre* (Paris, A. Dupret, 1887).

4 For biographical details of Siegfried, see A. Siegfried, *Mes souvenirs de la IIIe République: mon père et son temps: Jules Siegfried, 1836–1922* (Paris, Editions du Grand Siècle, 1946).

5 A. Siegfried, *Mes souvenirs*, p. 63.

6 For biographical details of Picot, see the obituary notice read to the annual assembly of the Académie des Sciences Morales et Politiques in 1909, by A. de Foville, *Notice historique sur la vie et les oeuvres de M. Georges Picot* (Paris, Firmin-Didot et Cie, 1909). See also the tribute by E. Cheysson in *BSFHBM*, 19 (1909), pp. 253–63; pp. 264–6 of this issue give a list of Picot's main

activities and initiatives in relation to housing. For Cheysson, a biographical note and bibliography are included in E. Cheysson, *Oeuvres choisies* (2 vols., Paris, A. Rousseau, 1911).

7 At the time of Robert's birth in 1827, his father was involved in the construction of a new quarter in Mulhouse, which included housing, and the premises of the recently founded Société Industrielle in the town.

8 For biographical details of Robert, see A. Trombert, *Charles Robert, sa vie, son oeuvre* (2 vols., Paris, Chaix, F. Alcan, 1927, 1931).

9 From the statutes of the Office, published in Office Central des Oeuvres Charitables, *La France charitable et prévoyante* (93 parts, Paris, E. Plon, Nourrit et Cie, 1896–1900), part 1, p. I.

10 From a note on the founding of the Alliance, in *BSFHBM*, 15 (1904), p. 214.

11 From the statutes of the Musée, quoted in P. M. Wolf, *Eugène Hénard and the Beginning of Urbanism in Paris, 1900–1914* (The Hague, International Federation for Housing and Planning, and Centre de Recherche d'Urbanisme, 1968), p. 77.

12 E. Levasseur, *Questions ouvrières et industrielles en France sous la IIIe République* (Paris, A. Rousseau, 1907), p. 375.

13 For a biography of Le Play, see M. Z. Brooke, *Le Play: Engineer and Social Scientist* (London, Longman, 1970); See also Zeldin, *France*, vol. 2, pp. 953–9.

14 Further reformers who were members of the Société d'Economie Sociale included Emile Muller, Emile Cacheux, Arthur Raffalovich, Dr Jules Rochard, Eugène Rostand and Charles Lucas.

15 Zeldin, *France*, vol. 2, pp. 1016–17; Guerrand, *Origines*, p. 65.

16 Cahen, *Logement dans les villes*, pp. 260–1.

17 E. Cacheux, *L'économiste pratique* (Paris, Baudry, 1885), p. 77.

18 Raffalovich, *Logement*, pp. 331–4.

19 Zeldin, *France*, vol. 2, p. 1017.

20 Raffalovich, *Logement*, pp. 287–8, 290.

21 Ibid., p. 289.

22 Ibid., p. 334.

23 Dr J. Rochard, 'La maison de l'ouvrier', *Revue des Deux Mondes*, LXXXVII (1888), pp. 415, 420.

24 E. Levasseur, *Histoire des classes ouvrières et de l'industrie en France de 1789 à 1870*, 2nd edn (2 vols., Paris, A. Rousseau, 1903–4), vol. 1, p. 282.

25 Rochard, *Revue des Deux Mondes*, LXXXVII (1888), p. 420; Raffalovich, *Logement*, p. 299.

26 Cheysson, *La question des habitations ouvrières*, p. 48.

27 G. Picot, 'Exposition Universelle Internationale de 1889 à Paris; rapports du jury international, économie sociale; rapport sur les habitations ouvrières', *BSFHBM*, 2 (1891), p. 303.

28 Picot, *BSFHBM*, 2 (1891), p. 298.

29 Siegfried, *La misère*, p. 49.

30 Simon, *L'ouvrière*, p. 334.

31 Dr A. Penot, 'Projet de caisses de retraites et de prévoyance', *BSIM*, XXI (1847–8), p. 394.

32 Just over 30 years later, in 1849, Delessert was to be among the founding shareholders of the Société des Cités Ouvrières de Paris.

33 Levasseur, *Histoire des classes ouvrières*, 2nd edn, vol. 2, pp. 686–90.

34 Simon, *L'ouvrière*, p. 335.

35 J. Siegfried, 'Les habitations à bon marché', *BSFHBM*, 3 (1892), p. 121.

36 Simon, *L'ouvrière*, p. 334.

37 Cheysson, *La question des habitations ouvrières*, pp. 42–6.

38 J. Gaumont, *Histoire générale de la coopération en France* (2 vols., Paris, Fédération Nationale des Coopératives de Consommation, 1924), vol. 2, p. 124.

39 A. Casimir-Périer, *Les sociétés de coopération: la consommation, le crédit, la production, l'amélioration morale et intellectuelle par l'association* (Paris, Dentu, 1864), p. 8.

40 Quoted in C. Gide, *Les sociétés coopératives de consommation*, 2nd edn (Paris, A. Colin, 1910), p. 257.

41 Gaumont, *Histoire générale*, vol. 1, p. 468.

42 Ibid., vol. 2, p. 77.

43 E. Rostand, 'La coopération appliquée à la construction des habitations à bon marché, *BSFHBM*, 1 (1890), pp. 325–56; this paper had been presented by Rostand at the International Cooperative Congress held in Marseilles in 1890.

44 Quoted in Gaumont, *Histoire générale*, vol. 2, p. 574.

45 Guerrand, *Origines*, pp. 83–97, 183–202, 232–57; I am indebted to these passages for the material throughout this discussion of socialism.

46 Ibid., p. 91.

47 The comments on housing in these reports are summarized in ibid., pp. 92–4.

48 Ibid., p. 202.

49 Ibid., p. 241.

50 Quoted in ibid., p. 242.

51 Zeldin, *France*, vol. 1, pp. 753–4.

52 *Documents Parlementaires*, Chambre des Députés (1882), No. 1299, p. 2360.

53 Raffalovich, *Logement*, pp. 313–20; Cacheux, *L'économiste pratique*, pp. 65–70. The political debate in the early 1880s is considered in more detail in Chapter 24, 'The Société Française des Habitations à Bon Marché, and housing legislation'.

54 Guerrand, *Origines*, pp. 255–6.

55 Raffalovich, *Logement*, p. 313.

56 *BSFHBM*, 1 (1890), p. 16.

57 See A. Siegfried, *Mes souvenirs*; Sutcliffe, *Towards*, pp. 137–8, 146–50.

58 Raffalovich, *Logement*, p. 309.

17 Housing and hygiene

1 See Pinkney, *Napoléon III and the Rebuilding of Paris*.

2 'Ordonnance concernant la salubrité des habitations, Paris, le 23 novembre 1853', reprinted in *Congrès International d'Hygiène 1878*, vol. 1, p. 565. The earlier documents of 1848 are bound together in the volume of official publications relating to hygiene, in the British library: CT. 436/4: Conseil de Salubrité, *Instruction concernant les moyens d'assurer la salubrité des habitations*, 10 novembre 1848; Préfet de Police, *Ordonnance concernant la salubrité des habitations*, 20 novembre 1848.

3 Shapiro, 'Working class housing', p. 83. The Prefect of Police did have a role of inspection in relation to the lodging houses (*garnis*), but this was related more to the need to ensure public order than to enforce standards of hygiene; there were no specific sets of hygiene regulations relating to *garnis* before 1878, and those introduced after this date were limited in effect. See *Congrès International d'Hygiène 1878*, vol. 1, p. 562; and Shapiro, 'Working class housing', p. 267.

4 Shapiro, 'Working class housing', p. 94; Sutcliffe, *Autumn*, p. 102; 'La commission des logements insalubres de Paris', *GAB*, IV (1866), p. 230.

5 A. Lance, *Rapport fait au conseil de la Société Centrale des Architectes au nom*

de la commission nommée sur la proposition de M. Harou Romain pour étudier les moyens propres à assurer l'assainissement des habitations insalubres (Paris, E. Thunot, 1850), p. 30.

6 Sutcliffe, *Autumn*, pp. 262–8; G. Jourdan, 'De l'assainissement des habitations dans la ville de Paris', *Congrès International d'Hygiène et de Démographie 1889* (Paris, Bibliothèque des Annales Economiques, 1890), pp. 354–6.

7 Sutcliffe, *Autumn*, p. 103. Sutcliffe notes that part of this fall was more apparent than real, owing to the effect on the statistics of the incorporation of suburban areas in the enlarged city boundaries from 1860.

8 One of the housing reformers had particularly direct experience of the problems associated with the besieged city; Emile Cheysson was in charge of the mills set up in Paris to provide flour for the population. The exhaustion of grain supplies in the city was one of the major factors contributing to the city's eventual capitulation.

9 *RGA*, XXIX (1872), col. 94.

10 Ibid.

11 Guerrand, *Origines*, p. 203; Sutcliffe, *Autumn*, p. 103.

12 Guerrand, *Origines*, p. 202; Shapiro, 'Working class housing', pp. 103–6.

13 See the reports by A. Paul, and E. Trélat, in 1876 and 1878 respectively: *Congrès International d'Hygiène, de Sauvetage, et d'Economie Sociale 1876* (2 vols., Paris, Germer Baillière et Cie, 1877), vol. 2, pp. 487–539; *Congrès International d'Hygiène 1878*, vol. 1, pp. 538–52.

14 *Congrès International d'Hygiène 1878*, vol. 1, p. 585. For du Mesnil's report, see pp. 552–63.

15 *Congrès International d'Hygiène 1878*, vol. 1, p. 596.

16 Ibid. p. 593.

17 J. Alphand, 'Note sur la situation du service des eaux et égouts, et sur les mesures à proposer au Conseil Municipal', quoted in *RGA*, 4th series, XI (1884), col. 68.

18 Commission Technique de l'Assainissement de Paris 'Résumé des travaux et résolutions adoptées', *Annales des Ponts et Chaussées, Mémoires et Documents*, 6th series, X (1885), p. 461.

19 *RGA*, 4th series, X (1883), col. 184.

20 For a brief biography and bibliography of Durand-Claye, see A. Choisy, 'Notice nécrologique sur Alfred Durand-Claye', *Annales des Ponts et Chaussées, Mémoires et Documents*, 6th series, XVI (1888), pp. 505–22.

21 Commission Technique de l'Assainissement de Paris, *Annales des Ponts et Chaussées, Mémoires et Documents*, 6th series, X (1885), pp. 458–76.

22 Shapiro, 'Working class housing', p. 279.

23 Ibid., p. 141; Pinkney, *Napoleon III*, p. 23.

24 Sutcliffe, *Autumn*, pp. 103–7; Shapiro, 'Working class housing', p. 141.

25 Sutcliffe, *Autumn*, p. 105.

26 Dr E. Clément, 'Des moyens propre à pourvoir les bâtiments de lumière et de chaleur solaires', *Internationaler Congress für Hygiene und Demographie zu Wien 1887* (37 Hefte, Vienna, Verlag der Organisations-Commission des Congresses, 1887–8), Heft 11, p. 34; the emphasis is Clément's.

27 Sutcliffe, *Autumn*, p. 264.

28 E. Trélat, 'Moyens de pourvoir les bâtiments de lumière et de chaleur solaires', *Internationaler Congress für Hygiene und Demographie zu Wien 1887*, Heft 11, p. 43.

29 Guerrand, *Origines*, p. 226.

30 Shapiro, 'Working class housing', p. 267.

31 Ibid., p. 271; P. Juillerat, 'Sur le casier sanitaire des maisons de Paris', *Congrès International d'Hygiène et de Démographie 1900* (Paris, Masson et Cie, n.d.), pp. 360–1.

32 P. Juillerat and Dr A. Fillassier, 'La statistique sanitaire des maisons. Le casier sanitaire des maisons de Paris', *Internationaler Kongress für Hygiene und Demographie 1907* (4 vols., Berlin, Verlag von August Hirschwald, 1908), vol. 3, p. 1376.

33 Juillerat and Fillassier, 'Statistique', p. 1377.

34 See Shapiro, 'Working class housing', chapter 7, to which I am indebted for the following discussion of the revision of the 1850 law.

35 15 fevrier 1902: Loi relative à la protection de la santé publique, article 1.

36 E. Dennery, *La question de l'habitation urbaine en France* (Geneva, League of Nations, Health Organisation, 1935), pp. 47–52.

37 The process of expropriation under the 1850 law, and its successor in 1902, was governed by the expropriation legislation enacted in 1841.

38 Sutcliffe, *Autumn*, pp. 109–14.

39 Guerrand, *Origines*, p. 228.

18 Housing and urban growth

1 M. Daly, 'L'Association Française pour l'Avancement des Sciences: session de Rouen 1882–3', *RGA*, 4th series, X (1883), col. 185.

2 N. Williams, 'Paradise and the bourgeois villa, the architecture of the Parisian suburbs 1850–1914', Department of Architecture, University of Cambridge (unpublished dissertation, 1980), pp. 5–25.

3 *Congrès International d'Hygiène 1878*, vol. 1, pp. 556, 589–90.

4 See du Mesnil, *L'habitation du pauvre*; du Mesnil's study includes records of visits made, in the course of his work for the Commission des Logements Insalubres, to the Cité Jeanne d'Arc, built between 1869 and 1872; and housing in the Avenue de Choisy, built in 1882.

5 Sutcliffe, *Autumn*, pp. 80–3; N. Evenson, *Paris: A Century of Change, 1878–1978* (New Haven and London, Yale University Press, 1979), pp. 76–82.

6 *Congrès International d'Hygiène 1878*, vol. 1, pp. 557, 580.

7 A. Boulanger, 'Sur les habitations ouvrières dans Paris; considérations sur la salubrité du quartier Saint Gervais', *Congrès International d'Hygiène 1878*, vol. 2, p. 336.

8 Cheysson, *La question des habitations ouvrières*, p. 31.

9 Sutcliffe, *Towards*, p. 137.

10 Raffalovich, *Logement*, pp. 313–17.

11 Ibid., p. 319.

12 E. Cacheux and A. Rendu, *Congrès International des Habitations à Bon Marché 1907* (Orléans, Imprimerie Auguste Gout et Cie, 1908), p. 84.

13 *Internationaler Kongress für Hygiene und Demographie 1907*, vol. 1, p. 255.

14 G. Hottenger, 'La cité moderne et ses fonctions', *Bulletin de la Chambre de Commerce de Nancy*, No. 53 (1913), pp. 132–65; R. de Souza, *L'avenir de nos villes. Nice, capitale d'hiver* (Paris, Nancy, Berger-Levrault, 1913).

15 G. Risler, 'Les plans d'aménagement et d'extension des villes', *Bulletin de la Chambre de Commerce de Nancy*, No. 53 (1913), p. 126.

16 G. Hottenger, *L'habitation populaire et l'extension des villes, d'après les récents congrès* (Nancy, Imprimeries Réunies, 1913), p. 7.

17 Cacheux and Rendu, *Congrès*, p. 84.

18 M. Dufourmantelle, 'Les cités-jardins, leur portée sociale, leur caractère, leur organisation', in Société Française des Habitations à Bon Marché, *La question de la reconstruction des villes et villages détruits par la guerre* (Paris, 9, Rue de Solferino, 1916), p. 87. Dufourmantelle's paper had initially been delivered to the National Congress of Housing Societies held in Lyons in 1914.

19 M. Dufourmantelle, *La réforme de l'habitation populaire par les cités-jardins* (Brussels, Revue Economique Internationale, 1910), p. 20.

20 Dufourmantelle, in Société Française des HBM, *La question*, pp. 110–14.

21 Report by J. Dépinay, reprinted in Sellier, *La crise du logement*, pp. 898–917.

22 Sellier, *La crise du logement*, p. 239.

23 Wolf, *Eugène Hénard*, p. 75.

24 This total area of about 1,200 hectares was a considerable area for any French city to contemplate owning or controlling; but it can be compared with the areas owned by some German towns in 1910: Strasbourg, 4,590 hectares; Munich, 4,660 hectares; Frankfurt am Main, 5,260 hectares; Berlin, 17,930 hectares. See Sellier, *La crise du logement*, p. 240.

25 Cahen, *Logement dans les villes*, p. 177.

26 Quoted in J. F. Chiffard and Y. Roujon, 'Après les fortifs et la zone, la ceinture', *Architecture Mouvement Continuité*, No. 43 (1977), p. 11. This article gives detailed consideration to the history of the fortification land.

27 Cahen, *Logement dans les villes*, p. 188.

28 E. Hénard, *Etudes sur la transformation de Paris, Fascicule 2. Les alignements brisés; la question des fortifications et le boulevard de grande-ceinture* (Paris, Librairies-Imprimeries Réunies, 1903). See Wolf, *Eugène Hénard*.

29 Wolf, *Eugène Hénard*, p. 77.

30 E. Cacheux, 'Extension méthodique du territoire à bâtir dans les villes', *Bulletin du Comité des Travaux Historiques et Scientifiques. Section des Sciences Economiques et Sociales. Congrès des Sociétés Savantes de 1908* (Paris, Imprimerie Nationale, 1909), p. 75.

31 *BSFHBM*, 21 (1911), p. 450.

32 T. Garnier, *Une cité industrielle, étude pour la construction des villes* (Paris, Massin et Cie, 1917); E. Hénard, *Etudes sur la transformation de Paris* (8 'fascicules', Paris, Librairies-Imprimeries Réunies, 1903–9).

33 Sutcliffe, *Towards*, pp. 150–2.

34 Ibid., pp. 152–4; Wolf, *Eugène Hénard*, pp. 81–90.

35 The following organisations which started the teaching of *urbanisme* were founded during or just after the war: Institut d'Histoire, de Géographie et d'Economie Urbaine (1916); Ecole Supérieur d'Art Public (1917); Ecole des Hautes Etudes Urbaines (1919).

36 Gide, *Les sociétés coopératives de consommation*, pp. 127–8.

37 Dufourmantelle, in Société Française des HBM, *La question*, p. 78.

38 Sellier, *La crise du logement*, gives details of the initial founding and early projects of the Office. For later discussion of the Office's work, see: 'Les cités-jardins de la région de l'Ile de France', *Cahiers de l'Institut d'Aménagement et d'Urbanisme de la Région de l'Ile de France*, No. 51 (1978); O. Nicoulaud, 'Cités-jardins', *Architecture Mouvement Continuité*, No. 34 (1974), pp. 10–25; F. Laisney, 'Quand les HLM étaient roses', *Architecture Mouvement Continuité*, No. 35 (1974), pp. 79–104; J. Read, 'The garden city and the growth of Paris', *Architectural Review*, CLXIII (1978), pp. 345–52; G. Baty-Tornikian, *Un projet urbain idéal typique. Agglomération parisienne 1919–1939* (Paris, Institut d'Etudes et de Recherches Architecturales et Urbaines, *c.* 1979).

19 Architectural reform

1 C. Daly, 'Adresse à nos lecteurs', *RGA*, VII (1847–8), col. 450. For a discussion of Daly's activity at this time, see H. Lipstadt, *Architectural Design*, 48, No. 11–12 (1978), pp. 18–29.

2 Guerrand, *Origines*, p. 27.

3 For the list of architects appointed, see *Encyclopédie d'Architecture*, III (1852–3), cols. 5–7.

4 Lance, *L'assainissement des habitations insalubres*.

5 Ibid. pp. 33, 50.

6 N. Harou-Romain, 'Des cités ouvrières', *Annales de la Charité*, V (1849), pp. 737–46.

7 N. Harou-Romain, 'De l'assainissement des villes et de l'amélioration des habitations rurales au moyen d'une modification dans l'impôt de la propriété bâtie', *Annales de la Charité*, VI (1850), pp. 713–32.

8 Gourlier, *Des voies publiques*, p. 22; Gourlier notes that certain towns, notably Rennes and Strasbourg, actually had more coherent regulations than Paris at this time.

9 See entries under Harou-Romain in *La grande encyclopédie* (31 vols., Paris, Société Anonyme de la Grande Encyclopédie, n.d.), and Romain (Harou) in P. Planat, *Encyclopédie de l'architecture et de la construction* (6 vols., Paris, Dujardin et Cie, n.d.).

10 See entry under Rohault de Fleury in *Encyclopédie de l'architecture et de la construction*; Guerrand, *Origines*, p. 66.

11 *RGA*, VIII (1849–50), col. 210; G. Teyssot, '"La casa per tutti": per una genealogia dei tipi', introduction to Italian edition of Guerrand: *Le origini della questione delle abitazioni in Francia (1850–1914)*, ed. Georges Teyssot (Rome, Officina Edizioni, 1981), pp. li–lii.

12 Teyssot, '"La casa per tutti"', pp. liv–lv; Guerrand, *Origines*, pp. 77–8.

13 Teyssot, '"La casa per tutti"', p. lv.

14 See entry under Delbrouck in J. Maitron, *Dictionnaire biographique du mouvement ouvrier français* (18 vols., Paris, Les Editions Ouvrières, 1964–); *RGA*, VIII (1849–50), cols. 209–10; IX (1851), col. 138; X (1852), col. 157.

15 C. Questel, *Notice historique sur le service des travaux et sur le conseil général des bâtiments civils* (Paris, Imprimerie Nationale, 1886), p. 160. The first part of this *Notice*, covering the period from 1795–1848, consists of a reprint of the original *Notice historique* written by Gourlier, and published in 1848 (Paris, L. Colas).

16 Gourlier, *Des voies publiques*, pp. 27–31.

17 *RGA*, XI (1853), col. 259; *Encyclopédie d'Architecture*, VI (1856), col. 27; Gourlier, *Des voies publiques*, p. 33.

18 *Encyclopédie d'Architecture*, III (1852–3), cols. 94–5.

19 H. Roberts, *Des habitations des classes ouvrières*, traduit et publié par ordre du Président de la République (Paris, Gide et Baudry, 1850), p. 6; Guerrand. *Origines*, pp. 103–4.

20 *Encyclopédie d'Architecture*, II (1851–2), cols. 107–8; IV (1854), col. 16; the competitions in Saint Quentin, Amiens and Lille are discussed in Chapter 22, 'Housing societies'.

21 *RGA*, X (1852), cols. 51–3; *Encyclopédie d'Architecture*, XII (1862), cols. 79–80, 90–2.

22 *Nouvelles Annales de la Construction*, II (1856), cols. 78–80; III (1857), col. 112.

23 *RGA*, XXIV (1866), cols. 38–40. The workers' representative was Chabaud, who in 1862 had been president of the workers' delegation to the London exhibition of that year. In 1867 he was also involved in the workers' committee which organised the construction of one of the full-size blocks of flats exhibited at the Paris Exposition, and which subsequently established a co-operative to construct further housing. This co-operative is discussed further in Chapter 23, 'Housing and Co-operation'.

24 *RGA*, XVIII (1860), col. 3.

25 GAB, II (1864), p. 189.

26 See entries for Trélat, father and son, in the biographical dictionaries of Curinier, and Vapereau; Agulhon, *1848*, p. 26.

27 E. Trélat, *L'école centrale d'architecture* (Paris, A. Morel et Cie, 1864), p. 21.

28 Ibid., p. 30.

29 For further details of the founding of the Ecole Centrale d'Architecture, and particularly of Viollet-le-Duc's role, see R. D. Middelton, 'Viollet-le-Duc's academic ventures and the Entretiens sur l'Architecture', in *Gottfried Semper und die Mitte des 19 Jahrhunderts*, Symposium vom 2 bis 6 Dezember 1974 (Basel, Stuttgart, Birkhäuser Verlag, 1976), pp. 239–54.

30 *La grande encyclopédie*, vol. 15, p. 450.

31 From the statutes of the school, quoted in *Bulletin de la Société des Architectes Diplomés de l'Ecole Spéciale d'Architecture*, No. 8–10 (1965), p. 9.

32 *RGA*, XXIII (1865), col. 77; in addition to Viollet-le-Duc and Trélat, the 12 architects listed by the *Revue* included Viollet-le-Duc's son and son-in-law.

33 For the list of founding shareholders, see *GAB*, III (1865), p. 23. The Dollfus family and Viollet-le-Duc had links which predated the founding of the school, as Viollet-le-Duc had designed a house for Jean Dollfus (fils), near the family's factory, in the mid-1850s; see R. D. Middelton, 'Viollet-le-Duc and the rational gothic tradition', University of Cambridge (unpublished thesis, 1958).

34 For a discussion of the links of the Ecole Centrale d'Architecture with Saint-Simonists and Fourierists, see B. Marrey, 'Saint-Simoniens, Fouriéristes et architecture; les réalisations architecturales des socialistes quarante-huitards', *Archives d'Architecture Moderne*, No. 20 (1981), pp. 74–99.

35 For details of the courses and teachers, see *RGA*, XXIII (1865), cols. 76–85; and *GAB*, III (1865), p. 240.

36 Trélat, *L'école centrale d'architecture*, p. 13.

37 From the school's programme of courses, printed in *RGA*, XXIII (1865), col. 84.

38 *GAB*, V (1867), p. 149. In 1855 Cole had been instrumental in founding the museum of applied art in South Kensington, which formed the basis of the Victoria & Albert Museum. In his address at the Ecole Centrale d'Architecture in 1867 he indicated a parallel between the work of the Ecole and his work in Kensington, suggesting that the principles taught at the Ecole were the same as those put into practice in Kensington; see Middelton, 'Viollet-le-Duc's academic ventures', pp. 251–2.

39 A. de Baudot, 'L'architecture à l'Ecole des beaux-arts et à l'Ecole centrale', *GAB*, VI (1868), p. 10.

40 The programme was based on a proposal by Jules Siegfried in 1868, to finance a Working Men's Club in his home town, Mulhouse.

41 From a manuscript presented to the South Kensington Museum by the Ecole Centrale d'Architecture; the manuscript introduced reproductions of student projects, including designs for the Working Men's Club. These documents are now held in the Victoria and Albert Museum Library: 86.PP.1.

42 Critical reviews appeared in *RGA*, XXVIII (1870–1), cols. 132–8, 168–80; and *Moniteur des Architectes*, V (1870–1), cols. 161–5, 193–8. The *Moniteur des Architectes* even went so far as to reprint the correspondence between Garnier and Trélat, in VI (1872), cols. 170–5, 181–92, 195–6.

43 Middelton, 'Viollet-le-Duc's academic ventures', p. 253. For de Baudot's involvement in architectural education, at this period and subsequently, see special issue on de Baudot, *Architecture Mouvement Continuité*, No. 28 (1973), pp. 8–14.

44 E. Trélat, *Ecole Spéciale d'Architecture, ouverture 1879–80, discours du directeur* (Paris, 136, Boulevard Montparnasse, 1879); after being temporarily known as the Ecole Centrale et Spéciale d'Architecture, the school was now simply titled the Ecole Spéciale d'Architecture.

45 *Nouvelles Annales de la Construction*, 3rd series, IV (1879), col. 144. Muller

and Cacheux's study was published as *Les habitations ouvrières en tous pays, situation en 1878, avenir* (Paris, J. Dejey et Cie, 1879).

46 E. Muller, *Habitations ouvrières et agricoles, cités, bains et lavoirs, sociétés alimentaires, détails de construction, formules representant chaque espèce de maison et donnant son prix de revient en tous pays. Statuts, règlements et contrats* (Paris, Victor Dalmont, 1855–6), p. 10.

47 *Nouvelles Annales de la Construction*, II (1856), col. 85.

48 Muller, *Habitations ouvrières*, p. 12.

49 In the previous year, Muller had contributed a series of plans for two schools, to Clavel's *Traité d'éducation physique et morale* (2 vols., Paris, V. Masson, 1855).

50 E. Cacheux, *Etat des habitations ouvrières à la fin du XIXe siècle* (Paris, Baudry, 1891), p. iii.

51 Houses were illustrated from England, Austria, Belgium, Denmark, Spain, Holland, Italy, Norway, Russia, Sweden and Switzerland; there were also examples from America and Japan.

52 Picot, *BSFHBM*, 2 (1891), p. 408.

53 This society is discussed in more detail in Chapter 22, 'Housing societies'.

54 Cacheux, *Etat des habitations ouvrières*.

55 Quoted in Raffalovich, *Logement*, p. 362.

56 Cacheux, *L'économiste pratique*, p. 71.

57 S. Ferrand, *Systèmes de construction économiques. Les maisons de grand rapport et les loyers à bon marché* (Paris, l'auteur, 1871), p. 22.

58 This society is discussed in more detail in Chapter 23, 'Housing and Co-operation'.

59 P. Wolf, 'City structuring and social sense in 19th and 20th century urbanism', *Perspecta*, No. 13–14 (1971), pp. 227–31.

60 *La Semaine des Constructeurs*, X (1885–6), p. 353.

61 Détain, *RGA*, XXV (1867), cols. 219–31.

62 C. Lucas, *Etude sur les habitations à bon marché en France et à l'étranger* (Paris, Aulanier et Cie, n.d. – c. 1900), pp. 92–102: A. Dubois, 'Les avantages de l'adoption du système lyonnais de construction par les sociétés d'habitations à bon marchè', *BSFHBM*, 7 (1896), pp. 67–82.

63 Lucas, *Etudes sur les habitations à bon marché*, pp. 103–10.

64 Ibid., pp. 57–68: E. Cacheux, 'Les habitations ouvrières exposées en 1889', *Congrès International d'Hygiène 1889*, p. 432.

65 *Nouvelles Annales de la Construction*, 3rd series, IV (1879), cols. 4–9. Cacheux, *Etat des habitations ouvrières*, gives details of the medals awarded in 1889; A. Raffalovich and A. Roulliet, *Bibliographie des habitations à bon marché* (Le Mans, imprimerie E. Monnoyer, 1889), pp. 3–4, list the members of the 1889 housing committee.

66 Trélat, *Congrès International d'Hygiène 1878*, vol. 1, pp. 538–69.

67 E. Trélat, *Influence exercée par la porosité des murs sur la salubrité des habitations* (Geneva, Imprimerie Charles Schuchardt, 1883); *Régime de la température et de l'air dans la maison* (The Hague, Imprimerie Sud-Hollandaise, 1886); Moyens de pourvoir les bâtiments de lumière et de chaleur solaires, *Internationaler Congress für Hygiene und Demographie zu Wien 1887*.

68 E. Trélat, *Images et figures résumant les règles et preceptes professés par l'auteur pour assurer la salubrité dans les édifices* (Paris, Imprimerie de Delalain frères, 1886); *Aérage et chauffage des habitations* (Paris, G. Masson, Editeur, 1886).

69 C. Lucas, *Conférence sur l'habitation à toutes les époques* (Paris, Imprimerie Nationale, 1879), p. 8.

70 *RIBA Journal*, XII (1904–5), p. 635; the Journal also published a short biographical note on Lucas, written by another corresponding member of the Institute, A. Choisy: *RIBA Journal*, XIII (1905–6), pp. 18–19.

71 Lucas, *Etude sur les habitations à bon marché.*

72 The Boundary Street housing was one of the major projects of slum clearance and rebuilding carried out under the 1890 Housing of the Working Classes Act; built between 1895 and 1900, it provided more than 1,000 flats. See A. Wohl, *The Eternal Slum, Housing and Social Policy in Victorian London*, Studies in Urban History, 5 (London, Edward Arnold, 1977), pp. 270–3, p. 362.

73 *Congrès International des Architectes 1900* (Paris, Chaix, 1906), p. 217.

74 B. B. Taylor, 'Sauvage and hygienic housing, or the cleanliness revolution', *Architèse*, No. 12 (1974), pp. 13–16, 55.

75 Hénard, *Etudes sur les transformations de Paris*, fascicule 2.

76 For the basis of the following discussion, in particular of the Groupe des Maisons Ouvrières, and of Emile Cheysson's comments on comfort in popular housing, I am indebted to J. Taricat and M. Villars, *Le logement à bon marché. Chronique. Paris 1850–1930* (Boulogne, Editions Apogée, 1982); see notably pp. 96–115.

77 E. Cheysson, *Le confort du logement populaire* (Paris, Chaix, 1905), p. 4.

78 Ibid. p. 9.

79 Text taken from a plaque on the housing in the Rue de Prague.

80 *La Construction Moderne*, 2nd series, X (1904–5), p. 483.

81 C. Pawlowski, *Tony Garnier et les débuts de l'urbanisme fonctionnel en France* (Paris, Centre de Recherche d'Urbanisme, 1967), pp. 116–22.

82 Taricat and Villars, *Le logement à bon marché*, p. 115.

83 For example, the housing built by the Fondation Rothschild at 10 Rue Mathurin Regnier, and 117 Rue de Belleville; or the housing built by the Société des Logements Economiques pour Familles Nombreuses at 23 Rue Falguière, and 90 Rue Moulin Vert, all in Paris.

84 A. A. Rey, 'Street widening in close built areas by successive stages', *Town Planning Review*, V (1914–15), p. 44.

85 Ville de Paris, *Le concours pour la construction d'habitations à bon marché* (Paris, Préfecture du Département de la Seine, 1913), p. 16. The jury also noted particularly the importance of through ventilation in flats.

86 Taricat and Villars, *Le logement à bon marché*, p. 130.

87 Ibid., p. 126.

20 The reformers and the housing market

1 E. Cacheux, 'Habitations ouvrières en tous pays', *BSES*, VII (1880–1), p.111.

2 *BSES*, VII (1880–1), p. 135. The society had already considered the problem of French population growth in 1877, in its session of 28 January; see *BSES*, V (1875–7), pp. 472–515.

3 Dr O. du Mesnil, 'Les logements des ouvriers dans les grandes villes; garnis', *Congrès International d'Hygiène 1878*, p. 556.

4 Muller and Cacheux, *Habitations ouvrières*, pp. 59–62.

5 Cacheux, *BSES*, VII (1880–1), p. 123; Cacheux, *L'économiste pratique*, pp. 23–6.

6 A. Mangin, 'La question du logement et les maisons d'ouvriers à Paris', *L'Economiste Français*, VII, 1 (1879), p. 630.

7 P. Leroy-Beaulieu, 'Le développement des grandes villes et la spéculation sur les immeubles urbains', *L'Economiste Français*, VII, 2 (1879), pp. 497–500; P. Leroy-Beaulieu, 'La construction des maisons de luxe et des maisons à bon marché à Paris', *L'Economiste Français*, X, 1 (1882), pp. 437–9, 469–71.

8 E. Cacheux, letter published in *L'Economiste Français*, X, 1 (1882), pp. 416–17.

9 The society was the Société des Habitations Ouvrières de Passy-Auteuil, which will be discussed further in Chapter 22, 'Housing societies'.

10 E. Cacheux, letter published in *La Réforme Sociale*, V (1883), p. 168.

11 Projects by the Péreire brothers, and by a society headed by de Heeckeren and Kennard were implemented in reduced form; see Chapter 22 'Housing societies'. Emile Muller had experience of a developer foregoing the subsidy altogether, in a group of housing which he planned for construction in Paris; see Muller, *Habitations ouvrières*, pp. 37–8.

12 Picot, *BSFHBM*, 2 (1891), p. 294.

21 Housing for industry

1 Détain, *RGA*, XXVIII (1870–1), col. 69.

2 Levasseur, *Histoire des classes ouvrières*, 2nd edn, vol. 2, p. 668.

3 Raffalovich, *Logement*, p. 323.

4 When the Comité d'Economie Sociale of the Société Industrielle de Mulhouse investigated workers' housing already built in Alsace, in preparation of the report which Dr A. Penot presented in 1852, it was Zuber's housing which came closest to the committee's ideal; see Penot, *BSIM*, XXIV (1852), pp. 136–9. For the housing at Blanzy, Le Creusot and Anzin, see Détain, *RGA*, XXVI (1868), cols. 258–61; XXVIII (1870–1), cols. 66–71. For André Koechlin's housing, see Dr A. Penot, 'Les institutions privées du Haut-Rhin; notes remises au comité départemental de l'Exposition Universelle de 1867', *BSIM*, XXXVII (1867), p. 87. For the Hartmann company, see A. Audiganne, *Les populations ouvrières et les industries de la France dans le mouvement social du XIXe siècle*, 2nd edn. (2 vols, Paris, Capelle, 1860), p. 170. More recently, the housing at Le Creusot has been considered in detail in C. Devillers and B. Huet, *Le Creusot, naissance et développement d'une ville industrielle, 1782–1914*. (Seyssel, Champ Vallon, 1981).

5 Détain, *RGA*, XXVIII (1870–1), col. 67; Devillers and Huet, *Le Creusot*, pp. 48, 50, 223; it is interesting to note that the demolition of the last of these blocks coincided with the period in which the housing reformer Emile Cheysson was a director of the Schneider company in Le Creusot.

6 For a summary of this survey, see Guerrand, *Origines*, pp. 126–34.

7 *Moniteur des Architectes*, IV (1869), col. 189; V (1870–1), cols. 205–6; Guerrand, *Origines*, pp. 127, 131.

8 Détain, *RGA*, XXVI (1868), col. 209.

9 Ibid., cols. 209–11; Dr A. Penot, 'Les cités ouvrières du Haut-Rhin', *BSIM*, XXXXV (1865), pp. 427–31; Muller and Cacheux, *Habitations ouvrières*, plate 11.

10 Guebwiller: Penot, *BSIM*, XXXV (1865), pp. 415–27; Guerrand, *Origines*, p. 132; Muller, *Habitations ouvrières*, plate 23. Colmar: Penot, *BSIM*, XXXVII (1867), p. 86.

11 Détain, *RGA*, XXVIII (1870–1), col. 69.

12 Guerrand, *Origines*, p. 127.

13 Détain, *RGA*, XXVIII (1870–1), col. 66; Cheysson, *Oeuvres choisies*, vol. 1, p. 29; Levasseur, *Questions ouvrières*, p. 815.

14 Picot, *BSFHBM*, 2 (1891), p. 411.

15 Blanzy: Détain, *RGA*, XXVIII (1870–1), cols. 69–71; Muller and Cacheux, *Habitations ouvrières*, plate 13. Carmaux: Détain, *RGA*, XXVII (1869), cols. 261–3.

16 Détain, *RGA*, XXVI (1868), cols. 258–61; Muller and Cacheux, *Habitations ouvrières*, plates 8–10 show variants of the type exhibited in 1867.

17 Détain, *RGA*, XXVIII (1870–1), cols. 66–9; Muller and Cacheux, *Habitations ouvrières*, plate 14 shows another house type built at Le Creusot.

18 For a study of the development of Le Creusot, see C. Devillers and B. Huet, *Le Creusot*. For an analysis of typical *coron* housing, see O. Girard, 'Corons du Nord: l'espace industriel et l'habiter', *Architecture Mouvement Continuité*, No. 34 (1974), pp. 38–51; and E. Girard and J. P. Massenot, 'Corons du Nord 2: cité des Brebis (Mazingarbe)', *Architecture Mouvement Continuité*, No. 35 (1974), pp. 130–40.
19 Détain, *RGA*, XXVI (1868). col. 259.
20 Picot, *BSFHBM*, 2 (1891), pp. 299–300; E. J. Menier, 'Cité ouvrière de Noisiel' *BSFHBM*, 3 (1892), pp. 450–5; Lucas, *Etude sur les habitations à bon marché*, pp. 190–2; Muller and Cacheux, *Habitations ouvrières*, plate 19; Benevolo, *Origins*, p. 121.
21 G. Benoît-Lévy, 'La première cité-jardin de France: le village-jardin des Mines de Dourges', *BSFHBM*, 19 (1909), pp. 438–45.
22 Ibid., p. 439.
23 Rochard, *Revue des Deux Mondes*, LXXXVII (1888), p. 408; E. Cheysson, 'Rapport...presenté au conseil supérieur des habitations à bon marché au nom du comité permanent', *BSFHBM*, 16 (1905), p. 190; E. Cheysson, 'Rapport...presenté au conseil supérieur des habitations à bon marché au nom du comité permanent', *BSFHBM*, 18 (1908), p. 169.
24 Picot, *BSFHBM*, 2 (1891), pp. 303, 305.
25 Quoted in Levasseur, *Questions ouvrières*, p. 817.
26 Cheysson, *La question des habitations ouvrières*, p. 56.

22 Housing societies

1 Picot, *BSFHBM*, 2 (1891), p. 314.
2 Cheysson, *La question des habitations ouvrières*, p. 49.
3 Cacheux, *L'économiste pratique*, plate 5.
4 L. Puteaux, *Les constructions civiles* (Paris, Eugène Lacroix, 1873), pp. 15–16; Muller, *Habitations ouvrières*, pp. 37–8, 83.
5 Cacheux, *L'économiste pratique*, pp. 38–43, plate 1.
6 Ibid., p. 27, plates 5–6.
7 Puteaux, *Les constructions civiles*, pp. 12–14.
8 Muller and Cacheux, *Habitations ouvrières*, 2nd edn, pp. 143–4.
9 Muller, *Habitations ouvrières*, p. 81.
10 Puteaux, *Les constructions civiles*, pp. 14–15; Cacheux. *L'économiste pratique*, plate 7.
11 Muller, *Habitations ouvrières*, pp. 81, 83–5.
12 Cacheux, *L'économiste pratique*, p. 8; Muller and Cacheux, *Habitations ouvrières*, p. 63.
13 *Moniteur Universel*, 6 April 1854, p. 381; 27 April 1854, p. 461.
14 *Moniteur Universel*, 6 April 1854, p. 381.
15 For details of the Mulhouse society and its housing, see the reports by Dr A. Penot in *BSIM*, already cited: *BSIM*, XXIV (1852), pp. 135–41; *BSIM*, XXXV (1865), pp. 385–415; *BSIM*, XXXVII (1867), pp. 81–4; see also: Dr A. Penot, 'Rapport du comité d'économie sociale sur la construction d'une cité ouvrière à Mulhouse', *BSIM*, XXV (1853), pp. 299–316; Détain, *RGA*, XXV (1867), cols. 231–9; Picot, *BSFHBM*, 2 (1891), pp. 305–7; the various studies published by Muller and Cacheux, jointly and separately, also give valuable information and illustrations.
16 Picot, *BSFHBM*, 2 (1891), pp. 307–8.
17 *RGA*, XXIV (1866), col. 38.
18 These societies will be considered in Chapter 23, 'Housing and Co-operation'.
19 *RGA*, XXIV (1866), col. 90.
20 *RGA*, XXV (1867), col. 40; *RGA*, XXVI (1868), col. 45; C. Lavollée,

'Rapport au nom du comité de commerce, sur diverses communications relatives aux habitations ouvrières, *Bulletin de la Société d'Encouragement pour l'Industrie Nationale*, 3rd series, IX (1882), p. 487; Picot, *BSFHBM*, 2 (1891), p. 310.

21 *RGA*, XXX (1873), col. 185; Lavollée, *Bulletin de la Société d'Encouragement pour l'Industrie Nationale*, 3rd series, IX (1882), p. 484; Raffalovich, *Logement*, pp. 329–30; *La Réforme Sociale*, X (1885), pp. 430–32; Muller and Cacheux, *Habitations ouvrières*, plate 17.

22 Dunkirk: *GAB*, V (1867), p. 200. Reims: *Nouvelles Annales de la Construction*, 3rd series, IV (1879), cols. 4–9; Muller and Cacheux, *Habitations ouvrières*, plate 29.

23 Siegfried, *La misère*, pp. 206–10; Lucas, *Etude sur les habitations à bon marché*, pp. 199–204; Muller and Cacheux, *Habitations ouvrières*, plate 66; *BSFHBM*, 1 (1890), pp. 35–75 includes the statutes of the society, cost details of the houses, and a typical lease.

24 Bolbec: *Nouvelles Annales de la Construction*, 3rd series, III (1878), cols. 161–5; Nancy: Raffalovich, *Logement*, pp. 341–3; Chassignet, 'Enquête sur la condition des petits logements en France et à l'étranger: Ville de Nancy', *La Réforme Sociale*, 2nd series, VII (1889), pp. 330–40, 429–38, 480–8.

25 Quoted in Raffalovich, *Logement*, p. 342.

26 *BSFHBM*, 1 (1890), p. 39.

27 Détain, *RGA*, XXV (1867), cols. 158–63; E. Degrand and Dr J. Faucher 'Habitations caracterisées par le bon marché uni aux conditions d'hygiène et de bien-être', *Exposition Universelle de 1867, rapports du jury international*, (13 vols., Paris, Imprimerie Administrative de Paul Dumont, 1868), vol. XIII, pp. 910–14; Cacheux, *L'économiste pratique*, plate 4.

28 E. Dolléans and G. Dehove give estimates of the average daily wage for workers in industry in 1871 as 2.9 fr. in the provinces, and 4.98 fr. in Paris; see their *Histoire du travail en France* (2 vols., Paris, Domat Montchrestien, 1953, 1955), vol. 1, pp. 289–90.

29 Cacheux, *L'économiste pratique*, p. 59.

30 Ibid., p. 11.

31 Ibid., p. 83.

32 This, and the preceding quotation, from the statutes of the Société Anonyme des Habitations Ouvrières de Passy Auteuil, reprinted in ibid., p. 93.

33 From the statutes of the Société, in ibid., p. 93.

34 Lucas, *Etude sur les habitations à bon marché*, p. 173.

35 For details of the Société de Passy Auteuil, see Cacheux, *L'économiste pratique*, pp. 83–4, 93–107; Raffalovich, *Logement*, pp. 310–11; Lucas, *Etude sur les habitations à bon marché*, pp. 168–76; *BSFHBM*, 4 (1893), pp. 240–79 includes contractual documents relating to the sale of the houses, and a note by E. Cheysson on the history of the society and its financial position in 1892. See also coverage of the founding and early work of the society in *La Réforme Sociale*, and *L'Economiste Français*; notably, for a report on the competition held for the design of the houses, *L'Economiste Français*, X, 2 (1882), pp. 521–2.

36 Quoted in Lucas, *Etude sur les habitations à bon marché*, p. 176.

37 Lavollée had earlier discussed the work of the Compagnie Immobilière de Lille.

38 Lavollée, *Bulletin de la Société d'Encouragement pour l'Industrie Nationale*, 3rd series, IX (1882), pp. 492–3.

39 J. S. C. Huish, 'Speculators of the Second Empire', University of Kent (unpublished thesis, 1973), pp. 173–5; Détain, *RGA*, XXIV (1866), cols. 225–6.

40 Détain, *RGA*, XXIV (1866), cols. 226–8.
41 G. Picot, *Un devoir social, et logements d'ouvriers* (Paris, Calmann-Levy, 1885); Picot, *BSFHBM*, 2 (1891), p. 404; Raffalovich, *Logement*, pp. 347–50; Lucas, *Etude sur les habitations à bon marché*, pp. 103–10; *La Réforme Sociale*, X (1885), pp. 556–7.
42 Quoted in Lucas, *Etude sur les habitations à bon marché*, p. 57.
43 Picot, *BSFHBM*, 2 (1891), pp. 405–6; Lucas, *Etude sur les habitations à bon marché*, pp. 57–68; *BSFHBM*, 1 (1890), pp. 119–32 includes the society's housing commission report for the year 1889, and a technical note by the society's architect, W. Chabrol.
44 Lucas, *Etude sur les habitations à bon marché*, p. 58; Guerrand, *Origines*, p. 279.
45 Lucas, *Etude sur les habitations à bon marché*, pp. 92–102; *BSFHBM*, 1 (1890), pp. 204–23 includes the society's statutes, a description of its flats, and extracts from the society's report for 1889; *BSFHBM*, 3 (1892), pp. 337–75 includes extracts from the book by F. Mangini, *Les petits logements dans les grandes villes et plus particulièrement dans la ville de Lyon* (Lyons, A. Storck, 1891), giving details of the Lyons housing society.
46 Lucas, *Etude sur les habitations à bon marché*, pp. 110–16; *BSFHBM*, 10 (1899), p. 388. *BSFHBM*, 2 (1891), pp. 203–18 includes the report on the society's first year of activity, by its president, E. Rostand.
47 *BSFHBM*, 10 (1899), p. 507.
48 L. Flaus, 'Les fluctuations de la construction d'habitations urbaines', *Journal de la Société de Statistique de Paris*, LXXXX (1949), p. 187.
49 Picot, *BSFHBM*, 2 (1891), p. 308.
50 Picot, *BSFHBM*, 2 (1891), p. 406.

23 Housing and co-operation

1 Gaumont, *Histoire générale*, vol. 1, p. 477; for the general history of the co-operative movement, I have drawn on Gaumont's study throughout this chapter.
2 Détain, *RGA*, XXIV (1866), cols. 221–3; *RGA*, XXV (1867), cols. 226–31; *RGA*, XXVI (1868), cols. 110–13; Cacheux, *Etat des habitations ouvrières*, p.148; Raffalovich, *Logement*, pp. 306–7; Muller and Cacheux, *Habitations ouvrières*, plate 20.
3 Détain, *RGA*, XXVI (1868), col. 65.
4 Ibid., cols. 64–71.
5 Gaumont, *Histoire générale*, vol. 1, p. 539.
6 Ibid., pp. 565–6.
7 Cacheux, *Etat des habitations ouvrières*, pp. 147–8; Raffalovich, *Logement*, pp. 337–9; *BSFHBM*, 3 (1892), pp. 282–7 includes a note by E. Cacheux on the Union Foncière.
8 Picot, *BSFHBM*, 2 (1891), pp. 394–7.
9 Cacheux, *Etat des habitations ouvrières*, p. 147.
10 Gaumont, *Histoire générale*, vol. 2, pp. 568–70.
11 Raffalovich, *Logement*, p. 350.
12 Ibid., pp. 350–8.
13 Ibid., pp. 364–6.
14 Lucas, *Etude sur les habitations à bon marché*, p. 225; for details of the Oullins housing, see pp. 223–7.
15 Gaumont, *Histoire générale*, vol. 2, p. 574; E. Rostand, 'La coopération appliquée à la construction des habitations à bon marché', *BSFHBM*, 1 (1890), pp. 325–56.
16 Gaumont, *Histoire générale*, vol. 2, p. 579.

17 *BSFHBM*, 3 (1892), p. 13.
18 E. Cheysson, 'La Pierre du Foyer: société coopérative de construction à Marseilles', *BSFHBM*, 2 (1891), pp. 42–62, 428–74; *BSFHBM*, 4 (1893), pp. 158–78 includes the society's report on its first year of activity.
19 *BSFHBM*, 10 (1899), p. 397; *BSFHBM*, 16 (1906), p. 465.
20 Lucas, *Etude sur les habitations à bon marché*, p. 207.
21 Lucas, *Etude sur les habitations à bon marché*, pp. 206–11; *BSFHBM*, 10 (1899), pp. 390, 398. *BSFHBM*, 9 (1898), pp. 320–7 includes a note describing the aims and running of the society, and the society's report for 1897.
22 C. Gide, 'Economie sociale', *Exposition Universelle Internationale de 1900, rapports du jury international* (5 vols., Paris, Imprimerie Nationale, 1903), vol. V, p. 158.
23 Ibid., p. 155.
24 Ibid., p. 157.

24 The Société Française des Habitations à Bon Marché, and housing legislation

1 A. Fougerousse, 'La question des loyers; les diverses solutions proposées', *La Réforme Sociale*, IV (1882), pp. 166–71.
2 G. Picot, 'La question des logements ouvriers à Paris et à Londres', *BSES*, IX (1883–5), p. 527.
3 Shapiro, 'Working class housing', p. 210; A. Mangin, 'Les habitations ouvrières', *L'Economiste Français*, VIII, 2 (1880), pp. 627–9, 663–6.
4 Raffalovich, *Logement*, pp. 313–17; Shapiro, 'Working class housing', pp. 210–16; Guerrand, *Origins*, pp. 248–9.
5 Cacheux, *L'Economiste Français*, X, 1 (1882), pp. 416–17.
6 E. Cacheux, 'Les habitations ouvrières: réponse à M. Fougerousse', *La Réforme Sociale*, IV (1882), pp. 378–82.
7 Raffalovich, *Logement*, p. 309.
8 A. Mangin, 'La question des loyers', *L'Economiste Français*, X, 2 (1882), p. 289.
9 Leroy-Beaulieu, *L'Economiste Français*, X, 1 (1882), pp. 437–9, 469–71.
10 *Le Réforme Sociale*, 2nd series, VIII (1889), p. 5.
11 Conseil Municipal de Paris, *Rapports et Documents* (1883), No. 40, p. 7; Shapiro, 'Working class housing' pp. 218–47, discusses the various commissions and initiatives of the early 1880s.
12 Conseil Municipal de Paris, *Rapports et Documents* (1883), No. 8.
13 A. Fougerousse, 'Le projet du gouvernement pour la construction des petits logements', *La Réforme Sociale*, V (1883), pp. 401–7.
14 Conseil Municipal de Paris, *Procès-Verbaux*, 1 (1883), p. 562; 1 (1884), pp. 383–406.
15 Shapiro, 'Working class housing' pp. 228–31.
16 The history of this abortive attempt to lease public land was chronicled by A. Fougerousse, who took some satisfaction in the failure of proposals which he regarded as ill-advised. See his regular 'Chronique du mouvement social' in *La Réforme Sociale*, notably VII (1884), p. 347; IX (1885), pp. 368, 470–2; X (1885), p. 46.
17 Picot, *BSES*, IX (1883–5), p. 516.
18 Raffalovich, *Logement*, p. 288; Cheysson, *La question des habitations ouvrières*, pp. 34–42.
19 Rochard, *Revue des Deux Mondes*, LXXXVII (1888), pp. 418–19.
20 Picot, *BSFHBM*, 2 (1891), p. 426–7; for Picot's consideration of the role of the public authorities, see pp. 419–27.

21 Guerrand, *Origines*, p. 282; Brooke, *Le Play*, p. 128.
22 Raffalovich and Roulliet, *Bibliographie des habitations à bon marché*, pp. 3–4.
23 Guerrand, *Origines*, pp. 284–7; *BSFHBM*, 6 (1895), p. 541.
24 *BSFHBM*, 1 (1890), p. 34; this first issue of the Bulletin recorded the opening assembly of the new society, included the society's statutes, and gave a list of the founder members; it also gave details of the housing society founded by Siegfried, the Société Havraise des Cités Ouvrières.
25 *L'Economiste Français*, IX, 2 (1881), pp. 760–1; Guerrand, *Origines*, p. 284.
26 Lucas, *Etude sur les habitations à bon marché*, pp. 81–92, 178–80; *BSFHBM*, 2 (1891), pp. 85–108 gives an account of the founding meeting of the society, held at the Hotel Continental on 25 January 1891.
27 *Documents Parlementaires, Chambre des Députés* (1892), No. 1940, p. 539. For discussion of the passage of Siegfried's bill in parliament, see Guerrand, *Origines*, pp. 290–6.
28 Guerrand, *Origines*, p. 269.
29 *Documents Parlementaires, Chambre des Députés* (1892), No. 1940, p. 534. For the text of the law as finally passed, see Guerrand, *Origines*, pp. 319–24.
30 *BSFHBM*, 6 (1895), p. 410.
31 The major sources for this discussion of the achievement of the housing legislation are: the annual reports of the Conseil Supérieur des Habitations à Bon Marché, published in the *Journal Officiel de la République Française*, and also in the *BSFHBM*; the summary of the work of housing societies, assembled by A. Dubois, published in *BSFHBM*, 16 (1906), pp. 462–81; the summary table of investment by Caisses d'Epargne, published in *BSFHBM*, 16 (1906), pp. 285–6; parliamentary reports on proposals to revise the housing legislation, notably *Documents Parlementaires, Sénat* (1905), No. 81; (1912), No. 352 (report by Paul Strauss); and *Documents Parlementaires, Chambre des Députés* (1912), No. 1847 (report by L. Bonnevay).
32 *BSFHBM*, 16 (1905), p. 4.
33 Guerrand, *Origines*, p. 302.
34 The figures for the capital, and the investment in land and construction by the *sociétés anonymes* have been adjusted, to exclude from the figures in the Conseil Supérieur des HBM report the Groupe des Maisons Ouvrières, initially included as a *société anonyme*, but subsequently reformed as a foundation. The figure of 3,400 does not include houses whose cost had already been fully paid off by their occupants, nor those built by housing societies which had dissolved after completing a particular project. However, as the majority of the societies, founded under the 1894 law, were less than ten years old, the number of houses fully sold, and of projects completed, was still small, and would not have fundamentally affected these figures.
35 Gide, *Exposition Universelle*, vol. 5, p. 153.

25 The evolution of housing legislation 1

1 Guerrand, *Origines*, pp. 296–9; J. Challamel, 'Rapport...présenté au conseil supérieur des habitations à bon marché au nom du comité permanent', *BSFHBM*, 11 (1900), p. 20.
2 *Congrès International des Habitations à Bon Marché 1900* (Paris, Secrétariat de la Société Française des Habitations à Bon Marché, 1900), p. 297.
3 Guerrand, *Origines*, p. 301.
4 M. Dufourmantelle, report on question 5, 'Intervention des pouvoirs publics', p. 15, in *Congrès International d'Hygiène et de Démographie 1903* (9 vols., Brussels, P. Weissenbruch, 1903), vol. VII.
5 E. Rostand, 'Le mouvement d'amélioration des habitations populaires en

France. Etat de la question et quelques moyens d'avancer', *BSFHBM*, 11 (1900), p. 60.

6 Rostand, *BSFHBM*, 11 (1900), p. 66.
7 Picot, *BSES*, IX (1883–5), p. 527.
8 *Congrès International des Habitations à Bon Marché 1897* (Brussels, Hayez, Imprimeur de l'Académie Royale de Belgique, 1897), p. 424. The degree of intervention envisaged by du Mesnil was still only relative: his model was the legislation in Belgium, giving assistance to private societies, rather than the direct intervention of the English law of 1890.
9 *L'Economiste Français*, XXXII, 1 (1904), p. 244.
10 Conseil Municipal de Paris, *Rapports et Documents* (1903), No. 31; Conseil Municipal de Paris, *Procès-Verbaux*, 2 (1903), pp. 240–1.
11 Conseil Municipal de Paris, *Procès-Verbaux*, 1 (1904), pp. 1160–1.
12 Conseil Municipal de Paris, *Procès-Verbaux*, 2 (1903), p. 1928; Conseil Municipal de Paris, *Rapports et Documents* (1904), No. 71; Conseil Municipal de Paris, *Procès-Verbaux*, 2 (1904), pp. 612–15.
13 Conseil Municipal de Paris, *Procès-Verbaux*, 2 (1903), p. 1181.
14 Conseil Municipal de Paris, *Procès-Verbaux*, 2 (1904), p. 929.
15 Conseil Municipal de Paris, *Rapports et Documents* (1904), No. 127; Conseil Municipal de Paris, *Procès-Verbaux*, 2 (1904), pp. 1583–97.
16 Conseil Municipal de Paris, *Procès-Verbaux*, 2 (1904), p. 1144.
17 Conseil Municipal de Paris, *Rapports et Documents* (1905), No. 8.
18 Conseil Municipal de Paris, *Procès-Verbaux*, 1 (1905), p. 809.
19 Conseil Municipal de Paris, *Procès-Verbaux*, 2 (1905), p. 579.
20 *L'Economiste Français*, XXXIII, 1 (1905), pp. 911–12.
21 Among the other members of the Comité in the early 1900s were Emile Cacheux, Charles Lucas and Ambroise Rendu. As part of the campaign for the amendment of the 1894 housing law, the Comité organised a housing exhibition in Paris during 1904.
22 Alexandre Millerand, the Minister of Commerce, responsible for housing legislation when Strauss initially sent his letter in 1901, was the first socialist to sit in a French government; by 1903, however, when the issues raised by Strauss were taken up, Millerand was no longer Minister of Commerce.
23 *Documents Parlementaires*, Sénat (1905), No. 81, p. 331.
24 *Documents Parlementaires*, Sénat (1904), No. 80, p. 164.
25 *Documents Parlementaires*, Sénat (1906), No. 3, p. 1.
26 *Documents Parlementaires*, Chambre des Députés (1906), No. 439, p. 135.
27 Ibid.
28 Picot, *BSFHBM*, 2 (1891), p. 288.
29 Dr J. Rochard (ed.), *Encyclopédie d'hygiène et de médecine publique* (8 vols, 1890–5); Ministère de l'Instruction Publique, des Beaux Arts et des Cultes, Comité des Travaux Historiques et Scientifiques, *Enquête sur les conditions de l'habitation en France, les maisons-types*, introduction by A. de Foville (2 vols, Paris, Ernest Leroux, Editeur, 1894, 1899); Dr Baudran, 'Les petits logements dans les campagnes. Moyens pratiques de les améliorer', *Congreso Internacional de Higiene y Demografia 1898* (14 vols., Madrid, Ricardo Rojas, 1900), vol. 4, pp. 150–8; M. Pucey, 'Règles générales d'hygiène à observer dans la distribution, l'aération permanente et la décoration intérieure des maisons d'habitation', *Congrès International d'Hygiène et de Démographie 1900*, pp. 305–20.
30 *BSES*, V (1875–7), pp. 472–515; Dr J. Bertillon, *Le problème de la dépopulation* (Paris, A. Colin, 1897); in this booklet, Bertillon set out the programme of the recently founded Alliance Nationale pour l'Acroissement de la Population Française.

31 *Documents Parlementaires*, Chambre des Députés (1906), p. 135.

32 *BSFHBM*, 16 (1906), p. 472.

33 In the case of a co-operative housing society, the individual was effectively owner of his house as a member of the co-operative; but the deeds of the house remained with the co-operative until the member had paid in capital equivalent to the value of the house.

34 The option of life insurance under the 1894 law had in fact been little used.

35 In descending order of investment these ten were in Lyons, Marseilles, Paris, Compiègne, Chartres, Saint Etienne, Rouen, Bordeaux, Briey and Meaux. The major sources for this discussion of the achievement of legislation after 1906 are: the annual reports of the Conseil Supérieur des Habitations à Bon Marché; parliamentary reports on proposals to revise the housing legislation, notably *Documents Parlementaires*, *Sénat* (1912), No. 352, and *Documents Parlementaires*, *Chambre des Députés* (1912), No. 1847.

36 The cost of construction of a terraced house with land, in the early 1900s was typically between 4,000 M and 5,000 M in Germany; in France it was in the order of 5,000–6,000 fr. The German total thus represents a considerably higher investment.

37 Like several of the leading housing reformers, Risler had been born in Alsace while it was part of France; the fact that Alsace was part of Germany when Risler spoke in 1911, as when his fellow Alsatian Jules Siegfried made his patriotic call in presenting his housing bill in 1892, adds particular force to their appeal to national sentiment.

38 G. Risler, 'Rapport...presenté au conseil supérieur des habitations à bon marché au nom du comité permanent', *BSFHBM*, 21 (1911), p. 183.

26   The evolution of housing legislation 2

1 J. M. Flonneau, 'Crise de vie chère et mouvement syndical (1910–1914)', *Le Mouvement Social*, No. 72 (1970), pp. 49–81.

2 *Débats Parlementaires*, Chambre des Députés (1911), pp. 2810, 2838.

3 *Débats Parlementaires*, Sénat (1912), p. 1458.

4 In 1890 vacant dwellings constituted 4.6% of the housing stock; in 1911 they formed only 1%. Of the dwellings vacant in 1900, 60% had rents of 500 fr. or less; in 1913 only 24% did. See Cahen, *Logement dans les villes*, p. 190.

5 Ibid., p. 13.

6 F. Fourcade, 'Des diverses solutions pouvant être envisagées pour l'amélioration du logement ouvrier et plus spécialement du logement des familles nombreuses, à Paris', *BSFHBM*, 21 (1911), p. 397.

7 G. Risler, 'Rapport...presenté au conseil supérieur des habitations à bon marché au nom du comité permanent', *BSFHBM*, 22 (1913), p. 293.

8 *Débats Parlementaires*, Chambre des Députés (1911), p. 2810; (1912), pp. 435–6.

9 *Documents Parlementaires*, Chambre des Députés (1912), No. 1847, pp. 793, 804.

10 Conseil Municipal de Paris, *Procès Verbaux*, 1 (1907), pp. 1700–16; Conseil Municipal de Paris, *Procès Verbaux*, 1 (1908), pp. 926–32.

11 *Documents Parlementaires*, Chambre des Députés (1912), No. 2145, p. 1601; Sutcliffe, *Autumn*, pp. 111–14.

12 Conseil Municipal de Paris, *Rapports et Documents* (1911), No. 39 and No. 76; Conseil Municipal de Paris, *Procès Verbaux*, 1 (1911), pp. 1642–53.

13 G. Risler, 'Rapport...presenté au conseil supérieur des habitations à bon marché au nom du comité permanent', *BSFHBM*, 22 (1912), p. 286.

14 M. Dufourmantelle, 'Le IXe congrès international des habitations à bon marché', *BSFHBM*, 21 (1911), p. 319.

15 Fourcade, *BSFHBM*, 21 (1911), pp. 395–405.
16 G. Risler, 'Note presentée au nom de la Société Française des habitations à bon marché à la Commission des habitations à bon marché du Conseil Municipal de Paris', *BSFHBM*, 22 (1912), pp. 208–17.
17 *BSFHBM*, 22 (1912), p. 16.
18 *Documents Parlementaires, Chambre des Députés* (1912), No. 1847, pp. 786–9.
19 *Débats Parlementaires, Chambre des Députés* (1912), p. 112.
20 Ibid., p. 231.
21 Ibid., pp. 433–47.
22 Ibid., p. 434.
23 Ibid., p. 440.
24 Ibid., p. 444.
25 For the passage of the 1912 law, see the reports presented by Bonnevay in the Chambre des Députés, and by Strauss in the Sénat: *Documents Parlementaires, Chambre des Députés* (1912), No. 1847; *Documents Parlementaires, Sénat* (1912), No. 352; and the debates in the two chambers: *Débats Parlementaires, Chambre des Députés* (1912), p. 1999, 2259–74; *Débats Parlementaires, Sénat* (1912), pp. 1457–71, 1485–91.
26 *Documents Parlementaires, Chambres des Députés* (1912), No. 1847, p. 804.
27 Ibid., p. 793.
28 Ibid., p. 805.
29 Ibid., p. 805.
30 Ibid., p. 808.
31 *Débats Parlementaires, Chambre des Députés* (1912), p. 2268.
32 Large families were defined as those with at least three children under the age of sixteen.
33 *Documents Parlementaires, Chambre des Députés* (1912), No. 1847, p. 810.
34 *Débats Parlementaires, Sénat* (1912), pp. 1460, 1465.
35 Conseil Municipal de Paris, *Rapports et Documents* (1912), No. 31.
36 For the passage of the 1912 Paris law, see *Documents Parlementaires, Chambre des Députés* (1912), No. 2145; *Débats Parlementaires, Chambre des Députés* (1912), pp. 2251–6; *Débats Parlementaires, Sénat* (1912), pp. 1304–5.
37 Bastié, *La croissance de la banlieue parisienne*, pp. 264–77; for a general discussion of the growth of the *lotissements*, see pp. 227–340, Evenson, *Paris: A Century of Change*, pp. 226–31.
38 A. Gabillon and L. Boutillon, *Les cités-jardins au point de vue social. La cité-jardin du Petit-Groslay, près la nouvelle gare de Blanc-Mesnil* (Paris, 94 Boulevard Sebastopol, 1912), p. 11.
39 Bastié, *La croissance de la banlieue parisienne*, p. 301.

Conclusion: From Workers' Housing to Social Housing

1 Rostand, *BSFHBM*, 11 (1900), p. 66; Sellier, *La crise de l'habitation*, p. 183.

Bibliography

PART ONE: GERMANY

Official Publications

Reich and state
Statistisches Jahrbuch des deutschen Reiches, Berlin, 1873ff.
Statistisches Jahrbuch deutscher Städte, Berlin, 1891ff.
Stenographische Berichte über die Verhandlungen des deutschen Reichstages, Berlin, 1890ff.
Stenographische Berichte über die Verhandlungen beider Häuser des (preussichen) *Landtags: Haus der Abgeordneten*, Berlin, 1890ff.

Berlin
Statistisches Jahrbuch der Stadt Berlin (Stat. J. Berlin), Berlin, 1873ff.
Die Berliner Volkszählung vom 3 December 1861, Berlin, 1863
Die Resultate der Berliner Volkszählung vom 3 December 1864, Berlin, 1866
Die Resultate der Berliner Volkszählung vom 3 December 1867, Berlin, 1869
Die Bevölkerungs-, Gewerbe- und Wohnungs-Aufnahme vom 1 December 1875 in der Stadt Berlin, vols. 1–4, Berlin, 1875–80
Die Bevölkerungs-, Gewerbe- und Wohnungs-Aufnahme vom 1 December 1900 in der Stadt Berlin und 23 benachbarten Gemeinden, Berlin, vols. 1–2, 1901–2
Die Bevölkerungs-, Gewerbe- und Wohnungs-Aufnahme vom 1 December 1900 in der Stadt Berlin, Berlin, vols. 1–2, 1903
Die Grundstücks-Aufnahme vom Ende Oktober 1905, sowie die Wohnungs- und die Bevölkerungs-Aufnahme vom 1 December 1905 in der Stadt Berlin und 29 benachbarten Gemeinden, vols. 1–2, Berlin, 1910
Die Grundstücks-Aufnahme vom 15 Oktober 1910, sowie die Wohnungs- und die Bevölkerungs-Aufnahme vom 1 December 1910 in der Stadt Berlin und 44 Nachbargemeinden, Berlin, 1913

Periodicals

Architectural Review, London, 1896–
Archiv für Frankfurts Geschichte und Kunst, Frankfurt-am-Main (5th Series), 1948–
Archiv für Sozialgeschichte, Hanover, 1961–
Arbeiterwohl, Organ des Verbandes katholischer Industrielle und Arbeiterfreunde, Cologne, 1880–1914.
Concordia, Blätter der Berliner gemeinnützigen Baugesellschaft, Berlin, 1848–50
Concordia, Beiträge zur Lösung der socialen Fragen, Leipzig, 1860–1
Deutsch Land, Berlin, 1887–9
Deutsche Bauzeitung (DBZ), Berlin, 1867–1940.

591

Deutsche Konkurrenzen, eine Sammlung interessanter Entwürfe aus den Wettbewerben deutscher Architekten, Leipzig, 1891–1919.

Deutsche Rundschau, Berlin, 1874–

Deutsche Vierteljahrschrift für öffentliche Gesundheitspflege (VföG), Braunschweig, 1869–1914.

Jahrbuch der Bodenreform, Berlin, 1909–42.

Jahrbuch für Gesetzgebung, Verwaltung und Volkswirtschaft im deutschen Reich (Schmoller's Jahrbuch), Leipzig, 1877–

Janus, Jahrbücher deutscher Gesinnung, Bildung und Tat, Berlin, 1845–6

Mittheilungen des Centralvereins für das Wohl der arbeitenden Klassen, Berlin, first series 1849–55 (new series 1855–9), continued as *Zeitschrift des Central-Vereins in Preussen für das Wohl der arbeitenden Klassen*, Leipzig, 1859–6 and finally as *Der Arbeiterfreund, Zeitschrift für die Arbeiterfrage*, Berlin, 1863–1914

Preussische Jahrbücher, Berlin, 1858–1935.

Schriften der Centralstelle für Arbeiterwohlfahrtseinrichtungen (SCAW), Berlin, 1892–1914.

Schriften des deutschen Vereins für Armenpflege und Wohltätigkeit (SDVfAW), Munich and Leipzig, 1886–1914.

Schriften des Vereins für Sozialpolitik, Munich and Leipzig, 1873–

Der Städtebau, Monatsschrift für die künstlerische Ausgestaltung der Städte nach ihren wirtschaftlichen, gesundheitlichen und sozialen Grundsätzen, Berlin, 1904–29.

Sudhoffs, Archiv für Geschichte der Medizin und der Naturwissenschaften, Leipzig and Wiesbaden, 1929–

Vierteljahrschrift für gerechtliche Medizin und öffentliche Sanitätswesen, Berlin, 1844–1921.

Vierteljahrschrift für Sozial- und Wirtschaftsgeschichte, Leipzig, 1903–

Die Vierteljahrschrift für Volkswirtschaft und Kulturgeschichte (VfVK). Berlin, 1863–93.

Zeitschrift für Bauwesen, Berlin, 1851–1931.

Zeitschrift für Biologie, Munich, 1865–

Zeitschrift für Wohnungswesen (ZfW), Berlin, 1902–1940.

Zentralblat der Bauverwaltung, Berlin, 1880–1944.

Books and articles

Ackerknecht, E. *Rudolf Virchow: Doctor, Statesman, Anthropologist* (Madison, 1953)

Adickes, F., 'Die unterschiedliche Behandlung der Bauordnungen für die Innere, die Aussengebiete und die Umgebung von Städten', *VföG* 26 (1894), pp. 13–47

'Die Notwendigkeit weiträumiger Bebauung bei Stadterweiterungen und die Rechtlinien und technischen Mittel zu ihrer Ausführung', *VföG* 27 (1895), pp. 101–30

'Förderung des Baues kleiner Wohnungen durch die private Tätigkeit', in *Neue Untersuchungen*, vol. 2, pp. 275–302

Die sozialen Aufgaben der deutschen Städten (Leipzig, 1903)

Albers, G., *Entwicklungslinien im Städtebau: Ideen, Thesen, Aussagen 1875–1945, Texte und Interpretationen* (Düsseldorf, 1975)

Albrecht, G., 'Das Bremer Haus, ein Sonderfall in der deutschen Baugeschichte um 1850', in Niethammer, *Wohnen im Wandel*, pp. 233–51

Albrecht, H., 'Wohnungen für die Armen', *Deutsche Rundschau*, 65 (1890), pp. 265–78, 368–84

Die Wohnungsnot in den Grossstädten und die Mittel zu ihrer Abhülfe (Munich, 1891)

'Die Mitwirkung der Arbeitnehmer bei der Lösung der Wohnungsfrage', in *Die Verbesserung der Wohnungen*, pp. 29–52

'Bericht über die Ausstellung von Plänen von Arbeiterwohnungen', in *Die Verbesserung der Wohnungen*, pp. 191–2

Das Arbeiterwohnhaus (Berlin, 1896)

Fünf Jahre praktisch-sozialer Tätigkeit, aus der Versuchsstation der Centralstelle der Arbeiter-Wohlfahrtseinrichtungen, published as vol. 14 of the *Schriften der Centralstelle der Arbeiter-Wohlfahrtseinrichtungen* (SCAW) (Berlin, 1898)

'Bau von kleinen Wohnungen durch Arbeitgeber, Stiftungen, gemeinnützige Baugesellschaften und Vereine, Baugenossenschaften und in eigner Regie der Gemeinden', in *Neue Untersuchungen*, vol. 2, pt 1, pp. 1–88

'Die gemeinnützige Produktion', in *Wohnungs-und Siedlungsfrage*, pp. 278–96

Altenrath, J., 'Der preussische Wohnungsgesetzentwurf', *ZfW*, 11 (1912/13), pp. 137–48

'Der preussische Wohnungsgesetzentwurf nach den Komissionsbeschlüssen zweiter Lesung', *ZfW*, 12 (1913/14), pp. 335–9

'Die Reichs-Enquete über den sadtischen Immobilarkredit', *ZfW*, 12 (1913/14), pp. 121–8

Arnim, B. von, *Dies Buch gehört dem König* (Berlin, 1843)

Ascher, S., *Die Wohnungsmieten in Berlin von 1880–1910* (Bodenpolitische Zeitfragen, Heft 7) (Berlin, 1914)

Ascher, Dr, 'Über die gesundheitlichen Nachteile des Bewohnens feuchter Wohnungen und deren Verhütung von sanitätspolizeilichen Standpunkte', *VföG*, 25 (1893), pp. 178–205

Aschrott, P. F., 'Einrichtung und Verwaltung grosser Arbeiter-Mietshäuser in Berlin', *Schriften des deutschen Vereins für Armenpflege und Wohltätigkeit*, 11 (1890), pp. 5–27

'Die Arbeiterwohnungsfrage in England', in *Die Wohnungsnoth*, pp. 93–146

25 Jahre gemeinnützige Tätigkeit für Kleinwohnungen, Festschrift zum 25 jährigen Bestehen des Vereins zur Verbesserung der kleinen Wohnungen in Berlin (Berlin, 1913)

Banfield, T. C., *Industry of the Rhine*, vols. 1 and 2 (London, 1846–8)

Bangert, W., *Baupolitik und Stadtgestaltung in Frankfurt am Main: ein Beitrag zur Entwicklungsgeschichte des deutschen Städtebaues in den letzten 100 Jahren* (Würzburg, 1930)

Baumeister, R., 'Thesen über Stadterweiterungen', *DBZ*, 8 (1874), p. 265 and pp. 337–9

Stadt-Erweiterungen in technischer, baupolizeilicher und wirtschaftlicher Beziehung (Berlin, 1876)

Normale Bauordnung, nebst Erläuterungen (Wiesbaden, 1880)

'Die neue Berliner Baupolizeiordnung', *VföG*, 19 (1887), pp. 600–

'Bericht über die aus deutschen Städten eingegangen Mittheilungen, betr. Neuerungen auf dem Gebiete der Baupolizei', *VföG*, 28 (1896), pp. 9–12

Baumert, *Zum preussischen Wohnungsgesetzentwurf* (Berlin, 1905)

Beck, O., 'Förderung der gemeinnützigen Bautätigkeit durch die Gemeinden' in *Neue Untersuchungen*, vol. 2, pp. 172–272

Becker, F. W., MP, *Letters on the Cholera in Prussia* (London, 1832)

Berger-Thimme, D., *Wohnungsfrage und Sozialstaat* (Frankfurt am Main, 1976)

'Bericht über den ersten Verhandlungstag', *Verbesserung der Wohnungen*, pp. 159–60

Berlin und seine Bauten, published by the Architekten-Verein zu Berlin (1st edn, Berlin, 1877), vols. 1–2

Berlin und seine Bauten, published by the Architekten-Verein zu Berlin and the Vereinigung Berliner Architekten (2nd edn, Berlin, 1896) vols. 1–2

Berlin und seine Bauten, published by the Architekten-und Ingenieur-Verein zu Berlin (3rd edn):

Part II, E. Heinrich and F. Mielke (eds.), *Rechtsgrundlagen und Stadtentwicklung* (Berlin and Munich, 1964)

Part IV, vol. A. E. Heinrich and K. K. Weber (eds.), *Die Voraussetzungen. Die Entwicklung der Wohngebiete* (Berlin, Munich, Düsseldorf, 1970)
vol. B D. Rentscher and W. Schirmer (eds.), *Die Wohngebäude – Mehrfamilienhäuser* (Berlin, Munich, Düsseldorf, 1974)

Part X, vol. B. K. K. Weber, P. Güttler and D. Ahmadi (eds.), *Anlagen und Bauten für den Verkehr (1) Städtischer Nahverkehr* (Berlin, Munich, 1979)

Berthold, G., 'Die Wohnverhältnisse in Berlin, insbesondere die der ärmeren Klassen', in *Die Wohnungsnoth*, vol. 2, pp. 199–235

Bodelschwingh, F. F. L. von, 'Die Wohnungsverhältnisse der ärmeren Klassen in deutschen Grossstädten', in *Verhandlungen* (1886), pp. 61–76

Boese, F., *Geschichte des Vereins für Sozialpolitik, 1872–1932*, published as vol. 88 of the *Schriften des Vereins für Sozialpolitik* (Berlin, 1939)

Böhmert, V., 'Die sociale Frage im Reichstage und vor dem Reichskanzler', *Arbeiterfreund*, 14 (1876), pp. 1–15
'Materielle und ideale Lösung der socialen Frage', *Arbeiterfreund*, 24 (1886), pp. 20–8

Boldt, W., 'Das Interesse als Grundlage der Besteuerung', in *Einzelfragen der Finanzpolitik*, vol. 2, pt 1, pp. 85–138

Bollerey, F. and Hartmann, K., *Wohnen im Revier, 99 Beispiele aus Dortmund* (Dortmunder Architekturhefte No. 1) (Munich, 1975)

Born, K. E., *Staat und Sozialpolitik seit Bismarcks Sturz* (Wiesbaden, 1957)
'Sozialpolitische Probleme und Bestrebungen von 1848 bis zur Bismarckschen Sozialgesetzgebung' *Vierteljahrschrift für Sozial- und Wirtschaftgeschichte*. 46 (1959), pp. 29–44

Brakelmann, G., *Kirche, soziale Frage und Sozialismus* (Gütersloh, 1977)

Brämer, K., 'Die nützlichen Baugenossenschaften in England', *Arbeiterfreund*, 3 (1865), pp. 233–61
'Die Eisenacher Konferenz über die soziale Frage', *Arbeiterfreund*, 10 (1872), pp. 178–210

Brandts, F., 'Die Wohnungsfrage', *Arbeiterwohl*, 8 (1888): nos 11 and 12, pp. 233–42

Brandts, M., 'Aufgaben und Organisation der Wohnungsfürsorge insbesondere in den Städten', *Arbeiterwohl*, 16 (1896), pp. 272–7
'Beschaffung der Geldmittel für die gemeinnützige Bauthätigkeit' in *Neue Untersuchungen*, vol. 2, pp. 89–178
'Einige Bemerkungen zu den Entwurf des Gesetzes zur Verbesserung der Wohnverhältnisse', *ZfW*, 2 (1903/4), pp. 297–308

Braun, L., *Frauenarbeit und Hauswirtschaft* (Berlin, 1901)

Brinckmann, A. E. and Rath, B., *Die Margareten-Höhe bei Essen* (Darmstadt, 1913)

Bruch, E., *Berlins bauliche Zukunft und Bebauungsplan* (Berlin, 1870)

Brüggemeier, L. Niethammer, 'Schlafgänger, Schnappskasinos und schwerindustrielle Kolonie. Aspekte der Arbeiterwohnungsfrage im Ruhrgebiet vor dem ersten Weltkrieg', in J. Reulecke, W. Weber (eds.), *Fabrik, Familie, Feierabend, Beiträge zur Sozialgeschichte des Alltags im Industriezeitalter* (Wuppertal, 1978), pp. 153–74

Bullock, N., 'Housing in Frankfurt and the "neue Wohnkultur", 1925–1931', *Architectural Review*, 163 (1978), pp. 333–42

Busch, O. (ed.), *Untersuchungen zur Geschichte der früheren Industrialisierung vornehmlich im Wirtschaftsraum Berlin/Brandenburg* (published as vol. 6 of

Einzelveröffentlichungen der Historischen Kommission zu Berlin) (Berlin, 1971)

Cahn, E., *Die gemeinnützige Bautätigkeit in Frankfurt am Main* (Frankfurt, 1915)

Clapham, J. H., *The Economic Development of France and Germany 1815–1914*, 4th edn (Cambridge, 1968)

Cleary, E. J., *The Building Society Movement* (London, 1965)

Cohn, L., in *Die Wohnungsfrage und die Sozialdemokratie, ein Kapital sozialdemokratischer Gemeindepolitik* (Munich, 1900)

Collins, G. R. and C. C., *Camillo Sitte and the Birth of Modern City Planning* (London, 1965)

Crüger, H., *Einführung in das deutsche Genossenschaftswesen* (Berlin, 1907)

Damaschke, A., *Bodenreform, Grundsätzliches und Geschichtliches* (Jena, 1902)
  Die Aufgaben der Gemeindepolitik (Jena, 1902)
  Zur Geschichte der deutschen Bodenreformbewegung (Berlin, 1906), p. 20

'Danzig, seine Canalisation mit Rieselfeldern', *VföG*, 6 (1874), pp. 493–8

Dawson, W. H., *Social Insurance in Germany, 1883–1911* (London, 1912)
  Municipal Life and Government in Germany (London, 1912)

Desai, A. V., *Real Wages in Germany 1871–1913* (Oxford, 1968)

Dewsnup, E., *The Housing Problem in England, its Statistics, Legislation and Policy* (Manchester, 1907)

30 Jahre Wohnungsreform 1898–1928: Denkschrift aus Anlass des dreissigjährigen Bestehens herausgegeben vom Deutschen Verein für Wohnungsreform EV (Berlin, 1928)

Durm, J. et al. (eds.), *Handbuch der Architektur*, vols. 1–29 (Darmstadt, 1880–1906)

Eberstadt, R., *Städtische Bodenfragen* (Berlin, 1894)
  Der deutsche Kapitalmarkt (Leipzig, 1901)
  Rhenische Wohnverhältnisse und ihre Bedeutung für das Wohnungswesen in Deutschland (Jena, 1903)
  Handbuch des Wohnungswesens und der Wohnungsfrage, (1st edn, Jena, 1909) 2nd edn (Jena, 1910)

Ehmer, J., 'Wohnen ohne eigene Wohnung', in L. Niethammer (ed.), *Wohnen im Wandel, Beiträge zur Geschichte des Alltags in der bürgerlichen Gesellschaft* (Wuppertal, 1979), pp. 132–50

Einzelfragen der Finanzpolitik der Gemeinden (vol. 2 of *Gemeindefinanzen*, published as vol. 127 of the *Schriften des Vereins für Sozialpolitik*) (Leipzig, 1910)

Elvers, R., *Victor Aimé Huber, sein Werden und Wirken* (Bremen, 1874)

Emmich, W., 'Mittheilungen über Zwecke, Mittel und Wirksamkeit der Berliner gemeinnützige Baugesellschaft', in *Mittheilung des CVWaK*, Issue 7 (1850), pp. 38–45
  'Betrachtungen über Ursache und Abhülfe des Mangels an kleinen und mittleren Wohnungen in Berlin, nebst Ermittelungen über die Anlagekosten und die Erträge-Verhältnisse von Grundstücken verschiedenen Anfange, mit bürgerlicher Einrichtung', *Mittheilungen des CVWaK*, vol. 1 (neue Folge) (1855), pp. 249–57
  'Betrachtungen über den Stand des Unternehmens der gemeinnützigen Baugesellschaft und über neuere Vorschläge zur Abhülfe der Wohnungsnorth in Berlin', in *Mittheilungen des CVWaK* vol. 2 (neue Folge) (1859), pp. 195–201
  'Vergleichende Bermerkungen über die Bestrebungen zur Verbesserung der Wohnungsverhältnisse der arbeitenden Klassen in verschiedenen Ländern, namentlich England', in *Mittheilungen des CVWaK*, vol. 2 (neue Folge) (1859), pp. 145–9

Ende and Boeckmann, 'Über den Einfluss der Baupolizeivorschriften auf das Entstehen von Arbeiterwohnungen und deren gesunde und angemessene Gestaltung', *Arbeiterfreund* 3 (1865), pp. 210–19

Engel, E., *Die moderne Wohnungsnoth: Signatur, Ursachen und Abhülfe* (Leipzig, 1873)

Engels, F., *Zur Wohnungsfrage* (1872), translated by C. P. Dutt as *The Housing Question* (London, n.d.)

Die Entwicklung des Arbeiterwohnungswesens auf der Gussstahlfabrik von Friedrich Krupp zu Essen a.d. Ruhr (Düsseldorf, 1902)

Faucher, J., *Die Vereinigung von Sparkasse und Hypothekenbank und der Anschluss eines Häuserbauvereins also sozialökonomische Aufgabe unserer Zeit* (Berlin, 1845)

'Die Bewegung für Wohnungsreform', *VfVK*, 4 (1865), pp. 127–99; 5 (1866), pp. 86–151

'Über Häuserbaunternehmungen', *VfVK*, 2 (1869), pp. 48–74

Faust, H., *Geschichte der Genossenschaftsbewegung, Ursprung und Weg der Genossenschaften in deutschen Sprachraum* (Frankfurt am Main, 1977)

Fischer, A., *Geschichte des Deutschen Gesundheitswesens* (Hildesheim, 1965)

Flesch, K., 'Die Wohnungsfrage vom Standpunkt der Armenpflege', *Schriften des deutschen Vereins für Armenpflege und Wohltätigkeit*, vol. 6 (1888), pp. 212–64

Flesch, K. and Birndorfer, 'Das Mietrecht in Deutschland', in *Neue Untersuchungen*, vol. 1, pt 2, pp. 271–333

Flinn, M. W., Introduction to *The Medical and Legal Aspects of Sanitary Reform*, new edn (Leicester, 1969)

Flürscheim, M., *Auf friedlichem Weg* (Braunschweig, 1884)

Der einzige Rettungsweg (Dresden and Leipzig, 1890)

Fodor, J. von, *Das gesunde Haus und die gesunde Wohnung* (Braunschweig, 1878)

Freese, H. *Die Bodenreform, ihre Vergangenheit und ihre Zukunft* (Berlin, 1918)

Frick, D., 'Einfluss der Baugesetze und Bauordnungen auf das Stadtbild' in *Berlin und seine Bauten*, pt 4, vol. A, pp. 41–57

Fuchs, C. J. (ed.), *Die Wohnungs- und Seidlungsfrage nach dem Kriege* (Stuttgart, 1917)

Führer durch die Essener Wohnungssiedlungen der Firma Krupp (Essen, 1930)

25 Jahre gemeinnützigen Wohnungsbaus, Jubilaumsbericht der ABG, 1890 bis 1915 (Frankfurt am Main, 1915)

Gaebler, E., *Idee und Bedeutung der Berliner gemeinnützigen Baugesellschaft* (Berlin, 1848)

Gatliff, C., *Practical Suggestions on Improved Dwellings for the Industrious Classes* (London, 1854)

Gauldie, E., *Cruel Habitations, a History of Working-Class Housing 1780–1918* (London, 1974)

Geist, J. F. and Kürvers, K., *Das Berliner Mietshaus 1740–1862* (Munich, 1980)

Gemeindebetriebe, published as vols. 128 and 129 of the *Schriften des Vereins für Sozialpolitik* (Leipzig, 1906)

Gemeindefinanzen, published as vols. 126 and 127 of the *Schriften des Vereins für Sozialpolitik* (Leipzig, 1910)

George, H., *Progress and Poverty* (New York, 1879), translated as *Armut und Fortschritt* by C. D. F. Gutschou (Berlin, 1881)

Geschichte der gemeinnützigen Wohnungswirtschaft in Berlin (Berlin, 1957)

Goecke, T., 'Das Berliner Arbeiter-Mietshaus, eine bautechnisch-soziale Studie', *DBZ*, 24 (1890), pp. 501–2; 508–10; 522–3

'Verkehrsstrasse und Wohnstrasse', *Preussische Jahrbücher* 73 (1893), pp. 85–104

Göhre, P. (trans. A. D. Carr), *Three Months in a Workshop: a Practical Study* (London, 1895)

Goldthammer, Dr, 'Über die Kost- und Logirhäuser für die ärmeren Volksklassen', *Vierteljahrschrift für gerechtliche Medizin und öffentliche Sanitätswesen* (neue Folge), 28 (1878), pp. 296–333

Goltz, H. v., *Die Wohnungsinspektion und ihre Ausgestaltung durch das Reich* (Göttingen, 1900) (vol. 1 of the publications of the Deutscher Verein für Wohnungsreform)

Grävell, A., *Die Baugenossenschaftsfrage. Ein Bericht über die Ausbreitung der gemeinnützigen Bautätigkeit durch Baugenossenschaften, Aktienbaugesellschaft, Bauvereine, usw. in Deutschland während der letzten 12 Jahren* (Berlin, 1901)

Gretzschel, G., 'Wohnungsaufsicht und Wohnungsordnung', in *Wohnungs- und Siedlungsfrage*, pp. 111–27

Günther, A., 'Die Wohlfahrtseinrichtungen der Arbeitgeber in Deutschland', in *Die Wohlfahrtseinrichtungen der Arbietgeber in Deutschland und Frankreich*, published as vol. 114 of the *Schriften des Vereins für Sozialpolitik* (Leipzig, 1905), pp. 29–50

Günther, R., 'Krupp und Essen', in M. Warnke (ed.), *Das Kunstwerk zwischen Wissenschaft und Weltanschauung* (Gütersloh, 1970), pp. 128–74
  'Arbeitersiedlungen im Ruhrgebiet', in E. Trier and W. Weyres (eds.), *Kunst des 19ten Jahrhunderts im Rheinland, Architektur*, vol. 2 (Düsseldorf, 1980), pp. 465–95

Gumprecht, A., 'Die Arbeiterwohnungsfrage' *Arbeiterfreund*, 25 (1887), pp. 8–11

Gussmann, D., 'Die Kruppschen Arbeiterwohnungen', in *Die Verbesserung der Wohnungen*, pp. 138–55

Gut, A., *Das Berliner Wohnhaus* (Berlin, 1917)

Haberland, G., *Der Einfluss des Privatkapitals auf die bauliche Entwicklung Gross-Berlins* (Berlin, 1913)

Hammerow, T. S., *Restoration, Revolution, Reaction: Economics and Politics in Germany, 1815–1871* (Princeton, 1958)

Hansen, P. C., 'Der Arbeiterbauverein in Flensberg', *Arbeiterfreund*, 16 (1878), pp. 289–99
  'Das Dänische Arbeiterwohnungswesen', *VfVK*, 17 (2), (1879), pp. 112–48
  Die Wohnungsverhältnisse in den grösseren Städten (Heidelberg, 1883)
  'Der erste allgemeine deustche Wohnungskongress zu Frankfurt am Main', *Arbeiterfreund*, 42 (1904), pp. 362–3

Harms, 'Über die Arbeiterkolonie zu Friedrichsort', in *Die Verbesserung der Wohnungen*, pp. 108–118

Hartmann, K., *Deutsche Gartenstadtbewegung, Kultur und Gesellschaftsreform* (Munich, 1976)

Hecker, H., *Der Kruppsche Kleinwohnungsbau* (Wiesbaden, 1917)

Hegemann, W., *Das steinerne Berlin, die grösste Mietskasernestadt der Welt* (Berlin, 1930)

Heinrich, E. and Mielke, F. (eds.), *Berlin und seine Bauten*, pt 2 (Berlin, 1964), pp. 29–79

Heiss, G., *Wohungsreform und Lokalverkehr* (Göttingen, 1903) (vol. 7 of the publications of the Deutscher Verein für Wohnungsreform)

Henderson, W. C., *The Rise of German Industrial Power 1834–1914* (Berkeley, Cal., 1975)

Henrici, K., 'Arbeiterwohnungen', *Der Städtebau*, 3 (1907), p. 71
  'Arbeiterkolonien', in *Künstlerische Gestaltung*, pp. 59–70

Herzfeld, H., *Johannes Miquel, sein Antheil am Ausbau des deutschen Reiches bis zur Jahrhundertwende*, 2 vols. (Detmold, 1938)

'Die heutige Wohnungsfrage' and 'Zur Lösung der Wohnungsfrage', in *Arbeiterwohl, Organ des Verbandes katholischer Industrielle und Arbeiterfreunde*, F. Hitze (ed.) (Cologne, 1882) 2, Heft 7, pp. 117–28, Heft 8, pp. 139–52

Heyde, L., *Abriss der Sozialpolitik* (Heidelberg, 1949)

Höpker, H., *Denkschrift über die Verluste der Bauhandwerker und Baulieferanten bei Neubauten in Gross-Berlin in den Jahren 1909–1911* (Berlin, 1914)

Hoffmann, C. W., *Die Aufgabe einer Berliner gemeinnützigen Baugesellschaft* (Berlin, 1847)

'Die Berliner gemeinnützige Baugesellschaft' in *Die Wohnungen der Arbeiter und Armen*, Heft 1 (Berlin, 185?)

Huber, V. A., 'Eindrücke und Betrachtungen eines Reisenden: Manchester, das Proletariat', *Janus* (1845), vol. 2, sections 23 and 24, pp. 641–78, 705–26

'Über innere Colonisation', in *Janus* (1846), vol. 1, issues 7 and 8, pp. 193–222, 225–55

Selbsthilfe der arbeitenden Klassen durch Wirtschaftsvereine und innere Ansiedlung (Berlin, 1848), new edn: C. J. Fuchs (ed.), published as vols. 21–3 of *Genossenschaftliche Kultur* (Berlin, 1916)

Innere Mission und Association, eine Denkschrift (Berlin, 1853)

Die Wohnungsnoth der kleinen Leute in grossen Städten (Leipzig, 1857)

'Die Wohnungsfrage in Frankreich und England', *Mittheilung des CVWaK* vol. 2 (neue Folge) (1859), pp. 3–37; vol. 2 (neue Folge) (1860), pp. 123–96

'Die Wohnungsfrage: die Noth', in *Concordia, Beiträge zur Lösung der socialen Fragen* vol. 2 (Leipzig, 1861)

'Die Wohnungsfrage: die Hülfe' in *Concordia, Beiträge zur Lösung der socialen Fragen*, vol. 3 (Leipzig, 1861)

'Über die geeignetsten Massregeln zur Abhülfe der Wohnungsnoth', *Arbeiterfreund*, 3 (1865), p. 141

Hugo, C. (pseudonym for H. Lindemann), *Die deutsche Stadteverwaltung: Volkshygiene, Städtebau, Wohnungswesen* (Stuttgart, 1901)

Jäger, E., *Die Wohnungsfrage* (Berlin, 1902)

'Zur Beurteilung des preussischen Wohnungsgesetzentwurfs' *ZfW*, 11 (1912/13), pp. 169–71

Jacobi, D., *Die gemeinnützige Bautätigkeit in Deutschland, ihre kulturelle Bedeutung und die Grenzen ihrer Wirksamkeit*, published as vol. 167 of *Staats- und sozialwissenschaftliche Forschungen*, G. Schmoller and M. Sering (eds.) (Munich and Leipzig, 1913)

Janke, C. and Hilger, D. (eds.) *Die Eigenthumslosen, der deutsche Pauperismus und die Emanzipationskrise in Darstellungen und Deutungen der zeitgenössischen Literatur* (Freiburg, 1965)

Jones, T. J., *Every Man his Own Landlord, or How to Buy a House with its Own Rent* (London, 1863)

Kalisch, E., 'Zur Geschichte des Berliner Lokalvereins für das Wohl der arbeitenden Klassen', *Mittheilungen des CVWaK* (1848), issue 1, pp. 81–97

Kalle, F., 'Die Fürsorge der Arbeitgeber für die Wohnungen ihrer Arbeiter', in *Die Verbesserung der Wohnungen*, pp. 1–28

'Das Wohnhaus der Arbeiter', *VföG*, 23 (1891), pp. 153–78

Kampffmeyer, H., *Die deutsche Gartenstadtbewegung* (Berlin, 1911)

Kampffmeyer, P., *Die Baugenossenschaften im Rahmen eines nationalen Reformplanes* (Göttingen, 1900) (vol. 3 of the publications of the Deutscher Verein für Wohnungsreform)

'Die Kanalisation Danzigs', *VföG*, 1 (1860), pp. 168–212

'Die Kanalisation von Frankfurt am Main', *VföG*, 2 (1870), pp. 504–63

Kitchin, M., *The Political Economy of Germany 1815–1914* (London, 1978)

'Kleine Wohngebäude für invalide Arbeiter in Essen', *Deutsche Konkurrenzen*, 2: 6 (1893), pp. 1–32

Klette, R., 'Die Wohnungsfrage vom Standpunkt der Technik aus', *Arbeiterfreund*, 3 (1865), pp. 187–207

Knoblauch, S. E., 'Warum werden in Berlin nicht mehr Gebäude mit kleinen Wohnungen gebaut?', in *Mittheilung des CVWaK*, vol. 1 (neue Folge) (1855), pp. 246–9

Köllmann, W., *Bevölkerung in der industriellen Revolution* (Göttingen, 1974)

'Siebenter Kongress deutscher Volkswirte', *VfVK*, 2 (1864), pp. 223–40

'Achter Kongress deutscher Volkswirte', in *VfVK*, 4 (1866), pp. 186–206

'Neunter Kongress deutscher Volkswirte', in *VfVK*, 5 (1867), pp. 116–41

Kramer, H., 'Die Anfänge des sozialen Wohnungsbaus in Frankfurt am Main, 1860–1914', in *Archiv für Frankfurts Geschichte und Kunst* (Frankfurt am Main, 1978), vol. 56, pp. 123–90

Krieger, E., 'Über Kellerwohnungen in Berlin', *Mittheilungen des CVWaK*, vol. 2 (neue Folge) (1857), pp. 218–48

Krieger, L., *The German Idea of Freedom* (Chicago, 1957)

Krokisius, *Die unter dem Protektorat seiner Majestät des Kaisers und Königs Wilhelm II stehenden Berliner gemeinnützige Bau-gesellschaft und Alexandrastiftung, 1847 bis Anfang 1908* (Berlin, 1908)

Kuczynski, J., *Die Geschichte der Lage der Arbeiter unter dem Kapitalismus* vols. 1–38, (Berlin (East), 1961–79)

Kuczynski, R., 'Miete und Einkommen', *Wohnungs- und Siedlungsfrage*, pp. 29–33

Die künstlerische Gestaltung des Arbeiter-Wohnhauses, published as vol. 29 of the Schriften der Centralstelle der Arbeiterwohlfahrtseinrichtungen (SCAW) (Berlin, 1906)

'Kundgebung der Vereinigung Berliner Architekten betreffend die Mittel zur Lösung der Arbeiter-Wohnrage für Berlin', *DBZ*, 25 (1891), pp. 233–4

Landsberg, O., 'Die Entwicklung des Gemeindeabgabenwesens in den preussischen Städten unter der Herrschaft des Kommunalabgabengesetzes mit besonderer Berücksichtigung der östlichen Provinzen', in *Einzelfragen der Finanzpolitik*, pp. 1–42

Lange, F. A., *Jedermann Haus Eigenthümer* (Duisburg, 1865)

Latscha, J. and Teudt, W., *Nationale Ansiedlung und Wohnungsreform* (Frankfurt am Main, 1899)

Lehmann, K. B., 'Max von Pettenkofer und seine Verdienste um die wissenschaftliche und praktische Hygiene', *VföG*, 25 (1893), pp. 361–85

Lette, A., 'Zur Geschichte der Bildung und Wirksamkeit des Central Vereins in Preussen für das Wohl der arbeitenden Klassen', in *Arbeiterfreund*, 1 (1863), pp. 1–25

Liebchen, G., 'Zu den Lebensbedingungen der unteren Schichten in Berlin des Vormärz', in Busch (ed.), *Untersuchungen*, pp. 270–314

Liebrecht, A., *Reichshilfe für Errichtung kleiner Wohnungen* (Göttingen, 1900) (vol. 2 of the publications of the Deutscher Verein für Wohnungsreform)

Liedke, G. S., *Hebung der Not der arbeitenden Klassen durch Selbsthilfe* (Berlin, 1845)

Lindemann, H., 'Wohnungsstatistik' in Fuchs, *Neue Untersuchungen*, vol. 1, section 1, pp. 353–60

'Die öffentliche Produktion (Reich, Staat, Gemeinde)' in *Wohungs- und Siedlungsfrage*, pp. 297–311

Mancuso, F., *Le Vicende dello Zoning* (Milan, 1978)

Manega, R., *Die Anlage von Arbeiterwohnungen von wirtschaftlichem, sanitärem Standpunkte* (Weimar, 1871)

Mangoldt, K. von, 'Herr Oberbürgermeister Zweigert und der Verein Reichswohngesetz', *ZfW*, 2 (1903/4), pp. 149–52

Die städtische Bodenfrage, Eine Untersuchung über Tatsachen, Ursachen und Abhilfe (Göttingen, 1907) (vol. 8 of the publications of the Deutscher Verein für Wohnungsreform)

'Der deutsche Verein für Wohnungsreform 1898–1920', in *30 Jahre Wohnungsreform*, pp. 20–2

Marcuse, J., 'Beiträge zur Arbeiterwohnungsfrage in Deutschland', in *VföG*, 31 (1899), pp. 371–83

Marken, van, 'Der "Agnetapark", Arbeitersiedlung der Niederländischen Presshefe- und Spiritusfabrik in Delft', in *Verbesserung der Wohnungen*, pp. 119–22

Marx, Karl, *The Communist Manifesto* (London, 1847)

'Die Massregeln zur Bekämpfung der Cholera', *VföG*, 27 (1895), pp. 139–66

'Massregeln zur Ereichung gesunden Wohnens', *VföG*, 21 (1889), pp. 9–41

'Massregeln zur Ereichung gesunden Wohnens', *VföG*, 22 (1890), pp. 20–60

Miquel, J., 'Einleitung', in *Die Wohnungsnoth*, pp. ix–xxi

Monke, F., 'Einflüsse der Baugesetze und Bauordnungen auf das Wohnhaus', in *Berlin und seine Bauten*, pt 4, vol. A, (Berlin, 1970), pp. 41–57, 58–63

Munding, K., *Victor Aimé Hubers ausgewählte Schriften über Sozialreform und Genossenschaftswesen* (Berlin, 1894)

Muthesius, H., 'Die Entwicklung des künstlerischen Gedankens im Hausbau', in *Die künstlerische Gestaltung*, pp. 7–15
    Kleinhaus und Kleinsiedlung (Munich, 1918)

Muthesius, S., *Das englische Vorbild* (Munich, 1974)

'Nachricht für diejenigen, welche eine Wohnung in den genossenschaftshäusern zu mieten wünschen', in *Mittheilungen des CVWaK*, Issue 9 (1850), pp. 114–23

'Nachrichten welche die Tätigkeit des Central-Vereins betreffen', in *Mittheilungen des CVWaK*, Issue 7 and 8 (1850), pp. 1–11

Nathan, P., *Die Wohnungsfrage und die Bestrebungen der Berliner Baugenossenschaft* (Berlin, 1890)

Neefe, M., 'Hauptergebnisse der Wohnungsstatistik deutscher Grossstädte', in *Die Wohnungsnoth*, vol. 1, pp. 161–91

Neue Untersuchungen über die Wohnungsfrage in Deutschland und in Ausland, published as vols. 94 and 95 of the *Schriften des vereins für Sozialpolitik* (Leipzig, 1901)

Neuberger, M. and J. Pagel (eds.), *Handbuch der Geschichte der Medizin*, 3 vols (Jena, 1902–5)

'Neue Bauordnung für Berlin', *DBZ*, 5 (1871), pp. 297, 310, 313, 328, 329, 337, 345, 354

Neumann, S., *Die öffentliche Gesundheitspflege und das Eigenthum* (Berlin, 1848)

Niethammer, L., 'Wie wohnten die Arbeiter im Kaiserreich?', *Archiv für Sozialgeschichte*, 16 (1976), pp. 127–48
    'Ein langer Marsch durch die Institutionen. Zur Vorgeschichte des preussischen Wohnungsgesetzes von 1918', in *Wohnen im Wandel*, pp. 375–6

Niethammer, L. (ed.), *Wohnen im Wandel, Beträge zur Geschichte des Alltags in der bürgerlichen Gesellschaft* (Wuppertal, 1979)

Nörnberg, H. J. and D. Schubert, *Massenwohnungsbau in Hamburg* (Berlin, 1975)

Nosbisch, W., *Wohnungswesen in Frankfurt am Main* (Frankfurt, 1930)

'Die Notwendigkeit weiträumiger Bebauung bei Stadterweiterungen und die rechtlichen und technischen Mittel zu ihrer Ausführung', *VföG*, 27 (1895), pp. 101–30

Nussbaum, C., 'Grundsätze für die Einrichtung von Arbeiterwohnungen', in *Verbesserung der Wohnungen*, pp. 61–3
    'Bau und Einrichtung von Kleinwohnungen', *SCAW*, 20 (Berlin, 1901), pp. 6–16
    'Die Ausbildung der Küchen in kleinen Wohnungen', *Zeitschrift für Wohnungswesen*, 1 (1902), pp. 165–7, 178–9, 183–5

Parisius, L., 'Die auf dem Prinzip der Selbsthülfe beruhende Baugenossenschaft', *Arbeiterfreund*, 3 (1865), pp. 262–99

Petersen, R., *Aufgaben des grossstädtischen Verkehrs* (Berlin, 1908)
    'Die Verkehrsmittel in Fuchs (eds.), *Wohnungs- und Siedlungsfrage*, pp. 231–44

Pettenkofer, M. von, *Untersuchungen und Beobachtungen über die Verbreitungsart der Cholera* (Munich, 1855)

  Über die Beziehung der Luft zu Kleidung, Wohnung und Boden (Dresden, 1872)

Pistor, M., 'Über die Anforderungen der Hygiene an Kost- und Logirhäuser', *VföG*, 12 (1880), pp. 55–102

Prince-Smith, J., 'Die sogennante Arbeiterfrage', in *VfVK*, 4 (1866), pp. 192–207

Protokolle über die Verhandlungen des Parteitags der Sozialdemokratischen Partei Deutschlands zu Hannover 1899 (Berlin, n.d.)

Protokolle über die Verhandlungen des Parteitags der Sozialdemokratischen Partei Deutschlands zu Mainz 1900 (Berlin, n.d.)

Radicke, D., 'Die Berliner Bebauungsplan von 1862 und die Entwicklung des Weddings: zum Verhältnis von Obrigkeitsplannung zu privatem Grundeigentum', in G. Poeschken, D. Radicke and T. Heinisch (eds.) *Festschrift für Ernst Heinrich* (Berlin, 1974), pp. 56–74

Radicke, D., 'Die Entwicklung des öffentlichen Personennahverkehrs in Berlin bis zur Gründung der BVG', in *Berlin und seine Bauten*, pt 10, vol. B (Berlin, 1979)

Ranke, W., *Heinrich Zille, Photographien Berlin 1890–1910* (Munich, 1975)

Reclam, K., 'Die englische Gesetzgebung für Hygiene', *VföG*, 1 (1869), pp. 5–39

Reich, E., *Der Wohnungsmarkt in Berlin 1840–1910* (Munich and Leipzig, 1912)

Reichardt, E., *Die Grundzüge der Arbeiterwohnungsfrage mit besonderer Berücksichtigung der Unternehmungen, die Arbeiter zu Hauseigenthümern zu machen* (Berlin, 1885)

Reincke, J. J., 'Die Beaufsichtigung der vorhandenen Wohnung (inkl. Sanierung oder Beiseitigung ungesunder Quartiers)', in *Neue Untersuchungen*, vol. 1, pt 2, pp. 3–44

Reulecke, J. (ed.), *Die deutsche Stadt im Industriezietalter, Beiträge zur modernen deutschen Stadtgeschichte* (Wuppertal, 1978)

Riehl, W., *Die Familie*, vol. 3 of *Naturgeschichte des Volkes als Grundlage einer deutschen Social-Politik* (Stuttgart and Augsburg, 1855)

Roberts, Henry, *The Dwellings of the Labouring Classes* (London, 1850), translated by C. Busse as *Wohnungen für die arbeitenden Klassen* (Berlin, 1852)

Rohr, D. G., *The Origins of Social Liberalism in Germany* (Chicago, 1963)

Roscher, E., 'Der Berliner Spar- und Bauverein und die Herausarbeitung grossstädtischer Mietshaustypen', *Zeitschrift für Wohnungswesen*, 10: 8, pp. 109–15

Rosenberg, H., *Grosse Depression und Bismarckszeit* (Berlin, 1967)

Roth, E., 'Von Pettenkofer als populärer Schriftsteller', *VföG*, 25 (1893), pp. 386–96

Ruprecht, W., *Die Wohnungen der arbeitenden Klassen in England* (Göttingen, 1884)

Rusch, M., 'Die private Bautätigkeit', in *Wohnungs- und Siedlungsfrage* pp. 295–62

  'Die Förderung der Kleinwohnungsproduktion durch Reich, Staat und Gemeinden', in *Wohnungs- und Siedlungsfrage*, pp. 312–19

Sax, E., *Wohnungszustände, der arbeitenden Classen und ihre Reform* (Vienna, 1869)

Schäffle, A. E. and Lechler, P., *Nationale Wohnungsreform* (Berlin, 1892)

  Der erste Schritt zur nationalen Wohnungsreform (Berlin, 1893)

Schilling, B. and Stübben, J., 'Die Bauordnung', in *Neue Untersuchungen*, vol. 1, pt 2, pp. 189–248

Schinz, A., 'Das mehrgeschossige Mietshaus von 1896–1945', in *Berlin und seine Bauten*, pt 4, vol. B (Berlin, 1974), pp. 1–20

Schmidt, P., 'Der Spar- und Bauverein zu Hannover als Muster für die Lösung der 'Klein-Wohnungs-Frage' in den Grossstädten', *Arbeiterfreund*, 30 (1892), pp. 34–46

Schmitz-Cliever, E., 'Die Anschauungen vom Wesen der Cholera bei den Aachener Epidemien 1832–1866', in *Sudhoffs Archiv für Geschichte der Medizin und Naturwissenschaft* (Wiesbaden, 1943–53), vol. 36, pp. 261–76

Schmohl, G., 'Die Arbeitgeber', in *Wohnungs- und Siedlungsfrage*, pp. 263–77

Schmoll, G., 'Die Arbeiterhäuser in der Breite in Basel (1854–1857)', in *Basler Zeitschrift für Geschichte und Altertumskunde*, 76 (1980), pp. 125–65

Schmoller, G., 'Ein Mahnruf in der Wohnungsfrage', in *Jahrbuch für Gesetzgebung, Verwaltung und Wolkswirtschaft im deutschen Reich*, 11 (1887), pp. 425–48
'Die soziale Frage und der preussische Staat', in *Zur Sozial- und Gewerbepolitik der Gegenwart* (Leipzig, 1890), pp. 37–63

Schraepler, E. (ed.), *Quellen zur Geschichte der sozialen Frage in Deutschland*, vols. 1 and 2 (Berlin and Frankfurt, 1964)

Schultze-Naumburg, P., 'Die Gestaltung des Arbeiterwohnhauses', in *Künstlerische Gestaltung*
Kulturarbeiten: vol. 1, *Hausbau*, vol. 3, *Dörfer und Kolonien* (Munich, n.d.)

Schulze-Delitzsch, F. H., *Vorschuss-Vereine als Volks-banken, Praktische Anweisung zu deren Gründung und Errichtung* (Leipzig, 1955)
'Kapitel zu einem deutschen Arbeiterkatechismus', in Ernst Schraepler (ed.), *Quellen zur Geschichte der sozialen Frage in Deutschland*, 2 vols. (Berlin and Frankfurt, 1964), vol. 1, p. 182.

Schülke, H., *Gesunde Wohnungen* (Berlin, 1880)

Schwabe, H., *Berliner Gemeinde-Kalender und städtisches Jahrbuch* (Berlin, 1868)
'Einfluss der verschiedenen Wohnungen auf die Gesundheit ihrer Bewohner, soweit er sich statistisch nachweisen lässt', *VföG*, 7 (1875), pp. 70–7

Schwann, B. *Die Wohnungsnot und das Wohnungselend in Deutschland*, Berlin, 1929 (published as vol. 7 of the Schriften des Deutschen Vereins für Wohnungsreform)
Die Wohnungsverhältnisse der Berliner Altstadt (published as vol. 10 of the *Schriften des Deustschen Vereins für Wohungsreform*) (Berlin, 1932)

Sembritzki, 'Die Besteuerung', in *Wohnungs- und Siedlungsfrage*, pp. 128–35

Senftleben, H., 'Über gesundheitsgemässe Einrichtung ländlicher Arbeiterwohnungen', *Arbeiterfreund*, 3 (1865), pp. 171–86
'Die Bedeutung und der Fortschritt der Wohnungsfrage', *Arbeiterfreund*, 6 (1868), pp. 365–400; 7 (1869), pp. 82–98, 213–29, 376–405

Seutemann, R., *Die deutsche Wohnungsstatistik, ihre gegenwärtige Stand und ihre Bedeutung für die Wohnungsreform* (Göttingen, 1902) (vol. 6 of the publications of the Deutscher Verein für Wohnungsreform)

Shanahan, W. G., *German Protestants face the Social Question*, vol. 1 (Notre Dame, 1954)

Sheehan, J. J., *The Career of Lujo Brentano: a Study of Liberalism and Social Reform in Imperial Germany* (Chicago, 1966)

Sitte, C., *Der Städte-Bau nach seinem künstlerischen Grundsätzen* (Vienna, 1889)

Smiles, S., *Thrift* (London, 1875)

Soyka, J., Über Canalgase als Verbreiter epidemischer Krankheiten und über Richtung und Stärke des Lutfzuges in den Seilen', *VföG*, 14 (1882), pp. 33–77

'Stadterweiterung, insbesondere in hygienischer Beziehung', *VföG*, 18 (1886), pp. 9–39

'Die Stellung des Verbands der "Haus- und städtischen Grundbesitzvereine" zur Arbeiterwohnungsfürsorge', *Arbeiterwohl*, 18 (1898), pp. 289–91

Stier-Somlo, Dr, *Unser Mietrechtsverhältnis und seine Reform* (Göttingen, 1901) (vol. 4 of the publications of the Deutscher Verein für Wohnungsreform)

Strang, J., *Germany in 1831* (London, 1836)

Strassmann, W. and Haselberg, B. von, 'Anforderungen der öffentlichen Gesundheitspflege an die Baupolizei in Bezug auf die neue Stadtteile, Strassen und Häuser', *VföG*, 7 (1875), pp. 52–69

Stübben, J. and E. Zweigert, 'Handhabung der gesundheitlichen Wohnungspolizei', *VföG*, 21 (1882), pp. 57–107

Stübben, J., *Der Städtebau* (Darmstadt, 1890), published as the 9th half-volume of Durm et al. (eds.), *Handbuch der Architektur*

'Der Stadterweiterungsplan und seine Durchführung', in *Neue Untersuchungen*, vol. 1, sec. 2, pp. 155–67

Die Bedeutung der Bauordnungen und Bebauungspläne für das Wohnungswesen (Göttingen, 1902) (vol. 5 of the publications of the Deutscher Verein für Wohnungsreform)

Sutcliffe, A., *Towards the Planned City, Germany, Britain, the United States and France, 1780–1914* (Oxford, 1981)

(ed.), *Multi-Storey Living: The British Working-Class Experience* (London, 1974)

Swenarton, M., *Homes Fit for Heroes, the Politics and Architecture of Early State Housing in Britain* (London, 1981)

Täglichsbeck, O., 'Die Beförderung der Ansiedlung von Arbeitern der Staatsberg-, Hütten- und Salzwerke durch Gewährung von Bauvorschüssen und Bauprämien seitens des preussischen Bergfiskus', in *Verbesserung der Wohnungen*, pp. 98–107

Tarn, J. N., *Five Per Cent Philanthropy, an Account of Housing in Urban Areas between 1840 and 1914* (Cambridge, 1973)

Taylor, A. J., *Laissez-faire and State Intervention in 19th Century Britain*, Studies in Economic History (London, 1972)

Teale, T. P., *Dangers to Health: a Pictorial Guide to Domestic Sanitary Defects* (London, 1879)

Thiele, T. P., 'Über die Kolonie Leienhausen', in *Die Verbesserung der Wohnungen*, pp. 122–37

Thienel, I., *Städtewachstum im Industrialisierungsprozess des 19ten Jahrhunderts, das Berliner Beispiel* (published as vol. 39 of the *Veröffentlichungen der Historischen Kommission zu Berlin*) (Berlin, 1973)

'Industrialisierung und Städtewachstum, die Wandel der Hauptsiedlungsformen in der Umgebung Berlins 1800–1850', in Busch (ed.) *Untersuchungen*, pp. 106–49

Thompson, W., *Housing Handbook* (London, 1903)

Thünen, J. N. von, *Der isolierte Staat in bezug auf Landwirtschaft und Nationalökonomie* (Hamburg, 1826)

Trüdinger, O., *Die Arbeiterwohnungsfrage und die Bestrebeung zur Lösung derselben* (Jena, 1888)

'Über die hygienischen Anforderungen an Neubauten zunächst in neuen Quartieren grösserer Städte', *VföG*, 8 (1876), pp. 97–138

Uhlig, G., *Kollektivmodell 'Einküchenhaus', Wohnreform und Architektur zwischen Frauenbewegung und Funktionalismus 1900–1911* (Giessen, 1981)

'Die unterschiedliche Behandlung der Bauordnungen für das Innere, die Aussenbezirke und die Umgebung von Städten', *VföG*, 26 (1894), pp. 13–47

Unwin, R., *Town Planning in Practice, an Introduction to the Art of Designing Cities and Suburbs* (London, 1909)

Varrentrap, G., *Zur Gründung einer gemeinnützigen Baugenossenschaft in Frankfurt am Main* (Frankfurt, 1860)

'Über die neue Canalisation Frankfurts', *VföG*, 5 (1873), pp. 656–68

'Häuser der gemeinnützigen Baugesellschaft zunächst in Frankfurt am Main', *VföG*, 6 (1874), pp. 393–401

'Über die hygienischen Anforderungen an Neubauten zunächst in neuen Quartieren grösserer Städte', *VföG*, 8 (1876), pp. 97–138

Die Verbesserung der Wohnungen, Vorberichte und Verhandlungen der Konferenz vom 25 und 26 April 1892, published as vol. 1 of *Schriften der Centralstelle für Arbeiter-Wohlfahrtseinrichtungen* (Berlin, 1892)

Verhandlungen der am 24 und 25 September 1886 am Frankfurt am Main abgehaltenen Generalversammlung des Vereins für Sozialpolitik, in *Schriften des Vereins für Sozialpolitik,* vol. 33 (Leipzig, 1887), pp. 5–139

'Verhandlungen den Vereins für Sozialpolitik über die Wohnungsfrage', *Schriften des Vereins für Sozialpolitik,* vol. 98 (Leipzig, 1902), pp. 15–118

Virchow, R., *Über die Kanalisation Berlins* (Berlin, 1868)

Vogt, A., 'Über die Richtung städtischer Strassen nach der Himmelsgegend und das Verhältnis ihrer Breite zur Häuserhöhe', *Zeitschrift für Biologie,* 15 (1879), pp. 217–47

Voigt, A., 'Bodenbesitzverhältnisse, das Bau- und Wohnungswesen in Berlin und seinen Vororten', *Neue Untersuchungen,* vol. 1, sec. 1, pp. 152–260

'Die Bedeutung der Baukosten für die Wohnungspreise', in *Neue Untersuchungen,* vol. 1, pt 1, pp. 339–64

Voigt, A. and P. Geldner, *Kleinhaus und Mietskaserne, eine Untersuchung der Intensität der Bebauung vom wirtschaftlichen und hygienischen Standpunkte* (Berlin, 1905)

Voigt, P., *Hypothekenbanken und Beleihungsgrenzen* (Berlin, 1899)

Grundrente und Wohnungsfrage im Berlin und den Vororten (Jena, 1901)

Vormbrock, H., 'Die Landes- und Provinzial-Vereins für Kleinwohnungswesen', in *Wohnungs- und Siedlungsfrage,* pp. 320–8

Vossberg, W. *Die deutsche Baugenossenschaftsbewegung* (Jena, 1906)

Wagner, A., 'Communalsteuerfrage', in *Verhandlungen der fünften General-Versammlung des Vereins für Sozialpolitik* (published as vol. 14 of the *Schriften des Vereins für Sozialpolitik*) (Leipzig, 1878), pp. 5–26

Grundlegung der politischen Ökonomie (2 vols., Leipzig, 1894)

Wagner, H. von, *Die Tätigkeit der Stadt Ulm a. D. auf dem Gebiet der Wohnungsfürsorge* (Ulm, 1903)

Wagon, E., *Die finanzielle Entwicklung der deutschen Aktiengesellschaft* (Jena, 1903)

Weber, Adolf A., *Über Bodenrente und Bodenspekulation* (Leipzig, 1904)

Weber, Alfred, *Über den Standort der Industrien* (Tübingen, 1909)

Weber, A. F., *The Growth of Cities in the 19th Century, a Study in Statistics* (New York, 1899)

Weimann, K., 'Bevölkerungsentwicklung und Frühindustrialisierung in Berlin 1800–1850' in Busch (ed.), *Untersuchungen,* pp. 150–69

Weissbach, K. and Mackowsky, W., *Das Arbeiterwohnhaus* (Berlin, 1910)

Wohnhäuser (Stuttgart, 1902), published as vol. 2, pt 4 of Durm et al. (eds.), *Handbuch der Architektur*

'Weitere Behandlungen der Wohnungsfrage seitens des Centralvereins in Preussen für das Wohl der arbeitenden Klassen', *Arbeiterfreund,* 4 (1866), pp. 1–19

Weyl, T., *Handbuch der Hygiene* (10 vols., Jena, 1896–1901)

Wohl, A. S., *The Eternal Slum, Housing and Social Policy in Victorian London* (London, 1977)

Wohlfahrtseinrichtungen der Kruppschen Gussstahlfabrik zum besten ihrer Arbeiter und Beamten (Essen, 1876) (3rd edn, 1902, vols. 1–3)

Die Wohnungsfrage mit besonderer Berücksichtigung auf die arbeitenden Klassen (Berlin, 1865)

'Die Wohnungsfrage vom Standpunkt der Armenpflege', in *Schriften des deutschen Vereins für Armenpflege und Wohltätigkeit (SDVfAW),* 6 (1888), pp. 67–120; 11 (1892), pp. i–xxiv, 1–57; 13 (1894), pp. 67–79, 146–57

'Die Wohnungsfürsorge im Reiche und in den Bundesstaaten', in *Stenographische Berichte des deutschen Reichstages*, Session 1903/4, Appendices, vol. 4, no. 4

Die Wohnungsnoth der ärmeren Klassen in deutschen Grossstädten und Vorschläge zu deren Abhülfe, published as vols. 30 and 31 of the *Schriften des Verein für Sozialpolitik* (Leipzig, 1886)

Zeidler, H., *Geschichte des deutschen Genossenschaftswesen der Neuzeit* (Berlin, 1893)

Ziemssen, H. von and Pettenkofer, M. von (eds.), *Handbuch der Hygiene und der Gewerbekrankheiten* (20 vols., Leipzig, 1882–1910)

Zimm, A., *Die Entwicklung des Industriestandortes Berlin, Tendenzen der geographischen Lokalisation bei den Berliner Industriezweigen von überörtlicher Bedeutung sowie die territoriale Stadtentwicklung bis 1945* (Berlin (East), 1959)

Zweigert, E. 'Die Beaufsichtigung der vorhandenen Wohnungen', in *Neue Untersuchungen*, vol. 1, pt 2, pp. 45–112

'Der Entwurf eines Gesetzes zur Verbesserung der Wohnverhältnisse für die preussische Monarchie, *ZfW*, 2 (1903/4), pp. 57–61, 169–74, 297–307

'Zur Arbeiterwohnungsfrage', *Arbeiterwohl*, 9 (1889), pp. 99–125

'Zur Kanalisation von Frankfurt ans Main', *VföG*, 4 (1872), pp. 628–40

PART TWO: FRANCE

Official Publications

Conseil Municipal de Paris, *Rapports et Documents*

Conseil Municipal de Paris, *Procès Verbaux*

Conseil Supérieur des Habitations à Bon Marché, annual reports published in the *Journal Officiel* and the *Bulletin de la Société Française des Habitations à Bon Marché*

J. Duvergier, *Collection complète des lois, décrets, ordonnances, règlements et avis du Conseil d'Etat*

Journal Officiel, Documents Parlementaires, Chambre des Députés

Journal Officiel, Débats Parlementaires, Chambre des Députés

Journal Officiel, Documents Parlementaires, Sénat

Journal Officiel, Débats Parlementaires, Sénat

Le Moniteur Universel

Chambre des Deputés, Commission chargée de faire une enquête sur la situation des ouvriers de l'industrie et de l'agriculture en France, et de présenter un premier rapport sur la crise industrielle à Paris, *Procès Verbaux* (1884)

Commission d'Extension de Paris, *Aperçu historique. Considérations techniques préliminaires* (2 vols., Paris, Préfecture du Département de la Seine, 1913)

Commission Technique de l'Assainissement de Paris, 'Résumé des travaux et résolutions adoptées', *Annales des Ponts et Chaussées, Mémoires et Documents*, 6th series, X (1885), pp. 458–76

Ministère de l'Instruction Publique, des Beaux Arts et des Cultes, Comité des Travaux Historiques et Scientifiques, *Enquête sur les conditions de l'habitation en France, les maisons-types*, introduction by A. de Foville (2 vols, Paris, Ernest Leroux, Editeur, 1894, 1899)

Ministère du Travail et de la Prévoyance Sociale: Statistique Générale de la France, *Salaires et coût de l'existence à diverses époques jusqu'en 1910.* (Paris, Ministère du Travail et de la Prévoyance Sociale 1911)

L'Office Public d'Habitations de la Ville de Paris, 1937 (Paris, Office Public
    d'Habitations de la Ville de Paris, 1937)
*Rapport sur la marche et les effets du choléra-morbus dans Paris et les communes
    rurales du département de la Seine* (Paris, Imprimerie Royale, 1834)
Ville de Paris, *1e concours pour la construction d'habitations à bon marché* (Paris,
    Préfecture du Département de la Seine, 1913)
Various official documents relating to public hygiene in the late 1840s and early
    1850s, bound together in the British Library: CT. 436

Periodicals

Académie des Sciences Morales et Politiques: Compte rendu des séances et travaux
Annales de la Charité
Architecture Mouvement Continuité
Bulletin de la Société Française des Habitations à Bon Marché
Bulletin de la Société Industrielle de Mulhouse
Bulletin de la Société Internationale des Etudes Pratiques d'Economie Sociale
La Construction Moderne
L'Economiste Français
Encyclopédie d'Architecture
Gazette des Architectes et du Bâtiment
Le Moniteur des Architectes
Musée Social: Mémoires et Documents
Nouvelles Annales de la Construction
La Réforme Sociale
Revue Generale de l'Architecture et des Travaux Publics
La Semaine des Constructeurs
La Vie Urbaine

Exhibitions and congresses

Congrès International d'Hygiène, de Sauvetage, et d'Economie Sociale 1876 (2 vols.,
    Paris, Germer Baillière et Cie., 1877)
Congrès International d'Hygiène 1878 (2 vols., Paris, Imprimerie Nationale, 1880)
Internationaler Congress für Hygiene und Demographie zu Wien 1887 (37 Hefte,
    Vienna, Verlag der Organisations-Commission des Congresses, 1887–8)
Congrès International d'Hygiène et de Démographie 1889 (Paris, Bibliothèque des
    Annales Economiques, 1890)
Congreso Internacional de Higiene y Demografia 1898 (14 vols., Madrid, Ricardo
    Rojas, 1900)
Congrès International d'Hygiène et de Démographie 1900 (Paris, Masson et Cie.,
    n.d.)
Congrès International d'Hygiène et de Démographie 1903 (9 vols., Brussels,
    P. Weissenbruch, 1903)
Internationaler Kongress für Hygiene und Demographie 1907 (4 vols., Berlin, Verlag
    von August Hirschwald, 1908)

Congrès International des Habitations à Bon Marché 1897 (Brussels, Hayez,
    Imprimeur de l'Académie Royale de Belgique, 1897)
Congrès International des Habitations à Bon Marché 1900 (Paris, Secrétariat de la
    Société Française des Habitations à Bon Marché, 1900)
Cacheux, E. and Rendu, A., *Congrès International des Habitations à Bon Marché
    1907* (Orléans, Imprimerie Auguste Gout et Cie., 1908)

Congrès International des Architectes 1900 (Paris, Chaix, 1906)

Town Planning Conference, London, 10–15 October 1910 (London, Royal Institute of British Architects, 1911)

Congrès International et Exposition Comparée des Villes, Gand, 1913 (Brussels, Union Internationale des Villes, 1914)

'Exposition de la "Cité Moderne", 1913', *Bulletin de la Chambre de Commerce de Nancy*, No. 53 (1913)

Interallied Town Planning Conference, Paris, 1919 (Paris, La Renaissance des Cités, 1919)

Premier Congrès de l'Habitation tenu à Lyon du 9 au 12 octobre 1919 (Lyons, Imprimerie Noirclerc et Fénétrier, 1920)

Deuxième Congrès de l'Habitation du 10 au 14 mars 1920 à Lyon (Lyons, Imprimerie Noirclerc et Fénétrier, 1920)

Troisième Congrès de l'Habitation organisé à Lyon du 9 au 12 mars 1921 (Lyons, Imprimerie Noirclerc et Fénétrier, 1921)

Biographies and encyclopaedias

Curinier, C. E., *Dictionnaire National des Contemporains* (5 vols., Paris, Office Générale d'Edition, completed 1905)

Maitron, J., *Dictionnaire biographique du mouvement ouvrier français* (18 vols., Paris, Les Editions Ouvrières, 1964–)

Planat, P., *Encyclopédie de l'architecture et de la construction* (6 vols., Paris, Dujardin et Cie., n.d.)

Vapereau, G., *Dictionnaire Universel des Contemporains*, 6th edn (Paris, Librairie Hachette et Cie., 1893)

La grande encyclopédie (31 vols., Paris, Société Anonyme de la Grande Encyclopédie, n.d.)

Books and articles

Abriani, A., '"Lorsque l'ouvrier songe à se bien loger, il est sauvé"', *Lotus*, No. 9 (1975), pp. 136–45

Agache, A. D., Auburtin, J. M. & Redont, E., *Comment reconstruire nos cités détruites* (Paris, A. Colin, 1915)

Agulhon, M., *1848 ou l'apprentissage de la république, 1848–1852*. Nouvelle Histoire de la France Contemporaine, 8 (Paris, Editions du Seuil, 1973)

Anderson, R. D., *France 1870–1914. Politics and society* (London, Routledge and Kegan Paul, 1977)

Audiganne, A., *Les populations ouvrières et les industries en France dans le mouvement social du XIXe siecle* (2 vols., Paris, Capelle, 1854); 2nd edn (2 vols., Paris, Capelle, 1860)

Bastié, J., 'Capital immobilier et marché immobilier parisiens', *Annales de Géographie*, no. 373 (1960), pp. 225–50

   La croissance de la banlieue parisienne (Paris, Presses Universitaires de France, 1964)

Baty-Tornikian, G., *Un projet urbain idéal typique. Agglomération parisienne 1919–1939* (Paris, Institut d'Etudes et de Recherches Architecturales et Urbaines, c. 1979)

Baudot, A. de, 'L'architecture à l'Ecole des beaux-arts et à l'Ecole centrale', *GAB*, VI (1868), pp. 9–12

Bauer, C., *Modern housing* (Boston and New York, Houghton Mifflin Company, 1934)

Beddall, T. G., 'Godin's Familistère', *Architectural Design*, 46 (1976), pp. 423–7

Bellet, D. and Darvillé, W., *Ce que doit être la cité moderne, son plan, ses aménagements, ses organes, son hygiène, ses monuments et sa vie* (Paris, H. Nolo, 1914)

Benevolo, L., *The Origins of Modern Town Planning*, trans. J. Landry (London, Routledge and Kegan Paul, 1967)

Benoît-Lévy, G., *La Cité-jardin*, preface by C. Gide (Paris, H. Jouve, 1904)
    Cités-jardins d'Amérique, preface by E. Cheysson (Paris, H. Jouve, 1905)
    'La première cité-jardin de France: le village-jardin des Mines de Dourges', *BSFHBM*, 19 (1909), pp. 438–45
    La cité-jardin, 2nd edn (3 vols., Paris, Editions des Cités-Jardins de France, 1911)

Bertillon, Dr J., *Essai de statistique comparée du surpeuplement des habitations à Paris et dans les grandes capitales européenes* (Paris, Chaix, 1894)
    Le problème de la dépopulation (Paris, A. Colin, 1897)
    La dépopulation de la France. Ses conséquences – ses causes. Mesures à prendre pour la combattre (Paris, F. Alcan, 1911)

Bertocci, P. A., *Jules Simon. Republican anticlericalism and cultural politics in France. 1848–1886* (Columbia and London, University of Missouri Press, 1978)

Blanqui, J. A., 'Rapport sur la situation des classes ouvrières en 1848', *ASMP*, XIV (1848), pp. 317–36; XV (1849), pp. 5–29, 105–27, 237–313

Blumenfeld, H., *The Modern Metropolis: Its Origins, Growth, Characteristics and Planning* (Cambridge, Massachusetts Institute of Technology, 1967)

Boulonnois, L., *La municipalité en service social. L'oeuvre municipale de M. Henri Sellier à Suresnes* (Nancy, Paris and Strasbourg, Berger-Levrault, 1938)

Bouvier, J. (ed.), *L'ère industrielle et la société d'aujourd'hui (siècle 1880–1980)*, Histoire Economique et Sociale de la France, 4, 1 (Paris, Presses Universitaires de France, 1979)

Brooke, M. Z., *Le Play: Engineer and Social Scientist* (London, Longman, 1970)

Buret, E., *De la misère des classes laborieuses en Angleterre et en France* (2 vols., Paris, Paulin Libraire, 1840)

Butler, R. and Noisette, P., *Le logement social en France 1815–1981. De la cité ouvrière au grand ensemble* (Paris, La Découverte/Maspero, 1983)

Cacheux, E., 'Habitations ouvrières en tous pays', *BSES*, VII (1880–1), pp. 100–24
    Le philanthrope pratique. Première partie: habitations ouvrières – études, avec plans, sur les habitations isolées, maisons à étages, hôtels pour ouvriers (Laval, E. Jamin, 1882)
    L'économiste pratique (Paris, Baudry, 1885)
    Etat des habitations ouvrières à la fin du XIXe siècle (Paris, Baudry, 1891)
    'Le sacrifice de la propriété privée', *Bulletin du Comité des Travaux Historiques et Scientifiques. Section des Sciences Economiques et Sociales. Congrès des Sociétés Savantes de 1901* (Paris, Imprimerie Nationale, 1901), pp. 113–15
    'Intervention des municipalités dans la question des petits logements', *Bulletin du Comité des Travaux Historiques et Scientifiques. Section des Sciences Economiques et Sociales. Congrès des Sociétés Savantes de 1904* (Paris, Imprimerie Nationale, 1905), pp. 143–9
    'Extension méthodique du territoire à bâtir dans les villes', *Bulletin du Comité des Travaux Historiques et Scientifiques. Section des Sciences Economiques et Sociales. Congrès des Sociétés Savantes de 1908* (Paris, Imprimerie Nationale, 1909), pp. 69–75

Cahen, G., *Le logement dans les villes; la crise parisienne* (Paris, F. Alcan, 1913)

Cahen, L., 'Evolution des conditions de logement en France depuis cent ans', *Etudes et Conjoncture*, 12 (1957), pp. 985–1376

Canaux, J. (ed.), *Urbanization and planning in France* (Paris, International Federation for Housing and Planning, and Centre de Recherche d'Urbanisme, 1968)

Casimir-Périer, A., *Les sociétés de coopération: la consommation, le crédit, la production, l'amélioration morale et intellectuelle par l'association* (Paris, Dentu, 1864)

Castells, M., *The Urban Question, a Marxist Approach*, trans. A. Sheridan (London, Edward Arnold, 1977)

Chemetov, P. and Marrey, B., *Architectures, Paris: 1848–1914* (Paris, Dunod, 1980)

Chevalier, L., *La formation de la population parisienne au XIXe siècle* (Paris, Presses Universitaires de France, 1950)

Classes laborieuses et classes dangereuses à Paris pendant la première moitié du XIXe siècle (Paris, Plon, 1958), trans. F. Jellinek, *Labouring classes and dangerous classes in Paris during the first half of the nineteenth century* (London, Routledge and Kegan Paul, 1973)

Chevallier, A., 'De la nécéssité de bâtir des maisons pour loger les classes moyennes (les ouvriers); de la possibilité de faire des constructions, en retirant un intérêt raisonnable de son argent', *Annales d'Hygiène Publique et de Médecine Légale*, 2nd series, VIII (1857), pp. 100–12

Cheysson, E., *La question des habitations ouvrières en France et à l'étranger* (Paris, G. Masson, Editeur, 1886)

Cheysson, E. and Toqué, A., 'Les budgets comparés des cent monographies de familles publiées d'après un cadre uniforme dans "Les ouvriers européens" et "Les ouvriers des deux mondes"', *Bulletin de l'Institut International de Statistique*, V (1890), pp. 1–157

Cheysson, E., *Les cités-jardins* (Paris, H. Jouve, 1905)

Le confort du logement populaire (Paris, Chaix, 1905)

Oeuvres choisies (2 vols., Paris, A. Rousseau, 1911)

Chiffard, J. F. and Roujon, Y., 'Après les fortifs et la zone, la ceinture', *Architecture Mouvement Continuité*, no. 43 (1977), pp. 9–25.

Choisy, A., 'Notice nécrologique sur Alfred Durand-Claye', *Annales des Ponts et Chaussées, Mémoires et Documents*, 6th series, XVI (1888), pp. 505–22.

'Les cités-jardins de la région de l'Ile de France', *Cahiers de l'Institut d'Aménagement et d'Urbanisme de la Région de l'Ile de France*, no. 51 (1978)

Clapham, J. H., *The Economic Development of France and Germany 1815–1914*, 4th edn (Cambridge, University Press, 1968)

Clavel, A., *Traité d'éducation physique et morale* (2 vols., Paris, V. Masson, 1855)

Clément, Dr E., 'Des moyens propre à pourvoir les bâtiments de lumière et de chaleur solaires', *Internationaler Congress für Hygiene und Demographie zu Wien 1887* (37 Hefte, Vienna, Verlag der Organisations-Commission des Congresses, 1887–8), Heft 11, pp. 3–34

Considérant, V., *L'avenir, perspective d'un phalanstère ou palais sociétaire dédié à l'humanité* (Bordeaux, Imprimerie de H. Faye, n.d.)

Couturaud, E., *Guide pratique pour la reconstruction, l'extension, l'aménagement et l'embellissement des villes et des communes rurales* (Paris, Librairie de la Construction Moderne, 1915)

Daumard, A., *Maisons de Paris et propriétaires parisiens au XIXe siècle, 1809–1880* (Paris, Editions Cujas, 1965)

Degrand, E. and Faucher, Dr J., 'Habitations caractérisées par le bon marché uni aux conditions d'hygiène et de bien-être', *Exposition Universelle de 1867, rapports du jury international*, (13 vols., Paris, Imprimerie Administrative de Paul Dumont, 1868), vol. XIII, pp. 881–952

Denby, E., *Europe Re-housed* (London, G. Allen and Unwin, 1938)

Dennery, E., *La question de l'habitation urbaine en France* (Geneva, League of Nations, Health Organisation, 1935)

Dépinay, J. and Dufourmantelle, M., *Les offices publics d'habitations à bon marché. Etude théorique et pratique* (Paris, F. Alcan, 1918)

Detain, C., 'Un mot sur la question des habitations ouvrières à Paris à propos de l'Exposition Universelle de 1867', *RGA*, XXIV (1866), cols. 221–8

'Exposition Universelle de 1867. Habitations ouvrières', *RGA*, XXV (1867), cols. 158–63, 219–39; XXVI (1868), cols. 64–71, 110–13, 209–13, 256–61; XXVII (1869), cols. 214–19, 260–3; XXVIII (1870–1), cols. 66–71, 110–16.

Devillers, C. and Huet, B., *Le Creusot, naissance et développement d'une ville industrielle, 1782–1914* (Seyssel, Champ Vallon, 1981)

Dolléans, E. and Dehove, G., *Histoire du travail en France* (2 vols., Paris, Domat Montchrestien, 1953, 1955)

Dufourmantelle, M., *La réforme de l'habitation populaire par les cités-jardins* (Brussels, Revue Economique Internationale, 1910)

'Les cités-jardins, leur portée sociale, leur caractère, leur organisation', in Société Française des Habitations à Bon Marché, *La question de la reconstruction des villes et villages détruits par la guerre* (Paris, 9, Rue de Solferino, 1916)

Dupeux, G., *French Society 1789–1970*, trans. P. Wait (London, Methuen & Co. Ltd; New York, Barnes & Noble, 1976)

Duroselle, J. B., *Les débuts du catholicisme social en France, 1822–1870* (Paris, Presses Universitaires de France, 1951)

Duveau, G., *La vie ouvrière sous le Second Empire* (Paris, Gallimard, 1946)

Ecole Spéciale d'Architecture, *Projets d'élèves 1868–69* (manuscript and photographs held in the Victoria and Albert Museum Library, 86.PP.1)

'Ecole Spéciale d'Architecture 1865–1965', *Bulletin de la Société des Architectes Diplômés de l'Ecole Spéciale d'Architecture*, no. 8–10 (1965)

Engels, F., *The Housing Question*, ed. C. P. Dutt (London, Martin Lawrence, 1935)

Evenson, N., *Paris: A Century of Change, 1878–1978* (New Haven and London, Yale University Press, 1979)

Le familistère de Guise ou les équivalents de la richesse (Brussels, Editions des Archives d'Architecture Moderne, 1976)

Le familistère Godin à Guise, Habiter l'utopie (Paris, Editions de la Villette, 1982)

Fay, C. R., *Cooperation at home and abroad* (London, P. S. King and Son, 1908)

Ferrand, S., *Systèmes de construction économiques. Les maisons de grand rapport et les loyers à bon marché* (Paris, l'auteur, 1871)

Flaus, L., 'Les fluctuations de la construction d'habitations urbaines', *Journal de la Société de Statistique de Paris*, LXXXX (1949), pp. 185–221

Flonneau, J. M., 'Crise de vie chère et mouvement syndical (1910–1914)', *Le Mouvement Social*, no. 72 (1970), pp. 49–81

Foucher de Careil (Comte), *Les habitations ouvrières* (Paris, Eugène Lacroix, 1873)

Fourcade, F., 'Des diverses solutions pouvant être envisagées pour l'amélioration du logement ouvrier et plus spécialement du logement des familles nombreuses, à Paris', *BSFHBM*, 21 (1911), pp. 395–405

Foville, A. de, *Notice historique sur la vie et les oeuvres de M. Georges Picot* (Paris, Firmin-Didot et Cie., 1909)

Frégier, H. A., *Des classes dangereuses de la population dans les grandes villes et des moyens de les rendre meilleures* (2 vols., Paris, J. B. Baillière, 1840)

Solution nouvelle du problème de la misère (Paris, Amyot, 1851)

Gabillon, A. and Boutillon, L., *Les cités-jardins au point de vue social. La cité-jardin du Petit-Groslay, près la nouvelle gare de Blanc-Mesnil* (Paris, 94, Boulevard Sebastopol, 1912)

Gaillard, J., *Paris, la ville 1852–1870* (Paris, Editions Honoré Champion, 1977)

Garnier, T., *Une cité industrielle, étude pour la construction des villes* (Paris, Massin et Cie., 1917)

Gaumont, J., *Histoire générale de la coopération en France* (2 vols., Paris, Fédération Nationale des Coopératives de Consommation, 1924)

Gide, C., 'Economie sociale', *Exposition Universelle Internationale de 1900, rapports du jury international* (5 vols., Paris, Imprimerie Nationale, 1903), vol. 5

    Les sociétés coopératives de consommation, 2nd edn (Paris, A. Colin, 1910)

Girard, E. and Massenot, J. P., 'Corons du Nord 2: cité des Brebis (Mazingarbe)', *Architecture Mouvement Continuité*, no. 35 (1974), pp. 130–40

Girard, O., 'Corons du Nord: l'espace industriel et l'habiter', *Architecture Mouvement Continuité*, no. 34 (1974), pp. 38–51

Godin, J. B. A., *Solutions sociales* (Paris, A. le Chevalier, 1871)

Gould, E. R. L., *The Housing of the Working People* (Washington, Government Printing Office, 1895)

Gourlier, C., *Notice historique sur le service des travaux des bâtiments civils à Paris et dans les départements depuis la création de ce service en l'an IV (1795)* (Paris, L. Colas, 1848)

    Des voies publiques et habitations particulières à Paris (Paris, Librairie d'architecture de B. Bance, 1852)

    Salon de 1853. Architecture. Etudes de maisons ouvrières et de bains et lavoirs publics (Paris, E. Thunot et Cie., 1853)

Gourlier, C. and Questel, C., *Notice historique sur le service des travaux et sur le conseil général des bâtiments civils, depuis la création de ces services en l'an IV (1795) jusqu'en 1886* (Paris, Imprimerie Nationale, 1886)

Gray, G. H., *Housing and Citizenship, a Study of Low Cost Housing* (New York, Reinhold publishing corporation, 1946)

Grison, C., 'L'évolution du marché du logement dans l'agglomération parisienne du milieu du XIXe siècle à nos jours', Thèse pour le Doctorat de Sciences Economiques, Faculté de Droit, Université de Paris (unpublished thesis, 1956)

Guerrand, R. H., 'Aux origines de la cité radieuse: l'architecture phalanstérienne', *Architecture Mouvement Continuité*, no. 12 (1969), pp. 18–24

    Les origines du logement social en France, Collection 'L'évolution de la vie sociale' (Paris, Les Editions Ouvrières, 1967)

    Le logement populaire en France. Sources documentaires et bibliographie 1800–1960 (Paris, Centre d'Etudes et de Recherches Architecturales, 1979)

Guerrand, R. H. and Canfora-Argandona, E., *La répartition de la population, les conditions de logement des classes ouvrières à Paris au 19e siècle* (Paris, Centre de Sociologie Urbaine, 1976)

Guerrand, R. H., *Le origini della questione delle abitazioni in Francia (1850–1894)* (Rome, Officina Edizioni, 1981)

Halbwachs, M., *Les expropriations et le prix des terrains à Paris 1860–1900* (Paris, E. Cornely, 1909)

    La classe ouvrière et les niveaux de vie, recherches sur la hiérarchie des besoins dans les sociétés industrielles contemporaines (Paris, F. Alcan, 1913)

Harou-Romain, N., 'Des cités ouvrières', *Annales de la Charité*, V (1849), pp. 737–46

    'De l'assainissement des villes et de l'amélioration des habitations rurales au moyen d'une modification dans l'impôt de la propriété bâtie', *Annales de la Charité*, VI (1850), pp. 713–32

Haumont, N., Haumont, A., Raymond, H. and Raymond, M. G., *L'habitat pavillonaire*, 2nd edn (Paris, Centre de Recherche d'Urbanisme, 1971)

Haussonville, Comte d', *Etudes sociales. Misère et remèdes* (Paris, C. Levy, 1886)

    Etudes sociales. Socialisme et charité (Paris, C. Levy, 1895)

Hénard, E., *Etudes sur la transformation de Paris* (8 'fascicules', Paris, Librairies-Imprimeries Réunies, 1903–9)

Hottenger, G., 'La cité moderne et ses fonctions', *Bulletin de la Chambre de Commerce de Nancy*, no. 53 (1913), pp. 132–65
  L'habitation populaire et l'extension des villes, d'après les recents congrès (Nancy, Imprimeries Réunies, 1913)
Howard, E., *Garden Cities of Tomorrow* (London, Faber and Faber, 1965)
Huish, J. S. C., 'Speculators of the Second Empire' Kent University, (unpublished thesis, 1973)
Jaquemet, G., 'Belleville aux XIXe et XXe siècles: une methode d'analyse de la croissance urbaine à Paris', *Annales: Economies, Sociétés, Civilisations*, 30 (1975), pp. 819–43
Juillerat, P., 'Sur le casier sanitaire des maisons de Paris', *Congrès International d'Hygiène et de Démographie 1900* (Paris, Masson et Cie., n.d.), pp. 360–5
Juillerat, P. and Fillassier, Dr A., 'La statistique sanitaire des maisons. Le casier sanitaire des maisons de Paris', *Internationalen Kongress für Hygiene und Demographie 1907* (4 vols., Berlin, Verlag von August Hirschwald, 1908), vol. 3, pp. 1375–84
Juillerat, P., *L'hygiène du logement* (Paris, C. Delagrave, 1909)
Kulstein, D. I., *Napoleon III and the Working Class. A Study of Government Propaganda Under the 2nd Empire* (Los Angeles, Ward Ritchie Press, 1969)
Laisney, F., 'Quand les HLM étaient roses', *Architecture Mouvement Continuité*, no. 35 (1974), pp. 79–104
Lance, A., *Rapport fait au conseil de la Société Centrale des Architectes au nom de la commission nommée sur la proposition de M. Harou Romain pour étudier les moyens propres à assurer l'assainissement des habitations insalubres* (Paris, E. Thunot, 1850)
Lavollée, C., 'Rapport au nom du comité de commerce, sur diverses communications relatives aux habitations ouvrières', *Bulletin de la Société d'Encouragement pour l'Industrie Nationale*, 3rd series, IX (1882), pp. 481–96
Legge, T. M., *Public Health in European Capitals* (London, Swan Sonnenschein and Co., 1896)
Le Play, F., *Les ouvriers européens. Etude sur les travaux, la vie domestique et la condition morale des populations ouvrières de l'Europe précédée d'un exposé de la méthode d'observation* (2 vols., Paris, Imprimerie Impériale, 1855)
Leroy-Beaulieu, P., 'Le développement des grandes villes et la spéculation sur les immeubles urbains', *L'Economiste Français*, VII, 2 (1879), pp. 497–500
  'La construction des maisons de luxe et des maisons à bon marché à Paris', *L'Economiste Français*, X, 1 (1882), pp. 437–9, 469–71
Leuilliot, P., *L'Alsace au début du XIXe siècle. Essais d'histoire politique, économique et religieuse (1815–1830)* (3 vols., Paris, S.E.V.P.E.N., 1959, 1960)
Levasseur, E., *Histoire des classes ouvrières en France depuis 1789 jusqu'à nos jours* (2 vols., Paris, Hachette, 1867)
  La population française (3 vols., Paris, A. Rousseau, 1889–92)
  Histoire des classes ouvrières et de l'industrie en France de 1789 à 1870, 2nd edn (2 vols., Paris, A. Rousseau, 1903–4)
  Questions ouvrières et industrielles en France sous la IIIe République (Paris, A. Rousseau, 1907)
Lipstadt, H., 'César Daly: Revolutionary Architect?', *Architectural Design*, 48, no. 11–12 (1978), pp. 18–29
Lipstadt-Mendelsohn, H., 'Pour une histoire sociale de la presse architecturale: la *Revue Générale de l'Architecture* et César Daly (1840–1888)', Thèse de Doctorat en 3e Cycle, Ecole des Hautes Etudes en Sciences Sociales, Paris (unpublished thesis, 1979)
Lipstadt, H. and Mendelsohn, H. (eds.), *Architecte et ingénieur dans la presse: polémique, débat, conflit* (Paris, CORDA, IERAU, 1980)

Lough, J. and M., *An Introduction to Nineteenth Century France* (London, Longman, 1978)

Lucas, C., *Conférence sur l'habitation à toutes les époques* (Paris, Imprimerie Nationale, 1879)

    Etude sur les habitations à bon marché en France et à l'étranger (Paris, Aulanier et Cie., n.d., *c.* 1900)

Madre, Comte A. de, *Des ouvriers et des moyens d'améliorer leur condition dans les villes* (Paris, Hachette, 1863)

Magri, S., *Politique de logement et besoins en main d'oeuvre* (Paris, Centre de Sociologie Urbaine, 1972)

    Etude comparative des politiques du logement et de la main d'oeuvre. Paris et Londres 1890–1939 (Paris, Centre de Sociologie Urbaine, 1976)

    'Politique du logement et de l'état: exigences du capital et lutte des classes', *International Journal of Urban and Regional Research*, 1 (1977), pp. 304–20

    Les politiques municipales du logement dans le cadre des politiques de réforme sociale. Paris et Londres 1870–1914 (Paris, Centre de Sociologie Urbaine, 1980)

Mangin, A., 'La question du logement et les maisons d'ouvriers à Paris', *L'Economiste Français*, VII, 1 (1879), pp. 630–2

Mangini, F., *Les petits logements dans les grandes villes et plus particulièrement dans la ville de Lyon* (Lyons, A. Storck, 1891)

Marjolin, Dr, *Etude sur les causes et les effets des logements insalubres* (Paris, Masson, 1881)

Marrey, B., 'Saint-Simoniens, Fouriéristes et architecture; les réalisations architecturales des socialistes quarante-huitards', *Archives d'Architecture Moderne*, no. 20 (1981), pp. 74–99

Mayeur, J. M., *Les débuts de la IIIe République, 1871–1898*, Nouvelle Histoire de la France Contemporaine, 10 (Paris, Editions du Seuil, 1973)

Menier, E. J., 'Cité ouvrière de Noisiel', *BSFHBM*, 3 (1892), pp. 450–5

du Mesnil, Dr O., 'Les logements des ouvriers dans les grandes villes; garnis', *Congrés International d'Hygiene 1878* (2 vols., Paris, Imprimerie Nationale, 1880), vol. 1, pp. 552–69

    L'hygiène à Paris, L'habitation du pauvre (Paris, J. B. Baillière et fils, 1890)

du Mesnil, Dr O. and Mangenot, Dr, *Etude d'hygiène et d'économie sociale. Enquête sur les logements, professions, salaires et budgets* (*loyers inférieurs à 400 francs*) (Paris, Chaix, 1899)

Meuriot, P., 'Le livre foncier de Paris, 1911', *Journal de la Société de Statistique de Paris*, LIV (1913), pp. 364–407

Middleton, R. D., 'Viollet-le-Duc and the rational gothic tradition', (University of Cambridge, unpublished thesis, 1958)

    'Viollet-le-Duc's academic ventures and the Entretiens sur l'Architecture', *Gottfried Semper und die Mitte des 19 Jahrhunderts*, Symposium vom 2 bis 6 Dezember 1974 (Basel, Stuttgart, Birkhäuser Verlag, 1976), pp. 239–54

Muller, E., *Habitations ouvrières et agricoles, cités, bains et lavoirs, sociétés alimentaires, détails de construction, formules représentant chaque espèce de maison et donnant son prix de revient en tous pays, Statuts, règlements et contrats* (Paris, Victor Dalmont, 1855–6)

Muller, E. and Cacheux, E., *Les habitations ouvrières en tous pays, situation en 1878, avenir* (Paris, J. Dejey et Cie., 1879)

Muller, E. and du Mesnil, Dr O., 'Des habitations à bon marché au point de vue de la construction et de la salubrité', *Annales d'Hygiène Publique et de Médecine Légale*, 3rd series, XXII (1889), pp. 150–60

Muller, E., *Usines céramiques de Emile Muller*, 2nd edn (Paris, Chaix, 1889)

Muller, E. and Cacheux, E. *Les habitations ouvrières en tous pays*, 2nd edn (Paris, Baudry, 1889)

Muller, E. and Cacheux, E., *Les habitations ouvrières en tous pays, supplément par M. Emile Cacheux* (Paris, Ch. Béranger, n.d., *c.* 1903)

Murard, L. and Zylberman, P., 'Le petit travailleur infatigable', *Recherches*, no. 25, (1976)

Nicoulaud, O., 'Cités-jardins', *Architecture Mouvement Continuité*, no. 34 (1974), pp. 10–25

Nitot, H., *Les Cités-jardins. Etude sur le mouvement des cités-jardins, suivie d'une monographie de la cité-jardin de Trait (Seine-Inférieure)* (Paris, Presses Universitaires de France, 1924)

Office Centrale des Oeuvres Charitables, *La France charitable et prévoyante* (93 parts, Paris, E. Plon, Nourrit et Cie., 1896–1900)

Olchanski, C., *Le logement des travailleurs francais* (Paris, Librairie générale de droit et de jurisprudence, 1946)

Ostrowski, W., *Contemporary Town Planning from the Origins to the Athens Charter* (The Hague, International Federation for Housing and Planning, and Centre de Recherche d'Urbanisme, 1970)

Palmade, G. P., *French Capitalism in the Nineteenth Century*, trans. G. M. Holmes (Newton Abbot, David and Charles, 1972)

Passy, F., 'Un chef d'industrie alsacien, Jean Dollfus', *ASMP*, CXXX (1888), pp. 769–82

Pawlowski, C., *Tony Garnier et les débuts de l'urbanisme fonctionnel en France* (Paris, Centre de Recherches d'Urbanisme, 1967)

Penot, Dr A., 'Recherches statistiques sur Mulhouse', *BSIM*, XVI (1842–3), pp. 263–532
    'Projet de caisses de retraites et de prévoyance', *BSIM*, XXI (1847–8), pp. 386–417
    'Projet d'habitations pour les classes ouvrières; rapport presenté au nom du comité d'économie sociale', *BSIM*, XXIV (1852), pp. 129–41
    'Rapport du comité d'économie sociale sur la construction d'une cité ouvrière à Mulhouse', *BSIM*, XXV (1853), pp. 299–316
    'Les cités ouvrières du Haut-Rhin', *BSIM*, XXXXV (1865), pp. 385–432
    'Les institutions privées du Haut-Rhin; notes remises au comité départemental de l'Exposition Universelle de 1867. Section IV: logements, assurances', *BSIM*, XXXVII (1867), pp. 81–91

Picot, G., 'La question des logements ouvriers à Paris et à Londres', *BSES*, IX (1883–5), pp. 513–27
    Un devoir social, et logements d'ouvriers (Paris, Calmann-Levy, 1885)
    Exposition Universelle Internationale de 1889 à Paris; rapports du jury international, économie sociale; rapport sur les habitations ouvrières', *BSFHBM*, 2 (1891), pp. 286–315, 394–427
    Self-Help for Labour. Some French Solutions of Working Class Problems (London, Liberty and Property Defence League, 1892)
    La lutte contre le socialisme révolutionnaire (Paris, A. Colin, 1895)
    Notice historique sur la vie et les travaux de Jules Simon (Paris, Firmin-Didot et Cie., 1896)

Pinkney, D. H., *Napoleon III and the Rebuilding of Paris* (Princeton, NJ, Princeton University Press, 1958)

Piorry, P. A., *Des habitations et de l'influence de leurs dispositions sur l'homme en santé et en maladie* (Paris, Pourchet, 1838)

Plessis, A., *De la fête impériale au mur des fédérés, 1852–1871*, Nouvelle Histoire de la France Contemporaine, 9 (Paris, Editions du Seuil, 1973)

Puteaux, L., *Les constructions civiles* (Paris, Eugène Lacroix, 1873)

La question du logement et le mouvement ouvrier français (Paris, Editions de la Villette, 1981)

Raffalovich, A., *Le logement de l'ouvrier et du pauvre. Etats-Unis, Grande Bretagne, France, Allemagne, Belgique* (Paris, Guillaumin et Cie., 1887)

Raffalovich, A. and Roulliet, A., *Bibliographie des habitations à bon marché* (Le Mans, imprimerie E. Monnoyer, 1889)

Read, J., 'The garden city and the growth of Paris', *Architectural Review*, CLXIII (1978), pp. 345–352

Rebérioux, M., *La république radicale? 1898–1914*, Nouvelle Histoire de la France Contemporaine, 11 (Paris, Editions du Seuil, 1975)

La Renaissance des Cités, 1916–1935. Son utilité; ses travaux; sa fin active; sa continuité morale, (Gap, Louis Jean, 1936)

Retel, J. O., *Eléments pour une histoire du peuple de Paris au 19e siècle* (Paris, Centre de Sociologie Urbaine, 1977)

Rey, A. A., 'Street widening in close built areas by successive stages', *Town Planning Review*, V (1914–15), pp. 39–46

Risler, G., 'Note présentée au nom de la Société Française des habitations à bon marché à la Commission des habitations à bon marché du Conseil Municipal de Paris', *BSFHBM*, 22 (1912), pp. 208–17

'Les plans d'aménagement et d'extension des villes', *Bulletin de la Chambre de Commerce de Nancy*, no. 53 (1913), pp. 111–28

Roberts, H., *Des habitations des classes ouvrières*, traduit et publié par ordre du Président de la République (Paris, Gide et Baudry, 1850)

De la condition physique des classes ouvrières résultant de l'état de leurs habitations et des heureux effets des améliorations sanitaires récemment adoptées en Angleterre, traduit de l'anglais (Paris, Chaix, 1855)

Rochard, Dr J., 'La maison de l'ouvrier', *Revue des Deux Mondes*, LXXXVII (1888), pp. 393–421

'L'hygiène en 1889', *Revue des Deux Mondes*, XCVI (1889), pp. 54–85

Rochard, Dr J. (ed.), *Encyclopédie d'hygiène et de médecine publique*, (8 vols., 1890–5)

Rostand, E., 'La coopération appliquée à la construction des habitations à bon marché, *BSFHBM*, 1 (1890), pp. 325–56

'Le mouvement d'amélioration des habitations populaires en France. Etat de la question et quelques moyens d'avancer', *BSFHBM*, 11 (1900), pp. 48–66

Henri Sauvage 1873–1932, exhibition catalogue (Brussels, Archives d'Architecture Moderne; Paris, Société des Architectes Diplômés par le Gouvernement, 1976)

Schulze-Delitzsch, H., *Cours d'économie politique à l'usage des ouvriers et des artisans*, trans. B. Rampal (2 vols., Paris, Guillaumin, 1874)

Scolari, M., 'The origins of the working class house: design and theory', *Lotus*, No. 9 (1975), pp. 116–35

Sèche, L., *Jules Simon. Sa vie et son oeuvre* (Paris, A. Dupret, 1887)

Sellier, H., *La crise du logement et l'intervention publique en matière d'habitation populaire dans l'agglomération parisienne* (Paris, Editions de l'Office Public d'Habitations à Bon Marché du Département de la Seine, 1921)

Habitations à bon marché du département de la Seine (cités-jardins et maisons ouvrières) (Paris, C. Massin, 1922)

Sellier, H. and Bruggeman, A., *Le problème du logement. Son influence sur les conditions de l'habitation et de l'aménagement des villes* (Paris, Presses Universitaires de France, 1927)

Sellier, H., *Le socialisme et l'action municipale* (Paris, La Vie Communale, 1934)

Shapiro, A. L., 'Working class housing and public health in Paris, 1850–1902' (Brown University, USA, unpublished thesis, 1980)

'Private rights, public interest and professional jurisdiction: the French public health law of 1902', *Bulletin of the History of Medecine*, 54 (1980), pp. 4–22

Shaw, A., *Municipal Government in Continental Europe* (London, Unwin, 1895)

Siegfried, A., *Mes souvenirs de la IIIe République: mon père et son temps: Jules Siegfried, 1836–1922* (Paris, Editions du Grand Siècle, 1946)

Siegfried, J., *La misère. Son histoire, ses causes, ses remèdes* (Le Havre, J. Poinsignon, 1877)

Simiand, F., *Le salaire, l'évolution sociale et la monnaie* (Paris, F. Alcan, 1932)

Simon, J., *L'ouvrière* (Paris, Hachette, 1861)

De l'initiative privée et de l'Etat en matière de réformes sociales (Bordeaux, G. Gounouilhou, 1892)

Smets, M., *L'avènement de la cité-jardin en Belgique* (Brussels, Pierre Mardaga, 1977)

Société Française des Habitations à Bon Marché, *La question de la reconstruction des villes et villages détruits par la guerre* (Paris, 9, Rue de Solferino, 1916)

Société Industrielle de Mulhouse, *Histoire documentaire de l'industrie de Mulhouse et de ses environs au XIXe siecle* (2 vols., Mulhouse, Veuve Bader et Cie., 1902)

Souza, R. de, *L'avenir de nos villes. Nice, capitale d'hiver* (Paris, Nancy, Berger-Levrault, 1913)

Sutcliffe, A., *The Autumn of Central Paris. The Defeat of Town Planning 1850–1970*, Studies in Urban History, 1 (London, Edward Arnold, 1970)

'Environmental control and planning in European capitals 1850–1914: London Paris Berlin', *Growth and Transformation of the Modern City* (Stockholm, Swedish Council for Building Research, 1979), pp. 71–88

'Architecture and civic design in nineteenth century Paris', *Growth and Transformation of the Modern City* (Stockholm, Swedish Council for Building Research, 1979), pp. 89–100

Towards the Planned City, Comparative Studies in Social and Economic History, 3 (Oxford, Basil Blackwell, 1981)

Swenarton, M., *Homes Fit for Heroes* (London, Heinemann Educational Books, 1981)

Taricat, J. and Villars, M., *Le logement à bon marché. Chronique. Paris 1850–1930* (Boulogne, Editions Apogée, 1982)

Tarn, J. N., *Five Per Cent Philanthropy, an Account of Housing in Urban Areas between 1840 and 1914* (Cambridge, University Press, 1973)

Taylor, B. B., 'Sauvage and hygienic housing, or the cleanliness revolution', *Archithèse*, no. 12 (1974), pp. 13–16, 55

Teyssot, G., '"La casa per tutti": per una genealogia dei tipi', introduction to R. H. Guerrand, *Le origini della questione delle abitazioni in Francia (1850–1914)*, ed. Georges Teyssot (Rome, Officina Edizioni, 1981)

Trélat, E., *L'école centrale d'architecture* (Paris, A. Morel et Cie., 1864)

Ecole spéciale d'architecture, ouverture 1879–80, discours du directeur (Paris, 136, Boulevard Montparnasse, 1879)

'Cités ouvrières, maisons ouvrières', *Congrès International d'Hygiène 1878* (2 vols., Paris, Imprimerie Nationale, 1880), vol. 1, pp. 538–52

Influence exercée par la porosité des murs sur la salubrité des habitations (Geneva, Imprimerie Charles Schuchardt, 1883)

Régime de la température et de l'air dans la maison (The Hague, Imprimerie Sud-Hollandaise, 1886)

Aérage et chauffage des habitations (Paris, G. Masson, Editeur, 1886)

Images et figures résumant les règles et préceptes professés par l'auteur pour assurer la salubrité dans les édifices (Paris, Imprimerie de Delalain frères, 1886)

'Moyens de pourvoir les bâtiments de lumière et de chaleur solaires', *Internationaler Congress für Hygiene und Demographie zu Wien 1887*, Heft 11, pp. 35–43

La salubrité (Paris, E. Flammarion, 1899)

Trombert, A., *Charles Robert, sa vie, son oeuvre* (2 vols., Paris, Chaix, F. Alcan, 1927, 1931)

Union Féminine Civique et Sociale de Dunkerque, *L'habitation ouvrière dans l'agglomération dunkerquoise* (Lille, C.A.U.E. du Nord, 1981)

Unwin, R., *Town Planning in Practice: An Introduction to the Art of Designing Cities and Suburbs*, 2nd edn (London, Unwin, 1911)

Véron, E., *Les institutions ouvrières de Mulhouse et de ses environs*, (Paris, Hachette, 1866)

Villermé, Dr L. R., *Tableau de l'état physique et moral des ouvriers dans les manufactures de coton, de laine et de soie* (2 vols., Paris, Jules Renouard et Cie., 1840)

'Communication sur les cités ouvrières', *ASMP*, XVII (1850), pp. 225–39

Weber, A. F., *The Growth of Cities in the Nineteenth Century* (New York, MacMillan, 1899)

Weill, G., *Histoire du mouvement social en France 1852–1902* (Paris, F. Alcan, 1904)

L'Alsace française de 1789 à 1870 (Paris, F. Alcan, 1916)

Williams, N., 'Paradise and the bourgeois villa, the architecture of the Parisian suburbs 1850–1914' (Department of Architecture, University of Cambridge, unpublished dissertation, 1980)

Wohl, A. S., *The Eternal Slum, Housing and Social Policy in Victorian London*, Studies in Urban History, 5 (London, Edward Arnold, 1977)

Wolf, P., *Eugène Henard and the Beginning of Urbanism in Paris, 1900–1914* (The Hague, International Federation for Housing and Planning, and Centre de Recherche d'Urbanisme, 1968)

'City structuring and social sense in 19th and 20th century urbanism', *Perspecta*, no. 13–14 (1971), pp. 222–31

Zeldin, T., *France 1848–1945* (2 vols., Oxford, Clarendon Press, 1973, 1977)

Sources for illustrations

PART ONE: GERMANY

1 Reich, *Wohnungsmarkt*, pp. 124–5
2 *Die Resultate der Berliner Volkszählung vom 3 December 1864* (Berlin, 1866), pp. 3–8; *Die Bevölkerungs-, Gewerbe- und Wohnungsaufnahme von 1 December 1875*, Heft 1, Berlin, 1878, pp. 113–16; the data after 1875 are taken from the section on 'Bevölkerung' published in the annual digest of statistics for Berlin in the *Stat. J. Berlin*; the data on the population of the selected suburbs are taken from the summary of 'Die Volkszählung vom 1 December 1910 in den Vororten', *Stat. J. Berlin*, 32 (Berlin, 1913)
3 Thienel, *Städtewachstum*, fig. 2; and map by Reimer in the Landesarchiv in Berlin
4 Reich, *Wohnungsmarkt*, pp. 126–8, tables 3 and 4
5 Hoffmann, *Die Wohnungen der Arbeiter*, Plates I and II
6 *Facsimile Querschnitt durch den Kladderadatsch*, p. 62
7 Based on F. Monke, 'Einflüsse der Baugesetze und Bauordnungen auf das Wohnhaus'
8 *Berlin und seine Bauten*, pt IV, vol. A, p. 46
9 Adickes, Hinkeldyn, Classen, 'Die Notwendigkeit weiträumiger Bebauung', *VföG*, 24 (1892), p. 114
10 Varrentrap, 'Häuser der gemeinnützigen Baugesellschaft', *VföG*, 6 (1874), p. 401
11 Weissbach, *Wohnhäuser*, p. 270
12 Günther, 'Arbeitersiedlungen im Ruhrgebiet', p. 469; and Bollerey and Hartmann, *Wohnen im Revier*, Object 65
13 Bollerey and Hartmann, *Wohnen im Revier*, Object 57
14 Weissbach, *Wohnhäuser*, p. 257
15 *Führer durch die Essener Wohnungssiedlungen*, p. 45
16 *Führer durch die Essener Wohnungssiedlungen*, p. 47
17 *Führer durch die Essener Wohnungssiedlungen*, pp. 15 and 46
18 *Berlin und seine Bauten*, pt IV, vol. B, pp. 5–6
19 Eberstadt, *Handbuch*, pp. 232–3
20 Eberstadt, *Handbuch*, p. 231
21 *Berlin und seine Bauten*, 1st edn (Berlin, 1877), pt I, p. 450; and *Berlin und seine Bauten*, pt IV, vol. A, p. 2
22 Goecke, 'Das Berliner Arbeiter-Mietshaus', p. 501
23 *Centralblatt der Bauverwaltung*, 13 (1893, p. 446)
24 *Berliner Architekturwelt*, 2 (1900), pp. 315–21
25 *Berliner Architekturwelt*, 2 (1900), pp. 315–21
26 *Berlin und seine Bauten*, pt IV, vol. B, pp. 146–7
27 *Berlin und seine Bauten*, pt IV, vol. A, p. 123

28 Weissbach, *Wohnhäuser*, p. 228; 'Die Verbesserung der Wohnungen', p. 120, p. 196
29 Hecker, *Der Krupp'sche Kleinwohnungsbau*, pp. 11, 12
30 *Wohlfahrtseinrichtungen der Gussstahlfabrik der Firma Krupp*, 2, pp. 28, 31
31 *Führer durch die Essener Wohnungssiedlungen*, p. 49
32 Weissbach and Mackowsky, *Das Arbeiterwohnhaus*, pp. 157–8
33 Henrici, 'Arbeiterkolonien', Plates 41 and 42
34 Schultze-Naumburg, *Die künstlerische Gestaltung*, pp. 30–1
35 Vogt, 'Über die Richtung städtischer Strassen', p. 327
36 *Führer durch die Essener Wohnungssiedlungen*, p. 30; and Muthesius, *Kleinhaus*, p. 143
37 Ranke, *Heinrich Zille*, p. 133
38 Reich, *Wohnungsmarkt*, pp. 146–7, tables XXII C and D
39 A: Ascher, *Wohnungsmieten*, table 13; B and C: Reich, *Wohnungsmarkt*, table XV; D: Reich, *Wohnungsmarkt*, table XIV (column 6)
40 A1: Reich, *Wohnungsmarkt*, p. 127, table III; A2: Reich, *Wohnungsmarkt*, p. 128, table V; B: Ascher, *Wohnungsmieten*, p. 120
41 Based on the map of Gross-Berlin (1:40,000) published by the Bibliographisches Institut Leipzig, 1913
42 Schwann, *Die Wohnungsnot und das Wohnungselend in Deutschland*, pp. 136, 138

PART TWO: FRANCE

 1 Considérant, *L'Avenir*
 2 Taricat + Villars, *Le logement à bon marché*, p. 61
 3 Teyssot, Introduction to Italian edn of Guerrand, *Le origini della questiona delle abitazioni in Francia (1850–1914)*, plate 113
 4 Photo: James Read
 5 Muller + Cacheux, *Les habitations ouvrières*, plate 15
 6 Foucher de Careil, *Les habitations ouvrières*, plate 2
 7 Muller, *Habitations ouvrières*, plate 2
 8 Photo: James Read
 9 Muller + Cacheux, *Les habitations ouvrières*, plate 1
10 Société Industrielle de Mulhouse, *Histoire documentaire* vol. 1, plate 4 (20)
11 Picot, *Notice historique sur la vie et les travaux de Jules Simon*, frontispiece
12 Société Industrielle de Mulhouse, *Histoire documentaire*, vol. 1, plate 12 (15)
13 de Foville, *Notice historique sur la vie et les oeuvres de M. Georges Picot*, frontispiece
14 Cheysson, *Oeuvres choisies*, vol. 1, frontispiece
15 Trombert, *Charles Robert, sa vie, son oeuvre*, vol. 1, frontispiece
16 Evenson, *Paris: a century of change, 1878–1978*, p. 151
17 Muller + Cacheux, *Supplément*, plate XXXIX
18 *Internationaler Kongress für Hygiene und Demographie 1907*, vol. 3, p. 1382
19 Evenson, *Paris: a century of change, 1878–1978*, p. 205
20 *L'Office Public d'Habitations de la Ville de Paris, 1937*, p. 74
21 *Architecture Mouvement Continuité*, No. 43, p. 11
22 Hénard, *Etude sur les transformations de Paris*, Fascicule 2, p. 49
23 *Architecture Mouvement Continuité*, No. 43, p. 13
24 *Architecture d'Aujourd'hui*, June 1937, p. 43
25 Sellier, *La crise du logement*, p. 791
26 Cacheux, *L'économiste pratique*, plate 18
27 *RGA*, XXVI (1868), plate 11
28 Photo: James Read

29 Photo: James Read
30 a. *RGA*, XXV (1867), plate 55
30 b. *RGA*, XXVI (1868), plate 11
30 c. Foucher de Careil, *Les habitations ouvrières*, plate 1
31 Lucas, *Etude*, p. 109
32 *BSFHBM*, 1 (1890), between pages 120–1
33 Photo: James Read
34 *Henri Sauvage 1873–1932*, p. 23
35 Taricat + Villars, *Le logement à bon marché*, p. 100
36 Pawlowski, *Tony Garnier*, p. 120
37 *La Construction Moderne*, 2 September 1905
38 Ibid.
39 Taricat + Villars, *Le logement à bon marché*, p. 112
40 *Henri Sauvage, 1873–1932*, p. 165
41 Ville de Paris, *le concours pour la construction d'habitations à bon marché*, plates
    1, 3, 20, 21
42 Muller, *Habitations ouvrières*, plate 23
43 Muller + Cacheux, *Les habitations ouvrières*, plate 66
44 Ibid., plate 8
45 Benevolo, *The origins of modern town planning*, p. 121
46 *BSFHBM*, 19 (1909), p. 439
47 Cacheux, *L'économiste pratique*, plate 5
48 Muller + Cacheux, *Les habitations ouvrières*, plate 17
49 Ibid., plate 66
50 *RGA*, XXV (1867), plate 44
51 *BSFHBM*, 4 (1893), opposite page 248
52 Muller + Cacheux, *Les habitations ouvrières*, plate 20
53 Lucas, *Etude*, p. 208
54 Muller + Cacheux, *Supplément*, plate 9
55 Annual reports of the Conseil Supérieur des Habitations à Bon Marché; Paul
    Strauss report, *Documents Parlementaires*, Sénat (1912), No. 352

CONCLUSION

 1 Bouvier (ed.), *L'ère industrielle*, p. 33 (from a document in the possession
    of Michelle Perrot)
 2 *Das neue Frankfurt*, vol. 4. nos 4/5 (Frankfurt, 1930), p. 76
 3 Photo: James Read

We thank the following for permission to reproduce illustrations: Part One: The
British Architectural Library, RIBA, London for nos 3, 8, 12, 13, 18, 21, 26,
27 and 42; Part Two: The British Library for nos 11 and 14.

In part Two, nos 1, 5, 7, 9, 10, 12, 13, 15, 17, 18, 22, 26, 32, 41–4, 46–9,
51, 52 and 54 are photographed by the Bibliothèque Nationale, Paris.

Chronology

	England	Germany	France
1840			Dr L. R. Villermé, *Tableau de l'état physique et moral des ouvriers dans les manufactures de coton, de laine et de soie* *Revue Générale de l'Architecture et des Travaux Publics* founded by César Daly
1841	Foundation of the Metropolitan Society for Improving the Dwellings of the Industrious Classes	C. W. Hoffmann's first proposals for a non-profit housing association	Legislation on expropriation for public works projects
1842	*Report on the Sanitary Conditions of the Labouring Population and the Means of its Improvement*		
1843	Royal Commission on the Health of Towns	Bettina von Arnim. *Dies Buch gehört dem König*	
1844	Metropolitan Building Act Foundation of the Health of Towns Association Foundation of the Society for Improving the Conditions of the Labouring Classes (SICLC)	Riots by the Silesian weavers Foundation of the Centralverein für das Wohl der arbeitenden Classen (CVWaK)	
1845		*Janus, Jahrbücher deutscher Gesinnung, Bildung und Tat* founded by V. A. Huber Prussian legislation strengthening the powers, granted under the Allgemeine Landrecht of 1794, of the *Baupolizei* to determine street layout and building design and construction	*Annales de la Charité* founded by Armand de Melun

	England	Germany	France
1846		V. A. Huber, *Über innere Colonisation* The Verein zur Verbesserung der Arbeiterwohnungen founded by C. W. Hoffmann	Articles on workers' housing in England, France and Belgium published in the *Revue Générale de l'Architecture et des Travaux Publics*
1847		Riots in a number of German cities over the food shortages C. W. Hoffmann launches the Berliner gemeinnützige Baugesellschaft	
1848	Cholera Epidemic Public Health Act	The March Revolution Cholera Epidemic	February: the King, Louis-Philippe, abdicates May: official proclamation of the Second Republic June: the June days: violent suppression of rioting in Paris July: tax reliefs on new building introduced, including a special subsidy for workers' housing in Paris: Sous-Comptoir des Entrepreneurs founded December: Louis Napoleon elected President of the Republic Reorganisation of hygiene services in response to the threat of cholera J. A. Blanqui visits urban areas to study working-class conditions; submits report to the Académie des Sciences Morales et Politiques

622

1849	Model Dwellings, Streatham Street, for the SICLC, by Henry Roberts *(see 1850)*	First houses of the Berliner gemeinnützige Baugesellschaft opened on the Wollankstrasse	Paris: Société des Cités Ouvrières founded; the society finances the Cité Napoléon
			Government commission set up to study public baths and laundries
			Louis Napoleon sends a commission to England to study workers' housing
1850	Model Dwellings, Streatham Street, for the SICLC, by Henry Roberts	Prussian legislation further strengthens the powers of the *Baupolizei* to regulate building	H. Roberts, *The Dwellings of the Labouring Classes* translated into French under the patronage of Louis Napoleon
	H. Roberts, *The Dwellings of the Labouring Classes*		Legislation on housing hygiene
1851	Sir Titus Salt commences the construction of Saltaire		Legislation providing subsidies for public baths and laundries
	Lodging Houses Act, permits local authorities to erect buildings for lodging houses with finance from the Public Works Loan Commissioners		December: coup d'état organised by Louis Napoleon
1852		Translation into German of Henry Roberts' *The Dwellings of the Labouring Classes*	Dr A. Penot presents report on workers' housing to the Société Industrielle de Mulhouse
			Crédit Foncier founded
			Official patronage of housing: 10 million franc subsidy announced in January; competition for housing designs in Paris announced in May
			December: declaration of the Second Empire; the President Louis-Napoleon becomes Emperor Napoleon III
1853		New Building Regulations to control the form of development in Berlin by limiting the maximum height of buildings and the minimum size of court	Mulhouse: Société des Cités Ouvrières founded under the lead of Jean Dollfus
			Lille: the Scrive brothers found a housing society for their employees
			G. Haussman appointed Prefect of the Seine Department

	England	Germany	France
1854		Renewed outbreak of Cholera	
1855	The Metropolitan Management Act and the creation of the Metropolitan Board of Works	H. Schulze-Delitzsch, *Vorschuss-Vereine als Volks-banken*	Exposition Universelle held in Paris
1856		Prussian Municipalities gain the power to prepare city extension plans subject to approval by the *Baupolizei* Foundation of the Alexandra Stiftung in Berlin	E. Muller, *Habitations ouvrières et agricoles* Société d'Economie Sociale founded by F. le Play
1857		V. A. Huber travels to England (meeting Lord Shaftesbury); writes *Die Wohnungsnoth der kleinen Leute in grossen Städten* Foundation of the Kongress deutscher Volkswirte (KdV)	
1858			
1859	G. Godwin, *Town Swamps and Social Bridges*	V. A. Huber, *Über die Wohnungsfrage in England und Frankreich*	Guise: J. B. A. Godin starts building the Familistère for workers in his factory
1860		Foundation of the Frankfurter gemeinnützige Baugesellschaft	Guebwiller: housing society founded Lille: Bureau de Bienfaisance builds a block of flats Paris city limits extended
1861		V. A. Huber launches a new periodical *Concordia* Census for Berlin, giving, for the first time, detailed information on housing conditions Krupp builds housing for his supervisors	J. Simon, *L'ouvrière*

624

1862	George Peabody establishes the Peabody Trust	Publication of James Hobrecht's plan for Berlin / Foundation of the first mortgage bank in Berlin / Foundation of the Häuserbau-Genossenschaft von Schiffszimmern in Hamburg	Workers' delegation visits the Universal Exhibition in London
1863	Sydney Waterlow founds the Improved Industrial Dwelling Company	Krupp builds first (temporary) workers' housing estate on the Westend site / First publication of *Die Vierteljahrschrift für Volkswirtschaft und Kulturgeschichte*	Société de Crédit au Travail founded
1864	Octavia Hill begins her work with the management of slum property	First discussion of 'Die Wohnungsfrage' at the annual meeting of the KdV	Beaucourt: Japy frères found housing society / Caisse d'Escompte des Associations Populaires founded
1865		CVWaK sets up a committee to consider the Wohnungsfrage / Publication of CVWaK study *Die Wohnungsfrage* / F. W. Lange *Jedermann Hauseigenthümer*	Clichy: Mme Jouffroy Renault finances a group of workers' housing / Anzin: consumer co-operative founded for workers in the mines / Ecole Centrale (later Spéciale) d'Architecture founded / Paris municipal statistics department established
1866	Sanitary Act / J. Hole, *The Homes of the Working Classes with Suggestions for their Improvement* / Labouring Classes Dwelling Houses Act, establishes the right of local authorities to borrow from the Public Works Loan Commissioners to purchase sites and erect dwellings for the labouring classes	Renewed outbreak of Cholera / J. Faucher, *Die Bewegung für Wohnungsreform* / Austro-Prussian War	Colmar: housing society founded by A. Herzog / Amiens: Société Anonyme des Maisons Ouvrières founded / Saint Quentin: Société Académique holds competition for a study of housing

	England	Germany	France
1867	Foundation of the Artizans', Labourers' and General Dwelling Co.	KDV rejects the problem of housing as an issue of general concern	Lille: Compagnie Immobilière founded
		Construction of sewering and water supply systems started in Frankfurt to designs by Lindley	Paris: Société Coopérative Immobilière, and Société Coopérative Immobilière des Ouvriers founded
		Co-operative associations win legal recognition in Prussia	Exposition Universelle held in Paris; includes major presentation of workers' housing
		Formation of the North German Bund	Legislation on limited liability companies
1868	Torrens' Artizans' and Labourers' Dwelling Act		Dunkirk: Société pour l'Encouragement des Sciences, des Lettres et des Arts holds competition for a housing design
			Paris: Epargne Immobilière housing co-operative founded by the Association des Maçons
1869	The Improved Industrial Dwellings Co. begins the construction of the Bethnal Green Estate	First publication of the *Deutsche Vierteljahrschrift für öffentliche Gesundheitspflege*	Reims: housing society founded; architect, A. Gosset
	Foundation of the Charity Organisation Society	E. Sax, *Die Wohnungszustände der arbeitenden Classen*	
1870		Franco-Prussian War; victory for Prussia	Reims: Union Foncière founded
			July: declaration of War with Prussia
			September: end of the Second Empire declaration of a new Republic: siege of Paris begins
			October: 3-month moratorium introduced on rents due in Paris

1871		Unification of Germany Start of the campaign for national legislation to control the forms of new urban developments launched by the Versammlung deutscher Naturförscher und Ärzte Krupp starts building permanent workers' housing: Schederhof, Kronenberg, and Baumgarten estates K. Manega, *Die Anlage von Arbeiterwohnungen* Foundation of the Verband deutscher Architekten- und Ingenieurvereine	January: moratorium on Paris rents extended Armistice, and capitulation of Paris March–May: the Commune holds power in Paris Le Havre: Société des Cités Ouvrières founded under the lead of Jules Siegfried Emile Cheysson takes up office as a Director of the Schneider company in Le Creusot
1872		Foundation of the Verein für Sozialpolitik (VfSP); Ernst Engel presents one of the three papers at the opening conference on 'Die Wohnungsfrage' F. Engels, *Zur Wohnungsfrage*	Nancy: housing society founded Exposition Internationale et Spéciale d'Economie Domestique held in Paris
1873	Special Report by the Charity Organisation Society: *The Dwellings of the Poor*	Banking Crisis in Vienna and Berlin First publication of the *Statistisches Jahrbuch der Stadt Berlin* Foundation of the Verein für öffentliche Gesundheitspflege (VföG)	

627

	England	Germany	France
1874		VföG debates the form of control for urban development: *Anforderungen der öffentlichen Gesundheitspflege an die Baupolizei auf neue Stadtteile, Strassen und Häuser* *Verband deutscher Architekten- und Ingenieurvereine* debates the same issue: *Grundzügen für Stadterweiterungen nach technischen, wirtschaftlichen und polizeilichen Besiehung* Prussian *Enteignungsgesetz* provides municipalities with extended powers for the compulsory purchase of land and buildings for projects of public utility	Noisiel: construction starts on the workers' village adjacent to the Menier chocolate factory *Le Havre*: the Cercle Franklin workers' club set up under the lead of Jules Siegfried
1875	The 'Great' Public Health Act Cross', Artizans' and Labourers' Dwellings Act	Construction of sewering system for Berlin Prussian *Fluchtliniengesetz* The Gotha Programme: Unity of the 'Lassalleaner' and the 'Eisenacher' to form the SPD	
1876		R. Baumeister, *Stadt-Erwieterungen in technischer, baupolizeilicher und wirthschaftlicher Beziehung*	
1877	Circulation of the Model Bye-Laws by the Local Government Board		J. Siegfried, *La misère* *L'Egalité*, socialist newspaper, founded by Jules Guesde Société Française d'Hygiène, and Société de Médecine Publique et d'Hygiène Professionelle founded

628

1878		Foundation of the Flensburger Arbeiterbauverein by Christian Hansen Anti-Socialist legislation	Bolbec: housing society founded under the lead of Jules Siegfried Jules Siegfried becomes mayor of Le Havre Exposition Universelle and International Hygiene Congress held in Paris
1879		VföG debates the question of control of lodging houses	E. Muller and E. Cacheux, *Les habitations ouvrières en tous pays* Orléans: Société Immobilière founded The question of rent levels in working-class areas is brought up in the Paris municipal council
1880		R. Baumeister, *Normale Bauordnung* Foundation of Arbeiterwohl, Verband katholischer Industrielle und Arbeiterfreunde	Ministerial commission set up to consider waste disposal in Paris
1881	Appointment of a Parliamentary Select Committee on Housing Second Special Report by the Charity Organisation Society on the housing question: *The Dwellings of the Poor*	Translation into German of Henry George's *Progress and Poverty*	Proposal to revise the 1850 housing hygiene legislation submitted to Parliament
1882		Completion of the *Ringbahn* around Berlin	Paris: Société Anonyme des Habitations Ouvrières de Passy Auteuil founded Commission Technique de l'Assainissement set up to consider waste disposal in Paris Socialist congress leads to a split between the Guesdists and the possibilistes. The possibiliste Jules Joffrin is elected to the Paris municipal council; the Guesdists organise a petition for a reduction in rents

629

	England	Germany	France
1883	Cheap Trains Act Rev. A. Mearns, *The Bitter Cry of Outcast London*	*Krankenversicherungsgesetz* initiates Bismark's programme of social legislation	The Commission Technique de l'Assainissement reports in favour of the *tout-à-l'égout* system The Prefect of the Seine sets up an administrative commission on workers' housing The Government proposes a means of financing workers' housing through the Crédit Foncier The Paris municipal council sets up a special housing commission to study the Government proposal
1884	Appointment of a Royal Commission to investigate the housing of the working classes	Introduction of differential zoning regulations in Altona under Adickes	
1885	Publication of the Royal Commission's Report: *The Housing of the Working Classes* The Housing of the Working Classes Act, lowers interest rates for loans for housing from the Public Works Loan Commissioners	VfSP launches an enquiry into 'Die Wohnungsfrage' Foundation of the Hannover Spar- und Bauverein	E. Cacheux, *L'économiste pratique* G. Picot, *Un devoir social, et logements d'ouvriers* Lyons: Société des Logements Economiques founded Rouen: Société des Petits Logements founded; architect, E. Lecoeur Jules Siegfried elected to the Chambre des Députés First national congress of consumer co-operatives held

Year	Britain	Germany	France
1886		Publication of the VfSP's enquiry into the housing question: *Die Wohnungsnoth der ärmeren Klassen in deutschen Grossstädten und Vorschläge zu deren Abhülfe* G. Schmoller, *Mahnruf in der Wohnungsfrage* VföG calls for tougher controls on the form of new developments: Stadterweiterungen, insbesondere in hygienischer Beziehung Foundation of the Landliga (after 1898, the Band deutscher Bodenreformer) by Flürscheim Foundation of the Berliner Baugenossenschaft	Exposition d'Hygiène Urbaine held in Paris; Emile Cheysson delivers a paper on *La question des habitations ouvrières* Jules Siegfried submits a proposal to enforce public health regulations
1887		New building regulations for Berlin	A. Raffalovich, *Le logement des ouvriers* The Société d'Economie Sociale organises a survey of workers' housing The Government presents a proposal to revise the 1850 housing hygiene legislation
1888	Lever begins the construction of Port Sunlight	Foundation of the Verein zur Verbesserung der kleinen Wohnungen in Berlin The Deutscher Verein für Armenpflege und Wohltätigkeit first debates the housing question	Paris: the Société Philanthropique starts to build its first block of workers' flats in Paris; architect, W. Chabrol

	England	Germany	France
1889	First elections for the LCC	VföG debates the form of national housing legislation: *Reichsgesetzlichen Vorschläge zum Schutze des gesunden Wohnens* C. Sitte, *Der Städtebau nach künstlerischen Grundsätzen* Legislation introducing limited liability for co-operatives	E. Muller and E. Cacheux, *Les habitations ouvrières en tous pays*, second edition Marseilles: Société Anonyme des Habitations Salubres et à Bon Marché founded under the lead of Eugène Rostand Exposition Universelle held in Paris; includes a major presentation of workers' housing International Hygiene Congress, and the first International Congress of Cheap Housing held in Paris Société Française des Habitations à Bon Marché founded
1890	Housing of the Working Classes Act establishes the right of the local authority to build and manage housing for the working classes for the first time	T. Goecke's article, 'Das Berliner Arbeitermietshaus', initiates a discussion of the design of 'improved' tenement housing for Berlin First scheme for the development of the Weissbach'sen estate for the Verein zur Verbesserung kleinen Wohnungen by August Messel J. Stübben, *Der Städtebau* Extension of the invalidity and pension legislation to permit the use of the funds of the regional insurance boards to capitalise non-profit housing associations Foundation of the Aktienbaugesellschaft für kleine Wohnungen in Frankfurt by Karl Flesch	Dr O. du Mesnil, *L'hygiène à Paris. L'habitation du pauvre* E. Rostand delivers a paper on housing co-operatives at the congress of consumer co-operatives The Société Française des Habitations à Bon Marché organises a housing competition in Saint Denis Office Central des Oeuvres Charitables founded

1891	Introduction of differential zoning regulations in Frankfurt

VföG discusses the inspection of existing housing: Handhabung der gesundheitlichen Wohnpolizei

Foundation of the Centralstelle für Arbeiter-Wohlfahrtseinrichtungen in Berlin (CAW) | Marseilles: La Pierre du Foyer, housing co-operative, founded

Census; for the first time, statistics relating to dwelling size and occupation levels in Paris are collected

Proposal to revise the 1850 housing hygiene legislation submitted to the Chambre des Députés |
| 1892 | Introduction of differential zoning regulations in Berlin

(CAW) conference of workers' housing: 'Die Verbesserung der Wohnungen'

Foundation of the Berliner Spar- und Bauverein

Foundation of the first Beamtenwohnungsverein in Kassel

A. E. Schäffle and P. Lechler, *Nationale Wohnungsreform* | Reorganisation of the Paris hygiene services: Commission d'Assainissement et de Salubrité de l'Habitation set up under Dr A. J. Martin

Jules Siegfried submits a proposal for housing legislation to the Chambre des Députés |
| 1893 | Start of the development of the LCC's Boundary Street Estate

Reform of municipal tax structure through Miquel's Kommunalabgabengesetz | Bureau de l'Assainissement de l'Habitation set up in Paris; the technical section starts to collect information for the *Casier Sanitaire*

The Ville de Paris floats a loan to extend the city's water and sewer system |

	England	Germany	France
1894	Cadbury begins the construction of the Bournville Estate	R. Eberstadt, *Städtische Bodenfragen* / Housing for the Berliner Spar- und Bauverein on the Sickingenstrasse by A. Messel / VföG debates the application of differential zoning regulations: *Die unterschiedliche Behandlung der Bauordnungen für die Innere, die Aussengebiete und die Umgebung von Städten*	Musée Social founded / Legislation on housing: Habitations à Bon Marché (Loi Siegfried) / Legislation obliges proprietors in Paris to link their properties to the mains sewer
1895		Police regulations passed in the Düsseldorf area to permit inspection of existing housing / First debate on the housing question in the Reichstag / Expansion of the provision of funds for housing for those in Prussian State service	Roubaix: La Ruche Roubaisienne founded / Legislation on Caisses d'Epargne authorises them to lend money to finance cheap housing
1896		Max Brandts puts forward proposals for assisting the growth of the non-profit sector: *Aufgaben und Organisation der Wohnungsfürsorge insbesondere in den Städten*	
1897	Start of the development of the LCC's Millbank Estate (under Part III of the 1890 Housing Act)	Housing on the Proskauerstrasse for the Berliner Spar- und Bauverein by A. Messel / Foundation of the Rheinsicher Verein für Förderung des Arbeiterwohnungs-Wesens by Brandts	
1898	Ebenezer Howard, *Tomorrow: A Peaceful Path to Real Reform*	Damaschke takes over the leadership of the Bund deutscher Bodenreformer / Foundation of Verein Reichswohngesetz in Frankfurt	Société de Crédit des Habitations à Bon Marché founded as an intermediary between the Caisse des Dépôts et Consignations and housing societies

1899		VISP launches its second enquiry into the housing question Pastor Bodelschwingh raises the housing question in the Reichstag; appointment of a committee to consider the issue	Paris: Groupe des Maisons Ouvrières founded
1900	Formation of the National Housing Reform Council Housing of the Working Classes Act, amends Part III of the 1890 Act so that urban councils were allowed to erect housing outside their own districts Start of the development of the LCC's cottage estate at Totterdown Fields, Tooting	Introduction of *Erbbaurecht* in Frankfurt Foundation of the Beamtenwohnungsverein in Berlin	François Hennebique pioneers the use of a concrete frame structure for an apartment building Exposition Universelle held in Paris, together with various international congresses: Hygiene; Cheap Housing; and the Congress of Architects, which considers the question of cheap housing for the first time First part of the Paris Métro opened
1901	Rowntree begins the construction of New Earswick to designs by Raymond Unwin	Lex Adickes: introduction of legislation in Frankfurt making *Umlegung* possible Substantial increase in the Reichswohnungsfürsorgefonds Commitment to Prussian legislation on housing in the King's speech Extended debate in the Reichstag on the housing question VISP's second enquiry into housing published as *Neue Untersuchungen über die Wohnungsfrage* A. Grävell, *Die Baugenossenschaftsfrage*, the response of property interests to the growth of the non-profit sector	Tony Garnier's *Cité Industrielle* exhibited

	England	Germany	France
1902		Foundation of the Deutsche Gartenstadtgesellschaft First publication of the *Zeitschrift für Wohnungswesen*	Legislation on public health supersedes the 1850 housing hygiene legislation
1903	Foundation of the First Garden City Ltd and purchase of the Letchworth site W. Thompson, *Housing Handbook*	Publication of draft Prussian Bill on Housing E. Jäger, *Die Wohnungsfrage*	E. Hénard publishes the first of his *Etudes sur la transformation de Paris* Paris: Société des Logements Economiques pour Familles Nombreuses, and Société des Logements Hygiéniques et à Bon Marché founded The Musée Social sponsors Georges Benoît-Lévy on a visit to England to study the Garden City Interministerial commission set up to consider the role of local municipalities in the construction of cheap housing The Paris municipal council sets up a special housing commission
1904	T. C. Horsfall, *The Example of Germany*	T. Goecke and C. Sitte launch *Der Städtebau* First reading of the Prussian Housing Bill First Deutscher Wohnungskongress organised in Frankfurt by Verein Reichswohnungsgesetz Introduction of the Wertzuwachssteuer in Frankfurt	G. Benoît-Lévy, *La cité-jardin* Paris: Fondation Rothschild founded Alliance d'Hygiène Sociale founded First International Congress of House Cleansing and Hygiene held in Paris Jules Siegfried submits a proposal for legislation to ease the expropriation of unhealthy property

1905	Hampstead Garden Suburbs begun, to plans of Unwin and Parker	A. Voigt and P. Geldner, *Kleinhaus und Mietskaserne*	Paris: Le Progrès housing society, and the Fondation des Habitations Economiques des Employés de la Banque, du Commerce et de l'Industrie founded
		CAW Conference on the design of workers' housing: Die künstlerische Gestaltung des Arbeiterwohnhauses	Fondation Rothschild organises a competition for a housing development in Paris
			Henri Turot submits the report of the Paris council's special housing commission
1906		First Deutscher Wohnungskonferenz	Legislation on housing extends the scope of the 1894 housing law
			Jules Siegfried and Alexandre Ribot submit a proposal for legislation to aid rural housing
1907	Hampstead Garden Suburbs begun, to plans of Unwin and Parker		
	Victory by the Moderates in the LCC elections leads to a change in housing policy by the LCC		
1908	J. S. Nettleford, *Practical Housing*	Foundation of first German garden city at Dresden-Hellerau	Section d'Hygiène Urbaine et Rurale set up within the Musée Social
			Legislation on rural housing, introducing the Sociétés de Crédit Immobilier
1909	Housing and Town Planning Act, permits urban authorities to determine the layout of main streets, to designate areas of industrial and residential development and, to a limited extent, to control the form of new housing in these areas	R. Eberstadt, *Handbuch des Wohnungswesens*	The compagnie des Mines de Dourges inaugurates the 'first garden city' in France
			The demolition of slum areas is included as part of a major programme of public works in Paris
			Proposal for legislation introducing the principle of town extension plans

	England	Germany	France
1910		Berlin Town Planning Exhibition Reichstag imposes tighter limits on lending by the Regional Insurance Boards	Agitation in Paris due to the high cost of living
1911	R. Unwin, *Town Planning in Practice*	Second Deutscher Wohnungskongress	Demonstrations in Paris organised by the Syndicat des Locataires Ouvriers et Employés The question of high rent levels is raised in the Chambre des Députés and in the Sénat Comité d'Extension de Paris formed
1912		Extended debate in the Reichstag on the housing question, appointment of a new committee to consider the issue Doubling of the allocation of the Reichswohnungsfürsorgefonds after move to cut this funding to a non-profit sector Foundation of the Zweckverband Gross-Berlin to coordinate the physical planning of Berlin	Legislation on housing: a public housing programme introduced in Paris; Offices Publics d'Habitations à Bon Marché introduced The Ville de Paris organises a competition for housing developments to inaugurate its public housing programme Jules Siegfried submits a proposal for legislation on planning Commission du Plan de l'Extension et de l'Embellissement de Lyon formed
1913		Publication and first reading of the second Prussian Housing Bill Foundation of the Gross-Berliner Verein für Kleinwohnungswesen	Société Française des Architectes Urbanistes founded Planning exhibition 'La Cité Moderne' held in Nancy Commission des Habitations Ouvrières et du Plan d'Extension formed in the Seine Department
1914			R. Unwin, *Town Planning in Practice* appears in French translation International planning exhibition held in Lyons Office Public d'Habitations de la Ville de Paris formed

Index